THE BOOK OF
COSTUME

VOLUME II

XVIIc. Flemish.
Sir Anthony van Dyck: Marchesa Elena Grimaldi, wife of
Marchese Nicola Cattaneo. (*Widener Collection*)

XVIIIc. 1793. U.S.A. (see Ill. 2228).
Gilbert Stuart: Mrs. Richard Yates. (*Mellon Collection*)

XVIIIc. c. 1779, U.S.A. (see Ill. 2190).
Benjamin West: Col. Guy Johnson. (*Mellon Collection*)

XVIc. 1538. German (see Ill. 1154).
Hans Holbein, the Younger: Edward VI as Prince of
Wales. (*Mellon Collection*)

THE
BOOK
OF
COSTUME

BY
MILLIA DAVENPORT

New York
CROWN PUBLISHERS

Second Printing

CONTENTS

Volume II

LIST OF COLOR PLATES

(Photography for Color Plate No. 8 by Francis G. Mayer)

1240. Late XV-e.XVIc. Fran-co-Flemish. (Metropol-itan Museum.)

Tapestry. Country life: possibly scenes from a pas-toral play or poem.

Straw hats, hoods, pouches, sock-boots and tucked-up gowns perennial-ly seen in peasant costume; diagonal and laced closing of the transitional period.

1241, 1246. Late XV-e.XVIc. Franco-Flemish. (Metropol-itan Museum.)

The Unicorn Tapestries.

Anne of Brittany, whom Maximilian I had attempted to marry, became the queen of Charles VIII; upon his death in 1498, she assumed black, instead of the custo-mary white mourning of Queens Dowager, "reines blanches."

The research of James J. Rorimer has shown that these superb tapestries, from the chateau of Verteuil, celebrate Anne's marriage, in 1499, to Charles' succes-sor, Louis XII. In the "Start of the Hunt," the first and last letters of her name ap-pear, linked by the cor-delière of the Order of St. Francis, which Anne had established in 1498 for wid-owed ladies; and on the collar of one of the grey-hounds can be seen the words "FRNC REX."

Anne, whose motto was "Better die than be sullied" was intelligent, devout, nar-row-minded and rather bourgeois. She was plain, and because she had a short leg, a slight limp became court fashion. She was the founder of the modern court with its many maids of honor. Brantôme, whose aunt was one of these, tells of Anne's constant efforts to augment their numbers from all parts of France, and her scrupulous super-vision of their lives and training. She had, in addi-tion, a guard of 100 gentle-men, largely Breton, and the terrace at Blois, where

1242

1243

1244

1245

they waited to attend her, was named by Anne herself, "The Breton's Perch."

1241. *The Start of the Hunt*: Beaver hats with clustered plumes bound across crown and under chin; sometimes worn over small felt bonnets; these, when worn alone, may also be plumed. The jerkins of the gentlemen have sleeves of another material; skirts plain or pleated. Tights with upper portions striped. Shoes, square toed, fur-lined and of ankle height.

1246. *The Unicorn is Killed and Brought to the Castle*: Variety and combination of male hats (one slung back by its ties), and small caps with turned-up brims, which are now being slashed, knotted and pinned: the cap is turning into a bonnet. Collarless jerkins and short sleeveless gowns. High boots, or leggings worn with ankle-high shoes, have turned-down cuffs of another color. Anne and her ladies wear severe high-necked gowns with lapped-over bodices. Hoods are simple, long, not yet slashed, and not very richly trimmed. General absence of precious accessories, rings, chains, and pendants; replaced here by cords and sashes. Rosaries, here as elsewhere,

1246

until the Reformation.

1242-45. Early XVIc. French. (Paris, Bib. Nat.)

Hours of Anne of Brittany. Executed by *Jean Bourdichon*.

1242. Youths: in square-crowned bonnets, the brims of which are beginning to rake out from the perpendicular line shown in the Unicorn Tapestries.

materials, countercharged at the border. Shoes are broad and strapped.

A center-front closing has superseded the lapped fronts of Anne's earlier gowns.

1248. Late XV-e.XVIc. French. (Paris, Bib. Nat., ms. fr. 143.)
Le Livre des Echecs Amoureux. Music.

This is the book of music lessons studied by the children who became Francis I and Marguerite of Navarre.

The Muse, seated between a harp and an organ, plays a zither-like psaltery. Fanciful touches, like the headdress and flowing German sleeves, make her otherwise standard gown of the transition period suitable for an allegorical personage. The lady in the background wears a hood which dips in the center in a Franco-Flemish way (as opposed to the gabled English form of hood).

Behind the carved linen-fold panelling are seen flute and hautboy players, a bagpiper, and a boy's choir, in skull-caps and surplices, supervised by an ecclesiastic wearing a four-cornered biretta.

1249. XVIc. 1507. French. (Paris, Bib. Nat., ms. fr. 5091.)
Story of the Conquest of Genoa, by Jean Marot.

Marot offering his work to Anne of Brittany. The square neck is rising convexly, and sleeves shorten as they become definitely funnel-shaped. Overskirt has inverted V-opening. Girdle, necklaces, and border of hood are becoming richer, as a shorter, more sophisticated hood is set farther back on the head, over a cap with an exquisitely gauffered edge, usually of gold gauze. This is the beginning of the *French hood,* which supplants every other form, in the wear of the upper classes toward the end of the XVIc.

Waist-high hose with wide cod-pieces, laced to brocade doublets with lowering neckline.

1243. Gleaners.

1244. St. Lifar as a bishop: his pleated rochet will be shortened to knee-length, during XVIc.

1245. St. Catherine: in ermine-trimmed, ceremonial sideless surcoat of a queen, its skirt of brocade.

1247. XVIc. 1503. French. (Paris, Bib. Nat., ms. fr. 225.)
Unknown artist: School of Rouen. Petrarch's *Les remèdes de l'une et l'autre fortune.*

Louis XII, Anne of Brittany, and Claude of France.

Louis wears his crown set around his bonnet, and the collar of the Order of St. Michael. He is followed by a cardinal and peers.

The jerkins of the two little pages have low, square necks and carefully seamed and gored *bases* of two spinning wife has a fine hanging pouch and ring of keys; 4th, nobility: braided carpet, cushions under foot, fine leaded windows, impressive show of plate; familiar garments; bead necklaces, used in Italy since late XVIc., are new in France.

1254. XVIc. c. 1520. French. (Paris, Bib. Nat., ms. fr. 1537.)
Unknown artist. Chants royaux du Puy de Rouen.
Interior of a print shop.

Other illustrations in this ms. show masons, weavers, pottery-turners and armorers. The windows of a print shop now have leaded panes; marble paving slabs are increasing in size.

The scholars looking over proofs wear the expected rectangular cap, and a sleeveless closed gown with a collar and deeply curved front opening, for which the round-necked undergarment serves as placard: I believe this to be a specifically French form.

The foreman wears a jerkin with a standing collar, opening from the waist. The bearded printer's full shirt bulges between his short-sleeved doublet and slashed and gartered upper-hose; patterned caul-like cap; hair

1250-53. XVIc. 1510. French. (Amiens, coll. Jean Masson.)
The Four Estates of Society. Executed by *Jean Bourdichon.*

The 1st estate is savagery; 2nd, extreme poverty; 3rd, bourgeoisie: carpenter in his prosperous shop, its windows barred but without glass, wears cropped hair and a short-sleeved jerkin closed by knotted points; his

1257

1258

shorter; shoes broader, cut lower, with or without straps.

1255. XVIc. French. (Paris, Bib. Nat., ms. fr. 874.)

Unknown artist: *School of Rouen*. Ovid's *Heroides*.

The Red Chamber of the Danaïdes: Nightwear of both sexes; beds and hangings.

1256. XVIc. French. (Darmstadt Mus.)

Jean Clouet, d. c. 1541. Bath after Birth.

Many were bathed only at birth, as a preparation for marriage, and after their death; women bathed also after childbirth. To carry and heat enough water in a fireplace was difficult, and a bather had to be protected from the chill of a high-ceilinged, stone-walled room by a tent-like enclosure.

1257. XVIc. 1515. French. (Louvre.)

Clouet, probably Jean. Francis I.

Jean Clouet, called Janet, and his son François were both painters at the courts of Francis I and Henry II. Jean, probably a Fleming, married a Frenchwoman c. 1520 and died c. 1541. François died in 1571. It is difficult to attribute definite works to Jean, but he is supposed to have drawn many of the chalk portraits of his school, some of which bear Francis I's own witty comments on the sitters.

Francis, though "he had the longest nose of any man in France except his jester," Triboulet, was a handsome man, witty, high-spirited, intelligent and amiable; personally courageous, selfish, capricious and unstable. He was passionately devoted to sports and amusements. Tennis, which had been played in some form since time immemorial, was a favorite game of both the French and English courts; Francis

loved it, and his son, Henry II, became the finest player in France.

The competitive magnificence of Francis and Henry VIII in their interview in 1520, at the "Field of the Cloth of Gold," made it one of the greatest costume parades of all time and bankrupted many of their courtiers. The "Chronicle" of the contemporary English lawyer-historian, Edward Hall, gives a detailed description of its costume and pageantry; two paintings at Hampton Court, att. to Vincent Volpe, show the embarcation and the meeting place; magnificent pavilions and tents, impressive temporary buildings, were shipped from England like stage scenery for erection near Calais.

Hall tells us that "The French King and his band were apparelled in purple satin, branched with gold and purple velvet, embroidered with [Franciscan] friars' knots, and in every knot were pansy flowers, which together, signified 'Think of Francis.'"

In the Clouet portrait, the puffs and slashes of Francis' black and white, gold and silver costume are subservient to its vertical bands of e. XVIc. embroidery, in which cord is used in interlaced patterns and to edge scrolled and foliated appliqué. His jacket, like that of Henry VIII, is cut away to expose the bosom of his doublet; this is still collarless and has the bateau neck which Francis favored.

His overgarment is made from a rectangle, slit up the front and across at the neck in a T, forming flaps which turn back as revers; the sides of the rectangle are folded up and caught on the shoulders, giving them additional square width and exposing the doublet sleeve.

Francis carries gloves; rapier with a well developed guard around the hand and the XVIc. "pas d'ane" guard below the quillons.

1258. XVIc. 1566. French. (Paris, Bib. Nat.)

Jean du Tillet. Francis I.

This portrait of the king in robes of state was painted several decades after his death by an artist who specialized in official portraits. The familiar symbols, cloak and gown are worn with contemporary slashed sleeves and wide-toed, low-cut shoes.

1259. Last third XVIc. French. (Chantilly, Conde Mus., ms. fr. 1672.)

History by Diodorus of Sicily, translated by Macault.

Macault is reading his work to Francis I, his three sons, and a group of courtiers which included the Chancellor Antoine du Prat, one of the favorites of the king's early years, and the later favorites, the Admiral de Brion and Anne de Montmorency, afterwards the mentor of Henry II. Behind the king's pet monkey stands a group of scholars in gowns and quadrangular hats.

We have no date for this illustration. But the king, by his marriage with Claude of France, who died in 1524, had 7 children; the third was the Dauphin, who died in 1536; the fourth, born in 1519, became Henry II; the sixth was the third son. We know that there was another edition of this work in 1535, which was also the year of du Prat's death. We may therefore judge the children's ages, and with the evidence of the costume, date the picture at the start of the 1530's. The neckline is still low, but rising and edged with a ruffle; hair not yet cropped; extreme square width of the shoes.

We see three views of a gown similar to that worn by Henry VIII both with and without dependent sleeve; in the latter case, the puffed upper sleeve is horizontally cut and caught with aiglettes. As on the costume of Henry VIII, tiny puffs are drawn through apertures in the embroidery. Netted hair under hat, as in German examples; dagger now carries a huge tassel.

1260. XVIc. 1543. French. (London, National Gallery.)
Corneille de Lyon. Portrait of a Man.

Jerkins with short sleeves, and decorated in grouped parallel lines are characteristic of mid-XVIc., but the high Spanish collar with a lace edged ruff would not yet have appeared on this garment in England. Many jackets retain a full upper sleeve, but the sleeve is tending to become simple and close, vertically slashed or corded, in mid-XVIc.

1261. XVIc. c. 1555. Italo-French. (Florence, Uffizi.)
Unknown artist. Catherine de' Medici, Queen of France.

The orphan who, at 11, cut off her hair and dared the Roman senators to be seen carrying her off forcibly (dressed as she was like a nun) from the Murate Convent she loved, needed all her amazing self-conrol and intelligence in her life as Queen of France. She was 14 when her uncle, Pope Clement, himself officiated at her marriage to the future Henry II. Her Medici energy, taste, intellect and love of sports endeared her to Francis I, but despite her great dowry, the French resented her "bourgeois" origin. The deaths of her uncle and father-in-law left her alone and slighted in a court whose calumnies have injured her reputation almost to this day.

Catherine, childless for a decade, loved the heavy youth who was her husband; while Henry II, resenting her superiority, neglected her mercilessly for Diane de Poitiers, 20 years his senior, who referred to her as "the shopkeeper's daughter." Eventually Catherine had 9 children, of whom 3 became kings of France. Henry's character developed slowly, and

1261

Many arts we now think of as French were actually brought from Italy by Catherine: fine cooking, lace making, fans and parasols, and the distillation of perfumes. Catherine, who carried parsley seed with her from Italy, imported her own chefs, skilled in the age-old variety of Mediterranean cooking and the iced sherbets of the Orient. Their arrival was coincident with the new foodstuffs and seasonings which adventurers were bringing back from the New World and the Orient.

Cane sugar began to supplement honey, which had been the universal sweetener; rum and molasses appeared. From America, too, came turkeys, potatoes, squash, maize (which travelled on to South Africa and India from the Mediterranean, just as Marco Polo had brought back spaghetti, or at least noodles, from China), chocolate, pineapples, and tomatoes ("love apples"), a decorative curiosity, but still considered poisonous in our great-grandmother's time. Tea and spices from the Orient, long known, became relatively available, and cooking became an art in which royalty itself dabbled from the time of Louis XV.

The 7 great pearls which were the Pope's wedding present to her, and hers to her daughter-in-law, Mary Queen of Scots, were appropriated by Elizabeth, and were use in the coronation crown of Edward VII.

As a young woman, Catherine was notable for fine eyes, hands and complexion, and her tiny 16-inch waist. Brantôme, who would never return to court after her death, says that she dressed superbly, was an excellent companion, had beautiful easy manners, loved dancing and sports, and made light of her later infirmities. She was not the inventor of the side-saddle, with which she is often credited, but was an indomitable horsewoman and hunter until the age of 60, despite a broken leg, fractured skull, and a fall " in which, thank God, I was not much hurt, and am only marked on my nose, like the sheep of Berri."

Catherine's standards of court dress and etiquette were rigid and high. Her children, the neurotically subservient boys and the rebellious Margot, all held her in great respect and longed for the good opinion of the mother who had disciplined herself in enduring dignity.

Catherine's gown is of black velvet, embroidered with gold and lines of pearls, set with sapphires at their intersections; the underdress of pink satin.

A gored underbodice of heavy material (*vasquine, basquine*) used from late XVc., had been followed by a rigid, hinged corset of iron bands. Another of Catherine's introductions from Italy was the corset of flexible steel, such as she wears with the vertugale under this gown.

The bodice carries the turned-back fur sleeve of the time of Holbein, but its waist is very pointed; and its crimpled and jewelled gauze partlet has the ruff, a decade or two ahead of the rest of Europe, which had also been brought from Italy by Catherine: a gauffered lace ruffle, set on a turned-up collar.

With this, Catherine wears a French hood, now without the fall, which would interfere with the ruff; fan of ostrich tips with a fine handle; magnificent cross and girdle pendant.

improved; Catherine's admirably decisive actions, during the king's absence at the disaster of Pavia, won her his respect in the last years of his life. Henry was fatally wounded in the eye by a lance, during a tournament in which the victorious king had sent Catherine word that he "would try one more lance for love of her." The queen, for the rest of her life, wore heavy mourning, which she barely lightened, on such occasions as the wedding of her son, by exchanging black velvet or satin for her usual dull materials.

As Regent for 2 of her sons, and during the last 30 years of her life, Catherine labored with all her Medici tolerance and statesmanship to reconcile France's religious differences, and to improve her courts of justice. At 68, immensely heavy, and no longer able to ride because of rheumatism, Catherine continued to travel about France in a litter on her "journeys of pacification." At 70, she crept from bed in her last illness to try to undo the mischief of the assassination of Guise, leader of the Catholic faction, which had been instigated by Henry III.

Modern historical research tends to absolve Catherine of cruelties beyond those characteristic of her times; and the duplicity of which she was accused appears to have arisen from her tolerance, far in advance of her times, of both religions, which infuriated both.

1262. XVIc. 1558. French. (Metropolitan Museum.)
François Clouet. Equestrian portrait of Henry II.

The king wears a black and gold embroidered jacket with long skirts and pendant sleeves; doublet sleeves and unpadded, paned trunk hose of white and gold, pinked. Jack boots over embroidered boothose. Gloves with a turned-back cuff.

The trappings of the horse show the linked letters H and D, which Henry used on the façades of new buildings or wherever else possible, to signify his love for Diane de Poitiers.

1263-64. XVIc. 1562. French. (Metropolitan Museum, Print Room.)
Recueil de la diversité des habits, by François Descerpz, Richard Breton, Paris, 1562.

These illustrations, showing the difference between French and Flemish mourning, came from the first real book on costumes published in France.

The unmarried French girl, in mourning for near relatives, wears pleated cuffs to match her *barbe,* and a hood with an extremely long narrow fall which she carries over her arm. Gloves are now in common use.

In Flemish mourning, a very wide veil is wired out to frame the head, and tucked up in back to give a short, wide horizontal hemline.

Either black, white, or their combinations were used in mourning, though white was more commonly worn before Anne of Brittany's time. The pleated *barbe* was worn by widows, with a beguine or other hood, until the time of Catherine de' Medici, when it was replaced by a wired-out hood, dipping low over the forehead or carried out into a beak (Christine: Ill. 1290). For the white mourning (*deuil blanc*) of a young queen, a veiled hood over a tiny cap and a

pleated *barbe* under the chin, such as we associate with Mary of Scotland. (See Ill. 1359.)

Pleating and mourning were associated in costume. Francis I's widow wore a pleated white cambric gown, embroidered in white, and the black mourning gowns of Catherine de' Medici are pleated, although the *barbe* has been given up.

Beside the deep mourning of *grand-deuil,* the half-mourning of *petit-deuil* permitted the use of some color, though its use was restricted to skirts, petticoats, the underparts of bodices, and hose. Violet was often used; Brantôme says that beige and blue were also permitted, and that this was sometimes stretched to include flesh and chamois.

A girdle, rings and ropes of pearls were permissible but the use of cut stones was not.

Hooded mourning robes, completely covering the garments, were worn in funeral processions. Margaret Paston's will in 1482, directs that white mourning robes with hoods be provided for her tenants, at her funeral. With the advent of crepe in late XVIc., the crowns of hats were wreathed in twists of black mourning crepe. The dull textures of cotton and velvet were considered appropriate for mourning; silk was worn in Spain, and for a happy occasion like a wedding, Catherine de' Medici permitted herself to wear gleaming satin. (See Appendix.)

1265. Third quarter XVIc. French. (Metropolitan Mus.)
Corneille de Lyon. Portrait of a Widow.

Hood with a gold ridge, simple gold chains and pearls only. Velvet yoke: standing collar lined with white, informally pleated at top; puffed upper sleeve, white puffs above wrist; wide vertugale and lengthening V waist.

La damoiselle en dueil.

Le dueil de flandre.

1263

1264

1265

1266

1267

1268

1266. XVIc. 1548. French. (Chantilly, Conde Museum.)

François Clouet. Odet de Coligny, Cardinal de Chastillon.

The three Colignys, who played such important roles in the French wars of religion, were the Cardinal de Chastillon, and his Huguenot brothers: the Admiral Gaspard, assassinated on St. Bartholomew's Eve by the Guise, and Francis, known as the Sieur d'Andelot, who had led Gaspard into Protestantism.

Below his cardinal's hat, Odet wears the rich dress of a gentleman of the 1540's. His satin gown is lined and collared with lynx, which shows through slashes. His brocade jerkin shows a lengthening waistline and high collar, finished with a plain ruff, pleated but not rigidly set. He carries gloves with a slashed cuff.

Brocades of such large pattern have gone out of ordinary male use by end first third XVIc., and are retained here in ecclesiastical dignity. Plain materials pinked, braided, or embroidered in lineal or diapered designs replace brocade, in male use, until its reappearance in XVIIc.; and the brocades used in

women's dress take on smaller, all-over and diapered patterns.

1267-68. XVIc. c.1560. French. (Paris, Bib. Nat.)

François Clouet. Admiral Gaspard de Coligny. François de Coligny, sieur d'Andelot.

The crown of the flat hat is rising and decoration is now set about the band. The high crowned Italian bonnet, which rises to such heights in English use, is less frequently seen in France than a small French form of toque, or a high felt hat (like that worn by the Puritans of New England).

These drawings show in detail the cut, fastenings and decoration of high collared garments and the ruffs which accompany them in France. The braid trim of d'Andelot's collar is repeated, in picadill form, as a ruff-like edge and a piping at the base.

The fine goldsmith's work shows another influence attributable to Catherine de' Medici. Court intrigue, which Cellini recounts in his autobiography, interrupted his work for Francis I, in the 1530's, but he returned to France to design much of the jewelry of Henry II, and French goldsmith's work of the time was greatly influenced by his style.

1269-74. XVIc. French.

Pierre Woeirot (c. 1531-89). Engraved designs for rings.

Most of the early engravers had received their training as goldsmiths, and could work interchangeably as executors or designers of jewelry, armor decoration, or book illustrations.

Woeirot, primarily an engraver of ornament, did a series of the kings of France, pubished at Cologne, 1591.

Courtesy of Metropolitan Museum of Art, Print Room

1275. XVIc. French. (Chantilly Museum.)

School of Clouet. Marguerite of Valois, Queen of Navarre, France, b. 1553.

Catherine de' Medici maintained high standards for the dress of her court. The lovely, learned willful child who became the fabled Reine Margot sought for her mother's approbation in all things, and became, as Brantôme never tires of telling, the most imaginatively dressed woman in France.

Henry of Navarre, her husband, dressed very carelessly, and once said about his habitually sober clothes: "I am grey without, but inside all gold." He attempted, in several sumptuary edicts, to forbid "any of the inhabitants of the kingdom to wear either gold or silver on their clothes, except the *filles de joie* and pickpockets, in whom we do not take sufficient interest to trouble ourselves about their conduct." Marguerite's lavishness clashed with Henry IV's parsimony, but they remained loyal friends after their divorce and his marriage to Marie de' Medici. Henry's second wife brought the greatest dowery of any queen of France, and probably spent more money on clothes than any woman who ever lived.

The French hood persists in England after its abandonment in the country of its origin. By the 1560's in France the favorite headwear is a small cap, worn on the back of the head, over parted hair, usually with earrings. Brantôme, who once saw Marguerite's natural hair, says it was black like her father's, but usually covered by wigs of varying colors.

The neck unfilled by partlet is a conventional usage for young girls in second half XVIc.; its off-the-shoulder width, emphasized by sheer puffs, is specifically French. The second half XVIc. emphasis on the top of the close sleeve is given here by petal forms; otherwise attained by the use of rolls, picadills, a sleeve cap, or by exaggerated cut.

1276. XVIc. c. 1571. French. (Louvre.)
Att. to *Clouet*. Elizabeth of Austria, Queen of France.

The wife of Catherine de' Medici's second son, Charles IX, wears a brocade gown; tucker crimped and jewelled in a diapered design; sleeves with a full cap are caught in a spiral design. Her jewelled collar matches her bodice top and the band in front of her tiny cap. Matching ruffs at wrists and high collar.

The silhouette of this gown can be seen on full-length figures on the Quesnel tapestries; in these, the waist is a little more pointed and the partlet, slit up the front, is turned back to form an open ruff.

1277. XVIc. 1560-70. French. (Paris, Bib. Nat.)
Jean Clouet. Rénée de Rieux, demoiselle de Chateauneuf.

As in England, the masculine hat is set over the little cap on the back of the head, in which the coiled hair is enclosed. But in France, the parted front hair is rolled in stylized arches, over pads. The slashed and braided gown has the open front and standing collar of the Spanish surcoat.

1278. XVIc. 1568. French. (Paris, Bib. Nat.)
Jean Clouet. Madeleine d'Aubespine, wife of Nicolas de Neufville, seigneur de Villeroi.

The partlet, slipping off the shoulders, is gathered into a standing collar, finished with a ruff. With the reappearance of the ruff in the 1820's, almost identical forms will be found in drawings by Ingres.

1279. XVIc. 1569. French. (Vienna, Art History Mus.)
François Clouet. Charles IX.

Gold-embroidered black velvet cape and jacket, with high collar and ruff, dipping waistline and the beginning of the peascod swelling above, but with the long skirts of his father's time. The cape lining is horizontally striped. Pinked white doublet sleeves and paned and padded trunk hose, nether-hose and slashed shoes. Hat crown rising and banded; moustache; sword belt with fine catches.

1280. XVIc. Dec. 31, 1578. French. (Chantilly, Musee Conde.)

Guillaume Richardière. Henry III presiding at the first ceremony of the Order of the Saint-Esprit, founded by him.

Tiny toque with a centrally mounting ornament, characteristic of Henry III and his court, as is the king's haircut, and the moustache and small pointed beard which accompanied it.

Robes embroidered with the monogram of the collar, and the badge of the Order: a white and gold Maltese cross bearing a white dove with outstretched wings, ordinarily carried on a blue ribbon, *cordon bleu.* Wide double ruffs; very short paned hose; padded sleeves, approaching leg of mutton form, elaborately pinked, carry only a small turned-back cuff. On kneeling figures: short French cape, ermine lining and collar; pinked shoes with cork lifts, but as yet no heel. Cardinal, other ecclesiastics, and officials of the order wear falling band collars.

1281. XVIc. 1570. French. (Metropolitan Museum.)

Corneille de Lyon. Portrait of a Gentleman.

Scarves and rosettes coming into use, seen here around a sugar-loaf hat of gored fabric. Small ruff on high collar cut in one with jerkin, which is vertically slit and buttoned only at the top; rolls at shoulder of widening, slightly padded sleeves.

1282. XVIc. 1574. French. (Metropolitan Museum.)

Etienne de Moustier. Man in a white doublet.

Hat crown higher; ruff larger; doublet with the sloping shoulder seen in France, slightly peascod, and with short skirts; sword belt with tassel; hose much bombasted.

1283. XVIc. Flemish. (Antwerp, Mayer van der Bergh Collection.)

Att. to *F. Pourbus, y.* Prodigal Son.

There are many prints and paintings of people playing musical instruments, of musical parties and weddings, during second half XVIc.; they are apt to be called the Prodigal Son. This picture, attributed to Pourbus, y., shows the costume we would expect to find in a Franco-Flemish picture of about the period of Pourbus' birth: diapered yokes, with standing collars beginning to open, their linen barely edged with pleating; loose jackets with high-capped sleeves; bell-shaped skirts; masculine hats worn by women; and the French hoods and multiple, heavy chains which persist from first half of the century.

Accompanying the lutes, wind-instruments and singers, the maid picks with a claw at a two- stringed instrument; it looks deceptively like the thermometer, which will not be invented for another half century. On the floor, in front of the maid, is a ewer, set in a basin which may also be hung on the wall, as we still see them used in country houses on the continent, in a dining room or passage-way. There are knives on the wooden trenchers; in XVIc. forks are used only in Italy; Coryat saw them nowhere else in 1608; a knife and fork in a case will become a luxurious wedding present in XVIIc., but forks will not begin to be considered a necessity, even among the upper classes, until XVIIIc. Jester with his bauble, and Negro page in attendance.

Photograph courtesy of Metropolitan Museum of Art

1284-87. XVIc. c. 1575. Franco-Flemish. (Florence Uffizi.)

The Catherine de' Medici Tapestries designed by *François Quesnel,* executed in Brussels.

About 1575, Catherine ordered a great series of tapestries, which were completed in about 5 years, as a gift to her native city of Florence. Henry II, had loved fêtes and pageants, such as those with which he had celebrated the marriage of Mary Stuart with his eldest son. Many of these took place at the chateau of Chenonceaux, which Henry had given to Diane de Poitiers, and Catherine had exchanged with her for Chaumont, after his death. Chenonceaux had been developed out of a mill on the river Cher; its waters were ideal for displays of fireworks and for naval pageants, and the forest of Amboise was a perfect setting for courtiers dressed as figures from classical mythology.

The tapestries celebrate marriages and other notable events at the French Court, at about the end of third quarter XVIc. One tapestry in this series (given in Piton, p. 168) shows carriages and riders approaching the chateau of Anet, where Catherine's own marriage contract had been signed. The only three coaches in France belonged to the queen, Diane de Poitiers, and to René de Laval, an enormously fat nobleman. Three other Flemish tapestries,

also in the Uffizi, showing her marriage festivities at Marseilles, were sent by Catherine as a wedding present to her cousin Cosimo I in 1539.

In 1573, ambassadors from Poland offered its throne to Catherine's third son, Henry of Anjou. Before he reluctantly left the woman he loved, the Princess of Condé, and accompanied them back to Poland, a fête was given in their honor in the gardens of the Tuileries. A ballet was performed by the queen's maids of honor; a description of it by the Italian ballet-master, Baltazarini, is preserved in the Bibliothèque Nationale, together with the ballet music, the words and airs of the songs, and a drawing of the movable "property" rock, on which the musicians are seated. Charles IX died in 1574, and Henry succeeded in eluding his Polish subjects and escaping to France to become Henry III. In 1575, Henry was married to Louise of Lorraine; many entertainments were given in their honor: tournaments, naval battles, displays of exotic animals.

1284. The Polish Ambassadors. The figure of Henry III in the l. foreground shows the characteristic beard and hair form adopted by the French court, in contrast to the clipped Polish heads, clean shaven, with handle-bar moustachios or long beards (standing beside Catherine). Except for one behind

Catherine, who wears a slashed costume with peascod doublet and ruff, the Polish entourage wears long, low-necked garments with sailor collars, and tasseled closings, in large-patterned brocades; feathered turbans, or hats turned up in back; chains and pendants.

Henry wears a high, puffed Italian bonnet with a curled brim; peascod doublet; venetians braided down side seams and finished with picadills; shoes strapped over instep, but without heels.

The male dancers wear short French hose, with canions to or below knee; peascod doublets; short, circular capes; guarded rapiers, characteristically slung; pattern on these male costumes is applied, not woven; hats, in the present sense, appear with crowns, brims and bands. The same garments are worn by the crowds in the background, often without canions.

The dancing maids of honor show pattern, woven or applied. Their high-necked bodices carry closed ruffs, alone or combined with open ruffs. Pendant outer sleeves have reappeared, and are combined with the close sleeves shown on the ladies in the background; finished with a roll or puff at the shoulder. Rear views show the tiny cap worn with heart-shaped, rolled hair.

Catherine, in the center, wears severe mourning, with her cap drawn down characteristically in a point on the forehead; veil wired into a heart-shape; light colored gloves; ruff.

Musicians, with lutes, viols, and harps are dressed in allegorical costume.

1285. Attack on an Island: Henry III was a cultivated and intelligent person, incapacitated by neurotic instability and effeminacy. His slender elegance was marred by a facial tic; he hid in the cellar during thunderstorms; collected tiny dogs which he carried in a basket slung around his neck. The crowd of favorites, *mignons,* with whom he surrounded himself, and on whom he spent immense sums, followed his lead. Their hair, beards, moustaches and eyebrows were dyed, curled, plucked and scented; their painted faces and their hands were covered at night by masks and gloves impregnated with skin creams. At court fêtes they sometimes appeared in women's clothes and wigs, while the ladies wore male costume, with feminine hair and ruffs.

Henry wears the small toque with front ornament, fluffed hair and one earring which is almost his uniform; braided and pinked peascod doublet; short trunk-hose with canions.

The bride, Louise of Lorraine, shows the meticulously rolled French headdress over pads, *arcelets;* this is much more studied and artificial than the curled or frizzed hair of England. Her cap has a gauffered edge; a jewel at the part gives the new triangular front effect, which began in the dip, characteristic of the Mary Stuart caps, and is further developed in the widow's hood worn by Catherine de' Medici.

Her gown and underskirt are of bordered brocades. The French vertugale has never reached the enormous hem circumference seen in some English gowns, and there has been a general European reduction in the spread of the farthingale and in the width of the V-front, since mid-XVIc. The new hippiness, shown in this skirt, will soon reach proportions equal to the drum-shaped English skirt of the 90's, with its cartwheel ruffle from the waist, where the French skirt will usually remain untrimmed. The sleeves are of plain material, their pattern applied; with their great shoulder rolls and smocked stiffening they foreshadow the immense padded leg-o'-mutton sleeves to come with the wide-hipped skirt. Her wide decolletage carries an opening ruff of the Italian-French variety: a pleated edge on a standing collar, where the Elizabethan ruff is entirely pleated. The girdle is wider; its pendant reduced to a tab. She carries a marvelous example of the now indispensable feather fan.

Behind Henry III, Henry of Navarre, characteristically energetic, careless and comfortably dressed, wears loose venetians, smocked into diapered puffs, and a pinked doublet with a very plain band, instead of Henry III's high ruff.

The men-at-arms wear the German-Swiss unpadded *pluderhose,* which has the lining hanging full and loose between the panes, and bloused at waist.

1286. Combat at the Barrier: Henry of Navarre, on the l., and the king's younger brother, Alençon, at r., await their turn. Alençon was the suitor, 21 years her junior, whom Elizabeth called "Froggy," and for whom she and the English court wore mourning for a year after his death in 1584.

Both wear sumptuous armor, patterned in varicolored metals, and worn with brocade venetians, closed below the knee.

1287. Attack on an Elephant: Marguerite of Valois stands with her brothers, the Duke of Alençon and Henry III. Her *arcelet* hair arrangement is elaborated by a border of tight curls. The neckline is opening and widening; the shoulder roll is incorporated, by cutting, into the upper sleeve. As with Louise of Lorraine, the girdle pendant has become a tab; both skirts have bordered hems. She carries a handkerchief instead of a fan.

Henry's peascod doublet is split, over brocade which matches his sleeves and canions.

In this period of travel and discovery there is a growing interest in exotic animals, and peoples ancient and contemporary. The hysterical Henry III had destroyed Louis XI's zoo, but Henry of Navarre's small menagerie contained an elephant. Here, the elephant is being attacked by Orientals and defended by Romans, while a crowd of mercenary soldiers in *pluderhose* watches the battle.

But the first elephant ever seen by so curious an Englishman as Evelyn was in Holland in 1641; in a backward country like Scotland, an elephant was first shown in 1680. (Law: *Memorable Things,* 1638-84.)

1288

1288. XVIc. 1581. French. (Louvre.)

School of Clouet. Ball at the court of Henry III: called "the ball of the Duke of Joyeuse."

Henry III spent more than $2,500,000 on the wedding festivities of his *mignon,* Anne de Joyeuse, and the queen's sister, Marguerite of Lorraine. We see again, by these dancers at a court ball, that a gentleman of the XVIc., to first half XVIIc. is always cloaked in public and wears his hat at all times, even at home, replacing it with a cap for domestic comfort and bed.

The king sits under a red velvet canopy, with his mother in her familiar collar and widow's-peaked cap, and his wife in a flat, circular, open-front ruff and dramatically slashed sleeves. On the king's r. stands Henry, Duke of Guise, who will be assassinated in the king's own bedchamber seven years later.

The bride, in white and gold, with touches of red on her cap and under the lines of pearls which cross her inner sleeve, wears the French court version of the hip-bolstered skirt: circular, laid on in deep pleats and with a slight train. There is a new tendency, shown in the skirts of other ladies, to display the underskirt by catching up or turning back the outer skirt, which is no longer slit. The leg-o'-mutton sleeve is now elaborately decorated, in contrast to the plain fabric of the gown, and of the outer sleeve, where it is present. The bride's cap, analogous to the male hat of the court, has centrally placed, mounting decoration.

The groom has a white-plumed black hat; green cape, its rose lining to match the stockings, turned back to form revers and collar; green doublet, venetians and shoes.

There is great variety shown in the ruffs of both men and women.

François Roger de Gaignières, (1642-1715), squire in the household of the Duke of Guise, was already at 25 an art collector and man of erudition. He had to travel constantly in the provinces, and decided to keep a record of funerary and other monuments. As neither he, nor his valet-factotum (who was also a paleographer) could draw, an artist-engraver named Louis Boudeau was employed to accompany them from 1670-88. His talents were very modest, but his thousands of weak little drawings are all that remain to us of most of the material recorded.

Some of the drawings were given to Madame de Montespan, who loved antiques; eventually the entire collection, together with books and paintings was sold to Louis XIV for a small sum in cash and a pension and passed into government institutions.

French books on costume, with redrawn illustrations, like that by Quicherat, are greatly indebted to Gaignières. The Henry III balls, painted on copper, were part of Gaignières' personal collection. Some drawings by Boudeau are shown in Ills. 465, 658. The drawings, now in the Bibliothèque Nationale, Paris, have been listed: H. Buchot: *Inventaire des dessins exécutés pour Roger de Gaignières et conservés aux departements des estampes et manuscrits,* Paris, Plon Nourrit, 1891. Portfolios of loose plates have been published by the Bib. Nat.

Photograph courtesy of M. Jacques M. J. Manuel

1289. XVIc. 1581. French (Louvre.)

School of Clouet. Ball at the court of Henry III, called "the ball of the Duke of Alençon," d. 1584.

Henry, wearing the 8-pointed gold star of the Order of the Saint-Esprit on its blue sash (cordon bleu), stands at l. with his wife and mother. As in the other picture, the king's little dogs play in the foreground. Ladies sit on tabourets which accommodate their great skirts and have supplanted the cushions for merly used.

The bolstered skirt and leg-o'-mutton sleeve are at their most massive, now and at the French court. As the bodice has lengthened, the horizontal line of the yoke tends to disappear, under the influence of the collar-shaped ruff, which often begins its spread into revers upward from the point of the bodice.

With their peascod doublets, all the French courtiers now wear venetians; these usually have horizontal bands of narrow vertical slashing. The high-crowned hat, which we associate with the Puritans because it was commonly worn in their time, and was taken by them to America, appears, together with Henry's familiar bonnet.

Photograph courtesy of M. Jacques M. J. Manuel

1290-95. XVIc. c. 1595. Flemish. (Madrid, Prado.)

Unknown Flemish painter. Six princesses of Lorraine.

Christine of Denmark (1290), as a widow wears a veil wired in a peak, over a ruffled cap; the points of the veil caught together at the waist as a scarf. Gloves with slashed cuffs.

Claude of France (1291), Catherine de' Medici's daughter, is dressed in the costume of the period preceding her death in 1575.

CRESTIÈNE, ROYNE, DE, DEN-
NEMARCK, DVCHESSE DE.
LORRAYNE.

CLAVDE, DE, FRANCE,
DVCHESSE, DE, LORRAYNE

CRESTIÈNE, DE, LORRA-
YNE, DVCHESSE, DE FLORENCE

1290   1291   1292

ANTHOYNETTE, DE LORRAYNE,
DVCHESSE DE CLEVES

CATHERINE, PRINCESSE, DE
LORRAYNE

ELIZABETH, DE, LORRAYNE,
DVCHESSE, DE, BAVIERES

1293   1294   1295

Claude's daughter *Christine* (1292), brought up by Catherine, was her favorite grandchild; Catherine ceded her Florentine possessions and her claims to the duchy of Urbino to Christine, and provided a dowry of 600,000 crowns for her marriage in 1587 with the reigning Medici, Ferdinand I. Without special ability, Christine was a person of charm and utter goodness; she reformed the Florentine court; brought up well her son Cosimo II; was regent for her grandson, Ferdinand II; and had a great influence on Tuscany during the 50 years of her life there. Christine's brocade gown has the cut and pendant Spanish sleeve of the late XVI-e.XVIIc.; wired collar edged with magnificent reticella lace; hair worn in the mounting, unparted Spanish fashion; massive Spanish girdle; folding Italian fan.

The other princesses wear the French court dress and coiffure of the late XVIc. with beautiful and ever more elaborate ruffs.

1296. XVIc. French. (Paris, Carnavalet Museum.)

Unknown artist. Dance around an elm in a village square.

This picture, given to the Carnavalet by the painter Ingres, probably shows the "Orme St. Gervais," the elm on the square of the nunnery-hospital of St.

Gervais, under which the lord's justice had been meted since XIIc., and under which games are played and mummers and neighbors dance to the music of an orchestra perched in its branches. The costumes are even less pretentious than the simple dress shown in the "League" illustrations.

1297. XVIc. May 14, 1590. French. (Paris, Carnavalet Museum.)

School of Pourbus. Procession of the League.

Paris, always a stronghold of the League and Catholicism, had held out for a year against the siege of Henry IV, whom the Sorbonne had declared a heretic, inadmissible as king even though his excommunication were revoked. The death of the old Cardinal of Bourbon, whom the League had recognized as Charles X, left little alternative to a belated recognition of Henry.

But on May 14, 1590, as a last effort, the League organized a procession of the strength available to the religious establishments of Paris: 1300 inflamed and militant Chartreux, Carmelites and Capuchins regular and secular, in all sorts of bits and pieces of armor and weapons, gathered in the Church of St. Jean-en-Grève. The Benedictines, Celestines and the Canons of St. Germain and St. Victoire refused to join them. Before Notre Dame, they were blessed by the Papal Legate, and in the excitement, a salute of

1298

welcome let off by novices, killed two members of his entourage.

A most detailed contemporary account of the proceedings has been left in the "Satire Menipée," which purported to describe a procession three years in the future. Three paintings of the procession at different points in its passage, hang in the Carnavalet, and the Museum's "Guide explicatif" of 1903, (to which I am largely indebted) gives a full and fascinating account of the events, personages and localities.

In this picture we see the procession pouring from St. Jean-de-Grève (Gothic towers in the background, of a church which disappeared after the French Revolution) through one completed arch of the Hôtel de Ville (begun in 1532), where Parisian disorder traditionally begins, into the Place de Grève, where it so frequently also ended, since public hangings took place there from 1310-1832. The Grève (= river bank) had been a main port of Paris since Gallo-Roman days and remained much as we see it here, until it was first enlarged in 1673. At that time, the Gothic Cross, on the eight steps of which the unfortunate prayed, was set close to the bank. Between the first light building and those adjoining the Hôtel de Ville ran the narrow rue de la Mortellerie, where throats were cut nightly and dead bodies found every day. In front of it stood the Mast of St. Jean with its ladder-like cross pieces, before which (by a tradition antedating the Romans) a civic leader or the king himself appeared on June 23, in great state and wreathed with flowers, to burn a cask, a sack and a basket full of cats, while a salvo was fired; this was eliminated in the remodelling. Across the river we see the Ile de la Cité, with Notre Dame, the Hôtel des Ursins and the opening of the Port St. Landry, where a wooden bridge, built in 1623, brought the number of bridges up to eight. Far up the Seine we see the Convent and Quai of the Bernardins and in the mid-

dle, the Ile St. Louis, which was not built upon until XVIIc., covered with lines of washing.

During the siege, food and drinking water were scarce; on the l. we see a water carrier and an outdoor kitchen, where a thin, salted oatmeal gruel was sold "as dearly as it had been milk." On the r. a butcher is selling the donkey and horse meat to which the city had been reduced.

The group of onlookers, to the r. in front of the inn, includes the dukes of Nemours and Mayenne, Governor of Paris and Lieutenant-Governor of the State respectively, with their wives and children and the duchesses of Guise and Montpensier. The costume of these French Catholic aristocrats shows us that what we think of as Puritan costume was simply the current dress of the middle and upper classes at the time of our ancestors' emigration to America: truncated conical hats, plain bands, easy knee-length breeches, plain capes, shoes with a tongue; women's small caps and arched hoods, plain bodices and sleeves, skirts of ground length with farthingale fullness. Complexions and hands are protected by masks and gloves. The soldier on guard wears a cabasset; one of the boys at play has the morion of another soldier on his head.

The procession of embattled churchmen is led by Dr. Rose, Bishop of Senlis and Rector of the Sorbonne, who has exchanged his ecclesiastical for his scholar's robes; and the Curé of St. Jacques in a violet gown and halberd, who tries to regulate the crowd; both we learn, freshly barbered for the occasion.

1298, 1299. XVIc. May 14, 1590. French. (Paris, Carnavalet Museum.)

French School. Procession of the League.

Also in the Place de Grève; standard of Saint-Michel in the background.

(The dual illustration above accounts for both 1298 and 1299.)

1300

1301

1300-01. XVIc. 1499-1503. Italian Umbrian. (Orvieto Cathedral.)

Luca Signorelli. The Fall of the Antichrist (1300) and The End of the World (1301).

Among the biblical personages, the youth in the r. foreground (Ill. 1300) wears the typical laced brocade doublet of the transition period.

In Italian male costume, both the use of brocade and these open-front garments will be supplanted by absolutely plain fabrics and austere cut. There will be an almost total avoidance, in Italy, of the rich embroidery used in England and France, and their cut-out jackets, exhibiting the bosom of the doublet. The extreme slashings and puffings of the German-Swiss styles will be avoided; hose will be notably unaffected, but will be more elaborately striped in Italy than anywhere else. Hair is enclosed in a netted caul in Italy, as in Germany and to some extent in France, but not in England.

The soldiers wear doublets striped in many

1302

colors, to match their hose, which are gartered and have prominent cod-pieces.

1302. XVIc. c. 1500. Italian-Venetian. (Venice, Academy.)

Gentile Bellini. Miracle of the True Cross: Catherine Cornaro, ex-Queen of Cyprus, Crowned.

Bellini, one of a dynasty of distinguished Venetian painters, shows Catherine in the last decade of her life, her crown set over one of the veiled headdresses which should be compared with those of XVc. Spain. We see small caps on the back of the head; loose hair at the sides, bound into a pigtail (in this case, wound around the head); a veil enclosing the face (here, bead-edged and caught together in back to fall as a replacement of the pigtail).

The laced bodice worn by G. Albizzi (Ill. 780) has become lower- and wider-necked, more cut out. The completely separated sleeves are knotted on, well below the shoulder, over draperies which go far beyond the original puffs of the shirt.

Earrings are worn which, like the necklaces, are related to the diapered patterns used in the plastrons and sleeves.

1303. XVIc. 1500-10. Italian-Venetian. (Venice Museum Civico.)

Vittore Carpaccio. Two Venetian Courtesans.

Carpaccio sees, understands, loves, and poetically transmutes all the life of Venice, even "the women whose faces are too heavily painted, with heavy mops of dyed hair" who "signal him from a balcony. He goes up. And here he is in the company of filthy little dogs, obscene monkeys, and cooing doves, and is confused by the thick perfume and the shining eyes." (Elie Faure: *Renaissance Art.*)

Near the peacock stands a pair of pattens with very high platforms, which remain characteristic of Venice through the XVIIc. Little caps set like topknots; interesting way in which sleeve puffings are tied at the back of the shoulder; ring worn on thumb.

The accounts given by the English travellers, Fynes Moryson (1566-1629) in his "Itinerary," and Thomas Coryat (1577-1617) in his "Crudities," describe the persistent differentiations of Venetian costume from the varied but always more modest styles of the rest of Italy.

Evelyn's diary notes the continuity, after a century and a half, of Venetian ways: chopines, and hair dyed in streaks and sunned on balconies. A print by Bertelli shows the *solana* sunshade brim used in this hair bleaching. (See Appendix.)

The Venetian gowns leave the heavily powdered neck and breast bare, sometimes exposed almost to the stomach. The coarse locally-produced linen of the shirts of Italy is stuffed about the body to make it desirably bulkier. The heavily rouged Venetian women, with their blonde hair (dyed if necessary), require assistance to walk on foot-high pattens in their gowns with trains. Moryson translates the proverb which describes them as "tall with wood, fat with ragges, red with painting, white with chalk."

From Christmas to Lent, Venetian courtesans might be seen on the street in men's doublets and breeches, light colored and carelessly buttoned. Italian ladies, as well as girls, continue to ride astride, dressed in men's clothing, but with women's headdress.

1304. XVIc. c. 1500. Italian Paduan. (Washington, Nat. Gall. of Art.)

School of Mantegna. Triumph of Chastity.

1305. Early XVIc. Italian-Venetian. (Carrara, Accademia.)

Vittore Carpaccio. The Birth of the Virgin.

Slight change, during a century, in simple domestic dress, often trussed up at hips.

Oriental carpets, imported and distributed by the Venetians, at first used as decorative furniture coverings rather than carpets; in Venice, hung over balconies during open air festivities. Patterned swaddling bands being prepared for baby. Platform footwear with folded and laced fabric tops, worn by old midwife.

1306. XVIc. c..1510. Italian-Sienese. (Washington, Nat. Gall. of Arts.)

Girolamo di Benvenuto. Portrait of a Young Woman.

Green, gold and white costume, with rubies and pearls. Border of interlaced cord design, of the sort used on costume (see Ill. 1257).

1307-10. XVIc. 1505-7. Italian, Umbrian. (Siena, Cathedral Library.)

Bernardino Pintoricchio and assistants. Scenes in the Life of Aeneas Sylvius Piccolomini (Pius II).

In 1502, the excellent Cardinal Francesco Piccolomini (who became Pius III a month before his death) commissioned from Pintoricchio a series of ten wall paintings, representing episodes in the very full life of his uncle, Pius II, shown in the dress of 1490-1510.

Born in 1405 of an impoverished aristocratic family, Aeneas Sylvius became secretary to a series of bishops, papal secretary, and secretary and official poet to the Emperor Frederick III. He refused holy orders until 1446, then advanced rapidly from bishop to cardinal and in 1458, pope. He preached a crusade, and died on his way to the Orient in 1464.

1307. Aeneas on his way to the Council of Basel, a lay secretary in a group of cardinals and other ecclesiastics, wears a great beaver hat, bound across the crown and under the chin; gown with a handsome gored collar with braided seams. Another layman (background) shows front of similar garment.

Attendants wear plainly cut doublets; parti-colored and striped hose; shoes with the favorite Italian turned-down cuff. This is an era of cords and tassels, which appear on the handsome pouch and dagger, as well as on the bridle of the mule.

1308. Aeneas, Bishop of Siena, marries Eleanor of Portugal to his former patron, the Emperor Frederick III in Rome, in front of the column which was (later) erected to commemorate the marriage. To the l. of Aeneas stands Agnes Farnese, who married his brother.

Her costume, like that of the bride and the other attendants, should be compared to Sp.XVc. and It. XVIc., in respect to characteristics, some of which will have an immense influence on the costume of the second half XVIc.-e.XVIIc.

The veiled cap will alter, and the netted pigtail headdress with its fillet will pass with first third XVIc., as will the Spanish extravagance of looped shirtsleeve.

We have seen sleeves becoming independent of garments. In the Spanish sleeve of Eleanor's black and gold gown, there is a further independence of the lower from the upper section; they are separately cut on opposite grains of the fabric, and will develop into one of the most important features of the Spanish-inspired "Elizabethan" costume. So, also, will the skirt supported by the stiffened farthingale. The sleeveless, open overgarment which we have seen on Isabella, is worn by Eleanor and her ladies, slipped off one shoulder; from it will come the severe, masculine, coat-like garments of the late XVIc.-e.XVIIc.

Frederick, who was crowned Emperor by Pope Nicholas, three days after his marriage, wears the imperial crown, fringed tunic, mantle, and magnificent anachronistic shoes with poulaine pattens.

1309-10. Aeneas, as Pope Pius II, canonizing St. Catherine of Siena. It was stipulated that the designs, their laying out on the walls and all the heads were to be done by Pintorricchio himself. The paintings contain many portraits; those in the foreground of this portion are portraits of Raphael, Pintorricchio,

and his assistants. They show doublets of the most austere cut; hose striped vertically, as well as horizontally in an effect of trunks; knotted cod-piece. Cloaks will disappear, and gowns shorten; brims of laced bonnets will become flatter. Hair is worn flowing or caught in a netted caul; cropped head is covered by an embroidered cap.

Behind them is a crowd of monks of various orders; above, the Pope, surrounded by cardinals; St. Catherine in her black and white Dominican habit.

1311. XVIc. 1512. Italian. (Siena.)

Baldassare Peruzzi. Alberto Pio di Carpi.

The learned ambassador, though bearded in the new fashion, wears his hair extremely long; this sort of protest is often seen at the start of a new trend. His hat is conservative in form; Italian caps and bonnets seldom show the excesses of slitting, binding and decoration seen elsewhere. His gown is lined with a variegated fur, which appears as a fringed edge, caught by loosely knotted, tasseled cords.

1312. XVIc. 1514-15. Italian. (Metropolitan Mus., Bache Coll.)

Raphael. Giuliano de' Medici, Duke of Nemours.

Lorenzo's admirable son, at about the time of his marriage in France to Francis I's young Italian aunt, wears his black bonnet tilted, as is the rule when used over the netted gold caul which foreshadows cropped hair.

His gown of neutral greenish brocade with a line of gold along the sleeve seam, is heavily furred in dark brown. Black jacket with deep, square neck of first quarter XVIc; the scarlet doublet has the lapped closing, seen in various forms since 1500.

1313. XVIc. 1510-20. Italian (Louvre.)

Titian. Man with a Glove.

Shortening bobbed hair; extreme simplicity of line and fabric; finely pleated shirt, its neckline rising to a ruffle; fine chain and pendant, ring worn on forefinger; unostentatious use of jewelry in Italian male costume.

1314. XVIc. 1514-20. Italian-Venetian. (Lugano, Baron Heinrich Thyssen-Bornemisza.)

Vittore Carpaccio. St. Eustace.

St. Eustace armor shows the rivets and fluting of the XVIc.; high collar; sabatons with moderate toes; sword without quillons has a double guard. The armet of the mounted knight gives good protection to the neck; shows no sign of the comb-like ridge which develops on most helmets during XVIc. Counter-charged striping of his costume.

1315. XVIc. 1520-30. N. Italian-Veronese. (Metropolitan Museum.)

Unknown artist. The Rape of Helen.

Striped doublets and hose, one leg and sleeve plain.

1316. XVIc. N. Italian-Veronese. (Florence, Uffizi.)
Giovanni Francesco Caroto (?) Elisabetta Gonzaga, duchess of Urbino (d. 1526).

Analogous countercharging in women's costume is shown by the daughter of Federigo I. Gonzaga; she married Guidobaldo, son of Battista Sforza and Federigo di Montefeltro, first duke of Urbino.

I give the genealogical information because her neck is edged in a pattern of letters, which may be a motto, and appears to have a device at the corners; gown, counter-charging and parti-color, and emblem on forehead are probably significant.

1317. XVIc. c. 1520. Italian, Lombard-Venetian. (Washington, Nat. Gall. of Art.)

Bartolommeo Veneto. Portrait of a Gentleman, called "Massimiliano Sforza."

Black and gold costume; doublet with c. front closing; medallion of St. Catherine. Gown similar to that of Francis I, slit and projecting, instead of tucked up at shoulders (see also Ill. 1257).

1318. XVIc. 1521. Italian. (Metropolitan Museum.)

Tommaso Fiorentino. Portrait of a Man.

Very large hats with upturned brims worn till c.1530; brim caught or tied at c. front, especially in Germany and Italy. Very plain black jacket with ballooning upper sleeve, gray lower sleeve; rising neckline, filled in by shirt with standing collar, common by 1525.

1319. XVIc. c. 1530. Swiss. (Metropolitan Museum.)
Unknown artist of Swiss School. Charles III, Duke of Savoy.

Nobleman in European dress. He wears the 15 gold love-knots and silver roses of the Order of the Collar, founded in 1362 by Amadeus VI of Savoy, for 15 companions. It is the principal Italian order. Its name was changed by Charles III to the Order of the *Annunziata;* its medallion represents the annunciation.

1320. XVIc. c. 1515. Italian-Milanese. (Washington, Nat. Gall. of Art.)
Bernardino Luini. Portrait of a Lady.

1321. XVIc. 1523. Italian-Venetian. (Madrid, Prado.)
Lorenzo Lotto. Portrait of a Bridal Couple.

1322. XVIc. Italian, Venetian. (Bergamo, Coll. Carrava-Morelli.)
Lorenzo Lotto. Portrait of a Lady.

The turbans which the Italians always loved, but had abandoned during the transition period for tiny caps covering only the back of the head, return in the e.XVIc. in huge round forms, ruffled, netted and knotted; very different in shape from the German headdress of equal size.

Instead of the funnel or close sleeve of English, French or German gowns, with their neat shoulder line, the sleeve of an Italian gown is apt to be voluminously gathered at the top, like the male jacket sleeve (Ill. 1052) of the boy in the Meyer Madonna.

In Italy, particularly in Venice, it is the female silhouette which is wide-shouldered and bulky; while that of the male is slenderer and more austere than in any other country.

Throughout XVIc. and in XVIIc., sable and marten skins are worn at the neck, or as in Ill. 1320, chained to hang from the girdle. We find them particularly in Italian and Spanish portraits, where they are frequently shown with jewelled muzzles and paws.

Italian men with cropped hair, like the bridegroom, often wear small turbans and caps, covered with pattern. The embroidered and ruffled high collar of the bridegroom's shirt is caught by a braided bar and loops, instead of the usual ties.

1323. XVIc. Italian, Venetian. (Florence, Pitti Palace.)
P. Bordoni. Portrait of a Woman.

1324. XVIc. 1523-7. Italian, Venetian. (Madrid, Prado.)
Parmigianino. Portrait of a Woman with Three Sons, called the wife of Lorenzo Cibo.

Milan and Naples, dependants of Spain, are more affected by the rigid, high-necked, large-ruffed Spanish garments, than is the rest of Italy, in which the breast often remains bare, the ruff small, and petticoats are used in place of the farthingale.

Moryson, who remarks on the simple unostentation of Italian male dress, notes that Italian linen is much coarser than that of Flanders, and that the Italians are not skillful at starching and gauffering the ruffs they do wear. Moryson describes the costume of Milan as decent; Naples, glittering and sumptuous; Genoa, neat and comely without laces or guards; Rome and Florence, modest: Ferrara and Mantua, proud of attire, wearing caps with gold buttons.

The characteristic Venetian bodice, long and pointed in front, pointed but short behind, is often cut extremely low and is fat-bodied. In the gown of this matron, the V is filled by a crimped and collared tucker.

Her netted headdress is drawn together in front; this spot is also the focus of interest in embroidered caps, such as that worn by the Lotto bridegroom (1321).

Delicacy of Italian chains; magnificent girdle with double pendants.

Knotted cord decoration of boy's high-collared jackets; cropped hair.

1325. XVIc. 1525-30. Italian, Florentine. (Washington, Nat. Gall. of Art.)

Bugiardini. Portrait of a Young Woman.

Gold fringed and embroidered white scarf used as a turban. Red gown, black velvet bands; full white shirt.

1326. Second quarter XVIc. Italian, Florentine. (Lucca Picture Gallery.)

Jacopo da Pontormo (1494-1557). Portrait of a Youth, wrongly called Giuliano de' Medici.

Italian version of the wide-shouldered gown with collar; complete absence of patterned fabric and jewels.

1327. Second quarter XVIc. Italian Venetian-Parmesan. (Naples National Museum.)

Parmigianino (1504-40). Portrait of a Man, wrongly called Amerigo Vespucci.

Embroidered collars with long points, finished with tassels, are seen in Italian and German portraits, first to second third XVIc.

1328. XVIc. c. 1553. Italian, Brescian. (Metropolitan Museum.)

G. B. Moroni. Bartolomeo Bongo.

This picture was probably painted c.1553 and the information and date of Bongo's death added after the death of both painter and subject.

Bongo was a doctor of both civil and canon law, apostolic pronotary, canon and dean of the Cathedral of Bergamo, rector of the University of Pavia, count and knight; his coat-of-arms is shown above.

He wears the square biretta and long, richly furred gown of an important ecclesiastic, academic or legal figure.

The Torre Communale of Bergamo is seen through the window.

1329

1330

1331

1329. First third XVIc. Italian, Florentine. (Frankfort-on-Main, Stadel Inst.)

Pontormo, or Bronzino. Portrait of a Young Woman with a Dog.

The common European male sleeve, puffed above, close and often of satin below, is little worn by Italian men but is characteristic of Italian female costume, and is often worn by German women.

Another of the imaginative Italian chains; knotted girdle with handsome netted tassel; center decoration of turban.

1330. XVIc. c. 1537. Italian-Venetian. (Florence, Uffizi.)

Titian. Eleonora di Gonzaga, Duchess of Urbino.

With her Italian turban, the duchess wears the Italian gown from which the rest of Europe, through Catherine de' Medici, will develop its standard costume of second half XVIc. Its characteristics will be exaggerated and elaborated elsewhere.

Its partlet is now less apt to be embroidered in vertical bands; its crimping will be emphasized in France and England by jewels set at the intersections of the smocking; its ruff will become more dramatic and standardized in those countries, while in Italy it remains relatively modest and individually varied. The standard sleeve of second half XVIc. will become clarified out of this sleeve with its upper fullness.

In her lap, the duchess holds a fur-piece with an entire head of goldsmith's work, which is fastened to her girdle. Girdle in the form of a knotted and tasseled cord; gown sewn with motifs of knots, in place of points; wonderful pendant cross on a chain; pendant earrings.

Clocks have been set in towers since XIIIc.; during XVc., they become elaborately mechanical, with processions of comic figures appearing on the hour. By XVIc., handsome small clocks, like the duchess', begin to appear in portraits, and are followed by watches at midXVIc.

1331. XVIc. c. 1540. Italian, Florentine. (Turin Picture Gallery.)

Bronzino. Portrait of a Lady.

Simple collar of cut-work, with long-waisted gown and loose, coatlike outer garment of Italian brocade, worn over petticoats instead of a farthingale, and fastened with horizontal cord catches (see Ill. 1161).

The jewels do not overwhelm the costume as they are apt to do in France and England, but are important in their freshness. The girdle has a reduced pendant, where the pomander of an English lady would bang her ankles if it were not for the protection of her farthingale; and in the unusual importance given to the c. front from which it hangs, can be foreseen the tab finish seen in the Catherine de' Medici tapestries. The pair of chain bracelets is also new.

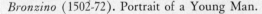

Bronzino (1502-72). Portrait of a Young Man.

1335. XVIc. c. 1550. Italian, Florentine. (Washington Nat. Gall. of Art.)
Pontormo. Ugolino Martelli.

1336. Second half XVIc. Italian, Florentine. (Metropolitan Museum, Frick Collection.)
Att. to *Bronzino*. Portrait of a Young Man.

The slope-shouldered, narrow-hipped Florentine male silhouette; sleeve without rolls or picadills at shoulder, widest below elbow; low standing collar, easy and often open with little display of elaborate linen; almost no jewelry. Aiglettes sparsely but functionally used. Cod-piece differs from tailored and decorated English-French forms. Short hair; smooth-shaven face.

1337. XVIc. c. 1540. Italian, Parma. (Naples Nat. Mus.)
Parmigianino. Portrait of a Young Woman..

Towards end first half XVIc., narrow, pleated, decorative aprons began to appear in rich bourgeoise costume in N. Italy, Germany, Switzerland, Flanders and parts of France. During second half XVIc. these, and other contemporary details, became integrated into "regional" costume, which persisted in some cases to XXc. and are well covered by the illustrations in the small edition of Hottenroth. (See key titles in Appendix.)

The apron is worn with a short-waisted bodice and full skirt, which is usually banded horizontally; or it is the apron which is banded when the skirt is finely pleated.

Simple parted hair with the coronet braids of Italy, and a centrally placed jewel; pendant earrings. Animal skin, "flea fur," chained to waist. Tabbed picadill finish, seldom seen in Italy, at wide cuff, which is filled by embroidered edge of wide shirt sleeve. Gloves now part of the wardrobe of all well-to-do people,

1332. Second quarter XVIc. Italian, Florentine. (Milan, Prince Trivulzio.)
J. da Pontormo. Portrait of a Youth.

1333. Second quarter XVIc. Italian, Florentine. (Cambridge, Fogg Art Mus. Loan of Chauncey D. Stillman.)
J. da Pontormo. Halberdier.

1334. XVIc. 1535-40. Italian, Florentine. (Metropolitan Museum.)

1338. XVIc. c. 1540. Italian, Brescia. (Washington, Nat. Gall. of Art.)

Moretto da Brescia. Portrait of a Lady in White.

This is a splendid example of the absence of stereotype, the personal touches, and the persistent, centuries-old interest in rolled coronets and the hair itself, in Italy.

Puffs of hair are drawn through loops in the headdress, and tasseled ends of the parure are brought forward as pendant earrings: this is a stylization of the free tuft or lock which finished the twisted hair arrangements in XVc. Italy.

The gown has the full-bellied Venetian bodice, long in front, and cut straight across, at a point well below the separation of the breasts. During the next quarter century, the partlet will split and be turned back, exposing the breasts and serving only as a base for the ruff, in the ground-length costume with a slight train, shown in the early fashion books, such as *J. J. Boissard: Habitus variarum orbis gentium,* 1581.

The old horizontal or rayed shirt decoration has retired, here, under a sheer, smooth partlet, tied on the shoulders; the partlet actually exploits the bosomy fullness of the shirt, which shows also in puffs and ruffles at the cuff.

Below the enchanting, modest ruff, the breast-parting is emphasized by chains and heavy pendant. Her feather fan hangs from a chain caught to a bracelet. She carries gloves and her hand rests on a Persian rug; still precious, such rugs are hung over tables, chests and balconies.

1339. XVIc. 1550-55. Italian, Venetian. (Washington, Nat. Gall. of Art.)

Titian. Portrait of a Lady, called Giulia di Gonzaga-Colonna.

With flowing hair and little wreath, the lady is informally dressed, as she might be at home. Under her green gown, with its slit and pendant Spanish sleeve, she wears only her wide-sleeved white shirt, edged with gold.

1340. XVIc. 1557. Italian, Brescia. (Metropolitan Museum.)

G. B. Moroni. Prioress.

The widow who became the prioress of the convent of the Nuns of St. Anna wears a cream colored headdress, horizontally pleated. A white kerchief is drawn about her goitre and tucked into the waist of her brown habit.

1341. XVIc. Italian, Parmesan. (Metropolitan Mus., Print Room.)

Enea Vico, fl.1541-67. Old Woman Spinning.

The need for getting their long skirts out of the way during active work is variously met in peasant costume. The classic plain Italian dress from Giotto's time has been short-waisted or belted just below breast, trussed up about the hips, and often has a fold above the hem. The apron covering this full-skirted garment cannot quite be deciphered: it surrounds the armseye, is included in the over- and underbelts of the dress, and is cut low or slit in front to permit passage of the distaff, which the over-belt helps to hold in position.

The most completely covered Italian head has always been that of an elderly woman of the lower classes: the cap and veil arrangement, in this case, seem to indicate widowhood.

Vico made a series of European costume plates, listed in Bartsch.

1342. XVIc. c. 1560. Italian, Brescia. (Washington, Nat. Gall. of Art.)

G. B. Moroni. Gentleman in Adoration before the Madonna (detail).

Around midXVIc., jackets were often short-sleeved, like this black one which shows the pinked sleeves of a red doublet, and a magnificently embroidered falling band. The second half XVIc. tendency toward beards is affecting the clean-shaven young Italian face.

1343. XVIc. 1553-5. Italian, Florentine. (Florence, Uffizi.)

Bronzino. Eleanora da Toledo, wife of Cosimo I, and her son Garcia or Ferdinand.

Cosimo I was the patron of Bronzino, whose companion portrait of Cosimo also hangs in the Uffizi.

Cosimo was fortunate in his marriage to the daughter of the Spanish Viceroy of Naples. She was rich, at a time when he needed money, was intelligent, and devoted to him and their eight children. While travelling with him for her health, the tubercular Eleanora and their favorite son,

Garcia, caught malaria and died within a few days of each other, in 1562.

The early Medici tradition of modest burial was completely altered by Cosimo; it would be interesting to know whether his great collection of Egyptian art influenced, as it might have warned him. Eleanora and the Medici after her were buried in their most magnificent clothes and wearing their jewels. A State commission, appointed in 1857 to examine the Medici tombs, which had been neglected and looted, was able to recognize Eleanora's body "with certainty by the rich dress of white satin embroidered with (black) 'galloon' trimming all over both the bodice and the skirt, exactly as she is depicted in the portrait painted by Bronzino which is in the Gallery of

the Statues (Uffizi), together with the same net of gold cord worn on the hair. Beneath this dress was an undergown of crimson velvet; and on the feet shoes similarly of crimson velvet." But the pearls and jewels had been looted.

Only the design into which partlets are smocked and jewelled, in continental Europe, is retained in the gold net yoke. There is no ruff or band; the low-necked Italian shirt barely shows as a line of embroidery beneath the yoke; its wide sleeves hang from the wrist in an unstudied ruffle.

The boy wears a beautifully embroidered shirt, its cuffs and falling band edged by a ruffle; long-bodied gown.

1344. XVIc. 1560. Italian, Venetian. (Vienna, Art History Museum.)

Copy of Titian by *Rubens*. Portrait of a Woman in White, formerly called the artist's daughter Lavinia.

The Venetian bodice, short in back, is beginning to be slit and laced over a decorative plastron, or voluminously gathered material; always thickened by shirt fullness or padding, it will be very susceptible to the influence of the male peascod doublet, in the last decades of the century. The very low decolletage is opening wider.

The fan is of a specifically Italian form, derived from Moslem lands, seen particularly in Venice: rigid and fixed to a stick. Used by all classes, it ranged from stark simplicity to elaborate decorativeness, but in either case was fringed and tasseled.

Coryat was much struck by the Italian fans: "Most of them are very elegant and pretty things. For whereas the frame consisteth of a painted piece of paper and a little wooden handle; the paper which is fastened into the top is on both sides most curiously adorned with excellent pictures, either of amorous things tending to dalliance, having some witty Italian verse or fine emblemes written under them; or of some notable Italian city with a brief description

thereof added thereunto. These fannes are of a meane price. For a man may buy one of the fairest of them for so much money as countervaileth with our English groat."

1345-46. XVIc. 1577. German.

Trachtenbuch illustrated by *Jost Amman,* publ. by Hans Weigel, Nuremberg, 1577.

1345. Woman of Verona or Dietterichbern: Theodoric the Great (Thiuda-reiks=Dietrich) was the hero of a confused German legend, of a Gothic king who emerged from Byzantium to conquer Italy and was dispossessed of his kingdom of Bern (=Verona), by his uncle.

The fashions of Southern Germany and Switzerland, passing through the Tyrol, affect N. Italian costume: high-crowned, white-covered headdress; severe lines of skirt and bodice, with completely closed high neck, globular and separated upper-sleeve fullness; apron with upper corners free of the waistband.

1346. Venetian noblewoman: Characteristic exposed breasts and rather blowzy, short-waisted fullness of Venice; with a great pleated and wired scarf, finished with tassels, used as a ruff.

1347. XVIc. c. 1580. Italian, Brescian. (London, National Gallery.)

G. B. Moroni. Portrait of a Lady of the Fenaroli Family.

Rose satin gown, short-sleeved like one form of male jacket; horizontally slashed, the edges whipped in gold thread. Underdress and sleeves gold. White standing collar, embroidered in rose. Fan is another of the rigid, tufted Italian forms.

1348. Last quarter XVIc. Italian, Florentine. (N. Y. Historical Society.)

Att. to A. Allori (Bronzino). Princess of Florence.

1349. XVIc. c. 1580. Italian, Roman. (Washington, Nat. Gall. of Art.)

F. Baroccio. Quintilia Fischieri.

In both Ills. 1348-49, we see severe, masculine Spanish styles; high collars; large formal ruffs; separation north bodice and skirt.

Quintilia's gold-embroidered bodice is green; her skirt blue. Fringed handkerchief.

The coat-like outer garment of the Florentine princess is of plum-red velvet brocaded on silver, its lapels and standing "Medici" collar faced with silver. Underskirt of shot silver, with red and gold. Handkerchief, lace edged, is an Italian usage, now spread through upper-class Europe.

1350. XVIc. c. 1580. Italian, Florentine. (Washington, Nat. Gall. of Art.)

A. Allori. Portrait of a Boy in Red.

Child's dress in Spanish fashion.

1351. Third quarter XVIc. Italian, Florentine. (Florence, Pal. Vecchio.)

G. Vasari. Scenes from the History of Florence: Assault of the Castle of Empoli.

Much of our information about Italian Mediaeval and Renaissance artists comes from Vasari's "Lives of the Painters." This wall-painting of the assault on a fortified castle gives us background material for military costume. The form and decoration of the tent has changed remarkably little from that shown in mss. illustrations of XIIc. Spain or XVc. France.

The tiny figures show halberdiers in *pluderhose,* and headgear of the morion and cabasset types.

After describing the costume of the Swiss guards at Fontainebleau, Coryat says: "The originall of their wearing of Codpieces and partie-coloured clothes grew from this; it is not found that they wore any until Anno 1476, at what time the Switzers tooke their revenge upon Charles Duke of Burgundie, for taking from them a Towne called Granson within the canton of Berne, whom after they had defeated, and shamefully put to flight, together with all his forces, they found there great spoyles that the Duke left behind, to the valew of three Millions, as it was said. (Commines lists the loot taken at Granson).

But the Switzers being ignorant of the valew of the richest things, tore in pieces the most sumptuous Pavilions in the world, to make themselves coates and breeches: some of them sold Silver dishes as cheape as Pewter, for two pence half-pennie a piece, and a great Pearle hanging in a Jewell of the Duke for twelve pence," (the Sancy diamond, 53½ grains, bought in 1835 by Prince Demidoff) "in memory of which insipid simplicity, Lewes the eleventh King of France, who the next year after entertained them into his Pension, caused them to bee uncased of their rich Clothes made of the Duke of Burgundies Pavillions, and ordained that they should ever after weare Suites and Codpieces of those varyegated colours of Red and Yellow. I observed that all these Switzers do wear Velvet Cappes with Feathers in them, and I noted many of them to be very cluster-fisted lubbers. As for their attire, it is made so phantastically, that a novice newly come to the Court, who never saw any of them before, would halfe imagine, if he should see one of them alone without his weapon, hee were the Kings fool."

1352. XVIc. 1570-75. Spanish. (Metropolitan Museum, Frick Collection.)

Doménikos Theotokópoulos, called El Greco. Vincente Anastagi.

The painter, whom we think of as Spanish, was a native of the island of Corfu, and was trained in Italy; in 1590 he became painter to the Spanish court.

Anastagi was a commander of both infantry and cavalry, and Governor of Malta during the siege. With armor bearing the white Maltese cross, Anastagi wears a high-collared Spanish ruff and the diagonal sash of a military commander, in green. Wide green velvet venetians of the 70's, galloned in gold; gartered white stockings; yellow shoes. On the floor, the combed morion of third quarter XVIc.

The World Widens: XVII Century

XVII Century Background

THE XVIIc. is a century of alteration, realignment, new strengths and energies, personal responsibility, and strain.

As royal prerogative gained over feudal power, the lord's responsibility for his own people was weakened.

The old, vertically-composed craft guilds, in which workmen, foremen, employers, merchants and shopkeepers shared (as crews, masters, and owners of fishing vessels still do in the proceeds of the catch), broke horizontally into commercial merchant-employers, and journeymen hired-help.

The new cleavage into capital and labor was strengthened by the rise of Protestantism.

The Catholic church, for all its rapacity, had never lost a real concern for the poor, and had never favored high interest rates. The Church completely controlled education, the law, medicine, and the administration of hospitals and all organized charity for the care of the poor, aged, and orphaned. These activities, which we now support by state and federal taxes, and the bequests of Rockefellers and Carnegies, were in those days paid for by the tithes of the church (one tenth of everyone's income, down to one out of a poor woman's ten eggs) as well as by additional funds from the rich and pious.

The dissolution of the monasteries was a redistribution of property as drastic as that being carried out in England today; the Church owned about one fifth of England's wealth, and administered it with the bureaucratic inefficiency of all over-large organizations. Protestants were enriched; and the charitable work of the Church, much of which had stemmed from the monasteries, was curtailed, while endless thousands of their former inhabitants were loosed into a world in which they were unfitted to compete; they starved, lawlessness increased, plague spread.

The invention of printing aided the rise of Protestantism. The Bible had been a possession of the higher levels of the Church alone; a monk or rich layman read his breviary; in order to read the Bible, he had to have permission of his religious superior. An unimportant layman could neither hope to own a manuscript Bible, nor be allowed to read it.

Printing provided cheap Bibles, which were critically read and pondered. People came to diverse conclusions: though disturbed, they might remain within the Church; but the tender, relaxed qualities of Catholicism were being impaired by the disunities, anxieties and struggles of the Counter-Reformation. Or they might join the Lutheran, Calvinist or other sects, which divided, competed and provided new tensions.

To forgive, or, worse, not to be able to forgive yourself is harder than to be periodically absolved of your burden by someone else. The ever-present Protestant concern with sin, and the austerity of a religion shorn of the Catholic graces and aesthetic satisfactions, drove the reformers, particularly the Calvinists, into industry for industry's sake. The rewarding money came to seem in itself good; God helped those who helped themselves. Calvin's ideals of service, more demanding than the tithes of the Church had been, were conveniently forgotten. The unfortunate and ineffectual tended to become objects of a determined, self-righteous charity, rather than part of the great body of the poor, weak, sinful children of God.

In the train of Reformation and Counter-Reformation went the devastation of the Wars of Religion. The states of present-day Europe were being formed, the limits of royal power defined, the part of the people in government explored, the courts freed of ecclesiastical rule.

The XVIIc. is France's century, as the XVIc. was Spain's. Least impaired by religious conflicts, she rises under the increasingly absolute rule of adroit Bourbon kings; her finances are established, agriculture and roads improved; industry, especially luxury industries, encouraged. She allies herself with the new power of the house of Vasa, under which the Swedes will go to the aid of Protestant Germany, and shoot to prominence and prosperity. France rivals a disunited Germany, of independent Protestant princes to the north (out of which Prussia will become preeminent in last third XVIIc.), and a weakened Empire, withdrawn around the Danube. But the end of the War of the Spanish Succession will see France's power suddenly controlled.

England, after nearly a century of internal preoccupations with Puritans and parliaments, Stuarts, revolutions and restorations, will emerge master of the Mediterranean and on her way to empire and world leadership, at the end of the century.

Spain has plummeted swiftly downward, her industrial potential self-destroyed, while she depends on her New World riches, her army and her proud tradition.

Italy is more disastrously disunited than ever, and Russia begins to emerge into Europe as Peter the Great combats Charles XII of Sweden suc-

504

cessfully for the Baltic, and the Turks, unsuccessfully, for the Black Sea.

DEVELOPMENT OF DRESS: 1620-1655

Spain's influence on European fashion weakened in the second decade XVIIc., but she evolved for her own use the style of the Infantas, painted by Velasquez from 1645.

Clothes outside of Spain lost their farthingales and became easy and flowing. During the 30 Years War, the military styles of the Low Countries and Sweden affected male costume, particularly that of middle-class Germany. However, men of all ages, stations and callings, everywhere, went booted and spurred, with swords, leather military jerkins, cocked hats and carelessly slung cloaks. As in second half XVIc., it was ill-bred to appear in public without a cassock or cloak, and the hat was seldom removed, even within doors.

This, in Kelly's words, is the age of long locks, lace and leather. The military usage of leather does not affect women's increasingly feminine clothes. Otherwise, their development parallels that of men's to second half XVIIc. As bombasted breeches go out, so do hip bolsters and farthingales. So long as male breeches retain their quilted linings the materials of women's gowns keep a fat, padded look. Women's necklines become low, but alterations in the important collars and methods of decoration are analogous with men's. Almost the only hats worn by women are of the high-crowned masculine variety; caps remain very important only in Holland. Hair is combed back, hangs loose at the sides, and gains bangs and length as men's grows longer.

Regional costume was retained, particularly, by the North German seaports: Danzig, Lübeck, Hamburg and Bremen; up the Rhine, in those cities where it had become very distinctive: Cologne, Frankfort, Strassburg, to Basel; along the Danube, from Swabia, past Ulm, Augsburg and Nuremberg into Bohemia. Much of this costume is preserved in W. Hollar: *"Aula Veneris"* and *"Theatre of Women."* The courts of Germany west of the Rhine quickly succumbed to French fashion.

England develops her distinct van Dyck "Cavalier" styles in second quarter XVIIc., as Spanish influence wanes.

Italy shows Spanish influences long after they are supplanted elsewhere. In 1644, Evelyn notes the "Spanish mode and stately garb" of Genoa and the persistence in Venice of fashions which have endured for a century and a half.

France, which has gained over the rest of Europe during the 30 Years War, develops a civilization and a fashion-sense which overwhelms all others in second half XVIIc., a lead which she has always since retained.

MEN'S DRESS, 1620-1655

Doublets: As the peascod belly disappears, c.1600, the fitted doublet develops a shorter waist, longer point in front, wider shoulder caps, and longer skirts which are now apt to be slit and overlapping. The garment is often slit half a dozen times, vertically, across the breast and shoulder blades. In second quarter XVIIc. skirts grow longer, the body easier and shorter. The slitting is reduced to the center front and back seams, both of which are furnished with a row of buttons, but are usually left open.

By 1640 the belt has disappeared; the body and skirts are cut in one, and the garment is scarcely longer than a vest. A great deal of blousing shirt shows below its hem and through its open front. In first quarter XVIIc. the upper sleeve is also apt to be slit, like the breast and back of the doublet; close-fitting below the elbow.

As the doublet alters in second quarter, the sleeve becomes closer above, easier below, and unified. The slitting is reduced to the inseam; like the front and back openings of the doublet, it is edged with buttons, whether used or not.

With the vest-like doublet of 1640, the sleeves are closed, except for a buttoned wrist opening; this is turned back, forming, in embryo, the all-important cuff of second half XVIIc.; showing fullness of the shirt's sleeve, to match the shirt's bloused fullness above the breeches; the doublet is becoming a coat. On this garment, wide linen collars cover the shoulder, and the shoulder-cap disappears.

Jerkin: The sleeves of the collarless jerkin had become dependant and useless in late XVIc. Now they tend to disappear; but when no doublet is worn, sleeves of another material are added, braided like a doublet sleeve. These are seen particularly on the military jerkins of yellowish-colored natural leather which are fastened by lacings through eyelets, sometimes by clasps, never by buttons. Around 1640, the jerkin takes on the same short, unbelted form as the doublet.

Breeches and Decoration: Breeches continue to be fastened to doublets until the advent of the short jackets of the 40's. But instead of being tied together underneath, the lacings are now brought through paired eyelets along the waistline, and are tied outside in decorative bows.

The ribbons by which aiglettes were hung in Spain during second half XVIc. have now become more important than the points themselves; their use increases in loops, bows, rosettes and in spaghetti-like, uneven, uncut fringes, no thicker than a shoelace and as insignificantly tipped.

Breeches: The full knee-breeches of late XVIc. supplant trunk-hose during first quarter XVIIc. They lose their interior quilting and become narrower. There are also loose, ungartered breeches hanging below the knee; similar forms, cut off above the knee, like those worn around the turn of the century, reappear with vest-like doublets of the 40's. Until this time, breeches are high-waisted and caught to the doublet; but by midXVIIc. they slip low on the hips, unattached. As breeches become more like shorts or trousers, they develop a fly-closing.

The trim of breeches agrees with that of doublet; when it is split at c. front and back, showing shirt, they may also be split, similarly edged with buttons, and show an underwear-like white linen lining. They are gartered with the same loops, bows and rosettes used on the rest of the garment. With the wide collars of the 40's, the breeches may be cuffed with lace to match, or trimmed at outseam and bottom with wide, lace-like braids matching those used on the underarm seams and edges of the short doublets.

Footwear: Legwear is also closely related to the rest of the costume, in first half XVIIc. Silk stockings are generally worn by the middle and upper classes. Several pairs are worn over each other, pushed down to show their differing colors, and deliberately wrinkled. Since they are still precious, they are protected by a variety of gaiters and linen boot-linings, which are sometimes worn with shoes alone, as well as with most boots. (A frame for the mechanical knitting of silk stockings had been invented in England in 1621.)

Shoes now have heels and heavy soles (both red, in court wear), and a strap over the instep, decorated with a ribbon rosette or bows. Toward mid-century, the toes lengthen and are cut square across the tip.

But this is primarily the era of boots. With heel and sole support, these now fit well around the foot. Their extremely wide tops are worn folded down and then up again, tending to become wider and folded lower in second quarter of century. The cuff thus formed is a receptacle for elaborate garters, hem decorations of breeches, or the elaborately lace-trimmed inner boot-hose, folded in unison with the folds of the boot-top. In second quarter XVIIc. a great quatre-foiled plaque of leather is held in place over the instep by the straps of the ubiquitous spurs. Boots are now worn by everyone, and the spur is an adjunct, quite devoid of function. This leather plaque becomes enormous in the 30's, and is retained when boots return to riding use in last third XVIIc.

Linen is becoming increasingly visible and important; it must be treated as part of the body garments, as well as a frequent part of footwear.

The wired-out flat whisk, or Spanish *golilla* of 1610, and the full but unsupported *falling ruff*, begin to be supplanted, in second quarter century, by the *falling band* collar. Cuffs with scalloped edges have already appeared, worn with the falling ruff; they continue in use, growing fuller as the falling band collar (usually with a scalloped edge) spreads over the shoulders of the short-waisted, long-skirted doublet, and ousts the shoulder wings, at end first third XVIIc. With the vest-like doublet of the 40's, the collar is reduced in size and loses its scalloped border; but now the fullness of the shirt appears between doublet and breeches, and below a sleeve, which is shortened by being turned back, later becoming a cuff.

Outer Garments: Cloaks and gowns are now indispensable outdoor wear. The slung mandilion fashions of second half XVIc. were developed in military use into longer, looser coats with easy, cuffed sleeves. The longer capes of the XVIIc. (often with pendant sleeves and square collars), are also worn slung about the body, and held in place by interior cords; these can sometimes be seen tied around the body, but are usually obscured by the great collar of the doublet, which is worn outside the cape or cassock.

For state and ceremonial wear, long gowns continued to be used as they are in England today. After 1620, trunk hose persisted only in livery or regalia wear.

Headwear: With the swashbuckling outer garments are worn dashing, plumed military hats, cocked at front, or on one or two sides for practicality; by last half XVIIc., they are often cocked into a tricorne. The other outstanding hat of the period is an essentially stiff one, with a narrower horizontal brim and a high, truncated cylindrical or conical crown. In last half of century there are low-crowned versions of this hat, typically trimmed with cord or loops, not feathers.

Hair: Hair has lengthened during the last decades of XVIc. Now all but the most dignified older men allow it to grow to natural length; at first c. parted; in second quarter of century, cut across the forehead in bangs; until parted hair reappears in the wig of the last half XVIIc.

Beards and moustaches are reduced in length as hair is allowed to grow. The upswept moustache of first third of century becomes smaller, as the beard changes to the Vandyke type and becomes very slight; in second quarter the beard disappears except on older men. Clean shaven faces are common from last half of the century, though tiny moustaches are worn till its final quarter; after that, hair disappears from faces until XIXc.

Accessories: The diagonal scarves worn by military commanders of second half XVIc. continue in use, and are now worn, as the beginnings of uniforms, by soldiers. Spurs and swords are seen on everybody; the slender rapier tends to be slung by a diagonal strap over the shoulder, in second quarter of century. Daggers pass out of ordinary wear. Umbrellas had appeared in late XVIc., but are still uncommon. Walking sticks come into fashion in first quarter XVIIc., and remain in use into XXc.

WOMEN'S DRESS, 1620-1655

The long-waisted, stomachered dresses of the turn of the century remain in use through first third XVIIc, with lowering necklines. However, the tendency is toward a shorter-waisted open gown or robe, for grander wear, worn over a corset-like bodice and skirt, supported by many petticoats beneath. This is a development of the Spanish coat-dress (see Ill. 1114: Vavasour), spreading wide to show the underbodice and skirt. Skirt fullness is attained by goring in front and gathering in back, or by gathering all around.

Stiff, heavily patterned fabrics are much less used. Underskirts are of ground length, and are usually lighter in color than the skirt of the robe. The robe may have a train, and when its skirt is looped up at the hips to show the underskirt, end first third XVIIc., it is apt to be of thinner material than the underskirt, with bright lining.

The stomacher of the underbodice is sometimes rounded, in first half of the century, but becomes pointed again in the second half; in Holland it is apt to be richly decorated.

Jackets: With the short-waisted male doublets of the end of the first third of century, short-waisted bodices with tabbed skirts appear on women. When the jackets have full, paned or leg-o'-mutton sleeves, they are tied around, between shoulder and elbow, with a rosetted ribbon. This matches a belt, fastened at side or c. front with a bow or rosette. Sleeves have a tall white cuff, which makes them seem shorter, and in second quarter century the sleeve does actually shrink toward the elbow, just as men take to turning back the bottom of their sleeve. When these jackets do not meet in front, they are usually hooked fast along the stomacher. There is another form of jacket, which is often of quilted or flowered stuff. When it is thick, like the military leather jerkin, it is apt to be laced together at front or back. It usually shows a simple, easy sleeve, slit up along inseam and cut off near elbow.

In English inventories of 1600, the jacket or bodice with skirt attached is called a *kirtle;* the skirt alone, a *half-kirtle;* jacket alone, a *jump.*

Gown or Robe: The outer gown of first half XVIIc. has a sleeve slit down the inseam, and caught with a rosette, where it is cut off above the elbow. This is the split Spanish sleeve of the end of XVIc., the bottom section of which was already almost truncated (Ill. 1238), and has now been dropped. During first third of century there are sometimes long strip sleeves, in addition, pendant from the armseye. With the short sleeve of the gown, the under sleeve of the bodice is cuffed, and tends to become fuller and shorter.

Necklines lower generally, into a rounded, then a squared form; this eventually widens and becomes rounder, as the bodice slips off the shoulders in the latter half century. The neckline is at first much higher in back to support the continuing ruff or wired-out collar; it becomes lower in back, though never so low as in front. Necklines alter as collars vary and combine.

The evolution of men's and women's linen and headgear in Holland (where it was most varied and influential) has been exhaustively charted by Fritjof van Thienen: *Das Kostum de Blütezeit Hollands,* 1600-60., Deutsche Kunstverlag, Berlin, 1930.

Linen: Ruffs at neck and wrists, and whisks persist through first third of century (the ruffs, particularly in conservative and bourgeois wear); both finish their careers, worn in conjunction with all sorts of falling collars and folded kerchiefs. These tend to spread, as shoulders are bared in latter half century, and kerchief becomes a drape around top of bodice, or disappears.

Hair is parted above the ears; the center section is drawn back and coiled into a bun above the nape, the curled sides hang loose and lengthen, as collars descend and widen. In first third of century there are clipped bangs; these tend to become curled locks and to rejoin the side hair in the '40's, while the bun becomes more conspicuous and is decoratively enclosed.

Head Coverings are always reduced or eliminated in proportion to elaborate attention given to the hair itself. This was as true of the XVIIc. as it has been of the 1940's. Caps almost disappeared, and were restricted to widows or conventional bourgeoises, except in Holland, their home, where they clung to the back of the head. Again as in our own time, kerchiefs and hoods covered the hair out of doors; the XVIIc. hoods are round in form, tied under the chin with ribbons, and are usually dark. At this time the black mantilla began to be worn in Spain. With these head coverings, and with the great hats which were worn for riding, ladies were now accustomed to wear masks.

Shoes followed male rules.

Accessories: With the increase in use of ribbons and lace, fine aprons come into style, and great pieces of jewelry go out. Pearls, modest in quantity, are retained in chains, bracelets, pendants, earrings and hair decorations.

As sleeves shorten, c. 1640, long gloves and muffs appear. Nightgowns begin to be used. Fans, hanging watches and mirrors continue in use.

"Women's Maskes, Buskes, Muffs, Fanns, Perewigs and Bodkins were first devised and used in Italy by Curtezans, and from thence brought to France and from thence they came into England about the time of the Massacres in Paris," according to Stow. In 1575, Van Meteren said that "Englishwomen go about the streets without any covering, either of heuk or mantle, hood, veil or the like. . . . Ladies of distinction have lately learned to cover their faces with silken masks or visards and feathers." Patches have now begun to accompany these headcoverings; but lowering necklines and loose curls brought with them a variety of outer garments: cloaks with collars, gored in front and full behind; ample "lap-mantles" which completely covered the figure; many shoulder capes and kerchiefs; and little loose *casaques* or *sacques,* worn particularly in Holland and France.

1353. XVIIc. c. 1606. Flemish. (Florence, Uffizi.)

Att. to *F. Pourbus, y.* Henry IV.

Collars of Saint-Michel and Saint-Esprit worn with ermine-lined and collared robes, semé France modern; delicately pinked doublet sleeves; short wide hose, the loose lining of which scarcely shows between the paned straps. In XVIIIc. Mme. du Barry will demand that Louis XV reward her female chef for a magnificent dinner with the *cordon bleu* of the Saint-Esprit.

1354. XVIIc. 1602. French.

Léonard Gaultier. Henry IV, Gabrielle d'Estrées, César duc de Vendôme and Catherine Henriette de Bourbon.

Henry of Navarre needed nearly ten years to subdue and consolidate the France of which he became king following the assassination of Henry III in 1589. Opposed by the plots of Spain, the League, the Guises, Mayenne, Nemours and Joyeuse, the Protestant Henry IV fought for his great cities, one by one. In 1593 he was converted to Catholicism; the following year even Paris capitulated; but his Edict of Nantes assured security of worship and belief to the Calvinists.

In little more than a decade of peace (before he, too, was assassinated in 1610 by a Catholic fanatic whose act horrified all factions), Henry proved himself perhaps the greatest of French kings. He reorganized France and strengthened her alliances (as well as the position of his own Bourbon dynasty) with immensely resourceful and courageous energy, patient commonsense and a sympathetic interest in people of all sorts. His indulgent and astonishingly informal good-heartedness and gaiety and the quick audacious Gascon wit which colors his every word make him one of the most appealing of kings.

The government, finances and army were efficiently reorganized by Henry and his devoted minister, Sully. Great attention was given to communications: canals, roads and bridges, and to sanitation (which was particularly scandalous in Paris, with its celebrated mud which sticks like glue). He aided agriculture and established factories: Gobelins tapestry, silk, glass; protected and aided industry by laws and by commercial treaties with his many new allies, from Sweden to Italy. He built or completed important projects in Paris: the Hotel de Ville, Tuileries, Louvre, Palais-Royal and the Pont Neuf.

Lest he should marry his mistress, Gabrielle d'Estrées, Marguerite of Valois refused to divorce Henry IV during the many years of their amicable separation, but she did so in 1599, after Gabrielle's death, to enable Henry to marry Marie de' Medici and provide heirs to the throne.

Female: bangs frizzed at forehead, hair dressed high with jewelled ornament; fan collars; leg-o'-mutton sleeve reduced in size; drum-shaped skirt, with or without cartwheel top, supported by hip bolster; shoes with high cork lifts. Daughter: bonnet with c. massed decoration, like that worn by Henry III; lace-edged apron; seams closed by the favorite paired braid catches.

Male: hair fluffed and combed backward; ruffs and falling bands; doublets with short skirts, cut and overlapping, worn with diagonal blue sashes carrying the cross of the Order of the Saint-Esprit; short circular cloaks; short paned hose, padded into a horizontal bottom line; with canions and rosetted garters (boy); sword slung through a wide, decorated holster; high-crowned felt hats; with centrally placed decoration and cord hat-band; shoes with tongue tied over instep.

Until the large Dutch *kas* and French *armoires* begin to be incorporated into buildings, as closets, in XVIIIc., storage space is at a premium; trunks and chests are still convenient seats for the wearers of wide bolstered skirts.

1355

1356

1357

1355. Beginning XVIIc. French. (Paris. Carnavalet Museum.)

Unknown artist. The Troupe of the Gelosi.

This troupe of Italian comedians, headed by the lovely, learned and virtuous Isabella Andreini, played several times in France between 1576-1604, under Henry III-IV. They were so popular that favorite preachers found themselves without congregations. After playing at Fontainebleau for Marie de' Medici in 1601, the Gelosi were pensioned by Henry IV.

The 7 characters, dressed in the costume of the turn of the century, are Oration and Isabella, la Pascalina, il Magnifico, Signor Pantalone, and a burlesque acolyte and valet.

The Italian comedy returned to Paris about 1622 with the company of Isabella's son, Giambattista Andreini.

Women had appeared in mediaeval miracle plays, but during Elizabeth's time, female parts were played by boys. Coryat had heard of women playing in public in London, but actually saw such a thing for the first time in Italy in 1611. The popularity of Italian comedy led to the general use of actresses on the English stage in second half XVIIc. Old women's parts were still sometimes played by actors in France in third quarter XVIIc., as occasionally happens in burlesque in our own time.

1356. XVIIc. After 1610. French.

Giles Rousselet, after *Grégoire Huret.* Gros-Guillaume.

1357. XVIIc. c. 1661. French.

Simonin. Molière as Sganarelle.

This engraving of Molière, acting the lead in his own play, is the only existing portrait of him made during his lifetime.

The great English theatre antedated the great French theatre by two generations. The first important theatre in Paris was the Hôtel de Bourgogne (1628), whose actors, trained in provincial fairs like the Foire Saint-Germain, became permanent members.

Gros-Guillaume (the fat Robert de Guérin) was one of the favorites of the *King's Company,* as the Italian troupe was called after 1610, in honor of Henry's inadequate subsidy, which was substantially increased by Louis XIII.

A rival troupe, Mondory's *Marais,* set up in 1629, took its name from one of a series of tennis courts*, successively burned down, on which they played.

* See Appendix.

1358

1359

1360

1361

Supported by Richelieu, they produced Corneille's plays until the death of their leading actor; eventually their remnant members were joined with the travelling company which Molière brought to Paris in 1658. The Petit-Bourbon Theatre, where they played his *Précieuses ridicules,* was to be demolished; they refurbished the marvellous private theatre which Richelieu had built in his Palais-Royal, and as the *Troupe de Monsieur,* under the patronage of Louis XIV's brother, opened in 1661 with *Sganarelle, or the Imaginary Invalid.*

Louis XIV made Molière one of his valets-de-chambre; but the actor was snubbed by the officers of the king's household because of his profession. One morning the king invited Molière to eat his "en cas" (the tray of food left by the bedside when the king went to bed) with him. Each had a chicken wing, served by the king, who announced to his following: "You see me engaged in entertaining Molière, whom my valets-de-chambre do not consider sufficiently good company for them." (Mme. Campan).

1358. XVIIc. 1609-11. French, Nancy. (Met. Mus., Print Room.)

Claude de la Ruelle. Engraved by F. Brentel.
Pourtraict du convoy fait en pompe funèbre de Charles III de Lorraine, Part II.

Engravings of whole processions, coronations and funerals, become common in e.XVIIc., conveniently accompanied by text identifying the personages. The funeral procession of Henry IV's brother-in-law, widower of Claude of France, shows the mourning robes with liripipes which have been used in all countries for many centuries (English: "doole" robes).

Herald's tabards worn with band collars over long robes; Swiss guards in loose *pluderhose;* Charles' superbly caparisoned horse accompanied by 2 squires and 4 footmen; the Rhinegrave Frederick with bare sword; another Swiss; the Grand Master with baton; the Grand Chamberlain with a gold key; another lord.

1359. XVIIc. After 1610. French. (Turin, Pinacoteca.)
Att. to *F. Clouet.* Marguerite of Valois.
White mourning of queens.

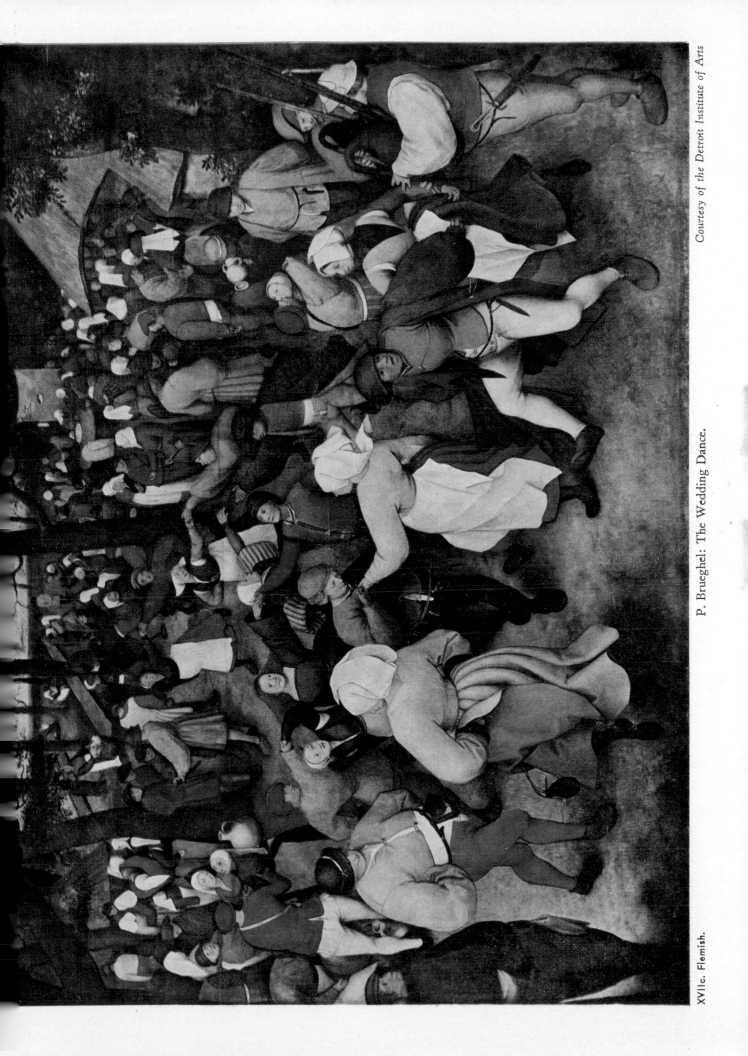

P. Brueghel: The Wedding Dance.

1360. XVIIc. c. 1615. Flemish. (Florence, Uffizi.)
F. Pourbus, y. Isabelle of Bourbon, Queen of Spain.

1361. XVIIc. Flemish. (Florence, Uffizi.)
F. Pourbus, y. Isabelle of Bourbon, Queen of Spain.

Henry IV's daughter, the 13-year-old bride of Philip IV, in French and Spanish dress.

French: fan collar; low-bosomed gown of delicately sprigged brocade pinked in a diapered pattern; simple modified leg o'mutton sleeve; shorter waisted bodice necessitated by cart-wheel topped skirt, which is typically without train; frizzed hair dressed high with jewelled ornaments; looped pearls.

Spanish: closed ruff; flowing brocade-lined outer sleeve; segmented puffing of inner sleeve; stomacher with long point; funnel-shaped skirt of large-pattern brocade with train, inverted-V opening over elaborately trimmed underskirt. Lace-edged handkerchief; magnificent jewels (which, as Regent, she later pawned to aid the armies of Spain).

1362

1362. XVIIc. Flemish. (Versailles, Nat. Mus.)
Unknown artist. Anne of Austria.

Philip III's daughter, married in 1615 to Louis XIII, was insulted and neglected during 20 childless years by her husband, by Richelieu, and by many of the great families of France. As Regent for her late-born son, Louis XIV, she banished many of these enemies, and through the tact of Richelieu's most able and charming successor, Cardinal Mazarin, lived in secure importance.

Marie de' Medici had 3 favorite dresses (Young: *The Medici*); among these was one which she wears in her portrait in the Uffizi and the Rijksmuseum, and which, in a refurbished form, served her daughter-in-law, Queen Anne (just as Anne of Denmark made use of the dresses left over from Elizabeth's wardrobe).

It was a blue velvet gown sown with gold fleurs-de-luce; its fleur-de-luce-shaped stomacher of ermine was decorated with amethysts surrounded by 4 clustered pearls; its plastron was filled by an immense amethyst cross with 3 pearl drops. With this gown, Anne wears a contemporary ruff, very wide and shallow, adroitly pleated out of petal-pointed lace; hair combed back and frizzed low over the ears in the new fashion.

1363

1363. XVIIc. 1610-17. Flemish. (Madrid, Prado.)
F. Pourbus, y. Marie de' Medici, widow of Henry IV.

The second Medici queen of France, brought up in the corrupt and murderous court of Francis of Tuscany and his unloved Austrian wife, carried an immense dowry to her marriage. She was a good-natured, stupid woman with a pink and blonde beauty (which Rubens admired) and beautiful taste in clothes. Regent 1610-1617 for her young son, Louis XIII, who was "as fit to reign as she," she was exiled by Richelieu in 1631. She escaped from Blois, fat as she had become, by being let down from a window; chose to live in poverty in Holland rather than to return to Florence; was chased out of Antwerp; and died in complete poverty in Cologne, a dependant of Rubens, whose patron she had been.

Widow's cap and veil in a reduced form of that worn by Catherine de' Medici, exquisitely pleated and wired out behind her petal-edged ruff, the same edging being used to border and fill in the decolletage of the bodice. The veil continues to be caught to the sleeve sections, as sleeves recede from the wrist and their paned fullness is formally caught about the arm. Skirt of delicately pinked satin shows the cartwheel top at about the end of its use. The ends of the veil, brought about the body from the elbow, are caught at the center of the skirt. Lace-edged handkerchief, and pearls.

1364. XVIIc. c. 1622. Flemish. (Metropolitan Museum.)

Rubens. Anne of Austria.

In the 1620-30's, the great fan-shaped ruffs are combined with flat kerchief and collar arrangements; following the same impulse, cuffs of deeply pointed lace emerge from behind straight-edged cuffs, both of which are in visible retreat away from the wrist. Uncovered hair loosening at the sides; pearl choker and ear drops; ribbon rosette at bosom; fur muff on lap.

1365. XVIIc. 1627-32. Flemish. (Metropolitan Museum.)

A. Van Dyke. Mlle. de Gottignies.

Painting in cosmopolitan Antwerp and in France, 1627-32, Van Dyke (or Dyck) produced portraits of German, French, English, Spanish and Flemish subjects.

This is the standard upper-class European gown, c.1630: loosening hair; fan-shaped ruff in process of falling into a lace collar; composite cuffs, double or triple, reaching high on the arm to give the appearance of a shortening sleeve; sleeve and waist tied about with ribbons, knots and rosettes; brocade less used, its patterns more delicate.

1366. Second quarter XVIIc. French. (Chantilly, Musee Conde.)

Philippe de Champaigne. Armand Jean du Plessis, duke-cardinal of Richelieu.

The Cardinal wears the Order of the Saint-Esprit; red biretta, mozetta and cassock, and lace-edged surplice, the fullness of which is finely pleated.

1367. XVIIc. 1629. French. (Boston, Museum of Fine Arts.)
Bosse after *St. Igny.* Cavalier.

1368. XVIIc. French. (Boston, Museum of Fine Arts.)
Bosse. Lady.

1369. XVIIc. 1633. French.

Bosse. Cavalier following the latest Edict.

Abraham Bosse (1602-76), son of a tailor and author of one of the first treatises on engraving, produced innumerable sets of illustrations, which are the great documents of French costume in second quarter XVIIc.: the history of the *Prodigal Son,* and other Biblical parallels; *Marriage in City and Country;* the *Five Senses;* and all manner of occupation, showing school rooms, artist studios, shoemakers, engravers, workmen and soldiers. In addition both Bosse and Briot engraved a great series of French male costume after St. Igny in 1629. Callot did such plates in 1617 and in 1632, and there are similar plates of Dutch cavaliers by Nolpe, after Quast, in the 30's. In latter half XVIIc., the costume plates of Picart, St. Jean, the three Bonnarts, Valk, Trouvain, and Arnoult are supplemented by information, both on costume and outdoor life, provided by the small figures in topographical scenes, maps and panoramas, views of celebrated buildings and gardens, fêtes and processions, such as those of Rigaud, Mariette, and the Perelles in France.

1367. Though the lace collar of the jacket is worn over the coat, the collar of this cassock is edged with an allied lacy scallop, since it is worn slung over the shoulders like a cape. The coat sleeve is set into the armseye in back, but is free of the body of the coat in front for ease, in the manner of the old pinned-on sleeve. Fur-edged and embroidered gloves; boots becoming more delicate, their heels and toes fitted into matching pattens.

1368. All the knowledge of wiring gained in the flowing veils and standing collars of the turn of the century culminates in this stylized headdress combined with collar.

1369. Four of Bosse's invaluable engravings show ladies and gentlemen before and after Louis XIII's edict of Nov. 18, 1633. This forbade the wearing, on shirts, breeches, cuffs, headdresses or any other linen, of cut work or embroidery in gold or silver thread, passementerie or lace, whether manufactured in or out of the kingdom. The edict had little effect, as Bosse's later engravings show. (See Appendix: Blum.)

The courtier's valet is carrying off his doublet with paned sleeves, his fine belt and ribbon-knotted breeches. These have been replaced by a short-waisted open doublet with sleeves open along the inseam, showing a good deal of untrimmed shirt-fullness; plain band collar, wide over the shoulders, trimmed only by its tasselled ties. A tiny rosette hangs, not from the ear, but tied to the hair; this favorite usage of the 20's, developed out of the hanging threads of the end of Elizabeth's reign, is continued in the rosettes tied to hanging locks of ladies' hair, particularly in the Low Countries. His boots have small reversed cuffs and plain boot-hose, but enormous spur leathers over the instep. Hat with low crown, its brim wreathed about with comparatively flat plumes, in a way which will become extremely important in the costume of Louis XIV.

1370. XVIIc. French. (Metropolitan Museum, Print Room.)

Bosse. "Marriage in the City": Return from the Christening.

1370. Fringed hair, combed back in the center into a bun at the back of the head, is much longer and beginning to cluster in curls at the sides. Lace nightcap and fur-collared dressing gown of the mother. Lady with muff (r.) clearly shows the remnant of the old pendant sleeve of the Spanish gown, slit up the inseam from elbow to shoulder (its lower half having been completely cut off), and its bottom corners caught together at the elbow by a bow, over the swollen inner sleeve; this gown has a wide lace-edged collar or kerchief, and is tied by a rosetted sash across a stomacher which matches the inner skirt. Woman with baby: lace-edged cloak with stiff collar must be worn back on the shoulders, since the kerchief or collar of the gown is always carried on top of the outer garment, by both men and women. Children: boy, still in diapers, wears skirts with a high-waisted doublet; his sister's hair and gown are miniature forms of adult wear.

1371

A. Bosse. Galerie of the Palace.

The Palais Cardinal, built by Richelieu, became the residence of Anne of Austria and her children after his death, and was henceforth known as the Palais Royal. It is constructed around a garden surrounded by galleries of 186 tiny shops, where books, jewelry and trifles are still sold as they were at the height of the Galerie's fashion. This print was inspired by Corneille's comedy, *La Galerie du Palais.*

The shop to the l. is that of the king's bookseller, Augustin Courbé; the book being sold is Tristan l'Hermite's *Marianne,* which the Marais troupe had offered with great success in 1636, in competition with the Théatre de Bourgogne production of the *Cid;* with frontispiece by Bosse, it has lately been published by Courbé.

In the middle is a mercer's shop, out of which grew our department store. The chartered fairs, of which Saint-Denis in Paris was the oldest (dating from VIIc.) had periodically supplied needs of all sorts, as merchants brought in the goods of Europe and even of the Orient, and the local shops were kept closed. By XIVc. it was impractical to allow great fairs within Paris. Various categories of meticulously licensed and regulated shops were set up; the mercers were allowed to sell a curious mixture of jewelry, notions, metal goods of all sorts, including swords and daggers, boxes and containers. Centuries of attrition have reduced *mercerie* from its original significance of general merchandise to its present level of small dry-goods and notions.

This was an age of reckless expenditure. Shopping became a major amusement, best in Paris; and best of all, in Paris, were the goods of these categories sold at the Galerie Mercière in the Palais. We see jewelry, fans, masks, gloves, muffs, caps, and the ribbon knots called *galants.* In the linen shop adjoining, are collars and cuffs and the band-boxes to hold them.

The edict of 1633 and that of 1634, which again forbade the use of satin and velvet, embroidery, and gold and silver stuffs, have obviously not been effective. But excess was beginning to bore the French. In 1645, the contrast between the Poles, at their embassy reception, and the simple ribbon-looped French costumes was noted by Mme. de Motteville.

Unknown artist. The Cries of Paris.

Permanent markets for all sorts of goods are being established, but the everyday needs of everyday people continue to be met by itinerant vendors, crying their wares, as only an occasional junk-man, or driver of an Easter flower wagon still does in New York. The Cries of cities like London and Paris will be popular subjects for prints for three centuries to come.

1372. 2: death to rats and mice. 3: cakes called *oubliés.* 4: hats. 5: hot pastries. 6: flints and steels. 8: handkerchiefs and collars. 9: sheet music.

1373. 1: Naples sand. 2: onions. 3: Holland cheese. 4. oranges and lemons. 5: hot chestnuts. 6: twig brooms. 7: vinegar.

1374. 1: stools. 2: iron utensils. 5: milk. 6: oysters. 7: grinder. 8: baskets.

1375. 7: *glands* tasselled band-strings for collars. 9: cherries. 10: broadsides.

1372

1373

1374

1375

1376. XVIc. 1643. Flemish. (Madrid, Prado.)

F. Pourbus, y. Anne of Austria as a Widow.

The mourning cap and enclosing veil, which we have seen wired out and drawn about the body in various ways, since Catherine de' Medici, is here gathered into the edge of the plastron of the bodice.

The drum-shaped skirt with a pleated top is retained, as majesty has always tended to retain effective old-established usages long after they have been given up elsewhere; but it is fastened by the currently fasionable ribbon bows and rosettes. The wired collar, too, has largely passed out of use, but is too effective, framed by the wired veil, to be given up by a widowed queen; it is set low on the neck, however, depressed by a pearl choker.

1377. XVIIc. French. (Turin, Pinacoteca.)

French School. A Daughter of Amadeo I.

Victor-Amadeus of Savoy, who had married one of

Louis XIII's sisters, had a number of daughters, the last of whom was born in 1636, and is probably the wearer of this gown, typical of the 1640-50's. Curls, massed at the sides, hanging low on the shoulders, are decorated like the gown with rosettes; neckline slipping low on the shoulders, horizontally banded bodice; sleeves short and cuffed; shirt sleeve caught with ribbon knot at wrist; as is often seen in male costume, ribbons of several widths are used, graduating down to the narrowest at the wrist; bodice point very long; skirts dragging in a train.

Loose bouquet of roses in a vase, at a time when paintings of flower and fruit arrangements begin to be seen.

PAINTERS OF MIDDLE AND LOWER CLASS DRESS, XVIIc.

Costume of the middle and lower classes is shown in the pictures prolifically produced by the brothers

Le Nain: Antoine, 1588?-1648; Louis, 1593?-1648; and Mathieu, 1607?-77; and by Michelin (1623-96). The French painter, Georges La Tour (1600-52), who worked in Holland as well, was chiefly preoccupied with the reflected glow of light, but his pictures show simple, middle-class French costume of great charm.

1378. XVIIc. French. (Paris, Pierre Landry.)
Georges La Tour. The Card Sharper.

The cut of costume is always explicit in La Tour's pictures, and even the simplest is apt to show a fine braid. These unusually elaborate Dutch costumes are full of rich, fresh detail: points hanging from the collar or as fringe from the armseye; beautifully embroidered shirts and collars; simple, wonderfully cut sleeves; unusual plumed turbans and hats. There is nothing quite like the clothing La Tour paints. I have always felt that, with the instincts of a great couturier, he eliminated a great deal of the clutter and impurity of line which actually existed.

1379. End of first half XVIIc. French. (Louvre.)
A. Le Nain. Family Reunion.

In these costumes, which show a strong Dutch influence, we see bows appearing, even on the instep of boots, toward the middle of the century. Both men and women show dangling side locks, which may be tied with bows, but women's hair is beginning to be wired out at the sides and hangs in corkscrew curls. Bands with tasseled strings no longer lie flat, but tend to rumple under the chin in the beginnings of the gathered cravat, as sleeves turn back into the beginnings of cuffs. The doublet grows shorter as the loose breeches of mid-XVIIc. are lavishly fringed with ribbon.

1380. XVIIc. French. (Paris, Paul Rosenberg.)
Mathieu Le Nain. The Feast of Wine.

1381. XVIIc. 1656. French. (Metropolitan Mus.)
J. Michelin. The Baker's Cart.

The costume of poor people is the least easy to date, based as it must be on comfortable garments of undramatic design, hand-me-downs from soldier days, and odd replacements, when it is not merely layers of rags.

Garments such as are shown in the Feast of Wine and in a companion picture (The Feast of the Bull), have been worn since the 30's, but the lacings around the breeches hem make it probable that they date from the end of the second third of the century.

1382. XVIIc. French. (Leningrad.)
Louis Le Nain. (Copy of The Bird Hunter.)

MEN'S DRESS, 1655-1715 (LOUIS XIV)

The doublet has only about another decade of life. It is now an open bolero-like garment, extremely short and with elbow-length cuffed sleeves. The shirt, full and soft, is bloused over the breeches (which now hang unsupported on the hips); below the short doublet sleeves, the shirt sleeve's fullness, pushed up and tied in puffs, is finished at the wrist by a ruffle. The collar hangs deep on the chest in an oblong which usually has rounded corners; it seldom lies quite flat and its tendency to buckle in the middle will become elaborated into gathered fullness; the collar turns into a cravat, *rabat*, by the 70's, worn with arrangements of ribbon bows above (later, underneath) or in the long negligent *steinkirk* form tucked into the vest in the 90's; *steinkirks* are worn also by women.

The breeches, already open, wide and decorated about the hem, are increased by gathering into several bulky forms of petticoat-breeches called *rhinegraves*: a petticoat, a divided skirt or full bloused pantaloons. These breeches are heavily decorated by ribbon loops, often hanging from the waistband below the bloused shirt, and characteristically massed at the hemline, particularly at the sides where the garter knot used to hang. There are elaborate combinations of these styles, as: a petticoat over longer pantaloons. The whole effect of multiplied horizontal ruffles is sometimes increased by another set called *cannons* (not the *canions* of XVIc.), fastened below the knee, reminiscent of the drooping boot-cuff and boot-hose, as boots are replaced by shoes with these garments. In the same spirit are stockings with very wide baggy tops, 1670-80.

Meanwhile the military cassock has been worn by almost everybody and has been found to be a most useful outer garment; about 1665 it begins to come into use as a collarless coat. The doublet, which has always been primarily an undergarment, now becomes a vest, at first sleeved; the sleeves may be long and tight, but are usually seen turned back in a cuff over the longer and wider cuff of the coat; as the vest tends to become sleeveless, its cuff effect may be retained as a piece of the vest material laid over that of the coat cuff.

With the new coats and vests of the 70's, narrower knee breeches, *culottes,* replace petticoat breeches; they become simple, closer fitting, closed by a few buttons or a buckled strap. Stockings are rolled to cover the knee strap or are drawn up smooth under it.

Coats, during their first decade of use, are cut rather straight like the cassock, reach to mid-thigh and are worn with waist-long vests; coat seams are unsewed below the waist though they may be closed by lines of buttons in the old ways. By the final quarter century, the coat is of knee length and increasingly shaped: a *justaucorps;* in the 90's its skirts are stiffened and widened by goring and by pleating at the seams.

The vest lengthens with the coat, though it is always a little shorter. While the coat stays open, the vest is closed throughout until the 90's when it opens to receive the ends of the steinkirk cravat; by mid-90's the vest is often buttoned only at the waist.

A vest, without the coat, is usual indoor wear; vests with sleeves are made especially for this purpose, and there are also dressing gowns. With all of these, the wig is apt to be doffed, and the clipped or shaved head protected by a *montero* or a nightcap.

The short coat sleeve of the 70's tends to lengthen, and to widen out below the shoulder, while its cuff grows wider, deeper and more important. Coat pockets originally followed the vertical or diagonal buttoned lines used on doublets; they come to be set horizontally, low on the skirts, and to climb higher, with heavy pocket-flaps, toward the end of the period.

Coats are of plain materials, increasingly edged and trimmed with metal galloon braids. Waistcoats and the turn-back to match them, which may appear on the coat cuff, are apt to be of brocaded material. Breeches are of the coat material or of black velvet.

With petticoat-breeches, boots are ousted by shoes, and rosettes by stiff bows. In final quarter of century, shoes close higher around the foot; round tongues become squared and very high during the 70's, tending to turn over and show another color. Square-cut toes, very long and narrow in the 70's, tend to shorten and the heavy red heels of the 70's to become higher and less clumping, as shoes become more delicate in the 80's and ribbon ties are replaced by small oval buckles, which in turn become squarer and larger in the XVIIIc.

Riding boots now have their cuffs turned up over the knee; the leg lengthens and becomes tubular; the tops tend to become smaller and to be cut away in back, and the quatrefoil stirrup-leather is replaced by a smaller rectangular one. The narrow *jack boots* are often closed by lines of buckles and there are similar *spatter-dash* leggings worn over shoes for riding. Cloaks go out of use, except for actual protection, as coats come into use.

Low-crowned, flat-brimmed hats begin to appear in latter half of century, growing wider-brimmed and more cocked in its final quarter; in the 90's, they become definitely tricornes, with an edge of metal galloon and an interior fringe of ostrich around the brim, replacing plumes. Caps continue to be worn in the home, and there are new fur-brimmed *montero* forms worn in the house or for riding.

Early in second half of century, parted wigs began to replace natural hair and are in universal use before the last quarter. These periwigs, at first imitating natural hair, become increasingly artificial; in the 70's their curls are carefully arranged; in the 90's they rise above the forehead in one or two peaks. During the century's final quarter they are sometimes seen tied out of the way in back, in the XVIIIc. fashion. Hair on the face disappears in last quarter of the century, not to be seen again until XIXc.

With the petticoat-breech costumes, ribbons are much used; in the final quarter century they still appear in a knot carried on the right shoulder. Wide sashes and baldrics continue in use to the XVIIIc., the baldrics becoming more elaborate.

Men's fashions are increasingly elegant, mannered and artificial. There is a great deal of what, on the stage, would be called "business," with wrist-ruffles and pockets. as hands manipulate handkerchiefs, snuff boxes, tall beribboned canes; men wear muffs hung by a scarf about the neck, and gloves become softer and simpler. carried as often as worn.

WOMEN'S DRESS, 1655-1715 (LOUIS XIV)

The analogies between male and female costume are much less evident during second half XVIIc., except in women's riding costume which is masculine in everything but its skirt.

While men are still wearing short doublets and petticoat breeches, women (although the little tabbed jackets lacing down the back still exist) re-appear in long-waisted bodices with a prolonged point in front.

Corsets are elaborately gored, and finished in a fringe of unboned tabs below the waistline: these are worn under the waistband of the underskirt, while the long-boned points of the front are carried out over the band.

Over these is worn a gown composed of a bodice and skirt. The neckline of the bodice becomes wider, more horizontal and tends to slip off the shoulders. Collars become a band of lace around the shoulders; and this formal band tends to become loose, draped and caught, scarf-like. Under the insistently moral influence of Mme. de Maintenon, shoulders become covered again, in the 80's, and the neckline approximately square. During the period of the beribboned male petticoat-breech, a ladder of ribbon knots, graduated in size, decorates the center line of women's long unified bodices. The bodice of the 80's is divided by its decoration into jacket and underbodice; the decoration, a collar or ruching, follows the front edges around the neck until they converge at a much shortened point a little below the normal waistline, and the V-opening thus outlined is filled by embroidery or brocade.

The full sleeves of the third quarter-century are often set on in careful pleats like those which join skirt to bodice; sleeves lose their inseam slit, tend to become shorter, showing more shirt puffs; but, again under the influence of Mme. de Maintenon, they become of elbow length, funneling from the shoulder and sometimes finished with a cuff, above increasingly lacy shirt frills.

The skirt of the third quarter-century, carefully pleated onto the bodice, has its center line marked by decoration, or open to allow the skirt to be looped up at the hips. Skirts had begun to trail in Van Dyke's portraits of the 90's; now both outer and inner skirts have trains, and these lengthen. The underskirt gains in importance and in flounced, petticoat-like decoration from the 80's. The caught-up overdress, heavier and more upholstered in the last decades, requires the support of whalebone, metal or basket-work *paniers* at the hips.

Women's shoes, with pointed toes and high, delicately shaped heels, are tied or buckled over the instep; they are often of embroidered or brocaded fabric.

As manners become freer, the "undress" worn at home receives more attention; loose uncorseted gowns, short fur-edged jackets and lacy capes are invented to be worn while receiving in boudoirs.

Loose hair at the ears tends to become bunched in curls in the 60's: these hang on the shoulders in the 70's and are heavily decorated with ribbon knots. There has always been a tendency to cover the bun of hair in back with some sort of cap; as the bunched ribbons now outgrow the hair in importance, they are combined with lace and fastened to the front of a sheer cap to form the fontange headdress of the 90's; the pleated height of this headdress increases so that it falls forward, in its late forms, to 1700. In e.XVIIIc., the cap, having lost its fontange front, becomes much smaller and concentrates on the ribbon lappets in back. Hair arrangement, at first wide, becomes higher and narrower as the fontange mounts, and like the periwig, is dressed in two horns in the 90's. In e.XVIIIc., hair arrangements are close and simple, and begin to be powdered.

Lacy hoods are worn in domestic undress, and hoods with shoulder-cape effects cover the elaborate fontange arrangements out-of-doors. Scarves, and shaped shoulder capes with long stole ends, are worn with the gowns of the last decades. Muffs continue in use. Aprons increase in importance and are worn through XVIIIc.; they may be white and lacy, but are often of colored silk or brocade, embroidered and trimmed with metal lace. Soft gloves of kid or silk in light colors become longer; mitts appear. Parasols are now common. Paint, patches, and perfume are used by both sexes. Elaborate jewels are largely supplanted by pearl chokers and eardrops; then, in French court use in the 90's, men's coats blaze with diamond buttons, and women's gowns are studded with immense diamonds.

The exquisitely put-together satin dresses of the third quarter-century are usually in pale colors: white, through ivory, to canary yellows. They are trimmed with white, gold, and a great deal of coral, in beads, gloves, and touches worked into gold bandings. These light colors were supplanted by darker, with the metal and fringe-trimmed, heavily upholstered brocade gowns of Mme. de Maintenon's time, which were, in turn, supplanted by light, pretty colors in XVIIIc.

The very large collections of Louis XIV costume plates in the Morgan Library and in the Museum of Fine Arts of Boston, include examples in which (thanks to an amusement of the Regency), the paper which represents fabric has been cut away, and the print backed by bits of contemporary brocades, of which we thus have many valuable samples.

1383. Second half XVIIc. French. (Paris, Carnavalet Mus.)

Fishermen's and Laundrywomen's Boats, Quai de la Mégisserie.

The Quai de la Mégisserie, built in 1369, got its name from the *mégisseurs* (lamb skin tanners) who then worked near-by. It is on the l. bank, above the Pont Notre Dame, with which Henry IV had bridged both branches of the river, across the upper end of the Ile de la Cité. In XVIIIc., water was still a commodity sold in the streets by 20,000 vendors, like the man we see, who will dip his buckets repeatedly in the river and dispose of 30-40 pails a day. (Saint-Evremond). Laundry was given out to be washed in the Seine and carried up the river to be dried on the Ile Notre-Dame, where it can be seen in Ill. 1297: the League procession. The sign on the fishermen's boat offers fat carp for 5 sols.

1384. Latter half XVIIc. French. (Paris, Carnavalet Mus.)

Fish sellers at the Halles.

The public markets had been removed from the Port de Grève, c.1135, to an open space; this became known as the Halles (halls) from 2 long sheds which were provided within a walled enclosure; and the fairs of St-Lazare and St-Germain were moved there by XIIIc. It had to be rebuilt in XIVc., when it changed from a market in which certain commodities were sold on given days, to the permanent market for all foodstuffs, which it still is.

In order to emphasize the importance of Versailles, Louis XIV visited Paris as infrequently as three times a year. Monsieur, his brother, illiterate and friendly, loved the Foire Saint-Germain and was adored by the common people, particularly the fish-wives of the Halles. He used the Opera as an excuse to visit his town house, the Palais Royal; actually, he was mad about ringing church bells. After Monsieur's recovery from an apoplexy, Saint-Simon tells us, "the fish-fags of the Halles thought it would be proper to exhibit their affection, and deputed four stout gossips to wait upon him (at Versailles). They were admitted. One of them took him about the neck and kissed him on both cheeks; the others kissed his hand. They were all very well received. Bontemps (first valet of the king) showed them over the apartments, and treated them to a dinner. Monseigneur gave them some money, and the king did also. They determined not to remain in debt, and had a fine Te Deum sung at St.-Eustache, and then feasted."

At the christening festivities of Louis XVI's first child, the boxes of the king and queen, traditionally assigned to the charcoal vendors and the fish women of the Halles, were found to be filled already; the indignant worthies were mollified by being seated on the stage with the rulers to watch the French comedians in *Zaire* and *Le Florentin*. (Mme. Campan.)

These traditions lasted as long as the monarchy. At the birth of the Dauphin, Marie Antoinette received a delegation of *dames de Halles,* though these were not fish-wives, in black silk gowns (the established full dress of their order) and diamonds, one of whom read off from the inside of her fan a speech written by La Harpe; they were dined, as in Louis XIV's day, with the maitre d'hotel presiding, wearing the king's hat. (Campan).

1385. Latter half XVIIc. French. (Paris, Carnavalet Mus.)

Farces in the streets of Paris, rue Saint-Antoine.

The rue Saint-Antoine was formed from the latter part of the Roman road leading S.E. out of Paris. This went from the Ile, by the Notre-Dame bridge and the market-port of the Grève, turned through the marshlands of the frequently inundated r. bank, to the higher land about Saint-Gervais, and out the great gate guarded by the XIVc. Bastille, the fortress from which the Grande Mademoiselle had fired the cannon which saved Condé's army in the rebellion of the Fronde, and in which the Man in the Iron Mask died in 1703.

Parisians have always loved to walk, observe and listen. As long as man can recall, they have lived and amused themselves on their streets, as in no other city; whether to saunter, to bargain, to dance, to watch fire-works, a balloon ascension, a public execution in the Place de Grève, or to follow a flogging at the tail of a cart, which would end at the pillory in the Halles.

The rue Saint-Antoine was the longest and widest dry and open space within the fortifications; it was therefore the favorite gathering place for crowds at tournaments, carnivals and masquerades. Saint-Gervais, the earliest part of the r. bank to be inhabited, had been settled in XIIc. by weavers, dyers, tanners and an overflow of Jews from the ghetto on the Ile; it has always had a working class and commercial population.

But the Knights Templar had settled there, and it had always had a connection also with the aristocratic heart of Paris, from which the road started, as well as with the port on which its industry depended. The old palace on the Ile had been outgrown as a royal residence in Charles V's time. Three kings had already lived in the XIVc. hôtel des Tournelles; but when Henry II was killed, in one of the tournaments which were held in the near-by rue Saint-Antoine during XV-XVIc., Catherine de' Medici ordered the Tournelles demolished. The site of the hôtel and its gardens became the Place Royale. (P. des Vosges.) The turbulence of the university students led many aristocrats to move there from the Ile. As the chateaux of the Loire were built, many moved away, but during XVIIc. the promenade of elegant carriages at carnival time was called the "cours Saint-Antoine." In XVIIIc. the bourgeoisie still gathered there to see the young people off on the 9-10 mile trip to the Bezons fair. (For dress description, see Ill. 1387.)

PICTORIAL FANS: XVII CENTURY

During second half XVIIc., fans painted with street scenes became fashionable. We reproduce 5 of 6 in the Carnavalet. Others, in the collection of Louis Serbat, are to be found in D'Allemagne (see Appendix). They show people in flight from a thunder storm at the chateau of Marly-le-Roi; the flower market on the quai near the Pont Neuf; and the bath-boats on the Seine, with the Louvre on the right.

The superiority of the standards of city life in mediaeval times, over those of the next three centuries, is not always realized. There was far more bathing in the Middle Ages than during XVIIc. Particularly in the German cities, there had been public bath houses since XIIIc.; these increased in number during XIVc., to 15 in Frankfort-on-Main, and 29 in Vienna, for instance. Coryat, in e.XVIIc., saw 13 inns in Lower Baden, with 300 hot baths, some of which had been in use since before the birth of Christ. The houses of the German bourgeoisie had bath rooms. In France, barber shops kept several tubs in the back room, and provided hot water, at least for male bathers.

Surgery became divorced from medicine in XIIc., when its practice was forbidden to the medical clergy. It was taken over by barbers, who also pulled teeth. The foundations of modern surgery and dentistry were the XVIIIc. schools of anatomy of the Drs. Hunter, who "helped to make" English surgeons "gentlemen," though Prussian officers of the XIXc. still expected to be shaved by the regimental surgeon.

Stow says soap was not made in London till about 1518, but there was imported Castile soap, or a "grey soap, speckled with white, very sweet and good, from Bristol, sold here for a penny the pound . . . and black soap for a halfpenny."

The mingling of sexes and ages at the public baths led to abuses, and they came to have a bad reputation, being attacked by both Protestants and Catholics during the religious fervors of XVIIc. As populations increased, supplies both of water and of the wood for heating it, became inadequate; syphilis was new and virulent; there were epidemics of plague and smallpox. Horror of the public baths became attached to the very act of bathing, and people lived in actual fear of water.

In third quarter XVII., tubs the size of a footbath began to be set in the small *entresols,* which made convenient dressing rooms. By second quarter XVIIIc., complete bath rooms began to be installed in chateaux, with tubs large enough for actual bathing, and comfortable arm-chairs with movable seats were set over chamber-pots. Water closets were a fascinating novelty to the provincial gentry, when the Cardinal-Archbishop de La Rochefoucauld, on a rare visit to his palace, had them installed at the end of a corridor.

Public hot baths began to be re-established in England in last quarter XVIIIc. (in England called *bagnios,* a word which, like the older word for hot baths, *stews,* came again to have disreputable connotations). But there had always been floating baths, wherever there were rivers, such as the curtained boats on the Seine (shown on a Serbat fan), or the baths established at the Porte Saint-Bernard.

1386

1387

1386. XVIIc. 1660. French. (Paris, Carnavalet Mus.)

Poultry and bread markets, Quai des Grands-Augustins.

The oldest of the Paris Quais was that of the Augustins, the "road on the Seine" of 1313.

1387. XVIIc. 1680. French. (Paris, Carnavalet Mus.)

Playing-card factory in a house on the Place Dauphine.

The Seine banks were constantly being restricted and raised, and the small islands consolidated. When the Pont Neuf was being thrown across the upper end of the Ile de la Cité, 2 small islands above it were filled in and incorporated with the Cité. In honor of the future Louis XIII, the new space was called the Place Dauphine; it is still lined with houses built in his time. The Ile Louviers, below the Ile Saint-Louis, was made part of the right bank in XIXc.

By 1698, the Place Dauphine teemed with itinerant quack doctors and dentists, and the pedlars and street musicians drawn by their customers.

In the factory, we see cards being glued and pressed, stencilled, dried, cut, packaged and sold. Through its open windows are the statue of Henry IV and the Pont Neuf; the Louvre on the right; the College Mazarin (now the Institut) on the left, occupying a site for which the Tour de Nesles was demolished.

The costume of midXVIIc., as shown in Ills. 1383-87, was good-looking and practical; the working people shown on these fans wear it with little alteration from the time of the Cries of Paris (Ills. 1372-75) through the century, at the end of which the fontange headdress appears on women, as on court ladies. The women, working out of doors, have always liked covered heads, and find the loose hoods pretty and useful, though many still wear a kerchief; they have worn aprons and tucked up their skirts, long before these usages became fashionable. Male hair lengthens; becomes wig-like; and, as wigs come into universal use (even by monks and priests, with a false tonsure), the coarse goat or horsehair wigs of working men may even be powdered, as we see in the playing-card factory. Hat brims widen and become cocked; coats lengthen and become narrower; and cravats with ribbon bows beneath are worn by the workmen as well as by the elegant customer buying a pack of cards.

1388

7 6 5 M A C L

1388. XVIIc. 1660. French. (Versailles, Nat. Mus.)
Designed by *C. Le Brun*. Gobelins Tapestry.
History of the King: Interview of Louis XIV and
Philip IV of Spain at the Isle of Pheasants.

In 1660, despite Louis XIV's infatuation with
Maria Mancini, niece of the cardinal, Anne of Austria was able to bring about her dream of the marriage of her son to the only daughter of her brother.

Philip IV, his court, and an immense procession
escorted Maria Theresa to the frontier, where they
were met by the French court on an island in the
Bidassoa. The Spanish ladies travelled in 18 horse-
drawn litters, the courtiers in 70 state carriages; there
were 70 magnificently trapped horses, 900 saddle
mules and 2000 other mules, 75 of which carried
Spanish fabrics and luxury items belonging to the
Infanta.

The dramatic contrast between the frizzed French
courtiers in their lace cravats and gay, beribboned
costumes and the dank-locked, somberly dressed
Spaniards, brought to a sudden end the parochial development of Spanish costume; henceforward Spanish dress, like that of the rest of the world, will be
basically French.

Wigs had been in use at the French court for 40
years. Louis XIII was bald, and adopted a wig after
the Abbé de la Rivière appeared at court in a long
blond one in 1620. A decade after his wedding,
Louis XIV starts to go bald in his turn, and finally
takes to the wigs he dislikes. Many of the courtiers
wear unmistakable wigs, with their beribboned
rhinegraves, so brilliant and unexpected in color that
they may well be itemized; c. to l.:

Louis XIV: gold costume, banded in darker gold;
cascades of cherry-colored ribbons; white shirt and

cannons; flesh stockings; yellow shoes with high
tongues, wide stiff pleated bows, soles and high heels
of red; brown hat, cherry plumes.

Cardinal: red.

Anne of Austria: green gown, gold lace at shoulders; white above caught with green rosette.

Monsieur (Louis' brother Philip, duke of Orleans):
gold cape; yellow costume; cherry ribbons; pink
stockings; yellow shoes with red ribbons; hat and
plumes of shaded pink.

5: Gold cape; light blue costume, banded in red-
selvaged gold, and laced with blue-green ribbon;
white shirt, gold lace wrist-ruffles; pink stockings;
brown shoes and bows, red heels; hat of neutral felt
with blue cock feathers.

6: White wig; blue coat laced with red-striped
gold, short-sleeved, with gold cuffs and gold lace
ruffles beneath; cherry-colored shoulder knots and
other ribbons; red petticoat over white petticoat
breeches; yellow stockings and shoes with blue
pleated bows.

7: Dark greenish-gold cape and rhinegraves; brown
ribbons; blue stockings; dark green shoes and bows.

On the Spanish side of the tapestry, Philip IV, blond
and wigless, is dressed in gold-laced blue-gray, lined
with deeper blue; wrist ribbons and stockings to
match; heelless pink shoe with a cork lift and a tiny
bow, such as is worn by all his courtiers. These are all
cloaked, with the green cross of Alcántara or the red
of Santiago, and wear natural hair, golillas or the old
ruff; close doublets; narrow breeches gartered with
small knots; some with wrinkled stockings and
square-collared capes of Flanders.

The bride wears a quilted white or silver gown
and coiffure familiar in so many Velasquez portraits.

1388 A

French Engravers: XVII Century

As the fashions in portraits change, showing
little more than hair and collars, a new source of
information fortunately appears. Prints of views
of gardens, fêtes, and architecture become extremely popular everywhere. They show in detail not only the costume but the means of trans-
portation and the entire outdoor life of the various quarters. They often celebrate new buildings
or important events; such things as the disappearance of former landmarks all help in dating the
costumes of the small figures which fill the foreground. The name of the engraver, of the publisher, and the address from which they were sold
may also be useful in dating costume.

However, there were whole dynasties of interrelated engravers, like the Perelles: Gabriel (1603?-
77); Nicolas (1631-aft. 1678) and Adam (1640-
95), and publisher-engravers like the Mariettes
(four generations, among them Jean (1654/60-
1742) and Pierre Jean (1694-1774), one of whom
married the widow of the publisher Langlois,
after his death in 1647, and continued business
under Langlois' name at the same address. Luck-
ily, the attendant text is often helpful.

1388A-1388B. XVIIc. c. 1660. French.

Jean Marot. Triumphal Entry of Their Majesties,
Louis XIV and Marie-Thérèse.

Through XVIc., ladies and ecclesiastics might
travel in carriages, but gentlemen rode on horseback;
when too ill to ride, they stayed at home rather than
be conveyed.

During the reign of Louis XIV, however, carriages
began to be more comfortably suspended on straps,
and in late XVIIc. on steel springs; male prejudice
against them began to vanish. Public carriages grew
rapidly in favor. London had them from 1625, and
the 50 permitted in 1635 had grown to 700 by 1694,
despite the competition of sedan-chairs. The French

1388 B

"fiacre" got its name from the Sign of St. Fiacre,
where carriages were first to be hired in midXVIIc.
Paris. In last half XVIIc. stage-coaches began to
make regular runs. By XVIIIc. carriages were becoming a luxurious necessity, and so personal, that one's
empty carriage with its coach- and foot-men could
be sent to funerals as a mark of esteem,

But into XIXc. some gentlemen always preferred
to ride, as Louis does on his entry into Paris after
his wedding.

1389. XVIIc. 1664. French.
Israel Silvestre. Les Plaisirs de l'Ile Enchantée,
Versailles: entry of Louis XIV as Roger.

1390. XVIIc. 1670. French.
"Festival ad capita annulumque de cursio a rege
Ludivico XIV:" armiger, Ephoebus, Americani.

LOUIS XIV AND VERSAILLES

Under Louis XIV, the woods in which his father
loved to hunt were transformed by Mansart and the
landscape architect Lenôtre into the great palace
and gardens of Versailles, which became the official
court in 1682.

$100,000,000 were spent on buildings, landscaping
and water supply. The water-works were inspired by
Fouquet's chateau at Vaux; but Versailles was so
poor in water that new water works were built at
Marly to collect water from as far away as Rambouillet (30 mi. from Paris) by 98 miles of aqueduct;
even then, all 1400 fountains could be played only
for the greatest fêtes. Fouquet was the minister under whom (as Colbert proved to Louis) only half
the tax revenue reached the Crown. In the king's
honor, in August 1661, Fouquet gave at his magnificent Chateau of Vaux one of the greatest entertainments in the history of France, at which Molière's
Les Facheux was performed for the first time, and
the banquet was supervised by the chef, Vatel. Three
weeks later, Fouquet was in prison for life, Lenôtre was Louis' gardener, and Versailles was to
come.

The Grand Canal, on which gondolas floated and
fire-works were reflected, was a mile long and 200
feet wide; smaller basins had fountains with 50-70
foot jets. Along the canal ran the *Tapis Vert,* the
endless lawn with its avenues of trees, off which
were groves of clipped yew.

Versailles was not the wanton extravagance into
which it deteriorated with Louis XV, but the perfectly executed expression of a profound philosophy.
With the aid of Versailles, Louis detached his court
from Paris and his nobility from their feudal, provincial roots. Here, each had his station below the
princes of the blood (as they were below the king)
but above someone else; constant effort was necessary to maintain and improve this position. Punctual
daily attendance on the king was required, service in

1390

his regiments, magnificent clothing and entertainment, gambling for high stakes. All this drained the
resources of the nobles, who were then dependant on
the king for preference, perquisites, pensions, ad-
vantageous marriages, and the advancement of their
children. Almost total support of the largely tax-exempt feudal nobles was assumed by the king. Tax
burdens of unimaginable weight and complication,
in addition to their feudal dues, were laid on the
common people. Much of France, owned by 25,000
noble families, mortgaged and bled by its absentee
owners, returned to wilderness. For lack of seed and
equipment, tenant farmers who looked more like
lumps of dung than human beings, starved on buck-
wheat (or even hay) and water; any amelioration in
their condition brought on fresh tax impositions.
Even farmers who owned land abandoned it to beg
in towns, or to emigrate, if they were not first caught
and sent to the galleys. Hordes of state functionaries

1391

took over the duties formerly performed by the feudal nobility, leaving them no occupation but daily hunting. Their exclusive hunting rights, originally ceded in return for their responsibility for the protection of their people from marauding animals, became fantastically distorted. Now, it is the animals who are protected and must be allowed to destroy crops, even kitchen gardens, without providing a mouthful of meat to the starving farmers.

Louis' policies gave France an efficient, centralized government, a uniformed and disciplined army, high standards of manners and elegance, and immense prestige abroad. The good and evil that grew out of these policies in the century which culminated in the Revolution are classically portrayed in Taine's "Ancien Régime," 1876.

"Who is he? He is a man that I never see," was a sentence which struck terror, as Louis intended. "The nobility has become another people with no choice left it but to crouch down in mortal ruinous indolence, which renders it a charge and contemptible, to go and be killed in warfare subject to the insults of clerks, secretaries of the state and the secretaries of intendants," said Saint-Simon.

To ameliorate the monotony of the rigidly disciplined court existence, Louis provided periodic shifts to other chauteaux, like Saint-Germain, and Marly (where one went only by invitation, and where etiquette was somewhat relaxed). There was much hunting, and all sorts of special entertainments in a court of which the manners and beauty were the wonder of the world. Since Marly was destroyed during the Revolution, Mme. Campan took pains to leave a description of its architecture, life and dress. Marly degenerated into an almost public gambling place. His hospitality, abused by all sorts of uninvited daily visitors, became an immense drain on the private purse of Louis XVI, who detested gambling. Marie Antoinette preferred the Trianon, and Marly was little used in last half decade of the reign.

Before Versailles was habitable, great fêtes began to be given there, in the finished portions of its gardens. One of the first was that of 1664, officially in honor of the king's mother and wife, but actually for the duchess of La Vallière, which was staged by Molière with music by Lully. In other pageants, the princes played Turkish and Persian potentates. In the 1670 illustration, we see the court version of another exotic, the American Indian (see Ills. 1389-90).

1391. XVIIc. French. (Met. Mus., Print Room.)
  J. Bérain (1639-1711), engraved by Ia. le Pautre

(1618-82). *Ornaments inventez par J. Bérain.*

This strange procession of fanciful costumes "invented" by Bérain shows dress suitable for court masquerades. We learn from the "Mercure" which describes the costume worn at court events, of Berain's difficulties in producing at short notice the 8-10 different disguises into which the Dauphin changed during one masquerade in 1683.

These clothes show a mixture of styles, some of which date from late XVIc. Odd slashings and puffings occur, with breeches of all sorts: loose, close-fitting and petticoat forms. The current long coat appears with others whose divided and diagonally finished skirts stem from those like Sir Philip Sidneys in Oliver's XVIc. miniature (see Ill. 1200). There are fan collars from e.XVIIc., falling ruffs, band collars wide on the shoulders, and collars never seen on any man before. The women's gowns have the tasseled, upholstered look of Louis XIV dresses.

1392

1392. Third quarter XVIIc. French. (Florence, Uffizi.)
Pierre Mignard. La Marquise de Sévigné.
For details of dress, see Ill. 1393.

Mme. de Sevigne and Her Times

The 1700 enchanting letters of Marie de Rabutin-Chantal, Marquise de Sévigné (1626-96), and the scandalous and witty *Histoire amoureuse des Gaulles,* of her cousin, Bussy-Rabutin, are among the greatest sources of information about French upper-class existence in latter half XVIIc.

The most accomplished letter-writer who ever lived (granddaughter of "Sainte" Chantal, the friend of St. Francis de Sales), the marquise was orphaned at 7. Fortunately, her guardian, an abbé-uncle, whom she called "Le Bien Bon," not only was an excellent business man who increased her fortune, but brought her up in a circle of important literary men. She was married at 18 to a Breton nobleman of no great fortune, whom she loved, and by whom she had two children; he spent her money, had many mistresses, but she never remarried after his death in a duel over one of them, "La Belle Lolo," when she was 25.

The marquise was affectionate towards her son, but doted almost insanely on her daughter, to whom she wrote daily letters whenever they were apart. The daughter married an elderly man who was for many years governor of Provence.

Madame de Sévigné's life was passed in the country at her husband's ancestral chateau, Les Rochers; after his death, much of her time was spent in the circle of the Hôtel de Rambouillet, and later in her own Hôtel Carnavalet, as the friend of Descartes, Pascal, La Rochefoucauld, Corneille, Saint-Evremond and of Mme. de La Fayette, whose *Princesse de Clèves* was the first great French novel.

Madame de Rambouillet, finding the life at court vulgar and dull, had begun, at 19, to gather around her the greatest literary men of Paris, mixed with the best of the aristocracy. She remodelled her hôtel for the purpose of holding great receptions, providing many smaller rooms for conversation, which she made the great art of the middle XVIIc. It was in satirizing her many and lesser imitators that Molière wrote his *Précieuses ridicules.*

Mme. de Sévigné, in those newspaperless days, recounts with the greatest gaiety, gusto, wit and detail, the occurrences, trivial or important, amongst servants, country neighbors, gossiping and intriguing courtiers, or the greatest philosophers; whether her transplanted Paris footman rebels at helping to get in the hay in the country; or Condé's chef, the great Vatel, commits suicide when the fish is late for dinner on Louis XIV's visit to Chantilly.

These were the days of great gardeners (like the English Tradescant) and chefs who were people of importance in their own right. Sauces were named after chefs, like Béchamel; dishes after great lords, who often collaborated in their invention: Soubise, or even the Earl of Sandwich, too busy as Lord of the Admiralty to eat more than meat between bread. With the Revolution, the gardens built for the aristocracy will become public parks, and the chefs whose masters have been guillotined, will work in inns or open restaurants, where any citizen with the price can and does, for the first time, eat like a lord.

Mauy important new usages date from Mme. de Sévigné's exact period. She was the first person to make coffee her beverage, although she underestimated its possibilities, since she indicated her preference for Corneille by saying, "Racine will pass, like coffee." The dramatic struggle of the forbidden painted India cotton fabrics was reinforced by her adoption of them.

In 1668, she bought her son Charles a commission in the Dauphin's Gendarmes, when service in Louis XIV's new companies of guards became an expensive fashion which it cost even more in royal favor to avoid.

Charles de Sévigné, like his father before him, and better men such as La Rochefoucauld and Saint-Evremond, had been the lover of the ageless and wonderful Ninon de l'Enclos, leader of fashion in her day, friend of Voltaire, Mme. de Maintenon and Mme. de La Fayette. After leaving the army, Charles and his childless wife became extremely religious, and both died cloistered. Mme. de Sévigné, the daughter who would not go to her mother for fear of infection, and the daughter's heir, all died of smallpox within a few years of each other.

1393. Third quarter XVIIc. French. (Metropolitan Mus.) *Unknown artist.* Hortense Mancini, Duchess of Mazarin.

The gown of third quarter XVIIc. (seen in Ills. 1392-93) is still frequently of satin, but brocade is also used, and brocade-like designs sometimes scroll the bodice, which is simple in cut and smooth. The pleating which connects the skirts to the bodice is turning into gathers.

A deliberate negligence affects the neckline and sleeves. The bodice, cut to expose the shoulders and breasts, is finished with an informally gathered lace frill, or may expose that at the top of the chemise. The ropes of pearls or the scarves which edge it are caught with increasing asymmetry, and frequently trail from one side. Sleeves lose their formal cuff and set pleating at the armseye; they are loose, turned-back, pushed-up, or caught by small brooches above an increasing display of puffed and ruffled chemise sleeve.

Hair widens at the ears and is eventually held out by wiring; a love-lock hangs on the shoulder. Ropes of pearls are negligently wound through the hair, which is generally uncovered. In France as plumes abound on courtiers' hats, headdresses of ostrich tips are seen on great ladies.

THE MANCINIS

Cardinal Mazarin had 5 beautiful nieces and a nephew, the Duke de Nevers. Laura, the eldest (1636-57), married Henry IV's grandson César, Duke of Vendôme, who became a priest in despair at her premature death. Olympe became the countess de Soissons. Marie, with whom Louis XIV had been so much in love, married the jealous Prince Colonna.

Hortense, the loveliest of all, was proposed by Henrietta Maria as a wife for Charles II, because of her dowry of 4 million livres. Both Mazarin and Charles refused the match, which the king found beneath his dignity. In 1661, at 15, she was married to a duke who inherited Mazarin's fortune, after assuming his arms and name. He, too, was frantically jealous and travelled constantly with his wife to keep her away from king and court. Leaving him, she continued to wander over Europe, travelling with her brother, with the Chevalier de Rohan, or with her sister Marie, in whose company she was arrested in Aix-en-Provence, both women dressed as men. Finally, she settled in England, where Charles wished to make her his official mistress, but she accepted a less royal lover.

For all her love of hunting, racing, cock-fights and gambling, Hortense Mancini was also the intelligent and witty friend of eminent philosophers. "Mme. de Mazarin is no sooner arrived in any place, when she sets up a house, and all the other houses are forsaken for hers. One finds there the greatest possible freedom; one lives there with like discretion" (Saint-Evremond). "She had, after all, balance and economy even in wasting her qualities and her gifts. . . . She lived and died a great lady" (Sainte-Beuve: *Causeries du lundi,* Oct. 28, 1849). French literature abounds in references to her, with "the longest, the finest, and the thickest hair in the world," attended by her little Negro page, Pompée, the thieving, drunken little rascal, pampered and torn by jealousy, who tried to keep everyone else away from her.

Hortense's fascination for Evelyn is visible through every disapproving entry in his diary, from his first dinner in the company of "the famous beauty and errant lady," at the Lord Chamberlain's in 1676, to her death in 1699.

Her youngest sister was Marie-Anne, the pet of the court of France, who married Turenne's nephew, the Duke de Bouillon. Her husband, too, had cause for jealousy, and she, too, travelled in Italy with her brother and visited her sister in England. Like Hortense, she was extremely intelligent and aided and encouraged literary men, notably La Fontaine.

DEVELOPMENT OF MILITARY UNIFORMS

Kings and great feudal nobles had always been surrounded by bodyguards composed of gentlemen. During the XVc., these will be seen, increasingly, wearing the badges and colors of their lords. Stow says that William Paulet, Henry VIII's treasurer, who died Marquis of Winchester in 1572 (at the age of 100), "kept gentlemen and yeomen in a livery of Reading tawney"; and Thomas, Lord Cromwell, "a greater number in a livery of grey marble; the gentlemen garded with velvet, the yeomen with the same cloth, yet their skirts large enough for their friends to sit upon them." "The late (16th) Earl of Oxford . . . within these 40 years . . . hath . . . ridden into this city, and to his house by London Stone, with 80 gentlemen in a livery of Reading tawny, and chains of gold about their necks, before him, and 100 tall yeomen in the like livery, to follow him without chains, but all having his cognizance of the blue boar embroidered on their left shoulder." By 1633, Evelyn's father, on becoming sheriff of Sussex and Surrey, will have his 116 servants and numerous gentlemen "every one liveried in the same garb" with green satin doublets, although this is a striking novelty, at that level.

The organization and subdivision of these bodyguards of the nobility began in XVc. Louis XI had married Mary of Scotland; Scottish archers, aiding France during the 100 Years War, were added to 2 companies of the *gardes du corps*. In England, Henry VII was establishing the Yeomen of the Guard about his person. In XVIc., Francis I increased his permanent guard to 8,000 and Henry VIII added the Gentlemen Pensioners (see Ill. 1467).

As the power of kings over feudal nobles increases, we see display, paid for by feudal lords, exploited for crown benefit. Matthias of Hungary's wedding invitation includes a "little pattern of a man" to be followed by the guests in outfitting their retainers, to give an impressive uniformity to the emperor's procession.

While Louis XIV sucks all France into Versailles and makes an army career almost a requirement for a young gentleman, troops are outfitted at the expense of their officers. In last quarter XVIIc., taxes begin to be levied to outfit and keep permanent standing armies at the expense of the population.

Coryat describes the various guards of the French king in 1609: 1600 foot-guards with musket, arquebus and pike, 200 of which are stationed at a time before the Louvre; 50 archers at the gate; a bodyguard of 400 archers and arquebusiers, of whom 100 are Scotch; 500 Swiss outside the gate and 100 with halberds and swords inside the hall. The archers of the bodyguard wore long-skirted, half-sleeved coats of white with skirts of mingled red and green, their bodies protected, fore and aft, by plain silver mail. The Swiss wore no coats, but paned doublets of red, yellow and blue, with puffs of yellow sarcenet between the panes, and colored cod-pieces.

The Scottish archers of the French crown were augmented in the 1630's by the *régiment d' Hébron,* raised by the Scotch Catholic soldier of fortune, Sir John Hepburn. Commanded by Ormond and other members of the Douglas family, these Scotch soldiers were returned to the British service in 1669, becoming the Royal Scots Fusiliers. Until disbanded in 1791, the Scotch guard in France was recruited, as far as possible, from Frenchmen of Scotch descent.

Aside from the *Suisses* in their traditional costume, Louis XIV's military establishment was dressed in the red, blue and white Bourbon colors: bodyguards in silver-laced blue coats, red breeches and black boots; blue companies of cavalry; red companies of light horse and gendarmes; mounted grenadiers; and the black and gray musketeers, who were named not from the colors of their uniforms but of their mounts. Officers, who had heretofore dressed pretty much after their own taste, began to wear scarlet uniforms with gold trim and silver scarves; color-bearers white; non-commissioned officers blue; soldiers gray trimmed with silver, with ribbon knots (differing in color by companies) on the shoulder—a usage out of which epaulettes developed. Hunting costume came under the influence of uniformity. Those who hunted the wolf with the Dauphin wore bright bright blue coats, laced with gold and silver, red waistcoats, blue breeches, boots, gold-fringed gloves and white-plumed hats.

Power had been consolidated in France while England was still recovering from civil war. The French army, both in the establishing of new units and forms and in their costuming, leads Europe by several years.

Red and blue, as common and fast colors, were most used in English uniforms. Anthony Wood noted quarrels between meanly dressed companies of russet and of blue-clad foot-soldiers at Oxford, October 2, 1642, and a reissue of smarter clothing in the next year.

The huge parliamentary army, though disbanded, was a constant worry to the restored Stuarts. They increased the number of troops they supported from 5,000 to 30,000, adding new regiments and categories of soldiers: Monk's Life Guards in scarlet tunics, blue collars and "bearskins," (later the Coldstream Guards); His Majesty's and the Duke of York's Guards, in red and blue respectively; the Queen's Own troop of cavalry; the Old Buffs (named from the buffalo leather of their accoutrements); the Scotch Fusiliers; the dragoons in "red coats and clokes" who, while in training at Oxford for service against the French, shot Dalby the tailor's wife through her privy door (Wood, January, 1679); and the "new sort of soldiers" described by Evelyn (June 29, 1678), destined to oppose those formed two years earlier in France, "called *Grenadiers,* who were dexterous in flinging hand grenades, everyone having a pouch full; they had furred caps with coped crowns like Janizaries, which made them look very fierce, and some had long hoods hanging down behind, as we picture fools. Their clothing being likewise piebald, yellow, and red."

Hitherto troops have lived off the land, been billeted on the populace, dressed by their officers, disciplined by and responsible to no one by law. The proliferation of these unsanctioned troops under James II caused Parliament, in 1688, to take over the control and support of the large army which was required overseas, and to formulate its discipline. Outside of this new militia, only the Yeomen of the Guard and the Gentlemen Pensioners remained as the king's bodyguard, unaffected by the new martial laws and Mutiny Act, which formed one of the basic changes in the British constitution.

DEVELOPMENT OF TEXTILE INDUSTRY IN FRANCE

Louis XIV's devoted minister, Colbert, envied the industrial development of England and Holland, and took the most energetic measures to encourage and improve French manufactures. Colbert listed the imported goods which could be made in France, encouraged foreign factories to move to France, and forbade French workmen to leave the country. About 100 establishments, including the Gobelins tapestry factory, were opened under the patronage of the crown. He set up rigid standards of quality, and punishments for failure to meet them. Duties on such goods as lace, fine materials, and knit stockings were doubled and tripled; eventually the import of Venetian lace and other goods which interfered (by being better) with the consumption of French manufactures, was completely prohibited. This enmeshed France in a governmental bureaucracy from which it has never escaped, but it did succeed in establishing France as a pre-eminent producer of textiles and of fine laces: needlepoints such as Point de France, d'Alençon, Argentan, Sedan, and pillow laces like Valenciennes.

Colbert also re-established in 1664 the *Compagnie des Indes,* which Richelieu had formed in 1642. It traded out of Pondicherry on the Coromandel coast, in amity with the nearby English, but hopelessly hampered by Colbert's endless regulations.

Its principal return cargoes were of India cottons, intended primarily for hangings and upholstery. These were a revelation to all Europe: so crisp and cool, easily cleaned, enchantingly pounced and painted, and in the early days so very cheap. Everyone fell in love with them, from their first appearance at the Foire Saint-Germain in 1658. The poor, in the hot port towns in the south of France where the *toiles* entered, wore nothing else. The aristocrats with a taste for the exotic (aped by Molière's *Bourgeois Gentilhomme* in 1670) had *Indiennes* made up into dressing gowns. Mme. de Sévigné brought some to her daughter from Marseilles in 1672. By the final quarter of the century they were universally worn by the bourgeoisie.

To protect the weaving industries, the importation or imitation of *toiles* was forbidden in 1681. They went temporarily out of fashion, as we learn from a poem in an almanac of 1861, in which a girl who has "retailed prints to small and great" laments that she must quickly find a place in the service of "the ladies created by her *toiles.*"

In 1685, however, the arrival of a shipload of India cottons ruined the woolen goods market, and sent the weavers out on strike. Except during 1695-8, when their import was allowed, by way of bolstering up the shaky *Compagnie des Indes,* the next seventy-five years provided 24 further prohibitions, with increasingly severe penalties of fines, jail sentences and confiscation. In 1736, in addition to the loss of the garment, there was a fine of 3,000 livres for wearing on the street a dress, coat, skirt, petticoat or apron of India fabric. The danger of losing their only dresses made it necessary for the townswomen of Southern France to do their marketing dressed in their husbands' clothes; people were even arrested for being seen through a window wearing *toiles.* As many convictions as possible had been urged by Colbert, for all crimes, or vagrancy, or merely for being a poor alien, in order to man the growing fleet of French ships with galley slaves.

Imitations of India fabrics had begun to be printed in France before 1685, and were as bitterly opposed by the weavers. With remarkable lack of vision, this new industrial possibility was suppressed. Reserve printing, alone, was allowed, since its technique offered a chance to quibble over the definition of printing. These prohibitions, together with the revocation of the Edict of Nantes, drove many of the best printers to England, Switzerland, Alsace and Holland, where cotton printing of superb quality soon flourished with a head start over what was finally to become one of the great industries of France.

Louis XV's court preferred *toile* to silk, and *toiles* remained for years the principal bootlegged, black-market commodity of France. The demand for them was too great to be controlled by the weavers; and the dishonesties of the system were so flagrant that in 1759 their manufacture was finally made legal. A government official, privy to the proposed change, set up the German brothers Oberkampf in a factory at Jouy, which was to become the greatest of all textile printing factories in late XVIII-e.XIXc. (See Appendix.)

French Fashion Plates, XVII Century

The fashion magazines of the XVIIIc. were preceded by series of single plates often purporting to show noble or newsworthy people, but always indicating the latest fashions. These were produced by I. Dieu de St. Jean during the 1670-80's; by members of the Bonnart family of engraver-printsellers: the brothers Nicolas (1636-1718), Henri (1642-1711), Robert (1652-1729) and Jean-Baptiste (1654-1686), and the sons J-B (1678-1726) and Henry. Also by J. Valk, the printseller, A. Trouvain (1656-1708), and N. Arnoult, who worked in Paris, c. 1680-1700.

The Morgan Library has one of the largest collections of these plates, some cut away contemporaneously, and backed by actual fabrics of the period. This collection, to which we are greatly indebted, is supplemented by the small but beautifully chosen collection in the Print Room of The Metropolitan Museum of Art.

The Elizabeth Day McCormick Collection of costume material in the Museum of Fine Arts of Boston includes a great mass of costume plates, much of it unique, from which the Museum has been good enough to make photographs for our use. Among their material can be found Trouvain's plates of Louis XIV's *appartements,* and their amusements; games of *trou-madame,* billiards and cards, dancing and refreshments; a collection of about 250 Bonnart plates bound together, and a large number of loose plates, among which are very early examples by St. Jean; late plates of Italian comedy by H. Bonnart and by Martin Engelbrecht; about 25 piracies (in reverse position) of Larmessin's plates of the trades; several of Pluvinel's *Manège royal;* original water-color plates of sets of theatrical costumes; and all manner of other material, such of which is still being catalogued (in 1947).

1394-97. Latter half XVIIc. French.

I. D. de St. Jean. Abbé in soutane (1394); Suit worn with a sword (1395); Suit worn with a sword (1396); *N. Bonnart.* King's page (1397).

In these transitional costumes of the 1670's, we see ribbon loops beginning to succumb to plumes, fine gathered lace, edgings of metal lace braids, and an increase in the use of fringes and fur.

Interest is drawing away from flat-brimmed hats with truncated crowns and ribbon trim, to hats with swinging brims, edged with metal lace and an interior fringe of ostrich, into which the crown disappears. The short wig, characteristic of an abbé, and that of No. 1395, are frizzed in the older way; those of No. 1396 and 1397 hang in corkscrew curls.

Coats have buttons down the entire front, although only the uppermost are closed, so that in No. 1394 and No. 1396, the old bloused shirt and ribbon loops at a low waistline, continue to be seen. Coats flare as they lengthen, with the open side seams in their skirts stressed, like the front opening, by braids. Pockets are horizontal but still set low. Short, narrow sleeves grow longer; the turned back cuff, still split, begins to flare into real importance. Fur-edged gauntlets have been worn for half a century, but their cuff increases in importance until the cuff of the coat flares sufficiently to replace them, as it is beginning to do in No. 1396.

Between petticoat or loose breeches and the important garters at the knee, we see cannons or the embroidered edge of a flaring stocking top, turned up and tacked, or falling free at the side. Clocked stockings, with the characteristic shoe of the 1670's: heavy heels, long, narrow square toes; high, square tongue, which tends to turn downwards above small buckles. No. 1395 shows the old bows on the shoe, persistent, but set on the side of the shoe.

The costume of the king's page shows the newest trends. Lace is used, in profusion for these times: in the double rows of his cravat (the ribbon bows of which are on top, and appear to tie it, but will presently retreat and become merely a backing for the lace); in the ruffle (in memory of the bloused shirt) drawn through the bosom of his long coat (still without vest), and finished with the cross of the Saint-Esprit on a blue bow; in the ends and borders of the wide sash about his hips; in his shirt sleeves and the lingerie backing (developed from the wide stocking top seen on No. 1396) which backs the ribbon bunches at the side of his still baggy breeches. His shoes, too, have the new, more delicate heel, and high, glove-fitted look.

In Louis XIV's time, a coat profusely covered with braid about the upper arm and chest has a connotation of livery and service whether worn by the queen's groom, or by a page of the king, both nobly born.

Even a century later, D'Héziques, in *Souvenirs d'un page de Louis XVI,* says that on his arrival at Versailles in 1786, "there were 150 pages not including those of the princes of the blood who lived at Paris. A page's coat cost 1,500 livres" (crimson velvet embroidered with gold on all the seams, and a hat with a feather and Spanish point lace).

1398-99. Latter half XVIIc. French.
I. D. de St. Jean. Peasant from the Neighborhood of Paris (1398), Peasant Woman from the Neighborhood of Paris (1399).

The heavy, Italian-inspired laces, so suitable for high cuffs, and collars wired out or spread over the shoulders, are supplanted in third quarter XVIIc. by much more delicate needlepoint or bobbin laces, made of finer threads, in France and the Low Countries. Their designs flow in perpendicular candelbra or delicately scrolled and flowered patterns, attractive when gathered into cravats and ever deeper flounces. In late VII-XIXc., lace is furnished in large-shaped pieces, circular capes, triangular scarves, hoods with lappets, fans and round parasol covers. Italian lace, though always characteristic, is revolutionized by the filmy designs of the Northern lace makers.

The peasants have not yet been ruined by the court. Since it is they who make the lace as a part-time home industry, under the tutelage of the nunneries, the peasants can and do wear lace on their best clothes as beautiful as that of the greatest ladies. Women of all classes embroider; the bodice front and skirt borders of a peasant costume may be as fine as any other.

The woman's delightful lace hood is worn under a plain one of linen. A cape-like lace collar stresses the wide horizontal neckline, though the bodice, with its embroidered stomacher, has a square opening; its sleeves are short and wide, the cuff disappearing, with much display of chemise sleeve and its lace ruffle. Under a plain apron (for any other would detract from the lace and embroidery at the top and bottom of the costume), the outer skirt is tucked up and caught in back, over a skirt with an embroidered band. Women's slippers have high heels, much more delicate than men's, and toes barely, if at all, squared.

The wig of courtiers has not yet made its way down to peasants, even in their best clothes; the hair of this man is worn at its full natural length. His cravat is tied with ribbon loops, which also trim his wide-brimmed hat and petticoat breeches. His coat, while still buttoned only at the top, is longer, beginning to flare, while its pockets are rising; sleeve is longer; cuff united. Shoes with high tongues and heels and square toes are worn with clocked stockings.

Courtesy of the Morgan Library

1400. XVIIc. After 1674, (Morgan Library.)

N. Bonnart. Winter Coat, called a Brandenburg.

Modern Germany began with the union of Prussia and Hohenzollern Brandenburg, led by the Great Elector, Frederic William, and with his new standing army, nucleus of the Prussian army to come. They formed an important part of the coalition forces which defeated Louis XIV's plans for expansion. During France's invasion of the United Provinces in 1674, however, the Elector's army of 20,000 was defeated in Turenne's brilliant campaign to reconquer Alsace for France.

The greatcoats worn by the Brandenburgers made a deep impression on the French, who adopted them and called them by the invader's name. The writer of the appended verse admits that this is a funny looking coat, but argues that in addition to keeping the body warm, it protects the clothing. The Brandenburg is characteristically decorated by a braid trim, made into loops on one side and braided buttons on the other, for closing, used into latter half XIXc.

The cocking brim and its feather edging conceal the crown of the hat. Throughout the 1670's, wigs retain a natural look and are often finished with long, knotted lovelocks. The cravat is folded over, but now the ribbon knot, which used to be tied around it, is either eliminated or has become a stiff bow set beneath the fall.

1401. XVIIc. Jan. 1676. French. (Metropolitan Museum, Print Room.)

N. Bonnart. Man in a Dressing Gown.

A wig was hot and uncomfortable. The head beneath it was usually shaved, sometimes clipped, although as changes in wig form exposed the neck, hair was left at the nape to be mingled with that of the wig.

In the privacy of the home, the wig was not usually worn; the shaved head was covered, both for protection and looks, by an embroidered cap or fur *montero.* The coat, too, was usually removed; the sleeveless waistcoat and shirtsleeves sufficed, although a dressing gown was often worn over breeches, vest and shirt. Painted India cottons were favorite materials for these dressing gowns, *banyans,* and for a sleeved form of vest, especially made to be worn without a coat; these show a little decoration, in places which would be unseen and made of plain material in an ordinary waistcoat. Waistcoats of this sort were also made of embroidered linen, like many of the accompanying caps. Shoes were exchanged for *pantoufles* with equally high heels and long square toes, but no back; lace-bordered handkerchief and cravat.

Louis XIV, who had beautiful hair, would not

1400   1401

wear a wig until he began to grow bald at 35. Even then, he refused to have his hair shaved. Special wigs were made with holes through which his own hair could be drawn and mingled with that of the wig.

It was far from necessary to be dressed in order to receive, in second half XVII-XVIIIc. It was a mark of intimacy, and the *lever* or *coucher* of a king like Louis XIV was attended by any courtier who could contrive to get in. The king dressed by stages, first putting on a special short wig, and a dressing gown over his nightshirt, to breakfast among high ecclesiastics and peers. These gentlemen then removed their gloves and handed the king's garments and accessories, one by one, to his valet who warmed them if necessary. The king then exchanged his short wig for a long one, and was ready to go out.

The entire routine is described in minute detail by Saint-Simon. In order to occupy quantities of courtiers, the royal wardrobe was subdivided, to be handled by as many people as possible, and the royal body even apportioned for service into right and left sides. Mme. Campan, first lady of the bedchamber to Marie Antoinette, was about to hand the queen her chemise, when, one after another, there entered (removing gloves and in turn taking the chemise), a lady of honor, the duchess of Orleans and the countess d'Artois, while the queen sat up in bed, shivering, with her hands crossed over her breast, enraged at their insistence on their superior rights. (Mme. Campan: *Memoires.*) The *Enfants de France* fared worse. Their wet-nurse might suckle but not touch them. Specific persons performed certain functions at stated times. If the baby was stuck by a pin, or soiled its diapers immediately after being changed, it had to lie screaming for three or four hours, until the return of the person authorized to perform the proper service. (Barbier: *Journal,* Oct. 1670.)

1402. XVIIc. 1678. French. (Morgan Library.)

I. D. de St. Jean. Man of Quality in Winter Dress.

1403. XVIIc. French. (Morgan Library.)

N. Bonnart. Man in Winter Dress.

The verse below the Bonnart print says that the fur is attractive, and any man so well covered will not be taken by surprise, no matter how cold it may become. Men as well as women now wear black patches. The ribbon bow is now stiff and set beneath the fall of the cravat. His coat is completely closed down the front; its skirts have a definite flare. Breeches are becoming close-fitting and are rolled around the garter at the bottom. Knots decorate hat, sword and stick. His gloves have a fur border to match the costume; a tasseled handkerchief hangs from his pocket.

The neck of the collarless coat is usually covered by the wig. The man whom we see from the back wears an extremely simple wig, which will not interfere with the marvellous stole of fur and embroidery slung over his shoulder and held in place by a wide scarf about the hips. The split cuff of his sleeve has an interesting partial cuff of fur set into its upward fold. The split cuff of his gauntlet is also fur-edged; and it is possible that the fur we see below is that of a matching muff. The fine ribbons with a fancy colored border, used in his sword-knot, are probably a result of Colbert's concentration on French luxury trades. Today we still import such fine ribbons from France.

A fascinating plate by N. Bonnart, dated 1678, shows a man in heavy mourning, with a long veil trailing from his hat. (Museum of Fine Arts, Boston, not shown here.)

1404. XVIIc. Jan. 1678. French. (Boston, Mus. of Fine Arts, Print Room.)

J. J. Bérain, e. Interior of a Needlework Shop, from the *Mercure,* Jan. 1678.

All publication within the kingdom was regulated and supervised; not even the costume plates of Bonnart appear without *avec Privilège du Roy* (some-

times abbreviated to *A.P.D.R.*), just as the tasseled hat of a cardinal on the title-page of a Spanish book indicated the required sanction of the Church. The French genius for getting one's way within the law was formed by centuries of over-regulated existence; questionable material was apt to be sent to liberal countries like Holland or Switzerland to be printed.

The first French periodical was the weekly *Gazette,* started in 1631 under Richelieu's patronage. The *Gazette* of 1650-65 was in rhyme, much more informal and amusing. Colbert, who founded the Observatory and the Academy of Sciences (now the Institut de France) was also the patron of the learned *Journal des Savants,* which began in 1665 and is published still.

The *Mercure Galant,* founded in 1672, became the *Mercure de France* in 1728, and did not go out of existence until 1792. One of its editors was Thomas Corneille, the much younger brother of the playwright; many great literary men served and were served by it.

Like its predecessor, the *Mercure* published official bulletins of the court and state, foreign and local news. It also reported society news, reviewed openings, sermons and publications, printed the latest songs, showed the latest fashions and described the costumes worn at court functions by notable people. A lady of quality, seated on a canapé, reading the *Mercure Galant* in 1688, is shown in a plate by Bonnart in the Elizabeth Day McCormick Coll., Museum of Fine Arts, Boston.

On the men's side of the shop we see boots and shoes; wigs and cravats with their strings in ready-made bows; scarves, sashes and knots; petticoat breeches looped with ribbons; shallow crowned hats and gloves. On the women's side, slippers and gloves; ruchings and ribbons; caps and bows; bandings, laces; ready-made scarves such as the lady wears, and everywhere, bolts of patterned fabrics.

1405. XVIIc. India. (Metropolitan Museum.)

Tree of Life: Wall-hanging of Painted Polychrome Cotton.

India cottons were first used as wall and bed hangings, curtains and upholstery; then for dressing gowns, aprons and petticoats; and eventually for gowns of great pretensions.

Indian patterns were copied in Europe quite literally at the beginning, though the wood-blocks familiar to European printers were substituted for the Indian method of pouncing the outline and painting in the color. The Indians, in their turn, adopted this European invention, as the Europeans went on to the use of engraved copper plates and rollers.

"Inventions" on the motifs of classic Oriental themes, like this Tree of Life, such as the wonderful pattern books of *Baroque* and *Idéal* flowers and *Chinoiseries,* published in the 1770's by Jean Pillement, had an immense effect on the design of European fabrics (woven as well as printed, silk as well as cotton) and laces.

1406. Early XVIIIc. French. (Metropolitan Museum.)

Dressing gown of painted India cotton.

The early *Indiennes* were of such extraordinary quality in respect both to fabric and dye-stuffs, that many garments made of them have survived 250-300 years in exquisite condition, despite wear, washing and sunlight. This garment, although it actually dates from late in Louis XIV's reign, is characteristic of the fabric and cut of these first dressing gowns of cotton.

Borders of compound strips of running pattern, such as originally surrounded hangings like the Tree of Life, were cut up to make such edgings as we see on this garment; in Louis XV's time, gowns of *Indiennes* were additionally embroidered in metal thread.

1407. XVIIc. 1682. French.

Nicolas Bazin, after *J. B. Martin*. Queen Maria Theresa.

For riding and hunting in second half XVII-XVIIIc., court ladies wear a costume of male hat, wig, cravat and coat, with a trailing skirt. These are cut from small-patterned brocades instead of men's plain materials, or are laced with an extraordinary amount of metal braid; the hat is apt to be larger and more exaggeratedly plumed, and there is some exaggeration in the size of the masculine shoulder knot worn by the queen (from which the army epaulette developed). A superb example of such a riding costume (French, last quarter XVIIc., in gold-embroidered velvet) is 43. 1618 in Elizabeth Day McCormick Collection, Mus. of Fine Arts, Boston.

Umbrellas have been seen occasionally for a hundred years past but c. 1680, long-handled parasols begin to open over every woman of fashion. These are usually edged with fringe or tassels; in XIXc., great circles of lace will be especially made as parasol covers.

The queen's page wears his own long hair as he runs behind her; if his service were in the palace, he would doubtless wear a wig. "When the king goes to shoot, four pages of the Great Stables are sent to His Majesty, and they call them the four ordinaries. They follow the king and take charge of his dogs. Six pages from the Little Stables follow also. If any ladies go with the king, pages from the Great Stables accompany the ladies. The six pages from the Little Stables have the honor of carrying His Majesty's guns, and the game shot by the king is frequently distributed among them. In other hunts, when there are ladies mounted on horses from the Little Stables, a page of the Little Stables accompanies each lady." (*Etat de la France,* 1712; describes the different functions of the two stables, and the education given the young gentlemen serving there.)

The page's livery coat is distinguishable from that of an ordinary gentleman at court by its heavy braid stripings, covering the upper sleeve and chest, where the ordinary coat is untrimmed. If the tail of the horse did not interfere, we would probably see his forearm, below the wide cuff, encased in a close-fitting doublet sleeve, instead of full shirt sleeves. Such sleeves are sometimes seen in the costume of gentlemen around the '90's, but are common on mu-sicians, hairdressers, valets, and others who would find the white fullness of a shirt sleeve difficult to manage, or keep clean while at work. This close sleeve is also apt to be heavily striped in braid, in lengthwise or chevron patterns. (See also Ills. 1424, 1417.)

1408. XVIIc. French. (Boston, Museum of Fine Arts, Elizabeth Day McCormick Coll.)
Boissevin. Lady Singing from a Book of Music.

1409. XVIIIc. French. (Met. Mus., Print Room.)
I. D. de St. Jean. Lady in Town Dress.

1410. XVIIc. French. (Morgan Library.)
I. D. de St. Jean. Lady Walking in the Country

1411. XVIIc. 1683. French. (Morgan Library.)
I. D. de St. Jean. Lady in Morning Déshabille.

1412. XVIIc. 1683. French. (Met. Mus., Print Room.)
G. Valk. Lady in Summer Déshabille.

1413. XVIIc. 1683. French. (Met. Mus., Print Room.)
H. Bonnart. Young Lady of Quality.

In 6 of the most delightfully feminine informal dresses ever worn by women, we see ribbon loops (so consistently worn as long as hair is bunched at the sides) beginning to lose ground as hair arrangements mount. But ribbons are such a perfect trim for cotton and lace garments that their use is continued in in-formal summer dresses like that shown by Valk. Ribbons, however, are changing their manner. They are carried around a long boned bodice at the natural waistline, and finish with a freshly tied bow rather than the old *chou* of loops.

At Louis XIV's court, manners are being discov-ered, practiced and codified; style is all-important in conduct and costume, as in conversation and letters (see text, Ill. 1392). Saint-Simon says of Louis: "Never was a man so naturally polite, nor of such circumspect politeness, so nice in its shades, nor who better discriminated age, worth and rank, both in his replies and deportment. . . . His salutations, more or less marked, but always slight, were of incomparable grace and majesty. . . . But especially towards women, there was nothing like it. Never did he pass the most indifferent woman without taking off his hat to her; and I mean chambermaids whom he knew to be such."

The old Marshal de Richelieu, who had lived under three courts, said to Louis XVI: "Sire, under Louis XIV no one dared utter a word; under Louis XV, people whispered; under your Majesty, they talk out loud." All will become studied and oppressive, by the end of Louis XIV's reign. During his and succeeding reigns, it is an actual ordeal to carry the weight of a dress suitable for appearance at court, and ladies will lie about their private apartments without "dressing," except for the few hours or even minutes of their official appearances. So regulated was court life under Louis XIV that everybody knew exactly where the king might be found at any hour of any given day. On his return, an apparently deserted court would suddenly be flooded with people who drained away, as suddenly, after his passage. Louis' own manners, dress and punctuality were flawless and he demanded no less of his court. Under Louis XV, we read of strange makeshift costumes, thrown on in unexpected crises: no such deviations would have occurred or been tolerated under his great-grandfather. With the much wider range of amusements in Louis XVI's reign, costumes will be changed four or five times a day, as ladies attend a *lever* at Versailles, play at milkmaid in muslin at the Petit Trianon, go to the Opera, and walk after it on the left side of the Palais-Royal.

In Ill. 1413, even the gown of the young lady of quality still keeps some of the charming freshness of the other informal dresses.

The legend under Bonnart's young lady stresses the protection of a fine skin against freckles, which is implicit in all the adjuncts of all these costumes: parasols; lacy hoods and sheer scarves, veiling the décolletage; long gloves of thin kid, or of elaborately knit silk, to the elbows; masks and fans.

There is lace everywhere. The singer practices in a hood of pleated black lace and the least utilitarian of lace aprons. The lady in town dress wears it, in the manner of the old horizontal collars, but it also edges her skirts and overlies the boning of her bodice. In the dress of beautifully mitred and arranged stripes, the entire shirt sleeve is of lace. In the morning undress, it borders the little combing jacket, apron and hood, and bracelets one arm, tied with a ribbon bow. The gown of Bonnart's young lady (which shows the beginnings of the stiffness of late Louis XIV styles) is based on the magnificent band of heavy point lace which finishes the under (and more important) skirt. Where there is already sufficient pattern in fabric or lace, fine net is used in scarf or hem flounce.

All accessories show great finish. Handkerchiefs have tiny acorns or lace bells at the corners; walking sticks, secured by a loop and bow, and parasol handles are as beautifully inlaid and engraved as busks; there are exquisite patch and snuff boxes; small mirrors; *chatelaine-nécessaires* full of tiny toilet and sewing and lace-making aids; *étuis* to hold sticks of wax which seal the letters everyone sends by someone's hand; and fans, which will be at their most elaborate in the XVIIIc.

1414. XVIIc. French. (Metropolitan Museum, Print Room.)

H. Bonnart. The Well-dressed Cavalier.

The coat, which began by being buttoned down the chest, is opening to expose the waistcoat. Both coat and vest are furnished with buttons and buttonholes throughout their length. The coat is now likely to be buttoned only at the waist and may even hang completely open; the vest is closed, as the coat used to be, but eventually it, too, may be fastened only at the waist.

The buttoned-back cuff, still split, is becoming much more important; here, it falls in circularly-cut extra fullness. The pockets, while vertical in the old fashion, are increasingly stressed by decoration, as are the seams of the armseye and sleeve. Breeches have lost most of their old fullness. Gauntlets are heavily edged with fringe.

1415. XVIIc. 1684. French. (Morgan Library.)

I. D. de St. Jean. Man of Quality in a Surtout.

There have been dictionaries and encyclopaedias since Greece and Rome but this is the century of the great dictionaries, as the XVIIIc. is of great encyclopaedias. The dictionary begun by the French Academy in 1639 took more than half a century to complete; meanwhile, many modest dictionaries are appearing. Guy Miege's 1 vol. French-English dictionary, published in London in 1679, can be immensely helpful to-day, as much for the words it does not contain as for its current, slang or obsolete words. (Chamberlayne. See Appendix.)

The *justaucorps* has been worn long enough for definition as a close-fitting coat, but such fashionable garments as the *Brandenburg* and *surtout* have not yet managed to enter a dictionary. The new surtout (literally *over-everything*) was, as it is today, an easy-fitting top-coat. We see it here, plainly trimmed, furnished with great patch pockets, buttoned down over everything, muffling the cravat; it is a real top-coat, and must have been a welcome garment in the bitter winter of 1683-4, which Evelyn tells us was felt "even as far as Spain and the most southern tracts."

Another top-coat with easy skirts and pockets, called a *pichena,* is shown in No. 7 of the bound volume of 250 Bonnart plates: Elizabeth Day McCormick Coll., Museum of Fine Arts, Boston. It is worn by a sea-captain, but the caption tells us that it is suitable for a rider, and for city and country wear, in rain or shine.

1416. XVIIc. 1684. French. (Morgan Library.)

A. Truvain. The Chevalier de Bouillon.

Research by the Morgan Library indicates that the Chevalier de Bouillon was a young adventurer at court. The Duke de Bouillon, father of the great Turenne (whose mother was William the Silent's daughter), had an illegitimate son whose descendants long contrived and eventually succeeded in being allowed to use the family name, de La Tour d'Auvergne. Possibly this young man is a left-handed nephew of Turenne, though he little resembles that modest Protestant Marshal of France, of whom Mme. de Sévigné said that he received congratulations on his victory at Turckheim, looking "a little more shamefaced than usual."

This is a young person of the most ostentatious and daring elegance, who may well be making his way on his looks and imagination.

Cleanliness is becoming a necessity, and the man who buttons himself up above the waistline is now accused of trying to conceal soiled linen. The chevalier, in the hot summer weather, dispenses with a waistcoat entirely, and transfers its attributes to his exposed breeches. These match the coat, instead of being the usual, barely-seen necessity; they carry the waistcoat's horizontal pockets, elaborately trimmed to match the side seams; the few buttons we would expect to see closed at the waistline of the vest are frankly set on the fly.

His light summer coat has a shawl collar, very startling in the day of collarless justaucorps. There is a great knot of fringed ribbon, matching his sword-knot, on the right shoulder of his completely new raglan sleeve, which is much less close-fitting in the arm, and has great, low-set, closed cuffs.

The expanse of sheer shirt front is partly filled by a very long, unusually pleated oval cravat, set on a soft band. Since he wishes to show off his coat collar, he dispenses with the customary stiff cravat strings and carries his wig down his back, out of the way. His shoes have shorter toes, the new delicately fitted look, and tongues turned down over larger buckles. His hat, with an interior fringe of ostrich, is definitely cocked into a tricorne.

1417. XVIIc. 1687-8. French.

Nicolas Arnoult. The Family of Monseigneur the Dauphin.

Although Louis XIV had only one legitimate son, three grandsons seemed to assure the succession.

The Dauphin was a colorless person, "drowned in fat and sloth," and completely overshadowed by his father. He was distinguished only by his prowess as a boar-hunter, and by the exceptional taste with which he furnished his apartments, which were the showplace of Versailles. He lived on good terms with the Dauphine, a Bavarian princess, not at all beautiful but intelligent, charming and good, who spent as much time as possible with music and books, apart from the court she disliked. Their children, the *Enfants de France,* were Louis, duke of Bourgogne, b.1682; Philip, duke of Anjou (later Philip V of Spain), b.1683; and Charles, duke of Berry, b.1686. The Dauphine died in 1690; in 1711, the Dauphin died of smallpox; the extraordinarily promising duke of Burgundy and his duchess died within a few days of each other, in 1712, of measles; in 1714, the duke of Berry was killed in a hunting accident, leaving as the aged king's only heir the unpromising youth (born 1710) who became Louis XV.

Monseigneur, the dutiful son, sits with his family beneath a portrait of his father. Not until 1690 will the need to raise money for the wars force Louis to

set an example to his lords by melting down 2,000 pieces of the carved and gilded solid silver furniture of Versailles, replacing it with carved wood, trimmed with copper-gilt. The silver furniture in the king's own quarters had diamond-studded drawer knobs. Most of Monseigneur's furniture was made by Boule, but there was a table of carved silver, made by Balin, which cost about $70,000; it may, for all I know, be the one seen here. The Dauphin and his wife sit, as is their right, in high-backed chairs; were his father in the room, the Dauphin would stand (see text, Ill. 1419).

All are clothed in metal-laced brocades. The coats are still rather straight-cut, capable of being buttoned down the front, and have vertical pocket slits. A wide, shallow cuff is buttoned to the narrow, short outer sleeve, and exhibits the lower arm in a close sleeve belonging to the waistcoat. The cravat is less important than the bows beneath. Shoes very high and close, with turned down tongue and jewelled buckle. All wear handsome sashes and the *cordon bleu.* The duke of Burgundy has fringed gloves, stick, miniature sword and a short wig. The babies, too young for wigs, wear beribboned and plumed turbans. The younger, dressed as a girl in boned bodice and lace apron; the elder, still in skirts, has the sleeves and neckwear of his father and big brother.

The Dauphine's dress is richly conservative, transitional between the standard low-necked dress of second half XVIIc. and the costume we associate with Louis XIV's court. Her hair, with long love-locks and small corkscrew curls at the temples, is begin-

1418

ning to be dressed higher, and its ribbon decoration is mounting. Lace handkerchief.

1418. XVIIc. c. 1689-90. French. (Morgan Library.)
N. Arnoult. Charles of France, Duke of Berry.

Berry himself said that his grandfather and the tutor of his eldest brother "thought only of making me stupid and stifling all my powers; I was a younger son; I coped with my brother. They feared the consequences; they annihilated me. I was taught only to play and to hunt and they have succeeded in making me a fool and an ass, incapable of anything, the laughing stock and disdain of everybody." He was, as a matter of fact, a pleasant, witty, and popular prince, who had the misfortune to marry the fifteen-year old eldest daughter of the Regent; she was intelligent and charming, vicious and reckless, drank herself into insensibility, and died young after child-birth.

The infant of No. 1417 is now in leading strings, but still in skirts, i.e. diapers.

At the age of seven, royal children were turned over to male tutors, usually a duke and a prelate. Until that time, the *Enfants de France* were in charge of a governess, at this time the Maréchale de la Mothe, herself a duchess. Like their elders, royal children were served only by gentlefolk.

When the king dined in public, *au grand couvert,* any well-dressed person in his kingdom might enter and watch. Ordinarily he dined alone (surrounded, as always, by a crowd of familiar courtiers) at a table in the room where he also slept; occasionally he invited another person, such as his brother, to sit down with him. His own old nurse and the governess of his grandchildren were among the few women who centered his chamber at this time; Saint-Simon says the Maréchale was the only woman he ever saw invited to sit with the king at the *petit couvert.* The king ate supper every night with his

family; about three times a week there was a court reception, *appartement,* with dancing, billiards, gambling for high stakes, other games very much like the pin-ball machine of today, and a buffet to be "pillaged" by the courtiers.

The nurse, however grand a lady, is dressed for the part in a silk apron, which has a sleeved top with diagonal trimming to match, related to the banding of her handsome gored underskirt. The new tendency of the bodice neckline to rise is indicated by the lingerie frills on her bow-trimmed bodice; ribbons tend to disappear from more formal dresses, except on headdresses and muffs. Sleeves are still short but their future length and funnel shape begin to show in the frills of the sleeve. The ruffles of her delightful bonnet are not yet formalized into the pleats of the fontange, universally worn in the 90's, with hair dressed high. Fan, patches and pearl choker, with a fine chain and jewelled pendant.

MME. DE MAINTENON AND THE LOUIS XIV COURT

We may well view the latter part of the 72 years of Louis XIV's reign through the life of Mme. de Maintenon, the most interesting woman involved in it.

Françoise d'Aubigné (1635-1719), granddaughter of the great Protestant leader, daughter of a trivial, improvident father (imprisoned for Protestant trouble-making) and a Catholic mother, was born in her father's jail. After his release, the family emigrated to Martinique, where he died penniless. Little Françoise was taken by her aunt, Mme. de Villette, whom she adored, and brought up as a Protestant. She was removed to the custody of her Catholic godmother to be reconverted: "I will believe anything, so long as you do not oblige me to believe my aunt is damned." In a family with a carriage and six horses, the girl went neglected, barefoot or in sabots, given shoes only when there were guests.

She was befriended by the comic dramatist, Scarron (whose name is commemorated in New York's Schroon Lake), a 42-year old invalid hunchback, who "has drawn many pleasantries from the irregularity of his shape, which he describes as very much resembling the letter Z. He diverts himself likewise by representing to his reader the make of an engine and pulley, with which he used to take off his hat" (*Spectator,* i, 17). Françoise chose, at sixteen and a half, to marry him. For a decade she lived in the most brilliant society, nursing him faithfully until his death in 1660.

To avoid scandal about the king's involvement with his new sister-in-law, soon after his own marriage, it had been arranged that he should court one of her maids-of-honor. The 17-year old Louise de La Vallière (1644-1710), whose name is preserved in that of a type of jewelled pendant, was exquisite and graceful despite a short leg, gentle, innocent and religious. She and the king both fell unexpectedly and deeply in love; they had a number of children, one of whom, Mlle. de Blois, became the princess de Conti.

At about the time when Mme. de Montespan was supplanting Mlle. de La Vallière as the king's official mistress, she met Mme. Scarron and had her installed at court as governess of the duke de Maine, Louis' beloved son by Montespan.

The *Mesdames* and *Mlles. de Blois* of these days can be very confusing. Louis XIV's son, the Dauphin, was *Monseigneur;* Louis' brother, Philip, duke of Orleans, was *Monsieur,* and the latter's second wife, the Princess Palatine, was *Madame,* to whom Mme. de Maintenon did not chose to be lady of honor. Louis' daughter by the duchess of La Vallière was *Mlle. de Blois,* until she married the prince de Conti; a younger daughter of Louis', by Mme. de Montespan, was then called *Mlle. de Blois,* until her marriage to her cousin, the duke of Chartres (later the regent Orleans), son of *Monsieur* and *Madame;* the young couple were called *Monsieur le duc* and *Madame la duchesse.*

There were three grades of palace service for noblewomen: *dame d'honneur; dame d'atours* (who took care of the wardrobe and knelt with a salver to receive the jewels removed at the *coucher*); and *dame du palais.* With her customary self-effacement, Mme. de Maintenon refused the post of lady of honor to Madame, and suggested a suitable person to replace Mme. de Richelieu.

Meanwhile, another of Madame's ladies-of-honor, a person of completely different character, had determined to supplant La Vallière. Mme. de Montespan (1641-1707) was equally blonde and beautiful, but proud, vain and intriguing; witty and intelligent, although she resorted to witchcraft to gain and hold the king, and was supposed to have poisoned a temporary rival, Mlle. de Fontange (whose name lived after her death in 1681, in the headdress for which she was responsible). In 1667, Montespan became the *maîtresse tonnante et triumphante,* as Mme. de Maintenon described her, of the king. Her husband went about court wearing mourning for his lost honor, but accepted a pension and was sent off to distant service.

In late XVII-e.XVIIIc., we learn from d'Argenson, only blue-eyed blondes were accounted beautiful. Black hair was disliked and red ridiculed. But its nearness to blonde gradually led to the acceptance of red hair; during last quarter XVIIIc., it even took the lead, and powders were used to redden hair.

La Vallière, who wished to become a nun, was forced to remain as official mistress for half-a-dozen hideous years. When she was finally allowed to enter the convent, she told Mme. Scarron: "When I am hurt by something at the Carmelites, I will always remember what those two people (Louis and Montespan) have made me

suffer." The queen's affection led her to visit Sister Louise de la Miséricorde in the convent where, until her death, she washed the sisters' linen.

Everybody confided in the discreet, charming and dignified Mme. Scarron. Her high character at first alienated the king. When he was amusing himself tipping court ladies in their armchairs back to the ground, he passed by Mme. Scarron, saying: "Oh, with that one, I wouldn't dare," at which a courtier said he'd sooner try to pinch the queen's *derrière* than Mme. Scarron's.

Louis, however, came to respect her, making her Marquise de Maintenon. The queen, who eventually died in her arms, said she had never before been so well treated by the king, and that she owed it all to Mme. de Maintenon.

During the eight years of her liaison with the king, Montespan had born him nine children, legitimized (as had been those of La Vallière) by Louis; among them the duc de Maine, Mlles. de Nantes, de Tours, de Blois, and the count of Toulouse.

Mme. de Maintenon's influence increased; Montespan failed to get rid of her by plotting her marriage to another hunchback, the elderly duke de Villars. The temper, scenes and activities of Montespan became increasingly distasteful to Louis. She was not invited to the court fête of 1679, but rather than shame their children, Louis allowed her to remain at court until 1691 when she, too, retired to a convent; at her death, he forbade her children to wear mourning for her.

After the queen's death, Mme. de Maintenon and the king were secretly married by the Archbishop of Paris, in the presence of the king's confessor, the Jesuit Père La Chaise and a number of others. The tone of court life was raised and became much less amusing, its gowns less revealing. Louis had always had a very real religious feeling. Under his second wife's influence, this increased, although as she said, while he would never miss a sermon or a fast-day, no one could make him understand what was mean by humility or repentance. Her own piety was true but not aggressive; and the greatest mistake of Louis' life, the Revocation of the Edict of Nantes, for which the Church had longed, was not due to her influence. The Protestants, who were among France's most worthy and industrious citizens, were driven to sympathetic neighboring countries; some of the most prosperous districts of France were depopulated and reduced to poverty, as weavers, and printers, watchmakers and goldsmiths set England, Switzerland, Alsace, Holland and Germany on the road to rivalry and supremacy in these arts.

Mme. de Maintenon, who had always made her way discreetly and unostentatiously, devoted herself to easing and simplifying the final thirty years of Louis' life. She spared him much routine business, sacrificed her own deep interests in other matters to the tedious restrictions of court and etiquette, and never let herself appear to the king otherwise than in good health and spirits, no matter what her real feelings.

She said he never saw her cry, even during his final illness, when he was 77 and she 81. Instead, they went through his papers, and the pockets of all his coats, laughing at their memories of what they found, and burning what might prove embarrassing. He said he regretted the wars he had waged, and that he had not made her happy. "It's true that he loved me more than anyone else, but even then he loved me only as much as he was capable of loving," she said, adding that without the aid of her religion, she could not have stayed on at court.

When the doctors told her that Louis, dying of gangrene, would never regain consciousness, she did not wait until his death, but drove off to St. Cyr, for fear of being molested and insulted on the way after the king's death. On a pension granted her by Orleans, she finished her life there in retirement.

1419. XVIIc. Before 1690. French. (Versailles, National Museum.)

Att. to *L. F. Elle*. Mme. de Maintenon and her Niece.

The wife of the king was a born teacher and social worker; the childless woman, whose own girlhood had been so insecure, loved children. One after another, she brought up young women like her cousin, who became Mme. de Caylus, and this namesake-niece, the only child of her only brother. Little Françoise, b.1684, was married at 14 to an old friend of her aunt's, the Marshal de Noailles, and inherited the Chateau de Maintenon, which is still owned by the Noailles family.

With the first increase in her fortune, Mme. de Maintenon had founded a home of girls, which developed into the famous school of St. Cyr. She spent as much time there as the routines of court permitted. When the court was at Versailles, she could go each morning to St. Cyr; when it was at Marly, she could not get there at all. Her letters recount the constant frustrations of court life. "My little finger tells me that the news from England is good. One must console oneself by that for the other little contradictions one finds on the way. I was dining with my *cabale*." (Her niece Noailles, cousin Caylus and five others, making a pleasant eight at table, joined twice a week, from five to ten, by the king, for supper). "The king prevented it; he should be coming here at 2 o'clock. Perhaps he will not come so early. He should be going out at four; perhaps he won't be going out. He is counting on a game at night. Perhaps we won't see him? I have absolutely no idea what I am doing tomorrow. All I know is that I am very trying to others and myself."

From the drive to St. Cyr, Mme. de Maintenon was apt to return without headdress or scarf, given to some poor woman picked up on the way in her carriage. Her taste in dress was very simple, and her bodice always cut so high that it was rumored to cover a defect. The duchess of Richelieu was astonished, one hot day, to find that her bosom was actually very handsome. Her linen was always exquisite and fresh. Her confessor at St. Cyr thought there was too much material in her dresses. When she protested, he said, well, it looked like too much when he saw it all spread about her as she knelt.

Her feelings about clothes are expressed in a letter of 1705, asking Mme. de Caylus to buy a short summer robe and petticoat to wear in getting out of bed when she was ill but still had to make a good appearance, since the king disliked the unadorned black costumes to which she inclined. She asks for a black and white petticoat of at least six widths of material, and a black and gold gown, neither of rich stuff. Violet and gold, or a "very Turkish blue" would do. "One must adorn the personage, while the person should only be thinking of the coffin."

Mme. de Maintenon's simple gown with train is collared to the throat with point lace. Her hair, which is beginning to be dressed high with a small curl on either side of the forehead, is covered with a scarf of sheer black bobbin lace, worn with a black *fontange*. This headdress, almost universal by 1690, came into being nearly a decade earlier when the hair of the girl for whom it was named fell down during the hunt and was put up with the help of her lace-edged garter. Though it reached almost unmanageable heights by 1700, it began as a standing ruffle of lace.

The little niece, though still in leading strings, wears the trained satin gown of a grown person, the bottom of the bodice finished with a line of stones; and her hair, though uncovered, is dressed on top of the head with a love-lock and tiny curls on the temples; by 1695, even children wear a fontange.

Through the window we see the buildings of Maintenon's beloved school, for which Racine wrote "Esther," first performed there in 1689 before the king; and where, in her old age, she deprived herself of her nightly cup of chocolate, fearing the effect of luxurious example on her 250 young gentlewomen.

The furniture is typically late Louis XIV. The chair with its curved, richly carved arm, is upholstered in velvet, bordered with metal galloon, fringed and tasseled, as is the cushion, set on a table with carved Baroque swags.

"The etiquette of seating is in this period the philosophy of royalty. Thus in order of importance range the arm chair, chairs with backs, joint stools, folding stools, hassocks with gold gimp, hassocks with silk edging. The Louis XIV throne chair was majestic—solid silver, draped with crimson velvet. The back was eight feet high, draped with gold embroidery carried by caryatids, fifteen feet high." (Aronson: *The Encyclopedia of Furniture*.)

Court life consisted of endless standing. Men almost never sat down, except at the card tables; women did so by permission. To sit on a seat not commensurate with one's rank, even though it were the only one available, led to "confusion," and was deplored (or worse) by the king, who noticed the least deviation from precedence.

The king, who had an extraordinary constitution, and could stand anything but tobacco and perfume, had no patience with human frailty. He endured the lack of all privacy, the three pairs of hands through which the least glass of water was handed him, the cold which froze the wine in its glass at dinner, or the heat engendered by crowds of candles and hundreds of courtiers. Ladies dared not faint in his presence. His coach never stopped on the road for the convenience of the queen, Mlle. de La Vallière, and Mme. de Montespan, as they rode together with him through Flanders, and the peasants thronged to get a look at the "three queens." Ladies who had lapsed from the king's standards of manners, withdrew from court, sometimes permanently to a nunnery.

French Court Life Behind the Scenes

Mlle. de Blois (b.1677, who became the duchess of Orleans), and Mlle. de Nantes (b.1673, later the duchess of Bourbon), two of the king's daughters by Mme. de Montespan, appear in "La Charmante Tabagie" (Ill 1422). The print represents an event described by St.-Simon, which took place at Marly, in the fall of 1695.

Everybody took snuff, and snuff boxes had become the conventional handsome present. Louis gave many of them, but detested tobacco personally; and smoking was considered extremely vulgar. The bored, spoiled girls teased the Swiss Guards into getting them pipes. They are shown in aproned magnificence and great fontanges, at a table under a grape arbor, playing cards, drinking and smoking amongst empty bottles and more cooling, smashed glasses and broken pipes. They were surprised by the Dauphin, punished next day by the king, and the story spread.

Of his half-sisters, the Dauphin much preferred the princess of Conti. She was even lovelier than the mother who had been named in her legitimatization; Montespan's daughters were at the disadvantage of having been merely declared legitimate. There was so much ill-feeling between the various half-sisters that Louis once threatened to have them locked up in their respective chateaux. The princess of Conti called the duchess of Orleans *sac-à-vin*, for she was always one to drown her annoyances. In return Mme. de Conti was called *sac-à-guenilles* (rag-bag). Montespan's high-spirited daughters felt that, as the king's daughters, they were condescending in marrying his mere nephew, and Condé's grandson.

Madame, the Princess Palatine, who had slapped her son's face in public in her rage at his marrying Mlle. de Blois, had a tongue as well as a temper beyond any other. She never forgave the gentle reprimand for some excessively indiscreet letters of hers, which had been put into Mme. de Maintenon's hands to deal with, by the secret police. She called her *"cette vieille ordure, ce méchant diable, cette ripopée* (mixture of all the leftover sauces dumped together, i.e. a mess), *cette ratatinée de Maintenon"* (meaning withered like an old apple). In fact, a great part of Mme. de Maintenon's reputation for hypocrisy comes from the hatred of the Princess Palatine and her competence at expressing it in the marvellous letters which were her constant occupation.

Name-calling increased at court with the XVIIIc. It might be in the form of nicknames as affectionate as Louis XV's *Coches, Loque, Graille,* and *Chiffe* for his daughters Victoire, Adelaide, Sophie and Louise; or as mocking as his courtiers' for his illegitimate son, the count de Luc, called the *demi-Louis*. It might be a "little language" of intimacy and affection, of discretion, of studied insult, or of simple vulgarity. Mme. de Lauraguais, herself known as *la rue des Mauvaises Paroles,* because of the names she made up for other people, called the Cardinal de Rohan the "broody hen," and d'Argenson, the "sucking calf." Mme. de Pompadour, in the circle of her *petits chats,* called the duke of Chaulnes "the pig," and called others the equivalent of "slut" and "pot-rag."

But *Madame* loathed the court as much as did Mme. de Maintenon when she wrote the princess des Ursins in 1707: "I find the women of today unbearable; their senseless and immodest clothing, their tobacco, their *gourmandise,* their coarseness, their laziness, all are so opposed to my taste, and it seems to me, to reason, that I cannot endure it."

1422

the painter's daughter put the ermine-lined mantle over the marquise's shoulders, Mme. de Sévigné's letters tell us that Louis said: "Yes, Sainte-Françoise well deserves it."

1421. XVIIc. French. (Versailles, National Museum.)

Pierre Vignon. The Duchess of Orleans and the Duchess of Bourbon.

1422. XVIIc. 1698. French. (Boston, Museum of Fine Arts, Elizabeth Day McCormick Coll.)

N. Arnoult. La Charmante Tabagie.

These two smokers (Ill. 1422) are not the young women to be influenced by the example of a stepmother they find stuffy.

In Ill. 1421, bodices, in the spirit of allegorical portraits, slip off one shoulder and breast, and are negligently caught or garlanded by flowers (of the same natural sort which Mme. de Maintenon holds, in the portrait with her niece). The hems of their dresses, however, are finished with heavy fringes. With tassels, such as hang from the pillows, these fringes are handsomer and more elaborate at the turn of this century than ever before or since.

Their hair is dressed very high, in twin peaks, as men's wigs of the time are, with paired scallops, *favorites,* on the temples, repalcing the old corkscrew curls.

Jewelry is reduced to lacy, sprig-like brooches, allied to the small patterns of the brocade used in their gowns; small clasps and studs in the hair, chains of stones at the waistline or catching the bodice, or a line of pearls. Decorative and quite useless aprons are an indispensable part of negligée, and even of "dress" costume in late XVII-e.XVIIIc.

The little Negro page they are fondling wears pearl earrings and a slave's collar with his livery coat and loose, fringed cravat.

1420. XVIIc. c. 1694. French. (Louvre.)

Pierre Mignard. Françoise d'Aubigné, Marquise de Maintenon.

In these days of portraits of ladies as half-naked allegorical personages, like Diana with a bow and a leopard skin, the modestly covered Marquise, whom Louis often addressed as "your Solidity," was painted by Mignard rather as a sainted Roman lady. When

1423 1424 1425

1423. XVIIc. 1688. French. (Metropolitan Museum, Print Room.)

N. Arnoult. Lady of Quality at her Toilet.

1424. XVIIc. After 1692. French. (Metropolitan Museum, Print Room.)

R. Bonnart. Lady of Quality at her Toilet.

In its early form, the lace of the *fontange* is a mere ruffle, backed by ribbon loops, and subservient to a cap, also looped with ribbon, the lappets of which hang down the front of the shoulders.

As the hair mounts, the *fontange* or *commode* headdress becomes higher, stiffer, tiered, formally pleated and backed by wired ribbon loops. The cap and its trim are reduced to a crown and the ribbon tied around it; the lappets become two long strips falling down the back, which may be pinned up to the crown in various ways.

The Arnoult lady wears a little combing jacket of wide point lace and a petticoat which may well be of *Indiennes*. She sits on a fringe-trimmed stool, with late Renaissance turnings, at a dressing table which is still utilitarian.

Her maid wears an apron with a lace-trimmed pocket, and a belt full of dangling utensils, over a charming gored skirt. Great ladies are seen in such gored skirts when their clothes must be easily manageable, as in the shooting costume worn by the countess of Toulouse in Arnoult's print of 1678. (in the Print collection of the Bibliothèque Nationale, Paris.) Her lace is naturally less splendid than that of her mistress. But lace has become so completely a necessity that many inexpensive approximations were soon provided. There were drawn-work effects on thin muslin; in other cases, the muslin was starched to hold a lacy pricked design, and pointed up with white paint. Cooper Union Museum has several examples; two are reproduced in Miss Marian Hague's article on "Comparisons in Lace Design:" *Chronicle of the Museum,* Vol. I, No. II, Dec. 1945.

As a little page holds a silver basin and ewer, the hard-hearted Bonnart lady washes her hands—as she will of any evil passions her beauty may inspire, we are told by the accompanying verse.

Under her combing jacket, we see the handsome placard of her corset and her petticoat trimmed with bands of galloon and fringed gimp.

The page wears a braid-striped livery coat but no wig. Like the hairdresser, his undersleeve is close-fitting. They both wear the *Steinkirk* form of cravat. In the 1692 battle from which this took its name, William of Orange was defeated by the French under Luxembourg, although the French officers went into action without time to finish dressing. They knotted their cravats about the neck and tucked the long ends into a buttonhole. This fashion was adopted by women as well as men, and being very comfortable, had a long life; it is occasionally seen into the third quarter XVIIIc.

The dressing table is becoming more elaborate; lace-edged cover; larger and handsomer mirror; many charming boxes for patches, cosmetics and jewelry.

By 1687, merchants' daughters are also shown at their toilette.

1425. XVIIc. 1694. French. (Metropolitan Museum, Print Room.)

A. Trouvain. Duchess of Humières in a Ball Gown.

Great balls were given during marriage celebrations and many masked balls were held at carnival time. The *Mercure* of 1683 tells of five balls given that winter "in five different *appartements* at Versailles, all so grand that no other royal house in the world can show the like. Entrance was given to masks only, and no persons presented themselves without being disguised unless they were of very high rank. People invent grotesque disguises; they revive old fashions, they choose the most ridiculous things and seek to make them as amusing as possible . . . The Dauphin . . . sometimes had double masks, and under the first a mask of wax so well made that, when he took off his first mask, people fancied they saw his natural face and he deceived everybody."

The duke of Chartres' masquerade at Marly in 1700 "represented the Grand Turk and his menagerie. He was carried by slaves in a palanquin, and preceded by a great number of animals as natural as life. There were ostriches, cranes, apes, bears, parrots and butterflies. In his suite marched the officers and slaves of the seraglio, and the sultanas, who, together with the animals, danced an entrée pleasant and new." The *Mercure* lists the parts played by the various members of the nobility whose "costumes were magnificent. All the animals were as natural as possible. The apes, who were professional mountebanks, were wonderful."

The duchess, daughter-in-law of the not very effective Marshal who apparently remained in favor because of Turenne's affection for his rich and lovely wife, carries a mask and long gloves. She is dressed in a costume of Eastern inspiration, whether Polish or Turkish, with a high turban and cockade. Her loose gown is turned back with triple bars of galloon, each ending in a tassel, and is bordered with passementerie; it is worn with a vest-like corset, braided and tasseled.

All these forms of decoration are at a height which will not be approached again, even in the Victorian era. Passementerie is silk or metal lace, often spangled. Gimp, being braided, is more closely related to passementerie than to galloon, which is woven in ribbon-like bands. The various techniques are often combined, as when openwork gimps are woven into galloon; and all are combined with wonderful fringes and tassels.

Cooper Union has a rich collection of books of these trimmings, including livery galloons woven with the arms of a lord, a city, or the insignia of a cardinal. Some of these are shown in the article on trimmings in the *Chronicle of the Museum*: Vol. I, No. 7, Sept. 1942. The Museum's collection includes not only laces, woven and printed fabrics, buttons and trimmings, but a remarkable number of contemporary pattern books and artists' original designs for these, and such allied arts as jewelry, sedan chairs and coaches, furniture and wall decoration, architecture and gardens.

1426. XVIIc. 1694. French. (Morgan Library.)

A. Trouvain. Jean Bart, Ship's Captain.

This fisherman's son, a common sailor at 12, was prevented by his birth from making rank commensurate with his worth, until his audacity at blockade-running in the Channel brought him to the king's attention in 1679. From that time, his exploits in carrying war supplies, his speedy escape from English prison, his revengeful raids on English soil and shipping, the destruction of six enemy ships by his *Glorieux* alone, and his leadership of one hundred wheat-laden ships to famished France, caused Louis to ennoble him in 1694.

Trouvain's engraving commemorates his invitation to Versailles. Despite his magnificent clothes, his rough plebeian ways (indicated by pipe smoking) made the courtiers nickname him "the bear." In 1702, as a result of overwork and exposure, he died of pleurisy.

As the attributes of the waistcoat, when it is not worn, are transferred to the breeches (as in the case

1426

1427

of Bouillon, Ill. 1416), those of a coat, when it is worn widely opened, are assumed by the waistcoat. Here it carries the pockets, heavily trimmed by braid and fringe. The narrow coat sleeve is longer, widening below the elbow, its cuff set lower, so that little of the shirt sleeve is now seen except its wrist ruffle. His *steinkirk* is twisted before it is drawn through the buttonhole. Hat elaborately laced and plumed.

The table is of the new console variety, set on two (or sometimes one) front legs only, and braced against the wall.

1427. XVIIc. 1694. French. (Morgan Library.)
H. Bonnart. Madame la Duchesse.

The disparate views of the duke of Saint-Simon and the Princess Palatine focus to show the wife of the future regent as a big, dignified, lazy hypochondriac; lop-sided, long of tooth, over-painted but handsome enough, with her fine skin and chestnut hair; intelligent but with a slow, blurred speech, a great timidity towards her father, Louis XIV, and a fantastic arrogance toward the rest of the world, for which her husband nicknamed her "Madame Lucifer." She ate lying down, and "would like larks ready roasted to drop in her mouth. She is so vain that she thinks she has more sense than her husband, who has a great deal." (*Memoirs of the Duchess of Orleans*).

These are the words of Madame La Duchess' mother-in-law, Charlotte Elizabeth of Orleans, the Princess Palatine (on whose behalf, though without her desire, Louis' claims to the Palatinate led to the invasions of 1688). She was a violent and masculine German, a strange mixture of rusticity and stiff-necked pride of race. She despised the French court and everyone in it (with the definite exception of the king), beginning with his brother, her husband (a polite, painted little man who tottered on his high heels), and the king's daughter, her son's wife.

To the 800-odd, forthright, 20-30 page letters which the Princess Palatine wrote from 6 a.m. to 10 p.m., with time out only for dressing, prayers, mass, and a quick dinner, we owe much of our knowledge of her times. Other sources are the memoirs of Saint-Simon, d'Angeau, Mme. de Caylus, and the letters of Mme. de Sévigné.

The court preoccupation with style is manifested, not only in clothes and manners, but in speech and writing. It is possible for a noblewoman to be almost completely illiterate (like Mme. de Coislin, former mistress of Louis XV, in whose hôtel, in her great age, Chateaubriand and his wife rented a floor, and whose incomparable sense of form in speech is recorded in "Les Mémoires d'outre-tombe.") Madame's youngest granddaughter, for a brief time queen of Spain, was such an illiterate. But an excellent education is equally possible, in another sister of the same family; letter writing has become a great art; daily records are kept by people of both sexes, on which will be based the endless memoirs of the XVIIIc.

The letters of the visiting German baron de Pöllnitz in e.XVIIIc. describe a hurried call of the young duchess of Berry (eldest daughter of Mme. la Duchesse) on Madame, dressed in a scarf and constantly asking the time. Upon questioning, it turned out that she was not going for a walk by torchlight, but to visit the king. Louis XV was still a child; but Madame was outraged by the lack of respect shown by the duchess' costume. "Give the king the respects due him and you will have the right to exact from others those due you. You certainly can get yourself dressed, the few times that you go to see the king, since I, your grandmother, dress myself every day. A princess should be dressed like a princess, and a soubrette like a soubrette." The little duchess, furious but remembering her breeding, made a silent reverence and withdrew. (See Appendix.)

Under the influence of "Goody Scarron," as the Princess Palatine called Mme. de Maintenon, formal court dress became high-necked and rigid late in Louis XIV's reign.

The low neckline of the final quarter XVIIc. will continue to be seen through first half XVIIIc., as kings' daughters act or are painted as allegorical or mythological characters. This gown always displays a good deal of chemise top and sleeve, even a shoulder and breast. But in e.XVIIIc., even the Princess Palatine considers a decorous form of this gown suitable for herself, wearing it with just such an ermine-lined mantle. (See Appendix: von B.)

The very cold winters of 1683-4 and 1688-9, were followed by warm ones, ending with the extraordinarily mild winter of 1693-4.

The winter of '83 is illustrated by many plates in the bound Bonnart in the Museum, Boston. No. 40 shows a lady *en écharpe;* 58, a man carrying a muff and wearing an unusual cape with embroidered front edges longer than his coat; 59 has an overcoat hung, cape-wise, over his shoulders. There are several later plates of ladies huddled at fireplaces with their feet on the fender; No. 106, *December,* shows one shielding her face with a firescreen, held in a hand the back of which is protected by a sort of stiffened mitten, reaching only to the knuckles, leaving the fingers free.

In 1694-5, the Thames again froze solid (Evelyn), and the Princess Palatine tells us that the intense cold at Versailles froze water and wine in the glasses at table. 1696-7 was another bad year; but the worst within living memory, in France, was that of 1708-9. Mme. de Maintenon sat in an especially constructed chair, like a sentry-box, which protected her from draughts from all directions. It was impossible to heat the great, high-ceilinged rooms of Versailles during any winter; in these particular years we see court ladies draped in ermine-lined oblongs, as large as comforters.

Gowns are beginning to be impressively studded with jewels, but the costume worn by Madame la Duchesse, with its lappeted and shaped corset-edge, and her uncovered hair, has a Bérain-like theatricality, not far removed from the frankly professional costumes of Watteau's *French Comedians.* Madame la Duchesse had a stately bearing but an indistinct speech. This is probably a gown to be worn at a fête. The days of court ladies appearing in private theatrical performances have begun, but will not become notable until the advent of the spirited duchess of Bourgogne.

1428. XVIIc. 1694. French. (Morgan Library.)

N. Bonnart. Lady of the Court in an Ermine Skirt.

Another court lady attempts to outwit the cold of 1694 by a gored skirt of ermine, a muff trimmed with a fringed bow, gloves and a lace scarf long enough to be knotted at the throat, hanging from her increasingly high *fontange* or *commode,* with the curls called *favorites* at the temples. There are all manner of names for the components of the headdress. Regnard's comedy of 1694, "Wait for me beneath the elm," explains that the *mouse* was "a small bow of ribbon which is placed in the *wood.* I must tell you that a knot of frizzled hair which trims the lower part of the fontange is called the *little wood.*" (Lacroix: *Eighteenth Century*). Her cuffs are laced back by a cord, the tassels of which match those which fasten her bodice to the embroidered corset.

1429. XVIIc. 1695. French. (London, National Gallery.)

N. de Largillière. James Francis Edward Stuart and Princess Louisa Maria Theresa Stuart.

During his early exile, Charles II's brother James had proved himself a brave and brilliant military commander under Turenne and Condé. After his return, his honest and efficient administration of the Admiralty was admired by Pepys. In 1660, he secretly married Clarendon's daughter Anne, by whom he had eight children, two of whom, Mary and Anne, became Protestant queens of England. In 1662, he was converted to Catholicism; and the next year took as his wife a hated Catholic princess, Mary of Modena, vulgarly called "the Pope's eldest daughter." The Test Act, to prevent Catholics from holding office, was passed, and he lived on the Continent for some time, until restored to the succession.

James was a better man than his brother, but as a king, he was politically inept and blinded by the successful results of his early firmness. Neither the marriage of his daughter Mary to the Protestant prince William of Orange in 1677, nor Mary of Modena's apparent inability to have more children after a long series of miscarriages, dispelled fears of a Catholic succession. James' alliance with France; his approval of the Revocation of the Edict of Nantes; his persecution of dissenters while showering very high-church men with patronage, because he believed that such persons were already half Catholic; his punishment of the Tory opposition; and his setting aside of the Test Act, resulted (as Rome and even the most devoted English Catholics had foreseen), in uniting factions which James believed to be safely at odds.

The son born to Mary of Modena in 1688 was supposed by many (including Bishop Burnet), to be an impostor planted to insure a Catholic succession. James' Protestant son-in-law was invited to succeed him as William III, and accepted in order to save England from being brought in on the French side in the wars which Louis was about to undertake. James fled to France, and after an inept Irish campaign in which he showed none of his old courage, crept back to die, broken and devout, at Saint-Germain under Louis XIV's protection.

"The Old Pretender," whom we see here with the sister born after him at the French court, was proclaimed king of England by Louis XIV after his father's death, and lived under Louis' protection. He

1428

1429

failed in his attempt to regain the throne from the Hanoverian succession, by way of Scotland in 1715; was one of the possible kings of Poland by virtue of his romantic marriage with the daughter of John Sobieski; and died in 1766 in Rome where he and his wife lived as king and queen of England at the Pope's expense.

He wears his own hair; a series of bows behind his cravat; and a brocade waistcoat, the sleeve of which is seen in a turned-back band over the deep cuff of his wide-skirted coat. He wears the Garter and shoes with a high tongue turned down to show its red lining. His sister, still in leading strings, wears an apron of lace, matching that of her corset, pleated cuffs, and the *fontange* which her mother will be influential in bringing to its end.

1430. XVIIc. Nov. 4, 1696. French.

From an almanach of 1697. Reception of the Princess of Savoy at Montargis.

Louis XIII's sisters, Christina and Henriette, had married, respectively, Victor-Amadeus I of Savoy and Charles I of England. The latter's daughter, Henrietta Maria, was the first wife of *Monsieur;* their daughter had then been married to Victor-Amadeus II. His child, the 11-year old Marie Adelaide of Savoy, was found suitable as a wife for Louis, duke of Burgundy, eldest son of the Grand Dauphin. In 1696 she was sent to live at the French court, in preparation for marriage.

From Louis XIV's time to the Revolution, separate establishments were set up for each member of the royal family in childhood, as they were for husband and wife of the great nobility. The contempt in which the nobility held the bourgeois functionaries of the crown led any concern with expenditures to be considered, increasingly, ill-bred; until the wealth amassed by these busy servants led the ruined nobility to "manure their fields" by marrying their daughters. Everybody lived at the expense of someone else and intrigued for more money to throw away. The advice of an experienced courtier to a novice was, "Speak well of everybody, ask for every vacant place, and sit down when you can." For signing his name once a year, a great lord would receive a percentage of the duties of a seaport; at the king's death, the thousands of horses in the royal stables fell to the Royal Equerry; so, too, the house servants sold for their own benefit any candle which had been lighted, and any left-over food (for the purchase of which commissions had already been

paid). In 1780, by "great reformations of the table," the expenditure for the food of *Mesdames,* those three aged ladies, is brought down to 600,000 livres a year (Taine).

Louis XIV went in state to meet the Princess of Savoy at Montargis. The illustration shows the little princess with her fiancé (who was not actually present); the duchess de Lude, who had been selected as *dame du palais* of the Princess' establishment; the count de Brienne, the ambassador who had taken delivery of the princess; and the marquis and marquise d'Angeau, the gentleman and lady of honor of her household. The king has his brother on his right, the Dauphin on his left, and is followed by his sons, by Mme. de Montespan, the count of Toulouse and the duke du Maine; and his sons-in-law, the dukes of Chartres and Conti.

The little princess was not at all pretty and had bad teeth, but was graceful and had been carefully tutored by parents familiar with French ways. "She did not fail in anything," Louis said, in writing Mme. de Maintenon of his delight at her manners and spontaneous charm. She became the freest and happiest personal contact of the old king's entire life, Mme. de Maintenon's doll, and the pet of the court. "Everybody is now becoming a child again," the Princess Palatine wrote wryly, having found herself, with three of her ladies, playing *"colin-maillard"* (blind man's buff), with the little princess.

"In private, she clasped the king around the neck at all hours, jumped upon his knees, tormented him with all kinds of sportiveness, rummaged among his papers, opened his letters and read them in his presence, sometimes in spite of him; and acted in the same manner with Mme. de Maintenon," whom she called "aunt." "Despite this extreme liberty, she never spoke against anyone; gracious to all, she endeavored to ward off blows from all whenever she could; was attentive to all the private comforts of the king, even the humblest; kind to all who served, and living with her ladies, as with friends, in complete liberty, old and young; she was the darling of the court, adored by all; everybody missed her when she was away; when she reappeared the void was filled up; everybody, great and small, was anxious to please her; in a word, she had attached all hearts to herself . . . The king really could not do without her. Everything went wrong with him if she were not by. She had measured his disposition to an inch"; her tact and discretion were flawless. She never came or went without seeing the king, and after even the latest party, "nevertheless adjusted things so well that she went and embraced the king the moment he was up, and amused him with a description of the fête." (Saint-Simon)

Although the marriage was not allowed to be consummated for two more years, the twelve year old princess and 15½ year old duke were married December 7, 1697. She wore a costume of silver cloth, edged with precious stones: she could scarcely walk when she put it on a few days later to show her schoolmates at St. Cyr, which she had attended, under the name "Mlle. de Lastic," and where, in the January before, she had played in *Esther,* at its first performance. At the marriage the duke had worn a gold-embroidered black mantle, lined in rose, over a white costume with diamond buttons.

Her young husband did immense credit to the efforts of his tutors, Fénelon and the duke of Beauvilliers. They had transformed an adolescent of brilliant intelligence, who was also a monster of uncontrolled violence, cruelty, arrogance and stubbornness, into an almost unrecognizable 20-year-old model of goodness, courtesy, and devotion to deeply-felt responsibilities. "A king is made for his subjects, not the subjects for the king," he said at Marly within the hearing of Louis XIV, who felt it a criticism of his own life. His young wife helped to correct the rather excessive new austerity, which made him go without a desk, in a room which needed regilding, in order to spend the money on charity.

The death of his father, in 1711, gave France as the new Dauphin, a poised and friendly man, of quick, inquisitive, instructed intelligence. But a year later, within days, both he and his wife were dead, probably of measles, though poisoning was also suspected. A few weeks later, their oldest surviving son died, and the heartbroken king was left with no heir but the sickly child who was to become Louis XV.

Louis XIV had always insisted on perfect dress, but the brilliant costumes of his younger days were given up after his remarriage. "He was always clad in dresses more or less brown, lightly embroidered, but never at the edges, sometimes with nothing but a gold button, sometimes black velvet. He had always a vest of cloth, or of red, blue, or green satin, much embroidered. He wore no ring and no jewels, except in the buckles of his shoes, garters, and hat, the latter always trimmed with Spanish point, with a white feather. He had always the *cordon bleu* over

his coat, except at fêtes, when he wore it under his coat, with precious stones, worth 8 or 10 million livres, attached." (Saint-Simon)

In this illustration, we see men's costume in all stages of transition, from coats of plain material patterned with braid, to those made of all-over patterned brocades, perhaps diamond-studded, but otherwise trimmed mainly along the seams and pocket edges. A coat of the plainest fabric now has cuffs of embroidery or brocade to match the elaborate vest.

Dress and masquerade costumes remained a passion with *Monsieur,* Louis' brother. We see him here, as Saint-Simon describes him: "A little round-bellied man, who wore such high-heeled shoes that he seemed mounted always upon stilts; always decked out like a woman, covered everywhere with rings, bracelets, jewels; with a long black wig powdered and curled in front; with ribbons everywhere he could put them; steeped in perfumes, and in fine a model of cleanliness. He was accused of putting on an imperceptible touch of rouge." *Monsieur's* one military command had been so successful that Louis took care he should never have another; according to his soldiers, he feared sunburn more than ball and powder.

His wife said, "As *Monsieur* loved to be covered with diamonds, it was fortunate that I did not regard them, for otherwise we should have quarrelled about who was to wear them." He danced well, she said, but not "like a man, because his shoes were too high-heeled." He is shown here in the longest wig and the highest heels of all, gloved, his coat sewn over with his diamonds.

Wigs are now universally worn, even by priests and monks, whose wigs have false tonsures. When they first came into use, under Louis XIII, their color was apt to be light or that of the natural hair. Darker perukes came into use; powder began to be used. Perukes are at their longest and fullest, now, at the turn of the century. As powder tended to litter the coat, wigs became smaller or were made of white hair, in a variety of subtle tints. There is already a good deal of variation in length, volume and form: in XVIIIc. wigs will become specialized by professions, and will last be worn by bishops in XIXc.; though they are still assumed in English official and legal wear. Diderot's *Encyclopédie* says that a wig might cost as much as 1,000 écus, but there were cheap wigs of goat's hair, and horsehair wigs which retained their curl. Wigs had to be dressed every two weeks, and preferably much more often; strenuous sports, like tennis, declined in popularity while wigs were in fashion.

Coat sleeves are longer and wider; skirts of coat full, with additional width pleated in at side-seam. Ambassador wears a shoulder knot of fringed ribbon.

The king had never liked the fontange headdress. On this state occasion the decorously gowned and gloved ladies wear it only as a backing for hair dressed in twin, diamond-studded peaks. In 1699, as fontanges two feet high seem to topple, d'Angeau's diary tells us that the king's distaste was so marked that the wife of the exiled English king, James II, gave up the fontange, and "in the twinkling of an eye, the ladies went from one extremity to the other." (Lacroix: *Eighteenth Century.*) Paris was less quick to follow Versailles, but the fontange was doomed.

1431. XVI-XVIIc. English. (Boston, Museum of Fine Arts.)

Needlepoint Bag:

Multicolor on Silver Ground.

1432. XVIIc. French. (Boston, Museum of Fine Arts, Elizabeth Day McCormick Coll.)

Brocade Pocket Book.

1433. XVIIc. French. (Boston, Museum of Fine Arts.)

Brocade Purse, showing the "Four Quarters of the Globe"; multicolored brocade with silver camel.

1434. XVII-XVIIIc. Spanish. (New York, Cooper Union Mus.)

Card Case.

1435. XVII-XVIIIc. Spanish. (New York, Cooper Union Mus.)

Card Case.

1436. XVIIc. English. (New York, Cooper Union Museum.)

Purse.

1437. XVIIc. American. (Brooklyn Mus.)

Corset of Natural Linen.

1438. XVIIc. c. 1620. French. (Boston, Museum of Fine Arts, Elizabeth Day McCormick Coll.)

Corset: blue silk damask, over wood; printed linen lining, brown on white. Built-in front pocket to hold a bottle of water to keep a bouquet fresh.

1439. XVIIIc. French. (Brooklyn Mus.)

Corset of Brocade. (See Appendix.)

1440

1441

1444

1445

1446

1442   1447

1440. Early XVIIIc. Italian. (Boston, Museum of Fine Arts.)
   Embroidered Stomacher: white silk ground, polychrome silk embroidery.

1441. Early XVIIIc. English. (Metropolitan Museum.)
   Embroidered Stomacher: silk embroidery on linen.

1442. XVIc. French. (Metropolitan Museum.)
   Busk: steel with engraved inscription.

1443. XVIIc. French. (Metropolitan Museum.)
   Busk: engraved ivory.

1444. XVIIIc. 1700-50. Italian? (Metropolitan Museum.)
   Busk: wood inlaid with ivory, mother-of-pearl and tortoise shell.

1445. XVIIc. c. 1685, French. (Boston, Museum of Fine Arts, Elizabeth Day McCormick Coll.)
   Embroidered Apron: yellow taffeta.

1446. XVIIIc. French. (Boston, Museum of Fine Arts, Elizabeth Day McCormick Coll.)
   Gold Lace Apron (see Ill. 1455.)

1447. XVIIIc. French. (Boston, Museum of Fine Arts, Elizabeth Day McCormick Coll.)

White Taffeta Apron: multicolor embroidery and gold bobbin lace edging.

In 1711, when Swift sent Stella silver lace for an under-petticoat, the entry of bullion lace had already been forbidden on pain of forfeiture and a £100 fine.

"Whereas two pieces of Silver Bone lace was brought to a shop in Winchester Street to be weighed, the Lace being suppos't to be stol'n, is stoped."† Mechlin and Brussels lace appeared in England under Anne.

1448. XVIIc. c. 1680. French. (Boston, Museum of Fine Arts, Elizabeth Day McCormick Coll.)

Woman's Shoe: light tan leather, dark olive green satin, and yellow straw appliqué simulating gold, seen also on bodice (Ill. 2084).

_____

† see Appendix.

1449. XVIIc. French. (Metropolitan Museum.)

Woman's Shoe: white kid and polychrome silk embroidery.

1450, 1452. First half XVIIIc. French. (Boston, Museum of Fine Arts, Elizabeth Day McCormick Coll.)

Woman's Brocade Shoe and Matching Clog: taupe satin ground, design white, yellowish green, pinkish red, pink, blue, and light tan; bound with dark brown.

1451. XVIIIc. c. 1750. English. (Metropolitan Museum.)

Woman's Shoes: these came to light during excavations in London, together with a quantity of men's knit hats and shoes. Heels covered with tan taffeta, narrowly edged with silver braid; vamps of leather and canvas, covered with green silk damask, and embroidered in silver. Similar pair dated c.1750, London Museum Catalogue of Costume, p.184,pl.LV.

1453. XVIIc. French. (Morgan Library.)

J. Mariette. Mlle. de Pons.

In her difficult days as the widow of Scarron, Mme. de Maintenon was loyally admired by Bonne de Pons, who became Marquise d'Heudicourt, and her sister. With sufficient research, one could undoubtedly discover a good reason, and a date, for Mlle. de Pons' appearance here; it seems probable that she was a relative of these old friends, and sponsored at court, like so many other girls, by Mme. de Maintenon. She may have become the abbess, sister of Prince Camille de Pons, who as Mme. de Marsin was governess of Louis XV's children, and like her father and brother received an income from the king.

Whatever the date of the plate, Mlle. de Pons' muff and wrap indicate one of the very cold winters, while the persistent bows on her corset, and the unexaggerated fontange, which are about all we can see of her dress, suggest a date not later than 1694.

1454. XVIIc. 1696. French. (Morgan Library.)

A. Trouvain. Madame la Princesse de Bade.

1455. XVIIc. French. (Morgan Library.)

A. Trouvain. Madame la Duchesse de Chartres.

1456. XVIIc. c. 1697. French. (Morgan Library.)

A. Trouvain. Charlotte, Landgrave of Hesse Cassel, Queen of Denmark.

In the costumes of Mlle. de Pons, the princess of Baden, and Madame la Duchesse, we see the steps by which line is transformed into motion, like that shown in the dress of the queen of Denmark.

Stiff brocaded fabrics, in large patterns, are giving way to plain materials, gathered flounces and horizontal lines. The uncluttered gored skirt worn by the first two ladies has been given additional fullness (and motion), in the gown of the duchess by the three great pleats set on either side. Mlle. de Pons' skirt is of a large-patterned material, unadorned except for a hem binding, but the brocade of her very new fringed wrap is lightly patterned. The princess' skirt is of plain material; its bandings, wide but delicate in pattern, are set in predominantly vertical lines, related to the goring. But there are underlying horizontal lines, and both are combined to form the newly important wide band around the hem.

The duchess' costume is of delicately striped brocade. Its vertical lines are swamped, on the underskirt, by two wide horizontal bands, sparkling with diamonds and shaking with fringe and tassels. A third band is furnished by the metal lace apron; it is only a step to the three gathered flounces of metal lace worn by the queen. Purely decorative aprons, like the metal lace one worn by the duchess, will be so universally worn that "low as a lady's apron strings" will be the Tatler's description of a gallant bow in society.

In its old form shown on the state ceremonial dresses worn at Montargis (1430), the overskirt was drawn back in a smooth flowing line and clasped at intervals to the underskirt; now it is being bunched up, in ways which culminate in the actual bustle worn by the queen. On the princess, its corners stick out; on the duchess, they are edged with passementerie; on the queen's gown, of perfectly plain material, they are edged with gathered lace. The skirt edges are now caught together at the center-back; and the frilled corners cascade below the bustle into which the top of the skirt is puffed.

1454. Prince Louis of Baden is actually in command of the Imperial forces opposing France in Italy, in 1696. But there are reasons for his wife's appearance here and now. Prince Louis, head of the Catholic branch of his house, is the hero who vanquished the Turks in 1689 and 1691. Louis XIV, not a bad Catholic, but a better Frenchman, had not entirely rejoiced with the rest of the Catholic world when a menace was removed from his enemy's back; and even Villars had opposed France's wanton devastation of Baden. John Sobieski III, who had saved Vienna from the Turks, has just died. There are eighteen candidates for the vacant throne of Poland; among them, Prince Louis vies with the duke of Lorraine, the prince of Conti, and Don Livio Odescalchi, nephew of Pope Innocent. In the end, the Elector of Saxony will win, by 8,000,000 florins and the renunciation of his Lutheranism, but at the moment it appears that the princess of Baden may well become the new queen of Poland. What the princess did become is an ancestor of Philippe-Egalité. Her daughter, not yet born, will be the adored wife of the Regent's scholar-naturalist son, for love of whom he will renounce the world, after her death in her second childbed.

1456. The court of the dissolute Danish king was a lavish imitation of Versailles; its amiable queen had the just sympathy and admiration of all Europe. Colored examples of this print show a fontange of red, blue, and gold; a red bodice with a gold *gourgandine,* a corset lacing over the fullness of the chemise (see Illus. 1465) like that of the duchess; a red overskirt, lined with blue, and flounced with white lace; an underskirt with alternating gold and silver *falabas,* the lace flounces which were introduced by Mme. de Maintenon.

Galloon is used on all these costumes; since metal galloon was wiry, it is pleated and bent, rather than cut, except where a band of fringe or another galloon would prevent fraying. It appears in the belt around the natural waistline of the queen; in bows on her muff and that of Mlle. de Pons; and hanging from the duchess' fan, always in combination with elaborately tasseled fringes.

Diamond earrings and a choker of huge pearls are standard with all who can afford them; obviously Mlle. de Pons cannot, and in any case she is unmarried. A cord, closed by a diamond slide, may be dropped into the corsage or display a diamond cross like that of the duchess. A profusion of immense diamonds is also sewn on the skirt bandings of the king's daughter; and the Danish queen has a huge brooch pinned on her muff.

Mlle. de Pons stands on rough ground in front of the walled garden of a very modest country house, although it probably passed muster as a chateau. The royal ladies appear on marble-paved terraces, against suitably formal gardens, complete with fountains and wrought balustrades.

1457 1458 1459

1457. XVIIc. 1695. French. (Morgan Library.)

A. Trouvain. The Duke of Savoy.

The father of the proposed bride of the duke of Burgundy is shown in clothes which are handsome but not of the cut current at the French court. Unless we are being given the artist's idea of foreign styles, the sleeve would appear to have remained close in Italy, so that there is a marked difference between the width of the brocade cuff and the forearm of the sleeve. In France, the sleeve is easier at the top and increases in width to the cuff, which is scarcely wider than the bottom of the sleeve. The underarm seam has the old emphasis, and the skirts have little flare. He wears a *Steinkirk* and a magnificent scarf of fringe and passementerie; this holds in place the diagonal ribbon and its pendant ornament, which is probably that of a knightly order although it might just conceivably be a watch. Shoes have the old square toe and high tongue.

1458. XVIIc. French. (Boston, Museum of Fine Arts, Elizabeth Day McCormick Coll.)

N. Bonnart. Spanish Dress.

Bonnart's plate of Spanish dress no doubt antedates Trouvain's of Italian, but it is convenient to set them together as French pictures of foreign fashions.

The proud Castilian is somberly dressed as what may now be a sort of stage figure of a Spaniard: flat-crowned, wide-brimmed hat; his own lank hair, with a lock in front of the ear, specific form of moustachio and goatee; golilla and wrist ruffles on a jacket which retains the Spanish shoulder-cap; long cape; Spanish rapier; rosette-trimmed shoes of comparatively natural shape, without heels.

1459. XVIIc. 1696. French. (Morgan Library.)

A. Trouvain. Charles de Lorraine, Count de Marsin.

The house of Lorraine had long been alienated from France. Charles of Lorraine, who passed his life, Voltaire said, in losing his estates, had sold the succession of Lorraine and Bar to Louis XIV against a life income. His subjects would have none of this arrangement; Charles abdicated in favor of his brother, the cardinal-bishop of Toul, and fought against France in the army of his brother-in-law, the emperor Leopold. His brother, who had never taken orders, was enabled to marry his cousin, Claude of Lorraine. Their son, Charles, whose title was recognized everywhere but in France, helped to defeat the Turks and was one of the candidates for the Polish throne; he failed to seize Lorraine in 1676, and refused its restoration in partial form. It was finally returned to

his son, Leopold, who ruled it admirably. Upon the marriage of Maria Theresa to Leopold's heir, Francis of Lorraine, Louis XV arranged to keep prosperous Lorraine from being joined to the Empire, by exchanging it for the Grand Duchy of Tuscany, which the heirs of the Empire ruled well. From his genial and learned little court at Nancy, Louis XV's Polish father-in-law administered Lorraine and Bar, which prospered under the legendary "good king Stanislas," until it reverted to France on his death at 89. Nothing endeared Stanislas more to his people than his original method of taxation. He went to church, rose after the sermon, waved his hat for attention, and mentioned the sum he needed. Men would sneak the linen out of the house and sell it to augment their share, since the king returned any surplus. (Mme. Campan).

Marsin or Marchin, a property of the House of Lorraine, was a name used by its cadet branch, to which the Chevalier de Lorraine belonged; he was a dissolute crony of "Monsieur," and gossip credited him with having poisoned the latter's first wife, Henrietta Maria.

As we see in the garments of the count of Marsin, the coat which is intended to be worn open, displaying a handsomely laced waistcoat, is still of the older, straighter cut; its lining is important, its inner edge is braided, and its buttons remain small. The old running braids are largely replaced by scalloped, lace-like passementerie. His shoulder knot is of cord, finished with points. The influence of the *Steinkirk* is seen in the less formal cravats, the pointed or rounded ends of which are merely folded over.

1460   1461   1462

1460. XVIIc. French. (Morgan Library.)

A. Trouvain. Monsieur le Duc de Chartres.

The eventual regent Orleans (nephew and son-in-law of Louis XIV), was a greatly gifted man with an extraordinary memory, and another victim of the conditions of court life. He had distinguished himself at Steinkirk, but was shunted off upon his return to Versailles. He combined a dissolute life in Paris with serious study of chemistry, painting and music.

Suspected of intriguing to replace Philip V as king of Spain, he was called back by Louis from brilliant military successes in Spain. Upon Louis' death he became regent by right of birth, succeeded in breaking Louis' will and attempted many liberal reforms. He gave back to Parliament rights which Louis had suppressed, attempted to enlist the services of the nobility which Louis had wasted, reduced taxes, liberated the Jansenists, and dreamed of revoking the

Revocation of the Edict of Nantes. But as an alternative to the bankruptcy of the state, which he had received in frightful financial condition, he became involved in the theories of the Scotch economist, John Law. Law's state banking system collapsed in 1719 after sensational beginnings and reckless speculation by all classes, who completely blocked traffic outside the offices of his Mississippi Company in Paris on the rue de Quincampoix. After this debacle and the suppression of the duke and duchess de Maine's conspiracy to replace him by Philip V, the Regent returned to the old governmental ways, serving as first minister from the majority of Louis XV, until his own death in 1723.

Chartres' costume, like that of the duke of Burgundy (1461), shows the increasing fullness of the skirts of the coat gored and pleated in at the hips. Coats are now, as often as not, made completely of brocade, which is more apt to be in a smaller repeated pattern than in the large, scrolled lace patterns used in the embroidery on the cuffs. When braid is used, its patterns are broken up, as in the zig-zag on Chartres' coat; the old block patterns in which braid was formerly applied are used by Burgundy in the placing of his sets of diamond buttons; these are now of immense size and Chartres uses scarcely smaller ones on his waistcoat as well.

Both wear hats cocked into definite tricornes. These have lost the lace edging which still appears on the hat of the prince of Savoy, and the plumes he shows have been reduced in France to a bare fringe of feathers, which will become a line of binding.

Burgundy's court costume, like those worn at Montargis (No. 1430), shows a square-edged cravat, but all are now folded over informally. Wrist ruffles are merely a fine finish to an unseen shirt sleeve. Shoulder-knots appear very generally; like sword-knots and the bows worn on muffs, they are finished by handsome, tassel-trimmed fringes. Shoes high, close, and delicate have a reduced tongue and a larger buckle than those worn by the duke of Savoy.

1461. XVIIc. 1697. French. (Morgan Library.)
Trouvain. Duke of Roquelaure.
Military life seems to have made Roquelaure, who became Marshal in 1724, extremely inventive about comfortable outer garments. This tasseled cape with a turned down collar is the forerunner of a loose, buttoned greatcoat with capes and pockets, which was still called a *Roquelaure* in midXIXc.

1462. XVIIc. 1695. French. (Morgan Library.)
Berey. Louis, Duke of Burgundy.
This engraving celebrates the marriage in December, 1697, of the Dauphin's eldest son to the little princess of Savoy (see Illus. 1430). He holds a portrait of her (wearing a *gourgandine*) propped on a carved table against a background of painted wall panels.

He is still the boy whose paroxysms of ungovernable rage, if crossed by no more than the weather, seemed to endanger his life and filled the court with apprehension at the prospect of his reign.

It is winter, although the fountains are still playing, as they do below the parterre on which Marsin walks in his summer clothes; Burgundy carries a muff suspended from his sash by the ribbon called a *passe-caille.* His breeches, like those of Chartres, are close and simple, without the obvious garter still worn by his father-in-law (1457).

DEVELOPMENT OF TRADES

The early craft guilds were composed of workmen, foremen, employers, merchants, and shopkeepers. In XIVc. the guilds began to split into trade and handicraft groups. Within these, major and minor guilds struggled for power. Should the blade- or the handle-maker control the knife trade? If weavers can dye, why cannot dyers weave?

The handicraft groups split into masters, and journeymen, many of whom could never hope to become masters. After an apprenticeship of 3-6 years, it was necessary to produce an expensive "master piece," pay a high entrance fee, and provide a banquet, even when guild membership was not limited to the children of masters.

Craftsmen within the livery companies were split into first and second class members: masters, and yeomen-bachelors, whose functions were defined. By end XIVc., shoemakers work with new leather; cobblers mend but do not make. Traders do not manufacture; masters do not do journeymen's work; journeymen are not supposed to do masters' work.

By 1405, the clothing trade had become divided into doublet-makers, who provided ready-made garments, and tailors who made to order. Fabrics were provided by the merchant guild of drapers; they considered the stock of trimmings kept by tailors as an infringement on their trade, and had them taxed.

Journeymen began to evade the control of the guilds by moving from their jurisdiction; great suburbs arose outside the city limits of London and Paris. In Germany, which was made up of small principalities, the journeymen were particularly hard to control, and took up the wandering careers which were still characteristic of itinerant German printers in America, into XXc.

Such conditions weakened the craft guilds by XVIc. The merchant-trader's guilds became richer and more powerful; they began to cut in on the trade guilds by their control of supplies; they brought in competing foreign goods. Guilds of merchants and artificers began to combine, always to the advantage of the merchant members.

The cap makers and hat merchants combined into the Merchant Haberdashers of 1500. The "linen armourers," tailors, and merchants were re-incorporated in 1503, as the Merchant Taylors, with Henry VII as an honorary member. The separately incorporated Fullers and Shearmen of 1507 were amalgamated in second quarter XVIIc. into the Clothworkers; they grew rich; many of their members became aldermen, and one, Lord Mayor; they rivalled the Drapers Company, one of the great original twelve.

The craftsmen of the early guilds, and the trading masters and yeomen of the XVc. were further split, in Elizabeth's time, into shipping merchants, merchant employers, small masters, and journeymen. The merchant employers became wholesale traders or large masters; the interests of small masters and journeymen began to coalesce in Stuart days.

The breeches-makers of Paris (equivalent to the Merchant Taylors of London) had acquired large interests in cloth production; in 1575 they combined with the drapers to control cloth (as the Merchant Taylors and Clothmakers did in London). The poorer masters were reduced to peddling breeches on the streets. Haberdashers and felt-makers combined in Paris in e.XVIIc.

In Paris in 1655, the *maîtres-marchands-tailleurs* (made-to-order) and the *marchands-pourpointiers* (ready-made) combined into the *maîtres-marchands tailleurs-pourpointiers* to control the clothing trade. By 1660, new statutes prevent *marchands, fripiers,* and *drapiers,* who are not members of the tailors' association, to make or sell any new garment.

A legacy from the old scramble to annex power can be seen in the variety of merchandise which may be sold in shops of a certain category. In the illustrations of Diderot's "Encyclopédie" we see that the XVIIIc. *boursier* manufactured not only purses, but certain sorts of caps, parasols, and Bavarian leather breeches. (See Appendix.)

1463-64. XVIIc. French. (Boston, Museum of Fine Arts, Elizabeth Day McCormick Coll.)

After *Nicolas de Larmessin, e.*

1463. Shoemaker.

1464. Tabletier.

Two of 25 hand colored plates which are contemporary piracies (in reversed position) of the enormously popular series of costume fantasies, based on occupations, by Larmessin, the elder, (1640-1725). The shoemaker exhibits among his footwear a man's shoe with a high platform sole and heel, clogs, *pantoufles,* boots, and shoes. A *tabletier* provides games, made from ivory, bone, horn, and ebony; and as the plates in the "Encyclopédie" show, makes other objects like combs and small boxes from the same materials. *Trou-madame* was one of the standard amusements at Louis XIV's *appartements;* unfamiliar game-accessories can be looked up in D'Allemagne. (See Appendix.)

1465. XVIIc. 1697. French. (Metropolitan Museum, Print Room.)

N. Arnoult. The French Tailor.

Since tailors had developed out of the *pourpointiers* and linen-armorers who provided padded and boned garments, corset-making was considered as part of tailoring; in any case, the corset was often a visible integral part of the gown.

1466. Paris Chez F. Guerard vis a vis la fontaine St Severin a l'image Notre Dame.

The five sets of plates of *Corps,* under *Tailleur* in Diderot's "Encyclopédie," show corsets for court and horseback, for pregnant women, boys and girls, as well as the difference between the long-bodied, straight-sided English corset, plain in front and laced down the back; and the curving lines of the French corset with its laced V-front.

1466. End XVIIc. or Early XVIIIc. French. (Morgan Library.)

F. Guérard. Cries of Paris.

As the easiest short-cut to an air of fashion, the *fontange* is quickly adopted by young women of the people. It is worn by the sellers of iced *tisane,* carp, tender root-vegetables, and by the girl with bouquets of jonquils, whose skirt hem is embroidered and apron edged with lace. The rather well-dressed young woman with the milk-jar on her head can only wear a cap with falls. The old women with baskets of artichokes and celery have bundled up their heads in the age-old kerchief.

The comfort of workingmen's clothes is slowly affected by fashion. Except for the young melon seller, they wear smocks; hand-me-down coats, long and straight; outmoded rabats, a knotted strip of something white, or no linen at all; comfortable full breeches; and flapping felt hats or cast-off *monteros.*

It seems to be a rule that for some time before privilege is about to be lost, those who enjoy it actually begin to lose their taste for it, whether or not they are conscious of the change, and whether or not they will fight to hold their privilege.

In XVIIIc., milkmaid styles begin to be worn as an alternative to oppressively panniered gowns. Style-consciousness increases among the lower classes. The pretty way in which the market women of Coventgarden manipulate a silk handkerchief as a head and neck covering will be copied by a famous procuress, adopted by her girls, carried by them to Ranelagh, and as the "Ranelagh Mob," will be worn by the aristocracy. (See Appendix.)

1467. XVIIc. June 16, 1600. English. (Sherborne Castle, Lieut. Col. Wingfield-Digby.)
Marcus Gheeraerts, e. Visit of Queen Elizabeth to Blackfriars.

In describing the wedding of Lord Herbert and Lady Anne Russell, R. Whyte wrote Sir Robert Sidney: "The bride met the Queen at the waterside, where my Lord Cobham had provided a lectica made like a litter, whereon she was carried to my Lady Russell's by six knights." The last of these is the groom, dressed in white, as are his father (2nd from left), the Queen, and the bride who follows. The gentlemen preceding the Queen wear the Garter and its Collar, with pendant miniature of the Queen; black cloaks embroidered in gold; and costumes for the most part in combinations of pale shades of rose, gray and green; with ruffs of many layers worn high. Lord Cobham, sword in hand, precedes the litter, dressed in peacock blue.

Dark colors, preferred earlier in Elizabeth's reign, "only white excepted which was then much worn at court," are beginning to alter to the light colors preferred in "King James his Reigne" (Moryson). From late Elizabethan times, short velvet capes, in their grandest form are often made of beaver, like the costumes of the ambassadors sent to France to arrange Charles I's marriage: "cloak and hose of fine white beaver, richly embroidered with gold, particularly the cloak within and without, nearly to the cape. The doublet was of cloth of gold, embroidered so thick that it could not be discerned, and the whole beaver hat was full of embroidery both above and below."

The Virgin Queen and bride wear open ruffs, and have huge pendants pinned to their left sleeves. The attendant ladies wear the closed ruffs of married women, very wide, full, and lacy, but carried lower on the neck.

In the background are the Gentlemen Pensioners with their halberds; their rich costumes are uniform only in their black and gold color. They were established by Henry VIII at his accession as the second oldest English royal bodyguard, antedated only by Henry VII's Yeomen of the Guard, which stand behind the litter in this illustration, wearing the union rose (gold on silver) and skull-caps instead of bonnets. Norris suggests that this may be a concession to their age, in a bareheaded procession. (See Appendix.)

The Yeomen of the Guard "were wont to be 250 Men of best quality under the Gentry, and of larger Stature than ordinary (for every one of them was to be Six Feet high) . . . of later Times reduced to 170 . . . at present no more than 100. These wear Scarlet Coats down to the Knee, and Scarlet Breeches, both richly guarded with black Velvet, and rich badges upon their Coats, before and behind; moreover, black Velvet round broad-crown'd Caps (according to the Mode used in the Reign of Henry VIII), with Ribbands of the King's Colour: One Half of them formerly bore in their Hands Harquebuses (but ever since the Reign of King *William* the Harquebuses have been disused); and the other Half, Partizans, with large Swords by their sides." (Chamberlayne)

1468. XVIIc. c. 1600. English. (Metropolitan Mus.)
Unknown artist. Queen Elizabeth.

The new tendency of bodice and skirt to separate can be seen in the different materials used in this example of Elizabeth's standardized personal costume, towards the end of her reign. (See Appendix.)

Where her head is framed by the loops of her wired headdress, lesser ladies may show a quivering, aigrette-like hair decoration, allied to the spray at Elizabeth's breast.

She shows looped bracelets of pearls, caught to sleeve and little-finger ring, and the new naturalism and asymmetry in the rose buds fastened to her ruff.

1469. XVIIc. c. 1611. English.

Renold Elstrack. James I and Anne of Denmark.

A number of engravings show the new king and queen after his accession in 1604. In one by Wierix c. 1605, the king wears truncated conical hat, falling band, cuirasse and scarf, and short open breeches, from under which hang gathered garters. The queen is dressed with comparative simplicity; much less hair, combed up into a point, love-locks in front of each ear, skirt without cartwheel top, falling in gathers over a small bolster.

Theirs was not the elegant court of Elizabeth. James had grown into an ill-proportioned slovenly man, who, though an accomplished rider, had to be tied in the saddle. "He never washed his hands, only rubbed his fingers' ends slightly with the wet end of a napkin." (Sir Anthony Weldon)

The luxury, masques and amusements of the English court were a revelation to the king of poor Scotland and his provincial Danish queen. But James never cared about his own dress, except that the doublets be quilted against his fears of assassination; on his clumsy body nothing looked well. Though we see him here in rosetted shoes, he protested their making a "ruffe-footed dove" of him.

James poured out luxury, however, on his handsome favorite Buckingham whom he called "Steenie," while signing himself "the old purveyor." In the

"little language" of the royal family we find James' detestation of pigs, and his characterization of Steenie as a dog preserved. Buckingham impudently calls James "His Sowship," and Anne of Denmark writes Steenie to "lug the sow by the ears." Buckingham writes from Spain (where he had accompanied Charles I on his fruitless, romantic quest for the Infanta) for more jewels: the king's best hat band, the Portugal diamond and the rest of the pendant diamonds, to make a necklace for the princess, and some rich chains for himself, else "your dog will want a collar."

"The wisest fool in Christendom," as Henry IV called James, had great pedantic learning, a quick coarse tongue, and a stubborn belief in absolutism, which embattled him with Parliaments and Puritans.

One of James' literary works was his "Counterblast to Tobacco," in 1610. Brought back, perhaps by Hawkins, in the third quarter XVIc., the use of the herb spread rapidly. Harrison in 1573 says: "In these daies, the taking-in of the smoke of the Indian herbe called 'tabaco' by an instrument formed like a litle ladell, whereby it passeth from the mouth into the hed and stomach, is gretlie taken-up and used in England, against Rewmes and some other diseases ingendred in the longes and inward parts, and not without effect."

The king and queen, standing below the arms of their countries, show the reduction in the use of braid and of all-over patterned brocades, which are being replaced by embroidered patterns running up from the hem.

The King's plumed bowler has a slightly cocked, wider brim; hair no longer cropped close; pleats shaping collar to neck show transition of open ruff into falling band collar; cape lengthening; pendant of the lesser George hanging by a scarf; doublet with slit, overlapping skirts; full breeches with padding and fabric cut and gathered as one; lace edged garter bow and the Garter on right leg; shoes with heels and rosettes.

The Queen's hair is padded very high and wide, with large, sparsely set decorations and a great brush-plume; frizzed curls along the hairline will soon become a straight fringe; slashing of sleeve just below the shoulder will be developed; pearls strung baldric-wise (like a military scarf); very wide drum skirt with elaborate cartwheel top; increasing importance of the skirt of the kirtle. Anne had inherited the 3,000 gowns in Elizabeth's wardrobe, many of them magnificently embroidered, and usable. (See Appendix).

1470. XVIIc. 1604. English. (London, Nat. Port. Gall.)
M. Gheeraerts. Somerset House Conference.

As King of Scotland, James had not been at war with Spain. The agreeable Juan de Tassis, sent by Lerma to congratulate James on his accession, had ingratiated himself and bested the French ambassador with many gifts of perfumed Spanish leather and gloves. Hostilities were suspended by James, who wished to see an end to the religious conflicts.

In 1604, after weeks of negotiations, during which the Spanish grandees were entertained by James at Somerset House at a cost of £300 a day, and after extensive bribing of the Howard faction by the duke of Frias, Constable of Castile, who headed the delegation, a peace was signed which left Holland alone, finally to conclude her struggles with the Archdukes in 1609.

Against tapestried walls, the Spanish plenipotentiaries on the left of the council table, which is covered with a fine rug, have the nearly identical somber costumes, neck and wrist ruffs, and beards as those painted by El Greco. There is more variety in the English negotiators: in the cut of their hair and beards, little caps on old bald heads near the open window, more complicated ruffs, braided and buttoned light doublets, short capes, and the preponderant absence of wrist ruffs.

1471. XVIIc. 1603. English. (Metropolitan Museum.)
Unknown artist (formerly att. to *Gheeraerts*). Henry Frederick, Prince of Wales, and Sir John Harington. (See Frontispiece, Vol. I.)

The lumpish, effeminate and timorous king, who had no taste at all, and his disdainful, masculine wife who had a great deal of taste, all of it bad, were the parents of two children in addition to Charles I, of the most luminous grace, dignity and taste. Henry, Prince of Wales and Elizabeth of Bohemia (who was called the "Queen of Hearts," because of her gallantry in exile) were, after all, grandchildren of Mary Queen of Scots.

From earliest childhood, Henry promised to become perhaps the greatest English king. He was already one of the four or five greatest book collectors of his time, and had formed an unsurpassed collection of coins and medals; he was a perfectionist as an athlete and horseman; he had his father's wit in a more attractive form; his was the most popular court, gay, intelligent and completely decorous. Young as he was, Henry championed Sir Walter Raleigh in the Tower, saying: "No King but his father would keep such a bird in such a cage;" and the realization of Henry's compassion, as Phineas Pett (Illus. 1485) knelt before the king during his entire trial for incompetence, led the old shipbuilder to name his next great 1400 ton warship "The Prince."

Henry's hunting companion is the son of Lord and Lady Harington, who had charge of his sister; their arms hang above them. Whether or not Henry was poisoned, before they were 19 both boys were dead. As he had for Elizabeth, James forbade the court to wear mourning for Henry.

Ruffs, originally of linen, were later made of lawn, and were sometimes dipped in colored starches. Ruffs of colored net, and collars of dyed batiste, edged with white lace (like the blue one the Prince wears here), are now occasionally seen. Yellow ruffs are constantly singled out for attack by writers and preachers in late XVI-e. XVIIc., and were forbidden in the Cathedral by the dean of Winchester. Their use came rather quickly to an end, when a physician's wife, Mrs. Turner (the leading yellow-starcher of her day, who was supposed to have brought the method from France), was condemned to be hung wearing one of her own abominable yellow ruffs; at the instigation of Lady Essex, she had poisoned Sir Thomas Overbury, while he was already imprisoned in the Tower for writing "The Wife," an attack on the liaison of his friend, the favorite Rochester, with the already infamous countess.

In latter half XVIc. lacy embroidery had begun to be used on high-crowned, plumed hats; replacing braid, it is now used only on edges and on the most important seams. The prince's doublet with overlapping skirts retains only a hint of the peascod belly.

He had been invested with the Garter in June and

wears the pendant of the lesser George on its blue ribbon; his sword and hunting horn hang by two other crossed scarves. High boots with cuffs reversed. Cropped hair, with tiny lovelocks.

1472. Early XVIIc. German. (Hampton Court, H. M. the King.)

Unknown artist. Christian, Son of Henry, Duke of Brunswick.

Entire costume gored; seaming replacing braid decoration. Style comes as often out of limitations, as from any other factor: the cut of military leather garments was dependant on the size and imperfections of hides; new ways of cutting then affected non-military garments cut from cloth.

Around the turn of the century, there was a tendency to separate doublets and breeches completely, by color and decoration; the same impulse is followed in women's dress. During first half XVIIc., the costume will become completely unified. Both impulses are shown in this costume, in which the doublet of a dotted fabric, and breeches of plain, are both gored. The breeches, full, but gored and narrowed

into the waist by additional interior gores, require a fly-closing; this is made of the dotted fabric of the doublet.

The collar, gored and standing like a ruff, is turning down into a band; it has the tasseled cords which have hung from band collars throughout second half XVIc., and which will continue to be used, but knotted, in XVIIc.

1473. XVIIc. 1608. English. (New York, Knoedler.)

M. Gheeraerts, y. Portrait of a Boy.

Embroidery began its rapid development in England during the latter part of Elizabeth's reign. The bold and fabulous growths, predominantly blue-green and rusty-red to yellow, familiar on the "crewel" embroidered white linen bed-hangings of second half XVIIc., stem from such work as Elizabeth's skirt in the Hardwick portrait, and the garments of this boy.

1474   1475

1476   1477   1478

1474. XVIIc. 1611. English. (London, Christie sale, May 1, 1925.)

M. Gheeraerts, y. Frances Howard, Duchess of Richmond.

"Flowers and fanciful attire indicate festivities in connection with a wedding." (Morse: *Elizabethan Pageantry.*)

But, during the 100 years of her life, Frances Howard was always what in the U.S.A. today, would be called a "character." She gave supper parties with a great show of silver and plate, but no food, and ate alone later. She was immensely proud of the Dukes, her grandfathers, both dead on the scaffold; and lorded it over the Earl of Hertford, second of her three husbands, who used to take her down by asking: "Frank, Frank, how long is it since you were married to Prannell?" (Her first husband, a certain Prannell, had been, inexplicably, a London vintner of no pretensions whatever.) On the death of her third husband, Ludovic, Duke of Richmond, she announced that she would never again marry or eat at table with anyone less than a king.

Courtesy of the Frick Art Reference Library (1474)

Between 1610-20, necklines were occasionally cut much lower than on this bodice, even exposing the breasts entirely; male portraits in fancy dress show a doublet bosom cut almost away in the same manner.

With this neckline, a flat wired lace whisk is usually worn under the chin; its tasseled white ties hang down, over a black neck-cord falling between the breasts.

The lace-edge white bodice is scrolled with floral embroidery. The kirtle skirt, dark green, decorated in gold, is of the 1610-20 ankle length.

Her red cloak is worn in the currently beloved diagonal fashion; it is lined with white brocade; caught on one shoulder with a black bow; its embroidery is no longer in a band, but rises from the hem in patterns derived from reticella lace edgings.

White shoes with immense gold rosettes, airy decoration of the hair which is descending at the sides.

1475. XVIc. 1594. English. (Ditchley, Viscount Dillen.)

M. Gheeraerts. Capt. Thomas Lee.

This picture of male fancy dress is set, out of strict chronological order, as a parallel to Illus. 1474; the

1479

1481

1480

1482

shirt open low on the bosom will also be seen in the Oliver miniature (Ill. 1491).

Capt. Lee wears a slightly peascod doublet open over a superbly embroidered shirt with a great lace collar; the length of the shirt is curiously rucked up and padded to simulate upper hose. With this vulnerable costume and bare legs and feet, he wears a pistol and dagger and carries a morion and shield.

1476. XVIc. English. (Boston, Museum of Fine Arts.)
Gloves with Embroidered Cuffs, said to have belonged to Queen Elizabeth.

1477. XVIIc. English. (Boston, Museum of Fine Arts.)
Gloves with Embroidered Cuffs.

1478. Early XVIIc. English. (Boston, Museum of Fine Arts.)
Embroidered Gloves.

1479. Late XVIc.-Early XVIIc. French. (Boston, Museum of Fine Arts, Elizabeth Day McCormick Coll.)
Man's Doublet: white leather, slashed and punched, trimmed with gold braid; olive green velvet (probably modern) under slashes; front padded in style known as *cosse des poies;* sleeves separate from rest

of doublet, but sewn to linen guimpe.

1480. Late XVIc.-Early XVIIc. French. (Boston, Museum of Fine Arts, Elizabeth Day McCormick Coll.)
Man's Leather Boots: light greyish white leather trimmed with appliqué of white leather; tops slashed with olive green velvet (possibly modern) under slashes.

1481. XVIIc. 1600. Bohemian. (Metropolitan Museum.)
Man's Pourpoint: cream satin, embroidered in colored silk.

1482. XVIIc. c. 1603-25. English. (Metropolitan Mus.)
Woman's Embroidered Jacket.

A guest at Elizabeth of Bohemia's wedding in 1613 wrote, "The Lady Wotton was reported to have a gown that cost 50 pound the yard for embroidery; and the Lord Montague bestowed 1500 pound in apparel upon his two daughters."

Photographs of a similar jacket, the actual garment painted in Ill. 1502, is reproduced with notes in A. F. Kendrick: *Book of Old Embroidery,* and *Embroidery,* part I, p. 17, fig. 10 and frontispiece.

1483. XVIIc. c. 1613. English. (Malmesbury, Charlton
Park. Margaret, Countess of Suffolk and Berk-
shire.)

Daniel Mytens, e. Sir Edward Sackville, Fourth
Earl of Dorset.

There is a companion portrait of his brother
Richard, standing in the same setting; he wears one
tasseled earring; his doublet, unbuttoned half way
from the bottom, shows his full shirt, and has a baldric-like band disappearing into a slit in the bosom
and crossing the shoulder underneath the garment;
his lace-edged garters make a pattern against his
stockings, and hang half way to the immense lace
rosettes across on his shoes.

The Sackvilles were still children when Elizabeth
died: Leicester and his elegance were gone before
their birth. But their clothes are the last extravagant
manifestation of the preceding period, and worn by
no decadent courtiers, either. The Sackvilles, for all
their personal beauty, were a family notable for wide
interests, cultivation, courage, and competence. Edward was Bacon's defender, twice Ambassador to
France, and privy-councillor to Charles I. It was he
who retook the royal standard at Edgehill, after re-
fusing Charles' order to conduct the young princes
out of the battle, since "he would not be thought a
coward for ever a King's son in Christendom." From
Charles' execution until his own death, he never
went out of Dorset House.

"The English," wrote Moryson at just about this
time, "are more sumptuous than the Persians, because despising the golden meane, they affect all ex-
tremeties. For either they will be attired in plaine
cloth and light stuffes (always provided that every
day without difference their hats be of Bever, their
shirts and bands of the finest linnen, their daggars
and swords guilded, their garters and shooe roses of
silke, with gold on silver laces, their stockings of
silke wrought in the seames with silke or gold, and
their cloakes in Summer of silke, in Winter at leaste
all lined with velvet) or else they daily weare sumptuous doublets and breches of silke or velvet, or cloth

of gold or silver, so laid over with lace of gold or
silke, as the stuffes (though of themselves rich) can
hardly be seen."

The brothers wear almost identical great lace-edged
whisks; hair longer and fluffed; beards and moustaches reduced.

Edward's gloves deserve attention. They have the
gauntlet cuff of the XVIIc.; but it is so related to the
doublet in fabric, matching embroidery, and lace-
edged scallops like those of the whisk, as to appear
part of the doublet; a tiny wrist-ruff, set over the
seam between leather hand and fabric gauntlet, adds
to the illusion of a short glove worn with an extravagantly cuffed doublet. The ungloved hand shows
the actual cuff to be a flat one of straight-edged lace.

"Milloners or haberdashers," Stow says in his
varied spelling, "had not then any *gloves imbroiaered,*
or trimmed with gold or silke; neither gold nor im-
broidered girdles and hangers, neither could they
make any costly wash or *perfume,* until about the
15th yeere of the queane, the Right Honorable Edward de Vere, Earl of Oxford, came from *Italy,* and
brought with him gloves, sweete bagges, a perfumed
leather jerkin, and other *pleasant things*: and that
yeere the queene had a *pair of perfumed gloves* trimmed only with four tuffes or *roses of coloured silke.*
The queene tooke such pleasure in these gloves, that
she was pictured with these gloves upon her handes,
and for many years after it was called 'The Earl of
Oxford' perfume."

Both brothers have heavily embroidered capes with
wide collars slung over a shoulder; and wear immense, loose, embroidered slops. Edward is gartered
below the knees; his silk stockings have embroidered
clocks which almost surround the ankle; shoes with
high heels and great choux on the strap are embroidered to match the doublet.

1484. Start of XVIIc. English. (London, Nat. Port. Gall.)
P. van Somer (copy of). Charles, tenth Earl of Nottingham.

The Lord High Admiral, Howard of Effingham,
who vanquished the 149 great ships of the Armada

with his 80 small ones, by "plucking their feathers one by one," was made Earl of Nottingham in 1596. He had advised Elizabeth to sign Mary Stuart's death warrant, and it was to him on her death bed that Elizabeth designated Mary's son as her successor. The Admiral retained his post under James I until charges of corruption, (in which the courteous and estimable old man of 82 had no part) brought about his resignation and the reorganization of the navy.

The admiral wears a cap indoors: quantities of these delightful caps, as well as the embroidered gloves of the period, are still in existence in our time. His hat stands on a table covered by a fine carpet; imported rugs are still luxury articles, although they have begun to be manufactured in England, in last quarter XVIc., and are the models for small pieces of tufted "Turkey work." Fringed velvet covers, often embroidered (Ill. 1486), tend to replace rugs as table coverings.

Scarlet peer's robes are worn with the Garter and its collar and blue sash. Doublet is slightly peascod; paned trunk hose will be retained with ceremonial robes. Shoes have high cork soles, raised in back, which preceded heels; ribbon ties over a tongue. Walking stick.

1485. XVIIc. 1613. English. (London, Nat. Port. Gall.)
Unknown painter. Phineas Pett, Master-builder of the Navy.

Ships had been built along the S.E. coast of Eng-

possible, so great and so casual were the movements of English armed shipping, whether independent or the Queen's own.

Despite the corrupt and lax administrations of the Admirals Effingham and Buckingham, and his own inadequate resources, James I showed great interest in maintaining his fleet.

Under his master-builder, Phineas Pett, naval construction advanced from a knack of science.

In 1641, Evelyn, saw the launching of Pett's "glorious vessel, the Royal Sovereign," (the first to be taxed and a contributing cause of the Great Rebellion). He banqueted with Pett at his country house, with its statues and gardens, and calls Pett "the most skillful shipbuilder in the world . . . the inventor of the frigate-fashion of building." By 1660, ships could be built of such size that an hereditary Royal Navy was no longer possible; Charles II had to levy taxes for their support. Evelyn had been impressed by the pleasure boats he saw in Holland; in 1661, the Dutch East India Company presented Charles I with the first yacht to be owned in England.

In his office above the shipyards (which we see through the window) Pett wears the embroidered cap which any man of the XVIIc. would have worn indoors in a less draughty place.

Pett's wired whisk shows a few of the pleats of its ancestor, the open ruff. Its dangling cords are now knotted.

The shorter-waisted pinked doublet shows sleeves

1485 1486

land, under expert Genoese supervision, since e.XIVc. Men-of-war were, however, a personal possession of the king, until second half XVIIc. No ruler before the Tudors had enough wealth for naval expansion. Henry VIII in his 5th year, "built a Ship, then accounted the biggest that ever had been seen in England, and named it Henry Grace de Dieu, or the Great Henry; it was 1000 tons." (Chamberlayne)

Until Henry VIII, privateers and merchant adventurers, exempt from admiralty control, had largely to look out for themselves and the defense of their own part of the coast. Under Elizabeth, incentives of piracy and trade expanded shipyards enormously. The Emperor's agent found effective espionage im-

caught along the inseam by bows; full baggy breeches, braided along the outer seam. Sword slung in the old manner. Rather full beard of a worthy man, neither young nor elegant.

1486. XVIIc. 1618-21. English. (London, Nat. Port. Gall.)
School of P. van Somer. Francis Bacon, Baron Verulam, Viscount St. Alban.

The impatient, ambitious intelligence of Burleigh's nephew, and his eloquence, of which Ben Jonson said "the fear of every man that heard him was lest he should make an end," alienated Elizabeth from utilizing Bacon's services. Under James I he rose quickly to the Lord Chancellorship, and aroused the fears of the favorite, Buckingham. Bacon was accused of corruption (of a sort generally accepted in his day), acknowledged his conviction to be "just, and for reformation's sake, fit," and retired from government to continue his philosophical and scientific writing. These works helped to free science from theology and laid the base for modern experimental investigation. Bacon's death resulted from an experiment; he took a fatal chill when he got out of his coach to pack a chicken carcass with snow, so that he might study the effect of refrigeration on putrefaction.

The hat with truncated cylindrical crown, seen last quarter XVIc., is wider brimmed, wreathed with a crepe twist. Hair longer; beard like that which Evelyn's father in 1620 "wore a little peaked as the mode was." The Chancellor's gown has a hanging sleeve strip and braid trim; he leans on a walking stick.

Braid is changing its character from flat, woven, running bands into rounded, braided open forms used with braided buttons, knotted, looped and fringed into frogged fastenings and patterns.

1487. XVIc. 1566 Dutch. (Metropolitan Museum.)
Quilted Cap of White Linen.
The parchment which was preserved with this cap is dated "Bruxelles, anno MDLXVI," and announces in Latin that it was made by Margaret of Parma's own hands, and is ordered by her to be given to Antonio du Granvelle, described as a most eminent and trusty servant of Philip, king of Spain. The Cardinal, her chief counsellor, seems to have revered it too much to wear it.

1488. Late XVIIc. Italian. (Metropolitan Museum.)
Man's cap: Knitted green and white silk.

1489. Early XVIIIc. English. (Metropolitan Museum.)
Man's Cap: White linen, embroidered in colored silk. Early XVIIc. versions of this embroidered cap have been seen in Ills. 1470, 1484, 1485.

When Miss Molly set out to marry old Isaac Bickerstaff, we are told (Tatler, #91, Nov. 8, 1709). "Things went so far that my mistress presented me with a wrought night-cap and a laced band of her own working."

The head of a well-born male is seldom seen uncovered. The hat is worn indoors as well as out, although it may be replaced by one of these caps. As heads are cropped for wigs, such caps, and heavier fur-edged monteros, become indispensable.

John More, the eccentric rector who turned Baptist in 1699 "went through Worcester with a handkerchief on my head, resolving never again to wear a wig ... A neighbor objecting against my white cap I said the mountains and hills wear white caps, I am in the mode." (Ponsonby: *English Diaries*).

1490. XVIIc. English. (Dulwich College Gallery.)
Unknown artist. Nathaniel Field.

One of the three great acting troupes of the Elizabethan theatre was that of the Children of the Royal Chapel; its necessarily frequent replacements were made by the most brutal means. Field (1587-1633), who became the most brilliant young actor of his time, was the son of a Puritan preacher, violently opposed to the stage, who died shortly after Field's birth, and the brother of a later Bishop of Hereford. He was kidnapped into the company in early adolescence, in 1600. Field wrote two good plays, one with Massinger, with whom he was imprisoned for debt. He later became a member of the King's Players which had developed out of Burbage's troupe; Ben Jonson wrote "Which is your Burbage now? .... your best actor, your Field?" Before 1625, he had retired and died in 1633.

Shirts still are, as Stubbes wrote in 1583, "either of cambric, holland, lawn, or else of the finest cloth that may be got. And of these kind of shirts everyone doth now wear alike ... wrought throughout with needlework of silk, and such like, and curiously stitched with open seam, and many other knackes beside. Shirts .. cost .. ten .. twenty .. forty shillings, some five pounds, some twenty nobles . . and some ten pounds apiece."

This shirt with a falling band collar, and tie strings fluted to match the cuffs, is embroidered on the lines along which a doublet would be braided; earring cord; goatee and small moustache.

1491. XVIIc. Before 1617. English. (London, Victoria and Albert Museum.)
Isaac Oliver. Young Man.

Against a background of flames, the young man in this miniature wears a single earring, chain and pendant, with his beautiful shirt open almost to the waist. Women's bodices are seen, c.1615, cut out to below the midriff, barely containing the points of the breasts within the sides of the bodice. At the same period, this female U opening is seen, with bare legs and feet, in male fancy dress; the same impulse is responsible for this open shirt. (See also Ill. 1475.)

1492. XVIIc. English. (Northampton, Ecton Hall.)
Isaac Oliver, d.1617. Anne of Denmark.

1493. XVIIc. English. (London, Victoria and Albert Museum.)
Isaac Oliver. Anne of Denmark.

1494. XVIIc. 1617 Flemish. (Hampton Court, H. M. the King.)
Paul van Somer. Anne of Denmark.

James thought armed hunting "a thievish kind of sport," but chased with a pack to the exhaustion of the court. The queen's hunting costume, worn with gauntlets and a male hat, is a severe version of ordinary dress. The hair and hip bolster are reduced to comfortable size; the low neck is filled with a lawn partlet; and a manageable wired whisk of bobbin lace, through which wind will pass easily, is buttoned together in front.

The note of dangling black is now often tied into the hair, on one or both sides; it is worn by both men and women, particularly on the Continent, and progresses from a thread-like cord to a ribbon ending in points, and, eventually, in tassel-like bows.

The miniatures by Oliver show two unusually interesting collars, above the low-cut bodice so characteristic of England, 1610-20; the frizzled hair and love-lock; and the clutter of ornaments, in which the costume of Elizabeth came to an end, as described in "Lingua, or the combat of the tongue," by Thomas Tomkis. (Quoted by Morse.) ". . . Five hours ago I set a dozen maids to attire a boy like a nice gentlewoman; but there is such doing with their looking glasses, pinning, unpinning, setting, unsetting, formings and conformings, painting blew veins and

cheeks; such stirr with sticks and combs, cascanets, dressings, purls, falls, squares, busks, bodies, scarfs, necklaces, carcanets, rebatoes, borders, tires, fans, palisadoes, puffs, ruffs, cuffs, muffs, pulses, fusles, partlets, frislets, bandlets, fillets, crosslets, pendulets, amulets, annulets, bracelets, and so many lets (hindrances) that yet she is scarce dressed to the girdle; and now there's such a calling for fardingales, kirtles, busk-points, shoe ties, etc., that seven peddlers' shops —nay all Stourbridge fair—will scarce furnish her: A ship is sooner rigged by far, than a gentlewoman made ready."

The androgynous character of Elizabethan costume is most striking in this moment of its decadence. Women's parts are acted on the stage by boys; women add to their more severe and rigid costume the hat which is the most masculine feature of male clothing; and men in long love-locks, wide loose breeches, and rosettes assume, on occasion, the extremely exposed breast which is the most feminine part of women's dress.

The two miniatures show Anne, "so low she went bare all the days I had the fortune to know her," as Osborne said, describing James' ostentatious farewell, "kissing her sufficiently to the middle of her shoulders," as he left her coach to hunt.

In her frizzed and love-locked hair, and over her gowns and the two interesting ruffs, Anne has pinned or hung a clutter of lockets and brooches, keepsakes, posies and animals. This is merely the tasteless cul-

1498　　　1499　　　1500

mination of Elizabethan ways.

Burleigh's son, the Earl of Salisbury, though a cripple on crutches, was a delightful man. A letter written Sept. 18, 1592, by the Earl of Shrewsbury says: "Young Lady Derby, wearing about her neck in her bosom a picture which was in a dainty tablet, the Queen (Elizabeth) espying it, asked what fine jewel that was. The Lady Derby was curious to excuse the showing of it; but the Queen would have it; and opening it and finding it to be Mr. Secretary's (Salisbury's), snatched it away, and tied it upon her shoe, and walked long with it; then she took it thence and pinned it to her elbow, and wore it some time there also." Salisbury wrote verses about this, which Elizabeth heard of, and insisted should be sung to her.

(Intended Ills. 1495-97 did not arrive from European sources in time to be included in the book.)

1498. XVIIc. 1619. English. (Northampton, Lamport Hall, Gyles Isham.)

C. Janssens van Ceulen, e. Portrait of a Lady.

The excessively low-cut neckline is being filled in, and the ruff is declining. Attempts to give it fresh interest result in colored ruffs, of varying width, with contrasting edges, overlaid with points of bone lace. The Mary Stuart cap is also renewed by its covering of prickly points of lace.

1499. XVIIc. 1621. English. (London, Sir Osbert Sitwell.)

Cornelius Jansens (signed). Portrait of a Lady with her Daughter.

This portrait shows many specifically English characteristics in common with that of Margaret Laton's (No. 1502). Both women wear caps, of the Mary Stuart shape, which will recede and widen to frame the head, as hair becomes wider, longer and develops a fringe in the 1630-40's. On all three figures we see falling ruffs and whisks being transformed into the collars which will soon cover the shoulders. The child's whisk has developed long kerchief-like points; the neckline is set eccentrically in her mother's ruff; Margaret Laton's falling ruff is patterned along the sides of its central division.

Both ladies show the separation of skirt from bodice, the scalloped borders of which precede the long, tabbed skirts on the low-necked jackets of the 30's. The outer robe is reduced to a skeleton; sleeves shorten, cuffs become less close fitting; little scarves

and bracelets are clasped around the wrist. Earrings on cord.

The child in an apron has a scarf tied about the upper arm, prophetic of an important usage to come. From John Manningham's diary we learn that in 1601-2 "the play of shuttlecocke is become soe much in request at Court that the making of shuttlecockes is almost growne a trade in London."

1500. XVIIc. 1624. English. (London, Lord North.)

C. Janssens van Ceulen, e. Hon. Elizabeth North.

The steady rise of distinguished citizens into the nobility is well illustrated by the Norths. An eminent lawyer and clerk of Parliament became the first Lord North in 1554; the second was a soldier and courtier of Elizabeth; the third, father of the Hon. Elizabeth North, was a poet, an athlete, and friend of Prince Henry, an upholder of the Commons, and of Parliament in the Civil War.

The curative powers of the mineral springs at Tunbridge Wells were discovered by him in 1606, yet in 1630, Henrietta Maria and her suite had to live in tents while she took the waters after the birth of Charles II. A few houses and amusements were then provided, and with the visits of Charles and Catherine of Braganza, and of James with his family, Tunbridge became fashionable. It was favored by Puritans and has to this day an Evangelical flavor. Anne loved it, long before she was queen or it was paved, which was done in her honor; Tunbridge and Bath became the fashionable watering places of the XVIIIc. The springs at Epsom, also discovered by Lord North, were favored by people from East London, whom Pepys, on his visit, considered common.

The petal shapes, in which the lace of caps is finished, have been used in the metal leaves which replace lace on her headdress.

1501. XVIIc. English. (New York, Knoedler.)

M. Gheeraerts. Lady of the Lenox Family.

Characteristic of costume of the first quarter XVIIc., particularly in England, is the narrow bit of black cord, dangling somewhere. It may be caught under a finger and twisted about a wrist, as the Lenox lady wears it. One portrait of Elizabeth of Bohemia shows it trailing along a ruff, from a pierced ear. Small pieces of sentimental, keepsake jewelry are much seen now, like the pansies for thought in the hair of the Lenox lady. In the same category are Elizabeth North's earrings, of hearts pierced by arrows. They might well hang by a black thread, like Margaret Laton's, except that the motif is used only once in each costume, and she already carries a keepsake ring hanging on a black thread, above her rose breast-pin enamelled in the combined colors of York and Lancaster.

1502. First third XVIIc. English. (London, Lord Harmsworth.)

Unknown artist. Margaret, wife of Francis Laton of Rawdon.

Sir Hugh Brawn's daughter, wife of the Yeoman of the Jewel House to James I, Charles I and II, is shown wearing a tunic which was bought, together with the portrait, from one of her descendants in 1929 for £4200; it is the best preserved and executed garment of the period remaining to us, and is reproduced with notes and photograph in Kendrick (see Ill. 1482).

The photograph shows the jacket to be of hip length, with shoulder wings, and a sleeve ending in a point which turns back to form a cuff, and is closed along the outer seam above the wrist. The jacket is of white linen, embroidered in gold, silver and colored silks, on a spangled ground, and edged with gold and silver lace. (See text, Ills. 1499, 1501.)

1503. XVIIc. Dutch-English. (Northampton, Lamport Hall. Gyles Isham.)

Mierevelt. George Villiers, First Duke of Buckingham.

James' favorite, "raised from a Knight's fourth son to that pitch of glory, and enjoying great possessions, acquired by the favour of the King upon no merit but his beauty and prostitution" (Lucy Hutchinson), was by 1616-18, the second richest nobleman in England. He eloped with the greatest heiress in England, the duke of Rutland's daughter, with whom he lived on the most affectionate terms, endowing her with his own immense estates.

Buckingham was a person of the most dazzling charm and beauty; intelligent, well-intentioned, pleasant to his inferiors, arrogant, reckless, no statesman, and unfitted for the power he wielded. Despite the opinions of Lucy Hutchinson, the Protestant Colonel's wife, Buckingham was liked and respected by far more estimable old gentlemen than Bishop Good-

man who insisted he was "inwardly beautiful as he was outwardly."

Twenty-six years younger than James, Buckingham was only eight years older than Charles, over whom he had great influence. After the favorite's assassination at thirty-six, Charles brought up Buckingham's children with his own; during his exile and for some time after the Restoration, Charles II, and the second duke of Buckingham, two years his senior, will be inseparable companions.

Lucy Hutchinson said: "It was common for him at any ordinary dancing to have his clothes trimmed with great diamond buttons, and to have diamond hat bands, cockades and earrings: to be yoked with great and manifold knots of pearl. . . . At his going over to Paris in 1625" (when Louis XIII called Buckingham one of the few English gentlemen he had ever seen), "he had twenty-seven suits of clothes made, the richest that embroidery, lace, silk, velvet, gold, and gems could contribute, one of which was a white, uncut velvet, set all over, both suit and cloak, with diamonds, valued at £14,000, besides a great feather, stuck all over with diamonds, as were also his sword, girdle, hatband and spurs."

The "knots of pearl," such as we are more accustomed to see, from the time of Elizabeth through first quarter XVIIc., worn by the greatest ladies, are tucked into the bosom of his jacket through slashes edged with small pearls, opposed to large ones as buttons. Trailing, thread-like lovelock on great whisk of bone lace.

1504. XVIIc. c. 1623. Dutch-English. (England, T. W. Fitzwilliam.)

D. Mytens, e. The First Duke of Buckingham as Lord High Admiral.

In official dress, he wears the otherwise outmoded trunk hose. As a gentleman of the period, he would have worn breeches gartered like those shown on Charles I. (Ill. 1505), midway in fullness between those of James I (Ill. 1469) and Charles, and probably boots.

His lace whisk is worn with the new jacket, slashed at the bosom, and carrying the breeches knotted through its pointed waistline; and the new sleeve, full and slashed above, close below the elbow. Garter and its insignia on a ribbon, cape, shoes with high heels and rosettes, walking stick.

1505. XVIIc. 1629. Dutch-English. (Metropolitan Museum.)

Daniel Mytens, e. Charles I.

In 1623, at Buckingham's instigation, "Baby Charles"—still Prince of Wales, and "Dog Steenie" set out secretly, as "Mr. John and Mr. Thomas Smith," on a fantastic quest for the Infanta of Spain whom Charles hoped to marry. Their small party dressed in "fine riding coats, all of one colour and fashion, in a kind of noble simplicity." (Howell's "Letters.") They spent one night in Paris, "disguised" in periwigs; Charles saw the French princess, Henrietta Maria, at a masked ball, and was recognized by a servant-girl from London. In Spain, magnificent entertainments were improvised; the Infanta was driven in a carriage, with a bow tied on her arm, so that she and Charles could look at each other from a safe Spanish distance. The people discovered that the English were not half-man, half-beast, as their priests had told them; presentation was made of the gifts James had provided: "a good looking glass, with my picture on it to be hung at her girdle, diamonds set like an anchor, three goodly peak pendants diamonds whereof the biggest to be worn at a needle on the middle of her forehead and one in every ear" (Hardwicke's "State Papers"); and more were sent home for. The decorum of the court was upset by Buckingham; Charles could not be converted to Rome; and after endless delays, the pair went home with a marriage contract which was never meant to be fulfilled.

In the couple of years which separate this portrait of Charles from another painted by Mytens in 1627, the king has grown a long lovelock; his doublet has developed bosom slashing, reduced shoulder caps; straight edged open cuffs have replaced pointed lace ones; and the boot, cuffed just below the knee in 1627, is now turned down much lower on the calf.

1506. XVIIc. c. 1628. Dutch-English. (London, Nat. Port. Gall.)

G. van Honthorst. Henrietta Maria, Queen of Charles I.

The year after his Spanish failure, Charles was married to the daughter of Henri IV and Marie de' Medici. Henrietta Maria, "a numble and quiet, black-eyed, brown-haired, and, in a word, a brave lady, though, perhaps, a little touched by the green-sickness" was taller than Charles had supposed. She lifted her foot to show: "Sir, I stand upon mine own feet. I have no helps of art. Thus high I am, and neither higher nor lower."

Priest-ridden and bitterly suspect because of her Catholicism and her Gallic gaiety, the queen had no one familiar with England to advise her; her own French entourage left her one dress and two undershirts, and a list of debts to them, padded to £19,000, on their flight back to France. She was a gay, brave, loyal and always beautifully dressed wife to the dignified, tasteful, well-intentioned, and calamitously unwise Charles. Yet she played a great part in the downfall of the king, who said he thought he could earn a living at any trade but tapestry-weaving, but who failed at the business to which he was born.

Satin is a favorite material in the new soft styles, increasingly untrimmed as it gains in popularity; here it is still embroidered in pearls. The neckline is wide and low, the remnants of the ruff appearing in the lace edge. A loose string of pearls is tied across the pearled outline of the old, long stomacher at a short waistline. Short, puffed sleeves finished with many ruffles, gathered together. Hair in tiny arranged curls against the cheeks and forehead. Pearl crown, earrings and choker; bracelets, folding fan.

1507. XVIIc. 1628. Dutch-English. (Chatsworth, Duke of Devonshire.)

G. van Honthorst. Elizabeth of Bohemia,* Countess of Devonshire, and her Children.

These are fashionable clothes, the daughter's showing later styles. But where Henrietta Maria's dress of the same year looks forward, these relate to old usages in many of their details.

The spray which the countess wears in her hair is the end of an Elizabethan fashion, done in newer pearls. Her ruff has the varied width seen in its widest, late forms; it is combined with the new spreading neckline of the short-waisted gown, emphasized by a kerchief-like collar, and jewels strung in an elaboration of a baldric. Across the tab of the stomacher, it is belted by a ribbon, to match the ribbon tie, called a *virago,* which catches the full paned sleeves between shoulder and elbow; these are short, finished with a ruff matching that at the throat. Her kirtle has the new all-over spot patterns, but a good deal of the old braiding is used on all the garments, though often in fresh ways. Fan tied to belt ribbon.

The boy at l., who grew up to be one of the original members of the Royal Society, wears his lace collar out, over the crimson cloak of a Knight of the Bath; jacket and breeches of a dot-patterned stuff.

The boy with the crossbow shows the doublet waist shortening; its overlapping skirts very long. Braid is used in patterns which emphasize goring and slashing. The continuation of sleeve slashings below elbow is unusual. Narrowing breeches, slit along outer seam and edged with buttons, show gartered underwear-like white beneath, as do the slashes of bosom and sleeves. Shoe toes squaring.

The daughter's flat collar is developing out of a fan-shaped ruff. Her sleeve finish, rows of ruffles gathered together, is newer than the pleated ruffs worn by her mother. Braid is used to give importance to the kirtle, and a diagonal border to the gown.

---

* There is a 1632 portrait (by Miereveld, in the National Portrait Gallery, London) of Elizabeth of Bohemia, with a black cord dangling from her earring over a similar ruff, graduated and very high in back of the head. It is, however, of a very different lady—the gay and gallant daughter of James the 1st—who bore thirteen children to Frederic, the Elector Palatine (among them Rupert and Sophia), and who lived on charity, sometimes a vagrant, after his death.

1508-09. XVIIc. Flemish-English.
Anthony Van Dyke.
1508. Henrietta Maria, Queen of England (1634). (Windsor Castle H. M. the King.)
1509. Henrietta Maria, Queen of England (1632-40). (Dresden Museum.)

Portraits by Rubens' pupil, Van Dyke, are wonderful costume documents. Beginning about 1618 in the Netherlands he painted the prelates and nobility of Italy from 1621-7; returned to Flanders where he and his master were court painters to the Infanta; went to England in 1629, returning to the Netherlands during 1634-5; thereafter, until his death in 1641, lived in London where he married an English noblewoman and was himself knighted. Differences in costume in the various countries, and their alterations in repeated portraits of the same personages, can be seen in the 537 chronologically arranged examples in the tremendously useful *Klassiker der Kunst* series; *Van Dyck,* Deutsche Verlags-Anstalt, Stuttgart, 1909.

"The portraits of this Fleming are so frequent in England that the generality of our people can scarce avoid thinking him their countryman, though he was born at Antwerp in 1598." (Horace Walpole: *Anecdotes of Painting in England, 5 vols.,* 1782). Van Dyke painted so many pictures of Charles' family and court, that we call their styles by his name.

One of his pictures of Henrietta Maria with her dwarf, in 1633, shows her walking in a great, romantic plumed hat, and a braid-edged, high-necked masculine jacket, with a spreading collar. In 1634, her gown is of the plainest satin, low-necked, short-waisted, and laced with pearls across a stomacher, which is scalloped like the long skirts of the jacket; hems of skirts are also finished with such scalloped edges. Soft, full sleeves, finished with a ruffle at the elbow, show lace-edged undersleeves. Precious baldric; pearl choker, earrings, and strand around knot of hair. The little scallop of hair, of 1628, and the lovelock, are becoming corkscrew curls.

1510. XVIIc. 1632-40. Flemish. (Metropolitan Museum, Bache Coll.)
A. Van Dyke. Robert Rich, Earl of Warwick.

The son of Lady Penelope Rich, Sir Philip Sidney's lovely "Stella," wears a silver brocade doublet and crimson breeches, edged with gold braid; both are open and edged with buttons along the main seam. Crimson cloak, pink stockings, white shoes, black hat in hand.

1511. XVIIc. 1638. Flemish. (London, Lady Louis Mountbatten.)
A. Van Dyke. Lord John and Lord Bernard Stuart.

The younger sons of the king's cousin Esmé, Earl of Lennox, are shown here at 17 and 15; within half a dozen years both will be killed fighting for the Royalists.

Lord John, at left, wears a yellow doublet and crimson breeches; Bernard, a white satin doublet, blue cloak lined with white and blue breeches. Clogs protect toes of his boots, which have high red heels.

1512. XVIIc. 1632-41. Flemish. (Metropolitan Museum.)
A. Van Dyke. James Stuart, Duke of Richmond and Lennox.

John and Bernard's older brother, dressed in black. has the Star of the Garter on his cloak, and the lesser George on its blue ribbon.

1513. XVIIc. 1632-40. Flemish. (London, Duke of Grafton.)
A. Van Dyke. William Villiers, 2nd Viscount Grandison.

Grandison, who was killed in the civil wars in 1643, was the father of Barbara, Duchess of Cleveland; he wears gauntlets with embroidered cuffs; ribbon knots on immense leather plaques over the instep.

Red, blue, yellow, black, white and metallic colors are the favorites of this period, the reds running from pink, to deep crimson, to brightest scarlet.

"It is usual to turn back the cloak to display the rich lining, and where the doublet and breeches do not match it is common to find the lining of the cloak matching the doublet and the cloak matching the breeches." (Kelly & Schwabe: *Historic Costume*).

In these pictures we see the collar (always worn over the cape or cassock) spreading until the shoulder cap disappears; doublet beoming shorter-waisted and more vest-like; decoration in openwork braids applied along the seams of underarm, sleeve and breeches; breeches narrowing and higher-waisted, often long, tubular and finished by gathered ruffles or spaghetti-like fringe. Lace-edged inner boot-hose of linen show in cupped cuff of boots, as the cuffs slip lower on the calf; heels become higher, and the leather plaques more enormous. Hair is lengthening, beards disappearing.

1514

1514. XVIIc. c. 1639. Flemish-English. (Metropolitan Museum.)

Van Dyke. Earl of Arundel and his Grandson.

Arundel, Earl Marshal and Constable of England, of whom Clarendon said there was "nothing martial about him but his presence and look," was the first great English antiquarian. He collected beautiful small objects and Greek and Roman sculpture; he was the patron of Van Dyke and Hollar, the friend of Evelyn and Sir Robert Cotton. He was responsible for the new use of brick in English building.

For a century, property had been changing hands and fine things in England destroyed or barely saved from destruction. Manuscripts acquired by Cotton, after the dissolution of the monasteries, were the foundation of the present Cottonian Library. Arundel's marbles went to Oxford; his library was dispersed between the College of Heralds and the British Museum, but his collections suffered during the civil wars.

There are many accounts, like Dowsing's, of destruction proudly performed under warrant; in 1643-4, at Clare: "We brake down 1000 pictures superstitious; I brake down 200; three of God the Father and two of Christ and the Holy Lamb, and three of the Holy Ghost like a Dove with Wings; and the twelve Apostles were carved in Wood on the top of the Roof which we gave orders to be taken down; and the Sun and the Moon in the East Windows, by the King's Arms, to be taken down." (Ponsonby: *English Diaries*). Evelyn says that at Lincoln in 1654, "the soldiers had lately knocked off most of the

brasses from the gravestones . . . with axes and hammers . . . until they had rent and torn off some barge loads of metal, not sparing even the monuments of the dead, so hellish an avarice possessed them; beside which they exceedingly ruined the city."

Arundel was a general in the First Bishop's War, when the diary of Charles I's Privy Chamberlain, John Aston, tells us: "I had a cuirassier's armes for myselfe, close caske, gorget, back and breast culet, pauldrons, vambrance, left hand gauntlet, and cuisses and a case of pistolls and a great saddle." (Ponsonby: *Eng. Diaries*).

Falling band over gorget; baton of office. Grandson: doublet with small band, longer skirts; knee-breeches with garter bows; pearl baldric; shoe tocs lengthening and squaring.

EFFECTS OF PURITANISM IN XVII-E.XVIII CENTURY

There were only two sorts of people in XVIIc. England: Dissenters and Royalists. The division, based on religion, was vertical, splitting families and comprising all classes. The excesses of each intensified the opposed feelings and behavior of the others, and there was much confusion of thought within each division. Under stress, Puritanism evolved from its Elizabethan reasonableness, and reached its most extreme form in the American colonies. But there were, within the party at any one time, persons of every degree of bigotry, often as opposed to the extremists in their own party as to people of the other persuasion.

There was much ambivalence in individuals, such as Cromwell's "overeager" General Harrison; who said that "gold and silver and worldly bravery did not become saints," when Colonel Hutchinson wore what his wife called "sad colored cloth, trimmed with gold and silver points and buttons . . . pretty rich, but grave, and no other than he usually wore"; but who, himself, waited upon the Spanish ambassador the next day "in a scarlet coat and cloak, both laden with gold and silver lace, and the coat so covered with clinquant (foil) that one scarcely could discern the grounds," while Hutchinson and others wore plain black. (Lucy Hutchinson: *Mem. of Col. Hutchinson*).

Puritans dressed and behaved like their contemporaries, but in a much toned-down way. The loyalist Anthony Wood said that at Oxford "they would avoid a tavern or alehouse, but yet send for their commodities to their respective chambers, and tiple and smoake till they were overtaken with the creature. And yet, of all men, none more than these were ready to censure the boone Royallist or any person they saw go in or out of a tavern or alehouse. Some, I confess, did venture, but then if overtaken would in their way home counterfeit a lameness, or that some suddaine paine came upon them." Generally speaking, their heads were cropped as though they were ready for the wigs they avoided; they wore dark clothes, with small plain bands instead of lace, and worsted stockings in place of silk. (A. Wood, *Life & Times*. Oxf. Hist. Soc. 1891.)

Wood, who had found the Presbyterians and Independents saucy, troublesome, conceited and rude to the "old stock," and their sermons interminable, attests, after the Restoration, to their diligence. He finds "nothing well done but by those who had their breeding during the intervall ... The truth is they (i.e. the returning Cavaliers) have lost their learning," and have no aim but "to live like gent., keep dogs and horses, to turn their studies and coleholes into places to receive bottles, to swash it in apparell, to wear long periwigs." On Charles' visit to Oxford in 1666, Wood thought the courtiers "neat and gay in their apparell, yet very nasty and beastly ... rough, rude, whoremongers, empty, careless"; not only were they insolent to great scholars "who had parted with their chambers and conveniences," but they had committed nuisances in their chimneys and studies (as, indeed, courtiers did in the great rooms of Versailles, for lack of accommodations).

Members of a dissenting minority are apt to be as contentious, but as thoughtful, earnest and literate as Wood found their Oxford students. Their numbers increased to a majority on a flood of leaflets, satires and periodicals. The Dissenters may be credited with much of the general improvement in education, which was particularly noticeable among middle and lower class townswomen, at a period when Royalist ladies were taught only graceful accomplishments, and were sometimes even more illiterate than the "beautiful and accomplished" widow of the sixth duke of Norfolk, who wished Pepys to accept delivery for her of "a parsell of Scotch plad of ten or a leven peses ... I am encoreged to give you thes trubell ... becaus now in my abcenc I have letell entreist in town." (Pepys).

The Puritan mistrust of art, music, the stage, and popular amusements impoverished English life, in which a good deal of taste had developed under Charles I. After the period of Rubens, Van Dyke, Honthorst, van Somer, Janssens, Mytens, and the English court miniaturist William Dobson, English painting consisted of such miniature painters as Samuel Cooper, and of the Dutch painter who became Sir Peter Lely, to whom Cromwell and a few other Puritans did sit. As Walpole said, "The restoration of royalty brought back art, not taste." Lely's even duller successor was the German, Godfrey Kneller. At propitious intervals, Flemish, Dutch, and French artists did make trips to England. But neither William nor Mary had taste, and Anne avoided court life as much as possible, leaving her ministers to preside at her drawing-rooms. Theirs is, on the whole, one of the most difficult periods in which to find illustrations of costume.

The Plague aided the Puritans in closing the theatres and public gathering places. Until the Restoration, the English theatre consisted of the private masques at court (in which Anne of Denmark and Henrietta Maria had delighted, for which Ben Jonson wrote, and the architect Inigo Jones provided the décor).

With the Restoration, comes brilliant, licentious comedy like that of Wycherly, heroic drama such as Dryden's "Conquest of Granada," and the first English opera, by the great Purcell. People flocked to the watering places like Tunbridge Wells and Bath, to the many pleasure gardens like Vauxhall and Ranelagh; to fashionable drives like the Ring in Hyde Park; and to the endless coffee houses which served as office and club, where for a fee a gentleman could read all of the new flood of periodicals and hear all the latest gossip.

The XVIIc. is that in which the King James translation made the Bible available, to become the keystone of the lives of millions. In another level of society, stage people begin to mingle on equal terms with the great world, noblewomen fight duels over actors, and Charles II, since he apparently must share Lady Castlemain's favors, advises her to let Harry Jermyn, the lady killer, go in favor of Jacob Hall, the wonderful rope dancer.

1515-17. XVIIc. 1638. English. (Kent, East Sutton Church.)

Monumental brass, signed Ed. Marshall. Sir Edward Filmer and his Wife, Elizabeth.

Sir Robert, eldest son of Filmer's eighteen children, became a political writer. His theory that government was, by God's decree to Adam, based on the authority of the father, naturally made him an ardent supporter of the king against Parliament; his house was despoiled ten times by his opponents. One wonders whether some of the younger sons may have reacted differently to authority, and profited by rebellion.

Sir Edward's short-waisted cuirasse has long skirts, as high boots with spur leathers replace plate protection of the legs. Frog fastenings of outer seam of loose knee breeches.

The elderly Lady Filmer also clings to a ruff, which widens in back; a wired-out veil and a long-waisted stomacher. Cuffs do not surround the wrist and are not scalloped.

Robert wears a cassock with cuffed sleeves over his armor, his widening falling band spread over the shoulders of the cassock. Other sons show a variety of jackets, garters, shoes and boots.

The daughters, all with caps, wear their hair loose at the sides and with a fringe. Collars lowering and spreading. Slashed sleeves, knotted around above the elbow, in the tie called a *virago*.

Vnder this rest in certaine hope of the resurrection the bodies of S.ᵗ Edward Filmer Knyght and dame Elizabeth *together Fortie foure yeares and had issue Eighteene Children viz. nine sonnes and nine Davghters He depated this*

his wife Davghter of Richard Argall Esq.ʳ they lived

1518. XVIIc. 1641. Flemish-English. (Amsterdam, Rijks-museum.)

Van Dyke. William of Orange and Mary Stuart.

The Dutch *stadholder,* whose son will become William III of England by virtue of his father's and his own marriages to English princesses named Mary, holds by the hand his little bride, dressed in greenish-gold brocade, in the exquisite taste of her mother.

The Rijksmuseum also owns a piece of the actual lace of the collar which spreads over the coppery satin of William's gold-embroidered costume. He wears stockings of a paler shade, which hang in deliberate wrinkles, and red-heeled shoes which are knotted, like his breeches, with loose gold, in scarf rather than ribbon form, as it will later be used. He carries a black hat, banded in jewels instead of the usual cord, in a buff-gloved hand, over the sword belt which passes underneath his jacket.

1519. XVIIc. c. 1642? English.

M. Gheeraerts, y. Beata, Countess of Downe and her Children.

This picture presents time-consuming complications, which often occur and which it may, for once, be interesting to outline.

It is one of four related pictures which had remained in the Pope family until it was sold at Christie's, July 11, 1930 (#63). It is accepted by Cust as the work of Gheeraerts, who died in 1636. According to Burke's Peerage, Beata Poole was married April 20, 1636 and Thomas, the heir, was baptised Sept. 20, 1640. The picture must therefore be c.1642-3, if the names shown are contemporaneous with the figures, as appears to be the case. In that case, the painting would seem to have been the work of another artist, who painted costume as beautifully and hands as badly as did Gheeraerts.

The Countess' costume is of white satin with multicolored silk and metal embroidery, and a blue scarf. Her short-waisted jacket has the widening

Photograph Courtesy of Frick Art Reference Lib. (1519)

1518

1519

neckline, gored peplum, short sleeves and wide cuffs of the 40's.

The children are dressed in olive green. The boy wears a masculine doublet, with skirts since he is still in diapers, and carries a plumed and tasseled hat. The diary of Sir Henry Slingsby (1601-50) relates that he got his son "the first breeches and doublet he ever had and made by my tailor Mr. Miller; it was too soon for him to wear them being but five years old, but that his mother had a desire to see him in them, how proper a man he could be—(Ponsonby: *English Diaries*). Lady Slingsby was an invalid and was dying.

1520-25. XVIIc. 1639-40. Bohemian-English. (Metropolitan Museum, Print Room and Boston Museum of Fine Arts, Elizabeth Day McCormick Coll.)

Wenzel Hollar. Ornatus muliebris.

Hollar is one of the world's great fashion artists. He was a Bohemian, born in 1607, driven from Prague and the profession of law by the Thirty Years War. He worked as an engraver under Merian in Frankfort in 1627-9, and in Strassburg and Cologne. There in 1636 he met the antiquarian, Arundel, who loved exquisite workmanship and the company of artists. He went with Arundel on his embassy to Vienna and Prague and returned to live with him in London. He passed into the service of the Duke of York when Arundel fled the Civil Wars, but eventually joined Arundel in Antwerp, where Hollar spent his most productive years, 1644-52. He returned to London, lived with the engraver Faithorne for a time, and died there in the greatest poverty in 1677.

Working by an hourglass at 4d. an hour, Hollar produced 2740 plates: architectural drawings, views of cities (particularly of London before and after the Great Fire of 1666), book illustrations, portraits, and his wonderful drawings of costume. These have been catalogued by Parthey, Berlin, 1853.

The *Ornatus muliebris* illustrations are of English costume c.1640. These are not great ladies in grand clothes, but the daily wear of the middle classes.

1520. Side locks and bun arrangement of the central portion of the hair, seen from the back. Collar edges cover the shoulders; waistline very short; skirt looped up over a handsome petticoat.

1521. Street costume of hood and mask, scarf, muff, and a chatelaine of some sort. French prints of Louis XIV's time often show ladies huddled over the fire, with their feet on the fender, partial mitts on their hands, screening their faces with long-handled fans. This fur-edged one, which may have had a mirror center, must have been a comfortable accessory to hold on a visit in a chilly drawing room.

1522. Muffs occur in late inventories of Elizabeth's wardrobe and rapidly increase in use, being carried by men as well as women, even by army and naval officers during latter half XVII-e.XVIIIc. This wide-brimmed, truncated conical hat is almost the only one now worn by women; when a cap is worn, the hat is set over it. The ruff still persists in bourgeoise use, but is elliptical in shape, and, in this example, is reduced from a triple to a double ruff, and narrowed, over the bare breast of the laced bodice.

1523. Kerchief collar, over a dropped shoulder line, to avoid interference with the full, short sleeve; apron; skirt tucked up over a handsome short kirtle, showing handsome high-heeled slippers with rosettes.

1524. Simple home costume with a lovely cap and hanging embroidery scissors.

English embroidery has been notable since Tudor times and will remain so into the XIXc., although in the general dissolution of the XVIIIc., it begins to be neglected and we find the Spectator (#606, 1714) proposing:

I. That no young virgin whatsoever be allowed to receive the addresses of her first lover but in a suit of her own embroidering.

II. That before every fresh servant she be obliged to appear with a new stomacher at the least.

III. That no one be actually married till she hath the childbed pillows, &., ready stitched, as likewise the mantle for the boy quite finished.

But Sir Walter Calverly's diary, Nov. 27, 1716 says: "My wife finished the sewed work in the drawing room it having been three years and a half in doing. The greatest part of it has been done with her own hands. It consists of ten panels" (which still hang in Sir George Trevelyan's bedroom at Wallington). (Ponsonby: *English Diaries*).

1525. Marketing in pattens, with the embroidered hem of her jacket costume looped up out of the mud. The basket holds fine artichokes (cultivated in England for two and a quarter centuries), and some parsley and root vegetables for seasoning soup. Carrots and beets, as agreeable vegetables to eat, are the XIXc. creation of the French plant breeder, Vilmorin. Until his work, the carrot was a stringy, whitish-yellow root, unlike the wild parsnip (probably brought to England in Roman days), which Pliny knew could be transformed by several seasons of good tilth into a good vegetable.

1526

1527

1528

1526-27. XVIIc. 1643-4. Bohemian-English.

W. Hollar. The Four Seasons: Winter, and Autumn.

Scarcely a trace remains of the old rigidity of costume. There are black hoods and masks over loose curls; fichu-like collars; fur pieces and muffs; full, fashionable aprons; objects like fans, watches, mirrors or *nécessaires* of sewing or toilet articles hang from the waist; gloves lengthen as sleeves become short and wide. Background of the city views at which Hollar excelled.

Men, too, carry little kits of toilet articles, which it is gallant to use in public and in society. "Will you be combing your wig, playing with your box, or picking your teeth?" Steele asks in the Tatler, (#38,July7,1709). Before his execution, Charles I had given his gold toothpick case to Col. Tomlinson. Among the inventory of the effects of a fop (Tatler,#113,Dec.29,1709), appears "a very rich tweezer case, containing twelve instruments for the use of each hour in the day"; snuff, with three gilt boxes, one with a mirror in the lid, and "two more of ivory, with the portraitures on their lids of two ladies of the town."

1528. XVIIc. 1647. Bohemian. (Metropolitan Museum, Print Room.)

W. Hollar. Muffs.

While living in Antwerp, Hollar produced a wonderful series of etchings of muffs and accessories, of which this is one.

Masks are fast coming into fashion all over Europe. Pepys mentions them first, June 13, 1663, when he sees Cromwell's daughter, the Countess of Falconberg, "when the house began to fill . . . put on her vizard, and so kept it on all the play: which of late is become a great fashion among ladies, which hides their whole faces." He stops to get his own wife a mask, at a milliner's (Jan., 27, 1663-4). At the theatre again (Feb., 18, 1666-7), he scarcely sees the play for overhearing a charming, teasing, witty conversation between Sir Charles Sedley and two masked ladies obviously of quality and virtue, whom he did not recognize. One "did give him many pleasant hints of her knowledge of him, by that means setting his brains at work to find out who she was, and did give him leave to use all means to find out who she was, but pulling off her mask."

By 1712, masks have become the mark of prostitutes, and are worn by respectable women only at the first night of a play. However, the advertisement (in *Spectator* #546), of the opening of the "Blind Beggar of Bednal Green" at Punch's Theatre, says "No persons to be admitted with masks or riding hoods."

Muffs are coming into male use, also. On Nov., 30, 1662 Pepys "first did weare a muffe, being my wife's last year's muffe; and now that I have bought her a new one, this serves me very well . . . in this month . . . of great frost."

The fantastic Salter, "eminent barber and antiquary," as well as musician and inkeeper, ridiculed by Steele as "Don Saltero" (*Tatler*,#34, June 28, 1709), could be recognized a quarter of a mile away, as he held his horrible old grey muff to his nose, according to Babillard.

1529

1530

1529-30. XVIIc. 1645. English. (Oxford, Ashmolean Museum.)

De Critz. John Tradescant in his garden (1529), Hester and John Tradescant (1530).

In the age of discovery and colonization, and of quite general European travel by gentlemen imbued with the new spirit of inquiry, experiment and recording, begins the great interchange of plants between continents. About 1602, many new fruits and vegetables appeared in England from the Continent. They were taken to the New World, which had already given Europe the potato, tomato, tobacco, and pumpkin.

John Tradescant, jr., was the keeper of Charles I's Botanical Garden at Chelsea, in whose honor a three-petaled blue flower from America was named *Tradescantia virginica.* His father, a Dutchman living in England since 1600, had been gardener to the duke of Buckingham; he left a collection of North African curiosities, enlarged by the son with material from his own trip to America in 1637.

The will by which Tradescant's collections were left to his friend Elias Ashmole, was bitterly and fruitlessly contested by Mrs. Tradescant. Evelyn visited Ashmole at Lambeth on July 23, 1678, to see the collection which Ashmole had just given to Oxford. He noted particularly "a toad included in amber." Twelve wagons were required to remove the natural history specimens to the newly erected Ashmolean, the first great scientific museum, which had been completed from Sir Christopher Wren's design. On Feb. 17, 1683, Ashmole's diary says: "The last load of my rarities was sent to the barge, and this afternoon I relapsed into the gout." The Ashmolean is now an archaeological museum.

Tradescant gardens in an open shirt and easy, furlined coat. Mrs. Tradescant, sharing one of the botanical illustrations from the collection with her step-son, wears the high-crowned hat, familiar from the Hollar illustrations, set over her cap, and an enchanting embroidered petticoat, with a pendant watch at the waist. The interior of the cuff becomes important, as sleeves grow shorter and wider; the cuff is not folded, but is doubled back from a lace edge.

1531. XVIIc. English. (Oxford, Sir Kenneth Clark.)
Daniel Des Granges. The Saltonstall Family.

1532. XVIIc. 1648. English. (Northampton, Lamport Hall, Gyles Isham.)
C. Janssens van Ceulen, e. Mary, Daughter of Sir Eusebius Isham of Pytchley.

The lady, married first to Edward Reade and later to Sir Fleetwood Dormer, is shown as a widow; lace is replaced by composite collars of sheer-bound lawn; pearls are caught by black bows; heart-shaped chatelaine pinned at the waist.

1533. XVIIc. 1654. English. (Croome d'Abiot, Wostershire Parish Church.)
Tombstone by unknown artist. Second Wife of Lord Coventry.

The first nightshirts of the XVIc. did not differ much from day shirts; now they are coming to have a specific character and to be supplemented with dressing gowns and slippers. The bedroom has always been the most comfortable room; as houses are cut up into smaller, better heated rooms and large windows admit more sunlight, the bedroom increases in use for all but the most formal entertainment. Delightful caps (men's embroidered and women's lacy) and a dressing gown, over a corset and petticoats, or breeches and vest, tend to become informal wear in the morning hours, during which, regardless of sex, there is a great deal of visiting back and forth, during XVII-XVIIIc. In 1683, Evelyn sees the Duchess of Portsmouth "in her dressing room . . . in morning loose garments, her maids combing her, newly out of bed, His Majesty and the gallants standing about her."

Wood calls it, in 1663, "a strange effeminate age when men strive to imitate women in their apparell, viz. long periwigs, patches in their faces, painting,

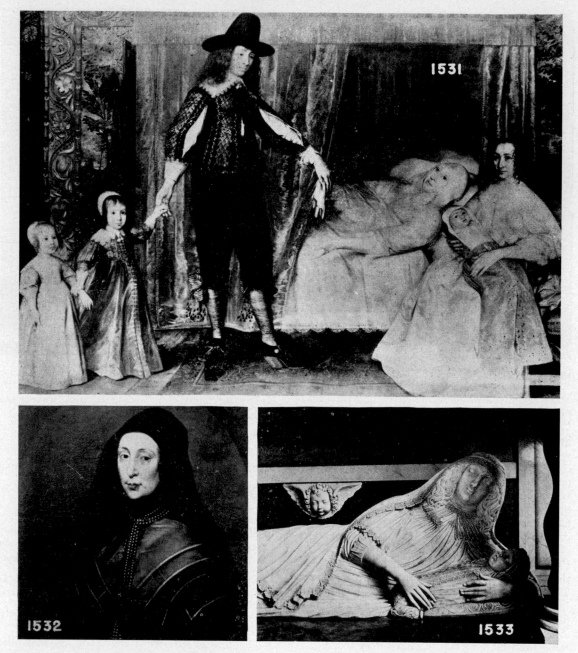

short wide breeches like petticotes, muffs, and clothes highly sented, bedecked with ribbons of all colours. And this apparell was not only used by gentlemen and others of inferior quality, but by souldiers, especial those of the Life Gard to the King, who would have spanners hanging on one side and a muff on the other, and when dirty weather some of them would relieve their gards in pattens. On the other side, women would strive to be like men, viz., when they rode on horseback or in coaches weare plush caps like monteros, either full of ribbons or feathers, long periwigs which men use to weare, and riding coate of a red color all bedaubed with lace which they call vests, and this habit was cheifly used by the ladies and maids of honor belonging to the Queen, brought in fashion about anno 1662 . . . at their being in Oxon."

In Dec. 1674 Wood notes: "A great excess in apparel in men, women and children of the common sort: lace, fals hair, lace whisk, aprons, petticotes, lac'd shoes, fals towers of hair. This in Oxford . . . The decay of study, and consequently of learning, are coffy houses, to which most scholars retire and spend much of the day in hearing and speaking of news, in speaking vily of their superiors."

In the *Spectator's* time, 1711, young lawyers appear at coffee houses near the Temple in "nightgowns with our stockings about our heels, and sometimes but one on," to breakfast in dressing gown and slippers (#320). "Ladies likewise brought up the fashion of receiving visits in their beds. It was then looked upon as a piece of ill-breeding for a woman to refuse to see a man because she was not stirring; and a porter would have thought unfit for his place, that could have made so awkward an excuse." (#45).

On May 11, 1654, Evelyn says: "I now observe how the women began to paint themselves, formerly a most ignominious thing, and used only by prostitues." By 1673, "the imprudence of both sexes (was) become so great and universal (that) persons of all ranks (keep) their courtesans publicly," and the increase of lawlessness is continually noted until a late entry in 1699, of "such horrible robberies and murders as had not been known in this nation, atheism, profaneness, blasphemy among all sorts," as well as insensate gambling, after a century of dissension and civil war, plague and fire.

Mrs. Saltonstall and Lady Coventry show delightful new forms of caps, night- and dressing-gowns. The babies, swaddled tight under their long gowns, wear caps which convert into bibs. The child whose hand Mr. Saltonstall holds shows the bows by which breeches would be tied to the short waist of his jacket, if he were out of diapers and skirts. The younger child in an apron is probably a sister.

Mr. Saltonstall's vest-like jacket, unfastened from the neck, has openwork braid along its seams. He wears the most wonderfully gauzy garter-ribbons, finished with tassel-dotted lace, and the highest heels on square-toed shoes. Light as all this is, we see a hint of the tasseled and fringed upholstery-like styles of Louis XIV, which are still with us today in hotel lobby decoration. His stocking wrinkles are akin to the flopping, turned-down cuffs and the folds of the inner hose, which are characteristic of the boots of the period.

TOBACCO AND SNUFF

For a century after its introduction into England, tobacco was smoked in large clay pipes. Despite the "Counterblast" of James I, and Charles I and II's prohibition of tobacco-growing in England, smoking became habitual in XVIIc. Because of its supposed fumigant and medicinal properties, its use increased during the Plague of 1665. Jorevin says that in Worcestershire, during the reign of Charles II, children were sent to school with pipes, which they smoked at recess, while the teacher showed the novices how. A French traveller of 1671 noted Englishwomen smoking a great clay pipeful after dinner. At Garroway's Coffee House in Leeds, in 1702, a sickly child of three smoked three pipes, like the veteran he was, since he had been doing so for the year past.

In France and Spain, tobacco was used in the form of snuff, and carried in handsome boxes in Louis XIII's time. Louis XIV disliked most odors, and none more than tobacco. But snuff boxes had begun to rival (and eventually surpassed) watches as presents to mark appreciation or to honor visiting dignitaries. Louis XIV made many gifts of the beautiful snuff boxes of his period.

The English became snuff users in 1702, by an accident which is recounted by Charles Lillie, the perfumer and tobacco seller, whose name appears so frequently in the *Tatler* and *Spectator*. During the Spanish war, English ships commanded by Sir George Rooke raided Fort St. Mary, where among other great booty they took quantities of cochineal and some thousands of barrels of the finest Spanish snuff, each cask containing four tin canisters. On their return, in Vigo harbor they destroyed a fleet of galleons just in from Havana, loaded with rawhide bales of rough snuff to be manufactured in Spain. Officers and men received their shares of the fifty tons of snuff, as spoils of war; wagon loads of coarse "Vigo" snuff were sold in Portsmouth and Plymouth by the sailors for 3-4 d. a pound.

Snuff, "taken with pipes the size of quills out of small spring boxes" had been a luxury in England, known only to returned travellers and foreigners. Spanish Jews living in England recognized the quality of the Fort St. Mary snuff and bought it up. They, and the officers who kept their shares, eventually realized fortunes.

Snuff immediately became fashionable, and excise duties on it a rich source of government revenue as well as an incitation to smuggling. The tobacco was twisted into ropes. It was at first rasped with ivory graters, attached to a small box which was provided with a spoon; the name "rapee" (from *râper*) remained for coarse snuff. Graters were separated from boxes and snuff was taken with the fingers, as fine prepared snuffs were bought by connoisseurs with as much discrimination as vintage wines.

From Swift's *Journal to Stella* (whose companion, in his "little language," is M.D. or Dingly) we learn a great deal about the taking of snuff, 1710-11. In letter IV, he has "the finest piece of Brazil tobacco for Dingly that ever was born"; XXI: "I have left off altogether. I have a noble roll of tobacco for grating, very good. Shall I send it to M.D., if she likes that sort?"; XXIV: "Are you as vicious in snuff as ever? I believe, as you say, it does neither hurt nor good; but I have left it off, and when anybody offers me their box, I take about a tenth part of what I used to do, and then just smell to it, and privately fling the rest away"; XXXIII: "Then there's the *Miscellany*, an apron for Stella, a pound of chocolate, without sugar, for Stella, a fine snuff rasp of ivory, given me by Mrs. St. John for Dingly, and a large roll of tobacco, which she must hide or cut shorter out of modesty, and four pairs of spectacles for the Lord knows who"; LII: "You may keep the gold-studded snuff box now; for my brother Hill, Governor of Dunkirk, has sent me the finest that ever you saw. It is allowed at Court that none in England comes near it, though it did not cost above twenty pounds." To hold this, the Duchess of Hamilton made him a "pocket," like a woman's, "with a belt and buckle (for, you know, I wear no waistcoat in summer)."

An amusing bit of publicity by Steele in No. 138 of the *Spectator,* says: "The exercise of the Snuff Box, according to the most fashionable Airs and Motions, in opposition to the Exercises of the Fan, will be taught with the best plain or perfumed Snuff at Charles Lillie's, Perfumer, at the Corner of Beaufort Buildings in the Strand, and Attendance given for the benefit of young Merchants about the Exchange for two hours every day at Noon, except Sundays, at a Toy Shop near Garraway's Coffee House. There will likewise be Taught The Ceremony of the Snuff Box, or Rules for offering Snuff to a Stranger, a Friend, or a Mistress, according to the Degrees of Familiarity or Distance: with an Explanation of the Careless, the Scornful, the Politick, and the Surly Pinch, and the Gestures proper to each of them."

In No. 344 (1712), the affected "modesty" of snuff-taking women has been outgrown: "The Women, the fine Women (are) lately fallen into (the Custom) of taking Snuff. This silly Trick is attended with such a Coquet Air in some Ladies, and such a sedate Masculine one in others, that I cannot tell which most to complain of. . . . *Flavilla* is so far taken with her Behavior in this kind, that she pulls out her Box . . . in the middle of the Sermon, and to shew she has the Audacity of a well bred Woman, she offers it to the Men, as well as to the Women who sit near her."

By 1773, "smoking has gone out," Dr. Johnson says; he and his cronies, Garrick, Reynolds, and Goldsmith all take snuff. Eighty per cent of the trade of XVIIIc. tobacconists in London was in snuff. But in the first decades of the XIXc., cigars began to come in use; matches were invented; and by the middle XIXc., snuff formed only ten per cent of the tobacco business, and had become a plebeian habit.

The passion for giving, receiving, and collecting snuff boxes outlasted the habit of taking snuff. Boxes of Louis XV's period are less beautiful than those of Louis XIV, and less precious than the diamond-studded boxes of Louis XVI, which you were supposed to give back. The necessity of luxury was becoming insupportable, and reduced to a gesture; Mirepoix paid a rental of £240 for a suit to be worn once at Court; dukes began to go spectacularly bankrupt.

Even the poorest had snuff boxes, whether of wood, horn or tortoise shell, pewter, brass or silver, lacquer, or the pretty, commercially produced Battersea enamels. French jewellers made a fortune at Maria Theresa's long-expected death by selling black shagreen snuff-boxes bearing a framed medallion of Marie Antoinette and the words *Consolation en chagrin.*

The finest snuff boxes were French. Like watches and engravings, they were produced by a relatively small number of dynastic and interrelated artists.

Frederick the Great loved tobacco in every form. He carried it in pockets especially lined with leather, and a receptacle to hold snuff stood in every room. These were often in the form of a "mull," a ram's horn with silver mountings. Thrifty though he was, Frederick left a collection of 1,500 snuff boxes; the prince of Conti had left 800, a decade before.

Napoleon took snuff habitually, and collected boxes. But the fashion was beginning to wear out. His brothers, the Kings of Westphalia and Holland, sometimes disappointed visiting dignitaries who expected a handsome snuff box.

Although George IV did not like snuff, he ordered it in 12 varieties for the snuff boxes he always carried; he paid £8205-15-1 for snuff boxes, as gifts to visiting ambassadors at his coronation.

Talleyrand said snuff was essential to diplomacy; it gave a man time to compose his features and collect his thoughts, while opening his box and taking a pinch.

The last of the great collectors was also one of the most impassioned. Lord Petersham (1780-1851), was a connoisseur of teas and snuffs. He dressed his household in snuff-colored liveries, and left a choice variety of snuffs which brought £3000 at auction, and a collection of snuff boxes for every day, and appropriate to every season of the year. (For sources of information, see Appendix.)

1534. XVIIc. French
Box: mother of pearl, tortoise shell, gilt metal.

1535. XVIIIc. 1740-50. French.
Box: agate and gold.

1536. XVIIIc. 1778-9. French.
Snuff box by Jean Joseph Barrière (app. 1750; master, 1763; still working, 1793): gold and enamel.

1537. Early XVIIIc. French or English.
Pendant: sardonyx cameo, set with smaller cameos in gold.

1538. XVIIIc. 1757-8. French.
Snuff box: carved gold, encrusted with floral designs and enamel; portrait of Queen Anne on cover.

1539. XVIIIc. 1759-60. French.
Snuff box: by Mathieu Coiny (master, 1755-88): carved gold panels, reserved and painted with genre scenes, jewelled and enamelled.

1540. Late XVIc. c. 1600. German.
Pendant: ship; gold, enamel, pearls, and rubies.

1541. XVIc. Italian, Venetian. (Metropolitan Museum.)
Mirror Frame: wood inlaid with metal and ivory.

1534 1535 1536

1537 1538 1539

1540 1541 1542

1543 1544 1545

1542. XVIIc. French. (Metropolitan Museum.)
   Mirror Frame: red leather, bead and passementerie, fake jewels.

1543. XVIIc. English? (Metropolitan Museum.)
   Mirror Frame: champlevé enamel and coral.

1544. XVIIc. French? (Metropolitan Museum.)
   Mirror: silver filigree.

1545. XVIIc. Italian. (Metropolitan Museum.)
   Mirror: silver frame, partly gilt.

1546. XVIIc. English. (London, Victoria and Albert Museum.)

John Hoskins. Lady Catherine Howard.

Hoskins, called by Walpole, "a very eminent Limner in the reign of King Charles I, whom he drew with his queen and most of his court . . . was bred a face-painter in oil, but afterward taking to miniature, he far exceeded what he did before." (*Anecdotes of Painting.*) Hoskins, d.1664, was the uncle and teacher of Samuel Cooper (1609-72), the greatest English miniature painter. Other fine English miniaturists were Alexander Cooper, d.1660; David Des Granges (1611-75); Thomas Flatman, d.1688; and David Loggan, d.1692, the engraver of Oxford, who worked as a miniaturist in plumbago. While Elizabethan miniatures often show whole figures or even groups, like Oliver's Brothers Brown and their Servant, XVIIc. miniatures are unfortunately apt to be of bust length only. (For Miniature Painting sources, see Appendix.)

Lady Catherine, daughter of the Earl of Suffolk, led a blameless life as the wife of George Stuart, Seigneur d'Aubigny, who died in 1642, and of James, Viscount Newburg, who lived many years after her death in 1650.

Pale as death, she is the pattern of the new trends of mid-XVIIc.: curls wired out from the head, pearls, and a low, bright blue satin bodice, swathed and draped in scarves.

1547. XVIIc. c. 1660. Flemish. (Windsor Castle, H.M. The King.)

Hieronymus Janssens (1624-93). Charles II at a Ball at the Hague.

The romantic story of Charles II's flight, exile and return is largely spoiled by the Restoration, as "Bonnie Prince Charlie" tarnishes into "Old Rowley," nicknamed after a lecherous old goat in one of the palace enclosures.

After the defeat at Worcester, Charles and his lifelong crony, the second duke of Buckingham, became separated. Whether at White Ladies, or in the priest's hole at Boscobel, recognized by half a hundred people, but never betrayed for the £1000 reward, Charles went disguised as a woodsman, in the clothes of "trusty Dick," one of the children of Penderell, the miller; whose descendants, even in America, enjoy their shares of some £3000 a year, settled on them in perpetuity after the Restoration. Charles's

costume consisted of a "leathern doublet with pewter buttons; a pair of old green breeches, and a coat of the same green; a pair of his own stockings, with the tops cut off, because embroidered, and a pair of stirrup stockings lent him at Madeley; a pair of old shoes, cut and slashed to give ease to his feet; an old gray greasy hat without a lining; a noggon shirt of the coarsest linen; his face and hands made of a reeky complexion by the help of the walnut tree leaves." Various such costumes, worn during the escape, are described in the king's own account, dictated to Pepys in 1680, and in the *Boscobel Tracts.* (See Appendix.)

The course followed by Buckingham (who had been Charles' sole companion during his jail-like existence as King of Scotland) had the audacity which was repeatedly shown in the life of:

"A MAN so various that he seemed to be
Not one, but all mankind's epitome.
Stiff in opinions, always in the wrong,
Was everything by starts, and nothing long;
But in the course of one revolving moon,
Was chemist, fiddler, statesman and buffoon.
Then all for women, painting, rhyming, drinking,
Besides ten thousand freaks that died in thinking.
Blest madman, who could every hour employ,
With something new to wish, or to enjoy.
Beggar'd by fools, whom still he found too late,
He had his jest, but they had his estate."

Dryden: *Absalom and Architophel*

Buckingham actually made his way back to London, and set up on the street as a mountebank. "He caused himself to be made a Jack Pudding's coat, a little hat, with a fox's tail in it, and adorned with cock's feathers. Sometimes he appeared in a wizard's mask; sometimes he had his face bedaubed with flour, sometimes with lampblack, as the fancy took him. He had a stage erected at Charing Cross, where he was attended by violins and puppet-players. Every day he produced ballads of his own composition upon what passed in town, wherein he himself often had a share. These he sung before several thousands of spectators, who every day came to see and hear him. He also sold mithridate and his galbanum plaister in this great city, in the midst of his enemies, whilst we were obliged to fly, and to conceal ourselves in some hole or other." (Mme. Dunois.) Buckingham was an incomparable mimic; his waddling imitation of the progress of his enemy Clarendon, bellows swinging as purse, and preceded by a crony holding the fire-tongs as a mace, was as amusing as anything that had happened at court since the jester, Archie Armstrong's feud with the archbishop, and his grace at a dinner attended by his enemy: "Great praise be to God, and little LAUD to the devil."

There was a great deal of this sort of thing. Rochester, during his disfavor, performed as the famous German doctor, Alexander Bendo. The queen went to the fair at Audley-end with her ladies, disguised as country girls, to buy a pair "of yellow stockens for her sweet-hart." Two of her ladies, the Misses Price and Jennings, sold oranges in a playhouse under the very eyes of the court, and ran into a great deal of trouble, returning in their coach.

During Charles' various exiles, spent wandering through France and the Low Countries, he lived at The Hague during 1648; after his exclusion from Holland, by the treaty of 1654, he made a secret visit to The Hague, which would not have been celebrated by a ball. It was, however, at The Hague that he received the commission from England, inviting his return as king.

We see the six-foot Charles with his shining black hair, as he was described by Mme. de Motteville, a year or so earlier, when his early good looks were already beginning to fail, "well-made, with a swarthy complexion agreeing well with his fine black eyes, a large ugly mouth, a graceful and dignified carriage, and a fine figure." He was always a fine dancer, rider, and tennis-player.

Full and difficult as the picture is, for comment, it shows the transitional costume of mid-XVIIc., with valuable rear views (l.) of a woman, and a man in a long military cassock (the garment from which the coat of latter half XVIIc. came), worn with the sword slung by a broad baldric. He wears the wide, tubular form of petticoat breeches, their hems laced with ribbon; wrinkled stockings; and cannons, gathered on a band below the knee.

Charles shows the new, wide hat; the standard costume of beribboned petticoat breeches and loose, vest-like jacket; worn with high-heeled shoes, the elongated toe of which spreads, c. 1650, just before it is cut square across. Bands have lost their irregular edges and are beginning to shrink back from the shoulders. Although periwigs had already appeared in Paris at the time of Charles' father's overnight stay there on his way to Spain, natural hair is worn here in the long form which preceded the general assumption of wigs.

The ladies' hair is lengthening, bunched at the sides in curls, the twist in back surrounded by a little Dutch cap. They carry gloves and fans, and show little bow-knots at the front or back of bodices, along the waistline (c., dancing), or on the outseam of long gloves (extreme l., and seated c.). They wear the dragging satin dress which tends to become looped in a bustle in second half XVIIc.; with long, corset-like bodices; horizontal necklines, deeply caped in lace and veiled in knotted scarves; and combinations of inner and outer sleeves of the utmost variety of finishes.

The room, with its heavily carved, gilded, and painted Dutch ceilings and walls, and high windows, is lighted by candles on the dividing pilasters, and by one of the great Dutch brass chandeliers, whose original form was that of clustered, pronged antlers.

1548-49. XVIIc. April 23, 1661. Bohemian-English. (Metropolitan Museum, Print Room.)

W. Hollar. Coronation Procession of Charles II.

This is a small section of Hollar's panorama of the whole procession. There is a 4-page account of it in Evelyn's diary; and the *Mercurius Publicus,* May 24, 1660 (q. by Malcolm, 1811, v. I, p. 295-304) describes the various groups and the colors of their costumes.

The high-crowned hats, which we are inclined to think of as Puritan because they were the hats worn to America by our ancestors, were worn by both factions alike, as these Royalist illustrations show; Puritans differed only in an avoidance of extravagances.

This hat, now ringed with feathers, will become low-crowned in a decade. Hair, parted and very long, now begins to be shaved off and replaced by periwigs which at first resemble natural hair.

The falling band will retain its oblong shape on the chest until final quarter XVIIc. It follows the old rule of appearing over the outermost garment: cape or the new coats which developed out of the cassock

---

England After the Restoration

Fashions are now, and will remain, French.

The horse ridden by Charles at his coronation belonged to Fairfax (No. 1550), the Parliamentary general who had defeated his father.

The invention of gunpowder altered not only war and armor but horsebreeding. Armor disappeared and the heavy knight's charger with it. Speed became desirable. As carriage building became more expert in latter half XVIIc., four fast light horses could draw a coach, though a fine horse remained the quickest and the most elegant means of transport for anyone able to ride.

The best European stock had always been Spanish with some admixture with fast Arab horses during the Crusades; but heft was still necessary until XVIIc. Two Arab stallions had been imported under James I, and one under James II. Three more, brought back from the siege of Vienna, greatly impressed Evelyn (Dec. 7, 1684): "Such a head . . . in all regards beautiful, and proportioned to admiration; spirited, proud, nimble, making halt, turning with that swiftness, and in so small a compass, as was admirable." He is probably describing the Stradlington Lister Turk. Under William III were brought into England the three Arab stallions whose blood is in every race horse today: the Byerly Turk, and the Darley Arabian and Godolphin Barb.

Charles, his brother James, Duke of York, and the Earl of Oxford, gave the suits they had worn at the coronation as theatrical costumes for Betterton, Haines, and Price, who played Prince Alonzo, Prince Prospero, and Lionel, son of the Duke of Parma in "Love and Honour," by Shakespeare's reputed son, Sir William D'Avenant. Mrs. Barry received the wedding dress of her pupil, the Duchess of York, and her coronation robes after the Duchess became queen, to be used as theatrical costumes.

With the Restoration, Charles had licensed two acting companies, the actors of which, like himself, had had the opportunity to see the magnificently set theatrical productions of France. Killegrew, manager of the King's Men, and D'Avenant, of the Duke of York's company, became the most powerful theatrical producers of history, until our own days. Their respective theatres, the Drury Lane (after 1663); and the Lincoln's Inn Fields and later Dorset Gardens houses, rivalled

and have as yet little shape.

Narrow knee-breeches and full Rhinegraves are shown, worn with ruffled cannons below the knee, or with sharp bows which have replaced soft bows, loops and rosettes at garter and shoe.

Kings of arms and heralds in armorial tabards. The formerly elaborate trappings of the horse are being reduced, even for parade use, to a saddle blanket. (Coronation procession of James II [1687] was similarly reproduced by Francis Sanford.)

---

each other in the changes of movable scenery, which had been first instituted for D'Avenant by Inigo Jones' pupil, Webb. Killegrew's company was made up of Hart and Kynaston (originally actors of women's parts), Mohun, Lacy, and Mrs. Hughes, the sisters Marshall, Pepys' adored Mrs. Knep, and eventually Mrs. Boutell and Nell Gwynn. It was opposed by D'Avenant's Betterton (the greatest English actor of his age), and his brother, the two Noaks, Cave Underhill, Joseph Harris, and the Mrs. Davenport, Davies and Sanderson (the last of whom became Betterton's devoted wife), and later by Mrs. Barry and Mrs. Bracegirdle. Betterton, who managed the Dorset Gardens company after D'Avenant's death, was sent by James II to study stage productions in France. His lavish sets and costumes eventually forced the company to amalgamate with the King's Men in 1682, which remained the only company in London until 1695.

The Dorset Gardens, pleasantly set facing the river, was built from Wren's designs, with carvings by Grinling Gibbon. It deteriorated with the neighborhood until, in 1698, it was being used for lottery-drawings. Opera was briefly played there; then it was torn down and its second-hand building materials advertised in the Daily Courant in 1709.

The Queen's Theatre in the Haymarket was built by Killegrew in 1704 from Sir John Vanbrough's designs, specifically as an opera house; its acoustics were terrible and its roof had to be altered. There is a great new interest in music; silver tokens (designed by such artists as Hogarth) are issued to season subscribers to the concerts at pleasure gardens like Vauxhall; the tradition of concert and opera subscriptions begins. The £3000 required to build the Queen's was raised in £100 life memberships. So many of these were taken by members of the Kit-cat that Cibber says: "Of this Theatre I saw the first Stone laid, on which was inscrib'd *the little Whig,* in Honour to a Lady of extraordinary Beauty, then the celebrated Toast and Pride of that Party" (Lady Sunderland, Marlborough's daughter).

The institution of toasting arose in Anne's day, the Tatler (#24) says, from the ancient custom of dropping a roast apple or hot toast into mulled ale or wine. In Charles II's reign, when an admirer dipped and drank from the water in which a beauty stood at Bath, a fuddled bystander "offered to jump in, and swore, though he liked not the liquor, he would have the Toast." The Toast of a London club was elected by balloting. "When she is so chosen, she reigns indisputably for that ensuing year; but must be re-elected anew to prolong her empire a moment beyond it. When she is regularly chosen, her name is written with a diamond on a drinking glass. The hieroglyphic of the diamond is to shew her that her value is imaginary; and that of the glass to acquaint her, that her condition is frail, and depends on the hand which holds her."

During Anne's reign, some of the four theatres of London were open at the same time. There were not enough patrons to fill the cheaper seats, and servants were admitted free to the galleries. When Anne Barwick, "who was lately my servant . . . committed a Rudeness last night at the Play-house, by throwing of Oranges, and hissing when Mrs. l'Epine, the Italian Gentlewoman Sung," Mrs. Tofts apologised to Christopher Rich, manager of the Drury Lane, in a notice in the Daily Courant, Feb. 8, 1709.

The elaborate new scenery and mechanical effects at performances of "Dick Whittington and Cat" and the Opera, with Rinaldo, at the Haymarket are contrasted by the Spectator (14): "We had also but a very short allowance of thunder and lightening, though I cannot in this place omit doing justice to the boy who had the direction of the two painted dragons, and made them spit fire and smoke. He flashed out his rosin in such just proportion and in such due time . . . As to the mechanisms and scenery, everything indeed was uniform and of a piece, and the scenes were managed very dextrously. At the Haymarket, the undertakers forgetting to change their side scenes, we were presented with a prospect of the ocean in the midst of a delightful grove; and though the gentlemen on the stage had very much contributed to the beauty of the grove, by walking up and down between the trees, I must own I was not a little astonished to see a well-dressed young fellow, in a full-bottomed wig, appear in the midst of the sea, and without any visible concern taking snuff."

PURITAN AND CAVALIER

Fairfax, like his father, general of the Parliamentary forces, was succeeded on his resignation in 1650, by his lieutenant, Cromwell, and retired to Nun Appleton in Yorkshire on a £5,000 a year pension. Fairfax had pursued Charles I, to force on him a petition to listen to Parliament; had refused to sit as judge at his trial, since his fate was foreordained; and had led the commission to Holland, inviting Charles II's return.

Fairfax (1613-71) and his wife Anne, daughter of his superior officer, Lord Vere, at the time of their marriage in 1637, are a surprisingly youthful couple. Soest (1637-87) could scarcely have painted them before the Restoration, and they wear the costume of the 60's. Three generations later, the

Baron Fairfax descended from them will inherit great estates in Virginia from his Culpepper mother, will die there, a friend of Washington; and collateral descendants in Virginia will hold his title in XXc.

Another of their children will figure in the most fantastic exploit of the interregnum. George Villiers, the younger Buckingham, tired of exile in France on the proceeds of his father's pictures, conceived the idea of recovering some portion of his confiscated estates by marrying the only daughter of the man who had most benefited from his loss. Practically unconcealed, he arrived in England to court Mary Fairfax, whom he had never seen. Fairfax had no prejudice against an aristocracy to which he also belonged; he was an honorable man who felt bound to make such restitution, and a brave one, who must have been taken by Buckingham's sheer audacity. Cromwell, who had intended to marry one of his daughters to Buckingham, quarrelled with Fairfax; and Buckingham retired to Nun Appleton with the Fairfaxes, playing to perfection and enjoying the role of amiable country squire, until the Restoration brough him back to fortune.

The marriage was childless and the duchess dull. In a duel, in which two combatants died and the other four were wounded, Buckingham killed the Earl of Shrewsbury over the latter's wife (who is supposed to have dressed as a page and held his horse during the encounter). He then went to bed with the lady in his blood-stained shirt out of bravado—and because the demarcation between day and night shirts was not yet firmly fixed. Eventually he brought the "duchess dowager" to his own house. The outraged legal duchess found he had arranged in advance to have a coach waiting to take her back to her family.

The duke alternated brilliant speeches in the House with repeated imprisonments in the Tower, once for treason against Charles, who pardoned him. He wrote "The Rehearsal" a burlesque of the heroic drama which put the style of Dryden entirely out of fashion. "The Rehearsal" was imitated by Sheridan in "The Critic." The duke then tried to recoup his failing fortunes by founding the glass house at Lambeth, whose products Evelyn so much admired (Sept. 19, 1676). He wittily worsted the Jesuits sent for his conversion by James II; and finally retired, with £140,000 debts, to country life. The news of this Sir George Etheredge said he had heard "with no less astonishment than if I had been told the Pope had begun to wear a periwig, and had turned beau in the 74th year of his age." Buckingham died of a chill after hunting, but in circumstances far less squalid than recounted by Pope's poem.

The sober Fairfax, so dark that he was called "Black Tom," does not yet wear a wig, although under Cromwell, May Day, 1654 "was more observed . . . than for divers years past, and indeed much sin committed by wicked meetings, with fiddlers, drunkenness, ribaldry and the like. Great resort came to Hyde Park, many hundreds of rich coaches, and gallants in attire, but most shamefully powdered hair; men painted and spotted women." (*Cromwelliana.*)

Wood, who was no beau, but no Puritan either, paid "2s 6d for powder and mending of my periwige," when settling his quarterly accounts with his Oxford barber. He reports that Dr. John Owen, "the deane of Christ Church, had as much powder in his haire that would discharge eight

1550. XVIIc. German-English. (London, Nat. Port. Gall.)

Gerard von Soest. Thomas, Third Baron Fairfax and his wife.

Soest (1600-87), who came to London in 1656 and died there, was so ill-mannered and personally untidy that fewer women than men sat to him.

Fairfax, the humblest and most unpretentious of men, except in battle when "scarce anyone durst speak a word to him, and he would seem more like a man distracted and furious than of his ordinary mildness," wears a modest band, as befits a general of the rebellion; but as a rich gentleman, his band is fashionably cut and handsomely stringed, and worn with the satin-smooth, rather skimpy coat, usually quite untrimmed, which we see in so many Lely and Kneller portraits of Englishmen in latter half XVIIc.

His wife wears the beginnings of the studied satin negligence of the third quarter century, her ringlets now falling forward over the shoulders. The cut-and-fitted-together look has left the outermost garments; they appear to be rectangles, slung about the body, rather than gored capes. The cape-like lace about ladies' shoulders is disappearing in favor of an edge of shirt-frill, or scarves, knotted or caught with small brooches, and allowed to trail.

1551. XVIIc. 1660. Flemish-English. (Metropolitan Museum.)

Janssens van Ceulen. Dorothy Percy, Countess of Leicester.

Dorothy Percy, daughter of the ninth Earl of Northumberland, had fifteen remarkable children by her marriage in 1616 with Sir Philip Sidney's cousin. Of her daughter Dorothy, the Tatler (#61) says, "The fine women they shew me now-a-days are at

canons . . . and being a vaine person weared for the most part sweet powder in his haire," as well as lawn boot-hose tops, "in opposition to a prelaticall cut." Pepys, under less compulsion than the Oxford ecclesiastics to indicate his politics by his costume, first tries on wigs at Jervas, his barber's, May 9, 1663, balancing their trouble against their advantages; eventually buys two, at £3, and at 40s., and fails to make the stir he had expected when he appears at church in the better one, Nov. 8, 1663.

best pretty girls to me who have seen "Sacharissa" when all the world repeated the poems (by Waller) which she inspired." One of her sons was Algernon Sidney, "that man of great courage, great sense, great parts," author of the "Discources concerning Government," which upheld resistance to oppression by the crown, and reaffirmed the importance of both Houses of Parliament in its restraint. He was executed on Dec. 7, 1683, on what Evelyn calls "the single witness of that monster of a man, Lord Howard of Escrick, and some sheets of paper taken in Mr. Sidney's study, pretended to be written by him, but not fully proved, nor the time when, but appearing to have been written before His Majesty's Restoration, and then pardoned by the Act of Oblivion." The Sidneys were handsome and cultivated anti-Tory aristocrats, too Protestant for Laud, too moderate for the Puritans. Their eldest son was another judge, who, like Fairfax, refused to take part in the farce of Charles I's trial, and was pardoned at the Restoration for the important part he had played, as Lord Lisle, in the Civil Wars.

Dorothy Percy is faultlessly dressed for the role of a handsome and high-minded, middle-aged Protestant of great position; everything is perfectly sober and suitable, rich and becoming. While the lovely Lady Isabella Thynne and Mrs. Fanshawe appear at chapel at Oxford during the interregnum "half-dressed, like angels," the countess is covered to the ears by exquisite sheer lawn and lace, the whole effect of which hangs by the thread of black below the sweep of her great hat, and leading to the bow on her bosom.

1552

1552. XVIIc. c. 1661. English. (Bratton Fleming, Basil Fanshaw.)

Sir Peter Lely. Sir Thomas and Lady Fanshawe.

The Fanshawes, for three generations remembrancers to the king's exchequer, were a family whose second and third generations were ruined by civil war.

Sir Thomas, the First Viscount; his brother Richard (the diplomat, translator of the *Lusiad,* and husband of the memoir-writing Lady Anne); and his son Thomas, the Second Viscount, were all in the loyalist army, and disabled to sit in parliament. The brothers "compounded" for the restitution of their estates, but were largely ruined. The second Thomas had to sell Ware, the family seat, for £26,000, after the death of his mother (daughter of Sir William Cokayne, Lord Mayor of London). One of his younger brothers, "a witty but rascally fellow, without a penny in his purse," was a great trial to Pepys (Feb. 23, 1667/8). He was asking "what places there were in the Navy fit for him, and Brisband tells me, in mirth, he told him the Clerke of the Acts, and I wish he had it, so I were well and quietly rid of it; for I am weary of this kind of trouble." Among James I's new devices for raising money had been his institution of baronetcies; first granted May 22, 1611 to seventy-five knights. Ninety receiving that honor, March 13, 1614, paid £1090 to maintain thirty foot-soldiers three years in Ireland at 8d a day. Powerful places in the government, with their valuable perquisites, were frankly sold. Now an English aristocracy pauperized by war (as that of France by the demands of court life under Louis XIV), was, like young Fanshawe, scrambling for places.

The younger Sir Thomas' first wife, Catherine Ferrers, "a very great fortune and a most excellent woman," had died in 1660. Since he had by his second wife (Sara Evelyn, widow of Sir John Wray) a daughter, who was herself married in 1675, Fanshawe must have remarried almost immediately. This portrait by Lely, (who also painted Sir Richard Fanshawe and his lady) probably celebrates the new marriage.

Like the miniature of Lady Catherine Howard, this shows the characteristic costume of the third quarter of the century, against which ministers were launching such attacks as Richard Baxter's "A just and seasonable reprehension of naked breasts and shoulders."

This loose informality also affects male costume; gentlemen begin to be painted in handsome shirts, barely showing under a great deal of slung drapery; then they will be painted in shirts and dressing gowns (see Ill. 1581); and by XVIIIc., in dressing gowns and caps.

1553. XVIIc. 1664. Flemish-English. (Windsor Castle, H. M. the King of England.)

Jacob Huysmans (1633-96). Frances Stuart, Duchess of Richmond.

Henrietta Maria's physician during her exile was one Walter Stewart. His daughter Frances came to England in 1662 as maid-of-honor to Charles' Portuguese queen, despite Louis XIV's promise to see her married "as well as any lady in France," if she remained at Versailles.

"It was hardly possible," Count Hamilton said, "for a woman to have less wit or more beauty. . . . She was very graceful . . . well bred, and possessed to perfection that art of dress . . . which is rarely attained unless acquired while young in France."

Charles made love to her for many years with little success, and even considered divorcing in order to marry her. Pepys' diary, 1663-7, is filled with entries about the king's infatuation, and comparisons of her beauty with that of the king's official mistress, the dazzling Lady Castlemain.

When the court went into mourning, April 23, 1666, "forcing all the ladies to go in black, with their hair plain, and without spots," Pepys finds Lady Castlemain "not so pretty as Mrs. Stewart"; on Oct. 30, he decides that "plain natural dress" becomes neither lady. But on Nov. 14, Mrs. Stewart is "a glorious sight . . . in black and white lace, and her head and shoulders dressed with diamonds," exceeding Lady Castlemain, "at least now." On Feb. 27, 1666/7, Pepys sees the King's "new medall," the copper penny, on the reverse of which Rotier had represented Mrs. Stewart as Brittania, as she appears to this day.

On April 26, 1667, "she was come to that pass as to

1553

1554

venience. The scurrilous pages devoted by Wood (May 1, 1661) to the villainies of Tom Clayton, the new warden, (who had taken a fancy to the rooms while calling on the lady), can surprise no one who has ever lived through a row in a chaste institution like a college or museum. The heavy furniture which had been "well liked by Dr. Goddard, Brent, Savile &c., being disliked by that proud woman (Lady C.) because, forsooth, the said goods were out of fashion . . . all must be chang'd and alter'd to the great expence of the college . . . A very large looking glass, for her to see her ugly face, and body to the middle, and perhaps lower . . . and which cost, as the bursar told me, about £10," Wood accuses the Claytons of carrying off to their private country house, among other stylish new objects of which the college had kept no inventory.

1554. XVIIc. After 1660. Dutch. (London, Sir Philip Sassoon.)

H. Danckerts (1630-78). The Pineapple Picture.

This picture, by a Dutch painter who had studied in Italy, belonged to Horace Walpole. His notation on the back says that it shows Mr. Rose, the king's gardener, presenting to Charles the first pineapple grown in England. The scene is the landing from the Thames at Dawnay Court, Sussex, where the pits in which the palms were grown for protection still exist. (Sacheverell Sitwell: *English Conversation Pictures.*) Pineapples were still a rarity when the king gave Evelyn a slice of one from the Barbadoes from his own plate (Aug. 19, 1668); Evelyn was disappointed. "It has yet a graceful acidity, but tastes more like quince and melon" than any of the fruit to which it had been likened in Capt. Ligon's mouthwatering descriptions of travel.

Charles' "good-natured condescensions" were legendary. When the mayor, Sir Robert Viner, tried to drag the king back bodily for one more bottle at the Lord Mayor's banquet, Charles said, "He that's drunk is as great as a king" and returned. (*Spectator,* No. 462.) On a visit from America, Penn stood covered, after the Quaker fashion, in the king's presence. Charles took off his own hat. Penn asked, "Friend Charles, why dost thou not keep on thy hat?" and was told by the king, "'Tis the custom of this place for only *one* person to remain covered at a time." (Gray's *Hudibras.*)

The amusing and quick-witted Charles had been defectively educated, but was an adroit politician of great natural gifts. "If this king loved business as well as he understood it, he would have been the greatest king in Europe," Sir Richard Bulstrode said. Bishop Burnet says Charles "told Lord Essex that he did not wish to be like a Grand Signor, with some mutes about him, and bags of bow-strings to strangle men; but he did not think he was a king so long as a company of fellows were looking into his actions, and examining his ministers as well as his accounts." After a life of poverty and exile, Charles wanted to stay at home, be king, and amuse himself. He had a considerable interest in science and the arts, and, Pepys, says, "a transcendant mastery of all maritime knowledge."

In this picture, Charles, who "delighted in a bewitching kind of pleasure called sauntering," and who walked every day in St. James' Park to feed the

have resolved to have any gentleman of £1500 a year that would have had her in honour . . . for she could not longer continue at court without prostituting herself to the king, whom she has so long kept off."

Since the king opposed her marriage she eloped with the rich but dull Duke of Richmond. Charles expelled her from court; she sent back the jewels he had given her. But returning to court as the Queen's first lady of the bedchamber, she did eventually become Charles' mistress, retaining her influence despite a disfiguring attack of smallpox in 1668. Dying childless in 1704, she directed that an estate should be bought and called "Lennox-love to Blantyre," as a gift to her favorite nephew.

Frances Stewart was a superb horsewoman. Wood tells us that male red coats were worn as ladies' riding dress at Oxford, 1660-5. On Aug. 26, 1664, Pepys went "to see some pictures at one Huysman's, a picture-drawer, a Dutchman, which is said to exceed Lilly; and indeed there is both of the Queens and Maids of Honour, particularly Mrs. Stewart's, in a buff doublet like a soldier, as good pictures, I think, as ever I saw." On June 11, 1666, "walking in the galleries at White Hall, I find the Ladies of Honour dressed in their riding garb, with coats and doublets with deep skirts, just, for all the world, like mine; and buttoned their doublets up the breast, with periwigs and with hats, so that, only for a long petticoat dragging under their men's coats, nobody could take them for women at any point whatever: which was an odde sight, and a sight that did not please me."

Frances Stewart's "buff doublet," harking back to the cavalier styles of the civil wars, has the laced closing which has been characteristic of XVIIc. leather military garments. With her great sense of style, she uses the knot of ribbons which we would expect to find on the shoulder of a contemporary man's coat, as a more effective finish to the front lacing.

After a royal visit to Oxford, poor Mr. Fisher was never able to get back the lodgings in Merton from which he had been ousted for Mrs. Stewart's conbirds, is shown with the little spaniels which went everywhere with him. Their breed is still called by his name.

> "His very dog at Council Board
> Sits grave and wise as any Lord."

Both Charles and Mr. Rose wear wigs and long, easy-fitting coats with shoulder-knots, and sleeves caught back by bows. Charles' coat, with the Garter star on its breast, is still buttoned at the top, and has a pocket in its early form, barely above the hem; from it hangs a tasseled handkerchief. In 1667, when his mistress, Lady Castlemain, was losing £25,000 a night at the cards Charles himself disliked, Pepys says (Sept. 2), the king had "at this time no hand-kerchers, and but three bands to his neck," for lack of money to pay the linen-draper £5,000, "the grooms taking away the king's linen at the quarter's end as their fee . . . let the king get more as he can."

(For data on intended Ill. 1555, see Appendix.)

1556. XVIIc. 1674. English. (London, National Gallery.)
Unknown painter. Martha Horton, née Binns.
The widow of Joshua Horton of Sowerby was probably painted by a member of the de Critz family, in her weeds.

1557-58. XVIIc. 1670. U. S. A. (Charleston, W. Va., Mrs. Alexander Quarrier Smith.)
Unknown artist. Margaret Gibbs and Henry Gibbs.
Among the earliest American portraits of children are those of the Gibbs children, and of Madame Freake and Baby Mary, of Boston mercantile families. (See Appendix.)
All show the expected provincial time lag of several decades. Margaret Gibbs' gown is of red velvet, with red ribbons and fine lace; apron embroidered in blue-black; silver beads; wonderful square-toed white shoes with red soles and ribbons. Henry, who became the pastor of East Parish, Watertown, and married the daughter of the Rev. Nathan Appleton of Cambridge, wears a red cap banded in lace, a brown gown with red-brown cuffs, laced in gold and white galloon; plain white pinafore and band collar; and yellow shoes with red soles and bows.

1559-78. XVIIc. 1675. English. (Metropolitan Museum, Print Room.)

David Loggan. "Oxonia Illustrata."

Sheldonian Theatre (1559), Academic Costume (1560-78).

The passion for recording which is characteristic of the XVIIc. led Oxford to make Loggan "public sculptor of the University," and to give Anthony Wood access to the records of the various colleges for his "Hist. & Ant. Univ. Oxon." Their books, with Hyde's catalog of the Bodleian, became Oxford's official presents to visiting dignitaries (with the addition of a pair of embroidered gloves on a visit from the king; festivities and processions attending such visits are minutely described by Wood: see Appendix.)

The new architectural and topographical plates of second half XVIIc.-first half XVIIIc. need figures and carriages in the foreground to give them scale. Useful costumed figures are found on such plates as Speed's *Map of the Kingdom of England,* 1646, Sanford's *Coronation Procession of James II,* in the various *Surveys, Annals, Almanachs* and *Cries of London* of the period, as well as in book illustration, which is becoming important. Loggan followed his *Oxonia* by *Cantabrigia Illustrata,* 1690, one plate of which shows country folk harvesting the surrounding fields.

The Sheldonian Theatre, designed by Sir Christopher Wren, was built and endowed by Gilbert Sheldon, Archbishop of Canterbury, and opened with the "great" Act of 1669. Its basement housed the university press, and the theatre with its painted ceiling was henceforth used for the degree-granting ceremonies of the Act, early in July. Throughout Act Saturday, Act Sunday and Act Monday, specific functions are held, while at the same time (and during this week alone), professional actors, rope-dancers, jugglers, and freaks were allowed to perform. Wood had paid 1s. 8d. for refreshments and to see the play given at the "Blewe Anchor," July 6, 1657, and went twice to see the "Turke" dance in 1658.

After the Restoration, "to spite the Presbyterians," both morning and afternoon performances were given at the "King's Armes in Halywell." Crowds thronged to Oxford to see one to three showings of ten different plays, "wherein women acted" (among whom was Roxilana, married to the Earl of Oxon) "making the scholars mad, run after them, take ill courses."

Elizabeth Davenport, called "Roxilana" after the part in the "Siege of Rhodes" in which Pepys found her incomparable, had indignantly refused to become the Earl of Oxford's mistress, but was tricked by him into a "marriage," performed by his herald, dressed as a priest. Wedding festivities have become so expensive that the fashionable trend is toward the smallest possible weddings, held in the country or at midnight. Children, wards, and their fortunes have been manipulated with so little heart or conscience, especially in England, that the era of clandestine, runaway, irregular marriages is beginning. Footmen, in their master's clothes and well-observed manners, court masked women who may be ladies or adventuresses; heiresses are abducted by fortune-hunters; marriages, legal or not, are performed in the "lawless" churches, or in prison chapels, which do not require banns, by equivocal ministers, often themselves prisoners, or by court clerks, impersonating their superiors, and giving forged certificates. Sion Chapel at Hampstead required a license, but advertised in the *Postboy* in 1710, that you could be married there free, if you had your wedding dinner in its gardens.

Wood's descriptions and Loggan's plates (which Wood often refers to as "the cuts" to his book), show academic costume at Oxford, just as the common, dignified dress of the Middle Ages, anachronistically retained in ecclesiastical wear, is becoming stylized and fixed into its modern form. (See Poole: Appendix.)

Wood mentions in 1649 the neglect of the old rules of academic dress under the "new comers," who "mostly were very meane and poor at their first comming" having gotten into good fellowships, "became wondrous malapert and saucy, especially to the old stock remaining. They went in half shirts, appearing at their brest and out at sleeves, great bands with tassel band-strings, and Spanish leather boots with lawne or holland tops," all avoiding "cassocks, or canonical gownes or coates, or curcingles, because they smelt too much of the prelaticall cut." Gowns with sleeves "as wide as those of surplices, a fashion brought into the Universitie by the Cantabrigians" were worn until 1666. Square or round academic caps, and hoods were not "woren in publick," and often not at Congregation and Convocation. Commoners often wore the gowns of gentlemen commoners, while the latter might appear in velvet faced gowns. The sleeves and facings of formal gowns of doctors of divinity were of velvet; of medicine, satin; of law, taffeta.

In 1660, "the next matter was to restore formalities and habits, totally in a manner neglected in the intervall, but sleeves and caps were not reformed to their exact size until Dr. Fell became vice-chancellor." Meanwhile (1663) "gentlemen commoners and other idle scollars" followed the courtiers' fashion of singing and whistling "in a careless way as they went too and fro . . . to the disgrace of the gown."

Dr. John Fell changed all that on Aug. 27, 1666. The new rules were printed in English as well as Latin "for the benefit of taylours:"

1. Servitours' gownes to have round capes and sleeves hanging behind the shoulder without any buttons.

2. The battelars' gowne altogeather the same with the servitours', excepting that the cape be square. [This is the type of gown now worn by commoners.]

1560. Undergraduate student of Civil Law, who has finished 4 academic years.

1561. Bachelor of Music.

1562. Bachelor of Arts.

1563. Bachelor of Arts, degree to be granted at Lent.

1564. Collector of Bachelor's degrees.

1565. Bachelor of Medicine.

1566. Proctor of the University.

1567. Proctor in an ermine hood (caputio ex minutio vario).

1568. Bachelor of Theology.

1569. Doctor of Medicine.

1570. Doctor of Sacred Theology.

1571. Doctor of Sacred Theology, in a scarlet cappa (capa coccinea).

1572. Doctor of Sacred Theology in a scarlet gown (toga coccinea).

1573. Members of the lesser nobility, Knights and Baronets.

1574. Sons of Viscounts, Marquises, Dukes and Earls.

1575. Superior bedells.

1576. Chancellor of the University.

1577-78. Attendants.

3. The commoners' gowne to be distinguished from the former by having half a dozen of buttons on each sleeve, not exceeding 5s the dozen nor the bigness in the public patterns.

4. The gent. commoners' gowne to be half-sleeved, and, if they please, to have buttons not exceeding 4 dozen nor the rate of 5s the dozen nor the bigness in the public patterns.

5. A baronet's and knight's gowne, the same with the former, only distinguisht (if they please) with gold and silver buttons.

6. Noblemen to weare (if they please) coloured gownes, of the same form as the former.

7. Bachelaures of Arts and Foundation men that are undergraduats to weare wide-sleev'd gowns, the sleeves not reaching beyond the fingers' ends nor above an ell in compass. The Bachelaurs' sleeve to hang at length; the Foundation men turn'd up to the wrist.

8. None to weare mourning gownes, unless upon a cause approved by the head of the house and to be allowed by the vicechancellor and proctors. [The day before the burial of Dr. Oliver, president of Magdalene College, Oct. 27, 1661, "the university bellman went from college to college with the doctor's scarlet and square cap on, according to antient custome in these manners, to give notice when he should be buried." This custom had been prohibited by the Parliamentary Visitors, 1647-8. In 1675, "moorning gownes woren, as for thes 5 or 6 yeares past, by all sorts of scholars, and especially in the winter. Strange that no course is taken." In 1680, the vice-chancellor did not take the votes, at convocation, of

"those in mourning that would not vote for him; those that did, he took." Loggan's complete plates show these mourning gowns.]

9. Servitours, batlars, commoners, gentlemen-commoners of all conditions, being undergraduats, to weare round caps; gentlemen to have a hatband upon them; knights, baronets, and noblemen being undergraduats to have velvet caps with silver or gold hatbands. [Our phrase "tuft-hunter" comes from the academic climbers who tried to become intimate with men of higher social rank, with gold tufts on their headgear.]

10. That persons studying the law being above 4 yeares standing in the University and being entred into the law-book be permitted to weare a half sleev'd gowne without buttons and a square cap.

"Which being published, all taylours, brokers, haberdashers and others whatsoever were warned not to make or sell any gowne or cap contrary to the patterne before mentioned next after S. Michael's day following. If any were found culpable then for the first offense, he was to pay 10s, halfe wherof was to goe to the University and tother half to the company of taylers. If the second time he offends, then 20s to be bestowed as aforesaid. If the third time, public discommoning, or dispriviledgd without hopes of restoration." (Wood)

Academic dress was formal, varying in color; or ordinary and black; with an intermediate form of convocation dress; red like the formal gown, worn by doctors.

The chancellor was an archbishop like Laud or Sheldon, or a great nobleman like Leicester, Pembroke, or Ormonde; his formal gown was of black silk laced with gold lace.

The vice-chancellor was the resident, acting head of the University, appointed for one year, but frequently reappointed. His power over Oxford was widespread. As an ecclesiastic, he controlled its pulpits and the conduct of heresy trials. His civil power gave him the discipline and jurisdiction over the night-watch and the streets, coffee, ale, and playhouses, markets and the prices of wine and ale, coaches and carriers, barber-shops, booksellers and censorship of the press. He supervised examinations, regulated academic dress, administered the finances of the University, and received the goods of felons and suicides.

The bedells were university officials, who did processional duty, and served as the vice-chancellor's messengers. They were six in number, an esquire and a yeoman bedell for each of the three faculties of theology, law, and arts and medicine. The esquire bedells wore gold chains and carried embossed silvergilt maces or staffs, which they must surrender to the king when he visits Oxford; the yeomen bedells, plain silver-gilt maces. The vice-chancellor's accounts show that during XVIIc. there was also a "bedell of beggars," for whose gown £1 15s 9d was paid in 1693-4, and £2 in 1695-6. "Rebellious and seditious books," condemned by the convocation (including Thomas Hobbs' "Leviathan" and works by Thomas Cartwright), were thrown on a bonfire in the school quadrangle in 1683 by Gigur, the University bedell of beggars, before the vice-chancellor, bishop, and doctors in their "formalities."

Wood's diaries and compilations furnish an immense mass of information about such dress as is worn by the gentlemen in the lower corner of the sheet. Like Wood, they probably paid their barbers by the quarter; they might still wear their own hair, or wigs, costing at Oxford from 20 to 32s 6d. Their broad-brimmed castor (beaver) or demi-castor hats probably cost 11 to 24s; their bands, plain or laced, from 1s 5d to 13s 6d a pair. Their shirts were always made to order, probably by a woman. Wood once bought "3 ells and a quartern at 8 groats an ell" for a shirt which cost him altogether 8s 6d, and paid his sister Kit 7s 6d for another.

In the same way, the material for suits was never provided by the tailor who made up and kept the suit in repair. On April 24, 1665, Wood "bought a black shaloone suit (i.e. the material for it) of Mr. Fifeild and a studying gown of nectarello which cost me out of the shop £2 15s 9d.," and on May 4 paid "Mr. Hieron (Hearne) the taylor for making my suit 5s 6d; for making my studying gowne, 1s 6d." Wood's suits were apt to be black or sad colored. As his income increases, his costumes become more elegant and he rides a great deal more. On May 7, 1678, he puts on "a new riding camlet coat out of Mr. Fifeild's shop, £1 18s; making 4s; sising 1s; sum £2 3s," and on June 16, 1690 he has a new "white demity shuit; making 4s 9d."

In his least affluent days, gloves seem to have been a necessity; they were usually tan, wash leather or dog-skin and cost 1s to 1s 6d a pair. As cold weather set in, in Oct. 1661, Wood buys gloves to wear while writing. Wood's stockings were of black, pearl or sadcolored wool and cost from 3s to 5s 6d a pair; he is constantly paying "Bessie Creke for loyning and lengthening my new yarn stockings, 3d" or giving "Gooddy Gale" 6d for mending them. Shoes of russet or "liquored black Spanish leather" are made to order at Oxford for about 4s, and are kept in repair by their maker, or by the cobbler. With the growing interest in personal cleanliness, tooth brushes begin to appear in Wood's accounts about 1690.

In these straight, long-skirted coats we see the pockets in their early position, just above the hemline; the use of ribbon reduced to knots at shoulder, cuff, knee and shoe. The shirt, bloused above petticoat breeches, is beginning to disappear, as vests lengthen and coat buttons are fastened lower.

1579

1579. Last quarter XVIIc. English. (Metropolitan Museum.)

School of Lely. Barbara Villiers, Duchess of Cleveland (Lady Castlemain).

The daughter of that "faultless person," Grandison, was, Burnet says, "a woman of great beauty, but enormously vicious and ravenous." She was married in 1658 to Roger Palmer, went with him to Charles' court in the Low Countries, and returned as Charles' mistress at the Restoration. She turned Catholic in 1663, and was treated with every consideration by Louis XIV's ambassadors, while she intrigued against the Chancellor, Clarendon, who would not permit any social relations between her and his wife. Her unpleasant husband was made Earl of Castlemain in 1662, and Duke of Cleveland in 1670. As James' ambassador to Rome he was the darling of the Jesuits, but was never allowed to complete his mission at the Vatican; at every audience, Innocent was siezed by a fit of coughing and had to withdraw, just as Castlemain began to speak; and, at his threat to leave Italy, Innocent said: "Only recommend him to rise early, that he may rest at noon; it is dangerous in this country to travel in the heat of the day."

Charles, childless by his Portuguese wife, had about 15 children by seven mistresses; six of Lady Castlemain's were perhaps his. She was "foolish but imperious, very uneasy to the king, and always carrying on intrigues with other men, while yet she pretended she was jealous of him. His passion for her, and her strange behavior towards him, did so disorder him, that often he was not master of himself, nor capable of minding business . . . in so critical a time," the bishop continues. Her lovers included leading actors, like Hart and Goodman; Jacob Hall the rope dancer; the playwright Wycherly; and the handsome duke of Marlborough.

Lady Castlemain lost immense sums at basset but could afford to gamble because of a large income: "£10,000 more a year to the Duchess of Cleveland; who has likewise near £10,000 a year more out of the new farm of the county excise of beer and ale;

£5,000 a year out of the Post Office; and, they say, the reversion of all the King's leases, the reversion of all the places in the Customhouse, the Green Wax, and indeed, what not! All promotions, spiritual and temporal, pass under her cognizance." (Andrew Marvell.) Clarendon, however, never allowed the Great Seal to be affixed to any paper on which her name appeared.

Her influence lasted about 10 years. She had always resented the superior beauty of Charles' son, born to Lucy Walters in exile, over her own children. Her position was weakened, after the marriage of "La Belle Stuart" who did not care to gamble, and laughed and built card-houses with Buckingham, while Lady Castlemain was losing her house and its contents at cards. It was further impaired by her behavior over her rivals. Nell Gwynn, the delightful actress, had refused a title and settlements. Charles, "so pleasant a man," even on his death-bed, asked the court to forgive him for being so long a-dying, and asked his heir, James, to "take care of Carewell (Querouaille, his last mistress), and let not poor Nelly starve," before he was hustled with horrifying lack of ceremony into his grave.

The duchess of Cleveland had gone to France in 1670; there in 1705, she married the beautiful but brutal "Beau" Feilding (whose footmen flaunted fantastic yellow liveries, slashed and plumed in black, and who turned out to have a wife already). In 1709, at 70, she died of dropsy.

Like the duchess of Mazarin, Lady Castlemain wears the simple, careless dress of the turn of the third to final quarter XVIIc., the underlinen of which overflows the neckline of the bodice, and forces its way out between the tiny jewelled clasps of the center-front, and is pushed up, with studied negligence, at the elbows. Her cloak is the new, informally draped and caught rectangle, unshaped by any bias cutting.

Walpole calls Lely's clothes "a sort of fantastic nightgowns, fastened with a pin." (*Anecdotes of Painting.*)

1580. XVIIc. German-English. (Marquis of Tweedale.)

Gerard von Soest. Lady Margaret Hay, Countess of Roxburgh.

"Lord Roxbrough . . . one of the flowers of this nobility," was one of the naval officers, whose loss, at the wreck of the Gloucester, is recorded by Pepys, May 8, 1682.

1581-82. XVIIc. 1687. English. (London, Messrs. Leygatt.)

J. M. Wright. Sir Willoughby Aston (1581), Lady Aston (1582).

The Astons were staunch Royalists, who had lived in Cheshire and served the Crown since the XIIc. Willoughby Aston was the only son of the heiress of Sir Henry Willoughby, Sheriff of Chester, and of that "stout and learned man," Sir Thomas Aston (a devout Churchman whose *Remonstrance against Presbytery, exhibited by divers of the nobilitie, gentrie, ministers, and inhabitants of the County Palatine of Chester,* was written in answer to "some brain-sick Anabaptist").

Wood records, with almost servile satisfaction, that Aston's cousin, Sir Henry Purefoy, had passed over an uncle to make Sir Willoughby heir to his estate of Wadley, the year before this picture was painted. Perhaps Purefoy appreciated fine manners more than did Sir Robert Newdegate, an extravagantly prodigal host, who mutters in his diary of "Sir W. A.'s ingenious but most abominable complimentall letter" of thanks for hospitality at Arbury. The bequest cannot have been unwelcome: Aston and his wife, Mary Offley, had eight sons and thirteen daughters to settle in life. (See Appendix, Newdegate.)

Sir Willoughby appears in the informal shirt and handsome dressing gown which is beginning to be fashionable indoor wear and which by XVIIIc. will appear on the streets, early in the morning.

Lady Roxburgh (Ill. 1580) and Lady Castlemain (Ill. 1579) wear approximately the same gown: its developing informality, as bunched-up and wired-out hair loses its artificial supports and begins to fall, is shown in the dress of Lady Aston. Its final form, the draperies of a goddess of antiquity, is worn by the Duchess of St. Albans.

1583. Late XVIIc.-Early XVIIIc. German-English. (Hampton Court, H. M. The King.)

Sir Godfrey Kneller. Lady Diana de Vere, Duchess of St. Albans.

The daughter and heir of Aubrey de Vere, the last Earl of Oxford, married Charles Beauclerk, Duke of St. Albans, son of Charles II and Nell Gwynn. He was a soldier, "a gentleman in every way de bon naturel, well-bred, doth not like business, is well affected to the constitution of his country" which he served under Charles, William and Anne. His wife was Lady of the Bedchamber and of the Stole to Queen Caroline, when she was Princess of Wales, while Charles was Grand Falconer.

There had been a decline of interest in falconry after James I's time. Its revival after the Restoration could not be maintained in face of the general use of firearms and the increase in agricultural enclosures. The "day" of falconry held on Oct. 1, 1828, by the Hereditary Grand Falconer of England, descendant of one of St. Albans' eight sons, was notably unsuccessful.

1584

1585

1586   1587

1584. Early XVIIc. (Boston, Museum of Fine Arts, Elizabeth Day McCormick Coll.)

Dress: grayish brown silk brocaded in gold; trimmed with gold and silver bobbin lace. Hem and back width are made of another (probably cheaper) material: brown ground, narrow stripes, warp figured, of minute geometric figures in blue, yellow and white; probably covered originally by some sort of loose panel or train.

1585-86. XVIIc. c. 1690. English. (Metropolitan Museum.)

Dress in Louis XIV style: gray wool, striped in indigo blue and henna, embroidered throughout in silver gilt in late XVIIc. conventionalized flower and scroll pattern done in satin and stem stitches. Belonged to the Wodehouse family, Kimberly House, Norfolk. (See Appendix.)

1587. XVIIIc. 1700-50. French. (Metropolitan Museum.)

Suit: mauve silk, all-over design of white flowers and green stems.

THE "CORRUPTED TOTTERING BISHOPS"

Cartwright was the very pattern of Mrs. Hutchinson's "corrupted, tottering Bishops." He was the grandson of that Thomas Cartwright (1535-1603), "head and most learned of that sect of dissenters then called puritans," whose original distaste for vestments and ritual was extended by Cartwright into a concern for the entire originzation of the church. He was ousted from his Lady Margaret professorship, and served as Rector of the University of Geneva. Always impetuous, he declared, during his prosperous and respected old age, back in England, that he wished he could relive his life "to testify to the world the dislike he had of his former ways" which had caused so much trouble.

The grandson of the old Puritan had no difficulty in obtaining a vacant fellowship at Magdalen during the interval, but at the Restoration he turned ardently loyal and got the post of chaplain to the duke of Gloucester. He then began the collection of preferments and lucrative sinecures, which became one of the scandals of an age not easily disturbed by such things: Prebendary of St. Paul's, Vicar of St. Thomas', Prebendary of Wells and Durham, Dean of Ripon. When senility made two vacant bishoprics, "they resolved to fill them," Bishop Burnet says, "with the two worst men who could be found. Cartwright was promoted to Chester. He was a man of good capacity, and had made some progress in learning. He was ambitious and servile, cruel and boisterous, and, by the great liberties he allowed himself, he fell under great scandals of the worst sort. He had set himself long to raise the King's authority (which) ... was from God, absolute and superior to law ... So he was looked upon as a man that would more effectively advance the designs of popery, than if he should turn over to it. And indeed, bad as he was, he never made that step, even in the most desperate state of his affairs," when he fled with James on the arrival of William, followed him to Ireland, and there died. Cartwright's sycophancy is clearly shown in the 1686-7 fragment of his diary, published by the Camden Society, 1843.

Cartwright had thanked James for the Declaration of Liberty of Conscience in 1687, and in the next year, the Catholic James, who felt that the High Church was half Catholic anyhow, made his favorite, Cartwright, head of the Ecclesiastical Commission of 8 "to take cognizance of all defaults in both Universities," after Canterbury had refused to serve. "Everyone understood," Wood says, "that the design of the commission was to introduce a Roman hierarchy which assumes a power over the temporal, in order to the spiritual, good; yet here this commission grants the temporal power," to the Lord Chancellor and two others, such as the Lord Treasurer and Chief Justice with "power of excommunication, which is a purely spiritual act." The ecclesiastical visitors expelled 25 from their fellowships at Magdalene.

James, the bigoted Catholic, like many others, mistook the conscientiously tolerant William Penn for "a concealed Papist." "Penn is no more a Quaker than I am," the king declared of the Lord Admiral's son, who had returned from Louis XIV's court with what Pepys thought (Aug. 30, 1664) "a great deal, if not too much, of the vanity of the French garb and affected manner of speech and gait." Penn, imprisoned in the Tower and in Newgate as a Quaker preacher, was freed on the strength of his own speech in court. On the death of his father he came into a fortune, and was granted land in America against Charles II's debt of £16,000 to the admiral. Penn provided his American property with a remarkably liberal constitution which guaranteed complete religious freedom and, in 1682, made the first of a number of trips to Pennsylvania. While Penn was in England, he attempted to negotiate with William III in Holland, on James' behalf; there Penn met and was disliked by Burnet, as "a talking, vain man" who "had a tedious, luscious way, that was not apt to overcome a man's reason, though it might tire his patience." Dean Swift, on the contrary, thought Penn "spoke very agreeably and with much spirit."

1588. Last Quarter. XVIIc. German-English. (London Nat. Port. Gall.)

Gerard von Soest. Thomas Cartwright, Bishop of Chester.

In protest against the "prelaticall cut," during the interregnum, wigs, bands with tasseled strings (together with boots and lawn boot-hose), and refusal to wear the academic hat, had emerged as literally "protest-ant" wear. The arch-prelaticall Cartwright, therefore, wears the square hat without a wig, a small austere band, and the cassock, to which his grandfather had been so opposed, with ostentatiously full lawn sleeves.

The life of a clergyman, with a good living or two, was a cheerful and not at all onerous one, in the rollicking days of Charles' Restoration. On the road to his induction at Chester, Cartwright dined with the Marquess of Winchester at Bolton "from one at noon till one in the morning" (an invention of Winchester's to enable him to avoid matters he disliked). The journal of the Rev. Giles Moore, rector of Horsted Keynes, Sussex (Ponsonby: *English Diaries*) which he kept from 1655-79, lists purchases which, to our watered-down and perhaps canting sobriety nowadays, seem extraordinary every-day wear for a clergyman.

I bought two payre of gloves for which I payed 2s 3d the payer. I had them faced with my own fringe which cost me 1s 4d.

I bought a levitacal girdle containing 4 oz. of silke, 10s & ½ a yd of velvet; two worsted canonical girdles 5s.

I bought 2 yards and ½ of Devonshire red bazes to make me a waistcoat for which I paid 7s 4d and I bought a payre of silk stockings for which I paid £1:1; for silken tops 6s 6d and for a payer of black worsted stockings I gave 5s.

I bought of my countryman Mr. Cooke a shaggy demicastor hat of the fashion for which I payed 16s 6d.

I carried Mat (his god-daughter) up to London buying for her a new riding suite for which I payed 28s.

I gave Mat 1s to play withall and I gave her 2s towards a payr of stockings which she is to knit for herselfe. I also gave her 1s which she is to spend on dancings.

I sent for Mat's board for six weeks at Mistress Chalmers during which time shee made mee shirts and bands £1:10 and I gave her to buy a hood at the faire 5s.

THE HOUSE OF COMMONS TAKES CONTROL

Once rid of James, the House takes the bit in its teeth. It executes a series of moves more revolutionary than any until our own day. It establishes itself as the preeminent power in England, and the training ground for the brilliant political figures of the XVIII-XIXc. Taxes are elaborated, the coinage revised, and the ground work laid for the modern banking and financial systems of the country.

First, the Civil Lists are revised; the indignant William finds the Crown now less well off than at the time of his predecessor.

The army is removed from Crown control. It must now look to Parliament for pay and maintenance, and it is, for the first time, regulated and disciplined by the Mutiny Act, which, together with the Bill of Rights, the Toleration Act, and the Oath of Allegiance required by all office-holders, are passed by the 1690 Parliament.

The French wars require immense sums to be raised at a time when French privateers are destroying English trade. The happily tax-free England of Elizabeth, which so amazed the Venetian ambassador, will never again be seen.

The simple money-raising devices of James' baronage and Charles I's fines on all persons worth £40 a year who refuse knighthood, now seem childish. "Tunnage" and "poundage" excises on both imported and exported commodities had been levied in 1644. Under Charles II, there are many other devices, the most hated of which is probably the tax of 2s levied on each chimney in 1662. People had begun to be comfortable under Elizabeth; chimneys had multiplied. The rate of acceleration is now slowed. As an educational institution, Oxford feels it should be tax-exempt. Influential men are begged to lobby towards that end; but the Sheldonian continues to be taxed for three hearths in the theatre and seven in the basement print-shop.

In 1666 comes a 1% income tax, increased in 1694 to 4s on the £, and doubled for non-jurors (to the Act of Allegiance). A poll tax of 1s is levied on each subject, with an additional £1 for each gentleman, and £5 more for doctors of all university faculties. Poor prissy-genteel Wood, so proud of his cousins worth £2000 a year who have several times been offered a baronetcy, cannot forbear from declaring himself a gentleman, although he is outraged that an industrious person like himself should have to pay £1 more than the "idle scollars," amusing themselves at Oxford.

"Chimney money," repealed on William's promise as he came to the throne, was merely replaced by Halifax' window tax. There is none too much sun in England. Now houses are built with fewer windows; existing windows are blocked up; teeth, and the tuberculosis rate do not improve.

French wines and goods have been taxed off the market since 1668; customs and excise taxes are increased in 1670. By the final quarter century, smuggling, adulteration and substitution become common. Home-made gin replaces imported liquors; home-brewed beer follows beer taxes in e.XVIIIc.; and brews are fermented out of all sorts of strange substances after the malt tax which tries to control home brewing. Salt and sugar, tea, coffee, chocolate, tobacco and spices, soap and candles, paper, parchment and leather, textiles, glass, and hackney coaches are in turn taxed, and wine sellers and keepers of public houses are licensed. By 1695, there are taxes on birth, marriage, death and burial, and for widows and bachelors. To encourage its raising, wool is made tax-exempt, and an act for "burying in wool" is passed, while hemp and flax acreages are taxed. By 1701, all beasts of burden and peddlers are licensed.

Because tea is easy to smuggle, the English become a nation of tea-drinkers. To save a dying industry, the glass tax has to be repealed in 1697. The poll tax is replaced by a stamp tax. But stupid and venal tax collectors enable the rich to pay less than their share of this and of the new land and property taxes. It was even proposed to confiscate and melt all the silverware in England, at about the time that Louis XIV was melting up his silver furniture at Versailles.

English banking was far behind that of such early commercial civilizations as Italy and the Low Countries. Large sums were originally deposited for safety at the Mint, where they brought in no interest. After Charles I's requisitioning of this money, it became the custom to leave money with the goldsmiths, who advanced it at 8% to the government, against tax receipts, and paid their depositors 6%. Government obligations, backed by no current funds, had fallen to half their face value, so the government was actually paying 16% interest. In 1672, Charles II closed the Exchange without warning, confiscating the principal saved by some 10,000 people. This money, the foundation of the National Debt, did not begin to receive the promised 6% until five years later.

Montague was one of our preeminent Whigs forming the "Junto," which was the beginning of the modern cabinet. He became Chancellor of the Exchecquer after shares in the new Bank of England, which he had fostered, were quickly subscribed, and after the Bank provided funds with which to regularize the National Debt. The strength of the Bank of England was assured by provisions which, until 1826, prohibited the establishment of other banks owned by more than six people.

With the air of Sir Isaac Newton, now director of the Mint, Montague set about the long overdue revision of English currency. Confusing coins, dating from early English history, and later coins, halved, quartered or deliberately debased by clipping, and which caused England to pay a premium of 20-30% to get foreign exchange, were all called in. During May-June, 1696, Evelyn notes the disruption of trade caused by the lack of coins. "All was on trust . . . tumults are every day feared . . . for . . . want of current money to carry on the smallest concerns, even for daily provisions

in the market," until the Mint, working without closing, made up the deficiency by August.

Stow had devoted 6 pages to the complications of English coinage, up to 1598. Bad money had its uses. When Horace Walpole was escorting a lady from an evening party at Twickenham, they were held up and the lady gave the highwayman a purse of bad money, which she carried just for that purpose. A farmer in Yorkshire was afraid to receive 100 guineas in good coin, "lest he should be sent to prison as one of the gang of counterfeiters thereabouts." (Walpole: *Letters*.)

———

1589. Last quarter XVIIc. German-English. (London, Nat. Port. Gallery.)

Sir Godfrey Kneller. Charles Montague, Earl of Halifax.

Montague, one of the greatest figures in English finance, was a friend of Sir Isaac Newton since Cambridge days, and the patron of literature, "fed all day long with dedications" who, in his later arrogant vanity, was caricatured by Pope as "Bufo."

With the cravat worn after the battle of Steinkirk, 1692, and a mounting wig, Halifax wears a sleeved waistcoat, another form of the negligée attire favored at the turn of the century. Its slit sleeves are turned back, as in theory they always were, to form the trim of the coat sleeve, although the ordinary waistcoat was sleeveless. The waistcoat, skimpily cut, is caught together after the manner of women's bodices, but with braid frogs. This trim will be a favorite during the early decades of XVIIIc., and will reappear later in that century as well as in XIXc.

1590. XVIIc. 1605. German. (New York Public Library.)

T. De Bry. "Voyages to the East Indies," first published 1590. (1st Ser., Germ. ed., 1605.)

The King of Kandy and Admiral van Spilbergen.

Vasco da Gama brought back from his 1498 voyage to Calicut (from which is derived the word "calico") a letter from its ruler to the king of Portugal, which said that da Gama's visit had "given me great pleasure. In my kingdom there is abundance of cinnamon, cloves, ginger, pepper and precious stones. What I seek from thy country is gold, silver, coral and scarlet."

Trade with India was a Portuguese monopoly throughout the XVIc., but was lost to them by midXVIIc., as a result of Dutch and British pressure, combined with their own excesses of religion and arrogance.

Freed of Spanish rule, the Dutch embarked on the search for new passages to India. Barents attempted a Northwest passage to the Orient in his Arctic voyages, 1594-7. The way around Cape Horn was discovered in 1616 by the Dutch. And Dutch sea power enabled the Netherlands East Indies Co., founded 1602, to outstrip Elizabeth's English E. India Co. of 1600. The rivalry grew fiercer as the Dutch and English fought at home and England began to build her great ships, but it was resolved in 1689 under the rule of William of Orange.

Spilbergen's alliance with the King of Kandy was concluded in 1602, but it was a third of a century before their joint efforts managed to displace the Portuguese by the tolerant Dutch regime.

The king's pleated costume shows the exquisitely patterned sheer cotton materials which will become an important part of India's trade with Europe: their importation in the XVIIc. and their production in Europe during the XVIIIc., will be bitterly opposed by the wool and silk industries, but much of French and English prosperity at the turn of XIXc. will be founded on cotton.

The admiral wears the standard costume of the turn of the century: beard and ruff; pinked doublet; full, rosetted breeches; shoes with ties and heels; a commander's baldric; sword slung from a narrow belt.

1591. Early XVIIc. Dutch.

Crispin de Passe. Prodigal Son.

In one of his series of illustrations of the story of the prodigal son, de Passe shows transitional forms of men's and women's clothes.

Ruffs are open, turning into falling bands, or wide and closed, sometimes still supported, but often worn

low and flowing with the body lines around the neck.

Doublets are shorter waisted and easier; worn with long, full unpadded breeches, which often have the outer seam decorated, and fringed garters. Shoes are in transition; rosettes and heels appear as slashing goes out of use. Truncated high flat hats.

Women's hair is dressed high into a center point, studded with jewels and an aigrette; or little raked-back caps, pointed like the hair arrangements are worn, especially 1610-20. Gowns are of two types: the bolstered cartwheel skirt, which is seen to 1620, and the Spanish gown, the sleeve of which is cut across above the elbow.

Wall coverings are also transitional between tapestry and wall-paper. Paper is still made in sheets and will not become popular as a wall covering until it can be manufactured in rolls in XVIIIc. Meanwhile block printed linen is hung or stamped leather is glued to the walls. Raised plaster decoration of ceilings.

Chairs are now less severely rectangular; their arms had begun to be shaped in latter half XVIc. Spinets had developed a recessed keyboard, midXVIc.; originally box-like, they are now being mounted on legs. Typical hanging "goodly branches of brass for tapers" which Evelyn so admired in Holland in 1641.

1592. XVIIc. 1608. Flemish. (Metropolitan Museum.)

Unknown artist. The Dwarf, Hans Voorbrueg.

Household dwarfs retain their XVIc. popularity through XVIIc., and are frequently painted, with their owners or alone.

1593. XVIIc. c. 1609. Flemish. (Munich, Alte Pinakothek.)
Rubens. Self-portrait with Isabella Brant.

Rubens, shown with the beautiful bride of whom he painted so many portraits during the 17 years of their marriage, wears a black hat and cape, which is lined with wine-lees brown. His wide lace collar has the informality of an unsupported open fan collar. His beige doublet is corded in brown, with prominent shoulder caps and yellow sleeves, its lower buttons unfastened; "suntan" stockings.

With her Dutch costume, Isabella Brant wears a mannish hat of straw, faced with greenish-gold satin, set over a turned-back lace cap. Her blue-black braided jacket with revers is worn over a white and gold brocaded stomacher; wine colored skirt trimmed with gold; blue underskirt edged with gold. Bracelets on both wrists as sleeves prepare to retreat upwards.

1594. XVIIc. Dutch. (Berlin, Museum.)
Willem Buytewech. Bister drawing.

The Dutch etcher Buytewech (c.1590-c.1630) made a number of delightful drawings of Dutch costume of the first quarter century.

1595. XVIIc. 1608. Dutch.
Jacob de Gheyn (illustrator). "Maniement d'Armes," Amsterdam, 1608.

The musket was a heavier and more powerful development of the arquebuse which needed support for firing. "The armes of a Musquetier offensive are a Musquet . . . Bandoleer with 12 charges at the least, primer, bullet bag and pruning yron, with a rest of a length proportionable to his stature, and a sword. As for the defensive armes, he hath none,

1595

although in some parts I have seene them wear a Headpeace." A plumed hat was commonly worn, and a sword. (See Morse, Appendix.)

Earrings; falling band; trousers decorated across outer seam with parallel lines of fringed braid.

CHANGES IN ARMOR, XVIIc.

The character of war changed during the Wars of Religion, when men fought less for glory than for personal conviction and survival; French and English fought against their brothers and the militia of the Low Countries staved off the superb Spanish professionals.

The invention of firearms had first made necessary the production of armor "proof" against them. Then soldiers became increasingly specialized and disciplined, as firearms improved and the use of each required training; armies moved faster, offense gained over defense, infantry over cavalry, and armor became a drawback.

The heavy cavalry alone wore the close helm; light cavalry wore burgonet, cuirasse, some plate protection of shoulder and upper arm, one gauntlet, and carried pistol and sword.

Rows of pikemen still preceded the increasingly important arquebusiers and musketeers; they carried ever-longer pikes, up to 18 ft., and wore morions, with upper bodies still completely armed.

They were followed by the more lightly armed and mobile arquebusiers, in morions and brigandines with mail sleeves, in front of musketeers with little plate protection.

The halberdiers, to mop up after the shooting, came last.

During XVIIc. armor became more disadvantageous, but was worn by the cavalry until it largely disappeared by XVIIIc.

The comb morion of the infantry was supplanted by the high Spanish morion-cabasset, and this, in XVIIIc. by round topped lobster-tail burgonet, iron hat and pikeman's pot.

With the invention of grenades, latter half XVIIc., groups of grenadiers were increased to companies in the Régiment du Roi by 1668, and on June 29, 1678, Evelyn says: "Now were brought into service a new sort of soldiers, called Grenadiers, who were dexterous in flinging hand grenados, everyone having a pouch full; they had furred caps with coped crowns like Janizaries, which made them look very fierce, and some had long hoods hanging down behind, as we picture fools. Their clothing being likewise piebald, yellow and red." These fur caps developed into the familiar Bearskin. By Dec. 5, 1683, "The King had now augmented his guards with a new sort of dragoon" (cavalry trained to fight on foot), "who also carried grenades, and were habited after the Polish manner, with long peaked caps, very fierce and fantastical."

1596

1596. XVIIc. 1613. Swiss-Papal.

Francisco Villamena. The Papal Officer, Jean Gros of Lucerne.

The Swiss Guard of the Pope was instituted in 1506 by Julius II. It consisted originally of 150 men, dressed at the Pope's expense, but not uniformly. Under Adrian VI, they dressed in white, green, and yellow, although these were not his colors. When 42 of its survivors capitulated in battle in 1527, they were all dressed alike in yellow, blue and red, the personal colors of Clement VII, which were retained. The red and yellow costumes of the Suisses appear in the description of Holy Week festivities, about which Pepys' nephew, John Jackson, wrote him from Rome, Dec. 25, 1699. (See Appendix.)

Another portrait of a Papal guard by Villamena actually shows the same person; during the ten year interval, Gros changed his name to Alto.

Gros was a non-commissioned officer. His halberdier's costume shows the beginning of the degradation of the Papal Guard uniform; but it is full of interesting detail of fullness, often inserted into gores, and of the removal of fullness, by goring at breast and sleeve. The full, long breeches are no longer paned, but a reminiscent effect is gained by the use of sections of pleating. His high-crowned hat carries the excess of plumes loved by Swiss soldiers since Holbein's time.

Gros stands by the base of a column, of the colonnade originally flanking Trajan's column, seen rising behind his right arm.

1597. XVIIc. Flemish. (London, Nat. Gall.)

Hans Jordaens II (fl. 1620-43). Interior of an Art Gallery, detail.

Arundel was the greatest of innumerable amateurs of *articles de vertu* in his time. Evelyn's diary is a catalog of the great collectors of all Europe, their possessions, and the shops which catered to them. Evelyn was himself an incurable shopper, whether for maps and atlases at Hondius & Bleau's shop in Antwerp, or the wares of the gallery of the Palais-Royal. Nor was collecting any longer an interest confined to the nobility; in 1654, he went to see "one of the rarest collections of agates, onyxes and intaglios that I have ever seen either at home or abroad, collected by a conceited old hatmaker at Blackfriars, especially one agate vase, heretofore the great Earl of Leicester's." In 1661, he dined at Mr. Palmer's in Gray's Inn, "whose curiosity excelled in clocks and pendules . . . also good telescopes and mathematical instruments, choice pictures and other curiosities." Mr. Palmer would have been a good customer for the globes and chronometers, cameos and minatures, illustrated books, prints and paintings which these gentlemen are examining with the aid of spectacles, dividers, folding rule and magnifying glass.

The Royal Academies of Science, founded in Paris and London in the 60's, grew out of discussion groups of long standing. Tycho Brahe's and the other observatories of the XVIc. were privately supported, but Royal observatories were set up in Paris in 1667 and Greenwich in 1675; there is a print by Leclerc of Louis XIV's visit (in petticoat breeches) to the new Paris Observatoire.

Bouquets of natural flowers begin to replace the standing cups and jewelled objects which stood on tables in XVIc. portraits. Still lifes of fruit and game, and flower pieces, like that hanging high on the right, come into favor. An age which loved dwarfs and exotics was charmed by monkeys. A troupe of fashionably dressed monkey acrobats was one of the features of the Southwark Fair in 1660.

Standard costume of pinked satin; unrelated doublet and breeches, with seam and pocket decoration; garter bows; stockings tending to wrinkle; shoes with rosettes.

1598. XVIIc. 1615. Dutch. (Metropolitan Museum.)

J. A. van Ravesteyn. Arent Hermansz.

Costume of plain and pinked satin with brocade sleeves. Ruffs, even when pleated, take on an informal gathered look and may have irregular edges. Slit seam of sleeve edged with buttons and tiny loops. Gold trim of breeches-seam and garters. Cuff of gauntlet embroidered in a lace design. Plumed helmet and gauntlets.

COACHES AND CONVEYANCES

The word "coach" is derived from Kocs, the Hungarian town in which rude coaches were first built. Their use, at first by women only, spread to royalty, great ecclesiastics, and the infirm, in Germany and Italy. Sumptuary laws tried to control their use. Like all luxuries, they were then carried to the rich seaport cities of the Low Countries; by 1560, there were 500 coaches in Antwerp. Thence they were introduced into France and England.

The three coaches in Paris in 1550 belonged to the Queen, the King's mistress, and a nobleman too fat to ride; the queen's coach had leather curtains in place of the windows which did not appear until midXVIc.

About 1555, coaches began to be made in England. Elizabeth had a coach which could be opened to the air, built by Walter Rippon in 1564 for her state progresses about England. Her 2-horse coach, built in the eighth year of her reign by her Dutch coachman, William Booren, "was a strange monster in those days, and the sight of (a coach) put both horse and man into amazement." (*Harl. Misc.*,v.IV,p.218, and John Taylor, the Water Poet: *Works*, 1630.)

The first coach which we might recognize as such was brought to England by Fitzalan, Earl of Arundel, in 1580, Stow says. In 1611, the bride of Matthias of Hungary rode to her wedding in a coach of perfumed leather.

By midXVIIc., coaches "of the new fashion, with glasses, very stately; and . . . pages and lacquies . . . of the same livery" began to appear. Steel springs replaced leather straps c.1670. Grammont says ladies "were afraid of being shut up in (coaches): they greatly preferred the pleasure of shewing almost their whole persons, to the convenience of modern coaches." Between 1658 and 1758 the coaches of Paris had increased from 310 to over 14,000. (Saint Foix.)

Buckingham was the first person to be carried about London in a sedan chair, a conveyance just brought to England and patented by Sir Sanders Duncombe. This was bitterly resented, as his coach had been, by the common people. These new modes of travel threatened the monopoly of the Thames watermen. Coryat's enemy, the waterman-poet, John Taylor (1580-1653) wrote:

Carroaches, coaches, jades and Flemish mares
Doe rob us of our shares, our wares, our fares.
Against the ground we stand and knock our heels
Whilest all our profit runs away on wheels.

The Thames became a coach road during the great freeze of 1683-4 but in spite of the boatmen's fears, the river remained a favorite way of travel through the XVIIIc. Vauxhall Stairs, in 1750, was "a terrible confusion of wherries" as bawling watermen competed for fares.

Everyone is coach-conscious. There is rivalry in handsome equipages; citizens could identify coaches by their coach-work, the number and color of the horses, and the liveries of the men on the box, as readily as any small boy in the U.S.A. does his neighbor's green Plymouth sedan or black Buick convertible. Coaches become projections of and substitutes for their owners; they may be sent, quite

empty, to "swell a progress," or do honor at funerals.

1599. XVIIc. c.1616. Dutch. (Metropolitan Museum, Print Room.)

J. van der Velde. May.

By the spring of 1616, a drive about the countryside is merely a pleasant pastime for Dutch ladies and gentlemen: the only excitement will be among the hounds as the coach clatters away; the swineherd goes about the business of getting his animals past the 2-horse carriages ahead with their coachmen on the box. The 4-horse coach is driven by a man riding postilion; glass windows have not yet replaced curtains, but there are doors, and the whole nail-studded leather body with its canopy and wheel guards has a certain elegance, far removed from the glorified farm-wagon of a half century before.

The two following engravings have been particularly chosen to show unaristocratic costume; but no dress of the first years of the XVIIc. has a longer, more stylized line than the Dutch cavaliers with their highest of hats, and their ladies whose lean, corseted waists are emphasized by looped-up skirts, immensely wide ruffs, and raking headdresses. These are best seen in the bistre drawings by William Buytewech (Berlin Museum) and in the engravings of the van der Veldes: Esias, c. 1590-1630; Jan, c. 1593 to after 1641; and Adriaen, 1635-72.

FOODSTUFFS, OLD AND NEW

Until Tudor times, the English appear to have lived on bread, meat, fish, honey and malt ale. Many of the vegetables and fruits introduced during the XVI-XVIIc. came to them from the Low Countries, which had either received them as a result of their trade with the Mediterranean and the East, or had long cultivated them. Cabbage varieties, including brussels sprouts, had been sold in Belgian markets in 1213, when the English had perhaps not yet discovered that their wild sea-cabbage was edible. Katherine of Aragon had to send to Flanders for the salads, turnips and carrots she was accustomed to eat at home.

The cherries planted by the Romans, 100 B.C. had been forgotten; cherries first reappeared in a Kentish orchard laid out in 1540. Pippins were planted in Sussex in 1525 by Leonard Mascall; grapes and currants arrived in mid-XVIc. Dr. Linacre, Henry VIII's physician, brought back musk and damask roses and Lord James Cromwell, musk roses and plums, from their travels. "Unknown" flowers were planted in Norwich by the Flemish weavers who arrived in 1567: gillyflowers, carnations, and Provence roses. The first tulips came from Vienna in 1578.

Old herbals, like that of the surgeon, John Gerarde, gardener of William Cecil, Lord Burghley, in 1597, tell us what vegetables were known and what they looked like then.

Leeks had been a Welsh badge since 544 A.D.; Treveskis' herbal of 1526 recommends onions. Parsnips, brought to England from Germany by the Romans, had gone wild; no vegetable responds faster to simple good tilth, so parsnips were the standard root vegetable. Beets were pale and woody, and carrots a seasoning, scarcely edible. Spinach was grown in England in 1568; tomatoes from America were cosnidered unwholesome. Gerarde's is the first English description of horseradish, and he was mad about parsley, which had come from Sardinia in 1548. Cucumbers arrived from N.W. India in 1573. Peas, wild and bitter, were eaten during the famine of 1555. Gerarde lists two varieties of potatoes, which Raleigh planted in Ireland in 1588, and which were grown in Wales and Scotland, where plots were fenced, before England, where land was held in common.

Asparagus and cauliflower arrived in the first decade XVIIc. and England played an important part in the improvement of the cauliflower. Gerarde tells how to boil and butter haricot beans, but scarlet runner beans received from S. America in 1633 were raised for their flowers. Watercress and 12 varieties of salad are shown in herbals of 1710-15, but watercress was first sold in London in 1808.

Flax and hops were imported from Artois in 1520, but hops were not grown in sufficient quantities in England for beer to become an important beverage until XVIIc. Bread was not made with yeast until 1650.

Melons, brought from Spain by Sir George Gardner, were a royal gift from James I to Buckingham; and then became a luxury costing 5 to 6s.

1600. XVIIc. c. 1616. Dutch. (Metropolitan Museum, Print Room.)

J. van der Velde. December.

The boats are almost frozen in the canal of this little Dutch town; beyond the bridge we see a farm wagon. A sailor in characteristic long trousers is walking from the left. The chimneys of the brick houses smoke, as women covered by long *"heuke"* buy the last vegetables. School is letting out. The children, well bundled up and shod, run past the inn with their lunch baskets and books, while the poor schoolmaster, who has had to keep his dog with him, walks almost barefoot, his legs and feet covered with a sort of combination legging and spat, which is buckled at the back of knee and ankle.

1601. XVIIc. Dutch. (Metropolitan Museum, Print Room.)
J. van der Velde, after *W. Buytewech.* Earth.

The characteristic *"heuke"* headdress of the Low Countries is seen in various beaked forms, or wired out like an Elizabethan veil, mounting the Rhine to Cologne. Its length varies; hanging to the ground in Holland, to half way below the knee at Antwerp, and to the elbow in Belgium. It is often worn with hats of an inverted-basket shape, as well as the

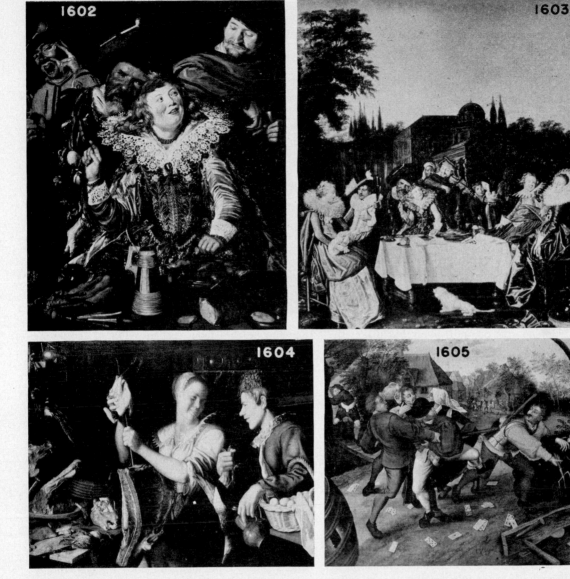

flat, knobbed plates shown here, and the tiny "tip-hoike" seen in Hollar's plates.

The dress beneath is apt to have a full skirt of ground length, worn with a close-fitting bodice beneath a short, fitted spencer.

The utilitarian apron may appear anywhere at any time; but the decorative apron which has been a feature of German-Swiss costume in final quarter XVIc., will not become an important part of European dress until final quarter XVIIc., when it will been made of gold lace or embroidered taffeta.

Until XIXc., long trousers such as we see on the figure to the r., will be worn only by farmers and sailors. The knee breeches derided by the class-conscious *sans-culottes* of the French Revolution will remain the mark of a gentleman, and a required part of formal court wear, down to our own time, more than a century after passing out of general use.

1602. XVIIc. c. 1615. Dutch. (Metropolitan Museum.)
Frans Hals. Merry Company.
The roistering, improvident Hals, who was given house, fuel and an annuity by the city in his bankrupt old age, was an enormously prolific painter of portraits and groups of all classes of society; and of banquets of military and governing associations, termagant fishwives and drunken gamesters.

The new impulse to portray natural, everyday objects is shown in the plate of pig's feet and sausages, the tankard and the bagpipe.

The loose lady's fan collar is not only double but has an interior edge of lace. It is worn with an embroidered doublet and skirt; satin inner sleeves and outer-sleeve lining; knots at throat and waist.

As in Brueghel's day, spoons and pipes are thrust through the cocked brim of the hat.

1603. XVIIc. Dutch. (Louvre.)
Dirk Hals. Rustic Feast.
The plagiarized central figures are not very successful, but in the full-length figures at the side, Hals' son shows some pleasant examples of the dress sketched by Buytewech.

1604. XVIIc. Flemish. (Metropolitan Museum.)
Adraen Nieulandt (1587-1658). Kitchen Interior.
The cook's little close cap and lace collared shirt might be worn at almost any time between 1620-50,

1606

but the flopping ruff of the delivery boy makes the late part of first quarter XVIIc. more probable.

Baskets of eggs, kitchen utensils, game and meat, now lovingly painted..

1605. XVIIc. 1619. Flemish. (Metropolitan Museum.)

P. Brueghel, the younger. Gamblers Quarreling.

Peasant costume changed little since the time of the elder Brueghel; tailored codpieces affixed to flap-codpieces. Separate sleeve persists in Flemish and Italian women's use.

1606. XVIIc. 1616?. Dutch. (Amsterdam, Rijksmuseum.)

W. C. Duyster. Fete in Honor of the Marriage of Adriaen Ploos van Amstel and Agnes van Byler.

Wonderful costumes (either very prophetic or questionably dated a decade too early), shown from all angles, and with every sort and combination of collars. The whorls of the wire support of a fan collar worn with another unsupported one (No. 2); unsupported collar worn with stiff ruff (No. 12); small round collar with stiffened fan in addition (No. 7); wide single ruffs; falling ruffs and bands. Cuffs

funneling to the elbow give an effect of shortening sleeves; this is actual on the scalloped sleeve of (No. 5); and on the turned back cuff of (No. 1). Turned-back caps, large on (No. 2, 5, 12).

The classic Dutch women's costume of first third XVIIc. is shown on (No. 5): jacket with stomacher emphasized by a scalloped border; underskirt patterned (also 8, 10); skeleton overdress with emphasis around the shoulder cap.

The gartered gentlemen in great hats so floppy that they will soon have to be cocked, show lengthening doublet skirts; slashed bosom and upper sleeve; watch at belt; breeches narrowing (11); and the long leather military jerkin, with lacings up the front and hanging from the tabbed shoulder caps; doublet sleeves barred across the open inseam with braid (as on musician, No. 13); outer seam of breeches open and edged with buttons (No. 9). Boy (No. 4) shows the increasingly fashionable wrinkled stockings, button trim on hat band to match shoulder caps, skirts and open front of doublet and studded belt.

Ladies, gentlemen and musicians alike wear curious cut-out heelless sandals.

1607. XVIIc. Dutch. (Metropolitan Museum.)

M. J. van Miereveld. Portrait of a Woman.

Wide cap of the early decades of the century worn over tiny close cap. Small interior collar of lace over a ruff with graduated pleats.

1608. XVIIc. 1618-21. Flemish. (Washington, Nat. Gall. of Art.)

Van Dyke or *Rubens.* Suzanna Fourment and her Daughter.

Four years after the death of Isabella Brant, Rubens married a lovely 16-year-old-girl named Helena Fourment, of whom he painted many portraits. This picture of her sister Suzanna, whether painted by Rubens, or more probably by his former pupil, Van Dyke, shows the same chain worn by Helena in the

portrait by Rubens.

Suzanna's pearl choker stresses the tendency of ruffs to sink lower on the neck. Stomachered jacket of small-patterned golden brown brocade; underskirt of rose and gold Italian brocade in the classic pineapple pattern, banded in rose-flecked gold; gold and white slippers; black overdress; white lace; tiny embroidered and jewelled dark cap of Flanders set over the bun of hair.

Her daughter wears a brown velvet hat, edged in white, set over a cap with rose and gold ties; little doublet with fan collar, picadill shoulder caps and tabbed border, of rose brocaded in white with gold lines; crossed by a baldric of purple; skirt of rosy-gold shot taffeta.

1607

1608

1610. XVIIc. 1628. Dutch. (Metropolitan Museum.)

M. J. van Miereveld. Dutch Lady.

The brim of the cap, seen on the older woman painted by the same artist, begins to be turned back in the first decade XVIIc., and to be worn farther back on the head as it tends to become smaller in the third decade. The ruff worn with this gown remains uncluttered, but the cuffs succumb to the general tendency to grow higher and to duplicate. The divisions of the peplum of the doublet become increasingly scalloped and foliated in lace-inspired patterns. The overgarment may be a jacket like that of Isabella Brant, or a long gown, cut straight with the torso to the waist and there gored wide over the hips; here it is loosely girded by a chain.

Gauntlets embroidered on the seam of fingers as well as on tasseled cuff.

1609

1610

1609. XVIIc. c. 1625. Flemish. (Munich, Alte Pinakothek.)

Cornelis de Vos. The von Hutton Family.

The parents are in standard Flemish black with cartwheel ruffs; the mother's is the somber Dutch gown which sets off a blazing gold stomacher, longer, rounder, more decorated and importantly edged than that of any other country. Elsewhere the stomacher will be a doublet with matching sleeves, which appear below the shoulder cap or truncated sleeve of the gown; but in Holland the stomacher is a vest, and the close sleeve agrees, not with it, but with the rest of the outermost garment. The ruff worn with these stomachers is always severe.

Boy by father: gray doublet and skirts, seamed in black and silver; petticoat with black embroidery.

Red-headed baby: cream dress and slippers; white cap and apron; coral necklaces, bracelets and shoe ribbons.

Oldest child, still wearing a baby cap, has her red hair drawn over it (as women's hair is drawn back) and a tiny gold headdress like her mother's set over hair and cap; the same impulse is shown in the center lock of the other children. She wears coral earrings and bracelets, flat wired ruff, brown bodice brocaded in silver, yellowish-green satin apron over a golden yellow skirt banded in blue-green.

1611. XVIIc. 1623. Dutch. (Metropolitan Museum.)

Frans Hals. Yonker Ramp and his Sweetheart.

The construction of military jerkins is dependent on the shape and imperfections of the skins used; they are usually cut in 2 to 4 front and 2 back sections. To avoid strain, seams are left open where possible. Horizontal seaming around the waist is avoided by goring the sections out into skirts which overlap to conceal weak spots in the leather; actual closing is by flexible leather laces. Reinforcement of edges and cuts is made decorative by embroidery, or, where no strain will be put upon them (as in this case), by buttons which fasten through scallops with pinked edges; their diagonal lines simulate a breast slit and the direction which the current waistline of the civilian doublet is taking, as it creeps up under the arms. The jerkin when not worn over a doublet has sleeves of the doublet type, made of a different material.

His companion has double collars and cuffs, of which the wide outer set is the sheerer.

1612. XVIIc. 1625-30. Flemish. (Florence, Pitti.)

Joost Sustermans. The General Leopold, Count of Tyrol.

1611

1612

1613

Leopold V, brother of Emperor Ferdinand II, married Christine of Lorraine's daughter Claudia, efficient Regent of the Tyrol after his death.

His lace-edged whisk is worn with a gorget which matches the blue and white plumed helmet beside him, and a magnificently embroidered jerkin of yellow leather. Boots wth square plaques of the same leather are drawn high over lace-edged boot-hose. Sword carried by a baldric-like band; baldrics are already very handsome and will become wider, more elaborate, often edged with fringe, into XVIIIc.; lace fringed sash. Goatee and moustache with lengthening hair.

1613. XVIIc. 1626. Dutch. (Budapest, Museum of Fine Arts.)

N. Eliasz. Portrait of a Man.

The pleating of ruffs is increasingly subtle; the effect of multiple horizontal rows is gained here by vertically set pleats.

This doublet, of the dotted stuff we have seen throughout first quarter XVIIc., owes much in cut to the military leather coats. But as it is a true doublet, its sleeves are of the same stuff. The lower buttons of the row on their outseam (which is becoming more important then the old braid-trimmed inseam) will soon begin to be left open and the cuff turned back. Full breeches with buttoned side slit. Chain worn baldric-wise with pendant medal; dagger now seldom carried except in military use. These are the days of the volunteer militia companies organized during the 30 Years War, such as the St. George and the St. Adrien Arquebusiers, very differently dressed from the other companies of governing burghers, to which the same men probably belonged, and whose banquets were also painted by Hals.

1614. XVIIc. c. 1630. Flemish. (Metropolitan Museum.)

Van Dyke. Portrait of a Lady.

This Flemish lady wears the characteristic dark caul cap and lace-edged double ruff (where the Dutch cap is white and the single ruff severe when worn with the important stomacher). Elaborate chains cross

the less conspicuous Flemish stomacher, with its braided doublet sleeves; these show below the pendant Spanish sleeve (cut in a $+$ across the bend of the elbow) of the brocade overdress, which has simulated breast slits.

Deviations are the surprisingly long sleeves with ruffs instead of cuffs at the wrist, and the form of the handle of the fan.

1615. XVIIc. 1631. Dutch. (Amsterdam, Rijksmuseum.)

W. Geest, e., Portrait of a Little Boy.

Falling ruff, on the standard costume of a boy who is still in diapers: skirt fastened, as breeches would be on an older boy, by knots through the doublet waistline. Braid trim in random zigzags instead of the old parallel ways.

1616. First to second third XVIIc. Flemish. (Vienna, National Museum.)

Brussels Tapestry. Country Life series: Lute-playing Cavalier with Lady.

With the swashbuckling male cavalier styles, female costume begins to lose its rigidity. The romantic portraits of Helena Fourment painted by Rubens in the 30's are closely akin to this lady in her great plumed hat; soft, low-kerchiefed, high-waisted bodice with sleeves repeatedly tied about the arm.

Rugs and tapestries continue to be thrown over balconies on gala occasions. Architecture is approaching the XVIIIc. Baroque; but the "excess of superfluity" of this Flemish decoration lacks the delicate grace of Grinling Gibbons' carved garlands and fruit.

Exotic animals and fruits increase. Small monkeys and parrots are now fairly common; the first rhinoceros (unicorn) and W. Indian crocodile appeared in England in 1684.

1617. XVIIc. 1632. Dutch. (Metropolitan Museum.)

Rembrandt. Volkeravan Beresteijn.

Rembrandt van Rijn, b. 1606, son of a miller, studied painting in his native Leyden. In 1631 he moved to Amsterdam and immediate preeminence as a painter of group and single portraits during the next decade. In 1634 he married a beautiful blonde and well-to-do Frisian girl called Saskia, whom he frequently painted until her death in 1642. The Portuguese Jews living on the same street with Rembrandt served as models for some of the paintings of his second period. In 1656 as times grew hard in the Netherlands, Rembrandt went bankrupt, but never ceased painting until his death in 1669.

Flat lace collar just showing under a ruff, slightly edged with lace, since it is not worn with the old sort of greatly exploited stomacher, but with the new short-waisted, belted gown with puffed sleeves. Stomacher subordinated to a belt finished with ribbon loops instead of the usual rosette. Jewelled stud in hair, behind which only the edge of the cap shows at the bottom.

1618. XVIIc. c. 1632. Dutch. (Berlin, Kaiser Friedrich Museum.)

N. Eliasz. Catarina Hoeft, wife of Cornelis de Graef, Bürgermeister of Amsterdam.

Few illustrations so clearly show the upper sleeve, completely truncated, and the widening inner sleeve (matching the underskirt and stomacher) showing below, but not yet tied in puffs around the arm. Very wide compound kerchief-collar and double cuffs; very short waist, belted with a side rosette matching those

which catch an asymmetric chain to the collar; fan chained to belt.

1619. XVIIc. 1635. Dutch. (Metropolitan Museum. Frick Coll.)

F. Hals. Portrait of a Woman.

1620. XVIIc. 1636. Dutch. (Metropolitan Museum.)

Isaac Luttichuijs. Portrait of a Young Woman.

One elaborate double form of cap of third decade XVIIc. does enclose the hair and ears; worn with wide shallow ruff and gown of black brocade and satin. The young woman has beautiful fringe-trimmed white gauntlets, and bag patterned with black lace; dark lace is similarly used on stomachers, boldly patterned in horizontal bands like that worn by Hals' Woman (Ill. 1642); "housewife" carried on a running chain from her belt.

1621. XVIIc. 1634. Dutch. (Paris, Gustave de Rothschild.)

Rembrandt. Martin Day.

Narrow braids used to give over-all pattern and gored effect, big beaver hat, lace collar spreading over shoulders and cape, waistline rising under armpits, knotted tags turning into formal rosettes, narrowing breeches, pleated garters, wrinkled stockings, largest possible rosettes on shoes cut out below strap.

1622. XVIIc. 1636. Flemish.

Van Dyke. Rupert, Prince Palatine.

This German prince, grandson of James I, was born in 1619, brought up in Holland, first visited England in 1636, but returned in 1642 to become the greatest cavalry commander of the first Civil War and to die in England, unmarried, in 1683. His sister Sophia or her issue, as the closest Protestant Stuarts, had been made heirs to the English throne, if previous rulers died childless; in 1714 her son, a far lesser man than his uncle, became king as George I.

Rupert's clear-sighted and inventive intelligence concerned itself with science, improvement of military equipment and techniques. He was, in addition, a fine engraver and the pioneer worker in mezzotint.

Van Dyke and Rupert were both in the Netherlands in 1634-5; but these are English clothes such as Van Dyke painted in 1632-9, and Rupert's only visit to England during Van Dyke's lifetime was in 1636.

Small lace collar worn over gorget; military jerkin over vest-like doublet with shortening sleeve, and increasingly full, puffed linen.

1623. XVIIc. c. 1638. Flemish. (Washington, National Gallery of Art.)

Van Dyke. William II of Nassau and Orange.

William the Silent's grandson was married in 1641 at 15 to Charles I's 10-year-old-daughter Mary. The very able Dutch Stadholder died of smallpox at 24, as his great son, William III, was born.

He wears a steel cuirasse over a yellow doublet; this has the short sleeve, full bloused shirt sleeve with wide informal wrist ruffles, and small, square tassel-tied collar of the 40's. Walking stick and riding crop.

1624. XVIIc. c. 1636. Flemish. (Metropolitan Museum.)
Adriaen Brower. The Smokers.

Tobacco was brought to Philip II from Mexico in 1558; the generic name of the plant, *Nicotiana,* commemorates the French ambassador Nicot, who sent its seeds to Catherine de' Medici. Pipes came to England about 1565. Harrison described its use in 1573 and despite the "Counterblast" of James, the use of tobacco increased greatly during the troubled XVIIc.

The smoker is the artist himself. His painter friend, de Heem, is the man with a small wind instrument stuck through his hat, as we have seen the spoon or pipe used in Brueghel and Hals pictures. Wide square collar with tasseled ties; sleeve unbuttoned and turned back at wrist; tasseled finish of loose breeches; wrinkled stockings worn with pantoufles.

1625. XVIIc. 1637-43. Dutch. (Amsterdam, R. Pelzer Coll.)

Albert Eeckhout. Portrait of a Negro Chief in the Dutch Service.

This picture formerly att. to van der Helst is by a painter from Amersford, Holland, who accompanied Prince Maurice of Orange to Brazil in 1637, and returned to Brazil in 1641 and in 1643 with the landscape painter, Franz Post. The date of Eeckhout's birth is not known, and he disappears with a painting dated 1664.

The Negro Chief wears rich clothing of the 30's: pink plumed hat, nasturtium-colored jerkin with hanging sleeves; and a doublet of brocaded white satin.

1626-27. XVIIc. 1637. Dutch. (Amsterdam, J. M. van Loon.)

J. M. Molenaer, Family Gathering, (2 details).

These details are from a very long painting which is one of Holland's greatest costume documents.

MALE: Hats: wide sombreros or cocked; great plumes reduced to a shaggy fringe around the band (I). Lace collars at their widest, fastened with tasseled ties; cuffs of high lace (A), loose ruffles (I), plain (E). Doublet: short-waisted, long-skirted, beltless; lacy braid along seams (A, I) and edges. Superimposed garments= jacket and vest (A). Military jerkin with sword belt (E). Sleeves short (A) or turned back (E). Breeches open (reappeared second third XVIIc.), or closed, with decorated outer seams and edges. Braid of seam beginning to disintegrate into fringe as it approaches fringed hem; visibly buttoned fly closing of breeches (E). Boots of polished leather with sock-boots (A, E); or wrinkled stockings, elaborate garters and hugely rosetted shoes (J, L). Hair on shoulders; moustaches; some chin tufts. Page boy's livery elaborately braided (F).

FEMALE: Short-waisted jackets with tabbed peplums worn over a single full skirt, which is decorated down center-front seam and around hem. Overgarment eliminated, but its old sleeve appears as the upper section, ending above the elbow and slit toward the shoulder; lower sleeve is increasingly full but not yet tied about the arm in puffed sections. Jacket, its belt finished at the side by loops or rosette, is actually low-necked; but the neckline is completely filled by a yoke-like collar, covered by a folded kerchief, and worn with multiple choker collar of pearls. In latter half XVIIc., the inner collar will shrink and the kerchief side off the shoulders in a fichu. Hair, fringed at the forehead and loose at the sides, is drawn back and dressed with a pearl band across the crown. Child: cape with aigrette; gored seaming stressed by braid; lines of braid with fringed ends cross the center-front seam. Maid (G): white cap and gathered white shoulder cape with flat collar; brocade jacket with close fitting sleeves and short peplum, apron and full skirt.

ACCESSORIES: Glass manufacture had been established in Flanders by Philip the Good; by third quarter XVIc., heavier and less elegant versions of Venetian patterns began to be exported to England from Flanders; during XVIIc. Flemish glass began to be cut and engraved and was one of the familiar objects which Flemish artists loved to paint. In final quarter XVIIc. England began to produce better glass at Greenwich and Lambeth than was made at Murano.

Oranges are a treat but no longer a rarity. Evelyn saw orange trees 120 years old at Beddington in 1700 and one of the most magnificent of orange trees, the Grand Bourbon at Versailles, which still bears 200 fruit at a time, was transplanted there from Fontaine-bleau by Louis XIV. It had belonged to Francis I and was planted in 1421 by a princess of Navarre. But pineapples from the Barbados were still a novelty when the King cut off a slice for Evelyn in 1668.

A roast peacock in its plumage has been a great banquet dish since before mediaeval days; carried by manservant (deleted figure, ext. r.).

1628-32. XVIIc. Bohemian. (Metropolitan Museum, Print Room.)

W. Hollar. "Aula Veneris."

1628. Lady of Quality of Antwerp (1643).

1629. Leading Townswoman of Antwerp in House Dress (1648).

1630. Wife of a Merchant Citizen of Antwerp (1650).

The *hoike* mantle and *tiphoike* tufted forehead plate are typical outdoor wear of Antwerp, Cologne and Bremen; with a turned-back lace cap, long loose hair, and double skirts, the uppermost tucked up, and the underskirt heavily banded. Muffs for outdoor use; apron, fan, and plumed hat worn indoors over a cap in the late XVIc. way.

1631. Daughter of a Citizen of Prague (1636).

1632. Wife of a Merchant of Prague (1636).

In Bohemia a single skirt is worn with a fur cape, the broad revers of which turn into a square "sailor" collar. Over this is worn either a wide ruff or a collar characteristically squared off across the front. Locks in front of the ears are small and short; even into XVIIIc., little hair shows below the fur hats of Swabian, Bavarian and Bohemian regional costume, since these hats, in a sense, replace hair. The traditionally uncovered head of an unmarried woman has a little pill-box cap over the bun, while a married woman wears the characteristically conical fur hat of Prague. (No. 1633 is omitted.)

1634-37. XVIIc. 1643-45. Bohemian. (Metropolitan Museum, Print Room.)

W. Hollar. "Runde Frauentracht."

1634. The Hollar catalog identifies none of this set of costumes. We can see that the cap, and the needle-point ending in a drop, are related to the *tip-hoike* which run north up the Rhine from Bremen and Antwerp to Cologne. It is worn with a sleeveless garment of which we unfortunately see little; it has one of the square fur collars which, originating in Bohemia, move west through Franconia and Frankfort-on-Main, to affect costume as far west of the Rhine as Luxemburg. These collars also appear along the coast of the North Sea, where it is probable that the wearer of this costume lived.

1635. In Bavaria the round fur hat is worn with one of the collars shown in the Prague illustrations above. Here it has moved west to meet the Dutch kerchief, come up the Rhine.

1636. Antwerp (1643).

1637. Augsburg or Nuremberg, worn with the square-cut Bohemian collar. The distribution of fur hats in Central Europe in XVIIc. may be thus roughly given:

Cap-shaped: Swabia, Basel, Strassburg, the Palatinate, Frankfort-on-Main, and Danzig.

Circular: Nuremberg and Augsburg, with a very wide form at Strassburg where hats have always been widest.

Square: Augsburg and Nuremberg, often with the squared-off collar which runs from Bohemia west to Hanau.

Conical: Augsburg, Nuremberg, from Bohemia. All these circular, square and conical fur hats have round headbands, rather than the curving bottom line of the Rhenish fur caps; and all are seen, simultaneously worn, in Bavaria.

High, spreading at top: Saxe-Altenburg.

1638. XVIIc. Dutch. (Amsterdam, Rijksmuseum.)
Frans Hals. Sara Wolphaerts van Diemen (1594-1667).

When the wide, plain ruff appears between 1620-30, it sways somewhat over the shoulder, and is apt to be elaborated, like other forms of collar, by notched lace. The cap slips back, until it merely frames the hair, by 1630.

1639. XVIIc. Dutch. (Metropolitan Museum.)
M. J. van Miereveld, d. 1641. Portrait of a Woman in a Lace Collar.

From 1620-30, the wide composite collars were still high in back; caps barely outlining hair, 1630-40.

1640. XVIIc. Flemish. (Metropolitan Museum.)
C. de Vos, e., d. 1651. Portrait of a Young Lady.

Hair with a fringe and longer, relatively uncovered; collars widest and flat on shoulders, c. 1635; wide, loose cuff with billowing ruffle.

1641. XVIIc. 1642. Dutch. (Metropolitan Museum.)
F. Bol. Portrait of a Dutch Lady.

Hair uncovered except the band around the bun; collar on sloping shoulder line; cuff shorter and wider; sleeve no longer tied around the arm at elbow.

1642. XVIIc. c. 1645. Dutch (Metropolitan Museum.)
F. Hals. Portrait of a Woman.

Black caps with a tongue running down the forehead, seen 1640-60. Shoulder more sloping, sleeve shorter, cuff wider; stomacher horizontally striped, with black predominating.

1643. XVIIc. 1655. Flemish. (Budapest, Museum of Fine Arts.)

A. Palmedesz. Portrait of a Woman.

Pointed black cap, combined with caul over the bun; bows on hanging side locks precede and foretell their turning into bunches of corkscrew curls.

The collar is slipping down shoulders, which are not yet ready to be bared completely; shirt as inner yoke. As the banding at the bottom of the collar becomes pre-eminent, the front closing is stressed in some way, often by an important pendant brooch. The sleeve itself is losing out to its cuff, which is in transition into ruffles. In bourgeoise use, especially, the skirt is often worn tucked up; in this case, the drape has been made an integral part of its construction.

1644. XVIIc. c. 1645. Flemish. (Metropolitan Museum.)
Unknown artist. Family Portrait.

Mother: kerchief closed high about the neck gives sloping shoulder line. Upper and lower sleeve unified, their former divisions and slits marked by braid, as is the center-front line of the closed skirt.

Boy with hawk on gauntlet: doublet open at bottom over puffed shirt; visibly buttoned fly of tubular breeches; band collars smaller, tending to lose scalloped edges.

All the seams of sleeve, trouser and skirt, formerly open, buttoned or trimmed, are closing and diminishing in importance. Cloaks grow longer and have square "sailor" collars.

1645. XVIIc. Flemish. (Metropolitan Museum.)
C. de Vos, e. (d. 1651). Mother and Children.

Hair bunched in curls at the ears. Kerchief collar, finished by a wide band of straight-edged lace, is softly gathered up in front; the stiff kerchief is turning into a soft fichu which will slip away from the throat and uncover the shoulders. Sleeves short and wide with full, puffed shirt-sleeves finished by a gathered ruffle.

The pin at her bosom shows the new trend toward faceted stones. Mediaeval jewels were polished round as star sapphires are today; Renaissance stones were carved and engraved; pearls followed in popularity. Jewel cutting had been established in Flanders by Charles the Bold in 1475; Antwerp and Amsterdam have remained the great diamond-cutting centers ever since. Diamonds had been mined in India since mid-XVIc.; they were brought back in quantity by the French jewel merchant, Jean Tavernier, from half a dozen trips to the East; his first trip to the great Golconda mines was in 1638-43. In 1725 the great diamond mines of Brazil were discovered. The XVII-XVIIIc. are times of sparkling, cut stones.

1646. XVIIc. 1661. Dutch. (Metropolitan Museum.)

G. Metsu. Visit to the Nursery.

Hair and costume of both men and women, now flowing, full, and soft. Mother in red velvet sacque and white satin skirt; visitor in black, edged with red at cuff-tops.

Wicker crib, fur blanket, fur-edged velvet canopy; maid with warming box; Ispahan rug as table cover.

1647. XVIIc. 1647. Dutch. (Leningrad, Hermitage.)

Bartholomeus van der Helst. The Presentation of the Fiancée.

Bun covered by an important, projecting cap. Lengthening side locks, tied with bows analogous to tassels seen on Bosse's Cavalier after Edict of 1733, or Morin's engraving of Count d'Harcourt, "Cadet La Perle" (von Boehn: *Die Mode,* XVIIc., p. 61).

1648

The round line of the bottom of the collar, and its rows of lace at the edge, establish the point at which scarves will be drawn around decolletage, when collar begins (as it soon will) to recede from the neck.

The simplified sleeve is set into the armseye, and the skirt onto the bodice, by carefully laid pleats. As the gown becomes more unified and less decorated, it will rely for the character of its satin elegance mainly on these pleats, which become exquisitely fine.

1648. XVIIc. 1648. Dutch. (Amsterdam, Rijksmuseum.)

B. van der Helst. Banquet of the Civic Guards in Honor of the Peace of Munster, detail.

This company of cross-bow men is meeting in the great hall of the St. Jousdoeln, through the windows of which can be seen the brewery "het Lam": the early architecture of New York was of this type, brought to Nieuw Amsterdam by its Dutch settlers.

Great variety of military (C, D) and civilian costumes; very fashionable young man (E) and conservatively dressed old man (B); his pinked black satin costume of full breeches and doublet worn with yellow stockings still carries a ruff, but in concession to fashion the ruff is loose and the doublet short-waisted, beneath the scarf which each member wears as sash on baldric. (C) In cuirasse, has a lemon yellow doublet, gray breeches, red stockingsg. (D) The Color Bearer, Jacob Banning, is in black, with a blue sash

and black and white plumes. (E) In pearl gray, laced in gold.

Band collars are becoming smaller (A, C), their edges straighter (A. C, D), with a tendency to be cut longer, squarer and to buckle slightly under the chin (E, G).

Doublet sleeves are being turned back into cuffs (C, E), showing more shirt sleeve fullness, finished with loosely gathered ruffles (A). Military jerkins (C), like doublets (E), have shrunk into vest-like forms. (A) shows the old multiple slitting.

Short tubular breeches make much of their front closing (C) and are in process of drawing their decoration from side seam to hem (E) showing the new interest in horizontal lines, culminating in Ill. 1673.

Boot cuffs wider, cupped lower on the calf, worn with elaborate sock-boots and stockings in bright colors (C, E). Garters are now less often rosettes than ribbon loops; as tabs of decoration at the sides of open shorts (E), they are often quite without function.

The old romantic hat is still seen, but is being replaced by more austerely blocked shapes (G, F) with higher crowns (E, above him) and brims straight (E), or curling and soon to be cocked (G, F); plumed or not (G, F). Hair, worn short by staid men (B, G, F), may be very long and worn with bangs (A, C). (See Appendix.)

1649. XVIIc. 1652. Dutch. (The Hague, Mauritshuis.)

C. van Everdingen. Diogenes Seeking an Honest Man.

Blocked hats with square-cut tapering crowns have band of feather fringe replaced by ribbon loops (child I, and men behind woman C). Longest hair on most fashionable men (F, E, B, A); bangs (E).

Cloaks, slung or not, are longer (B, E, F) and grow "sailor" and other collars of their own, as the great lace collars (which were always brought out over the capes) shrink to small plain collars with importantly tasseled ties. Cuffs are replaced by soft ruffles (F). Slitting of center-back of doublet (A).

Open breeches grow longer and much wider, and are heavily decorated with loops around the hems (E, F). As they descend, the boots are crushed lower, flaring very wide just above the ankle; boot hose are now multiple rather than lacy (E, F); these are also worn as gaiters, quite without boots (A). Shoe toes become long and narrow, cut square across the end (A, E, F).

Diogenes wears a hood, smock and bound leggings of a peasant (D). Hood of country woman (C), and regional costume and cap of woman (G) have scarcely altered since centuries.

1650. Third quarter XVIIc. Dutch. (Louvre.)

Karel Dujardin. Italian Charlatans.

Dujardin (1622-78) was a Dutchman, most of whose work was done between 1650-75. He made a great reputation in Rome, squandered his money and, returning to Amsterdam by way of Lyons, married an old heiress, whom he deserted after clearing up his debts. He died in Venice at 54.

Coryat explains that mountebank comes from *monta in banco*—to go up on a bench. He describes the 5 or 6 stages set up in St. Mark's Place, Venice, on which the mountebanks gave shows twice daily. Some wore vizards, or were disguised as fools, women, and characters in Italian comedy. While part of the troupe played and sang, others opened their trunks, took out drugs and cosmetics and with witty jests sold "oyles, soveraigne waters, amorous songs printed, Apothecary drugs, and a Commonweal of other trifles," at high prices which became lower by the end of the second show.

It was only a step from these "medicine shows" to the quack doctors who flourished all over Europe well into XVIIIc. The earliest quack doctors were apt to be Italian. Anthony Wood records the visits to Oxford of John Baptista de Succa in 1626-7, and of Dr. Vincent Lancelles of Venice in 1661. But Dr. John Pundeen came 4 times to Oxford between those dates, "set up his stage first in St. Marie's Churchyard by the diall; from thence he was removed to the Saracen's Head." Wood quotes the handbill of Professor James Themut, a "High Dutch Physitian . . . of Vienna in Austria," advertising his ability to cure all sorts of diseases "through God's mercy. . . . Within a month after . . . he rann away and cozenned his patients of a great quantity of money." Swift tells Stella (Journal to Stella, XX) of avoiding an invitation to go with Steele to Sir William Read's: "Surely you have heard of him. He has been a mountebank, and is the Queen's oculist; he makes admirable punch, and treats you in gold vessels. But . . . I will not go, neither indeed am I fond of the jaunt." Read's handbill advertised his successes with everything from dropsy to cancer, but its woodcut illustration shows an eye operation.

As Chamberlayne will be able to boast, a century later, "the poorest People in *England* wear good shoes of Leather; whereas in . . . neighboring countries, the Poor generally wear either Shoes of Wood, or none at all." (*Present State of Great Britain*, 1755 ed.) But Italian donkeys are beautifully dressed,

1651. XVIIc. 1656. Dutch. (New York Historical Soc.)
J. Van Goosen. Cornelis Steenwyck.

Above a view of Nieuw Amsterdam, the burgo-master of the Dutch colonial city which became New York, wears handsome garments which were in the latest mode at his last stay in Holland.

1652. XVIIc. 1655. Dutch. (New York, Cooper Union Museum.)
Cornelius Visscher. The Rat Catcher.

1653. XVIIc. 1656. Dutch. (New York, Cooper Union Museum.)

Cornelius Visscher. Gellius de Bouma.

Visscher's portrait of the noted ecclesiastic, and another of W. de Ryck, the opthalmist of Amsterdam, have always been known as "The Great Beards." "I find but few beards worth taking notice of in the reign of King James the First," wrote Eustace Budgell in Spectator, 331. But on these very old Dutch gentlemen in cap, gown, and the outmoded ruffs and beards of the days of their manhood, we see the beard at its greatest, just as it is disappearing until XIXc.

Photograph courtesy of the Metropolitan Museum of Art (1650)

1654. XVIIc. 1657. German.

Unknown artist. Procession of the Joiners and Cabinetmakers of Frankfort-on-Main.

A variety of doublets and coats worn with overflowing shirts and petticoat breeches; these are heavily beribboned below the bloused shirts and at the knees. Garters still appear with full breeches, but their knots are being transferred to the bottom of the outseam of the petticoat breeches; sometimes both forms are worn at the same time.

Baldrics are very wide and elaborate; hat crowns, squared off, are becoming lower; brims flat and wide, with plumes beginning to show a tendency to lie flat, surrounding the brim. Shoe rosettes supplanted by very wide stiff bows; square toes longer; heels higher.

Processions have an increasing quality of pageantry. Imaginatively costumed fabulous figures appear in the entertainments of Louis XIV, but the cabinetmakers of Frankfort stick to the old reliable fools and wild men; with a few American Indian headdresses added.

Tradesmen's houses, with shop or factory on the ground floor, and living quarters above. Guild members took great pride in beautifying their cities. Stow says, "The most beautiful frame of fair houses and shops that be within the walls of London, commonly called Goldsmiths Row . . . was built by Thomas Wood, goldsmith, one of the sheriffs of London in 1491. It containeth in number 10 fair dwelling houses and 14 shops, all in one frame, uniformly built 4 stories high, beautified towards the street with the Goldsmith's arms and the likeness of woodmen, in memory of his name, riding on monstrous beasts, all of which is cast in lead, richly painted over and gilt. This he gave to the goldsmiths, with stocks of money, to be lent to the young men having these shops, & . . . the front (was) again new painted and gilt over in the year 1594."

1655. XVIIc. c. 1660. Dutch. (Metropolitan Museum.)
Anton de Lorme, d. 1660. Figures painted by *G. Terborch.* Interior of a Church.

The male figures show the coat, at almost knee length, as well as the old circular cloak with square collar; breeches still loose but not full; lowered hat crown; one hat fringed with feathers and cocked into a tricorne.

Back view of hooded lady at l. shows looped and trailing skirts, tabbed jacket with short sleeves and much shirt sleeve, puffed above the elbow. The baby boy wears the new coat, very long, with very short sleeves and buttoned slits in its skirts; tiny sword slung by an important baldric.

Women and children of the people, in the garments shown by Brueghel.

1656. XVIIc. c. 1655. Dutch. (Metropolitan Museum.)
Gabriel Metsu. Artist and wife.

Ruffled boot socks, independent of boots, worn with shoes; knee-length coat has developed a closed cuff, buttoned back; horizontal pockets halfway up the skirts from the hemline.

Over her cap, his wife wears a hooded shoulder cape, pleated in around the neck, ingeniously folded up and carried in a semi-circle to cover the head.

Massive furniture of XVIIc. Netherlands, alternating square and turned forms; this is the type of furniture brought to New Amsterdam by the first Dutch settlers.

1657. XVIIc. c. 1660 Flemish. (Metropolitan Museum.)
Gilles van Tilborch. Visit of Landlord to Tenant.

Man, l.: rectangular collar hanging low on chest; jacket unbuttoned to show shirt; sleeves turned back in cuff: petticoat breeches with ribbon loops around waist; no boots, stockings beginning to be drawn up and rolled at knee. Musician, c.: hair of length immediately preceding the use of periwigs; voluminous shirt sleeve seen through and below short, slit doublet sleeve.

Women show headdresses and costume appropriate to their ages and positions. Young woman, l.: bunched curls falling on shoulders; fan. Necklines off shoulders, veiled in cape-like collars, combined with dark or light hoods, even on the baby; sleeves easy; short, puffed shirt sleeves tied with ribbons; aprons, light or dark, universally worn.

1658. XVIIc. Dutch. (Vienna, Czernin Gallery.)
Vermeer. The Artist in his Studio.

In his self-portrait, Vermeer shows one of the most extreme examples of slitting of the upper part of the doublet. Boots are being eliminated, but boot-hose are still seen, worn with shoes.

The beautiful maps, in the production of which the Dutch excelled, were favorite wall decorations in Holland. The cartouches of the borders contain panorama views, and often give important costume information as well.

1659. XVIIc. Dutch. (London, Earl of Northbrook.)
F. Bol. Married Pair at their Toilet.

During the 1650's and 1660's, painters like Rembrandt and Bol re-introduced late XV-XVIc. styles into their own costume, and that of their wives, particularly Rembrandt's Saskia; low-necked doublets, filled in with pleated shirts and band collars, which are often embroidered; soft beret-like hats, turbans and toques, quite unlike the current brimmed felts with blocked crowns. These romantic painters' usages had an effect on fashion.

Bol's wife wears the tongue-like headdress of the third quarter century, but some of the romantic style

1660

1661

1662

1663

is shown in the full shirt, and the embroidered band which finishes it, instead of the current collar or fichu-like band on the outside of the bodice, surrounding the shoulders. This show of pleated shirt coming up from under the bodice, and the baldric of pearls pinned from shoulder to sleeve across the bodices, are seen in Spanish costume.

1660. XVIIc. Dutch. (Metropolitan Museum.)
Terborch. The Toilet.

Little enclosed bun; hanging ends of hair tied with bows related to the tassels seen hanging from beneath male hair in the 30's. Back lacing of red corset bodice; sleeves of gown tied on by ribbon bows; yellow skirt.

1661. XVIIc. Dutch. (New York Metropolitan Museum, Frick Collection.)
Vermeer. Mistress and Maid Servant.

Little velvet jackets—yellow, red, blue, or green, edged with white fur, are characteristic domestic wear of the XVIIc. Netherlands. They appear repeatedly, outdoors and in, in pictures by contemporary Dutch artists: Gerard Terborch (1617-81) of Amsterdam and Haarlem, who traveled and painted all over Europe; Quieringh Gerritsz van Brekelenkam (1620-1680); Gabriel Metsu (c. 1629-1667) of Leyden and Amsterdam; and Jan Vermeer (1632-1675) of Delft, a much less prolific painter than the rest. Their pictures are seldom dated, and during this transitional period show a mixture of old and new fashions at the same time.

Ermine-trimmed yellow velvet jacket; sleeve fullness carefully pleated in at top, gathered at bottom; white skirt, trimmed with coral. Fringe in little curls becoming stylized and consolidated at the ears; bun covered by tiny decorative cap. Maid in gray with dark blue apron.

1662. XVIIc. Dutch. (Metropolitan Museum.)
Q. G. van Brekelenkam. Mother Amusing Child.

Mother with kerchief-like hood, wide double collar, and apron over fur-edged jacket. Mules with heels stand by the embroidered hem of her skirt.

Baby in embroidered cap, kerchief and apron is set safe in an enclosed high chair; rings to play with strung on a fixed bar.

1663. XVIIc. Dutch. (Metropolitan Museum.)
Vermeer. Young Woman with a Water Jug.

The jacket with tabbed doublet skirts continues to be worn; here, a yellow jacket, banded with the dark blue-black of the skirt, shows a new hood and cape.

Holland is the rich crossroads of all commerce. These pictures are full of interesting and precious things: Oriental rugs, Spanish boxes and chests, Venetian mirrors, native silver, brass, and pewter, and the fine maps which were first produced commercially in the Netherlands.

1664. XVIIc. 1659. Dutch. (Metropolitan Museum.)
G. Metsu. The Music Lesson.

The man at the window shows the new coat, in red, heavily braided in brown and silver; worn with a neckcloth instead of a band collar; and one of the romantic velvet toques, trimmed with little tips (red), which appear in Dutch pictures of the 50-60's, and are repeatedly shown in self-portraits by Rembrandt and Bol. Red and gray cravat; longer cane.

The musician: a sash at the waist of his brown and red ribbon-fringed petticoat breeches; the lowest of flaring brown boots with red linings, white bootsocks, red hose; fringed sword-belt on floor.

The lady: a hood, locks tied with bows at the ends; blue scarf tied in a soft fichu around the shoulders of the corset-shaped bodice of her orange and silver costume, trimmed with red ribbons. Tiny pointed shoe on a warming box of coals.

1665. XVIIc. c. 1660. Dutch. (Metropolitan Museum.)
Q. G. van Brekelenkam. Sentimental Conversation.

Short open doublet; much shirt fullness; extremely wide square collar; petticoat breeches, ribbon trimmed at bottom of outseam; gartered stockings, still wrinkled, worn with square-toed shoes with bows; elaborate fringed sword belt on table.

Gauzy dark cap from the bun fastened to earrings.
The high multiple windows of the Netherlands

admit a great deal of light; lower rank has the early form of sliding interior shutter brought to America by the Dutch, of which there is an example in the Metropolitan Museum's American Wing.

1666. XVIIc. Dutch. (Amsterdam, Rijksmuseum.)
P. de Hooch. Linen Closet.

There is a great deal of creature comfort in the XVIIc. houses of the Netherlands. They are excellent houses by any standards, filled with light from ranks of high windows, arranged for good ventilation. Their shining tile floors are easy to clean, pick up the warmth of the house in winter, and retain its summer coolness. The houses open on brick-paved courts with gardens, where it is pleasant to do the dinner vegetables or drink with friends.

Getting at things which are packed in a chest is complicated, as anyone learns who has a lid rather than a door-type freezing locker today. The Dutch were the first to evolve from chests these immense "kas," the first adequate closets; closets will not begin to be built into houses for more than a century.

Satin sleeves set with fine cartridge pleating at back of armseye and cuff; fine banded petticoat. Handsomer and better made laundry hamper than can be found in New York in 1948. Little girl practicing golf shots perilously near the Delft tile of the stair riser.

1668   1669   1670   1671   1672

1667. XVIIc. Flemish. (Carlsruhe, Picture Gallery.)

J. de Herdt. Woman Counting Money.

Spectacles, which were first scissored, and then tied in place, now pinch the nose. This Flemish equivalent of the Dutch velvet sacque is lined with fur and edged with embroidery; it is apparently part of a composed matching costume. Chain girdle with keys and pouch hangs on chair; many fine objects, including a standing piece of goldsmith's work.

1668. XVIIc. c. 1660. Dutch. (Washington, Nat. Gall. of Art.)

G. Metsu. The Intruder.

Seated lady reflected in Italian mirror with wings: gold and pearl decorated bun; green velvet jacket; lavender skirt trimmed in silver.

Lady arising: coral corset-bodice trimmed in silver; white satin petticoat; coral mules.

Maid: light brown dress; white cuffs; greenish-brown apron.

Intruder: gold-trimmed black coat; fawn hat.

On the Italian chair: the lady's coral velvet jacket and silver-trimmed matching satin overskirt.

Bed: still enclosed by curtains, has lost its wooden canopy as posts become more delicate.

1669. XVIIc. 1660-70. Dutch. (Washington, Nat. Gall. of Art.)

G. Terborch. The Suitor's Visit.

The suitor: black, white stockings, fawn hat; shoe toes square and spreading.

Lady: pearled cap and black bows; coral bodice; gold-trimmed white skirt.

Theorbo player: blue, silver hair bows.

Man behind: brownish gray.

1670. XVIIc. c. 1660-65. Dutch. (New York, Metropolitan Museum, Frick Collection.)

G. Terborch. Portrait of a Young Lady.

Black lace bands used on black satin, and as an edging over white satin banded in gold lace. Little ribbon knots at sleeves, bodice and in corkscrew curls.

1671. XVIIc. c. 1661. Dutch. (Berlin, Kaiser Friedrich Museum.)

A. van den Tempel. Nobleman and his Wife in their Park.

The nobleman's costume shows the favorite color combination of this period. His bronze satin doublet is worn with petticoat breeches lavishly looped below the belt and at the knee with variegated ribbons in reds, browns and beiges. The white shirt has green ribbons at the wrist and a wide green collar, edged with white lace. His baldric is black with an open-work emblem in silver; stockings sky blue. White boot-socks are worn, not with boots, but with black shoes, the red ribbons of which are halfway between rosettes and bows.

His wife wears the standard pale yellow satin gown, banded in gold lace, with a shaped white shoulder collar; black bows at the wrist.

Cattle (L. *capitale*=wealth, our "chattels") were

too valuable as draught oxen or milch cows to be lightly slaughtered, until a great deal of attention began to be given to cattle breeding in the XVII-XVIIIc. Venison was the predecessor of beef; the ownership of deer forests and parks and the right to hunt had been restricted to royalty and the great nobility. Limited park enclosures became naturally landscaped by the cropping and fertilization of generations of herds of deer and are now artfully planned; we are at the beginning of the great age of gardens and vistas. Property changes hands violently during the XVIIc. The old snob value of a deer park is reinforced by the increased demand for grazing land and a park, with or without deer, but certainly without cattle, is the desire of rich bourgeois or gentlemen of any pretentions.

1672. XVIIc. 1669. Dutch. (Carlsruhe, Art Gallery.)
B. van der Helst. Young Couple.

These are the classic costumes of c. 1670 at their most charming.

The man, whose hair is wig-like, wears the doublet in its last form, just before it is replaced for good by the coat and vest, and its rippling collar becomes gathered under the chin into a cravat.

The woman's gown leads directly into the satin-smooth low-necked dress of the early years of Louis XIV. Her hair hangs on the shoulders in ringlets clustered at the sides; even the fringe is in corkscrew curls. Her bodice has a row of graduated bows which will bring on the re-introduction of the V-front opening as necklines rise in Mme. de Maintenon's time.

1673　　　1674　　　1675

1673. XVIIc. Dutch. (London, National Gallery.)
G. Terborch. Portrait of a Gentleman.
(See also Color Plate, No. 7.)

There are German noblemen in rhinegraves more ruffled and beribboned but the culmination of elegance of this period is undoubtedly reached in the diamond-shaped silhouette of this gentleman. It is a triumph of diagonal and horizontal lines and of varied textures of black: polished leather, dull silk, and the deep richness of velvet.

The steeple-crowned hat and the circular cape are now almost old fashions, which are used with the utmost sophistication to reinforce the spread of the doublet opening, the petticoats, the flaring cannons. His hat is made new by the knot of ribbons on the crown; as the use of ribbons diminishes, such a knot will be retained on the shoulder of the coat. Here, ribbons of varied width are used at elbow and wrist; wide ribbons on the shoes, about the waist and massed at the sides of the petticoat breeches below the turn-back of the cape.

1674. XVIIc. Flemish. (Budapest, Museum of Fine Arts.)
P. van Lint (1609-1691). Portrait of a Man.

The coat, in its early form, worn with the old lace collar and without vest, over loose shirt and gathered breeches. It has pockets set low in the skirts; its cuffs are gaining in importance over those of the shirt, and the wrist ruffles of the shirt over the shirt's sleeves. Wig-like hair, hat brim rolling toward tricorne form, soft simple gloves, lace-edged handkerchief.

1675. XVIIc. c.1665-6. Dutch. (New York Historical Soc.)
G. Terborch. William, Prince of Orange (William III).

The posthumous son of the last great Stadholder and Charles I's daughter, married Mary, Protestant daughter of the Catholic James II. William and Mary were invited to replace James II in 1688, as Protestant discontent with the King was crystallized at the birth of a son to perpetuate the Catholic dynasty. William's precocious intelligence, chilled and sharpened by the difficulties of his childhood, endeared him less to the English during his lifetime than his noble plans and his diplomacy deserved.

William, born in 1650, appears to be about 15 or 16 in this portrait. His yellow and silver costume shows a laced leather coat, its sleeve finished with a ruffle of silver lace instead of a cuff; worn with a shoulder knot of silver and the new cravat into which the wide lace-edged collar has been gathered and reduced; full breeches; yellow stockings; brown shoes with a rounded tongue and small oval buckle; black and silver baldric; silver-fringed sash with tabs hanging at each side of waist. Hair is probably a wig. Black helmet with white plumes and red lining; breastplate; musket.

1676. XVIIc. Flemish. (Louvre.)
V. Boucquet (1619-1677). Standard Bearer.

An example of the combinations of two petticoats, the edges laced and the knees and sleeves looped with variegated ribbons. Baldric and sash wider and more fringed than ever; armor reduced to a cuirasse; stocking wrinkles carefully set around the calf; plumes laid around the brim of the hat will become a fringe of feathers as the hat becomes definitely cocked in the

final quarter century.

1677. XVIIc. Dutch. (Metropolitan Museum.)
Pieter van Slingeland. Portrait of a Dutch Burgomaster.

1678. XVIIc. Dutch. (Minneapolis, Institute of Arts.)
B. van der Helst. Portrait of a Burgomaster.

The collar of van Slingeland's worthy, black-clad burgomaster, has been tied into a cravat by red ribbons on the lavishly gold-trimmed black costume of van der Helst's proudly pleased sitter.

1679. XVIIc. 1669. Dutch. (London, Wallace Coll.)
Caspar Netscher. Lace Maker.

The lace maker, socially intermediate between the ladies and their servants painted by Metsu and Terborch, wears a less pretentiously trimmed sacque with her lovely little cap.

1680. XVIIc. 1673. German. (Frankfort-on-Main, Stadel Inst.)
T. Roos. Portrait of a Woman.

German regional costume changes with French influence in latter half XVIIc. Ruffs tend to be replaced by other forms of collar, sleeves to be shortened and cuffed, with more show of ruffled shirt sleeve. South of Frankfort-on-Main bodices become much longer, particularly around Strassburg, Nuremberg and Augsburg. From Luxemburg through Mainz, Frankfort and Hanau to Nuremberg, and south along the Rhine to Strassburg, these long waists often develop into skirted jackets, like fitted masculine coats or riding costume of women.

The great fur hats, particularly those of Strassburg, which least enclose the face, are worn over lace caps; and as they approach the end of their use, degenerate, with the lace invading the fur of the hat. With the southwest German leaning toward masculine styles, male neckwear, such as this collar and the later steinkirk cravat, will be seen on women's costumes.

1681. XVIIc. c. 1680. German.
Princess Louisa Hollandina. The Electress Sophia and Her Daughter, Sophia Charlotte.

This portrait of George I's mother, with her daughter who became Queen of Prussia, was painted by her sister, the Abbess of Maubuisson. The great mezzotint engraver Rupert, was their brother.

This is the smooth-bodied simple satin gown of the '60-70's, its neck slipping off the shoulders, unadorned or caught about by a gauze scarf.

EUROPE GROWS COLDER

As I examined thousands of pictures for this book, I began to feel that a marked change in the climate of Europe must have begun by final quarter XVIc. Elizabeth's muffs, at the end of her reign, might be attributed to failing power in old age of a woman who had heretofore felt cold less than other people. But Englishwomen, notoriously uncovered out of doors in all seasons during most of the XVIc., take to muffs, hoods, and capes with everybody else, by XVIIc. It was obviously more than mere fashion; and all of the evidence pointed to continued low temperatures during XVII and XVIIIc. (See Appendix.)

Wretched as life must have been in barn-like buildings and wattle-and-daub huts, the winter temperature of Europe during the Middle Ages seems to have been substantially higher than after third quarter XVIc.; and there was still wood, to warm a smaller population.

The thermometer was not invented until late in Elizabeth's time, but when wine freezes in its casks, and is sawed up in chunks and sold by the pound, or slow-growing trees like olives, whose lives are measured by centuries, even millennia, split open, the facts are apt to be recorded.

C. Easton has arranged chronologically all the records of Western European climate since 396 A.D. (C. Easton: *Les Hivers dans l'Europe occidentale,* E. J. Brill, Leyden, 1928.) These bear out a dramatic series of events shown by the records of the church at Grindelwald, Switzerland. (H. Hildebrandsson, in *Monthly Weather Review,* June, 1916.)

There were a few bad winters during first half XVIc., but the over-all picture is of mildness so great that, during 1528-33, it seemed the climate must have changed for good: there was no snow, no ice, and flowers bloomed in mid-winter. Then came the "Great Winter" of 1565, which froze European rivers solid and split its trees. This was the beginning of a series of cold, snowy winters.

At Grindelwald, the receding lower glacier began to descend. It covered the heads of gold and silver mines which had been worked throughout the Middle Ages. By 1584, its ice had overturned the chapel of St. Petronelle, the bell of which was supposed to date from 1044 A.D. By 1593, it had reached the village, wrecking two chalets and many barns; it altered the beds of two rivers, and covered the road to Oberwallis. During the period of glacial retreat of 1860-80, the road and the buried houses reappeared. The glacier ice, 25 metres deep in 1570, increased to 100 metres during XVIIIc., and was reduced to 40 metres by 1880.

Easton's compilation shows that after 1565, when even the canals of Venice froze, winters became generally colder. One of the two or three worst of all recorded freezes was in 1607-8, the "Great Freeze in the reign of King James," when the Thames became a coach road, the walnut trees of Montargis died by the thousands, and the pines of Vicenza were blasted, as Coryat noted the following year.

Although there were at least six intervening winters worthy of being called rigorous or worse, the coldest weather in England in Evelyn's memory since 1620 was that of 1683-4, which froze Europe, even Spain. For months, the Thames was used as a street by coaches which ran from the Temple to Westminster for 6d. A "Frost Fair" of theaters, inns, and rows of shops, was set up on the ice, "even to a printing-press, where the ladies and people took a fancy to have their names printed and the day and year set down when printed on the Thames. Fowls, fish and birds, and all our exotic plants and greens universally perished. Many parks of deer were destroyed, and all sorts of fuel so dear that there were great contributions to keep the poor alive. No water could be had from the pipes—nor could brewers and divers other tradesmen work." (Evelyn.) Weakened by a 24-hour exposure of cold, people dropped dead on the streets of France and Flanders. In London, smallpox deaths rose to 200 a week, so that two thirds of the congregation were in black on Sunday, and a gaudy costume in a crowd caused general attention.

The winter of 1694-5, particularly terrible in France, is dramatically reflected in French fashion plates.

From Stockholm to Cadiz and Naples, the winter of 1709 surpassed everything recorded between 1608 and 1830; Louis XIV sold his gold plate for 400,000 francs to relieve his people. 1740 was a very long, cold winter; and cold-to-rigorous winters, especially in France and Italy, reappear frequently till 1763.

Then a reverse can be sensed. There is a run of normal winters, broken by rigorous cold in 1784 and 1789 (which froze the sea off Holland and split the olive trees of the Midi); warm and cold winters alternate; 1820 is bad; 1830 is one of Europe's recorded worst, especially in Spain and Portugal; 1845 is long and snowy from Sweden to Morocco. About 1860, the winters become generally soft and mild.

The prolonged cold, combined with a decreasing wood supply and a larger population, was an important cause of emigration to the New World; in Europe, it forced the use of coal for heating, which had been known since Roman times, but forbidden in English cities because of smell and smoke.

1682-83. XVIIc. Flemish. (Metropolitan Museum, Print Room.)

Romeyn de Hooghe. "Figures à la mode," Amsterdam.

The Dutch gentleman, followed by his Negro servant, shows the coat in its early long, unfitted form, its pockets rising, its corners caught together out of the way. This is necessary since he continues to wear a ribbon-fringed petticoat over full breeches; the old wide-brimmed boots are filled with boot-hose, but with their cuffs beginning to turn upward.

The turned-up coat corners are, as it happens, one of the most momentous ideas in the history of fashion. It is so useful that it is adopted by riders and military men all over Europe, by 1700.

Ingenious alterations in turned-back usages are characteristic of English costume in XVIIIc., and lead to lapels. In France, the turned-back corners are cut away, resulting in the tailored frock (Fr. *fraque, frac*) coat, from which come our formal and dress clothes for men.

The sleeves of his shorter, fringed vest appear as a matching ruffle below shortening and widening coat sleeves. His linen, as is usual, corresponds in fullness to the width of the cuff. Knots of ribbon on the slightly cocked hat, the shoulders, behind the cravat, at elbows, and at the wrists to which the whip is fastened by a loop. The tasseled canes of the next century will be hung from a button by this loop, when hands need to be free.

Fond as the Netherlands have always been of skating and sleighing, a good freeze is not common there, and when it comes, in our day, offices close. Dutch ladies in masks, kerchief-hoods, little fur capes or pockets, are otherwise dressed as they would be indoors. One holds her slipper while her cavalier, wearing a bunch of ribbons on the side of his hat, laces skates over a foot protected by nothing but a stocking.

Both Lipperheide and Colas date the 12 plates of the *Figures à la mode* at "about 1700," which seems to me to be nearly a quarter of a century too late.

1684

1685

1686

1687

1688

1684. XVIIc. 1692. Dutch. (Metropolitan Museum, Print Room.)

R. de Hooghe, illustrator. "Relation de voyage de sa Majesté Brittanique en Hollande," by Tronchin du Breuil. The Hague, 1692.

Reception at the Westende Bridge to welcome William III. Europe now wears French costume, especially on ceremonious occasions and at court. Guardsmen; attendants in striped liveries.

1685. XVIIc. Dutch. (Detroit, Institute of Arts.)

G. Terborch. Young Man Reading.

The *montero* cap with a turned-up fur brim is worn as a riding hat, or within doors (where it is often worn in place of a wig) with a dressing gown. Hair is now replaced by an unnaturally woolly wig, separated over the shoulders.

The long coat of the 70's is frequently seen with a rather long, narrow sleeve, modestly cut and showing very little linen, with a small armseye and a tight-drawn look about the upper body.

Brown costume; *montero,* cherry and silver crown; yellow gloves.

1686. XVIIc. 1685. Dutch. (Budapest, Museum of Fine Arts.)

J. Weenix. Portrait of a Man.

Straight coat with narrow upper sleeve, worn with a long, closed brocade vest, which is probably sleeveless, although its material is used like a turned-back sleeve, to cover the wide coat cuff. No buttons on either garment, except at cuff. Knotted cravat with lace ends; full, unruffled shirt sleeve. Hair probably his own.

Negro servants replace dwarfs, except in Spain, and are frequently painted with their masters.

1687. Mid-XVIIIc. Flemish. (Cooper Union Mus.)
Rabat: bobbin lace; Brussels. Necktie end; one of pair; patterns opposed.

1688. XVIIc. Dutch. (Metropolitan Museum.)
Albert Cuyp (d. 1691). Cavalier and his Sons.
Long velvet riding coats, worn with turban or fur-trimmed *montero;* compare closing with gown of

Electress Sophia (1681). Boots, now restricted to riding use, are long, softer, and have their tops turned up to cover the knee. Retention of braid in sleeves and chest, in livery use.

1689-93. XVIc. Italian, Sicilian.
5-piece Set of Linen Underwear, embroidered in

silk and metal threads: *camisa* (underdress), shirt, stockings (without foot), and 2 pairs of underdrawers. Underdrawers, like most refinements of dress, originated in Italy. Moryson mentions "silke or linnen breeches under their gownes" as being characteristic of Italian townswomen's dress. He says that they are not worn at all in Germany; they were obviously none too common in his native England at end XVIc.

1694. XVII-XVIIIc. Italian.
Apron : linen, embroidered in red silk.

1695. XVII-XVIIIc. Spanish, Salamanca.
Peasant Sleeve: embroidered in black and colored wools.

1696. XVIIc. Italian.
Knitted Mitts: probably ecclesiastical, in light and dark brick pink, lemon yellow, green, cobalt blue, and natural color.

1697. XVIIc. Italian.
Knitted Jacket.

1698-1700. Early XVIIc. Italian.
Knitted Stockings.

1701-03. XVII-XIXc.
Knitted and embroidered stockings.

KNITTING BY HAND AND MACHINE

Knitting in Great Britain apparently began in Scotland and filtered down into England. The earliest English mention is of knit wool caps in 1488. "Knitte hose, knitte peticotes, knitte sleeves" are mentioned in an Act of Edward VI in 1553, and the trade of hosier in 1563. The first worsted hose knit in England were supplied to Lord Pembroke (executor of Henry VIII's will) by Thomas Burdet, "an ingenious apprentice of St. Magnus' Church." (Wade: *British Chronology*.)

Stow says that Edward VI had a "payre of long Spanish silke stockings sent him for a great present," the first seen in England, and that Henry VIII had only cloth or taffeta hose "or that by great chance there came a payre of Spanish silke stockings from Spain."

"In the second yeere of Queen Elizabeth 1560, her silke woman, Mistris Montague, presented her majestie for a new yeere's gift a paire of black knit silk stockings, the which, after a few days wearing, pleased her highness so well, that she sent for Mistris Montague and asked her where she had them, and if she could help her to any more; who answered, saying: "I made them very carefully of purpose only for your Majestie, and seeing these please you so well, I will presently set more in hand." "Do so (quoth the queene), for indeed, I like silke stockings so well, because they are pleasant, fine, and delicate, that henceforth I will wear no more cloth stockings."

Mary, Queen of Scots, at her execution wore "shoes of Spanish leather, the inside outward; green silk garters; watchet silk stockings, clocked and edged at the top with silver, and under them a pair of white Jersey hose." (Brummell, see Appendix.)

In Stubbes' time, cloth netherstocks were "thought too base" and were made of "jarnsey, worsted, crewell, silke, thred, and such like, or els . . . of the finest yearne that can be got, and so curiously knitte with open seame downe the legge, with quirks and clocks about the anckles, and sometime (haply) interlaced with golde or siluer threds, as is wonderfull to behold." They were still terribly expensive. "The time hath bene when one might have clothed all his body for lesse then a payre of these netherstocks will cost" People "will not sticke" at having 2 or 3 pairs, for which they have to spend their own earnings for a whole year.

A machine for knitting was invented in 1589 by the Rev. William Lee, a Cambridge graduate serving as a Nottinghamshire vicar. It was an excellent machine from the very start, and the entire stocking, jersey, and lace industry is founded upon Lee's machine, with refinements but no real alterations. He first made flat stockinet, but soon learned to "fashion" shaped garments. Nottingham was the heart of the later English machine lace industry, but since neither Elizabeth nor James showed interest in his invention, Lee took it to Rouen, under the patronage of Henry IV until that king's assassination.

There was no notable advance in knitting until 1758, when Jedediah Strutt of Belper attached a ribbing machine to Lee's frame. Ribbed stockings, often in blue and white, become common soon after, especially in France. Knitting was also enriched by the application of Jacquard techniques, in the beginning of the XIXc.

1704. Early XVIIc. Italian.
Border: cut-linen work: vine design in *punto reale* and *punto riccio* with figure motifs in *punto in aria;* edge of *reticella* lace of transitional type.

1705. Early XVIIc. Italian.
Alb: *punto in aria* on linen.

1706. XVIIc. Italian.
Handkerchief: reticella lace.

Courtesy of Museum of Fine Arts, Boston (1696-1703).
Courtesy of Metropolitan Museum of Art (1689-95, 1704-06).

1696

1697

1698   1699   1700   1701   1702   1703

1704   1705   1706

1707. XVIIc. Italian.
Handkerchief: bobbin lace.

Handkerchiefs were another refinement which originated in Italy, as did underdrawers. Unlike drawers, they became very popular in Germany.

The first laces were a sort of embroidery, based on the threads of fabric. The first *reticella* laces became less rectangular as workers gained skill. Their patterns had already begun to flow, even before the time when the basic threads of fabric had begun to be replaced by freely manipulated threads on bobbins.

1708. XVIIc. Italian, Genoese.
Collar: *reticella.*

1709. XVIIc. French?
Collar: embroidered linen; border in *punto in aria* and reticella.

1710. XVIIc. c. 1650. Italian.
Collar: Venetian point.

1711. XVIIc. Italian.
Collar: rose point.

1712. XVIIc. Italian.
Tassels for band-strings: bobbin lace.

1713. XVIc. Spanish.
Woman's Leather Shoe: brown on white, red heel.

1714. Early XVIIc. French.
Patten: wooden sole, leather strap and heel, iron ring.

1715. XVIIc. c. 1620. Probably Italian.
Woman's Shoe: white leather; brown leather toe strap; pink silk floss tassels.

1716. XVIIc. 1610. Italian, Venetian. (Metropolitan Museum, Print Room.)
Giacomo Franco. "Habiti dell donne venetiane."

Franco's costume book shows XVIc. fashions persistent in Venice. The man wears the costume of Goltzius' Standard Bearer. The horned hair arrangements of the lady are specifically Venetian. She retains the bodice seen in Venice throughout the XVIc., high-waisted in back, low in front and padded across the belly, from which the idea of the male peascod doublet seems to have come. It is, as always, extremely low cut, with the great wired fan collar of latter half XVIc.; interesting use of lace at the armseye, where the separate sleeves the Italians have long loved always tend to show the linen of the undershirt. A single skirt of brocade, undivided in the center and gathered all around into the waistline, is a Venetian usage, as is the fan chained to the girdle, which the rest of Europe took from Italy.

In 1645, Evelyn found Venetian garb "odd, as seeming always in masquerade." Some of their characteristic styles, like high chopines and hair deliberately streaked with dye, have persisted since Carpaccio's time. He describes their petticoats, "coming from their very armpits"; the "knots of points richly tagged about their shoulders," and their display of "shift" at the shoulders; the general look of nakedness which they "usually cover with a kind of yellow veil of lawn, very transparent"; and their enormous pearls.

On their chopines he says the Venetian ladies are "half-flesh, half-wood"; chopines are now forbidden wear for plain citizens and for prostitutes. Ladies continued to wear *chopines,* to the time of the daughter of the last Doge, Domenico Contarini. (Yriarte, see Appendix.)

Prostitutes wear great veils of shot taffeta (with broad, flat tassels of "curious Point de Venise" at the corners) which cover the entire body. "Out of (these) they now dart a glance of their eye, the whole face being otherwise entirely hid with it, nor may the common misses take this habit; but go abroad barefaced." Prostitutes are increasingly controlled: in Florence, daily tribute is exacted from them by the Medici duke, and though "not so much in value," by the Pope as well.

Gambling has become a passion with the Venetian nobility; masked players, "without speaking one word, come in, play, lose or gain, and go away as they please."

The typical "clarissimoe" gown of the Venetian citizen, with a flap over the shoulder which it had inherited from the Roman toga, and the colors which designated the wearer's status, are described in Coryat's "Crudities."

Tom Coryat's Crudities

Tom Coryat, a member of the household of Prince Henry, set out in 1608 to make a tour of Europe on foot and horseback. His account, published under the patronage of the Prince of Wales in 1611, notes the new and different things which struck an observant young Englishman.

In France, the windows are filled with glass or paper; there are wood shingles; parasols and fans are used. He describes the corps of uniformed guards at Fontainebleau, giving a plausible enough account of the origin of parti-color.

He finds that he cannot enter Venice without a bill of health from the preceding city. He describes the costume of Venetian men, women, courtesans and Jewesses; the superiority of their theater buildings and the inferiority of their performances in comparison to those of England; the appearance of women on the stage; "medicine shows" given by mountebanks; the use of forks, unknown elsewhere, umbrellas and lovely fans; the lace-canopied beds of Italian inns; the walls hung with stamped leather and windows filled with glass; the beautiful and costly straw hats of Piedmont; the Spanish sleeve which has reached female costume in Bergamo from Turin.

In N. Italy and Germany, the walls, even of inns, are hung with armorial bearings; Zurich, Basel and Strassburg have distinctive costumes; there are literally hundreds of public baths at Baden; stoves, and clock-towers with mechanical figures in Germany; the richest fair in Europe is held twice a year at Frankfort.

1717. XVIIc. 1602. Spanish. (Madrid, Descalzas Reales.)

J. Pantoja de la Cruz. Royal Baby.

With his brocade doublet and skirts the baby has a flat wired collar which is in process of becoming a falling band, and matching bibbed apron. By a cord about the neck is fastened a bar hung with crosses and reliquaries. In his hand and from his bracelet and belt he has all sorts of delightful playthings: bell, rattle, hand, a branch of coral for teething and a horn.

1718. Second decade XVIIc. Flemish. (Florence, Corsini Palace.)

J. Sustermans. Maria Magdalena of Austria.

The Emperor Ferdinand II's sister was painted not long after her marriage in 1609 to Cosimo II de' Medici, of whom there is a companion portrait in the same collection. Her brother Leopold presently married Cosimo's sister. The endlessly interrelated Florentine court was large, delightful and cultivated. Cosimo brought to Florence Galileo, the inventor of the pendulum, thermometer and sector, who invented the telescope and produced his philosophical studies of gravitation and astronomy under Cosimo's patronage, until the Duke's death at 30. Maria Magdalena and Christine of Lorraine served as co-regents of Tuscany, both dressed magnificently to do honor to Ferdinand II de' Medici, whom they represented.

Under a pearl choker, she wears a great lace whisk, which in its *golilla* form appears in Spanish portraits by Velasquez in the 60's. The excessively cut and decorated edges of the stomachers worn in the Netherlands are latent in the embroidered sections of the skirts of her doublet.

1719. XVIIc. 1609. Spanish. (London, Christie Sale.)

J. Pantoja de la Cruz. Margaret of Austria.

Philip III's wife was the sister of Leopold of Tirol and Maria Magdalena.

She wears the standard Spanish gown, hair dressed higher, its decoration mounting, ever wider ruff, lengthening bodice and point, cone-shaped skirt relatively unaffected by hip padding.

1720. XVIIc. 1620. Flemish-Italian. (Metropolitan Museum.)

J. Sustermans. Cosimo II de' Medici, Grand Duke of Tuscany.

The Grand Duke wears the extremely conservative costume now seen only in Spain and Italy; paned trunk hose in their long, wide first decade XVIIc. form; long skirted doublet; ruff; old form of matching short circular cape, with Maltese cross; heelless shoes with small bows; magnificently damascened helmet with umbril (eye-shade) which is now in the Metropolitan Museum's Armor Collection.

1721. XVIIc. Spanish. (Nantez, Museum.)

P. de la Cruz, d. 1610. Portrait of a Lady.

XVIIc. Dutch (see Ill. 1673). G. Terborch: Portrait of a Gentleman.

Courtesy of National Gallery, London

1722

1723

When the lacy white ruff had been made as wide as possible it began to be boring; ruffs then began to be made of colored material, edged with metal lace. Or, as in this case, embroidery replaces lace in a ruff, set, however, on a lacy supporting frame of wire loops and lattice.

1722. XVIIc. c. 1620. Spanish. (Madrid, Prado.)

Unknown Madrid painter formerly att. to *Pantoja de la Cruz*. Isabella of Bourbon, Queen of Spain.

Isabella (or Elizabeth), first wife of Philip IV, beautiful and beloved by the Spaniards, was aunt and mother-in-law of Louis XIV.

She wears a gray ruff with a gown of gray brocade sprigged with green. The inner sleeve of her Spanish gown has felt the tendency of European sleeves to grow shorter and wider.

The influence of the hip bolster on European costume did not outlast first quarter XVIIc.; Spanish and Italian costume was late in accepting it but retained it longer; in Spain it was eventually transmuted into the enormously wide skirt of Velasquez' portraits.

The point and tabbed skirts of her bodice are developing into the form of the important stomachers of the gowns of the Netherlands.

1723. XVIIc. 1622-27. Flemish. (New York, Metropolitan Museum, Frick Collection.)

Van Dyke. Paola Adorna, Marchesa di Brignole-Sale. (*See also* Frontispiece; of the same period.)

The Marchesa's white and gold costume, with a brown scarf and tinted ruff, shows the importance of the stomacher to be growing in Italian as in Flemish costume.

The growing boredom of all Europe with the ruff in second decade XVIIc. is being shown in many ways. Its width from front to side may be increased; it may be colored, embroidered or edged with metal lace. There is a tendency to replace gauffered, pointed lace by ruchings of tulle. These impulses are shown in this ruff; its border looks less like the lace it still is than like a more delicately fluted edge, on a more largely and loosely pleated ruff, worn with wrist ruffles of the old form, differing also in color. White cuffs are sometimes enlivened by being worn over a bright-colored cuff. (See Appendix.)

With her simply dressed Italian hair, the Marchesa wears a tiny pearled cap with a brown aigrette (a form of the quivering spray set in the hair since late Elizabethan days); sash worn baldric-wise; longest form of Spanish sleeve flowing down the train of her gown.

Photographs courtesy of Metropolitan
Museum of Art, Print Room

1724. First quarter XVIIc. French.

Jacques Callot. Bohemiens: Le vant-garde.

Jacques Callot (1592-1635), the son of a herald-at-arms of Nancy, and destined for the Church, ran away at 12 with a band of gipsies to study art at Rome. He was recognized there and sent back forcibly to Nancy. At 14 he ran away and was again recaptured. He was finally allowed to go to Rome in 1608-9 to study engraving. He worked in Florence under the patronage of Cosimo II from 1612 until the Duke's death in 1627, and then returned to Nancy, which he had visited in 1621. His 1600 plates illustrate costume, the life of vagabonds and gipsies, the grotesque figures of Italian comedy, the miseries of war. Many of his plates appear in several forms, engraved originally in Italy and reworked at Nancy after his return to France.

These gipsies in their bedraggled, swashbuckling finery, must be very like the cavalcade with which Callot first traveled.

1725-30. Before 1627. French.

Jacques Callot. Bohemiens: L'avant-garde.

These costume plates, produced first in Florence, show: swashbuckling military figures in plumed hats, draped capes, loose gartered breeches and high, stiffened whisk collars; priests or scholar in long garments; town and country women, the former in a male hat, sleeves pinned on at the shoulders, showing puffs of shirt, embroidered apron over tucked-up skirt, and heelless shoes; the latter in straw hat, kerchief over shoulders and an apron full of faggots.

1731. Early XVIIc. French.

Jacques Bellange. La Seconde Jardinière.

Another etcher from Nancy, whose work shows strong Italian influence, is Bellange (1594-1638). With her uncovered, braided hair, fringed shawl, fine straw basket, narrow embroidered apron, and Roman sandals, the "second gardener" is obviously an Italian peasant girl.

1732. XVIIc. 1682. Italian, Bologna.

Giuseppe M. Mitelli (1634-1718). Alfabeto in Sogno: E.

This little figure, by one of the early caricaturists, though produced much later in the century, is set here with the Callots from which it stems; such fanciful composite costumes are shown elsewhere in latter half XVIIc. Other engravings by Mitelli show the costume of Italian comedy characters.

Guatsetto. 1733 Mestolino.

Riciulina. 1734 Metzetin

Pulliciniello 1735 Sig.ª Lucretia.

Cap. Spessa Monti. 1736 BaGattino.

Scaramucia 1737 Fricasso.   Scapino 1738 Cap. Zerbino

1733-38. XVIIc. French.

Jacques Callot. Italian Comedy Figures.

The figures of the *commedia dell'arte,* descended from established characters in Roman farce, began to be developed in Italy early in XVIc. and are with us still. The action, largely comic and frequently bawdy, was improvised upon the skeleton of a prearranged scenario by troupes of strolling players and acrobats: ladies, and their pert or ribald maids; lovers, and their elders, Pantaloon and the Doctor; the boastful Spanish Captain; and all manner of servants, resourceful, witty or dull: Harlequin, Scapin, Scaramouche, Mezzetino, Pierrot and Punch, as we call them now. The companies were imported to France by Catherine de' Medici. Italian comedy had become part of the life of all Europe by the XVIIc. (See Appendix.)

Lucrezia is one of the many elegant names borne by the innamorata; she is always played without a mask, as are her lover and her maid. Ricciolina is a witty form of her companion-servant, allied to the soubrette, Harlequin's Columbine.

Of the male servants shown, Guatsetto and Bagattino are related to Harlequin and his alert impudence. The first is a rollicking fun-maker, the second a teasing juggler. Mestolino and Mezzetino are almost identical: quick-witted but dumb in spots. Pulcinello is a dope; Scapin, a rogue; Scaramouche has some of the swagger of the Captains, of whom Zerbino is one of the more elegant: he wears dark-rimmed Spanish spectacles over his flashing eyes lest their glance shame the sun.

Many of the little porcelain figurines of the XVIIIc. produced at Nymphenburg, Meissen and Vienna show the personages of Italian comedy in their characteristic costume.

1739. XVIIc. 1616. French.

Jacques Callot. Intermezzo, after Guilio Parigi's Sketch in the Stanzoni de' Commedianti, Florence.

Plays, whether of the traveling carnival sorts, grown out of the jongleurs and minstrels of the Middle Ages; the miracle and morality plays performed by guilds or townspeople; or the great processions of the Church or of princes like the Medici, originally took place in the open air, in public squares or palace courts.

Stages with a backdrop were at first set up on wagons or platforms. The theaters of Shakespeare's time grew out of the use of cloistered palace courts, multiplied into tiers of seats protected by a roof. They were open to the weather in the center where the standees massed to watch a performance played on a permanent stage, which projected into the clearing and was roofed over only in the rear. Obviously the standees got the best view of the performance. In late XVIc. completely roofed theaters with seats in the middle and scenery in perspective, began to be built in Italy. One of the first and finest was the Teatro Olimpico at Vicenza, designed by Palladio, and standing today; Coryat described its superiority to English playhouses.

During XVII-XVIIIc. playhouses were built from the plans of the greatest architects, like Inigo Jones, who also designed the scenery for Ben Jonson's plays. Theaters were included in palaces and private houses, but the old tradition of being seated at the side and up, safe from the weather and the riff-raff, was responsible for the retention, to this day, of boxes at the side, from which the most costly seats give the worst view of the stage.

For the entertainment of Callot's patron, Cosimo II, Parigi, who belonged to a great family of designers of spectacles in second half XVI-first half XVIIc., provides a pastoral set with the Renaissance's beloved long vistas.

The first textbook of theatrical design and lighting, end first half XVIc., was Italian. It describes the correct scenery for the three types of performances: tragedy, performed on a street of palaces in perspective; comedy, in a public square; and a rustic setting for dancing pastoral or allegorical figures. (See Appendix.)

The reversed crescent silhouette of the female body in 1616 swings from a fan collar, wired high in back, past pendant Spanish sleeves, to trailing skirt-ends.

New fashions of Europe affect the dress of male spectators more than that of their ruler in his official portraits (Ill. 1720). But the ()-shaped silhouette is typically Florentine: the plumed hat is high rather than wide, the flaring collar wider than the hat brim, the square-collared cape is bundled about the torso, while the breeches, full at the waist, are reduced at the gartered knee, and the body tapers to an inconspicuous foot. Even the standing postures are studied to emphasize the bulging center. (Male figs.: Foreground).

1740. XVIIc. 1622-7. Flemish. (Washington, Nat. Gall. of Art.)
Van Dyke. Marchesa Balbi.

The Antwerp-born Marchesa, who may have launched her fellow-townsman, Van Dyke, on his career in Genoa, wears a gold brocaded dark green costume. Its silver ruff is embroidered in gold; wrist ruffles of gauze so sheer that they appear to be of a lighter green than the costume.

1743   1744   1745

1741. XVIIc. 1630. Spanish. (Paris, Gustave de Roths-
    child.)
Velasquez. Queen Maria Anne of Hungary.

With her black and gold costume, Philip III's
daughter wears a sheer ruff of light brown tulle, gold-
edged wrist ruffles, and a handkerchief of gold gauze.

1742. XVIIc. 1624. Spanish. (London, Cassell Coll.)
Velasquez. Gaspar de Guzman, Count of Olivares,
Duke of St. Lucar.

Olivares, head of the household of the heir-appar-
ent, became on his accession Philip IV's devoted
minister, constant companion and alter ego, the most
powerful man in Spain until his fall from favor in
1643. He was a man of immense pride, who refused
to use the title of his acquired dukedom except in
combination with that of his inherited rank; a man
of bull-like power; a magnificent horseman. He
shared none of Philip's love of art and the theater, but
kept a great aviary, and carefully saw to the preser-
vation of a mass of the Spanish state papers.

He wears the green cross of Alcántara on his black
costume, together with symbols of his power, and
the collar out of which Philip devised his *golilla.*

1743. XVIIc. c. 1630. Spanish. (London, formerly Dor-
    chester House.)
Velasquez. Philip IV.

The King, of whom Velasquez painted so many
portraits, was a well meaning man, somber, indolent
and art loving, passionately devoted to the Spanish
theater in the great period of Lope de Vega and
Calderón. The Spain he had inherited from his far
lesser father was already ruined; he left its government to Olivares, who was, for all his qualities,
neither the economist Spain needed, nor any match
for Richelieu.

The king dressed beautifully, wearing the *golilla*
collar which was his own invention, and the moustaches which were carefully encased in a pomaded
leather form at night. His most effective costumes
were severe and dark, but their silhouette shows less
clearly than in similarly cut, lighter examples such
as those selected for reproduction.

Leather military jerkin with doublet sleeves matching the cuffs of his gauntlet and embroidered around
the seam of the thumb. Baton and diagonal lace-
edged sash of a military commander. Padded breeches
worn with high, soft boots, their tops slashed to show
a colored lining. Cocked hat with plumes and wide,
crushed crepe scarf. The lock of hair in front of the
ears is specifically Spanish. Spanish velvet table cover
with fitted corners, caught with braided gold frogs.

1744. XVIIc. 1631. Spanish. (London, National Gallery.)
Velasquez. Philip IV.

Brocade doublet has short buttoned openings below
throat and belt, outlined in heavy embroidery; matching diagonal pocket slits at its breasts and skirts. The
breeches, with vertical pockets, are padded, reduced
in width, buttoned along the outseam and gartered
with rosettes. Dark gauntlets have slashed cuffs
matching the doublet sleeves.

1745. XVIIc. c. 1633. Spanish (Madrid, Prado.)
Velasquez. Margaret of Austria on Horseback.

The queen wears a tall, plumed man's hat with her
riding costume. Women's dress in l.XVI-e.XVIIc. has
a severe masculinity. As it becomes more feminine in
latter half XVIIc., women's riding costume will retain or exaggeratedly ape masculine styles.

Court Dwarfs

A dwarf, with the word written over his head,
appears among the entourage of William the Conqueror in the Bayeux Tapestry. Dwarfs had been favorites in the noble houses of Europe since the Middle Ages. Nowhere were they more pampered, audacious, shameless, or ridiculous than in the somber,
religious, severely formal Spanish courts of the late
XVI-XVIIc.

Dwarfs might be witty, impudent and exaggerated,
in the tradition of court jesters, like Charles V's
Francesillo or Philip II's French buffoon, Brusquet.
Others were little gamecocks, like the matador, Juan
de Cazalla, who was accompanied by four scarlet-clad
Negro giants; or like Henrietta Maria's Jeffrey Hud-

son (18 inches high when nine years old), a cavalry captain in the Civil Wars, who fought two duels, the first with a turkey-cock and another with an opponent who met him with a squirt and was later shot dead by Hudson from horseback.

Many were endearing little companions and confidants, to be indulged (and sometimes bribed), who could perform small services, or take charge of the more helpless dwarfs: the mad, deformed or idiotic. These last served as butts for teasing, or as contrast and relief from the almost unbearably tense grandeur of the court, as they stumbled, smashed and misbehaved.

The more intelligent dwarfs were carefully educated. The most winning although often the most hideous, were as beautifully dressed and shod as their masters. Elizabeth's Tomasina got 12 pairs of shoes at a time. Some had tiny weapons and saddles, like Philip III's Polish dwarf, Estanislao, a skillful hunter.

Maria Theresa's Moorish dwarf delighted the French court: thereafter little Negroes begin to replace dwarfs in late XVII-XVIIIc. portraits.

The common people who loved the "merry drolls," gave them the name of their favorite food: Holland, Pickled Herring: France, Jean Potages; Italy, Macaronis; Great Britain, Jack Pudding. So says the *Spectator,* in bringing the matter through April fool jokes, to the practical jokers of the e.XVIIIc. called Biters. (See Appendix.)

1746. XVIIc. c. 1633. Spanish. (Madrid, Prado.)

Velasquez. The buffoon, Pablo de Valladolid.

Pablillo wears a collar which, like that of Olivares, is not quite a *golilla;* the cape without which a man was not properly dressed in public; brocade doublet; rather full, gartered breeches; and the heelless shoes, the short hair and the locks before the ears, characteristic of Spain.

1747. XVIIc. 1631. Spanish. (Boston, Museum of Fine Arts.)

Velasquez. The Infante Baltasar Carlos and his Dwarf.

This is the first of nearly a dozen portraits of the extremely promising young prince, often painted by Velasquez before his death at 17. We can see him, still in skirts in 1631; by 1635, breeched, in hunting clothes and boots with a miniature gun, or in magnificent court costume, or riding a prancing horse with the most assured proud dignity of any six-year-old boy who ever lived; or in tiny armor in 1639. But never are we without feeling some part of Philip's pangs at his loss, 300 years ago.

The Infante at 2 wears dark olive green velvet, embroidered in gold. With his steel gorget he carries the scarf of a military commander, in warm red; red hat with gray-white plumes, trimmed in gold.

The dwarf, Francesco Lezcano's brown dress is braided and cuffed in dark red; gray collar, edged in red-brown, surmounted by a choker of dark red beads; apron edged in gray lace, embroidered in dark gray; he carries a rattle.

1748. XVIIc. c. 1628. Spanish. (Madrid, Prado.)

Velasquez and assistant. Doña Antonia de Ipeñarrieta y Galdós and Her Son, Luís.

The stiffened collar of Doña Antonia's severely cut gown supports a series of white collars, flat and fluted, variously edged with color and bobbin lace. The old scheme of braided doublet sleeve issuing through pendant gown-sleeve is nicely varied here. Both are of the same stuff; the inner sleeve is reduced to a deep cuff over which the upper sleeve is puffed, and to which it is caught so that they move together. The close sleeve, barely cuffed, is shortening as elsewhere in Europe, to show a pair of fine bracelets. The austerity of such gowns is lightened by a pearl baldric and fine buttons.

The picture of the child, whom she holds by his pendant sleeve as by a leading string (which developed out of this usage), was added later to her portrait by another artist. He had the Spanish lock in front of the ears, a falling collar of lace, apron with an openwork bib and bobbin lace edge, and a bell hanging from his belt.

1749. XVIIc. Spanish. (New York, J. P. Morgan.)

Spanish School. Portrait of a Child.

The loving care lavished on Spanish ecclesiastical garments had brought to perfection methods of patterned pleating. The technique commonly seen on albs is transferred here to a child's apron. It is worn with a headdress related to the *bourelet* seen on so many XVIIIc. French children in pictures by Chardin and Boucher.

1750. XVIIc. 1635-8. Spanish. (Madrid, Prado.)

Velasquez. Infante Ferdinand of Austria Hunting.

Philip's brother, the Cardinal Infante, succeeded their aunt as Regent of the Netherlands. He was an able and energetic administrator and a formidable general, whose victory over Gustavus Adolphus saved S. Germany for Catholicism.

This picture of the Cardinal Archbishop of Toledo in hunting clothes must have been painted after Ferdinand's departure in

1633. Similar visored caps, long-skirted jerkins with hanging sleeves and brocade doublet sleeves, gauntlets, easy breeches, rosetted at the knee, and soft high boots with a reversed top, are also worn by Philip and Baltasar Carlos in Velasquez portraits in the 30's, with snaphance rather than the wheellock hunting gun which the Cardinal appears to carry.

The dogs favored by male Hapsburgs since Charles V are always immense; Baltasar Carlos had a mastiff as large as himself; only dogs of the Queen and her daughter were tiny.

1751. XVIIc. After 1637. Spanish. (Madrid, Prado.)

Velasquez. Surrender at Breda.

On his first trip to Italy, Velasquez traveled in the company of the Marquis of Spinola, younger son of an old Genoese family of bankers. Years later, from his memory of Spinola's account, Velasquez painted this picture, which the Spaniards call "Las Lanzas," and which is one of the great documents of military costume, as it varies between nations.

This picture shows the *condottiere* commander Spinola receiving Breda's second capitulation to Spain in 1625, after its long dramatic siege.

The difference between the slender Spanish silhouette and the clumsier one of Flanders is shown in the groups at r. and l. Spanish hair is short, though it may show the ear lock, neckwear smaller, waist long, breeches narrow; boots high, soft and tubular, with no plaque over the instep and the slightest of heels. The curling Dutch hair is longer, the collar spreads over the shoulders of a short-waisted doublet with shortening sleeves; wide full breeches fall into the spreading cuff of a boot with high heels and great stirrup leathers; military leather jackets in l. foreground.

1752. XVIIc. 1640-2. Spanish. (Louvre.)
Velasquez. The Conversation.
1753. XVIIc. 1647. Spanish. (Madrid, Prado.)
Juan Bautista del Mazo (figures by *Velasquez*). View of Saragossa, detail of foreground.

Spanish court costume continued to develop in almost parochial isolation until jolted by the impact of French fashion in 1660, at the marriage of Philip's daughter to Louis XIV.

But soldiering in Flanders affected the clothing of the Spanish army and, through them, the costume of Spain outside court circles.

The rapidity with which Flemish styles spread in less than a decade is shown by illustrations 1752-53.

In the "Conversation," locks are long, collars spread, waistlines short, and boots show reversed tops, boot-hose, stirrup leathers and higher heels, although the *golilla* and pendant sleeve persist and there is a certain restraint in the adaptations.

By 1647, in the "Saragossa" picture painted by his son-in-law, with figures by Velasquez, the men of military age wear flopping boots filled with boot-hose; short-waisted, mandilion-like jackets and military cassocks hung cape-wise on the shoulders; gold-laced capes.

The clericals and civilians wear long, somber, caped and collared cloaks, great rolled black hats without plumes, and small *golillas* or tiny band collars.

The women's back hair is caught up into a specifically Spanish cylinder instead of the little bun seen elsewhere; hair is falling loose on either side of the faces of all the women in Europe, but here it is concentrated in front of the ear, after the manner of the lock which began to separate from the rest of the hair in Spain in XVc. The Spanish bodice has a bateau or round neck banded with scalloped lace; easy, untrimmed sleeves which are often those of the shirt; and a peplum which covers the circumference of the Spanish farthingale (seen in its most exaggerated form in the court examples which follow).

1754. XVIIc. 1640. Spanish. (Chatsworth, Duke of Devonshire.)
Velasquez. Portrait of a Lady.

There are very few Spanish portraits of ladies who are not members of the royal family; theoretically they still lived in oriental seclusion, though a starving and seething Spain was greatly affected by the loose-living soldiers, returned from Flanders. Workmen wore swords like gentlefolk and a masked lady was not offended at being mistaken on the streets for one of Madrid's 30,000 prostitutes.

This wonderful creature, of whom he painted two portraits, may have been Velasquez' own daughter. As "The Lady with the Fan" in the London Wallace Collection, she is the timeless quintessence of our dream of the black-eyed, black-clad Spanish lady: mantilla and fan, bared bosom and rosary, as Goya, or even Zuloaga in the XXc. would dress her.

In the Chatsworth portrait, the gown worn with her black lace mantilla is a domesticated version of the court gown. The decolletage is masked with lace below the choker collar. The bodice has the dropped shoulder and divisions of the easy sleeve of Ills. 1626-27, stressed by braids with an uneven edge. The skirts of the bodice, divided like those of a doublet, extend over the supporting frame of the skirt.

1755. XVIIc. Italian. (R. Smith Barry.)
Florentine School. Saint Elizabeth of Hungary.

1756. XVIIc. Spanish. (New York Hispanic Society of America.)
Unknown artist. Portrait of a Spanish Lady.

1757. End XVIIc. Spanish. (London, Sir Charles Robinson.)
Carreño de Miranda (1614-85). Spanish Lady.

Like illustration 1754, these are no official Hapsburg portraits in state costume, though none could be more magnificent than the greenish-silver brocade gown (1756) pointed up with coral bows and jewels.

From the 40's we see the natural hair of unmarried Spanish girls parted at the side, looped across the forehead, caught with a pleated decoration, and combed out to hang free. The hair of the smaller princesses continues to be dressed in this way throughout Velasquez' day; but the frizzed hair of queens and their adolescent daughters flattens at the crown and widens at the sides into a decoration-studded creation of the utmost artificiality.

The bateau neckline of the 40's proceeds to become rounder and to be elaborated, both above and below the line of pearls, until it reaches the throat and covers most of the shorter-waisted bodice.

The sleeves of this Spanish gown are influenced to an unusual degree by the bombasted, paned and tied sleeves seen elsewhere from the 30's. The wrist ruffles with their fan-like sections are an interesting compromise between the old idea of pleating and the new sheer, informally gathered finish (1756).

The triangular earrings, characteristic of Spain since Moorish days, are elaborated like the tasseled cord-ends of a Spanish Cardinal's hat. The line of pearls at the neck is characteristic of important Spanish gowns. Pearl decoration gives the necessary emphasis to a dropped shoulder-line, which has to carry the spectacular sleeves. The accent of the massive brooches is repeated in the watches at the waist. The handkerchief of a lady becomes enormous in Spain by 1660.

1758

1758. XVIIc. Spanish. (New York, Metropolitan Museum, Frick Collection.)

Velasquez. Philip IV.

In this scarlet military costume and baldric, blazing with metal, which he wears in three Velasquez portraits, Philip makes his first concession to European fashion, except for his hair which he has gradually allowed to lengthen: wide scalloped collar, open button-edged jacket and slightly widened boot-tops over which lace is turned down.

Although in 1655-69 his dwarf, Antonio el Inglés, wears flowing hair, wide collar, short-waisted jacket, wide-topped boots with great spur-leathers, and a hat smothered in ostrich, Philip himself, depressed by the death of his wife in 1644 and of his son in 1646, reverted to his *golilla* and somber Spanish dress, which continued to be that of his tactful courtiers.

1759

1759. XVIIc. Spanish. (Boston, Isabella Stewart Gardner Museum.)

Zurbarán (1598-1664). A Doctor of Law at the University of Salamanca.

Modern academic dress has been codified from the mediaeval scholar's gown: cap fringed in green; brown gown with scarlet hood.

1760

1761

1762

A. Pièce du devant. — B. Pièce de dos. — C. C. Basques en deux pièces. — D. Manche formée de
bandes. — E. Fausse pièce du dos à laquelle sont fixés : 1° F. Le moucheron; 2° G. L'épaulette
et à la base H le pan retombant sur la jupe.

1763

1760-62. First quarter XVIIc. Spanish. (Paris, Worth
　　Coll.)
　Spanish court dress, and pattern.
1761. XVIIc. 1656. Spanish. (Madrid, Prado.)
　Velasquez. Las Meniñas.
1763. XVIIc. c. 1652. Spanish. (Metropolitan Museum.)
　Velasquez. Infanta Maria Theresa.
1764. XVIIc. Spanish. (Vienna, Art. Hist. Mus.)

Pupil of Velasquez. Mariana of Austria, Queen of
Spain.
1765. XVIIc. 1664. Spanish. (Madrid, Prado.)
　Velasquez. Infanta Margarita.
1766. XVIIc. c. 1680. Spanish. (Munich, Alt. Pinakothek.)
　Juan Carreño de Miranda. Mariana of Austria as
a Widow.

　The death of Baltasar Carlos made it necessary to
provide a new heir to the throne. In 1649, Philip
married his niece, Mariana of Austria, a 15-year-old
girl who had been intended for his son and was hardly older than his daughter, Maria Theresa.

　Mariana, her German attendants and ways, were
not beloved. When she shrieked with laughter at the
antics of the dwarfs, her horrified Spanish Mistress
of the Robes told her that etiquette did not allow
sovereigns of Spain to laugh in public. Mariana and
the King sat silent at the play, where he "did not
move foot, hand or head, only casting his eyes about
occasionally, nobody near him but a dwarf."

　The Meniñas, whom we see with Velasquez, the
German dwarf, María Bárbara Asquín and the
Italian, Nicolasito Pertusato, were the Maids of
Honor to whom was entrusted the care of the little
Infanta Margarita, born in 1851. The king and queen
are seen in the mirror, entering the room.

　Margarita was followed by Philip-Prosper, twice
painted by Velasquez, in skirts and in a miniature
version of the latest European style to reach Spain,
a decade or two late.

He lived only 4 years and was followed by Charles II, "the Bewitched," the calamitous end of too much Hapsburg inbreeding, who somehow contrived to exist for 40 years. Charles was so physically incapacitated that he had to be nursed until 6, could not be allowed to walk alone for years, and was always subject to fainting fits. He was too sickly to be educated, and it was impossible to keep him clean, but he was not actually unintelligent. When his illegitimate half-brother managed to have the Queen Regent banished to a convent and ordered the Infante's hair combed, Charles said, "Nothing is safe from Don Juan, not even vermin." It was during the Queen's two years out of power (during which she wore the nun-like mourning costume shown, c. 1680), that Spanish seamen in the Pacific, unaware of recent events at home, rechristened the Ladrone Islands as the Marianas in her honor.

The painter and male figures in the background of *Las Meniñas* wear the static costume of Philip's reign. Legend tells that Philip himself painted the red Cross of Santiago seen on Velasquez' breast; but the actual conferring of the decoration on the painter he faithfully loved for 36 years was delayed until 1659, while careful search discovered no Moor or Jew in the painter's ancestry and his position as royal painter was declared to be untainted by commercialism.

The development of the great Spanish gown from that of Isabel of Bourbon and Marie of Hungary, as the basque of its bodice spreads over the supporting frame of its skirts, can be seen in these examples and the Spanish ladies in Ills. 1754-57.

The ruff, which Isabel wore over an opened bodice in the 30's, disappears. The neck opening widens towards the shoulders, in a horizontal "bateau" neckline, seen particularly on young girls from the 40's. The neckline is stressed by a heavy edge of jewels or pearls above a deep hanging band of lace; a line of lingerie pleating (shirt) shows above the jewelled line. On women and adolescent girls, the neckline is apt to be more rounded, the inner pleating increased in width until it approaches the base of the throat; the lace band may be so deep as almost to cover the bodice.

The picadills at the shoulder become unified into a wing, which in turn is depressed into a dropped shoulder line.

The old +-slashed outer pendant sleeve is altered into a variety of vestigial pouch-like or strapped arrangements. The inner sleeve becomes fuller; its finish may be frilly, but in Spain it barely recedes from the wrist, although it is being shoved up toward the elbow elsewhere in Europe.

The cone-shaped Spanish farthingale becomes padded around the hips in the first quarter century to support the stiffened, shaped and extended skirts of the doublet. These are drawn out over an ever-widening frame, and the lines of the seams and divisions are dramatically stressed by asymmetrically edged galloon braids. On children's dresses, these braids are more apt to be tape-like, less differentiated from the gown material and applied in zigzag or diagonal patterns, or the gown may be cut on various grains of a striped fabric.

An appearance, at least, of superimposed skirts has always been favored in Spanish costume; this is still preserved as a fold or variation in direction of the pattern or trim at about knee height (1761-1765).

Below the accented line of the decolletage is set an immense jewelled medalion or brooch, often backed with ribbon or pleating. Caught diagonally across the bodice from sleeve to sleeve is a looped line of beads or pearls, related to the line on the decolletage, and often ending in another brooch caught on the sleeve. Folding fans, not gloves, are now indispensable.

The gowns of this period in Spain show a great deal of greenish silver with coral and darker greens, pointed up with black and gold. The *Meniñas*, for instance, are in silvery and darker green and in gray-green; the little Infanta in greenish silver; the female dwarf in blue-green; the male dwarf in red. In the 1664 portrait, Margarita wears a gown, the diagonal parts of which are of silver striped in coral, the horizontal parts in dark coral on light; the plume hanging down her hair at the right is coral; earrings, bows at neck and wrists and baldric of gold, with a line of black across the neckline. Other similar gowns are of silver and black, banded in gold at the neck, with a coral baldric and plum colored bows and plumes.

The Revolt of Minds and Men: XVIII Century

DEVELOPMENT OF DRESS: 1710-1795

Euroyean costume is henceforth French, except for a few years in the late XVIIIc. Even Spain succumbs, as the courts of Prussia and Saxony, Austria, Sweden and Russia slavishly copy France.

In England, characteristic and often very individual styles develop during XVIIIc. In the 1780's, possibly under the influence of great portrait painters, these styles take on a lovely simplicity which accords with contemporary French passion for Rousseau's naturalism. France is swept by a wave of Anglomania and English styles are supreme for the last two decades of the century. The differences between ceremonial or court dress, and ordinary wear, are defined. Our trousers, tailored cloth coats, and top-hats, make their appearance; elegance and good grooming actually go out of fashion among French and English men, as the Revolution approaches. Etruscan and Greek influences, felt in last quarter of century, will be reinforced by archaeological discoveries at Pompeii at the turn of the century, and by Napoleon's Egyptian campaigns in e. XIX.

The striking changes in costume during the XVIIIc. are seen in the heads of both men and women, and in the forms of women's skirts.

MALE DRESS

Hair. The full-bottomed wig, which dribbled powder over the chest of the coat and was a nuisance to active young men in the new military and naval services, is drawn back and got out of the way in a number of fashions. By the second third of the century, it is relegated to professional, or unfashionable elderly men. It continues to be worn by doctors, is last seen on bishops in mid-XIXc., although, like powder, it still appears in parliamentary and legal costume in England in XXc. But when, during a crisis in English affairs, Anne's brilliant young Secretary of State, St. John (Bolingbroke) appeared in a tie wig, the queen said he would probably come next to court in his nightcap.

Powder, used since Shakespeare's day, had begun to disappear long before it was taxed by Pitt, during the crucial flour shortage of 1795-1801. It last appears worn by an English eccentric of the 1840's.

Early in XVIIIc., the hair of the wig, which formerly stood in high points on either side of a part, begins to be brushed back from the forehead in a *toupet* (toupée), with "pigeon wings" from the temples: these develop into clusters of horizontal sausage-like curls by latter half century, the number of which is reduced to one by the final quarter. When the high padded and stiffened hair of women begins to collapse loosely, the hair of men's wigs (which have also grown high), loses its side rolls and turns into an analogous wide loose mass. Then, like women's hair, it is clipped into a combed out *hérisson* (hedge-hog) style.

The back locks of the lesser Ramilie wig are at first tied together at the nape of the neck by a black bow. Court style is always conservative. This fashion persists, as the successor of the full-bottomed wig, after the locks have become controlled in general wear.

Either they are enclosed in a black taffeta bag (*crapaud*) with a draw-string top; are braided or spirally wound about into 1-3 pigtails (which become very long c. 1740)—a favorite form in the army and navy; are clubbed into a *catogan,* at the end of third quarter; or fall into a couple of knotted locks.

Natural hair treated like a wig was not uncommon, and was often left unpowdered in everyday use; by 1765, this trend began to worry wigmakers.

Coats and waistcoats. The swelling which affects women's skirts, c. 1710, is accompanied by similar manifestations in men's costume during first half century.

Coats of knee-length, open or barely caught at the waist and worn with similarly cut, slightly shorter waistcoats, have already acquired a good deal of pleated side fullness in the skirts by the end of Louis XIV's reign. During first half XVIIIc., these skirts are held out by whalebone, horsehair, buckram or paper stiffenings.

In second half century, a profound change takes place in the cut of coats. It has been found convenient, at the very start of the century, to turn back and button up the corners of military and riding coats, after a XVIIc. Dutch fashion. This is exploited with great inventiveness in England, where coat fronts are affected and lapels also begin to develop.

In the final third of the century the skirts of all coats begin to be cut away in front, after this fashion, into a swallow-tailed frock coat (*frac*). The body of the coat hugs the torso; the side fullness of the skirts is reduced to a pleat or gore; the button, which has finished the top of the old fullness, retreats toward the back of the coat, as all the lines of the garment rake backwards.

Sleeves have grown longer in second half century. Their cuffs, large or small, open or closed, now become less conspicuous, as do the pocket flaps; and the neckline of the tail coat begins to rise into a standing collar. By 1778 the *frac* is adopted by Louis XVI, and persists far into XIXc. as official court dress, when it is otherwise quite outmoded by tailored cloth garments.

The waistcoat, following the lead of the coat, also becomes cutaway; but as the old correlation between coat and waistcoat lengths is abandoned, it is much shortened, into a vest.

Collars and lapels are emerging. In final quarter century, tailored cloth coats, often double-breasted, appear with lapels and turned-over standing collars. The waistcoat worn with these is a *gilet,* cut off square at the waist; it is also apt to be double-breasted and to carry lapels. The new short vests are sleeveless, their backs made of plain material, whereas the old long waistcoat, often sleeved and entirely embroidered, was worn at home as negligée with a nightcap, either alone or with a dressing gown.

The decoration of coat and waistcoat diminishes generally throughout the century, although the waistcoats of mid-XVIIIc. are often heavily trimmed with tassels and fringe. The long, back-slanting lines are particularly effective when completely untrimmed swallowtail coats are cut from narrowly striped satin. Plain cloths predominate from the 80's. Buttons increase in size and importance; earlier fabric-covered and embroidered forms are replaced by metal.

Overgarments. In addition to capes, there are many forms of loose buttoned topcoats and surtouts, such as the Roquelaure of the second quarter century. These tend to develop collars in second third of century, multiple capes during latter half, and to become fitted and double-breasted *redingotes* (i.e. riding-coats) in the period of English fashions, in final quarter.

The trend towards coachmen's clothes and ways in England is noted as early as Dec., 1738, when "Miss Townley" in the London Evening Post sees loose great-coats, called "wrap-rascals," dirty boots, and whips worn at the theater, not, as she had thought, by "a set of unmannerly, slovenly footmen sent to keep places," but by men she later saw paying for their box seats.

Breeches. The exposure of breeches as coats and waistcoats become shorter, and are cut away, requires a revolutionary method of cutting. Makeshift reductions of petticoat breeches had produced clumsily fitted, tubular breeches. These are now replaced by *culottes* cut on the bias, their legs springing apart like the open blades of a scissors. The diagonal cut is carried high in back for comfort. In front, the material which stretches across the thighs is sewed or buttoned onto a wide belt-piece, cut on the grain of the material to insure a trim waistline. The bottom of the breeches, which has been concealed by stockings rolled over the knee, is also made to fit; an outseam opening, buttoned like the front closing, or buckled by a band below the knee, allows the culotte to come down over the stocking, as it does almost universally in the latter half of century. As sleeves lengthen and cuffs become unimportant, similar buttoned slits will finish sleeve-bottoms, as they do today.

Smooth-fitting boots, reaching high on the calf, become an important component of English style in the 80's. Pantaloons of elastic materials, modelled on sailor's trousers, are drawn down to meet the boot-tops. It is difficult to tie them in place at the calf, and by 1793, they are extended to the ankle. On these pantaloons, a fly front or a pair of such openings replaces the buttoned closing of the culotte. A sharp division is being established between formal and informal garments. Boots and pantaloons were inadmissible at court. Their appearance at a coalition cabinet meeting in 1783 horrified Lord North, who was dressed in tail coat, culottes, and sword. The culotte, with its connotations of aristocracy, becomes a garment in which it is actually dangerous to appear among the pantalooned *sans-culottes* of the Revolution. It is retained as court wear in the XXc. Knee-breeches, instead of trousers, were still obligatory in small German courts, well into second half XIXc.

Footwear. The heavy jack-boot of XVIIc. goes out of use by second quarter XVIIIc., except on postilions who are constantly being called upon to help the coach out of the mire. They are replaced by closely fitted, delicate boots, and by many forms of fitted leather leggings, *spatterdashes,* and linen gaiters, buttoned up the outside of the calf. The old high tops, covering the knees, begin to be turned down, by the second third century, into an approximation of the boots worn by jockeys today.

The square toe of the Louis XIV shoe disappears by the first quarter century; its high tongue, during the second quarter, although red heels continue to be worn by the Macaronis of 1772. The shoe becomes a well-fitting pump of a natural shape. Its diamond, paste or silver buckles, larger in the third quarter, are retained in court wear, while what the manufacturers of Birmingham called "the unmanly shoe-string" began to replace buckles in everyday wear.

Hose. Stockings, with clocks embroidered in metal or silk, are commonly rolled over the knee of the culotte in the first half century and worn under the breeches in the second half. The mechanical stocking frame was modified, c. final quarter XVIIIc., to knit ribbed stockings, and striped hose, commonly in blue and white, begin to appear. The closing of the knee breeches over them may be laced, or finished with loops in the final quarter XVIIIc.

Hats. The hard, flat-crowned hat, cocked into a symmetrical tricorne, and commonly untrimmed except for a binding of metal braid, is carried in the hand or under the arm when the type of wig or toupet prevents its being worn. The Macaronis wore a minute tricorne slanting down their high-crowned wigs. The loops holding the cocks in place tend to relax, and the hard, flat hat to become much larger, higher and softer, degenerating into a bicorne in the final quarter, while one of the loops is elaborated into a pleated cockade. There have always been some round-brimmed, high-crowned hats: in final quarter XVIIIc., high-crowned hats, which develop into our top-hats, appear in England and are carried to France on the wave of Anglomania.

Linen. The Steinkirk has a long life in provincial wear, but is largely replaced, by the second quarter century, by a pleated muslin stock, fastened in back. The vertical gathers of the *rabat* are supplanted by the horizontally gathered *jabot* ruffles, matched by small wrist-ruffles. The waistcoat is open above the waistline, or only occasionally buttoned, in order to show the jabot ruffles. The *solitaire,* a black ribbon originating under the tie of the wig, is often folded about the neck, its ends crossed, pinned or knotted in front. The kerchiefs worn by women will be knotted about men's necks, late in the third quarter century, turning into *cravats.*

Accessories. Snuff boxes and toilet articles, muffs (enormous in final quarter century) and handkerchiefs, continue to be flourished and used in public. A gentleman still "pulls out his comb, curries his wig."

A sword is still a necessity in an inadequately policed and lighted world; it is commonly worn by gentlemen through the third quarter century; the shoulder-knot of ribbon which had helped to hold the XVIIc. sword-belt in place, disappears during first quarter XVIIIc. Gentlemen begin to tire of the sword in the third quarter, as legislation fails to prevent servants and workmen with egalitarian ideas from carrying swords. No longer worn in Parliament, swords went out of English use during the 80's except as part of court costume.

Canes, heavily knobbed with cloudy amber, become a mania c. 1710, and have a tasseled loop by which they can be hung from a coat button. Sword and cane are carried together, at first. Late in the century, quizzing glasses are often set in the head of a cane.

Utilitarian umbrellas of oiled fabric were used in bad weather in the Tatler's time; now they become fashionable. Appearing with the boots, great-coats, and top hats of the last decades they free gentlemen from dependence on coaches and sedan chairs.

Watches are still expensive, but in this era of conspicuous waste it becomes a fashionable necessity to carry them in pairs, or even as buttons, in series. Short vests allow pairs of fobs with dangling seals to be displayed against the long, pantalooned thigh; pantaloons begin to be held up with embroidered suspenders or braces.

Steel becomes more fashionable than precious metals during the 90's. It is used in buckles and fobs; it decorates buttons, in the fabrication of which all possible materials are exploited.

FEMALE DRESS

The extent to which the bondage of the *fontange* and the rigid gowns of late Louis XIV was resented can be seen in the rapidity with which they disappear c. 1710. This reaction is foretold by the flowing wraps of late XVIIc. The characteristic gown of the second and third decades XVIIIc. follows this impulse. It is a loose sacque (*contouche*) worn over a corseted bodice and underskirt; it is often open in front, sometimes sleeveless, and it flows behind in box-pleats from the shoulder. These pleats persist at the back of the bodice of the court *robe à la française,* and are even to be perceived in the back gorings of the bodice of the final quarter century's *polonaise,* two sections of which sometimes continue into the skirt.

But before discussing specific forms of XVIIIc. gowns, the outlines, determined by headdress and undergarments, must be defined.

Head. The death of the fontange was followed by nearly half a century of neat little heads, the hair cut 3-fingers long, powdered for ceremony, uncovered (especially in aristocratic use) or bearing tiny lappeted caps. Both cap and hair are surmounted, out of doors, by the pretty hoods so much admired by the *Spectator;* or from the 30's by pancake-like shepherdess hats.

Paniers and hair dressed low first appeared at Versailles in 1714, worn by two English ladies who were almost turned away from the king's supper because of their dress. Both styles appealed to the king; at mass the next day many headdresses had been reduced by three fourths in height. This amused uniformed persons, but upon the king's renewed compliments, was adopted by everyone at court.

In the 60's, both the hair mass and the caps covering it increase suddenly in size and elaboration. From 1740-85, *mob* and *fly* caps and the ruched *dormeuses,* enclose hair which, by the 70's, reaches a padded and powdered height, and an excess of decoration unheard of before or since. (See Appendix.)

The "head," pasted and pomaded over horsehair pads which may rise a yard high must be arranged by a professional. (An arrangement 72 inches from chin to top of hair, in 1772, is described by Lacroix.) As it remains untouched between the hairdresser's visits, one to three weeks apart, it usually becomes verminous.

The small shoulder curls previously seen in court wear now cover the shoulders. The back hair is clubbed into the Etruscan *catogan*. The crown of the head, feathered and looped with gauze, is topped by a fantastic clutter of decoration, which may include a sow with her litter, or a ship in full sail to celebrate the victory of *La Belle Poule* in 1778. These hair arrangements are protected out of doors by hoods like the *calash,* raised or lowered by fanwise supporting hoops, or by the gauzier *Thérèse*. In the daytime, equally ridiculous hats are worn, enormous or tiny and precariously tilted.

Differentiations are made between powdered formal or court coiffures, and the frequently unpowdered every-day arrangements; between the *bonnets* of ceremony, *chapeaux-bonnets* appropriate with both dress and walking costumes, and the equally elaborate but less formal hats, *chapeaux,* worn only in the daytime. An aristocrat of the second half XVIIIc. may find it necessary to change half a dozen times a day into costumes suitable for negligée at home, walking, riding, theater, supper, and the evening.

Large simple leghorn hats appear in England c. 1785, and largely replace caps. These wide straws arrive in France in the Anglomania of the last decades, together with beaver and other hats of masculine character. During the Revolution they are seen cocked, like men's, with the tricolor. Until the last decades, the tricorne is the hat commonly worn with riding habits.

In the 80's, the hair mass widens at the top and is squared off; then its support begins to be withdrawn. The hair, looser and wider in front, longer in back, may be a great mass of ringlets, in a *hérisson* (hedgehog), worn by men as well.

As powder reaches the end of its use, colored forms, blonde and red, appear briefly. By 1800, the head is again small, dressed in pseudo-Greek styles. Bonnets in poke shapes replace the great ruched hats which supplanted the all-enclosing ruched caps.

Skirt. The form of the skirt undergoes some five major changes during XVIIIc. The bustle and train of late Louis XIV are replaced, c. 1710, by a new form of the old farthingale. At first it is funnel-shaped and consists of a series of ever-wider hoops of wire, rattan, or whalebone, taped together from waist to hem, or run through slots in an ankle-length petticoat. Hoops come to be worn by women of every class, by working women, and even by nuns, of the more worldly sorts, such as canonesses of Remirement and abbesses. (Mme. de Genlis). These hoops, covered by gathered ankle-length skirts, swell to the roundest possible

form. It is almost impossible to gather up the hoops and skirts to pass through a door; stairs begin to be built wider to accommodate them. Around the middle of the century, hoops are often abandoned and replaced by stiff petticoats.

But mounting hair requires wide skirts for aesthetic balance. A new form of support is devised which gives an entirely different shape and motion to the skirt. It consists of narrow lateral wings, projecting over each hip. These *paniers,* made of several hoops, hinged and taped together, hang from the waist and do not fall much below the hipline. Seen from front or back, the skirts which fall vertically from this support are as wide as possible. From the side, the silhouette is very narrow. Pockets cut through the gathers of the skirts between the waist and the hips of the paniers, allow the wearer to slip in her hand, catch and raise the paniers. This method of support, seen early in Italy, is carried to its most extravagant six-foot width by Marie Antoinette from 1774. Its use in English court wear will be ended by George IV's command in the 1830's. All these supported over- and under-skirts are typically of ankle length; the split over-skirt of the *robe à la française,* worn with wide paniers, has a train. The short, gathered, white petticoat which serves as underwear is put on before the paniers and hangs close to the body.

The whole character of XVIIIc. dress comes from the limitations of motion imposed by wide paniers and top-heavy heads. The hooped petticoat gives a lovely, lilting movement to the skirts. The wide paniers give a more stately one, but the body must be swung to pass through a crowd or into the door of a coach. The roofs of sedans have to be hinged to enable the headdress to be got inside; the sedan can perhaps be closed again, if the angle at which the rigid lower bar of the panier can be tilted allows the lady to sink onto the seat instead of crouching. The head often had to be stuck out of the coach window, we learn from Mme. Campan. Even the motions of the arm are conditioned by problems of moving the elbows within the socket depression at the top of the skirt, between the waist and the rising tip of the paniers, and of removing them without clumsiness, when necessary. The most typical gesture of the XVIIIc. is the sweep of the bent arm in the carefully studied "exercise of the fan," while the elbows hug the body and appear to be supported by the paniers.

By 1780, the paniers grow smaller and c. 1785 are replaced, briefly, by hip-pads; then by the *tourneur,* a crinolined bustle, called the *cul de crin,* or, outside France, the *cul de Paris*. Although the *polonaise* worn with it is usually of ankle length, the bustle-supported skirts are, in general, longer and trailing.

Bodice. The bodice retains very much its XVIIc. form throughout XVIIIc. It usually has a stomacher, or an applied placard in that form, until the advent of the masculine coat styles of the last decades. The V may be filled, as in XVIIc., with a series of graduated bows; or be edged by a wide fold or ruching, running around the back of the high neck as a finish to the sides of the over-bodice, and continued down the front edges of the outer skirt, as it splits to accommodate ever-wider paniers. These bands, smoothly pleated *en platitude,* or shirred, may be laid on in straight or waving lines, on gowns which are apt to be of brocade or painted silk.

The bodice of the court *robe à la française* is actually fitted close to the body all around, but it appears to be corseted only in front. After the manner of the old *contouche* with its Watteau pleats, the fabric of the back of the bodice falls in pleats from the shoulder straight into the over-skirt. The short underskirt worn with this gown of the last half century is often quilted, or the petticoat has an embroidered border. The gathered lace *falabas* of late XVIIc. are a favorite trim of the first half XVIIIc., but the clutter of *pré-tentailles* tends to become *volants* of self material on the later petticoats.

The bodice is apt to fasten in front, under the fold which edges the outer bodice; but in latter half XVIIIc., back lacings in the manner of the English corset become common, and the lining of the bodice is apt to be boned along its gores, eliminating the corset. With the crinolined bustles, and multiple goring of *polonaise* bodices during the final quarter century, the waistline becomes shorter, aided by wide belts and fitted corselets.

Underwear has scarcely showed during XVIIIc. except as narrow ruffles. Tippets, scarves and fichus veil the bosom instead. This tendency increases during last half of century; great puffed and wired kerchiefs, *bouffantes,* appear with the short-waisted, trailing gowns inspired by English male styles. These are taken over by men, reduced to cravats, and in that form are returned to women's use.

By 1795, necklines are lower, shoulders more exposed, the waistline raised to a point just under the breasts; the sheer, naked gowns of the Classic Revival are beginning to be indicated.

Long, plain sleeves are seen at the beginning, and at the end, of the century; but the classic sleeve of the first half of century has an important cuff, pleated across the bend of the elbow or shaped; that of the second half replaces the cuff by ruffles, *engageantes.* In the final quarter century there are many deviations; puffed sections, *sabots,* appear which lead to the short, puffed cap-sleeve of the pseudo-classical gown.

Outer Garments. The hoods and scarves, tippets of sable or thin summer silk, capes, and long loose cloaks and coats like the *Joseph* of the first half century are apt to become elaborated during the latter half century. (See Appendix.)

There are elaborately gored short *caraco* jackets, pleated in back *à la polonaise;* fur tippets; *pelisses* edged with fur or eiderdown; and a great variety of greatcoats and *spencers,* based on riding or coachmen's coats in England, during the last two decades. These lead to coat-gowns of oriental inspiration: *lévites, circassiennes,* and to full, soft *chemises* of English muslin, which had been worn under them, but then appear alone. Combing jackets, short, completely enveloping, become a necessity and must also be charming; visitors of both sexes advise and admire, while the professional hairdresser, on his regular visits, spends hours on his combined work of hair arrangement and millinery, during second half of XVIIIc.

Shoes and Stockings. Shoe and stocking colors tend to become lighter, until the last decades. Red stockings, common early in XVIIIc., become pale pink or green, and later white. High-heeled slippers and mules are of light colored silk, brocade, velvet or kid, embroidered in metal and colors. In the latter half of century, slippers, beautifully buckled or knotted, lose their high tongues. With the masculine styles for women, plain shoes of natural shape, and even highlaced shoes with lower heels are worn, In the 90's, heelless satin ballet slippers with pseudo-Greek lacings appear; shoes are now apt to match the bright, light colors of yellow, blue or green gloves.

Accessories. Masks go out of English and French use during the first half of century, but continue to be seen in Italy. Patches continue to be worn throughout first half century.

The most characteristic accessories of XVIIIc. are the beautiful painted folding fans; and bands around the throat (analogous to the *solitaire* of men) which requires ruffles, ruchings, and artificial flowers when dresses become loaded with these decorations. Posies of real flowers, beloved since Elizabeth's day, are kept fresh at the corsage in a bottle of water, set in a pocket at the top of the corset.

The elaborate aprons of the late XVIIc. continue in use through first half of XVIIIc. For a brief period in the 1780's, while Marie Antoinette is playing milkmaid at the Petit Trianon, long, wide white aprons, with two big pockets and ruffles, are worn indoors and out.

Scarves, triangles and tippets, *palatines,* of lace or of very sheer gauze in dark colors, black, mulberry or deep green, embroidered in metal and colored silk, preceded the great white muslin bouffant kerchiefs and fichus of final quarter.

Muffs, worn since XVIIc., are seen throughout XVIIIc., and increase, both in use and size, from the last decades into XIXc.

Silk gloves are supplemented by gloves and mitts of silk net, from about 1740. Short leather gloves appear with the redingote styles of the 80's. Long kid gloves increase in use during latter half century. In final quarter and early XIXc., their color tends to agree with that of the slippers.

Drawstring purses, in netted *babila* work, or decorated with needlepoint, appear in e. XVIIIc.; purses, often beaded, increase in use and variety into XIXc.

Thin canes, grasped in the middle, and the knobbed or gold-headed canes and crops which accompany the English-inspired styles of the last decades, are joined by long-handled parasols. These are often small, much trimmed with ruffles and fringe, but in final quarter, large, umbrella-like forms are fashionable.

Servants and working people strive throughout the century to emulate the rich in everything. So much imitation jewelry is sold that the names of leading manufacturers are still synonymous with the gold-washed brass jewelry produced by Pinchbeck, and the paste diamonds of Strass.

Such rivalry is never one-sided. Diamonds are more favored than pearls, but jewels decrease in importance as accessories grow more luxurious. The watch anyone can afford it still a dream, but it will be realized within the lifetime of many of the ladies and gentlemen who show off their affluence by wearing watches in fobbed pairs in the final quarter century. Watches and perfume flasks form part of the equipment of *châtelaines* and *nécessaires*. Charming boxes in opaque enamel on copper, or carrying pottery cameos, are available to anyone. But the snuff, patch and comfit boxes of the well-to-do, and the *carnets-de-bal* of final quarter-e.XIXc. are apt to be decorated with the newly invented machine-turnings, glazed with transparent enamels, and edged and monogrammed with diamonds.

Greek influence, felt during second half XVIIIc. and through the first quarter XIXc., brings cameos, seals and medallions. With miniatures, silhouettes and cyphers they are used on bracelets, fobs and necklaces.

Buckles and buttons become larger; buttons, though made of increasingly varied materials (see button plates) become, in general, more metallic. Crucible steel, a product of mid-XVIIIc., is still very expensive, and is a very fashionable metal at the turn of the century.

Fabrics and Decoration. Legislation instigated by the wool and silk industries during first quarter XVIIIc. tried to bar India cottons (worn at home and in the country by the aristocracy, and almost universally by everyone else) from both France and England. Acts half a century old had to be repealed to permit printing of fine domestic cottons, machine-produced by the new techniques of the third quarter XVIIIc.

The importation of fine linen from Holland and Germany was permitted, to support the export trade in English worsteds; and a great deal of this was worked by its wearers with embroidered sprigs inspired by the patterns of India painted cottons. But wool and silk were the chief wear of the second and third quarters of the century, with some striped, checked or plain domestic linen. English cottons combined a linen warp with a weak cotton weft until final quarter.

Gowns, at first relying mostly on line, become trimmed with fur, lace, ruffles and ribbons. The line in which decoration is applied tends to alter from straight, to serpentine, to draped. Satins are plain or striped. Silks are plain; changeable; striped (changing, roughly speaking, from narrow, to wide, to compounded and elaborated, then back to narrow); painted or brocaded in patterns, which loosen from heavy *candelabre* designs into sprawled and sprigged patterns of greater delicacy (sometimes between straight stripes or serpentine garlands and ribbons), much used in the *robes à la française*.

The petticoat shown under a split underskirt is apt to be embroidered in patterns which become diluted as they rise from a dense border, ruffled or quilted. The wide court gown of Marie Antoinette's time is more apt to be made of plain material, draped, ruched and pleated with gauzy decoration like that of the immense headdress.

In final quarter of century there is a flood of muslin and cotton fichus and gowns, plain or printed, produced by machine spinning and weaving, and either hand-blocked or roller printed, if patterned. Loops and drapes change into simple, gathered, flowing skirts of cotton or cloth.

Fashion Magazines. The magnificent *Monument de costume* of Moreau le jeune at the beginning of final quarter is followed by periodical publication of fashion plates, such as the French *Galerie des modes* and Heidelhoff's *Gallery of Fashion* in London, forerunners of the deluge of periodicals, filled with the latest styles, embroidery patterns and culture, for which the XIXc. is remarkable. Engravers exploit the new field of book illustration with careful attention to costume detail.

1767

1767. First Decade XVIIIc. French.
Claude Gillot. Italian Comedy.

Gillot, (1673-1722), painter-etcher-engraver-illustrator, was specializing in pictures of Italian comedy early in XVIIIc., when Watteau and Lancret became his pupils, and soon his rivals. Some of his costume plates were published as "Nouveaux dessins d'habillements á l'usage des Ballets, Opéras et Comédies."

This is Italian Comedy in its most sophisticated surroundings, at end XVIIc., with the gentry in stage boxes. Additional chairs were often set on the stage, but this usage became extremely unpopular; one intended for the duchess of Queensbury at Drury Lane in 1729 caused so much commotion that it had to be removed.

The Italian Comedy troupe in Paris, though more popular than the French company, was again banished by Louis XIV because *La fausse parade* appeared to be a satire on Mme. de Maintenon. "You have no reason to complain that Cardinal Mazarin tempted you from Italy. You came on foot, and you have made enough to return in your carriages." Under the Regent in 1718, the Italian players returned; playing in French, they were more popular than ever.

Italian comedy could be played anywhere, on a tennis court, in the courtyard of an inn, or from the tail of a cart in a public square. In London at Bartholomew's Fair, June 25, 1700, all "interludes, stage plays, comedies, gaming places, lotteries and music-meetings" were forbidden. But you could still "see a wonderful girl of ten years, who walks backward up the sloping rope drawing a wheelbarrow behind

her; also you will see the great Italian Master, who not only passes all that has yet been seen upon the low rope, but he dances without a pole upon the head of a mast as high as the booth will permit, and afterward stands upon his head on the same. You will also be entertained with the merry conceits of an Italian Scaramouch, who dances on the rope with two children and a dog in a wheelbarrow, and a duck on his head." (Malcolm: 1810.)

We see in the boxes a forest of fontanges and of high-peaked, full-bottomed wigs, only one of which is not powdered. To accommodate their height, cocked hats have deep crowns.

The three worldly abbés all wear short, powdered wigs, curled up at the nape and rolled back from the face in a toupet. Abbés are all very worldly now, and a great many are, in fact, not abbés at all.

Everyone is searching for a place; even starving peasants try to become begging townspeople. Position goes by rank and influence, except, to some extent, among the educated bourgeoisie. A member of the ruined provincial nobility is often indistinguishable from the local blacksmith with whom he gets drunk, except by his sword and his hunting rights. Everyone gambles and is in debt. "It is very vulgar to mind being in debt; debts are a proof and a confirmation of a man's greatness. It may be assumed that a nobleman who owes 2,000,000 is twice as great as a nobleman who owes only a million," as the Abbé Coyer said in his ironical "Bagatelles Morales." A nobleman seeks to "manure his fields" by marrying money; it is acceptable that he marry the widow of a rich tax contractor, but not that his daughter marry her son; a daughter for whom there is no dowry is shoved into a convent.

The eldest son of a noble family is destined for the army or navy; the services have three times too many officer applicants with the necessary four quarterings of nobility; no one can hope to rise from the ranks by merit.

The second son is sent into the Church, to capture as many livings, granted by court favor, as are needed to keep him in the best society.

The cadets scramble as best they can. "Whoever would, was a Chevalier, and whoever could, an Abbé—I mean a beneficed Abbé." They try to make themselves charming to useful people at court, who may help them to become what they pass for. Gramont was both the one and the other at the siege of Trino, when his brother let him loose upon the town

to shake off his rustic air. He so thoroughly gained the manners of the world that he says: "I could not be persuaded to lay them aside, when I was introduced at court in the character of an abbé. All that they could obtain of me was to put a cassock over my other clothes . . . I had the finest head of hair in the world, well curled and powdered (i.e. no wig as yet) above my cassock and below were white buskins and gold spurs. The Cardinal, who had a quick discernment, could not help laughing. Mother said, Well, my little parson, you have acted your part to admiration and your parti-colored dress of the ecclesiastic and the soldier has greatly diverted the court"; but she said that he must choose. He renounced the church "on condition that I keep my abbacy," and that his brother consent to keep him at school. (Gramont: Mémoires.)

1768. XVIIIc. French. (Metropolitan Museum, Print Room.)

P. I. Drevet, after *Hyacinthe Rigaud*. Bossuet.

Bossuet, a profoundly religious man, the greatest preacher in France until he became tutor to the Dauphin in 1660, was a moderate who dreamed of re-converting the Huguenots and Calvinists. He opposed the Jesuits who had done much to combat Protestantism, and who, with worldly expediency, were prepared to mitigate punishments after confession that might alienate the rich and important from the Church.

Non-resident higher clergy, fat with plural livings, left the care of their parishioners to parish priests so illiterate that one was found to be praying to St. Beelzebub. Mission priests and Sisters of Charity were established by St. Vincent de Paul to serve the poor in their world, not from the cloister.

The need for reform which had led to Protestantism was also felt by many Catholics, who found in Jansenism a way to be "Catholic but not Jesuit, evangelical but not Protestant"; religion was discussed with passion in drawing rooms; Catholics read the Bible like Protestants, encouraged by Bossuet.

Jansenism was declared heretical in 1653; the Edict of Nantes was revoked in 1681; Jansenist nuns of Port Royal were forbidden to admit new members

after the death of their patroness, Louis XIV's cousin, Mme. de Longueville. Bossuet, who had influenced Mme. de Maintenon, died in 1704 and the old king fell under the absolutist and reactionary influence of the Jesuits, La Chaise and Le Tellier. The latter had the Jansenist nuns of Port Royal expelled, their buildings razed, and the bodies in their cemetery thrown to the dogs. The Jesuits will give up their fine schools, use their missionary activities to become a rich trading company, and through abuse of power, will themselves be suppressed and expelled from France within a half-century.

Bossuet, for all his worth and goodness, was a much less interesting and successful tutor to the dull Dauphin, than his disciple, Fénelon, was to the Dauphin's brilliant, erratic son, Louis of Burgundy, for whose instruction the archbishop wrote the "Fables" and "Télémaque," and in whom he implanted many of the ideas with which Rousseau will alter world thinking in the XVIIIc.

We see Bossuet, as Bishop of Meaux, holding his scarlet biretta. He wears a plain band with his scarlet-lined ermine *cappa magna,* and shows the increasingly deep band of lace, sometimes forming half the garment, with which surplices and albs are bordered in late XVII-XVIIIc.

The princes of the Church, drawn from the aristocracy, live like princes. Some are men of real heart, like the Bishops of Auxerre and Boulogne, who sold their plate to feed their people during the famines of the first XVIIIc. decade; or the Curé of St. Sulpice, who kept only three dishes and slept on a borrowed bed. But the Cardinal de Rohan, the dupe of the Affair of the Diamond Necklace, born a prince and with preferments worth 2,000,000 livres a year, had his kitchen furnished with silver pots, and the point-lace border of his best alb cost 100,000 livres. He was sent to Vienna as ambassador to arrange Marie Antoinette's marriage, but Maria Theresa was never able to have him recalled until after Louis XV's death. He spent immense sums, and dashed through Fête Dieu processions dressed in green and gold like the rest of his legation on the way to a hunt. The black market in smuggled silk stockings, operating from his secretary's office, sold more pairs in a year than Paris and Lyons together, Marie Antoinette told Mme. Campan.

1769. XVIIIc. 1708-9. French. (Metropolitan Museum, Print Room.)

Antoine Watteau. The Goddess Ki Mao Sao.

Watteau (1684-1721), son of a poor roofer of Flemish stock, came to Paris at 18. He was ill and poor from the start, never very well paid, and died early of tuberculosis. But he made fortunate contacts with painters and amateurs of broad knowledge, some of whom were very loyal; and the whole school of Louis XV painting: Lancret, Pater, Boucher and Fragonard, is based on his work.

After working with a scene painter who failed, and in a religious-picture factory, Watteau entered Gillot's studio during the latter's Italian comedy period. Forced out by Gillot's jealousy of his progress, Watteau began to study in 1708 with Audran, the curator of the Luxembourg Museum. Watteau's work was influenced by the architecture and gardens of the museum, and the Italian paintings in its collection, as well as by the graceful decorative *singeries* and *chinoiseries* in which Audran specialized.

The Goddess Ki Mao Sao is one of the characteristic products of this period in Watteau's work: its influence is felt by generations of designers, through Pillement to the textile printers of late XVIII-e.XIXc.

Watteau's pictures of camp life and soldiers, painted during a visit to his home at Valenciennes, also date from 1708-9.

1770. XVIIIc. French. (Metropolitan Museum, Print Room.)

N. H. Tardieu, after *Watteau.* Julienne and Watteau; cellist and painter.

Many of Watteau's paintings were preserved in the collection of the amateur, Jean de Julienne (c.1690-1766), and passed into the collection of the German emperor. Julienne is also responsible for the publication of Watteau's drawings, in the 4 vols. "Oeuvre." c. 1734, engraved by Cochin, J. & B. Audran II, Comte Caylus and Julienne himself.

The friends' wigs are reduced in size, less bushy, and end in curled locks. Coats tend to be plainer: in any case, these are specifically designed for work. The cuffs of the easy sleeves are closed except on Julienne's left arm. To eliminate friction as he plays, one sleeve is made without a buttoned cuff and is slit open.

1771, 1773-76. XVIIIc. French. (Metropolitan Museum, Print Room.)

Antoine Watteau. "Figures de différents caractères."

Two of the four volumes of Watteau's work published by Julienne are made up of 350 plates of the "Figures. . . ."

Watteau, better than anyone else, has preserved the spirit of the graceful, romantic, informal clothes worn between the periods of rigid formality of Louis XIV and the wired-out perkiness of Louis XV; the clothes shown in these engravings are, in any case, of the less formal type. These are young people at home, on a picnic in the country, walking or sauntering.

Hats are cocked, loosely and high, over deep crowns, because of wigs. But wigs flow in loose locks, ready to be tied back with a ribbon. Coats, with cuffs open or closed, hang loose and unbuttoned to display the waistcoat; this is still long, but grows disproportionately shorter as breeches are cut to fit. In some of the country scenes, amusingly gored and fitted short waistcoats with rippling short skirts, and long sleeves with slit ends, are worn with short capes, replacing coats: a sort of sports costume, worn with a short, almost bobbed wig.

In everyday use, the women's heads are covered by caps and turbans. There are little fur-bordered jackets. The material at the back of the bodice is laid on in characteristic "Watteau" pleats, flowing from the neckline into the skirt. In these flowing pleats, the informality of the loose sacques of the 1720's will remain, embalmed into XIXc., in the anachronistic formality of court gowns.

1772. XVIIIc. 1710. French. (London, Wallace Coll.)

Nicolas de Largillière. Louis XIV and family.

See also Color Plate on Box Label.

Nicolas de Largillière (1656-1746), though of French birth, lived with his merchant father in Antwerp and London during his childhood, and worked with Lely c.1674-8. He might have remained as court painter to Charles II, but fled an anti-Catholic outburst in England to become an enormously successful painter of some 1500 fashionable portraits, male and female, in Paris. A predestined Academician, he eventually became its chancellor.

The ample succession, about which the king boasts, quickly vanishes. The Dauphin dies in 1711; both Louis of Burgundy and his eldest surviving son, the duke of Brittany, in 1712. A sickly baby, born during the year in which this picture was painted, is a last unpromising hope as the old king dies in 1715.

The king wears a richly laced suit with the old vertical pockets; the waistcoat completely closed; the coat buttoned at the waist. On him we see the full-buttoned court wig, hanging in front of the shoulders as well as behind, at about the zenith of peaked, woolly height.

Louis of Burgundy, in natural looking ringlets, dressed low and beginning to recede to the back of the body, wears a coat which also shows new trends in its velvet simplicity. It has heavy, horizontal pocket flaps and large buttoned-back cuffs, matching the waistcoat, which will tend to retain its richness although the coat becomes plainer. As wigs are bulky or high, the hat is apt to be carried rather than worn.

If he were not uncovered in the king's presence, the duke would probably still carry his cocked hat, edged with white plumes, under his arm.

All wear cravats. Young Louis' steinkirk is drawn through a buttonhole of his partly open waistcoat. The knotted ends of his father's cravat hang on his exposed shirt, as its waistcoat is open to the waist.

Stockings are drawn up and gathered to mask the bottom of breeches which are not yet well fitted. Shoes have high red heels and shaped tongues, turned down to show the colored linings.

The fontange is disappearing. The XVIIIc. is full of charming hoods, in endless variety of color and texture, which often cover the shoulders. Mme. de Maintenon, who is 75, has chosen a gauzy black one, gathered to enclose the face and veil the neck.

Before the rigid, bustled and furbelowed dress of the 90's is replaced by hoop skirts or loose sacques, it softens and becomes simplified, and is made of plain materials, often of velvet. The accent is on the front closing of the bodice rather than the V-shape of a plastron, although the V-closing is not lost sight of, and reappears. On Mme. de Maintenon's gown, this line is discreetly clasped together; on other gowns its delicately embroidered edges part, sometimes in an informal diagonal or crossed-over line.

The child whose leading strings she holds is dressed almost exactly as his uncle had been.

1777. XVIIIc. French. (Former Coll. Sedelmayer.)

N. de Largillière. Lady and Child.

1778. XVIIIc. 1710-5. French. (Metropolitan Museum.)

N. de Largillière. Baronne de Prangins.

The Baroness and her husband were Swiss, who apparently lived for some time in Paris. A contemporary quatrain celebrates the luscious plumpness of the Baroness, amply demonstrated here in a white satin gown, with a gold-embroidered garnet girdle and red flowers. This is the large, serene, rather pop-eyed, goddess-like beauty of Louis XIV's period, soon to be supplanted by Dresden china delicacy and animation.

Hair continues to be dressed in high peaks with a curl at each temple for a time after the fontange is given up. It is dressed with jewelled clasps, a ribbon knot or flowers. Corsage bouquets are kept fresh by water bottles, in a pocket at the top of the corset.

Relatively undecorated gowns of plain fabric are caught about the body like dressing gowns, which that of the mother in Ill. 1777 may well be, as both sexes, all over Europe, spend much of their time, receive, and are painted, in negligée. The careless closing exposes the corset-lacings or a froth of lace on the chemise. The sleeves, too, are pushed up or clasped, almost at random.

1779. XVIIIc. c. 1715. French. (Versailles National Mus.)

R. Levrac Tournières. The House at Auteuil.

Levrac Tournières (1668-1752) was received into the Academy as a portrait painter in 1702, and an historical painter in 1716. He was an assistant professor in 1725; quarrelled with his colleagues, returned to his native Caen in 1750.

The cronies we see in this picture are (center) Prosper Crébillon (1674-1762), (right) Charles Du-fresny, Sieur de la Rivière (1648-1724), and (left) Bodin, the king's physician.

Dufresny, recipient of court sinecures from Louis XIV because of his illegitimate descent from Henri IV, collaborated with Regnard in a number of witty plays, and in 1705 wrote the "Amusements sérieux et comiques d'un Siamois," on which Montesquieu based his "Lettres persanes." Dufresny was uncontrollably extravagant, and instead of paying his washerwoman's bill, he eventually married her.

Crébillon père, son of a provincial notary-royal, had a period of great success at court as a tragic dramatist, followed by years of misfortune: the dowryless woman he had married died in 1707, leaving him with two children; his prosperous father died; his plays failed. He lived in bitter eccentricity, almost without food, endlessly smoking, in a filthy attic filled with animals and birds, until through the influence of Mme. de Pompadour, he was given various government posts (one of which was inherited by his novelist son) and a pension, and his later plays again became successful.

The full-bottomed wigs and clothes of Louis XIV's period are seen towards the end of their use. The crown of the full-bottomed wig is beginning to rake backward and flatten; its sides are breaking up into formal curls; it falls principally on the back of the coat. All three wigs are light brown.

The classic agreement in material of the waistcoat and the band trimming the coat cuff, arose from the usage displayed by Dufresny; his long gold waistcoat sleeve, slit at the bottom, is (or appears to be) turned back over the cuff of his gray coat. A red riding cloak is thrown over Crébillon's dark green coat. Bodin shows newer trends in his wig, and in his red-buttoned gray coat, the shaped fullness of which is massed farther toward the back. But all the breeches are cut in the clumsy old way. They agree in color with coats and stockings.

The serving woman, wearing a cap which is a modification of the old *fontange,* is dressed in red with dark green cuffs and a gray apron, in one of the simple wrapped-around gowns which preceded loose sacques; and a red and white petticoat of the stripes which are also much favored as overskirt linings in e.XVIIIc.

Green-painted walls with gilded mouldings; gilt chairs upholstered in darker greens.

English Coffee Houses and French Salons

Relationships between the sexes in society followed different courses in France and in England, during XVIIIc. The freedom of English women in Elizabeth's time had impressed foreign visitors; the implicit community of interest with men was not much affected by such tavern life as that of the "Mermaid" and Ben Jonson's club at the "Devil" where such women as appeared were of a different social level. But in last quarter XVIIc. Englishmen began to frequent the multiplying coffeehouses, which in the days of Queen Anne were largely monopolized by them. Coffee houses then became private clubs (some of which still exist), or remained as useful business adjuncts. Gentlemen go into politics, the military or naval service, or into business, and to the club and tavern, as never before. The segregation of the sexes increases; English women are left to the company of trivial men or of other women, as uneducated and without resources as they themselves usually are in XVIIIc. They pass the time with gossip and cards, tea and music, fashion and fine manners, shopping for clothes or china, and fall prey to the "vapors," an occupational disease of women who are bored and unoccupied to the point of hysteria. They have largely abandoned the fine sewing of their grandmothers but will be driven to other handiwork on the rather low level of *purfling* (unravelling), painting, cutting out, and pasting.

In France, increasingly repressive laws prevented any considerable unsupervised and unlicensed gathering of men, possible plotters against the monarchy. Large dinners could not be held, though small groups, like those led by Crébillon fils did meet at the *"Pelletier"* and the *"Caveau."* Cafés had begun to appear under the Regency but club life like that of England was never able to develop.

But a series of remarkable women appeared in France, after the death of the Regent, to carry on and perfect the salons which had begun in XVIIc. They were intelligent and competitive, witty or audacious, sometimes beautiful; many were born less to the aristocracy than connected with the higher administrative *gens de la robe,* the recently ennobled rich bourgeoisie.

There were completely aristocratic salons like the duke de Chartres' at the Palais-Royal, and the prince de Conti's at the Temple; salons of financiers like Grimaud de la Reynière, whose wife, nobly allied but not received at court, drew the court to her superb table. A salon filled with talent was presided over by a cook's beautiful daughter, Mme. Briffaud, whose husband was ennobled through the influence of Mme. du Barry.

The society which these women drew to their salons varied, but it was good of its kind, much of it risen by real capacity, and it was made up of both sexes. By the contrivance of women in salons, men became princes of the Church, ministers of state, members of the Academy, or were protected, as was Voltaire by Mme. de Richelieu to whom the Keeper of the Seals gave word of measures proposed against him.

One of the earliest XVIIIc. salons was that of Mme. de Tencin, d.1749, daughter of the president of the provincial parliament of Grenoble. She had been forced to take vows, but contrived to be released from them by 1714, and became a novelist. The suicide of one of her lovers in her own house broke up her earlier witty and dissolute salon. Literary men like Montesquieu, Marivaux and Fontenelle, whom she called "mes bêtes," and foreigners (like Chesterfield whom she was the first to entertain) enjoyed the good food and conversation of her later salon, in which she intrigued successfully to make her brother a cardinal.

Of Mme. de Geoffrin (1699-1777), who visited her death-bed, Mme. de Tencin said: "The cunning little woman has come to see whether she cannot inherit my property." In 1748 Mme. de Geoffrin, wife of a rich manufacturer, established a Monday dinner for artists and a Wednesday evening for literary men and the Encyclopedists at which the food was extremely simple; she entertained Walpole and Hume; the marvellous conversationalist, Mme. de Boufflers; and Mlle. de Lespinasse. Catherine of Russia tried to lure her to exhibit French intelligence and polish at St. Petersburg.

Her rival was the more aristocratic salon, from 1740, of the Marquise du Deffand (1697-1780), that intelligent "monster of wit," although her education had been "very irregular, very incomplete." Her original salon included Voltaire, Montesquieu, d'Alembert, the president Hénault, and the duchess of Choiseul. Becoming blind in 1754, she took Mlle. de Lespinasse as her companion, but broke with her on discovering that the companion was receiving her own friends at an earlier hour. The Encyclopedists

in a body followed Mlle. de Lespinasse. Whereupon Mme. du Deffand, bitter and spiteful, entertained no literary men until, at 68, she met Horace Walpole. It was to him, whom she loved with fantastic maternal tenderness, that she wrote her letters, in a prose that is "with Voltaire, the purest classic of its century, without even excepting any of the greatest writers." (Sainte-Beuve). To his care, she left her dog *Tonton,* who was "only vicious when beside his mistress."

There were others, like the overcrowded salon of Mme. Dupin de Forcalquier which Rousseau frequented; and that of old Mme. Doublet de Persan, who in 40 years never left her apartment in the wing of a convent, but learned everything, much of it "intolerably indiscreet," and sent it out over Europe in her "Nouvelles à la main," copied by her lackeys, despite the efforts of her nephew, the minister Choiseul.

1780. XVIIIc. 1718-9. French. (Metropolitan Museum.) *Antoine Watteau.* Le Mezzetin.

1781. XVIIIc. 1719-21. French. (Metropolitan Museum.) *Antoine Watteau.* The French Comedians.

Watteau's training with a theatrical scene painter and with Gillot gave him an abiding interest in the theater, dance and Italian comedy, which was perpetuated by his fellow-student Lancret, his pupil Pater, and the rest of his school.

Everyone is in love with the theater. From the court down, everybody acts. Every well-to-do merchant must have a private theater built into his house. Great ladies, who would not have spoken to an actor a century before, fight duels with each other over actor lovers, as ladies have already begun to do in England with the Restoration.

The Théatre Français is now installed in its own playhouse in the rue des Fossés; its sets and costumes in the style of Bérain with persistent and enormous court wigs and dramatic exaggeration. The wardrobe, as in England, is helped out by donations of royal robes of state.

In the center of the picture are the leading actors, Pierre Tronchin de Beaubourg (c. 1662-1725) and Mlle. Clairon (1670-1748), who still shout in the grandiloquent, posturing style detested by Voltaire, which will begin to disappear with Adrienne Lecouvreur and her successors.

To the left, the tragic figure of the Confidante weeps. Paul Poisson, as the comedy figure of Crispin, mounts the stairs to the right.

Mezzotino, one of the comedy servant-characters, whose costume is apt to be patterned, wears satin in the stripes which the e.XVIIIc. loved.

1782. XVIIIc. 1720. French. (Berlin, Charlottenburg Palace.)

A. Watteau. Gersaint's Signboard.

Gersaint was a picture dealer on the Pont Notre-Dame. It was in his arms that Watteau died, a year after painting him a signboard, of which we see both sides here.

It shows the costume of gentlefolk and of working people in all its grace and from many angles. Smooth little heads carry caps which are usually tiny. Flowing sacques, often sleeveless (4) hang in pleats or are bunched up in back (6). They are tied (9) or hang loose (13) in front. A low neck is apt to be filled in somewhat with a twisted cravat of the Steinkirk variety (9); the XVIIIc. is filled with scarves and tippets.

The locks of the gentlemen's wigs begin to be knotted at the bottom. Fullness in the coat-skirts is massed below a button at the waist of the side seam; an additional ripple between side seam and center back is provided by the cut (7). The skirts of both coat and waistcoat begin to flare (5). Pockets rise

1783

1784

1785

and are now always set horizontally.

The form of the shirt is shown on the workman (3). Coats worn by workmen are shorter and straighter, and their waistcoats almost vest-like (1). Béret-like striped caps, such as the one worn by (2) are seen on dancing gentlemen in the Lancret *fêtes champêtres* of the 30's.

1783. XVIIIc. 1722-4. French. (Madrid, Prado.)
   N. de Largillière. Infanta Anna Victoria.

1784. XVIIIc. c. 1724. French. (Versailles, National Museum.)

Att. to *A. S. Belle.* Anna Victoria, daughter of Philip V.

The bride intended for Louis XV was his cousin, the Infanta, b. 1718, who was sent to be brought up in France in 1722. She thought that the king was handsome, but that he talked no more than her doll. The young king's state was in every way so disquieting that it seemed advisable to marry him immediately to someone able to bear children; in 1725 the too-young infanta was returned to Spain.

We see her in a French gown of jewelled satin and lace, with her parted hair dressed high in points and *favorites* at each temple. The other dress is a modification of the heavily braid-trimmed basques of XVIIc. Spanish court costume.

The small uncovered head of the upper classes in e.XVIIIc. is trimmed with bouquets, delicate garlands and small bows; in court wear, a curl is usually brought over the shoulder.

1785. XVIIIc. French. (Versailles, National Museum.)

A. S. Belle. Catherine Elénore Eugénie de Béthisy and her brother, Eugene Elénore de Béthisy.

Mlle. de Béthisy wears a gauzy embroidered apron, its bib in the form of a stomacher, over a simply cut gown of brocade. Its heavy pattern shows an admixture of Far Eastern motifs. With hair dressed high and a fan, she is dressed like a grown woman.

Her brother, still in diapers, wears approximately the same braided gown we have seen on Louis XIV's grand and great-grandsons; the plumed turban has altered into a form of embroidered man's nightcap.

1786. XVIIIc. c. 1725. French. (Florence, Pitti Palace.)

J. F. de Troy. Louis XV and his sister.

Both *Vanloo* and *de Troy* belonged to dynasties of French painters.

Nicolas de Troy had sons, Jean and François; and the latter, a son, Jean-François (1679-1752), who studied in Italy and became an Academician on his return. The Cochins and other engravers have reproduced his paintings.

The Vanloos of Aix were Jacques; his son Louis; the latter's sons: Jean-Baptiste (1684-1745), and Carle-André (1705-65); and their nephews, Louis-Michel and François (the latter of whom died young while studying in Italy, together with his uncles). J.-B. Vanloo painted important portraits in England, 1734-42.

Carle Vanloo, while at Turin, married the daughter of a musician named Sommis. Mme. Vanloo had an enchanting voice and did much to popularize Italian music in France; a picture by Vanloo at Versailles shows the family group exercising their various talents. Diderot says that Vanloo, an Academician in 1634: "could neither read nor write; he was born a painter as one is born an apostle."

Louis' full-skirted court costume, of plain material, with small buttons and deep, open cuffs, is more elaborately trimmed than ordinary dress. Braided seams have almost completely disappeared except in livery wear; delicate embroidery now follows edges and outlines pockets, as it will continue to do on coats as long as embroidery is used, and on waistcoats and occasionally on vests, into XIXc. With the conservatism of court wear, Louis is shown in a full-bottomed wig; handsomely clocked stockings; square-toed, red-heeled shoes, buckled high over a square tongue. The wig and shoes of everyday wear are shown on the suitor in illustration 1788.

The little princess wears an embroidered and lace-edged gauzy apron with a stomacher-shaped bib, over a trained dress of heavily patterned brocade; hair drawn high and dressed with small flowers (1786).

1787. XVIIIc. French. (Versailles, National Museum.)

J. B. Vanloo. Maria Leczynska, Queen of France.

The health of the five-year-old orphan who became Louis XV was so poor that it was not considered safe to subject him to much education. He became a neurotic child, silent and willful, badly brought up and malicious, who tortured his servants and threw messy food at people who bored him. His chief amusements were hunting, cooking and embroidery.

His health improved at adolescence, but it was thought advisable to have him marry immediately. A census was made of 100 suitable persons; nearly half were over 24; about a third were too young; 10 were too poor. The list was narrowed to 17, and eventually reduced to the Regent's sisters and the English princesses; but Anne of England refused to become Catholic, and one of the Bourbon princesses became a nun.

A princess who had been discarded as too poor was the eventual choice. The 21-year-old daughter of Stanislas Leczynska, exiled King of Poland, had been hidden in an oven, lost and found again in a stable, during her parents' flight. Going to her wedding she was almost drowned in the mud through which her coach drove.

The population was starving, but the courtiers wore stockings of pure gold thread, costing 200 livres, at the wedding, and the king was dressed in gold brocade with diamond buttons and a mantle of gold *point d'espagne*. The new queen gave away the contents of a velvet coffer of jewels she had received, saying that it was the first time in her life that she had ever been able to give presents. (Comte Fleury: *Louis XV et les petites maîtresses,* Plon, Nourrit, Paris, 1899.)

Louis, who had never shown any interest in women, was charmed with his wife. Unfortunately, she was very inhibited and in her own way as neurotic as he. She was afraid of ghosts, had to be read to sleep, slept under so many comforters that the king could not endure it, and got in and out of bed all night long to look after her dog.

She was a worthy and devout woman but, as her father said, she and her mother were the two most boring queens he had ever met. While her father reigned as Duke of Lorraine, his daughter bore Louis some nine children, and lived as much as possible in the three little rooms of her private apartment. The king, when he had to visit her, killed flies on the window pane. The burden of trying to amuse the newly awakened boy, who was never amused by anything, fell on a succession of mistresses: the whole series of the sisters de Nesle; Mme. de Pompadour who succeeded longest; and Mme. du Barry, as the king's taste descended the social scale.

The queen passed her time with a clavichord, music, and books; a little print shop; painting and drawing materials; a spinning wheel, loom and embroidery frame. She once decided to make four panels for a Chinese room. She actually filled in only some of the simpler parts of the background; her teacher stood at her elbow, directing every stroke, and repaired her work while she was at mass. As "her

own work," she bequeathed the panels to the Countess de Noailles, who built a new pavilion to house them, and had written over the door, "The innocent falsehood of a good princess." (Mme. Campan.)

The queen's gown also shows court conservatism. It is of brocade in a heavy *candelabre* pattern, but while it is worn with hoops, its overskirt is caught back, though only once, in a way reminiscent of the bustled dresses of Louis XIV's court. A trailing cloak, semé France and lined with ermine, is carried by a turbaned attendant; braid applied on sleeves of coat below shoulder indicate its livery character.

Like the lady in the following illustration, the queen's very short cap sleeve is pleated into the armseye, although in court wear the lingerie of the lower arm is formally pleated. The fitted bodice of this period is smooth and round, with the form of the old stomacher sketched upon it, by a series of graduated clasps or bows, or, particularly in the case of children, by the transparent V-shaped bib of the apron.

1788. XVIIIc. French. (Berlin, Kaiser Friedrich Museum.) *J. F. de Troy*. Déclaration. (1724)

The lady wears a sacque of wide-striped brocade, falling loose from the shoulders in front pleats, and unbuttoned low to show the bow-trimmed corset: short sleeves cartridge-pleated into the armseye; flower studded hair; bracelet of black ribbon with a medallion; mules.

The suitor shows an interesting, deep, open cuff on a stiffly flaring coat with high-set pockets. The large buttons of Louis XIV are replaced on the plain coat and brocade waistcoat by a multitude of much smaller ones. Breeches finished with a band fit smoothly over the stockings. Shoes have a much reduced tongue and heel, and small oval buckles. The wig is tied back with a bow, from which the ribbon of the *solitaire* surrounds the stock.

1789. XVIIIc. French. (Met. Mus., Print Room.) *Jean Pillement* (1727-1808). *Chinoiseries.*

1789

1790. XVIIIc. French. (Metropolitan Mus., Print Room.)
J. J. Avril, after *Pillement*. Baroque Flowers.

1791. XVIIIc. French. (New York, Cooper Union Mus.)
Pillement. Fleurs Idéales.

1792. XIXc. 1830-70. English. (Metropolitan Mus.)
Roller printed cotton: pheasants and palms.

1793. XIXc. 1837-51. English. (Metropolitan Mus.)
Printed percale.

Persistence of the influence of Pillement, and of
the motifs which inspired his delightful designs, of
which the strange greens, brickish pinks, and yellows

should be looked at in their original form of raised
and colored engraving. Their effect, further debased,
is still visible in XIXc. cottons.

1794. XVIIIc. 1728. French. (Metropolitan Mus.)
B. Picart. "Enée et Lavinie," by de Fontenelle.

1795. XVIIIc. 1734. French. (Versailles National Mus.)
J. Raoux. Marie Françoise Perdrigion (Mme. Etienne Paul Boucher d'Orsay) as a Vestal.

In the course of a quarrel with the chevalier de
Rohan, Voltaire was imprisoned in the Bastille; on
his release in 1726, he exiled himself for two years in
England where he came to know all the important

literary and theatrical figures. The English stage of
the Restoration owed much to France; Voltaire returned with fresh ideas from England.

The tradition of boxes built and spectators seated
directly up on the stage as a part of the decor lost
force earlier in England than in France. A stage occupied only by actors was one of the English ideas
imposed on the French theatre by Voltaire; groups of
extras "dress" the sides of the stage in the tragic opera
by LeBovier de Fontenelle and Colasse, while the important action takes place in the center, against effects of belching smoke and fire, monsters and
emerging deities, which were a legacy from XVIIc.

But in the rivalry between Crébillon père, backed
by Mme. de Pompadour, and Voltaire, the exaggerated horrors of the former's tragedies were replaced
by the more reasonable stateliness of Voltaire's. A
whole generation of comparatively simple, natural
actors arose, and stage costume began to be affected
by the pretty simplicity of every-day dress. The stark
simplicity of Mlle. Perdrigion's satin gown is more
theatrically effective than plumes, scrolls, lace and
fringe inherited from Louis XIV.

1796. XVIIIc. French. (Metropolitan Mus.)
J. B. J. *Pater.* Comical March.

1797. XVIIIc. French. (Paris, G. Petit Coll., formerly J.
    Fairfax Murray.)
Nicolas Lancret. Danse champêtre.

1798. XVIIIc. c. 1730. French. (Washington Nat. Gall.
    of Art.)
N. *Lancret.* La Camargo Dancing.

1799. XVIIIc. French. (Detroit Inst. of Arts.)
N. *Lancret.* Breakfast of a Hunting Party.

Lancret (1690-1743) and Watteau were fellow students with Gillot. The enormously prolific lesser
painter outlived Watteau to become a successful
Academician.

Pater (1695-1736) was a pupil of Watteau, dismissed and then sent for again for a month's instruction when Watteau knew he was dying.

Marie Anne de Cupis (1710-70), who danced under the name of her Spanish grandmother, Camargo,
made a sensational debut at the Paris Opera at 16.
She had an enormous repertory and was the first
dancer to shorten the ballet skirt, to show her tiny
feet, which made the fortune of her shoemaker.
Everything she wore was copied; there was an epi-
demic of fashions *à la Camargo.*

The diagonal closing line, shown on the bodice of
Mlle. Perdrigion's bodice, is indicated on La Camargo's costume by a rope of its flowered trim.

Ladies' "sportswear" in the 30's is of three sorts:

Many wear jackets with slashed, flaring peplums
(1797,A; 1798,B). These usually have long, plain,
close-fitting sleeves; a wide, low neckline; and a bodice trimmed with a series of graduated bows. They
are worn with short, hooped skirts, which are usually striped in some way; woven stripes are used vertically (1797,A); braid stripes are applied horizontally at the hem or around edges (1798,B). When
two skirts appear, vertical stripes are used on the
underskirt (1797,E) or as a lining to the underskirt.

For riding, women wear men's coats and waistcoats, cut with an exaggerated flare, and men's tricornes.

Women also wear ordinary dress in the country: a

1800

smooth bodice, laced in back (1798,F); sleeves of elbow length, finished with ruffles (1798,F and K). A
ruche about the neck (1798,K) is often worn with
this dress. The hair is dressed up, formally, and may
even be powdered.

In "sportswear," men of the 30's often replace the
coat with a cloak (1798,A and G), worn over a but-
toned-up waistcoat with little skirts—almost a jerkin
(1798,E), often made of striped material (1798,G).

Or, coat and waistcoat are worn unbuttoned over
the full shirt, and easy breeches are actually laced
along the outer seams, with ribbons which are knotted above the knee (1797,C).

The hat most usually worn with these outdoor
country costumes is a sort of beret (1798,C), often
striped and finished with a rosette (1797,D; 1798,A
and G). Other hats are casually cocked (1798,E)
with a ribbon rosette, or trimmed with cock feathers
(1797,C; 1798,H). All forms are worn over short
wigs, usually not powdered, or over the bare, clipped head. In male riding dress, however, there is no
such informality; tricornes are worn with the wigs
and solitaires about the stock; fitted, flaring coats and
waistcoats.

1800. XVIIIc. 1731. French. (Louvre.)

J. Dumont. Mme. Mercier, nurse of Louis XV, and
her family.

A typical upper-class family in the XVIIIc. is fairly certain to have put some of its children into the
Church. The abbés and abbesses of Mme. de Genlis'
time mingle freely in society, keep carriages, entertain people of both sexes, and wear fashionable dress:
hoops, paniers, and powdered wigs, although usually
in a black-and-white, ermine-trimmed version. The
abbé is differentiated by his band collar and by his
comparatively short untied wig (E).

We see a variety of styles, appropriate to the ages
of the wearers.

The fashionable son (A) wears a wig with

pigeon's wings at the sides, and the long wound pigtail preferred by officers. His coat has the fullest possible stiffened skirts, their seam left open on the
right side to accommodate the sword, and caught together by occasional buttons (A,G). The edges of his
coat, and even its seams, are delicately embroidered.
But there is an unmistakable difference in the way
in which the XVIIc. braided style persists, almost as
a ghost, on the coat of this gentleman, while it is
heavily emphasized all over the livery coat of the
kneeling valet (K). Like his father (G), the young
man wears the muff of first half XVIIIc. slung from
his belt. His breeches close at the knee by tasseled
laces; handsomely clocked stockings are worn with
low-cut, low-heeled shoes of natural shape.

The youngest son (B) wears his solitaire tied under the chin in a bow, after a manner seen to 1750.
His waistcoat is stiffened, but as his coat is cut to
hang wide open in front, the sword does not have
to be stuck through its skirts. Pocket flaps have
mounted to the waistline.

The father carries both stick and sword, and
wears a dignified full-bottomed wig; but its top has
flattened, and its ends are knotted, whereas the wigs
of the younger men are drawn back and tied at the
nape.

Mme. Mercier (D), like her younger daughters
(F,I) wears a flowing sacque, open to the waist. The
sleeves of D and F have cuffs shaped at the bend of
the elbow by horizontal pleating; (I)'s sacque has
long, fitted sleeves.

The younger the woman, the more simple does the
treatment of her dress and head become. Mme. Mercier covers her hair with a cap; she wears a ruche
about her throat, and a fur tippet. The somewhat
younger woman (I) has a little frilled lappet hanging from hair dressed in curls at the side and a bun
in back. The ribbon with a jewel about her throat,
the embroidered scarf, the drawstring bag for her

1801

tatting, and her high-heeled, embroidered mules with peaked toes are characteristic of this period. Her gown is of a sprigged brocade; that of (H) is plain, but heavily trimmed with a garland. The hair of the youngest girl (F) is simply drawn up with a posy, and her completely plain sacque has a finished armseye. The sleeves we see are fastened to the undergarment.

1801. XVIIIc. French.

Nicolas de Larmessin, after *Lancret*. The Four Times of Day: Morning.

It is quite suitable to pour out the breakfast cup for a visiting abbé, in negligée: little cape or combing jacket, chemise, corset, brocade or embroidered petticoat and mules.

The maid brings a lace-lappeted cap. Servants, bourgeoises and older women now wear caps, but the cap is still primarily middle-class or domestic.

This is a well-to-do bourgeois household, but so young and pretty a mistress would wear a cap only with negligée. After she is dressed, her head will be bare, except for flowers.

The abbé, who keeps his hat under his arm, is almost certainly dressed in black, since he is probably making capital of his status. Except for his band collar and the comparative shortness of his toupeted wig he is dressed like any other man.

The floors are of inlaid woods; the walls hung with striped paper. The large sofa has the asymmetric back of Louis XV furniture. The dressing table, hung with sheer embroidery and littered with pretty toilet things, is here still essentially the table and mirror of Louis XIV. Inlaid tables with cabriole legs, drawers, and mirrors which fold down appear under Louis XV. Occasional tables appear with the advent of tea, coffee and chocolate, and pretty china cups, which do not yet have handles.

1802   1803   1804   1805

1802-05. XVIIIc. French. (Metropolitan Mus., Print Room.)

Bernard Picart. Costume plates.

1806-09. XVIIIc. 1735. French. (Metropolitan Mus., Print Room.)

Edmé Bouchardon. Cries of Paris.

Interest in exotic costume, aroused by explorations in late XVI-e.XVIIc., became extended to variations in costume in different parts of near-by countries, and by mid-XVIIc., to everyday life and common people near home.

Picart (1673-1733) was a Frenchman who worked in Amsterdam as well as Paris. He records such variations as the costume worn by pious girls under Jesuit supervision at Antwerp, who are dedicated to virginity until marriage and to the care of their parents during illness; a peasant girl in the costume of Brabant; a milk-seller on the outskirts of Paris; and a water-vendor of the city itself, in e-XVIIIc.

Nothing can equal the teeming life of London as Hogarth shows it, but at about the same time, Bouchardon's various series provide the best illustrations of the people of Paris streets.

The bewigged shoe mender is preparing to replace buttons on high spatterdashes which close by a series of pointed tabs.

The drink-vendor shows a diagonally closed coat. If left unbuttoned, its flaps would approximate lapels. These will not appear in France until late in the century, but the idea is germinating everywhere.

The poor Auvergnat knife-sharpener wears one old pair of thick stockings over another, thrust into backless slippers.

The hooded proprietress of the magic lantern carries a bodice, the boned goring of which is actually made decorative.

1810. XVIIIc. 1739. French. (Louvre.)
François Boucher. The Breakfast (detail).

1811. XVIIIc. 1743. French. (Metropolitan Mus., Frick Coll.)
F. Boucher. Portrait of his Wife (detail).

Boucher (1703-70), son of a designer of embroideries, was first trained as an etcher-engraver-illustrator, and executed some of the finest plates in Watteau's "Figures de différents caractères." His later studies in Italy affected not only his painting but the course of XVIIIc. book ornamentation. He became a successful painter on his return in 1731, was made Inspector of the Gobelins Factory, and in 1765, court painter. Besides portraits of Mme. de Pompadour, he executed large decorative projects to her order.

Both rooms show the charming interiors in which the well-to-do bourgeoisie live under Louis XV. The family breakfast takes place in front of a great mirror, panelled in blue-green and framed in gold, set over a pink marble mantle against coral-painted walls, and reflecting a blue-green door. The floors are inlaid parquet.

Furniture is light and comfortable, caned or upholstered; its lines are flowing and graceful; upholstery has lost the heavy brocaded patterns and colors of Louis XIV. Upholstered bergère armchairs or chaises longues with fat cushions and plump footstools have the same curved cabriole legs which are shown on an infinity of little night, tea, sewing and dressing tables, and on the chests of drawers, commodes, and consoles, which often have marble tops.

The breakfast chocolate is being drunk from a table in red and black lacquer. There are all sorts of standing and hanging shelves and cabinets to hold bits of oriental porcelain, trinkets and books. There are ormulu clocks and candles in scrolled gilt sconces.

Light screens fold in the old way, or are set on poles, particularly in England. They are papered, embroidered, painted or lacquered in bright colors and scenes, and are set against painted or papered walls.

A little girl plays with the toys which French middle-class children now enjoy, while the family breakfasts. Her beautifully dressed "baby" is propped against the cushioned footstool. The child wears a charming *bourrelet,* a padded cap, in lemon yellow, pink and white, and a bright, deep blue *robe à la française* with short cuffed sleeves (see Ill. 1810).

Watching her, a lady in white wears a short coral colored sacque and little black velvet hood over a lace cap set over a bunch of rosebuds. Baby in deep rose, sits on the lap of its mother in deep, rich blue; her

hair still cut rather short, and massed in rolled curls in back; black velvet bows at wrist and throat, tied with pink bow. Man with lightly powdered hair which appears to be his own, carefully dressed, wears a pistachio-green coat with an open cuffless sleeve, and a shirt in a greenish-yellow off-white.

Mme. Boucher lies in an enchanting white muslin negligée, with rose ribbons on cap and neck ruching, and a rose bodice trimmed with the shirred bands which are a characteristic decoration of second to final quarter century. A rose velvet workbag lies on the footstool, and her *chatelaine* watch is hung on the wall as a boudoir clock.

1812. XVIIIc. Before 1744. French. (Met. Mus., Print Room.)

P. L. Surugue, after *Chardin.* Card Tricks.

J. B. S. Chardin (1699-1779), son of a Paris woodworker, studied with Cazes, Coypel and J. B. Vanloo, and exhibited his wonderfully realistic still-lifes outdoors in the Place Dauphine. His first wife, who also came of working people, died in 1735, leaving him with two small children. In 1744, he married Marguerite Pouget, a well-to-do bourgeois widow, thrifty and intelligent. She took admirable care of his finances, and became like him, the intimate of Diderot, Rameau, Cochin and Aved. It was the latter fellow-artist who is supposed to have teased Chardin into portraiture, saying it was not so easy as painting sausages. Chardin became the most notable painter of the bourgeoisie in the intimacy of their homes; he became an Academician in 1728, and later its treasurer.

The bourgeoise will not join church and nobility in political power, as the Third Estate, until final quarter XVIIIc. It is now divided into three envious grades, many individuals of which are succeeding in rising above their original status.

The *gens de la robe,* judges and parliamentarians, administrators, tax-collectors and financiers, are rich and powerful. But even when recently ennobled or allied with the aristocracy by the marriage of their women, they are not received at court. Rather than risk rebuffs, they dine, discuss and play cards among themselves in a stiff, formal and rather heavy society. Their wives' imitations of Versailles fashions are apt to be tastelessly exaggerated. Because they are diligent, competent, respectable and home-loving, make money and pay bills, the thriftless and indebted aristocracy has mocked them from Molière's time: *Laissons les bons bourgeois se plaire en leur ménage.*

They are envied by the comfortable minor officials and tradesmen below them. These, in turn, are hated by the fermenting mass of workmen, servants, peasants and beggars.

In a household in the comfortable middle section of the bourgeoisie, we see the wig with pigeon's wings at the ears, tied high above the nape of the neck; that of the young man is encased in an oblong bag. His high tricorne has an irregular laced edge. The plain coat, trimmed only by buttons, has a standing collar, easy sleeves with large closed cuff, full skirts with the pocket flap set at the natural waistline. Breeches are closed both by buttons and by a buckled band with a long fringed end. The buckled closing is stressed on the shoe, its tongue and heel low.

The boy is just back from school, with drawstring bag and triangular striped apron tied about him, its bib-end caught in an upper coat button. His sister, in a ribbon-trimmed cap, shows the familiar reversed position in which the triangular bib is set on a girl's apron, following the line of a stomacher.

Typical light-weight, everyday chair of Louis XV, with decorative ladder-back slats and rush seat; tile floor; rug used as a table cover, in the manner of the past two centuries.

1813-14. XVIIIc. c. 1744. French. (Louvre.)

J. B. S. Chardin. Grace Before Meals (1813). The Industrious Mother (1814).

The typical bourgeoise head is always covered by some form of cap or hood. The child with folded hands wears the padded *bourrelet* (or *bourlet*), bound about the head by a protective sausage roll; it is usually brightly colored, and is worn over a close white cap.

Bourgeois women and children of both sexes wear aprons, often colored; those of women have a small square bib. White fichus cross at the bosom of plain

or striped dresses; cuffs are pleated across the inner elbow. While men's shoes are becoming plain, buckled black pumps, these housewives go about their work in pretty embroidered slippers and mules with pointed toes and the highest of heels.

The condition of children is greatly improved all over Europe, although the most fortunate probably belong to just such middle class French households as these. Children have many more toys. Dolls, called "babies" in the XVIIIc., drums, woolly animals to be dragged on a string, appear in almost every picture, and are as lovingly painted by Chardin as gleaming copper, pewter, silver and china, good furniture, and handsomely made odd pieces like the reel for the housewive's thread or the footstool she uses as a pincushion.

1815. XVIIIc. French. (Metropolitan Mus., Print Room.)

H. F. Gravelot. Pen drawing (detail).

The engravers of XVIIIc. find much employment in illustrations, vignettes and end pieces for the books which are seen lying open in so many French paintings. Everybody reads novels, which were first written in final quarter XVIIc. by Mme. de La Fayette and continued by Marivaux' "Marianne" and l'Abbé Prévost's "Manon Lescaut," and eventually by Rousseau's "Nouvelle Héloïse" and "Emile"; Voltaire's satires, plays, moral tales, fables and chansons.

Gravelot (1699-1773), a French draftsman-engraver, lived mostly in England c.1734-54, and greatly influenced English book illustration by his work for editions of Dryden and Richardson.

This pen drawing is one of a preliminary series for book illustrations, belonging to the Metropolitan Museum. It shows the carved and gilded *boiseries* of a rich Louis XV bedroom, an *ormulu* clock, one of the delicate three-legged pedestal tea tables, set on a carpet made in France.

The nurse wears a little flat hat tied over a close cap, neck ruche and apron, with the plain bodice, pleated cuff, and swelling, round skirt of midXVIIIc. The mother lies in the cap appropriate to her lacy, beribboned negligée.

1816. XVIIIc. 1739. French. (Louvre.)

Louis Tocqué. Louis of France.

Louis Tocqué (1696-1772), son of an architectural painter, studied with Rigaud, and became, with Lar-

gillière, the most successful painter of the rich bourgeoisie. Unlike Nattier, whose eldest daughter he
married, Tocqué managed his money very well. After
painting the queen, the Dauphin and Dauphines, he
made a triumphal tour of the courts of Northern
Europe, painting the Russian Empress in 1757, and
the Danish rulers in 1759 and 1769.

The wig of the Dauphin, father of Louis XVI,
shows the necessary court compromise between the
full-bottomed wig of Louis XIV and the neatly got-
ten-out-of-the-way wig of ordinary use. He wears the
cordon bleu over a red coat, the open cuffs of which
accord with the brocaded white satin waistcoat. The

heavy embroidery with which it is edged shows the
midXVIIIc. tendency toward massive decoration,
with edges of frogs and tassels. With the conservatism of court styles, his clocked white hose continue
to be rolled and gartered over the knees, and his dia-
mond-buckled shoes retain red heels, though they
approach the every-day form.

The Dauphin, the most intelligent of Louis XV's
children, encouraged his sisters to improve their de-
fective convent educations. The globe indicates his
interest in geography, an inherited passion of that
adept map-maker, Louis XVI.

1817. XVIIIc. French. (New York, Mrs. George F. Baker.)
N. Lancret, d. 1743. Park of the Petit Trianon.

Even at Versailles there had to be certain informal spots. Louis XIV had transformed his father's
hunting pavilion into a dairy-menagerie, where the
little duchess of Burgundy loved to have supper.
The Petit Trianon of Louis XV had a botanical garden; a little house of Sèvres porcelain was built there
for Mme. de Pompadour; and eventually the Hamlet, in which Marie Antoinette played at farmer's
wife.

Exotic modes of transport had always been provided at Versailles: gondolas; gilded barges; rolling
chairs like those on the Atlantic City boardwalk today, in which Louis XV was pushed as a weak boy.
Here we see ladies being drawn in a little gilded
chariot by four mastiffs.

The costume suitable for strolling or picnicking in
the woods remains substantially that shown in
earlier Lancret pictures. The skirts have become fuller. The hair, formerly bare or dressed with flowers,
now has a tiny cap or triangle of lingerie. Men wear
wigs, powdered and tied, unpowdered and flowing,
or the cropped head, in beret or high-crowned cap,
without any wig.

1818-20. XVIIIc. French. (Metropolitan Mus., Print Room.)

Jean Rigaud. Diverses vues.

1818. Chapel of the chateau of Versailles.
Rigaud (1700-54) specialized in engravings of chateaux and parks.

The courtyard in front of the palace of Versailles had been railed in blue and gold in 1680. Its entrances from three roadways were guarded by soldiers. The main entrance from the avenue leading straight to Paris was used only by the royal family and princes of the blood. Carriages of the nobility who had been granted the "Privileges of the Louvre" were admitted by the side gates, where we see a two-horse carriage approaching. Everyone else alighted and walked, or was carried for 6 sous in one of the "blue chairs" with blue-liveried carriers which were provided by a concessionnaire. There was coach service twice a day between Paris and Versailles, and carriages and horses for hire. Any respectably dressed person was admitted to the palace.

1819. Basin of Neptune in the gardens of Versailles.

There has never been enough water at Versailles to keep the fountains playing continuously, and the Basin of Neptune is only one consumer, although one of the largest, with its allegorical figures spouting between six 60-foot jets and 22 smaller ones. People have always turned out for the spectacle; just as two-wheeled carts working on the estate found reason, in the middle of the XVIIIc., to cross beautiful coaches with an outrider and two men on the box, and a crowd which is not entirely made up of courtiers.

The rider near the coach wears a double-breasted coat, the breast flap of which, opened up, can be buttoned back and so become translated into lapels. Women's skirts have reached the limit of round size, and are beginning to be flattened into greater width.

1820. Wing of the chateau of Fontainebleau, from the Court of Fountains.

Francis I had poured his joyous vitality into the building and wonderful interior embellishments of his palace at Fontainebleau; Henry IV extended it. Lenôtre designed the parterre, beyond the pond, but under Louis XIV, so preoccupied with Versailles, the court merely moved to Fontainebleau in the autumn, to play tennis and *mail,* as it moved to Compiègne in the spring to review army manoeuvres. Christine of Sweden lived there after abdication, in 1656-7, and eventually it became a favorite residence again under Napoleon I.

Undisturbed by the painted, gilded and canopied pleasure boat, the carp of Fontainebleau were as huge, old, greedy, and fun to watch and feed as they are today.

1821. Mid-XVIIIc. French-Polish. (London, Victoria and Albert Mus.)

Moreau le jeune. Lady in a Sedan Chair (detail).
The frame of this picture is surmounted by the arms of the Leczynski family. Its background may show the palace of Willanow, near Warsaw. Its figures wear Polish and French dress of midXVIIIc.

Liveried servants and chairmen: striped red and white coats, edged with gold; legs protected by spatterdashes.

Lady: pale pink with pale green overdress.

Man bowing to kiss her hand: white coat, gold brocaded edge; blue hose; ribbon and medal of an order.

Bearded man with clipped head and beard, facing chair: gray cloak, blue and yellow sash, brown boots.

Man wearing the Golden Fleece and looking very like John Sobieski, the Polish king who has been dead for about half a century: gold armor and gray boots under a dark green frogged coat with a brown fur collar. These coats, brought to Western Europe by the Hungarian hussars, will become a striking fashion of e.XIXc.

Courtier in French dress, at ext.r.: white-figured red coat, Order of the St.-Esprit, white hose, black shoes.

Negro page with leashed and belled pugs: white turban, gold doublet, blue-green hose.

1822-23. XVIIIc. 1745. French. (Paris. Bibl. de l'Arsenal.)
C. N. Cochin. Jeu de Roi (1822). Bal paré (1823).

The intimate family groups of early XVIIIc., give way to great, gregarious entertainments in mid-XVIIIc.

At Versailles, gambling is still restricted to those who have the entrée; less formal courts like Marly are degenerating into gambling-houses, thronged by black-clad chevaliers of Louis XIV's military order of Saint-Louis, and other uninvited men who drive out from Paris.

Walpole writes from Paris, 1739, that it is dishonorable in France not to be in the army, but "no dishonor to keep public gaming houses. There are at least a hundred and fifty people of the first quality in Paris who live by it. You may go into their houses at all hours of the night, and find hazard, pharaoh, etc. The men who keep the hazard-table at the duke de Gesvre's pay him twelve guineas each night for the privilege. Even the princesses of the blood are dirty enough to have shares in the banks kept at their houses."

Walpole notes at the same time the excessive use of a very dark shade of rouge, and at a later time, 1763, the "dissonance of parade and poverty" among the French nobility even at Versailles. The duke of Praslin's footmen are "powdered from break of day," but wait behind him with red pocket handkerchiefs about their necks.

The smaller rooms of Versailles overheated quickly with crowds and candles, so that ladies are always afraid of committing the unforgivable fault of fainting. But the great hall of mirrors remains glacial. Men carrying muffs show decoration, which reinforces the vent of spreading coat-skirts, carried up the c. back seam. Court wigs are usually untied, and show two long and one short center lock.

The small, flower-dressed head of short hair is giving way in French court use to caps with lappets falling over massed, trailing curls. Enormously distended hoops, becoming flattened, display a petticoat scalloped with ruching; the overskirt is reduced to a train matching the darker bodice.

1824. XVIIIc. 1746. French. (New York, Cooper Union Mus.)

Surugue, after *Ch. Coypel*. Mme.** in a ball gown.

1825. XVIIIc. 1748. French. (Neuilly-sur-Seine, Weill Coll.)

J. B. Perroneau (1715-83). Duchesse d'Ayen.

Mme. de Maintenon arranged a marriage between her niece Françoise and the Marshal de Noailles, brother of her dear friend the Cardinal.

Two sons born of that marriage became Marshals of France; their lives and those of their descendants show the various fates of the aristocracy during the Revolution.

Louis, the witty elder son, duke d'Ayen until his father's death in 1766, refused to emigrate, and died of old age the year before his wife (nearly a half century older than we see her here), his daughter-in-law, and one of his granddaughters were executed in 1794. His son returned from Switzerland as a peer, on the Restoration.

The younger son and more distinguished general, Philippe, duke de Mouchy, and his wife, first lady of honor to Marie Antoinette, were both executed in 1792. Both their sons had been members of the States General in 1789; both emigrated. The elder, the prince de Poix, returned to France in 1800. The younger, viscount de Noailles, had served under Lafayette in America, and was one of the young aristocrats who had voted for the abolition of privilege in 1789. He returned to America, worked in a bank in Philadelphia, then served the English in San Domingo under Rochambeau, and died in a sea battle off Havana in 1804.

Lafayette had married a Noailles, granddaughter of the duchesse d'Ayen shown here. He had designed the tricolor cockade of the Republic, had been offered the command of the newly formed National Guard, and had ordered the capture of the fleeing royal family at Varenne on his personal responsibility. But because he was a moderate, he was declared a traitor by the Jacobins, and had to emigrate in 1792.

Mme.**, in Coypel's pastel, is supposed to be Mme. de Mouchy, "virtuous, pious, charitable, and irreproachable," who was so concerned with details of the correct wearing of capes and cap-lappets, that Marie Antoinette nicknamed her "Madame Etiquette." "Arrange all these matters, Madame, just as you please, but do not imagine that a queen born Archduchess of Austria can attach the importance to them which might be felt by a Polish princess who had become Queen of France." Mme. de Noailles decreed that lappets should hang; when Mme. Campan did not understand her signals, it was the Queen who whispered: "Let down your lappets or the countess will expire." Marie Antoinette was a child of the age to come, in her impatience with minutiae of etiquette, and her attempts to live as a human being among friends. This freedom was bitterly resented at court, and helped to bring down the regime.

Madame Campan, whose Memoirs tell us so much about court life under Louis XV-XVI, and who loyally loved and served Marie Antoinette, was condemned, but was saved by 9 Thermidor, to become head of two schools which Napoleon established for the education of the young womenfolk of his heroes. Her republican brother, Girondist ambassador to the U.S., was recalled by Robespierre, but stayed in America as Citizen Genêt and married the daughter of Gov. Clinton of New York.

Mme. de Mouchy's ball gown shows a modification of the long sleeve of the second quarter century, with the passementerie, fringe and tassels so much used during the next quarter, and the black ribbon about the neck, which tends to become a lacy ruching in the latter period.

The little lacy triangle, *cornette,* of Lancret's day is commemorated in the point of the cap which grew from it, shown in Mme. d'Ayen's pastel portrait. Her loose dress, pleated at shoulder and cuff, opens over a *corps* with stepped bows. The low neck is generally covered or filled; in this case, by a froth of lace and a neckband. Taffeta apron. Cane backed chair.

1826

1826. XVIIIc. c. 1755. French. (Versailles Nat. Mus.— original at the Chateau d'Ew.)

L. M. Van Loo (copy). The Cup of Chocolate.

The Goncourts in "The Woman of the Eighteenth Century" have pointed out the comparatively cozy, homelike intimacy of group pictures of the nobility in first half XVIIIc., in contrast to the gay, glittering, cohesive conviviality of the third quarter century pictured by Saint-Aubin and Cochin, and the earnest, apprehensive, decomposed groups spotted through the same garlanded rooms, waiting for their fate, in the final quarter.

The duke of Penthièvre, the richest man in France, appears here with his son, the prince de Lamballe. The latter's wife (who returned from safety in England to share Marie Antoinette's imprisonment in the Temple, and whose head on a pike was paraded past the queen on Sept. 3, 1792); his daughter, Mlle. de Penthièvre, (later the duchess of Orleans, whose *pouf au sentiment* is one of the most famous of all extravagant coiffures); and his mother, the countess of Toulouse, widow of a natural son of Louis XIV.

We see two typical coats of the beginning second half century: Lamballe's of an all-over diapered pattern, relatively untrimmed, on which the emblem of the Saint-Esprit is embroidered. Penthièvre's on which hangs the Golden Fleece, has thick heavy embroidery massed in relation to buttons; this will soon become frogs, braid loops and tassels.

The waistcoat is sleeveless. Its connection to the coat, through the appearance of its fabric on the coat cuff, is being lost, and it is beginning to be cut away below the waist.

The "pigeon's wings" of the wig have become a series of formal rolls. Diamond buckles cover the shoe tongue and finish the knee closing.

The loose gown, with shirred or gathered edgings, is opened wide (to accommodate hoops which are approaching their limit of round width) over short petticoats trimmed with *volants* of self material. A bow, matching those on the ladder of the *corps,* is added to a self-frill and three deep *engageantes* of lace, as a sleeve finish, in place of the old pleated cuff. Brocades, often striped, are sprigged; their colors deep pinks and sharp light blues; the bows of the *echelle* often lavender.

Hairdressing begins to show a slight elaboration and height. That of an older woman of the aristocracy will now be covered by a pleated cap, dipping in front like the Mary Queen of Scots headdress of the XVIc., though the point is unrelated in its origin.

Walls painted and carved with loves and garlands of roses; parquet floors; graceful and comfortable upholstered chairs.

1827. XVIIIc. 1754. French. (Versailles, Nat. Mus.)
J. M. Nattier. Mme. Henriette playing the cello.

1828. XVIIIc. 1756. French. (Versailles, Nat. Mus.)
J. M. Nattier. Mme. Adelaide tatting.

1829. XVIIIc. 1758. French. (Versailles, Nat. Mus.)
J. M. Nattier. Mme. Adelaide Music Lesson.

Jean-Marc Nattier (1685-1766), son of a portrait painter and a miniaturist, and father-in-law of Tocqué, had none of the latter's astuteness in money matters. He was ruined by Law's speculations in 1720, gave up historical painting which had admitted him to the Academy, and applied himself to court portraits, which are the quintessence of Louis XV's period rather than expositions of individual character. His *Mesdames de France* are almost interchangeable. He died very old in miserable poverty.

Louis' first children were twin daughters, Elizabeth and Henriette, called "Madame Première" and "Madame Seconde." Elizabeth, the only daughter

1827   1828   1829

who married at all, became the unhappy wife of Elizabeth Farnese's son, the duke of Parma, and died young of smallpox while on a visit to Versailles.

Henriette and Louis, the young duke of Chartres were in love; Argenson favored and Fleury opposed the match which would have strengthened the Orleans faction. After Louis' marriage to the princess of Bourbon-Conti, Henriette simply died of grief at 24.

Following the birth of the Dauphin and the duke d'Anjou, came a series of five daughters, born between 1732-7. Only Adelaide, the eldest, and her father's favorite, after Henriette's death, remained at court. Victoire, Sophie, Thérèse, Félicité (who died at 8), and Louise (Madame Septième, who Louis vowed was Madame Dernière), were all packed off to the abbey of Fontevrault until adolescence, to save expenses.

The king had a considerable domestic affection for his daughters, though the "thrust of the hog's snout," as the court called his habitually unkind and disturbing remarks can be seen in the nicknames he gave his daughters; which translate into something like "tatters," "sow," "rook" (which has also a connotation of raucous spitting) and "rags."

In the morning, Mme. Campan tells us, he climbed up to the apartment of Adelaide with a pot of coffee he had made himself. She rang to notify Victoire, Victoire rang Sophie, who in turn notified the lame Louise, who scurried from the farthest apartment of all, to be kissed.

At the *débotter* of the king on his return from hunting, *Mesdames* interrupted Mme. Campan's reading to throw on a strange, makeshift costume: hoop and gold-trimmed petticoat, and hooked-on train, with the upper undress concealed under a great black taffeta cloak. They were kissed, rushed back and untied their strings, and within 15 minutes altogether, were again at their embroidery, listening to Mme. Campan.

Adelaide, whose insatiable desire to learn was encouraged by her brother, was as industrious as her mother. She learned to play every musical instrument, even the horn and jew's harp, not very well, but she was once able to play for a country girls'

dance when the orchestra failed to show up. Beaumarchais' talent as a harpist helped him to entrench himself at court as her teacher. For a very short time, she was pretty. But she was brusque and harsh; it was she who first called Marie Antoinette "L'Autrichienne," which by the change of a vowel became the epithet of the populace for "the other, the alien bitch."

Victoire was pretty and kind, pious and stupid, greedy and fat. Marie Antoinette found her the kindest of the aunts. She had suffered horrors at Fontevrault, forced to say her prayers for penance in a vault in which her sister lay buried, while an insane gardener of the convent died screaming outside. On fast days she stayed up till midnight to stuff herself at 12:01 A.M. When her sister became a nun, she cried, saying, "I shall never have Louise's courage. I love the conveniences of life too well; this lounge is my destruction."

Sophie was incredibly ugly and odd, silent and shy. She tore past people, and to avoid looking at them "acquired the habit of leering on one side like a hare." She was terrified of storms and was affable and even demonstrative to the humblest person around when it thundered, although she was not even civil until the next storm.

Louise, short and deformed, was very nearly a saint. At 12, she told Mme. Campan, she was "not mistress of the whole alphabet," and learned to read with the Dauphin's help, after leaving the convent. She went out early in the morning, alone and on foot, through rain and cold in any weather, trudging from hospital to police station on her charitable errands. (The Goncourts). She kindly plied Mme. Campan with sugar water, while exhausting her with five daily sessions of reading. Then the secret came out: she was finally being allowed to become a Carmelite, and wanted to learn all the history she could before she retired to Saint-Denis. Marie Antoinette had a doll dressed as a Carmelite to prepare her daughter for the sight of her aunt's costume when the royal family went three times a year to visit Louise, and found ambitious princes of the Church thronging about what the queen called "the most intriguing little Carmelite in the kingdom." Louise told Mme.

de Genlis that the most difficult part of being a Carmelite was getting down a circular back stair alone. "I was obliged to seat myself on the steps and slide down." She had never descended even the wide stairs of Versailles without the arm of an attendant gentleman.

All the sisters loved flowers, but they had only window boxes in which to grow them, and no private place to walk, until Louis XVI settled their first incomes on his 40-year old aunts and bought them the chateau of Belville. That it cost $120,000 a year, after attempts at economy, to feed three old ladies and their households was the sort of thing that first became general knowledge with the publication of Necker's "Compte-rendu" in 1781, the first itemized statement of French government expenditures, and one of the causes of the Revolution.

Madame Adelaide tatting shows the pastime of the second and third quarter century. It preceded *purfling* (*parfiler*=unravel) of precious gold thread from brocade, epaulettes and lace, for which gentlemen provided the materials and helped in the destruction of something far more valuable than its gold-salvage worth.

Her small head, lightly powdered, is dressed with lace in a compromise between the old, uncovered head of a young aristocrat and the ubiquitous cap of the future. She carries a little lace-frilled tippet and a *ridicule* (reticule) for her handwork, with a deep rose gown, sewn with silver motifs and trimmed with lace backed with pink. At the music lesson, she wears the narrow fur trim which is also seen on men's coats in the 60's. The old round hoops have been replaced by laterally spreading supports.

The Career of Pompadour

Mme. de Pompadour (1721-64), born Jeanne Poisson, and her brother were baptized as the children of a tarnished court official; their actual father was probably the rich tax-farmer, Le Normant de Tournehem. The "king's morsel" of beauty was specifically educated at Le Normant's expense to become the king's mistress, as had been prophesied by a fortune teller. She was taught every accomplishment by the most eminent masters: music by the opera singer, Jéliotte; declamation by Crébillon; she became a dancer, a fine horsewoman, an amusing story teller, a more than good etcher and engraver, and a woman with wonderful taste in dress.

A husband was necessary to her plan; at 20 she was married to her protector's rich nephew, Le Normant d'Etiolles. She had a superb private theatre and became a leader in the society of the *haute bourgeoisie*. But that was far from court. She could only come to the king's attention by accident. As he hunted, his path was constantly crossed by a lovely horsewoman, or by a lady in pink in a blue carriage, or a lady in blue in a pink carriage, sometimes by a lady driving her own equipage. She finally met the king at a masked ball given by the city of Paris, separated from her heart-broken husband, and, as the Marquise de Pompadour, became the official successor of Mme. de Mailly in 1745.

In the year or two during which she actually was the king's mistress, and for the following two decades, she concerned herself in every detail of French politics, foreign and domestic. All state matters, all

preferment passed through her hands before reaching the king. Even her enemy d'Argenson (whose colloquial French was considered vulgar by a court used to Corneille and Racine), said it was better to have a straight and lovely nymph governing than an ugly, squatting monkey like the old Cardinal Fleury, even though pretty ladies, like white kittens, caressed you, and then bit and scratched. She aligned France with Austria, involving her in the Seven Years' War; helped in the expulsion of the Jesuits. She drew about her, protected, and subsidized men of letters of all sorts, including Voltaire and the Encyclopedists and their cronies, like her own republican physician, Quesnay, thereby playing a large part in bringing on the Revolution. She employed many artists in the embellishment of her chateaux, and was the patron of fellow-engravers; she encouraged manufactures like the porcelain of Sèvres; disposed of a great deal of France's money; and made herself indispensable to the "old paper-shuffler, who could hardly walk" (as Voltaire called Louis XV, finding it ridiculous that he should have lived and she, died.)

To keep the king amused she supervised and appeared in the performances of the palace theatre, and retained power many years after they ceased to be lovers. At 42, she was dying of tuberculosis, and trying to conceal the loss of her beauty, while abetting the transient mistresses of the Parc aux Cerfs. Louis XV was a person of habit, as Mme. de Mirepoix understood when she told the Marquise that it was her staircase the king loved; he was used to going up and down it; but if he found another woman with whom he could talk about hunting and his other concerns, it would be all the same to him in three or four days.

When Pompadour was dying (which only the royal family was allowed to do in a palace), with her extraordinary courage she had herself dressed in full court costume, and was driven off in the rain. The typically callous cruelty of the king is commemorated in the report (though it seems to be false), that he merely said: "The Marquise will not have good weather for her journey." The funeral oration of the queen's late *dame du palais* was turned, by a clever Capucin, into a eulogy of the queen herself. It was Maria Leczynska, to whom the marquise had always behaved correctly, who was most shocked by the immediate obliteration of her memory, as though she had never existed. That was the world, the queen said, and she found it scarcely worth the trouble to love it.

Diderot said that what remained of the Marquise's extravagant expenditures and meddling in government was "the Versailles treaty, which will last as it may" (it admitted English goods duty-free); "Bouchardon's Amour, which will be admired forever; a few of Guay's engraved gems, which will astonish antiquarians still unborn; a good little picture by Van Loo which will be looked at once in a while; and a pinch of ashes." With her passing there also evaporated a good deal of the resentment felt during her lifetime towards an immensely courageous and hard-working woman whose whole life, as she said, had been a combat. There were lesser women to follow her.

1831

1830. XVIIIc. 1755. French. (Louvre.)

M. Q. La Tour. Marquise de Pompadour.

Maurice Quentin La Tour (1704-88) studied with a non-Academic painter, and took up pastels which the Venetian Rosalba Carriera had made fashionable in 1720. Enormously prolific and successful, he endowed art scholarships and charitable institutions in Paris, and in his native Saint Quentin, where he retired at 80. A bachelor, he was the faithful lover for many years of an exquisite singer, Mlle. Marie Fels.

Character, of all things, interested the free-speaking, independent La Tour: "I plunge into their depths, and I bring them out whole," whether Rousseau and Voltaire from the salons of Mme. du Deffand and Mme. Geoffrin, lovely actresses, bourgeois financiers, the royal family, or Mme. de Pompadour. But he had the secret of pleasing his sitters while exhibiting their living souls.

The life-sized pastel portrait, which La Tour exhibited in the Salon of 1755, shows the Marquise as 1st minister; at her feet, the famous portfolio of state papers which Choiseul spirited away under a great red cloak on the very warm day of her death. Her elbow rests on the new Vol. IV of the Encyclopaedia. An engraving, a globe, and music indicate other interests.

Her hair is lightly powdered; lace under-petticoat and ladder of ribbon of bows on corset with matching gown and petticoat; sleeves with pleated self-ruffle and 3 tiers of lace, below a shirred band; mules.

1831. XVIIIc. 1755. French. (Metropolitan Mus., Frick Coll.)

François Boucher. Winter.

This is one of the four "Seasons" painted for Mme. de Pompadour. The Frick Collection also includes a series of 8 panels which he provided for the octagonal boudoir of her chateau de Crécy, and armchairs of Beauvais tapestry, probably from his designs.

The sleigh is one of the fanciful means of transport constantly shown, and used, in pictures of the French court.

For winter, the shirred trim of summer gowns is replaced by ropes of fur, during the third quarter XVIIIc. Slippers, like the attendant's shoe to which curved skates are tied, are cut protectively high.

1830

1832. XVIIIc. 1761. French. (Versailles, National Mus.)

J. M. Frédon, copy of Van Loo. Louis XV in robes of state.

The king wears his robes over the anachronistic XVIIc. costume of majesty, and carries a XVIIc. plumed hat. His wig is a modification of the full-bottomed court wig of Louis XIV; his shoes are contemporary, with diamond buckles.

1833. XVIIIc. French. (Aix, Museum.)

Q. La Tour. Duke de Villars.

Villars (1702-70) was little more than the son of the old Marshal, that "fanfaron plein d'honneur" at whose death in 1734 he inherited many honors, acquiring the Golden Fleece he wears here. Villars' homosexuality was so flagrant that he was nicknamed "the friend of man."

The two coldest winters of the XVIIIc. were those of 1741 and 1760. During the latter, Walpole wrote Montague, "Whether you have the constitution of a horse or a man," you were equally in danger. Soldiers froze to death, sitting on their horses, on the Continent. Walpole, for all "his immortality" had had a fever for seven weeks, and listed the noble ladies who had died of septic sore throat, including the duchess of Bolton, Lavinia Fenton, the original Polly Peachum of the "Beggar's Opera." 1766 was the other Siberian winter, though Walpole obstinately refused to add "a grain" to his clothing.

Fur-lined coats are seen throughout this long period of cold. A courtier's life consisted of endless waiting about in great cold rooms and draughty, inconvenient corridors. Walpole could keep comparatively cozy in his toy house at Strawberry Hill. But a fragile courtier like Hervey, or a self-indulgent one like Villars, found a fur-lined coat a necessity. For his embassy at the court of Tuscany, Stainville had a sable-lined silver coat, trimmed in gold, which cost $5,000. A coat magnificent enough for Marie Antoinette's wedding in 1770 cost so much that Mirepoix preferred to pay his tailor a rental of $1,200 for one day's use. (Lacroix: *Eighteenth Century*)

1834. Last quarter XVIIIc. French.

H. Chefer, after *Drouais.* Comte Philippe de Vaudreuil (1724-1802).

The naval officer, pointing out the scene of his triumphs against the English in 1777, shows a late appearance of the fur-lined and collared coat. The coat has lost fullness; its lengthening sides are cut away. The decoration of tassels and frogs on the coat has been very much reduced, and is assumed by the

exposed waistcoat. The curls of the wig are being reduced in number.

1835. XVIIIc. French. (New York, Albert Blum.)

J. B. Greuze. Comte d'Augievilliers.

Jean-Baptiste Greuze (1725-1805), a Burgundian who became a painter against his father's wishes, was brought to the Royal Academy in Paris as a boy, by a provincial artist who aided him. He was so precociously successful that he had to prove that his work was entirely his own. He married the daughter of the bookseller Rabute shortly after his return from studying in Italy, 1755-7, and was at the height of his success c. 1765 on the wave of sentimentality brought on by Rousseau. He was so infuriated by his admission to the Academy as a genre, not as an historical painter, as he had intended, that he refused to exhibit. Between his own stubborn carelessness and the extravagance of an unpleasant wife, he was always in difficulties, was ruined by the Revolution, and died in poverty.

Augievilliers was director of the Crown Buildings. His redecoration of an unused room in the king's apartment cost 30,000 fr. Louis XVI, very distressed, said: "With that sum I could have made thirty families happy." Mme. Marchais was called "Po-mona" because of the beautiful fruit served at the suppers of her salon; it was sent by d'Augievilliers from the king's own gardens.

1836. XVIIIc. English.
Slippers: brocaded white silk.

1837. XVIIIc. Louis XVI. French.
Striped Floral Brocade.

1838. XVIIIc. French.
Floral Brocade.

1839. XIXc. 1837-51. English.
Printed Percale: floral motifs derived from XVIIIc. brocades.

1840. XIXc. 1830-70. English.
Roller-Printed Cotton: degraded derivative of Pillement's designs and the patterns of floral brocades.

1841. First half XVIIIc. French.
Needlepoint Flounce: Point de France; *candelabre* patterns.

1842. Mid-XVIIIc. French.
Needlepoint. Lappet: Point d'Alençon.

1843. XVIIIc. French.
Bobbin Lace Border: Valenciennes.

1844. Last half XVIIIc. French.
Point Lace: Argenta, worn by Queen Charlotte at her wedding to George III in 1761.

Courtesy of Metropolitan Museum of Art (1836-43); *Museum of Fine Arts, Boston* (1844)

1845. XVIIIc. 1757. French. (Metropolitan Mus.)
H. Drouais. Mme. Favart.

1846. XVIIIc. 1758. French. (London, Victoria and Albert Mus.)

F. Boucher. Mme. de Pompadour.

C. S. Favart, the dramatist, son of a pastry cook, became director of the Opéra Comique. With the assistance of the actress-singer-dancer-dramatist, "Mlle. Chantilly" (1727-72) whom he married in 1745, his productions became so successful that the rival Comédie Italienne contrived to have them closed. Favart was sent to the Low Countries with the army, by the Marshal de Saxe, to play impromptu comedy which was so brilliant that the enemy asked for an armistice in order to attend the performance. Saxe pursued Mme. Favart, whose recalcitrance, even after he had succeeded, led the Marshal to persecute both husband and wife until his death in 1750. From that time until her death, Mme. Favart was the leading actress of the Comédie Italienne. She altered its performances into the beginnings of true French comic opera, and was the first to play a peasant in an approximation of peasant costume, with bare arms and *sabots* instead of the customary gloves, jewels and paniers of a leading lady.

Mme. Favart's position allows us to see clearly the construction of the bodice of her turquoise-malachite green *robe à la française* and the pleats flowing from its shoulders; three lace ruffles below the self-ruffles of the sleeve. Hair powdered and lightly covered.

In many portraits (like one in Wallace Coll., London) Mme. de Pompadour is the epitome of the "Dresden china figurine" of the 50-60's, in pink, blue and lavender, ruching, ruffles and lace. Edges are now apt to be scalloped and shirred decoration to be laid on in serpentine lines.

Sitting in the woods with barely powdered hair, the marquise wears an absolutely simple, loosely fitted dress, laced at the throat, innocent of ruffles, and with pearl strands instead of her many bracelets.

1847-54. XVIIIc. French. (New York Public Library.)

Dictionnaire des Sciences. (Diderot's Encyclopédie).

A two-volume "Cyclopaedia" had been published in London in 1720 by Ephraim Chambers. While Zedler, the Leigzig bookseller, was producing his 64 vol. "Lexicon" in 1732-50, an Englishman and a professor from Danzig proposed a French translation of Chambers' work. There were heartbreaking complications with the king's printer and privileges; revision was necessary. Eventually Diderot and d'Alembert set out to provide a larger work, based on Chambers'. The first 2 volumes appeared in 1751-2; they were condemned as dangerous to church and state. Publication of the remaining 19 volumes was not completed until 1765. Society was split by its opinions of the anti-clerical Encyclopaedists. They were supported by the Minister, Choiseul, by Mme. de Pompadour, and by Malesherbes, director-general of the Librairie, who warned Diderot that the manuscripts were about to be confiscated and said: "Send them to me; they will not look for them here." Each volume was opposed, prohibited, and secretly circulated in France from abroad. "See how many philosophical writers there are at present," wrote d'Argenson (Dec. 20, 1750). "The wind from England blows over this stuff. It is combustible." This was even clearer to Voltaire by 1702: "All that I see is sowing the seeds of a revolution which will infallibly arrive, but which I shall not have the pleasure of witnessing. The light is spreading so from place to place, that it will burst out on the first occasion, and then there will be a fine row. The young men are very lucky: they will see many things!" (Letter to M. de Chauvelin, Apr. 2, 1762).

Louis XV's attitude toward the Encyclopédie vacillated with the various pressures brought upon him. He understood that it was dangerous, but had calculated that things would last out his time as they were. He seems not to have read it until a supper party at the Trianon. The duke de la Vallière suggested that Mme. de Pompadour's curiosity about how her rouge and stockings were made could have been answered by the confiscated Encyclopédie, and three servants brought in the 21 volumes.

The technical articles, as well as those on history, literature, grammar, and philosophy were written by Diderot, after painstaking study. The 10 volumes of the Encyclopédie published after 1765 were butchered by the printer, who took it upon himself to remove what he considered dangerous, after the last reading of the proofs. Diderot knew nothing about the deletions, until he consulted the books himself.

An extraordinarily complete picture of XVIIIc. life is provided by the Encyclopédie's 10 volumes of plates. They show us every industry, its men and women workers, its tools, and its products. We expect cheese-makers to wear smocks, but may not be prepared for the elegant attire of soap-makers. Pins are almost entirely the work of little boys. Goldsmiths sit on high stools, wearing gowns as long as a baby's christening clothes, perhaps to keep gold from slipping into pockets.

Do you need to know what an incubator for baby chicks, or a mechanical wheelchair looked like? How a ship of the line, or a royal galley differs from all the small sorts of boats in which the Dutch excel? The difference between a dozen sorts of carriages, like a *vis-à-vis, désobligeante, diable* or a *carrosse de jardin?*

You will find that *tabletiers* make not only chess

1847

and checkers sets, but combs, *carnets de bal* and card-cases of horn and tortoise shell, and that the women who make fans and feather-flower decorations for gowns are delightfully dressed themselves. You are shown how buildings are framed; how cotton and indigo are grown in the East, and stockings are knit in France. Soldiers in gaiters, with the skirts of their coats pinned together at the bottom, go through the manual of arms. Twenty-seven plates explain heraldry, blazonings and the orders of knighthood. You can even find the alphabets of all known languages, ancient and modern, from Abyssinia and Illyria, past the Malabar coast to Tibet—beautiful enough to be embroidered for their patterns alone.

1847. Cordonnier: Pl. II. Tome III, 1763.

Shoes, boots, leggings, and shoemaker's implements.

    30. boots
    43. shoes
    47. heavy bucket-top
        boots
    48. hunting boots
    49. hussar's boots
    50. dragoon's boots
    51. courrier's boots

1848-49. Gantier: Pls. II and IV. Tome IV. 1764.

Men's gloves and mittens.
Women's gloves and mittens.

1851. Tailleur d'Habits: Pl. V. Tome IX, 1771.

    1. coat
    2. vest
    3. breeches, *culotte*
    4. Bavarian breeches
    5. cassock, *soutane*
    6. abbé's long cloak
    7. abbé's short cloak
    8. redingote
    9. dressing gown
    10. court gown
    11. *gilet,* short vest
        without skirts
    12. frock, *fracque,* a
        new sort of coat.

1852. Pl. VI, Tome IX. Detailed patterns of a coat.

    1-2 coat front
    3-4. crinoline stiffening at
        seam of skirts
    5-6. piecing of skirts (H)
    7-8. crinoline stiffening of
        front to support buttons and button-holes
    9-10. coat back.
    11-12. crinoline stiffening
        to support seam of
        skirts in back
    13. collar
    14-15. pieces of sleeve
    16-17. pocket flaps
    18-21 crinoline stiffening
        pieces
    22-23. coat pockets
    24-25. cuffs

1853. Pl. VII, Tome IX. Vest and breeches.

1-2. front of vest
3-4. crinoline stiffening
of front
5-6. pieces of sleeves
7-8. pocket flaps
9-10. crinoline stiffening
11-12. back of vest
13. crinoline at neck
14-17. crinoline stiffening
18-19. front of breeches
20. front flap
21. back buckle
22-23. back of breeches
24-25. pockets
26-27. garter bands
28. button mould
29-31. method of making
covered buttons
32-33. belt of breeches

1854. Pl. VIII, Tome IX. Details.

1-2. French collar
3-4. German collar
5-6. English collar
7-8. pockets of a *fracque*
9-11. different styles of
cuffs for frock coats
12. vest with crossed-
over front
14-15. tools used to burn-
ish leather and flat-
ten seams of leather
breeches
16. flap closing of leather breeches
17-18. side pockets of
breeches
19-20. change pockets
21-22. front pockets

1855. XVIIIc. 1768. French. (Metropolitan Mus., Print Room.)

"Supplément de l'art de la coiffure des dames françoises," by the Sieur Legros, Enclos des Quinze-vingts in Paris, Plate 48.

Legros is the author of the first manual of hairdressing. No. 48, from a supplementary edition published three years later, shows an arrangement formed of "un rang de coque de devant & le deuxième rang est en rosettes & boucles, faites en marron; le chignon natté en quatre cordons, moitié en parquet & l'autre moitié à jour & les bouchons faits avec le bout de la natté."

Women's hair began to be dressed by men about 1740, when peruke-makers were called in to arrange small rolled curls like those on men's wigs.

One of the first coiffeurs was Frison, made fashionable by Mme. de Prie. He refused to teach; he recognized Guigne, the king's barber, posing as the man-servant of a customer, and outwitted him by doing an atrocious job.

Marie Antoinette's first hairdresser was Larseuer. She came to prefer the work of Léonard, but to spare Larseuer's feelings, she let him dress her hair, and then had it done over again by Léonard.

The great rival hairdressers of the 60's were Legros and Frédéric. Legros, originally a baker, opened an Academy of Hair, where ladies' maids and valets practiced on the hair of hired models. Dolls, dressed to show the latest Paris fashions, had been sent all over Europe from the beginning of the XVIIIc. Legros began to show hair fashions on these "babies" at the St. Ovide Fair, and in 1765, had 100 dolls on exhibition in his shop. Then he published his "Art of Hairdressing." Frédéric finally outstripped poor Legros, who was one of the vast crowds of unfortunates crushed to death in the Place Louis XV during Marie Antoinette's wedding celebration, to the relief of whose heirs the Dauphin and his new wife dedicated their entire income for the year.

In 1769 legal action was taken against the hairdressers, who now numbered 1200, by the Community of Master-Barbers, Wig-Makers, Bathers, and Washers. The victory was won by the *coiffeurs,* who argued that the *perruquiers* dealt with dead hair, on a block, but that the coiffeurs were artists, concerned with the embellishment of living hair, with the relationships of shape and color in hair, face, complexion, and with the millinery materials they used, which matched the gown.

The art of hairdressing reached its insane climax with Duppefort, Beaulard, Legard, and Léonard. It was to the last silly little man that Marie Antoinette entrusted her jewels, to be handed to her sister in Brussels, when Léonard emigrated with Choiseul. Léonard returned to France, and was listed among those guillotined and buried in a common grave with André Chénier, yet he turned up alive after a 20-year stay in Russia, and was Superintendent of Burials in Paris when he died in 1820.

Greatest of all hairdressing manuals was the French "Treatise of the Principles of Dressing the Hair of Women." Its 39 volumes showed 3,744 named fashions in use c. 1772.

As hair and its decoration mounted, Beaulard invented a push-button collapsible coiffure which enabled a woman to get into a carriage and sit upright.

Duppefort was playwright as well as hairdresser. His comedy "Les Panaches," describes a hair arrangement showing "the garden of the Palais-Royal with its fountain and the outline of its houses, without forgetting the great alley, the grille, and the café." (The Goncourts.)

The *pouf au sentiment* worn by the Duchess of Chartres in 1774 showed "in the rear, a woman seated in an armchair, holding a nurseling; this represented Monsieur le Duc le Valois and his nurse. At the right was a parrot pecking at a cherry, on the left a little Negro, the two pet beasts of Madame la Duchesse. And the whole was interwoven with locks of hair of all Madame de Chartres' relatives, her husband, her father, her father-in-law, the Duc de Chartres, the Duc de Penthièvre, and the Duc d'Orléans."

With the advent of professional hairdressers and the interrelationship of gown and hair trimming, the whole tradition of royalty being attended exclusively by gentlefolk, began to crumble. Marie Antoinette received her underwear from her ladies, and then withdrew to her closet to be finished by her dressmaker, the famous Rose Bertin, who could not be admitted to her chamber amongst her ladies. The Prince de Ligne says that reproaches against Marie Antoinette's luxurious dress were unfounded. Until the advent of Bertin, she was actually careless of dress, by court standards, and whenever possible, as at the Trianon, she wore the simplest muslins. The accusations seem to have arisen from the extravagant headdresses arranged by Léonard. The king detested them; the actor Carlin's daring burlesque with a peacock feather at a court performance was probably instigated by Louis XVI. Marie Thérèse returned a portrait sent by her daughter, saying: "It cannot be the likeness of a Queen of France, but that of an actress."

1856

1857

1858

Courtesy of Metropolitan Museum of Art (1856-57; 1859-61); Cooper Union Museum (1858)

1859

1860

1861

1862

1863

1864

1856. XVIIIc. French. Regency.
Reverse: kid leaf, painted in gouache; landscape; infoliated medallions, surrounded by birds, flowers and fauns; sticks and guards: pearl matrix, carved and pierced; guards gilded.

1857. XVIIIc. French? (Late Louis XIV or Regency.)
Ivory; decorated with vernis martin; guards painted and gilded.

1858. XVIIIc. 1730-50. German.
Fan leaf: engraved, hand colored; by M. Engelbrecht of Augsburg.

1859. XVIIIc. 1757. English?
Park scene: painted kid mount; sticks and guards ivory, carved, painted with fruit and flowers.

1860. XVIIIc. French. Louis XVI.
Obverse: scenes from comedy; painted silk mount; ivory sticks and guards; medallions on sticks.

1861. XVIII-e.XIXc. English.
Carved ivory; medallion in vernis martin.

1862. XVIIIc. French. (Boston, Mus. of Fine Arts, Elizabeth Day McCormick Coll.)

Embroidered Collar: sheer yellow silk muslin ground embroidered with polychrome silks.

These collars were frequently worked on a very dark ground: plum, raisin brown, or laurel green. There are a number of them in the Museum of Fine Arts collection, but the light grounds photograph more satisfactorily. (See Appendix.)

1863. XVIIIc. French. (Boston, Mus. of Fine Arts, Elizabeth Day McCormick Coll.)

Embroidered Kerchief: sheer yellow silk embroidered in polychrome silks and silver. Square in shape, made to be worn folded, as shown, with silver and silk border worked only on the under part. (Ill. 1867).

1864. Early XVIIIc. English. (Boston, Mus. of Fine Arts, Elizabeth Day McCormick Coll.)

"Babila" Bag: lavender, green and white stripes. The Museum of Fine Arts has a number of examples of the exquisitely fine XVIIIc. netting technique called "babila work."

1865

1866

1867

1865. XVIIIc. French. (Metropolitan Mus., Print Room.)

A. de Saint-Aubin. The Concert.

One of the large assemblies of the 60's, in the costume of Mme. de Pompadour's last years.

The skirts of the polonaise of the 70's will be looped, and in some cases actually drawn up by tasseled cords in a way derived from the form of curtain shown at windows of Mme. de Saint-Brisson's salon.

1866. XVIIIc. 1763. French. (London, Nat. Gall.)

L. C. Carmontelle. Leopold, Maria Anna, and Wolfgang Mozart.

L. C. Carmontelle (1717-1806), dramatic author and engraver, also made many completely delightful water colors of the rich in their most relaxed, informal moments: countesses sewing and talking together; Mlle. de Lespinasse with a book; Mme. d'Epinay's niece, Mme. d'Esclavelles, playing chess with M. de Linant while her old nurse looks on.

At 7, Mozart, the child prodigy, his older sister, and his violinist father made their second European tour. He charmed the French court as he had the Austrian, where the little boy had thanked Marie Antoinette in 1762 for picking him up when he fell, saying, "When I grow up I will marry you."

Wig tied in a bag; *solitaire;* coat longer and straighter in cut, but its skirts not yet cut away.

1867. XVIIIc. 1763. French. (Louvre.)

Olivier. Thé à l'Anglaise at the Prince de Conti's.

Mozart plays in the pink silk-hung white Gallery of the Four Mirrors, in the Temple; Jelyotte, the opera star, plays the guitar and sings. The host, who disliked being painted, is seen from the back talking to the finance minister, Troudaine. All the personages in the picture are known and are described by the Goncourts.

There are no servants. The ladies themselves serve tea and pass food kept warm in hot-water dishes.

Between Mlle. Bagarotti, in cerise and white stripes, and the Maréchal de Luxembourg in fur-trimmed white satin, are the Maréchale de Mirepoix in a fichu, her cap tied on by a black gauze kerchief, and Mme. de Virville in a sky-blue fur-lined pelisse. Behind their table stands Mlle. de Boufflers in pink, her bare head hardly powdered. The "delectable dowager," the elder Countess d'Egmont stands in a flowing red gown. The young countess d'Egmont, a "shepherdess on her way from the Opera to the Petit Trianon," wears a flat hat, lavender bows, and a lace apron. Behind her, Mme. de Boufflers, in rose, with a fichu and tulle-flounced apron plays maid. In the r. background the princess de Beauvau, in violet with a black scarf-collar serves a gentleman's glass.

1868

1869

1868. XVIIIc. 1766. Scotch-French. (Edinburgh, Nat. Gall.)

Alan Ramsay. Jean Jacques Rousseau.

Rousseau (1712-78) came of a family of French watchmakers who had emigrated to Geneva. The instability of his father left the child inadequately protected in France from the age of ten. His own "Confessions," begun during his English exile, tell the story of his life-long wanderings over Europe as a servant, secretary, musician of sorts and writer; of the mistresses and powerful friends who educated, supported, and protected him; of the endless quarrels of this man "born without a skin" (Hume); of his irresponsibility which sent his 5 children to the foundling hospital; and the madness of his last ten or fifteen years.

In 1761 appeared his novel, "La Nouvelle Héloïse"; in 1762, the "Contrat Social," which was anti-monarchical and had to be published abroad; and "Emile," a tract on education in the form of a novel. These revolutionized the life of the world.

The beauties of nature, simplicity, and feeling were discovered. Mothers began to nurse and educate their own children. Passionate friendships arose between women. Trustworthy middle-aged gentlemen trotted about, receiving confidences and furious if they found that something had been withheld. Everyone wrote diaries and confessions. Colloquial French words, such as d'Argenson had been ridiculed for using, replaced grandiloquent language. Powder seemed artificial; muslin and cloth replaced silk. Love became sentimental; keepsakes were exchanged, containing locks of hair and decorated with funeral urns, weeping willows and doves. Wild cliffs, ruined castles, broken statuary, were more beautiful than any cultivated parterre. Fashionable women's eyes were brimmed with tears, to indicate their agonizingly acute sensibilities. Rousseau did indeed "put the proud and weak on the wrong road." Whether in foolish innocence or bad conscience, aristocrats helped him to bring on their own downfall in the Revolution.

We see the professional child of nature in a sort of frontiersman's cap of shaggy fur like that of the collar of his cloak. Degrees of naturalness are being weighed in conversation; a cloak is "more natural" than a fitted coat, and such a rough fur would be called "more natural" than Villars' sables.

1869. XVIIIc. 1756. French. (Metropolitan Mus.)
Greuze. Broken Eggs.

1870. XVIIIc. French. (Metropolitan Mus.)
N. B. Lépicié (c. 1735-1834). Young Woman Knitting.

(For dress description of Ills. 1869, 1870, see "Cries of Paris," Ills. 1871-74.)

1870

THE GREAT FASHION ARTISTS OF FRANCE

The greatest of the many great engravers of costume and manners in the latter half XVIIIc. was *Jean Michel Moreau* (1741-1814), called *"le jeune"* to distinguish him from his painter brother *Louis Gabriel*. His designs for the "Chansons" of Laborde, Marie Antoinette's valet de chambre, show court life, c. 1773. He illustrated the "Complete Works of Rousseau" in 12 vols. (1774-83). But his culminating work is the "Suite d'Estampes pour servir à l'Histoire des Modes et du Costume des Français dans le XVIIIe siécle," of 1776-83. They are the finest of all costume plates.

Augustin de Saint-Aubin (1736-1807) is only below Moreau in his portrayal of French life and costume. His brother *Gabriel* (1724-80) was a fine, less prolific artist.

Charles Nicolas Cochin, II (1715-90) came of a family of engravers, his mother, née *Hortmels,* being one also. His "Jeu du roi" and "Bal paré" are among the great records of court entertainments.

There were many others, some designers, some engravers after the work of other men; such as *Noël LeMire* (1724-1800); *Nicolas Delaunay* (1739-92); *F. M. I. Quéverdo* (1748-98); and the great German, *Daniel Chodowiecki* (1726-1801) who produced 2,000 book and almanach illustrations, among them Lessing's "Minna von Barnhelm" in 1770.

Coloring the sporadically produced costume plates of late XVIIc. by hand, or cutting out and backing them with fabric, was an amusement of the Regency, sometimes well and sometimes atrociously done.

Plate engraving in color did not begin until second half XVIIIc. Into XIXc. it was often cheaper and, as in the case of *Heideloff's Gallery of Fashion,* more luxurious, to color plates by hand. The plates of the *Galerie des Modes* and *Costumes Parisiens* are numbered or dated. At the turn of the century begins a flood of periodicals of fashion and culture, from which magazines like *Vogue* and the *Ladies' Home Journal* clearly descend. The long-lived *Ackermann's Repository* contains pasted-in samples of actual fabrics, produced in English mills, in addition to a color-illustration of a leading industry—say, the showrooms of the Etruria pottery works, fashion plates, embroidery patterns, articles on finance, music, new books, etc.

1871-74. Last quarter XVIIIc. French.

Cries of Paris.

The caps of the middle and lower classes begin to be prettily fluted like those of the aristocracy as competition drives towards the Revolution, and servants buy the old clothes of aristocrats from dealers like Joseph Longprix on the rue Saint-Honoré. France has become prosperous under Louis XVI; tax burdens are lightened; trade has doubled between 1758-88. "Revolutions are not always brought about by a gradual decline from bad to worse. Nations that have endured patiently and almost unconsciously the most overwhelming oppression, often burst into rebellion against the yoke the moment it begins to grow lighter. The regime which is destroyed by a revolution is almost always an improvement on its immediate predecessor, and the most critical moment for bad government is the one which witnesses their first steps toward reform. A sovereign who seeks to relieve his subjects after a long period of oppression is lost, unless he be a man of great genius." (A. de Tocqueville: *The Old Regime and the Revolution.* Harper, N. Y., 1856, p. 214.)

In all these illustrations the clothes are ample, comfortable and attractive. The shoes are good; even the man selling vinegar from a wheelbarrow (1871) wears clocked stockings. Vests are warm, often double-breasted, their colored linings turned back in revers. Twisted scarves help to hold up breeches or long trousers. The soap dealer and the hot-pastry boy (1871) wear hats as smartly cocked as the well dressed Turpin (1874), with a beribboned wig and a watch hanging from his buttonhole.

Girl (1869) whose eggs are broken wears a pretty dotted and ribbon-tied cap; her straw hat is imaginatively wreathed with ribbon; her great muslin sleeves, fichu, and apron are fresh; her skirt has a colored edge. The street women's skirts are striped like that of bourgeoise (1870) and they, too, have a lace fichu or an approximation of one for Sunday wear.

FRENCH COSTUME PLATES
of Moreau le jeune and others.

(Note key letters which are referred to in the
following discussion.)

1875. (A) *Moreau le jeune*: "L'aveu."

1876. (B) *Moreau le j.*: "*Coucher de la mariée.*"
1767.

1877. (C) Helman, after *Moreau le j.*: "*N'ayez pas
peur, ma bonne amie,*" 1767.

1878. (D) *Moreau le j.*: "*C'est un fils, monsieur,*"
1767.

1879. (E) Helman, after *Moreau le j.*: "*Les délices
de la maternité.*" 1777.

1880. (F) N. de Launay, after *N. Lavreince*: "*La
toilette, 'qu'en dit l'abbé?'*"

1881. (G) P. A. Martini, after *Moreau le j.*: "*La
petite toilette,*" 1777.

1882. (H) A. Romanet, after *Moreau le j.*: "*La
grande toilette,*" 1777.

1883. (I) Carl Guttenberg, after *Moreau le j.*: "*Le
rendez-vous pour Marly,*" 1777.

1884. (J) Heinrich Guttenberg, after *Moreau le j.*:
"*La rencontre au Bois de Boulogne,*" 1772.

1885. (K) P. A. Martini, after *Moreau le j.*: "*Dame
du palais de la Reine,*" 1777.

1886. (L) Launay le j., after *Moreau le j.*: "*Les
adieux,*" 1776.

1887. (M) Patas, after *Moreau le j.*: "*La petite
loge,*" 1776.

1888. (N) *Moreau le j.*: "*La fin du souper.*"

1889. (O) *Matthew Darly*: "Flower Garden,"
(English, May 1, 1777).

The ceremonious French gown is now worn with
hair dressed high over pads, widened at the top by
sausage curls, and surmounted by plumes, gauze and
ribbons. (A, C, K, L, M, N, O.)

The smoothly rounded bodice follows the traditionally curved lines of the French corset. Its very
low neckline (A), spreading wide at its base, exposes
the breasts. It is edged with a little lace frill (L)
which sometimes mounts into a standing Medici collar. By way of emphasis of the breasts, a bow is set
at the top of the corset (the *parfait contentement*),
and a ribbon about the neck, or a necklace disappears
under it.

Sometimes (H, I) the Medici collar is transferred
to a sheer tucker, in walking dress; its fluted edges
run into the *parfait contentement*, after manner of
the necklace.

The English bodice remains open, exposing a V;
its edges are emphasized by pleats or shirred bands;
its neckline is higher, and is veiled in scarves and
handkerchiefs, which contribute to the V-appearance
of the bodice front.

In French dress (B, C, E, F), V-fronts and kerchiefs tend to be relegated to negligée wear of ladies,
and to the dresses of servants and housewives (D,
E, F). Even these have lost the rigidity of the old
placard-front with its busks. The bib of earlier aprons
is the mark of servants' aprons by latter half XVIIIc.

The characteristic new bodice stresses breasts, small
waists, and the roundness of the torso between them.
Decoration is usually carried artfully down the center line of the bodice from the *parfait contentement*.
But the fabric of the bodice tends to be rucked and
wrinkled into horizontal fullness, so that the eye is
carried around the body, below the springing breasts.

The ruffles at the elbows of close sleeves have a
tendency to become gathered together at the bottom
(E, I, N), and to turn into puffed bands, *sabots*.

The underskirt of negligée dress is usually flounced
at the bottom; that of more ceremonious gowns may
be trimmed with a flounce, with shirred bands, or
with a combination of these, related to the trimming
of the bodice and the sides of the overskirt.

As the paniers of court dresses are extended laterally to a great width (K), the underskirt becomes preeminent, and is garlanded with flowers, and looped
gauze, while the overskirt disappears from view in
front, and exists only as a long strip of train.

A series of new garments appears; *polonaises* (I),
caracos (F) (and the more flowing *circassiennes,
lévites* and *chemises* of the late XVIII.) for less ceremonious wear and for walking (to which all the
French world had been set by Dr. Tronchin). These
are coat-like, sometimes fitted in back *à la française*
(F). They are caught together at the throat, or more
usually at the *parfait contentement,* and are cut back,
like a man's frock coat, and spread over the *paniers*.

The *caraco*, the first to appear, is a jacket, extended
to cover the spread of the paniers. In a long form it
was already worn by the bourgeoises of Nantes, when
the duke d'Aiguillon passed through in 1768. Brought
back in this way to Paris, it was cut short to the
height of the pocket-slit of the skirt. It is edged with
a ruffle, or in the perky bustled form *à la polonaise,*
with puffed bands.

The back of the *polonaise* is gored and fitted; the
gored sections may extend into the skirt, or a full
skirt may be gathered onto a fitted bodice. In any
case, the skirt is looped up on either side in back,
in line with the two important gores, so that it is
gathered up in three puffed sections. The trim at the
bottom of the underskirt is often caught up in a
series of smaller loops.

The *polonaise,* worn for walking, or in the country,
was the forerunner of the tailored suit or sports dress.
Hats, rather than caps or *poufs,* and watches with
chains (later fobs) are worn with walking dress. For
winter, there are *polonaises* with pockets, and fur-
trimmed cloaks with collars, *pelisses,* which are accompanied by small muffs, as is the *polonaise,* but
may be worn with ceremonious caps.

There is a tendency to loop up the skirts of all but
the most formal garments (B, E, maid L). By the
final quarter of century the skirts of walking dresses
are often of less than ankle length.

Two impulses struggle for supremacy throughout
the century: negligée, informal dress, cotton, against
court paniers and silk.

Marie Antoinette's apologist, Mme. Campan, says
that the queen preferred to wear white dresses of
muslin, cambric, or Italian taffeta with muslin scarves,
straw hats, and unsupported skirts in summer at
Marly or the Trianon; until Rose Berlin's dressmaking was introduced at court by the duchess of Orleans
in 1774, the queen wore diamonds only at court and

on fête days like Christmas and Easter. Her simplicity was censured. "What misconduct might not be expected of a princess who could absolutely go without a hoop," and who wanted people to sit down where they liked at the Trianon, without regard to old distinctions of chair and stool. This simplicity was first criticized, and then copied. It would have been in step with the times and better for the regime if Rose Bertin's influence had preceded the queen's taste for simplicity. But the Revolutionary guards looked everywhere at the Trianon for furniture set with rubies and diamonds, a legend which arose from stories of Louis XIV's solid silver furniture, combined with glass-studded theatrical scenery left over from his reign and stored at the Trianon.

The flounced blue, rose and violet gowns introduced by Mme. de Pompadour turn into white court dresses. Their borders and decoration develop from shirred fullness of self-material (A, C,) into *barrières* composed of puffings (L) of silver and gold, white and rose tulle and gauze, caught with perfumed flowers of silk, chenille, and of feathers. Straight lines of decoration become serpentine (K, L), then sprawl asymmetrically or are looped. The large, heavy brocade patterns of first half XVIIIc. become loosely sprawled or delicately sprigged across light grounds. There are many fine stripes (H,I) or stripes combined with bands of flowers (F and actual textile photos).

These blue stripes, and pink and white flowered patterns are reinforced c. 1775 by strangely-named new colors, striking rather than pretty: *puce* (the purplish-brown color of a blood-filled flea which a very great lady caught and found beautiful); *caca d'oie* (goose-dropping green); *boue de Paris* (that most clinging of all muds, with which everyone was splashed anyhow); *cheveux de la reine,* from Marie Antoinette's ash-blonde hair, which suffered so from the birth of her first child.

The allusive names which every color, hairdress and fashion received, often helps to date them. The paired half-paniers of 1750 were called *jansénistes* from the religious dissensions which were splitting society. Galloons *du système* alluded to Law's plans of financial reform. The pet word of 1730 is commemorated in fans *à l'allure.* The appearance of a comet in 1742; of the first rhinoceros; the place of an army victory; the name of a new ambassador; the birth of a dauphin; *à l'inoculation* of Louis XVI's brothers for smallpox by Dr. Joubert (a dangerous notion from the northern courts, which was blamed on the queen); *à la débacle* in 1768, when the bed of the Seine is cleaned; a new song like *Malbrouck* in 1786; the balloon ascensions of Montgolfier—all give names to fashions.

The negligees of white muslin and pink ribbons and the every-day dresses of India cottons, which the XVIIIc. adored, have been less readily available since Louis XIV's time. During most of the century the import of their fabric was forbidden, and it had to be smuggled. Mme. de Pompadour refused to have anything in her chateau of Belleville which was not contraband. (Goncourts). Lesser folk had to go without cotton or chance severe penalties, until France began to produce her own cottons. English muslins, ribbons and fashions, pottery and carriages (as well as such subversive notions as Magna Charta and habeas corpus) were admitted duty-free after the Versailles Treaty of 1783.

The ideas of Rousseau and Dr. Tronchin affect everybody: the beauties of nature, physical labor, walking and riding in comfortable clothing; nursing and educating your own baby, become fashionable (E, H, I, J).

The trend had begun earlier. Mme. de Pompadour is painted sitting in the woods, not walking on a parterre. Childless herself, and returning from the porcelain factory at Sèvres, she went out of her way to spy out the secluded spot in the Bois de Boulogne where Mlle. de Romans used to go, in a lace negligée, to nurse Louis XV's baby son (later the Abbé de Bourbon.)

The *lever* and *coucher* of the ladies and gentlemen who are being dressed and undressed in Moreau's plates (B, C, F, G, H,) do not differ in essentials from those of Marie Antoinette, of which Mme. Campan has left minute descriptions.

Like Moreau's bride, the queen went to bed under a great *baldequin* or *impérial* (B), which was also used to curtain off her small portable tub. (Only at St. Cloud was there a bathroom.) Her nightdress consisted of a nightcap, lace-trimmed chemise with sleeves, ribbon-trimmed corset, white taffeta dressing gown, and embroidered slippers.

On bath-day she washed wearing a wide gown of English flannel, lined with linen, and was dried under it, just as French girls were still taught to do during my school-days before World War I; more modesty, but the same notions of the essential dangers of bathing were involved in e. XXc. To avoid catching cold, she went back to bed on bath-day, and sewed or read until the public toilet at noon.

This was a prolonged ceremony which required many people besides her hairdresser and her ladies. The queen's clothes had already been selected, by an intricate ritual too long to explain, and more complicated than the choices we see being made. Her clothes were brought in, done up in green taffeta sheets, in wicker baskets. They were handed to her by her own ladies, but a tirewoman, two pressers and folders, two valets and a porter were also required. The four ells (4 yds. 6") of ribbon for her dressing gown, and two ells of taffeta which covered the basket of gloves and fans, were renewed daily, and must have kept the tirewoman's whole family in green taffeta aprons, capes and beribboned caps.

Lesser gentlefolk still required maids, valets and hair dressers, tailors and dressmakers, and most of these find it necessary to have assistants of their own. Lavreince's (F) singer and musician try out a song while her hair is being dressed. Her doctor is concerned with her health; an abbé helps choose a length of striped floral brocade, brought in by a dressmaker and her assistant; two visitors chat.

The gentleman (G) holds an invitation which has just been brought by a liveried courier. He is swathed in night-shirt and dressing-gown, while a hairdresser takes a hot roller from an assistant, wearing an identical apron with a pointed bib buttoned to his coat. A tailor shows a new coat, held up by his assistant (whose striped stockings, like those of the abbé (F) were made on the new machine which knits ribs).

The nobleman (H), with the ribbon of his decoration across his chest, is now wearing his new frock coat. He pins on a nosegay; two fobs dangle from his breeches' pockets. With the sword and hat which wait on the chair, he will be ready to stroll with a friend, whose Order dangles on his breast, and the lady who waits in her walking costume of hat, fur-edged wrap, finely striped satin gown and rigid fan.

Gentleman in walking costume (I): a very cutaway frock coat, caught at the breast, just under the wide, rolling collar (male dress affected by female usages; the collar, equivalent to his companion's Medici collar, is caught at the point of her *parfait contentement;* the man's frock coat flows away from the button as her *polonaise* from its closing).

Lady's walking dress (I): parasol, plumed hat, braided hair clubbed up in back in a form of catogan; narrowly striped *polonaise* looped in gauze; petticoat shirred up in smaller sections; cord and tassel decoration of back gores. Another type of *polonaise,* even less formal, is very gauzy and summery.

Children with natural heads of hair play in the dirt, if they please, in pretty, comfortable wash dresses, with sashes about the waist. The waist and breasts have newly been discovered; the little girl has neither, so her sash is set high, in the trend towards the classic gowns of the turn of the century and Empire, which can already be discerned in the shorter waist and flowing outer garment of her mother's *polonaise.*

The groom wears a laced cocked hat; the gentleman, an informal riding hat cocked up softly into a shovel brim. Where a frock coat of ceremony would bare the breast, cutaway sports coats are closed for comfort at the throat.

Women's cutaway riding coats (J), almost indistinguishable from men's, closed with frogs, worn with sashes and skirts clear of the ground, plumed hats; one cocked behind by a button and loop, and worn with a long pigtail like a campaigner or sailor; the other, clubbed up behind.

A woman's riding costume, in the days when Tronchin set everybody to exercising, might have a gold-gallooned green satin coat and silver-trimmed pink skirt. A riding costume of 1786 is described as having triple collars on a coat of puce-colored shantung; ivory studs at front and pockets; a matching skirt with serpentine trimming in pink ribbon; pink doeskin boots; a canary yellow felt hat with green and white plumes; and hair clubbed into a *flambeau d'amour.*

Court costume (K): plumes, diamonds at the hair, ears, collar and necklace; overskirt reduced to a train, unseen from the front. A back view shows a method of attaching the train, drawn up with tasselled cords, after the manner of the *polonaise.* This court gown and the opera dress (L) show the elaborate *parement,* the demand for which can scarcely be met. Tulle, which got its name from the town where it was first made, appears during final quarter XVIIIc. Soldiers wove this net and worked on metallic trimmings in barracks and men-servants in livery embroidered while they waited in antechambers.

Courtiers and pages (K): In 1751 d'Argenson says: "The expense to courtiers of two new and magnificent coats, each for two fête days, ordered by the King, completely ruins them." Men's clothes are somewhat less elaborate now, but pages' coats cost 1,500 livres in 1786, and a lady's court gown like this might cost 10,000. (Taine: *Ancien Régime*)

Before and after the opera (L), ladies and gentlemen walked in full ceremonious dress in the Palais-Royal gardens and sat under the chestnut trees, until the galleries were built after the fire at l'Opéra in 1783.

The hair of the husband, who conducts the lady to her box, is dressed in a high *toupet* but falls loose behind in almost natural ringlets.

Her maid shows one of the inventive combinations of cap and kerchief from which great ladies begin to take suggestions.

Enrollment as a member of the companies of the Opéra or Comédie Française (M) was the dream of every little strolling player or pretty street girl. She became officially an *"artiste,"* was given independence from family control, and was spared from casual treatment by the police. She could make her way and marry into the highest circles, even after being kept. Upon marriage, she had to retire, but a royal order often allowed her to return to the stage.

A stage box had many uses. The occupant often paid no attention to the spectacle, but drew all the curtains and sat, unseen, comfortable in winter with fur wraps, feet on a charcoal warming box, in the company of visitors whom it might be difficult to receive publicly at home.

Dancer: last quarter XVIIIc. modifications of ballet costume established by La Camargo. Old woman: black and white cap and scarf; face enclosed by shell-shaped pleats of the cap.

Gentlemen: shorter double-breasted waistcoat forming sharp lapels; frock coat with deeply pointed collar and narrow inconspicuous cuff; wide curved shoebuckles covering entire instep.

People begin to tire of being waited on by a clutter of lackeys; they send them out and serve themselves at their ease (N). In Olivier's "Thé à l'Anglaise" (Ill. 1867) the countess de Boufflers, in an apron, replaces a servant while Mozart plays. Older ladies pour out tea. Chafing dishes and small stands make self-service comfortable. In France in XXc. that rare fruit, the pineapple, is still sliced from the bottom at table, and the remainder is set on a tall, handsome stand to await its next use.

Men's wigs are seen deteriorating toward natural hair; it may even be natural hair dressed as a wig in a careless style. Women's hair, clubbed up in back in braids, is set with the standard three plumes and gauze decorations of ceremony. *Polonaise* styles begin to affect more ceremonious dress, like this gown, banded with leopard between lines of plain fur (see also K).

All Europe is flooded with caricatures of extravagant fashions. This *pouf* (O), with its vegetable plots and gardener with a rake, is hardly more extravagant than many which were actually worn. Mme. de Matignon had her hair-dresser under contract at 24,000 livres a year, to supply her with a new headdress daily. (Taine: *Ancien Régime.*)

1890. XVIIIc. Louis XVI. French.
  Waistcoat: cream satin; chain-stitch embroidery in pastel colored silks.
1891. XVIIIc. French?
  Waistcoat: pounced and painted India cotton; part of male negligee.
1892. XVIIIc. French.
  Waistcoat.
1893. XVIIIc. French.
  Waistcoat: detail of embroidery.
1894. Early XIXc. French.
  Dress border: detail of embroidery.

1895. XVIIIc. 1774-92. French.
  Waistcoat: embroidery detail.

1896. XVIII-XIXc. 1785-1805. Italian, Venice.
  Waistcoat: double-breasted.

1897. XIXc. c. 1800. French.
  Waistcoat: linen; double-breasted. Washable white
dimities, twills, and corded cottons, embroidered in
silver and sometimes a little black, were made
especially for summer waistcoats in late XVIII-early
XIXc. Museum of Fine Arts, Boston, has a number
of examples.

1898. XIXc. c.1830. French?

Waistcoat: figured moiré.

1899. XIXc. English.
  Waistcoat: shawl collar; plum brocade, embroidered.

1900. XVIIIc. c. 1780. Italian, Venice.
  Coat and breeches: red grosgrain with satin stripe.

1901. XVIIIc. 1785-90. Italian, Venice.
  Coat: striped satin.

1902. Third quarter XVIIIc. French.
  Suit: black velvet coat, black satin waistcoat, blue
glass ornaments; breeches modern.

B   C   E   F   H

A   D   G

1903-06. XVIIIc. French. (New York, Cooper Union Mus.)
Sample card containing buttons of metal foil, metal thread and spangles. A contemporary note enclosed with this reads: "May, 1780, Notes of samples of buttons in gilding and silvering, sent to Messieurs An-toine Guillemot father and son of Thiers, and chez Garby, Manufactory of buttons at Clermont to be paid for with rebate for cash. From Nos. 1-30 all the buttons are (priced) at Ten livres the set of 30 large and 30 small."

Courtesy of Cooper Union Museum

1907. XVIII-XIXc. Various. (New York, Cooper Union Museum.) Buttons.

A. XVIIIc. French. Pearl, steel, glass, copper. B. XVIIIc. French. Pearl shell, metal foil, brass, rhinestones. C. XIXc. Dutch. Pearl shell, porcelain painted on blue, brass. D. XVIIIc. French. White paper, blue silk, glass, copper. E. Late XVIIIc. French. Insects, shells, sea-weed, tin, paper, copper, glass. F. Late XVIIIc. English. Stone ware mounted in copper. G. Late XVIIIc. Copper. H. XIXc. French. Steel, stained and cut out.

1908. XVIIIc. 1760-80. English, London.
Watch by John Witwer: gold, double case.

1909. XVIIIc. 1783-4. French, Paris.

Watch by Daniel Vauchez: back shows the Montgolfier balloon ascension, wreathed in wrought gold leaves, enamel and pearls; face black with white numerals, set around with diamonds; 2 hands; cylindrical escape movement. Only survivor of 12 balloon watches by Vauchez.

1910. XIXc. French, Paris. (Hearn Coll.)
Watch by Abraham Louis Breguet: gold with borders in *champlevé* enamel on front and back; painted pastoral scene.

1911. Early XIXc. Swiss.
Mourning watch and pin: gold and enamel, marked *Tiffany* for retailer.

1912. XIXc. Swiss.
Banjo watch.

1913. XVIIIc. c. 1790. French, Paris.
Watch by Vauchez.

1914. Late XVIIIc. French or Swiss. (Hearn Coll.)
Watch by Clary: gold face edged with pearls on blue enamel; back, enamelled portrait on white ground, studded with pearls.

1915. XVIIIc. French.
    Fob.
1916. Late XVIIIc. Swiss?
    Watch chatelaine; gold and enamelled steel.
1917. Late XVIIIc. English,
    Watch fob,

1918. Late XVIIIc. German.
    Fob, with seal and miniature.
1919. XVIII-XIX. German.
    Watch fob; silver and precious stones.
1920. XIXc. 1840-50. German.
    Watch fob; gold and enamel.

XVIIIc. c. 1780 French Colonial (see Ills. 1946-63.)
A. Brunias: Painted But-
tons.

*Courtesy of the Museum for
the Arts of Decoration of
Cooper Union.*

1921. First half XIXc. English.
Fob with seal.

1922. XVIIIc. 1777-8. French, Paris.
Carnet de bal: gold and enamel; *Souvenir* in brilliants.

1923. XVIIIc. French.
Etui for sealing wax, by Melchior René Barre (master, 1768-d.after 1791).

1924. XVIIIc. French.
Carnet de bal: Cotot enamel, *Je meurs ou je m'attache.*

1925. XVIIIc. English, Staffordshire.
Snuff box: Staffordshire enamel on copper; pastoral scene on white ground.

1926. Late XVIII-e.XIXc. French.
Bonbon box: Napoleonic symbols.

1927. Second third XIXc. English, London.
Snuff box: gold with cipher of William IV of England.

Containers are becoming increasingly specialized. Boxes to hold dance programs become a favorite in last quarter XVIIIc. Like everything else, they show the influence of Rousseau. Hard realism in love is turning to sentimentality, with weeping willows and funeral urns set on classic pillars.

The penny post is well established, with hourly

collections from 500 London coffee shops. Everyone writes letters, however badly spelled. There are no envelopes; letters are often written on the back of the latest printed news-sheet, which the recipient will not have seen; it is folded and sealed with wax carried in an *étui;* seals dangle from every fob and chatelaine.

Charming, inexpensive enamelled boxes began to be mass-produced by an offset process at Battersea in 1750-60, and later at Staffordshire. They hold patches and pins as well as snuff, which is beginning to lose ground. Since Charlotte of Mecklenburg-Strelitz loved snuff and royalty is slow to change conventions, her sons, George IV and William IV, carried snuff boxes and went through the motions of taking it, without actually doing so. To offer and to accept snuff was a traditional mark of courtesy.

1928. XVIIIc. 1770-75. French.
Floral print: polychrome woodblock in linen.

1929. XVIIIc. c. 1785. French, Jouy?
Floral print: polychrome woodblock with black lines on linen.

1930. XVIIIc. 1790. French, Nantes? or Rouen?
Balloon print.

1931. Late XVIIIc. French, Jouy.
Floral block-printed cotton, from the Oberkampf factory at Jouy, with their mark; designed by *Dubuison.*

1932-38. XVIIIc. 1778. French.

"Galerie des Modes et Costumes Français" (1778-87).

The plates in this publication are in color. Quoted material, here given, has been translated from the original captions.

1932. *Le Clere*. "Young Woman."
"*Caraco à la Polonaise* of vermicelli-patterned cotton, edged with a narrow band; the petticoat edged with a wide band with garlands of flowers on a white ground."

1933. *Desraies*. "Young Lady Lying on a Couch."
"Hair dressed in a round bonnet of corded linen with a headband tied informally around it; fur lined pelisse over undress."

1934. *Desraies*. "Pretty Dancer."
"Pleated, low-necked caraco of golden brown Italian taffeta; flowered batiste apron, trimmed to match the caraco; rose colored bows."

Rosettes and ribbon; pair of fobs; increasing size of ruffled white hats; apron with large pocket reappeared briefly c.1780.

1935. *Le Clere*. "Dressmaker and Girl Delivering Work."
Fashionable dress, gloves and fan, but dark apron with bib.

1936. *Le Clere*. "Ladies' Tailor Trying on a Corset."
"Nut brown coat (lined with green); black velvet collar with two gold buttonholes; similar buttons and buttonholes on the suit; vest of cerise tricot with gold tassels; black velvet breeches (banded and buckled in gold); gray silk stockings. The young woman wears only a simple petticoat and white stockings; and her breast is covered [*sic*] with a yellow-tinted cambric."

White *pouf* with red ribbons, red and yellow flowers and green leaves; pink slippers ruched in green; pink and red striped dressing gown with a green lining and white *sabots* (on right, not shown).

Courtesy of Metropolitan Museum of Art, Print Room (1932-38)

1937. *Desraies.* "Young Woman on Her Morning Walk."

"*Polonaise* with tubular trimming; two watches; her hair dressed in a new *pouf* elegant."

Tall, tasseled walking stick; pair of fobs.

1938. *Le Clere.* "Bourgeoise."

"Striped satin dress; fur-trimmed *pelisse,* and white muff."

1939. XVIIIc. March 30, 1778. French.

Moreau le j. The Crowning of Voltaire.

The exiled Voltaire finally bought an estate at Ferney on Lake Geneva, to which pilgrimages were made from all over the world. After twenty-eight years he was able to return to Paris in 1778 for the opening of his last play "Irène," at the Théatre Français. The old philosopher was acclaimed by the city; the other greatest citizen of the world, Benjamin Franklin, brought his nephew for Voltaire's blessing. The play was poor, but Voltaire was honored, a few weeks later, by a ceremony which was attended by most of the royal family—although not by the king.

Moreau shows Voltaire watching from a box. Actually, it was on Voltaire's own head, as he stood on the stage and the audience cried: "Let him be crowned!" that Mme. Vestris set the laurel wreath, while Voltaire's protégé, Lekain, declaimed, " 'Tis the people of France that send it."

The Théatre Français, run by its own members, the *sociétaires,* who paid for their own theatre, had become the most important in Europe. The first attempt to simplify the theatrical costume of Louis XIV, and relate dress to the play, was made in 1755 by the designer Leclere, and Sarrasin, the court costumer, for Voltaire's "Orphelin de la Chine." Lekain, whom we see on the stage in a long robe, gave up the tinsel cuirasse and plumes, and Mlle. Clairon played without paniers, for the first time on the stage since paniers were invented. Actors were dim figures on candle-lit stages; glittering sequins and waving plumes are not only a tradition, but will remain a necessity until theatres become well-lighted in XIXc. A personal pronunciation of Vestris' in declaiming words like *amour* as *amou—re,* still affects French dramatic acting. (Mme. de Genlis: *Mémoires.*)

1940. XVIIIc. 1778-85. French.

Paul Joilly. Franklin at the Court of France.

"Figure to yourself an Old Man, with grey Hair, Appearing under a Martin Cap, among the Powder'd Heads of Paris," Franklin said the year before his arrival as ambassador in 1778.

The king opposed French aid and recognition for America, even as he signed an alliance in 1778 after Burgoyne's defeat. But the wily old man in the brown coat of an "American agriculturalist," in his own unpowdered hair and his round Quaker hat, was already one of the world's most famous people. He was a member of all the important learned societies of Europe; his apparent modesty and mildness disarmed even anti-democratic courtiers; he was Catholic, Protestant or atheist, depending on the company in which he found himself; he ingratiated himself with every sort and condition of man and woman, young or old. "Such was the number of portraits, busts, and medallions of him in circulation before he left Paris that he would have been recognized from them by any adult citizen in any part of the civilized world." (F. C. Schlosser). (See Appendix).

At a reception for the democrat and Quaker, the court appears in simple, dark brocade gowns, not the pale, gauzy splendor of Moreau's *dame du palais* on a fête day; the headdress is also less extravagant, though it retains the three plumes required in court appearance. Men: muffs; widely ribbed stockings. Man (seen against arched doorway) shows the diagonally-set sprays of embroidery, which will develop into a massive gold form at Napoleon's court.

1941. XVIIIc. 1779. French. (Metropolitan Mus., Print Room.)

E. C. de Carmontelle. The Jeu de Bague.

In 1778, the duc de Chartres (later Philippe Egalité) bought a large property from Grimaud de la Reynière, seigneur de Monceau. Great gardens were designed by Carmontelle for the *Folies de Chartres,* as the park was then called. New city walls established by the Fermiers-généraux in 1784 reduced its size. It was nationalized in 1794 and rented as an amusement park where a chute-the-chutes was erected, and was variously disposed of by Napoleon and Louis XVIII. In 1852 it was reacquired by the city and redesigned by Alphand in 1861 into the present Parc Monceau.

The gregarious sparkle of the general assemblies of society of the 1760's at balls, gambling tables, or concerts, gave way to an era of waiting apprehension, aimless, witless gossip, relieved by bursts of mindless physical activity: games of hide and seek, and blind man's buff. (Campan).

The excavations of 1750 loosed a flood of styles *à la grecque.* Carmontelle had amused himself a decade before Hogarth's "Five Orders of Periwigs" (cf.) with the notion of constructing clothes composed from the five orders of classical architecture.

The playful spirit of Carmontelle and of his era is expressed here in a merry-go-round with Chinese attendants, and grown women in *polonaises* and *caracos* snatching at brass rings—the intermediate step between puppet shows and mechanical toys beloved of the midXVIIIc., and the huge chute-the-chutes of the First Republic.

1942. XVIIIc. 1765. English, Woolmer. (Boston, Mus. of Fine Arts.)

Printed Cotton Bed Curtain: pastoral scene.

1943. XVIIIc. 1783. French, Jouy. (Metropolitan Mus.)

"Les travaux de la manufacture": showing the Oberkampf factory at Jouy, designed by J. B. Huot; red copperplate on linen.

1944. XVIIIc. c. 1790. French, Nantes. (Metropolitan Mus.)

"Tombeau de J. J. Rousseau": from Petitpierre et Cie., Nantes; copperplate in mulberry.

1945. XVIIIc. c. 1800. English (Metropolitan Mus.)

"Penn's Treaty with the Indians": historical copperplate in mulberry. Most of these copperplates were printed in a variety of colors; red, brown, blue and mulberry.

1946-63. XVIIIc. c. 1780. French. (New York, Cooper Union Mus.)

A. Brunias. Painted Ivory Buttons.

(*See also* Color Plate, No. 8.)

These buttons, which are supposed to have belonged to Toussaint l'Ouverture, the Negro ruler of Haiti, and a similar engraving in the Cooper Union collection, are the work of an Englishman, Abraham or Auguste Brunias (as the engraving is signed), or Brunais (as given by Thieme-Becker). He exhibited in the Free Society in London, 1763-4, Society of Artists, 1770, and contributed subjects from the West Indies from 1777-79. The print is dedicated to Sir Francis Blake, who had returned to England but came of a family which had been connected with the West Indies for generations.

The extremes of French costume and headdress are enchantingly modified and transmuted in this unique record of colonial Negro dress. Until the

1946   1947   1948
1949   1950   1951
1952   1953   1954
1955   1956   1957
1958   1959   1960
1961   1962   1963

French Revolution, the prosperous island of Saint-Dominique, as it was still called, had a large population of well-to-do free mulattoes and Negroes. The white population's antagonism to the granting of French citizenship to the Negroes in 1791, and the repressive measures they took, led to the Revolution of Toussaint and to brief, fantastic grandeur of Christophe's court, which ended with his suicide in 1820. Christophe's great peaked mountain-top fortress, built by man-power alone, is one of the world's most astonishing engineering feats.

Cotton began to be printed all over France, Alsace and Switzerland by 1760. Nantes, where the dynasty of the Petitpierres worked, 1760-1866, was the great pre-Revolutionary center of cotton printing for the export trade with Africa and the Antilles. By 1789, it had nine factories, employing 4,500 workers and producing 120,000 pieces.

1964. XVIIIc. 1780. French. (Met. Mus., Print Room.)
P. A. Wille. The Petit Waux-hall.
Jean Georges Wille (1715-1808) was a South German engraver established in Paris after 1736, who reproduced paintings by Rigaud, Tocqué and Pesne. His less talented son, *Pierre Alexandre Wille,* was an officer in the National Guard, and died in poverty in 1815.

The success of the English pleasure gardens led to their imitation in Paris. Two Vauxhalls were opened. The Waux-hall Torre (later the Summer Waux-hall) was opened by an Italian whose name it bore, in the mixed Saint-Laurent quarter of pleasure houses and aristocratic hôtels; it provided fireworks and pantomimes, and after 1768, great fêtes in a ballroom which became too crowded for dancing.

The end of the Champs Elysées was still dirty or muddy, but it had begun to be filled with places of amusements and cafés like the Ambassadeurs. The $450,000 Rotunda and gardens of the Waux-hall Colisée, opened there in 1770 for dancing, gambling and spectacles, had a comparatively short success of about a decade.

The showily overdressed young person wears one of the newest hats, which will surpass even the larg-

est *pouf* hair arrangement in size and elaboration. She combines a Medici ruff with a shoulder-cape, on a long-sleeved *polonaise,* looped up almost as short as a *caraco;* immense nosegay. Old companion-duenna in a round cap with semicircles of pleating over the ears; elaborate silk *palatine.* Tasseled cane and obvious wig; quizzing glass and head which may be own hair powdered. Concentration of any fullness of coat-skirts into pleats below a button, set farther back in cutaway frock coat.

1965. XVIIIc. 1783. French.
von Göz. Supplement to Faded Charms.
The lady's aids are as outmoded as her looks: patches went nearly out of style under Louis XV; blood is still let to insure a pale complexion, and rouge is worn only by actresses, though a natural, healthy look is beginning to be valued. Paired *jansénistes* have been superseded by crinoline petticoats; and the new corset of 1778 can be seen in *Galerie des Modes.* (No. 1936).

1966-67. XVIIIc. 1781. French.
"Galerie des Modes."
1966. Le Clere.
"Dress worn by a lady of quality during the mourning for Maria Theresa of Austria, mother of the Emperor and the Queen of France: *Pelisse-lévite* with ermine collar, belt and edges; petticoat of black-dotted white satin; matching muff banded in ermine; *pouf* surmounted by batiste flowers and plumes."

The *lévite,* a fitted gown based on the tabernacle robes of the priests of Jerusalem, continues the trend

Courtesy of Metropolitan Museum of Art, Print Room (1968-69)

towards flowing garments. The point of the bodice is beginning to be lost under belts and sashes.

1967. *Le Clere.* "Half Mourning."

"White silk vest embroidered in black; black silk or cloth coat; white silk stockings; narrow ruffles."

Hair loosens and roughens; vest shorter, its edges cut away sharply from lowest button.

There is a "recrudescence of noblomania" just before the Revolution. Interest is revived in genealogy and heraldry; coats of arms and coronets are imposed on personal belongings. Shopkeepers' wives, who probably used "l'Autrichienne" as a curse after Marie Antoinette's marriage, appear in mourning, and answer commiserations at their loss by explaining that it is for the queen's mother. During Marie-Thérèse's last year of ill health, Marie Antoinette had sewed grave clothes for her mother; black shagreen snuff boxes, marked with the queen's initials and the legend *consolation en chagrin* were profitably hawked about the streets immediately after Marie-Thérèse's death.

1968. XVIIIc. c. 1783. French

Fr. Dequevauviller, after *Lavreince.* L'assemblée au salon.

The Goncourts point out the strict lines of classic architecture, leading to a few forgotten cupids; the absence of effervescence, glitter and conviviality in these last salons where a few friends pass the time together in broken groups. A girl reads by a window; alone; an abbé and a woman holding an ear-trumpet play a game of tric-trac; the conversation in the background is an earnest dissertation; the card game is time won from boredom without the old excitement in gambling.

The *polonaise,* shirred trimmings and cap of the deaf woman are giving way to the plain, trailing belted English gowns, kerchiefs and hats of the callers. Locks begin to trail; even the hair which we see from behind is no longer turned up in firm arrangements of braids.

1969. XVIIIc. French.

Augustin Legrand, after *Lavreince.* Jamais d'accord.

Intimate friendship and confidences go on between women, even though their pets do not agree. Not until now does a cat begin to rival a dog as a pet. Chaste mirror; console table which is almost a Greek altar; vase of cottage flowers; late Louis XVI chairs with pads on arms.

Cap into bonnet; falling curls into uncurled locks; huge feathered hats. Kerchief puffed to chin, elaborated into a series of collars. Striped gown showing vestiges of the former *caraco* (reduced to a frill over the bustle), and the *polonaise* (in the way in which the white muslin overskirt, which is merely an extension of the apron, is looped up out of the mud).

1970-72. XVIIIc. 1785. French.

"Galerie des Modes."

A decade after *Watteau's* death, his younger brother *Noël,* had a son, *Louis-Joseph,* b. 1731, who married, and was living at Lille in 1755; he and his son, *François,* are both designated by the name *Watteau de Lille.* Many other useful fashion plates appear in the "Cabinet des Modes," 1785-9, Paris.

1970. *Watteau de Lille.*

"The gleaming Nymph of the Palais-Royal; offering to the public the charm of face and elegance of figure which bring her merited praises; her head is dressed *à la Suzanne* with a *juste à la Figaro.*"

One of the most eminent architects of the Revolution was the son of a watchmaker named Caron. A watch which the younger Caron made for Mme. de Pompadour first brought him to court attention; he married money and bought a title. After changing his name to Beaumarchais, he became involved in lawsuits and imprisonment; his own brilliant defense freed him; he found himself a popular hero. While working in England as a secret agent of France, Beaumarchais became a violent partisan of the American cause which he supplied with arms, personally and through the government.

Beaumarchais wrote two audacious plays about a character as subtle and witty as himself, named Figaro. "The Barber of Seville" was staged after some years of delay in 1775; the queen and the king's brothers acted in it at the Petit Trianon. "The Marriage of Figaro" was prevented from being shown for half a dozen years by the king. His brothers were part of the audience which, in 1784, received deliriously this mockery of the king and their own society. The old, old duke of Richelieu, who had lived under three French kings, told Louis XVI: "Sire, under Louis XIV, no one dared to utter a word; under Louis XV, they whispered; under your Majesty they talk out loud." A Frenchman, returning after long absence, found the chief change was that "people are now saying in the streets what used to be said in drawing rooms."

The names of characters in Beaumarchais' plays were applied to everything, as we see in the case of the Brilliant Nymph's headdress and close-fitting jacket.

Curls and chignon now tumble, loose and free. Caps return to domestic use, as informal hats and the great decorations imposed on ceremonious heads merge, indistinguishable and extravagant. Even the mob cap turns into a huge lingerie hat. The tailored English style is preeminent. The bosom is enormously emphasized, not by exposure in the earlier French manner, but by extravagant *bouffants,* English muslin kerchiefs. *Polonaise* and *caraco* have passed, but their influence is seen in the long point at the back of the bodice, in its frilled peplum, and in the concentration of interest and skirt fullness into a high, humped bustle on trailing skirts. The reappearance of muslin from England is so welcome that any garment not made entirely of muslin is apt to have an apron as well as a kerchief; many dotted muslins in use.

1971. *Le Clere.* "Suit for the Lieutenant of Police at Audiences."

Marc-René de Voyer, Marquis d'Argenson, was father both to the modern police force and to d'Argenson of the Memoirs, "the best citizen that ever tasted the ministry." The peculiar efficiency of the Paris police today is based on techniques established by d'Argenson during his twenty-one years, from 1697, as Lieutenant General of Police. He spread a finely-meshed net which caught information at every level. A report of every word, every occurrence at the palace, in the intimacy of every salon, as well as in every gathering of thieves reached him, not later than next day, from informants of every class, from members of the royal family down. The marquis had every necessary quality of decision and discrimina-

tion, but he was also a man of breeding, humor and even of surprising heart.

This official costume is, as we expect, conservative in cut, and anachronistic in detail, like the attached mantle of dignity, and in place of a stock and ruffles, the *rabat* worn at the time when the office was first established.

1972. *Le Clere.* "Negligée of a young lady of quality.

"The dress is a sort of *chemise* in thin silk; round gauze bonnet; frilled *fichu;* muslin apron. The child wears a frock coat with his sailor's trousers and hat."

Round cap elaborated into a bonnet; dresses of sheer materials, full and easy; pleated decorations have deteriorated into mere fullness. The *sans culotte* trousers of sailors and working men appear on the children of French gentlemen; full, ruffled collar.

1973-76. XVIIIc. 1784. French.

"Galerie des Modes."

1973. *Watteau de Lille.*

"Lovely Dorine, brilliant as Venus, occupied by thoughts of what she has read in a note dictated by the most acute love. Robe *à la Malbrouk* and hat *à la Charlotte.*"

Proliferation of sentimentality—cottage nosegays, muslin, flounces and bustle. Anglomania: hat given the name of Queen Charlotte; everyone in France, including Marie Antoinette, sings "Malbrouk s'en va t'en-guerre." Shoe buckle turning into rosette.

1974. *Watteau de Lille.*

"Woman of quality lately risen from childbed walking at the hour of noon to take the air. The first fruit of a happy hymen is her sole occupation and augurs its durable happiness. She wears a large, lined satin *pelisse,* trimmed with two rows of martin, and her head is enveloped in a *Thérèse* of solid-color taffeta."

More hygiene, classical allusions, sentimentality and motherhood, together with warm cloak for the coldest winter since 1763, and an enveloping *calash* hood, which can be raised or lowered over the largest hat and headdress by the fanning hinged hoops which support it.

1975. *Watteau de Lille.*

"This English beauty, impressed by the rarities she has met with in Paris, but casting a proud air and in-

1973   1974   1975   1976

Courtesy of Metropolitan Museum of Art, Print Room (1970-76) different glance at the beauties she sees crowding the Palais-Royal, walks with a majestic mien, dressed in a great winter *pelisse* made of satin trimmed with martin, and a long gown with double trimmings and a muff of shaggy fur."

The last of the *catogan* is seen here in her clubbed-up longest lock, under the wide, plumed English hat. Muffs increase in size and elaboration. In 1794, English costume is pale, worn with bright-colored beaver hats, and muffs of eiderdown or fur in striped combinations of white, beige or gray. By 1797, dresses are darker, maroon or puce. Muffs, greatly enlarged, are of darker furs, tan and brown, worked into elaborate check and diamond patterns.

1976. *Watteau de Lille.*

"Mincing Marinette with her darling pet poodle on a public promenade dressed in a light morning robe and hat *à la Zazara.*"

It was a similar small dog, escaped from its mistress, which jumped on Louis XVI as he walked in the Tuileries, and was killed by him with his stick.

Increased size of hat and plumes (black and white, with striped olive-green ribbons to match the dog's leash); elaboration of kerchief into puffed section enclosing chin, and cape of white pleating, over compound capes of the pink fabric of dress and petticoat. The vestige of the *polonaise* point in back is usually suppressed, as by this wide black belt. Trailing overskirt, lined with white to match the white ruffle and petticoat, is bustled up in back, in walking costume.

1977. XVIIIc. 1787. French. (Versailles, Nat. Mus.)

Copy of *A. Girous.* Mlle. d'Orléans Receiving a Harp Lesson from her Governess, Mme. de Genlis.

Mme. de Genlis (1740-1830), poor, noble, spirited, well-educated, and an accomplished harpist, was the niece of a clever writer, Mme. de Montesson, who became the secret second wife of the old duke of Orleans. In 1770, through this influence, Mme. de Genlis was made governess of the daughters of his son, the duke of Chartres (Philippe Egalité). In 1780, in an unprecedented move, she was also made tutor of the boys of the family.

Mme. de Genlis' educational methods were far in advance of her time. A botanist accompanied the children on their walks; lantern slides enlivened their history lessons, and Mme. de Genlis later published a series of educational plays which she had written for them to perform. The people who served them were chosen for special knowledge from different nationalities; each spoke his native language with them. Mme. de Genlis was an expert book-binder, and the children became almost professional leather-workers; they learned to marble paper, make artificial flowers, weave ribbons, carpenter—even to make wigs. Any technique about which they read in the Encyclopédie they were taken to see in the factory. They constructed miniature chemistry and physics laboratories complete with tiny implements and glassware; these were exhibited in the *Galeries* of the Palais-Royal, and during the Empire Mme. de Genlis saw them still on exhibition in the Louvre. Mlle. d'Orléans started harp lessons, twice daily, at five, and was so expert at seven years of age that she played with three other instruments at a regular weekly concert, before an audience.

Mme. de Genlis' "adopted" daughter, the delightful Pamela, who was given in marriage by Philippe Egalité (Orléans) to the romantic, unfortunate Lord Edward Fitzgerald of the abortive Irish Rebellion, was probably Mme. de Genlis' own daughter by Orleans. Orleans represented a grave danger to the crown. He had married the greatest fortune in France; he associated with intellectuals; he was dissolute, but his manners were charming and very considerate. Court feeling against him became so intense and Marie Antoinette's enmity so particularly marked that Orleans spent a great deal of time in England between 1778-90. He became a crony of the sporting Prince of Wales, absorbed egalitarian ideas, and became the main channel through which Anglomania in ideas and clothes flooded France. He opened the gardens of his Palais-Royal to the public. Under his protection, orators inflamed its crowds; it was the incubation place and the heart of the Revolution. He renounced his title, became Citizen Egalité and a member of the Assembly, where he voted for Louis XVI's execution. He seems sincerely to have had no desire to be made king, but too many of his admirers wished it; his wealth and his popularity made him as great a danger to the Revolution as he had been to the Regime; in 1793 he too was executed.

Mme. de Genlis, like Orleans, suffered from the hatred of the royal family, and shared his republican sympathies, but not his fate. At the fall of the Girondist moderates, she fled to Switzerland with Mlle. d'Orléans and supported herself by her pen and brush until she was able to return to France on a pension from Napoleon. She wrote valuable ten-volume memoirs.

Soft, pseudo-classical *chemises,* hair-ribbons; striped, severe, long-sleeved costumes with jackets like a bobtailed frock-coat, the backward flow of which is emphasized by large, plain *fichus* crossed over the breast and tied behind; hems and sashes edged with fringe; high-crowned leghorn hats.

The results of excavation of the cities buried by Vesuvius in 79 A.D. has been felt since c. 1760. Herculaneum was sporadically dug, 1748-80, and Pompeii systematically from 1763. Their bronze and marble statues, Roman wall-paintings and furniture have drawn many travellers, and affect European architec-

1977

ture, decoration and costume. Interest is particularly intense in fermenting France; it turns from its own traditions, court-supported, and therefore corrupted by the Regime, to what it feels is the uncontaminated art of the classic democracies. This will result in a period of great archaeological activity in Italy under Napoleon. His Egyptian Campaign of 1798-1801 will arouse interest in the art of another ancient civilization, as will Layard's expedition to Nineveh and Babylon, 1845-51.

Classic revival influence in architecture and furniture; Roman tripod music stand.

1978. XVIIIc. 1787. French. (Louvre.)

A. Vestier. Mme. Vestier and Child.

Antoine Vestier (1740-1824) began exhibiting late in 1782, and did a number of portraits and miniatures of National Guard officers, 1795-1801. His wife, daughter of the master-émailleur Révèrend, was also a portrait painter.

High-crowned Leghorn hats; striped ribbons and plumes set on loosely fluffed, unsupported hair. Simply cut, almost untrimmed gowns; embroidered muslin ruffles. Shoes trimmed with ribbon ruching in place of buckle. Children now wear short-waisted muslin dresses, the neck finished with simple ruffles.

1979. XVIIIc. 1787. French. (Versailles, Nat. Mus.)

Vigée-Lebrun. Marie Antoinette, Madame Royale, the Dauphin, and the Duc de Normandie.

1980. XVIIIc. 1789. French. (Louvre.)

Vigée-Lebrun. Mme. Molé-Raymond.

Elizabeth Louise Vigée-Lebrun (1775-1842), daughter of a professor of painting at Saint-Luc, was aided by Greuze and Joseph Vernet. She married a picture dealer-artist named Lebrun; became Marie Antoinette's favorite painter. She foresaw the Revolution and went to Italy in 1789; she painted her saccharine portraits in the German principalities and during six years in St. Petersburg. She returned to Paris in 1802, then worked three years in London.

Both the queen and the actress of the Comédie Française show hair only slightly powdered, falling wide and loose, under immense hats or *poufs;* gowns simple in cut, of unpatterned material, and fur-trimmed or with fur accessories. Children's clothes simpler.

Mme. Molé-Raymond has a blue satin hat, with a gray plume caught by a lavender-violet bow; gauze scarf crossed and tied in back, over a lavender-violet satin gown with a blue skirt. Beige-tan muff, in the terrible winter of which Mme. Campan tells, when the fish froze in the sea, and olive trees split in the Midi.

1981. XVIIIc. 1788. French. (Versailles, Nat. Mus.)

A. Labille-Guiard. Elizabeth of France.

Adelaide Labille-Guiard (1749-1803) studied miniature painting with E. Vincent and pastel with Latour, and did portraits of Mesdames, Louis XV's sisters. She was received into the Academy of Saint-Luc in 1774 and that of Paris, 1783, in both cases in the same years as was Vigée-Lebrun.

As the Revolution approaches, French costume loses its national assurance and homogeneity. It is affected by the classical democracies of the past; by the growing English democracy of the present; by exotic garments and turbans from the East; and by romantic XVIIc. styles which have shown an influence in England.

Louis XVI's loyal sister, the decent and kind Madame Elizabeth, who will lose her head in half a dozen years for no more than loyalty, wears a hat straight out of a Rembrandt or Bols portrait; it carries their favorite tall, uncurled ostrich plume, though the toque of velvet has been expanded into a brim with a cocking loop and button. Standing collar of lace; stomacher decoration; hem laced with XVIIc. guards. The same influence is seen on the baby's long-waisted, trailing dress with leading strings.

These "Van Dyke" styles with long, straight plumes, collars and cuffs, slashings and peplums affect dress through first half XIXc.

1982. XVIIIc. 1787. French.

P. L. Debucourt. Promenade of the Palais-Royal Gallery.

There are many colored engravings of the packed, mixed crowds of that hotbed of *égalitairisme,* the Palais Royal, in the years around the Revolution. Among the most valuable records of costume and manners are the aquatints of Philibert Louis Debucourt (1755-1832).

L. to r.:

Caricature of a man in tall coachman's hat with immense cockade, striped coat covered with square buttons painted with race horses, fobs dangling almost to knees, tasseled Hessian boots worn with knee breeches and stockings.

Man facing him: coachman's coat with tight body and long full skirts, controlled by a tab in back; immense buttons; braided whip.

Three daughters preceding mama and papa: caps set on powdered hair dressed in the old sausage rolls; *robes à la française* to the ground; watches swinging at the side on long chains, about as outmoded as a pomander in comparison to the paired fobs seen to the r. of them; mitts.

Two young women: immense hats, fancy ribbons, plumes; bosom exaggerated; waist infinitesimal; dangling fobs; dotted muslin; large shaggy muff of pale fur.

Children: girl in Van Dyke style; boy in sailor hat, triple collar like English redingote on jacket, breeches with knee-strings, boots with reversed tops.

Young woman: slightly powdered *hérisson* with falling *catogan,* satin pelisse, and large muff. Tiny cylindrical muff accompanying the dark bonnet to the r. Man in wig and *frac* carrying a huge beribboned muff. Man and woman at ext. r.: patterned cylindrical muffs.

1983. XVIIIc. 1788. French. (Met. Mus., Print Room.)

P. L. Debucourt. The Bouquets: Grandmother's fête-day.

Boy: high-crowned, wide-brimmed hat, striped frock coat and trousers; collar, tripled and wider.

Young mother: powdered *hérisson* with long straight lock; *bouffant* kerchief to the chin; dotted black lace cape; long-sleeved, untrimmed coat-dress and petticoat; dark sash-belt.

Little girl: shepherdess hat, short-waisted muslin dress, elaborate sash.

Grandmother: cap, *caraco,* flounced petticoat.

Young woman: hair dressed with a ribbon.

1984. XVIIIc. French. 1787-9. (Collection Chaux d'Est-Ange.)

Boilly. The jealous old man.

Louis-Léopold Boilly (1761-1845), self-taught son of a wood sculptor in Northern France, came to Paris in 1779. He saved himself, when denounced for his morals by another painter during the Terror, by a picture of Marat after his acquittal by the Revolutionary Tribunal. Boilly's crowds awaiting the arrival or departure of the diligence, playing billiards and smoking in cafes, are delightful documents of the costume and manners of the Empire.

The dress, with paired fobs, worn by the accused young woman is essentially that of Mme. de Genlis. The replacement of the muslin kerchief by crossed ropes of fur might indicate the extremely rigorous weather of 1789.

Fullness controlled by rows of shirring on the lower arm of older woman, and on short-waisted muslin gown of child; bordered ribbon sash.

1985. XVIIIc. 1790. French. (Florence, Uffizi.)
Vigée-Lebrun. Self-portrait.

1986. XVIIIc. French. (New York, Morgan Coll.)
Vigée-Lebrun. Marquise de Laborde.

The artist, and a member of the family of the count, Marie Antoinette's valet de chambre, who wrote the "Chansons de Laborde," illustrated by

Moreau le j., show romantic-exotic styles. Muslin turban, full neck ruffle like a child's, with a muslin puff beneath; metal-edged sash. Braids, used like a fillet across a turban of metal-edged gauze; long-sleeved *circassienne* over full *chemise* of plain and skirt of dotted, gauze; wide belt fastened with an enormous antique cameo.

1987. XVIIIc. July, 1789. French. (Met. Mus., Print Room.)
A. F. Sergent-Marceau. The People Running Through the Streets with Torches.

1988. XVIIIc. 1793-4. French. (Met. Mus., Print Room.)
R. Knotel. Uniforms of Officers and Troops of the National Guard.

The news of Necker's dismissal and retirement to Basle did not reach Paris until Sunday, July 12, 1789. The Palais-Royal crowds, led by Camille Desmoulins, feared that German mercenaries would be ordered to massacre patriots. Crowds surged through the streets all that night with torches, building barricades, burning customs houses and pillaging. The mercenaries were attacked, fled, and refused to return. The French guards stood between them and the people that night, but joined the people on the 13th when Lafayette established a citizens' guard. Ammunition had not arrived. The Arsenal and warehouse were sacked for arms and ammunition to supplement 50,000 pikes which blacksmiths had forged during thirty-six hours. Torches flared again all that night. On the 14th, the Invalides and the inadequately guarded Bastille and their supplies were taken. The king, who knew nothing of events in Paris, and who had had an unsuccessful day's hunting, wrote *"rien"* in his diary and went to bed, to be awakened in the middle of the night and told about the Revolution.

On the 15th Lafayette established the National Guard of Paris and was acclaimed its commander; he will refuse the supreme command of the National Guard of France in 1790. He designed for it a cockade of the white of the king with the red and bluc of Paris, which, to the queen's indignation, Louis wore when he went before the Assembly on the 15th to promise cooperation, withdrawal of troops and recall of Necker. On June 12, 1792, Marie Antoinette will wear a tricolor and the King and Dauphin the Revolutionary red bonnet. The Assembly set to work on the Declaration of the Rights of Men and a Constitution, and the Revolution began to spread through the provinces; chateaux and religious establishments were pillaged and burned; there were agrarian riots, and taxes could not be collected.

On the 17th the emigration of the nobility began, and grew to 6,000 a day.

Food did not reach Paris. On Oct. 5, a starving population marched to Versailles in a cold rain, inflamed by reports of the quite routine entertainment given a newly-arrived mercenary regiment which Lafayette had ordered to Versailles. The mob ordered "the baker, the baker's wife, and the baker's little boy" to leave Versailles and accompany them back to Paris, to take up the first period of their imprisonment as luxuriously maintained hostages in the Tuileries.

Make-shift citizen guards and weapons of July 12-15, with one grenadier (1987). National Guard uniforms during the Terror; shoes closed by laces.

1989. XVIIIc. 1774-93. French.
H. Robert. Allegory of the Decadence of the du Barry Family.

Marie-Jeanne Bécu (1746-93), illegitimate and uneducated, lively, warm-hearted, and very pretty, began life as a milliner's apprentice. She was discovered in a house of prostitution by Count Jean du Barry, who first used "Mlle. Lange" to draw trade to his gambling-house; he then married her to his brother Guillaume, as a necessary preliminary to her introduction to court in 1769, and her installation as Louis XV's mistress. She stayed with the King as he lay dying of smallpox, but before he could receive the last rites of the Church, he was forced to dismiss her. She lived in her chateau of LucIennes until 1792, on a pension finally granted by that "fat, ill-mannered boy," as she had described Louis XVI. She went to England to raise money on her jewels; at her return, on the testimony of former servants, like her Senegalese Zamar, she was convicted of selling state property and of having worn mourning for Louis XVI in London.

People of origins very like her own reviled du Barry during her lifetime, with a malevolence they had never shown toward Pompadour, and rejoiced at her fall. She was still contemptible to them in death, because she was the only person of consequence who went to the guillotine without dignity, weeping and pleading.

1990. XVIIIc. 1790. French. (Versailles, Nat. Mus.)
David. Bertrand Barère de Vieuzac.

Jacques Louis David (1748-1825), the most important painter of the classical revival, studied in Rome with Vien at the time of Winkelmann's excavations. He returned to Paris in 1780 as painter to Louis XVI. David became a leading Jacobin and voted for the death of the King, of Desmoulins, and of Danton, whose execution he sketched. He was the designer of the Revolutionary *Festival of the Supreme Being,* and painted large group pictures of Revolutionary and Napoleonic scenes. At the Restoration he was exiled to Belgium, and died there.

The clever, temporizing Barère (1755-1841), one of the most unprincipled and contemptible figures of the Revolution, was the journalist-orator who declared that "the tree of liberty could not grow were it not watered with the blood of kings." He began as an attractive provincial delegate and tutor of Orlean's daughter Pamela. He veered from Girondist to supporter of Robespierre; was influential in Robespierre's downfall, and was himself imprisoned. He served Napoleon, then played royalist and died a pensioner of Louis Philippe.

Wigs and powder were first renounced by the Jacobins; their absence becomes a trademark of the younger, more violent revolutionaries. Neck swathed high in a colored kerchief with knotted ends, over a high shirt collar. Narrow coat with standing, turned-over collar and notched lapels, open over short double-breasted vest with prominent lapels and paired pockets. Breeches with double-closing.

1991. XVIIIc. 1790. French. (Louvre.)
David. Marquise d'Orvillers.
Short natural curls bound by ribbon fillet. Gown: compromise between oriental and close-buttoned English coat styles; cut very low. Full chemise with spread collar, like those now worn by little boys, replaces kerchief; waistline shortened by sash. Oblong, ruffled-edged scarves.

1992. XVIIIc. French. (Metropolitan Mus.)
Leonard Defrance. The Rope.
In XVIIc. women rope-dancers wore skirts over their tights. Early in XVIIIc., they began to drop off their skirts during their act. "The Pleasantry of stripping almost Naked has since been practiced (where indeed it should have begun) at Bartholomew Fair," the Spectator said (No. 51).

Mixed company of spectators, the gentry in the middle. An abbé studies the performer through a spyglass. Woman and man in English styles: high-crowned hats and plain cloth garments; coat with long skirts, large buttons, short striped vest, riding boots. Townspeople and servants: caps, aprons and flounced petticoats. Boy in frock coat and breeches has frilled shirt collar opening out over the shoulders like our sailor collar.

1993. XVIIIc. c. 1791. French.
N. F. J. Masquelier, after *Moreau le jeune*. Arrival of Mirabeau at the Elysian Fields.
Gabriel-Honoré Riquetti, Count of Mirabeau (1749-91), was the son of a fantastic marquis and political writer of Marseilles, author of the "Friend of Man." The marquis detested his son, who had been hideously pock-marked at the age of three, and refused to let him bear the family name at school. The marquis, although his own life was as disor-

derly and turbulent as his son's, repeatedly got *lettres de cachet* issued against him for his conduct. After much time in jail, and revolutionary activities in Corsica, Mirabeau returned to Paris in 1771, and was readmitted to his family and society. He stumped the South of France and was elected to the Assembly in 1789. His brilliant, agile oratory, his logic and practical statesmanship, his culture and breadth of experience, made him its undisputed leader, until his constitution, weakened by excess, collapsed from overwork in 1791.

We see the fat, ugly, awkward, over-dressed and over-eager man described by his friend, the count de la Marck, arriving among the Immortals. The Spirit of Liberty floats over his head bearing the inscription, *Free France,* while Mirabeau hands a copy of one of his works to Rousseau from those which the other little spirits carry. Franklin, in his unpretentious dress, crowns him with oak leaves. Montesquieu, Voltaire, Mably and Fénelon approach to receive him, and Demosthenes and Cicero, in the background, watch and discuss the French orator.

1994-95. XVIIIc. 1792. French.

Debucourt. Promenade of the Palais-Royal Garden (1994). The Public Promenade (1995).

1994. Striped stockings are worn combined with culottes in the stripes which the Macaronis had loved, to give a premonitory effect of long trousers.

The accompanying frock coat is patterned (N, R), striped vertically (I), or horizontally. Its skirts are slender; their pleats have retreated to the back, below enormous buttons. Its sleeves are narrow, with an inconspicuous cuff. The collar is very high, often turned over; chest flaps are turned back into pointed lapels, exposing a short and usually double-breasted vest with lapels. A neckerchief mounts to the chin; shirt ruffles show only between the lapels of the vest. High-crowned, almost "top" hats (G, N), or bicornes (R), with a stressed cocarde, accompany

these coats. English top hat, boots, sticks, and paired fobs (N).

Among the older men in the crowd we see every variation between this dress and the most conventional coat and wig, such as is worn by the gentleman in conversation with the nun.

Women's hats fall into four main categories. Very high-crowned, wide-brimmed Leghorn, trimmed with ribbon loops and bows which do not obscure the form of the hat-body (A, P, Q), are worn with the most dishevelled flowing locks and the most English garments. Hats with crowns concealed by masses of decoration are worn with more formally dressed hair (D, J), and English dress or a modification of it. Lingerie hats which developed out of caps (L) are worn with carefully dressed hair and frilly capes. Massed hair decoration of the *pouf* variety appears with the most conservatively French gowns. As *catogans* fall, the back hair is caught with a buckle.

Gowns of the English *redingote* style (A, J, P) have cape-like collars, wide lapels, long, tight sleeves, huge buttons, very wide belts which raise the waistline, fobs, crops, masculine neckwear (J), or puffed-out kerchiefs (Q). Fringe (A), enormous cameos (D), striped materials and crossed kerchief tied in back (M), dotted stuffs (Q), parasols (background, R. side). Child: sailor trousers and hat, frock coat with short sleeves and neck-ruffles.

1995. Where the catogan or falling hair, which is often topped only by ribbon loops (C, E), would be obscured by the brim of the hat, a scarf may flow from under the crown (A). Edges of kerchiefs (A and B), and the hem lines of short skirts (G), are becoming more insistently stressed. (A) is the perfect example of the type.

Multiple capes and collars, and buttoned tab fastenings (I). Male hair dressed like a wig, and falling into a collapsing *catogan* (I). Tricolor cocarde at knees (D, F).

Courtesy of Metropolitan Museum of Art, Print Room (1993-94);*Caisse Nationale des Monuments Historiques* (1995-96).

1996

1996. XVIIIc. 1794. French.
Boilly. La Marche Incroyable.

The population which marched on Versailles in sabots, and knitted while watching heads fall on the guillotine, gets a first look at the fashions which begin about 1795 and culminate in the XIXc. Lanté-Gatine plates of the Incroyables and Merveilleuses.

To our eyes, the costume seems much less likely to scare a horse than anything seen within a horse's lifetime. Immense headgear turns into small, simple bonnets with a scoop brim; hair has lost bulk and length, although its locks are shaggy, after years of careful dressing. The pouter pigeon bosom and crinolined *cul* are much reduced. As the back view of the preceding lady shows, it is less the gown, than the long narrow scarf drawn tight about the shoulders, and the muff, which continue to give the new dress some of the old aspect. Wide belts are completely eliminated, but the new, very short waist has been established at their top line.

Men's legs show a strong tendency to become covered. With fashionably delicate, pointed pumps without buckles, the man who is being driven wears culottes which have descended to mid-calf. Those of the driver are drawn down under his boot-tops, although they are still garnished with bunches of knee-strings. The soldiers (l.) has low boots with long hussar breeches; the shaggy mocker in striped stockings, high boots; the soldier-vendor, buttoned gaiters.

1997-98. XVIIIc. 1795. French. (Louvre.)
David. M. Sériziat (1997), Mme. Sériziat (Emilie Pécoul) and child (1998).

English fashions: Coachman's hat with buckled band and cockade. Very high, turned-over collar and prominent lapels on a coat which is becoming cut away above the waistline into a tail-coat. High, muffling kerchief; short double-breasted vest with lapels. The breeches are closed by a front flap. This was

sometimes shaped like an inverted square-bottomed U, did not reach to the waist, and was ostentatiously decorated all around by braid, with tassel-like elaborations in its pattern at the bottom. Paired fobs tend to replace these, as the flap changes character, and is carried up under the vest, appearing as two seams. Fobs lose ground, and are sometimes replaced by braided or quilted elaborations at the base of the openings.

M. Sériziat's breeches are closed both by buttons and knee strings, which have replaced uncomfortable buckles, as the breeches and boots begin to meet. Breeches are gradually drawn further down the leg, by lacing the knee-strings around the calf, until breeches of nearly ankle-length are attained. Then boots are often abandoned; the wearer walks about in stockings and low shoes with his ankles criss-crossed by the ties which hold down his breeches, while his lady's ankles are similarly criss-crossed by the ribbons from her Greek sandals. Materials become more elastic; the breeches are buttoned above the ankle, or they become wider and hang as trousers. (See Appendix.)

Leghorn hat trimmed with ribbon loops, and lined with a cap-like *valance* of lace, tied over tumbling locks, cut short over the head. Kerchief reduced to a V-opening beneath the round-necked bodice of a *chemise* dress. Waists are shortened and muslin fullness controlled between bands of shirring, or on the mother by a ribbon sash and folded over neck-edge, to stress vertical lines.

1999. XVIIIc. 1795-1800. French. (Louvre.)
David. The Three Ladies of Ghent.

Madame Morel de Tangry's standing daughter wears a *pelisse* over a very simple, classically-inspired gown, belted directly under the breasts with antique clasps. These pale gowns are worn with very elaborate, brightly-colored hats, which are becoming bonnet-like, set back on the head, framing the face; their under-brims are elaborately decorated with shirred, crumpled or ruched silk and lace ruffles, in addition to piled flowers and silk on the crowns. Fluted neck-ruches, *fraises,* are seen throughout first third of XIXc. They tend to become attached to the dress as the neckline closes higher during the 20's; and to spread into wide collars, as shoulders widen in the 30's. They are often edged with ric-rac or other severe, narrow braids, or are rigidly gauffered. Scarves are oblong, often light-colored India shawls with fringed and patterned ends. Mme. Morel's *pelisse* has a typical cape-collar. Necklaces of graduated chains; watches on fine neck chains, tucked into belt.

2000. XVIIIc. 1797. French. (Versailles, Nat. Mus.)
Attributed to *A. Yon.* Napoleon I.

The Constitution of 1795 put the government in the confused control of a Directory of five presidents and two houses, and disqualified the main body of the proletariat. Monarchists and Churchmen fanned discontent. An uprising attacked the Tuileries where the Convention was sitting but was put down by an obscure 25-year-old officer named Bonaparte, under command of Barras. In 1796, Barras married off his beautiful but troublesome mistress, Josephine Beauharnais, to the young officer, who left the same day for his Italian command.

After a brilliant success, he returned in 1797. He was young, ambitious and dangerous, and in 1798 was sent off on an Egyptian campaign. He came back from that to find a population which had been again disfranchised; corruption was rampant; a coalition of Europe was being formed against France. Napoleon staged the coup d'état of Brumaire by which the *Directoire* came to an end and, 1799, was replaced by a *Consulat* of three: Napoleon and two nonentities.

The shaggy man whom Aubrey, the military director in 1795 thought "the leanest and oddest object I ever cast my eyes upon," has gained assurance, but has not yet been polished by Josephine.

Extravagant collar on double-breasted coat which is being cut away into a knee length tail-coat. Its lines are accented by embroidery in a running Greek design, by which cuffs are given a new importance.

2003

2004

2005

2006

2007

2008

They have been buttoned close along the outseam; now they are turned back and open. Use of embroidery on dress garments will increase.

The wide-brimmed hat is cocked, square across the base, into a high-rounded bicorne. The cocking button is dropped to the forehead. The cocking loop, no longer attached to the crown, is drawn down decoratively to meet it, and encloses a huge cockade set high. Reappearance of gloves on men, with English styles.

Directoire chair, arm supported by a winged griffon. Fringe and gold embroidery in "classic" design on table cover.

2001-02. XVIIIc. 1799. French.
"Costumes Parisiens."
The periodical "Costumes Parisiens" was published from 1799-1831. Until about 1825 its plates were drawn by *Horace Vernet.*
2001. Man: high collar and wide trousers.
2002. Woman: veil in place of coiffure.
The "shaggy head" to which Walpole objected in the young English men of 1791, is worn in "dog's ears" with an English swallow-tail coat of cloth, the cuffs of which turn down to cover the knuckles (a usage which will reappear c. 1818), while the chin is buried in a knotted kerchief-cravat. English stick. High-crowned straw hat with a narrow rolled brim, is trimmed with a buckle, which has moved to the hat after leaving the shoe.

There are curious analogies between the rest of his costume and the current "classical" dress shown on the woman. In both, the waistline is raised high. His legs are draped in full, slit loose white cotton trousers (like his cuffs, this short, wide trouser will be seen c. 1818), as are her thighs in a muslin gown. He, too, wears heelless slippers, cut away to a minimum, which give the carriage and movement induced by the sandal of antiquity.

Her hair hangs in a shaggy fringe, her head is veiled like a Roman matron's, though in fashionable embroidered muslin. Whatever the climate of North Europe she continues to wear the thin draperies of Mediterranean antiquity into the first years of XIXc; and there were instances of women oiling their bodies to make their one thickness of draperies cling properly in the narrow dress of 1818-20.

Adaptation of Greco-Roman furniture; griffons as front legs of chair; severe rectangular pieces trimmed with wreaths and mouldings of gilt brass; Greek lyre.

2003. XVIIIc. English.
Racing scene: brown on white cotton.

2004. Late XVIIIc. French, Nantes?
"Diane chasseresse": brown copperplate on white cotton.

2005. XIXc. c. 1800. French, Nantes?
"Le Carrousel": red.

2006. XIXc. c. 1820. English.
Pictorial print: Hunting scene, mauve on white. Signed, *P. Pieter.*

2007. Early XIXc. French, Jouy.
"Monuments de Paris": designed by Hippolyte Lebas.

2008. XIXc. c. 1805. French, Jouy.
"Classic Medallions": mulberry copperplate, designed by Huot.

2009. XVIIIc. French. (Berlin, Kaiser Friedrich Mus.)
A. Pesne. G. F. Schmidt and Wife.
Antoine Pesne (1683-1757), a Frenchman, painted a good many portraits in Germany (1729-33), among them, this German engraver and pastellist (whose work was influenced by Pesne), and his wife.

Georg Friedrich Schmidt (1712-1775) wears a tasseled velvet turban, since he is without his wig, and a fur-lined velvet coat.

Women's costume in Germany and Flanders is more affected by French fashions than is English costume. Her short, unpowdered hair is dressed with flowers, without any sort of cap. She wears the new sort of bracelet, wide and set with medallions or cameos, and diamond earrings; a neck ruche, palatine of black lace; and a brocade gown, the sleeve ruffles of which are edged with ruching.

2010. XVIIIc. 1730. Flemish. (Metropolitan Mus.)
Peter Jacob Horemans (1714-90). Family Group.
A variety of nightcaps and turbans on men's clipped wigless heads; worn with unbuttoned garments, or rich dressing gown over a waistcoat. Older man—heavy wig with knotted locks; younger man—tie wig. The abbé on the balcony can be found living in every large Catholic household as secretary-companion-tutor, since there are not enough livings to go around and the best are plurally held by the aristocracy.

The elderly lady in the pleated, sheer black cap wears a brocade gown, apparently cut like that of Mme. Mercier (see Ill. 1800) but with a severely smooth stomacher in the Flemish tradition. The younger women are dressed in loosely and asymmetrically clasped plain satin gowns, with small powdered heads dressed with flowers.

The peasant costume of the woman servant was well established during XVIIc., but she wears slippers with tiny spike heels.

2011. Second quarter XVIIIc. German. (Vienna, Gall. Liechtenstein.)

H. Rigaud. Joseph Wenzel, Fürst von Liechtenstein.

Maria Theresa needed acknowledgment of her accession under the Pragmatic Sanction. Bavaria was hostile; England, the United Provinces, the Papacy and the Venetian Republic were friendly; Frederick II of Prussia falsely pretended to be.

Liechtenstein was sent as ambassador, c. 1740, to persuade France. He was reassured by the temporizing old Cardinal Fleury, but not until the Peace of Aix-la-Chapelle in 1748 did France finally acknowledge the Pragmatic Sanction.

Seven years after the end of the Seven Years War Maria Theresa's daughter, becoming the wife of the Dauphin, will experience the bitterness of France's continued hatred of Austria. But as the Revolution approaches there is a curious "recrudescence of *noblomania*"; at Maria Theresa's death mourning will be worn for the Queen's mother by French people far removed from court circles. (See Ills. 1966-67.)

Liechtenstein's ambassadorial robes show even more anachronistic characteristics than the French Royal Robes of State. He wears a modification of the XIVc.'s ceremonious dignified gown, and its chaperon with roundlet, together with a modified form of Louis XIV's full-bottomed court wig.

XVIII Century Venetian Dress

No costume is more dependent on the scale and perspective of its surroundings than that of XVIIIc. Venice. It is necessary to look at it in relationship with canals and squares, nearly empty or crowded with festival throngs, and with buildings and gondolas, as painted by Guardi and Canaletto; not only as it appears in the most detailed pictures by Longhi and Tiepolo.

Antonio Canale (1697-1768), called *Canaletto,* the son of a decorator, was a scene painter in his youth; studied in Rome for two years. Homesick for Venice, he returned in 1722 and never left his adored city for twenty-five years. He was hired by the year by the British consul, Joseph Smith, to produce a given number of pictures which Smith sold profitably to the English visitors who began to crowd Italy in XVIIIc. Meanwhile all the other artists of the last great resurgence of Venetian painting, including Canale's nephew, *Bernard Bellotto* (1724-80), (the other "Canaletto"), were travelling abroad, brilliantly rewarded. In 1746, Canale set off to London, which he revisited in 1751, after a meeting with his nephew at Dresden. His English perspectives of buildings and gardens (like Ranelagh and Vauxhall) and his nephew's of Vienna, Munich (where he was a court favorite) and Warsaw (where he died) are important for costume as well as for architectural panoramas.

Francesco Guardi (1712-93), Canale's pupil, was a rapid and prolific painter. His pictures show the great processions of Venice by water, the traffic of the Rialto, the crowds in piazzas and at theatres.

Giovanni Battista Tiepolo (1692-1769), a sumptuous fresco painter, has left precious costume documents on the walls of the Villa Valmarana (1737) and others.

Pietro Longhi (1702-85) painted in charming color with almost Hogarth-like fidelity many small pictures of the life of his contemporaries, rather than the glories of the city of Venice.

2012. XVIIIc. Italian, Venetian. (Toulouse, Mus.)
F. Guardi. The Departure of the Bucentaur.

By XVIIIc. the Doge had become a figurehead whose chief duty was to cast a precious ring from the State Galley, the Bucentaur, into the Adriatic at the yearly festival which symbolized the marriage of Venice and the sea.

As the Bucentaur leaves its moorings the shores are crowded with spectators and the basin of San Marco is filled with gondolas of every variety.

2013-16. XVIIIc. 1753. Italian, Venetian.
Gaetano Zompini: "Le arti che vanno per via della cittá di Venezia."
2013. Chair Maker. 2014. Old Clothes Vendor.
2015. Placing a Servant. 2016. Window Mender.
Short underskirts combined with even shorter overskirts are seen on young Venetian women of the people, and servants. Women's shoes are cut lower over the instep with lower heels and less exaggerated toes than in France.

Everywhere women's short hair began to be dressed like men's at the beginning of second third of century. "The Ladies of Norfolk universally wear periwigs and affirm that it is the fashion of London," Walpole writes Mann (Oct. 3, 1743). Wigs are not uncommon on women by midXVIIIc., and women's hair is usually dressed in this way with riding costume. Nowhere, however, does women's hair so completely imitate men's, with tie and pigtail, as with the masculine-influenced dress of Italian women of all classes. Their gowns are simple in cut, relatively untrimmed, with longer sleeves, the cuffs of which remain shaped or buttoned back. There is relatively less show of linen and almost none of ruffles below the cuff.

The boy (No. 2014) shows the netted cap of XVIc. persistent in Italy.

2017. XVIIIc. Italian. Venetian. (Venice, Coll. Brass.)

P. Longhi. Lady in Riding Costume.

Masculine hat, with pigtail, *solitaire* and jabot, coat and waistcoat, worn with matching skirt, braided like a military uniform.

2018. XVIIIc. 1756. Swedish. (Stockholm, Nat Mus.)

A. Roslin. Baronne de Newborg-Cromière.

Alexander Roslin (1718-93), a Paris-trained Swedish painter, worked in France, Sweden and Russia among the highest society.

The Baroness is as covered with ruchings, ruffles, lace and fresh flowers as Mme. de Pompadour, but her gown shows an interesting close sleeve on the forearm below the elbow ruffles.

2019. XVIIIc. Swedish. (Stockholm, Hallwylska Coll.)

Bernhardine von Diesbach. Gräfin von Hallwül (1728-79).

In 1920 Walter and Wilhelmina von Hallwyl gave their home, its complete contents, and funds for its upkeep to the Swedish crown as a museum which is never to be altered. Its contents, reproduced in fifty-odd magnificent volumes, includes portraits of Hall-

wül ancestors from XVIc. The collection is extra-ordinary, primarily, as a record of every personal possession of the clothing and household effects inherited or acquired by a rich Swedish gentleman born in 1839. Not only art objects, porcelain and silver are reproduced, but shoes and socks, underwear and galoshes; court, hunting, and everyday clothes of the family; and their every possession down to the meanest utensils from the kitchen, the boot boy's cleaning equipment, the family mending kit, hardware and screws.

Everyone is playing at shepherdess in XVIIIc., even before Louis XVI's accession in 1774 when wheat and cornucopias, symbolic of hoped-for plenty, decorate everything.

2020. XVIIIc. 1758. German.

D. Chodowiecki. The Sisters Quantin.

Daniel Chodowiecki (1726-1801) was a German engraver who illustrated "Minna von Barnhelm" (1770), "Werther," and "Lotte" (1775), as well as many almanachs.

Simple domestic dress and caps.

2021-24. XVIIIc. 1760-1765. Austrian, Viennese. (Vienna, Karl Meyer Coll.)

Viennese Porcelain Figures.

2021. Pilgrim with Staff and Wallet; cockle shells on hat and cape (1765).

2022. Skate Seller with Fur Hat, Fur-trimmed

2025

2026

2027

2028

2029

Coat and Muff (1760).

2023. Skate Seller with Ermine Muff (1760).

2024. Cavalier (1765).

Decorative figurines and groups are produced in the growing porcelain and pottery factories of Vienna, Germany, France and England in latter half XVIIIc. and first half XIXc. They are pastoral or genre, or pretty figures out of Italian comedy, like those dancing in Tiepolo frescos. (See Appendix.)

2025, 2027. XVIIIc. 1750. Italian, Viennese.

2025. Dress: green and white silk brocade.

2027. Matching stays and sleeves.

2026. XVIIIc. c. 1750. French.

Courtesy of Metropolitan Museum of Art (2025-27)

Bodice of Louis XV period.

2028. XVIIIc. French. (Boston, Mus. of Fine Arts.)

Headdress: quilted silk and brocade.

"The ladies have been for some time in a kind of moulting season with regard to (their heads) having cast great quantities of riband, lace and cambrick . . . What . . . would be substituted in place of those antiquated commodes. But (women) were all the last summer so taken up with the improvement of their petticoats, that they had not time to attend to anything else." (*Spectator*, 265, Jan. 3, 1711/12.) Now they begin to think of the other extremity. At the Opera, the Spectator notes the "prettiest coloured hoods that ever I saw," in blue, yellow, "philomot," pink, and pale green, like a bed of tulips.

2029. XVIIIc. Italian, Venetian. (Venice, Coll. Countess Adele Salom di Corrobio.)

P. Longhi. Masquerade at the Club.

2030-31. XVIIIc. 1756. Italian, Venetian. (Venice, Palazzo Papadopoli.)

G. B. Tiepolo.
2030. The Mountebank.
2031. The Minuet.

2032. XVIIIc. Italian, Venetian.

G. B. Tiepolo. Punchinellos.

2033. XVIIIc. Italian, Venetian. (Boston, Mus. of Fine Arts, formerly Oppenheimer Coll.)

G. B. Tiepolo (drawing). Milliner's Shop.

People of every degree, even children, masked at carnival time. Variety of masks: beaked *bauta,* worn by gentlefolk (never without domino); round and half masks; masks of Italian comedy figures, worn alone, or with the appropriate comedy costume.

The trade and costume of the entire world came together at mediaeval Venice. In XVc., loose trousers entered popular dress. Many Venetians bore the name of their patron, Saint Pantaleon; the rest of Italy mocked Venice and its garb, in the comedy figure of an old Venetian called "Pantalone." Italian comedy became familiar to the rest of Europe, and "pantaloon" entered language as the name for trousers. With the decline of Venice and the rise of English sea-power, loose trousers became part of sailor's dress.

Gentlemen's clothes, though covered by dominos, can be seen to differ less than ladies' from current European styles. Long full wigs persist in Italy (mountebank, older gentleman to right at club masquerade). Buttoned cloaks with collars worn by men who are neither gentlemen nor liveried servants. Muffs, carried by men as well as women in Italy. Ladies' cloaks and characteristic short flaring coats with striped hems. Slippers with pointed toes but comparatively low heels. Very short skirts; long, plain, pointed bodices; pretty, clocked stockings on maid servants.

2034-35. XVIIIc. c. 1760. Italian, Venetian. (Metropolitan Mus.)

P. Longhi. 2034. The Meeting. 2035. The Temptation.

Italian costume continued its familiar course of independent development during XVIIIc. It reached its most delightful and most specifically Italian form in the costume of carnival time, particularly in Venice.

Carnival lasted ten frantic bacchanalian days before Ash Wednesday. Walpole wrote West from Florence (Feb. 27, 1740): "Masqued, too, I have done nothing but slip out of my domino into bed and out of bed into my domino; all the morn one makes parties in masque to the shops and coffee-houses, and all the evenings to the operas and balls. . . . What makes masquerading more agreeable here than in England is the great deference that is shown to the disguised." No advantage was taken to be ill-tempered, gross or bawdy, yet the freedom of carnival gave Walpole opportunity to make new acquaintances.

The masculine tinge, seen in the less pretentious Zompini illustrations, affect the costume of Venetian ladies as well. A black tricorne hat is always the apex of their characteristic pyramidal silhouette. This is built up through a series of horizontal truncations and spreading vertical cuts into an apparently simple triangular form of immense subtlety. The cocked hat; the *bauta* mask, with its spreading nose; the flow of the black domino (half opaque, half lace) over the specifically Venetian cape which in its turn spreads over the widest of half-paniers; even the accompanying fan—all are necessary parts of the total effect, built up of V's.

The cut of the costume is pure and austere, completely uncluttered by flounces on the skirt. In Venice, it is the cape which spreads open; the skirt is not slashed up the front. In maid-servants' costume a short underskirt is worn with an even shorter overskirt, which is often banded at the hem. This may be thrown up over the head, but it is never cut vertically in front.

There may be a line of decoration on the shaped cuff and on the cape front, to emphasize its spreading edges. There is no ladder of bows coming from a corset beneath, in Venetian costume. A flat embroidered placard gives the V-shape of a lady's bodice-front its necessary emphasis. Sometimes it is laced across; often it is severely plain. It may have the little peplum of the Columbine costume.

In France three graduated lace frills finish the sleeve. What appears below the shaped Italian cuff is frankly an undershirt; the ruffles which finish it are primarily of its fabric. On the lady in Longhi's "Meeting" the cut of the ruffles adds to the angular forms of the whole costume.

There are wonderful combinations of dilute color. In Ill. 2034 the lady to the left wears a brick red bodice, tan skirt, green muff with blond fur and black. The man who bows wears a gray-blue domino; the man in back, a bricky-tan cloak. The lady is all in gold and silver, cream and lemon. Her maid (with pink and blue low-heeled slippers), has a green underskirt and throws her pink top-skirt over her head. The Metropolitan Museum has a collection of braided liveries such as that worn by the servant in "Temptation." His master wears negligée of yellow waistcoat, white dressing gown and blue and red embroidered slippers.

2036

2037

2038

Horemans the younger (1714-90), was one of a dynasty of prolific painters of Flemish genre scenes. Lower middle-class Protestant costume; men in unpowdered bob wigs; plain coats, vests of another fabric, trimmed only with ball buttons and buttonholes. Women in enclosing hoods with fluted edges, and fichus, are dressed in cotton prints. In "Autumn" the dress is of a large patterned scenic or floral print. The smooth-bibbed apron has an all-over motif; the petticoat is striped.

2038. XVIIIc. c. 1762. Flemish. (Metropolitan Mus.)

Raphael Mengs. Maria Louisa of Parma.

Raphael Mengs (1728-79) painted Charles III of Spain and his connections of Parma, Tuscany and Naples:

The wife of Charles IV of Spain wears a gown, the completely fitted bodice and skirt of which are cut in one piece. The construction of the skirt, to give fullness over the side wings, is made clear by the lines of the striped floral brocade. The pleats falling from the shoulders of the ordinary court gown are missing here. The lace sleeve ruffles, instead of falling over the forearm, are pleated and tacked back to the sleeve above the puffed finish. The bodice has no ladder of bows or embroidered plastron and carries no tippet scarf or palatine. They are replaced here by a bib of lace, as a background for the enamel and diamonds of the order pinned to her bosom.

2036-37. XVIIIc. Flemish. (Metropolitan Mus.)
J. J. Horemans, y. 2036. Winter (1761).
2037. Autumn (1762).

2039. XVIIIc. 1770.
French. (Metropolitan
Mus.)

H. Drouais. Emperor Joseph II of Austria.

Marie Antoinette's brother was an enlightened despot, sensible, amusing, forthright and tactless, who was unable to force acceptance of his liberal plans. As Count Falkenstein, he visited his sister in France, scolded her for her giddiness and rouge, was horrified by the booths in the palace stairs and galleries where shopkeepers sold souvenirs almost at the doors of the private apartments. He insisted on sleeping at an inn with his servants.

Coat, losing fullness, grows longer and more cutaway, waistcoat shortens. Wig in a bag, its side curls multiple.

2040. XVIIIc. 1771.
Swedish. (Stockholm, Nat. Mus.)

A. Roslin. Gustave III and His Brothers Discussing a Plan of Campaign.

2041. XVIIIc. Swedish. (Stockholm, Nat. Mus.)

P. Hilleström. Conversation at Drottingholm.

Per Hilleström (1732-1816) returned to Stockholm from Paris in 1750. He taught at the Academy in Stockholm of which he became director. His pictures also show the common people.

The King of Sweden and his brothers, whose mother was Frederick the Great's sister, were brilliant, learned and charming. Artists and people of distinction were beginning to make the tour of the new northern courts. They were both welcome, and delighted with the French atmosphere of the Swedish court.

Drottningholm, the Swedish summer court, was begun late in XVIIc. and finished in XVIIIc. by the son of the original architect. Its XVIIIc. theater had revolving scenery which is still of great interest to theatrical designers.

The life, interests and amusements of the court were thoroughly French, as are the metallically gleaming clothes of the King and his brothers. The costumes of the court ladies, however, are full of anachronisms dating from late XIVc. and XVIIc.: slashed and puffed sleeves and wired-out standing collars of lace are worn, without wide paniers, though they are accompanied by the high hair arrangement and the three plumes of latter half XVIIIc. court dress.

2042-49. XVIIc. 1780. German.
Daniel Chodowiecki. Figures From Almanachs and Book Illustrations.

Sword worn with more ceremonious clothes (2042); obligatory with court frock coat (2045); being given up in every-day wear (2043); or replaced by stick in clothes of English type.

Ceremonious snuff-taking; overcoat with wide collar, heavy top boots and pigtail; large muff and fur piece worn by gentleman (2042). The most ceremonious feather-topped "head" and gauze-draped court gown (2045). Umbrella and ermine cape carried by uniformed lackey; lady in negligée; gentlemen in Spanish *majo* costume; evangelical figure; business men with wide brims cocked high over deeper crown (2049).

English style: Round hat, own hair, wide collar, buttoned-back lapels, large plain buttons, stick, knee breeches and gaiters; short, square-cut vest, paired fobs (2043). English style with frock-coat and plain skirt (2044). "Head" dressed high (2044); plumes worn with *polonaise* as well as with *robe à la française, sabots* at elbow (2046). Raked-back *toupet* of Macoroni exaggeration; English garments: short vest, paired fobs with seals, breeches, soft high boots, stick (2047). Poor men in old-fashioned cast-offs; low-crowned cocked hats, long straight-cut coats and waistcoats (2048).

2050-52. XVIIIc. 1776-85. German. (Boston, Mus. of Fine Arts, Elizabeth Day McCormick Coll.)

Original Fashion Drawings.

2050. *Ein Kap*: gray-blue costume: a combination of *caraco* and officer's coat with buttoned-back edges, vest and wig, gray and white plumes, gold laced hat band, tasselled stick. 2051. *Herz Haube*: heart-shaped cap and matching kerchief; red gown; green apron, ribbons, and slippers. 2052. *Frisure à la Religieuse*: overhanging "Montgolfier" cap with green ribbon commemorates the first balloon ascension of the brothers Montgolfier in 1783. Pink cape-coat with gold buttons; collar, cuffs, and lapels of black fur, black slippers, white heels and stockings. Amazingly tasteless German version of the already fantastic French version of the long-waisted English style and cap.

2053. XVIIIc. 1776. German. (Frankfort-on-Main, Hauck Coll.)

Jean Noë Badger. Gogel Family.

2054. XVIIIc. c. 1780-5. Austrian. (Petraia, Villa Reale.)

Italian School. Family of Peter Leopold, Grand Duke of Tuscany.

When Maria Theresa married her cousin and friend Francis, duke of Lorraine, in 1736, his claims to Lorraine were exchanged for the Grand Duchy of Tuscany, whose last degenerate Medici ruler had died. Francis delegated Tuscan rule to Austrian regents until his son Leopold became eighteen.

Peter Leopold (1747-92) married Maria-Luisa of Spain and became one of the most progressive rulers of the XVIIIc. Until he became Emperor in 1790, the agreeable Tuscan court delighted the English visitors to Florence, although the natives resented its simplicity, after the Medici splendor which had ruined them. Leopold, enlightened but less aggressive than his brother Joseph, managed like him to alienate

2055

large blocks of his subjects: the nobility, by equalizing taxes and undermining feudalism; the church and its faithful, by attempts to control and rectify its faults, of which he had become aware during early studies for the priesthood; the people, by forcing a premature political maturity upon them. But he reformed government and law courts, and put them in Tuscan hands; replaced an expensive standing army by a citizens' militia; arranged free trade in food; drained swamps and improved agriculture for an underfed population.

German dress attempts to follow French fashions, but until the Congress of Vienna in 1815, Germany consists of many small, more or less provincial principalities, dependent on the taste of their courts and the physical difficulties of communication with Paris. Fashion plates begin to be sent out from Paris in final quarter century, and Bertuch of Weimar publishes the *Journal des Luxus und der Moden* in 1786, but intercourse is interrupted by the Revolution. Provincial England's notions of what was the current style of London, which had so amused the Spectator, are completely outdone throughout XVIIIc. by German fantasies about Paris fashions.

French style was most accurately followed at the court of Saxony; Frederick the Great was Francophile; the Austrian court was informed of French ways by its connection with Marie Antoinette.

The Tuscan court of her brother receives the world of Europe as it visits Italy; Leopold's thinking is affected by French philosophy, but the ceremonious dress of the court is a rigidly individual combination of Spanish, Austrian and French elements.

The Gogel family (2053) are in fairly good touch with France at Frankfort-on-Main, though the jackets and insistent trim of the three young females on the r., would not be seen in France in 1776.

The dress of the male figures of the Tuscan court (2054) is affected by that of Leopold's Spanish father-in-law, Charles IV. The younger boys wear the Spanish version of the open-collared, long-trousered costume: a closed tunic with a sash, *faja,* around the hips, rather than a coat open over a square-cut vest, as in England and France. The agreement of vest and breeches, and the insistent, repeated lines of heavy metal braid on the vests of the older males is a Spanish court fashion, repeatedly painted by Goya. The black stock, sometimes with a bow, is a lingering form of the *solitaire,* seen in Spanish and German dress of the final quarter century.

In this official group portrait hair is still powdered. That of the young girl (l.) is still dressed in a ceremonious cap as the Princess Royal's was in 1778, a fashion which had been abandoned for children of the same family by 1785.

The application of a ruffle, like that of a petticoat, to the outermost of two skirts, is seen both on the girl (extreme r.) of the Gogel family, and on the Tuscan princess (extreme l.); it would not be seen in France. The two older ladies of the Tuscan court wear standard, slightly outmoded French dress.

2055. XVIIIc. 1784. Spanish. (Metropolitan Mus., Bache Coll.)

Goya. Don Manuel Osorio de Zuniga.

Francisco Goya y Lucientes (1746-1828), was born in Aragón, son of a master-gilder and his wife who came of aristocratic family. Their turbulent son, audacious and headstrong, found it advisable to leave one place after another in a hurry. From Aragón, he went to Madrid, but soon set off with a band of bullfighters to make his way along the Mediterranean to Rome as a musician and bullfighter. He left Rome suddenly for Madrid, where he married the sister of the court painter Bayeu, his former teacher; by her he had twenty children of which only one son lived.

Bayeu started Goya on a long career as a tapestry designer in 1776. Mengs influenced him to begin

painting portraits in 1781. He made powerful friendships with the dukes of Osuna and Alba; was soon
on familiar terms with the royal family, and became
the lover of the duchess of Alba.

Many of his strange, satiric and terrible etched
series were done after an illness which left him stone-
deaf. His paintings, tapestry designs, drawings and
etchings show the entire life of Spain: the courts of
Bourbon and Bonaparte kings, officers and duennas,
peasants and bullfighters, *majas* and *majos,* bullfighters, courts of inquisition, the horrors of war.

His brothers-in-law, the Bayeus, and his follower
A. Esteve y Marqués show the same period in a
good deal of variety; and Vincent López y Pontaña
(1772-1850), the nobility of the following generation
or two.

Spanish child's costume: scarlet tunic and trousers
(see 2054): open collar with a gold and silver gauze
faja and slippers with bowknots.

The ceremonious dress of little boys of the early
XIXc. Bonaparte courts has a short jacket ending in
two long tasseled points; long, high-waisted trousers,

heavily embroidered like the jacket along the outseam and hem and on the thighs. It can be seen in
Victor Guye, page to King Joseph Bonaparte (Harding Coll., New York) and Pepite Corte (1813?-18?)
(Mellon Coll., Pittsburgh).

**2056. XVIIIc. 1786-7. Spanish. (Boston, Mus. of Fine
Arts.)**
Francisco Bayeu y Subias. Portrait of a Young Man.
Characteristic Spanish lapel, seen in a more exaggerated form on Bayeu's self portrait in 1769. The
earliest square-cut vests were bordered along the bottom.

**2057. XVIIIc. 1790. Spanish. (Washington, Nat. Gall. of
Art.)**
Goya. Marquesa de Pontejos.
The hair of lightly powdered heads is becoming
lower all over Europe, and spreads wider with the
lower locks falling, but the process is carried out with
more formality in Spain.

This gauzy gray costume with touches of pink has
long sleeves and a belted bodice with the round frilly
neckline which is preferred to the kerchief in Spanish
upper class dress. The round skirt is repeatedly caught

2056

2058   2057

with the loose bows seen in Spain. Characteristic Spanish slipper and heel cut low over the instep, with a tiny pointed toe.

2058. XVIIIc. 1795. Spanish. (Madrid, Duke of Alba.)
Goya. Duchess of Alba.

The greatest beauties at the Spanish court were the wives of Goya's patrons, the dukes of Osuna and Alba. Even children on the streets stopped playing to watch the "utterly graceful and completely beautiful . . . prodigy"—the duchess of Alba with her cloud of wonderful black hair. Her plain, round-necked muslin dress has a hem of Spanish fringe, bow and sash of scarlet, long sleeves caught down over the hand, and a bracelet of medallions on the upper arm.

2059

2059. XVIIIc. 1791. Spanish. (Madrid, Prado.)
Goya. Tapestry Cartoon: Blindman's Buff.

Goya dressed the figures of his Watteau-like pastorals in Spanish regional costume. The *majas* and *majos* he shows here were "gay members of Madrid's lower class who over-dressed in a fantastic manner." The tapestry weavers complained of "dandies and girls with so much decoration of coifs, fal-lals, gauzes, etc., that much time is wasted on them." (D. C. Rich: *Art of Goya*.)

1. Hat of blue ribbon, lightly powdered hair, pink dress, white lace, slippers and stockings. 2. Dark coif, blue gray bow; red jacket; black and yellow *faja;* golden yellow breeches trimmed in red; gray stockings, black shoes, silver buckles. 3. Blue gray net coif; coat and vest, dark and light brown; chestnut breeches; gray stockings. 4. Cream net coif, red jacket, brown-gold epaulettes, white skirt. 5. Dark greenish hat and cock feathers, brown gown, gold ruffles. 6. Gold coif; bluish jacket and breeches; greenish vest; gray stockings. 7. Gray net; yellow jacket trimmed in white puff; olive green breeches trimmed in silver. 8.

2060   2061

Dark greenish brown costume. 9. Black hat, gauze edged; powdered hair, white kerchief and apron; light yellow-green dress.

2060. XVIIIc. 1796-7. Spanish. (Metropolitan Mus., Print Room.)
Goya. San Lucar Sketch Book, India ink wash drawing: The Swing.

Goya spent six months in Andalusia with the duchess of Alba who had retired (or had been banished) to San Lucar at the beginning of her widowhood. This sketch book dates from that time.

2061. XVIIIc. Spanish. (Madrid, Prado.)
Goya. Wash drawing: Guitar Player and Dancer.

2062. XVIIIc. 1792. Spanish. (Metropolitan Mus.)
Goya. Don Sebastián Martínez.

Coats made of narrowly striped fabric are commonly seen in the last decade of XVIIIc. But the way in which these gay stripes are used to enhance the cutaway line and flapping lapel of a coat which remains open is characteristically Spanish. Large, ornate buttons, which preceded the large plain buttons of the English style of dress. Buttoned side pocket, partly seen on knee breeches.

2063. XVIIIc. 1796. Spanish. (Madrid, Prado.)
Goya. Francisco Bayeu y Subias.

A self-portrait by Goya's brother-in-law also shows this identical plain gray coat with characteristically cut and flapping Spanish lapels.

2064. XVIIIc. 1790. Spanish. (Washington, Nat. Gall. of
Art, Mellon Coll.)
Goya. Carlos IV as a Huntsman.

Very wide-brimmed hat turning into a bicorne. Spanish cutaway coat. Blue and white Ribbon of the Order of Carlos III over a tunic-like vest, belted at the hips at the low line of the Spanish *faja*. Until breeches are successfully drawn down below boot-tops, boot hose of the XVIIc. sort are often worn in the last decades XVIIIc. The king's boot top is also of the XVIIc. shape, in a peak which could turn up to cover the knee. The characteristic boot of the turn of XVIII-XIXc. is either the English jockey boot with a turned-down band and boot-straps, or a low, rather spreading black Hessian boot, cut down in front (i.e., at the line described by the colored turn-down of the king's boots).

2065. XVIIIc. 1799. Spanish. (Washington, Nat. Gall. of Art, Mellon Coll.)

Goya. María Luisa of Spain.

The little princess whom we have seen in a Mengs portrait has turned into the revolting, raddled and dissolute Spanish Queen. She wears Spanish national costume in sheer dotted black with repeated horizontal trimming; black lace mantilla, great knot of ribbon, and fan.

2066. XVIIIc. 1790. Spanish. (Madrid, Prado.)

Goya. General José de Urrutia.

2067. XIXc. 1800. Spanish. (Madrid, Prado.)

Goya. Infante Don Luis María.

Son of Carlos III's brother, the Infante Luis, as a Cardinal.

2068. XIXc. 1800. Spanish. (Madrid, Prado.)

Goya. Family of Carlos IV.

Court dress: embroidered frock coat and waistcoat; breeches, buckled shoes, tasseled sword. Spanish-Empire gowns with ceremonious tunic.

LIFE IN RESTORATION AND XVIIIc. ENGLAND

During years of poverty and exile, Charles I had ample opportunity to perfect the Continental pleasures of sauntering and looking on. This was one of many elements from which the subjects of "that pleasant man" constructed the new way of life peculiar to England in the XVIIIc.

"At this time," says Bishop Burnet, "the court fell into much extravagance in masquerading; both king and queen went about masked, and came into houses unknown, and danced there with a great deal of frolic . . . so disguised that none could distinguish them." The liberty afforded by masks was naturally abused and they began to fall into ill repute at the turn of the century.

Restless, pleasure-seeking and reckless, after years of war, people are constantly out of their own houses and about the streets, searching for amusements, which even courtiers fail to find in the stodgy, respectable courts of William and Mary and her sister Anne. Anne got out of attending her own receptions, leaving her ministers to do the honors; she sat silently gnawing her fan when she did appear. Swift went to court "to pick up a dinner" free. Anne's mourning for her consort was so prolonged that, after remonstrating, merchants managed to obtain a law limiting the duration of public mourning. Nor were the courts of the sensible Hanoverian Georges particularly amusing. George I arrived as a widower with a deplorable taste for undecorative German women; he spoke only German and cared nothing for dress. George II had some interest in fashion. Caroline of Anspach, his wife, was a tolerant woman of character and intellect, not without charm; she preferred the company of literary men, theologians and philosophers, and disconcerted the English court by the unseemly coarseness of her language. The English-born George III lived a happily domesticated life with the German Queen Charlotte, who bore him 15 children. He was an autocrat, long ill and for a time actually insane; neither of the couple had any taste or interest in art or literature. Their court was a stiff, uneasy horror, from which their sons revolted violently.

The luxury of transport by coach, sedan chair or barge has become a necessity. Licensed public conveyances, increasing in number each year, cater to those who do not keep liveried conveyances of their own.

Everyone goes by water or coach to Ranelagh, Vauxhall, or to innumerable other gardens, catering to all classes of society, as well as to take the waters at spas, like Bath, beloved by both Mary and Anne. Here they can gamble; listen to music and the new operatic performances; see spectacles like Mr. Winstanley's water works; watch exhibitions of horsemanship, gladiatorial combats, bull, bear, or dog-baiting, and cock fights; pick up new lovers; eat and drink in charmingly laid out gardens, while listening to nightingales. Coney Island is the debased end-form of this sort of amusement.

There is less and less real erudition. Men throng to coffee-houses and taverns to read the newspapers, gossip, meet their friends and do business. Newspapers have increased from the *Post Boy* of 1695 to 55 regular weeklies in 1709, usually issued to subscribers at 1d a sheet and printed on one side of the paper. Swift tells Stella that copies of the *Spectator* "never come my way; I go to no coffee-houses." The ½d Stamp Tax, which Swift predicts "will utterly ruin Grub Street," does kill the *Observator,* forces other papers to amalgamate, and while the *Spectator* has doubled its price and survives, it too will succumb late in 1712.

Most of the coffee we drink comes from Central and South America, to which the plant was brought in the e.XVIIIc., by way of Jamaica, from the Near East. A Greek scholar at Balliol had brewed his own coffee at Oxford as early as 1636, Wood tells us. But the first public coffee-houses in Oxford were those opened in Dec. 1650 by "Jacob, a Jew" and in 1654 by Cirques Jobson, a Syrian Christian. Coffee-houses immediately became enormously and time-wastingly popular. Their numbers multiplied and they took on club-like characteristics, as different houses served different colleges. Christopher Wren and the virtuosi and wits of All Souls', for instance, patronized the house opened in 1655 by the royalist apothecary, Arthur Tillyard.

The first coffee-house in London seems to have been the one established by a Greek in St. Michael's Alley, Cornhill, in 1652. The coffee-house serves as office, club, and post-office. Letters are left at coffee-houses for hourly collection, and many customers receive their mail at a coffee-house address; Swift's letters went to the St. James. Nearby inns are used as points of reference in addressing letters, since houses are not numbered. Men meet and entertain customers at coffee-houses, which usually cater to men of the same profession and political party, and become reduced to business use in the latter half of century. The different receptions with which the news of the death of the king of France would be accorded at 8 coffee-houses between the St. James and Garraway's is amusingly sketched in the *Spectator* (June 12, 1712).

Society is now aligned by political belief. Clubs, meeting at coffee-houses, are founded on eating or politics, usually both. The Beefsteak Club, of which the actress, Peg Woffington, was president and the only female member, was primarily an eating club. The October, which met at the Bell Tavern to drink "October Ale," was a Tory club. Kneller painted the portraits of the 40 Whig members of the Kit-Cat (named from Christopher Cat, who made their mutton pies), which met at the

Strand in winter and Hampstead Wells in summer.

Women are often downright illiterate, taught little but dancing, dress and manners. They, also, are so divided by politics that the *Spectator* (81) supposes that Whig and Tory ladies may come to indicate their politics by setting their patches on the right or left cheeks, and foresees difficulties with moles and pimples when "ladies patch out of principle." They visit constantly; send servants to inquire "Howdee" after each other's health—much as XIX-XXc. ladies leave cards. They have days at home; drink tea out of fine china, the collection of which becomes a mania. Tea and china are sold in the same shops, and are often bartered against used clothing, which brings good prices all over Europe.

Servants now dress with more luxury than their masters of the previous generation. Among their own class, they take rank from the rank of their masters, and dress as much like them as possible. They are accustomed to fine liveries, fresh gloves, and must meet a standard of cleanliness new even to those they serve. Gentlefolk who have eaten with their fingers all their lives are suddenly made ill by people too ill-bred to use forks; forks should not be wiped on a piece of bread but on a fringed napkin (furnished by Mr. Doiley, the linendraper, whose name they still bear), or they should be rinsed in a basin of water on the sideboard.

Ideas of politeness and cleanliness, though they had spread out over Europe from Louis XIV's court, become debased and diluted. Manners become gestures studied with French dancing masters. The middle half of XVIIIc. is, in actuality, one of the smelliest and dirtiest in modern history. Infrequently washed heads, caked with flour, housed vermin. The importation of the miraculously washable India cottons was prohibited in England and France.

Country people were crowding into towns, the old shallow wells of which were polluted and had lowered; they had not been adequate for a smaller earlier population. Improvement of the city's water supply had begun to concern public-spirited citizens in the XVIc.; Stow records sums given or willed by aldermen and good ladies towards this purpose, often requiring that an equal sum be laid out by the city. The earliest steam engines were those used to pump Thames water into the houses of the rich. Everybody else had less water than before, and perfume became almost a necessity.

Highwaymen, thugs and pickpockets infest the roads and cluster about fashionable meeting places. Bands of well-born young toughs called Mohocks, of which the *Spectator* and Swift's *Journal* complain constantly during 1711-1712, shove passersby into the gutter or "sweat" them in forced swordplay, roll old women down hill in barrels, but never take money. Dozens of such current names, signifying different categories of men—

wasted or useless, dissolute or dangerous, rich, climbing, gambling, or desperately poor—are explained in *Proteus Redivivus, the Art of Wheedling,* published *tempus* Charles II, and in the *Complete Gamester,* 1674 (Malcolm, 1811.) The more important pleasure gardens advertise that they provide armed guards to conduct their patrons, street lighting is improved (though mostly from park to palace), and, through the efforts of the Society for the Reformation of Manners, young baronets who run chaises through with swords or cut off people's noses are apt to be arrested.

Roads are improved and rewards posted for the capture of highwaymen, as a network of flying coaches crosses England at regular intervals, carrying the post and meeting packet boats. English people not only travel but live abroad, and the Grand Tour of a young English gentleman now lasts three years. The first of four lighthouses at wave-swept Eddystone is built after the design of Mr. Winstanley, who was lost in its collapse during the great storm of Nov. 3, 1703.

As in France, wild gambling played a part in the necessary new stabilization of government finances, and led to the beginnings of insurance. Life insurance companies, like "The Lucky Seventy, or longest livers take all," of 1709, became a mania of the first decade.

Fire insurance was provided by three companies: the Phoenix of 1682; the Friendly Society of 1684; and the Amicable Distribution of 1695, which became the Hand in Hand. The insuring companies maintained liveried men to put out fires, and fastened their own leaden plaques of identification to insured houses. Shallowly buried water pipes often froze. The fire at the Middle Temple in 1677, when the Thames froze over, had to be put out with 100 kegs of beer from the Temple cellar and the Devil Tavern.

Windows in new houses are reduced in numbers, because of the new tax, but become larger and let in more light. Individual panes remain small until new techniques produce large sheets later in XVIIIc., but they are now hung sash instead of casements. An advertisement of 1710 describes the typical new house: "To be Let, a New Brick House, Built after the Newest Fashion, the Rooms wainscotted and Painted, Lofty Stories, Marble Foot paces to the Chimneys, Sash Windows glaised with fine Crown Glass, large half pace Stairs that 2 People may go up on a Breast, in a new pleasant Court, planted with Vines, Jesamin, and other Greens, next door to the Crown, near the Sarazen's Head Inn in Carter Lane, near St. Paul's Church Yard, London."

Wallpaper and paint reflect the light, which used to be absorbed by dark tapestries and stamped leather hangings. Furniture, now clearly seen against light colors, becomes more delicate and elegant, in mahogany and lacquer, with new forms of tea-tables. Large mirrors and chandelier crystals catch and reflect candle-light. Fireplaces in England burn coal, and better water is now piped into subscribers' houses from the Thames and other waterworks by steam pressure.

Gardens, beautifully planned and kept, are part of English life, both in country and city. While Louis XIV's court, and those of his successors, make country life in France equivalent to exile and bankruptcy, so that its great estates are falling into neglect and ruin, the dullness of the English court allows country life, which has always appealed to the English, to increase in importance. Changing agricultural methods, fencing and improved firearms make shooting on foot as pleasant a sport, in its way, as hunting on horseback. The owner of a property, walking over it for game, has its condition always under his eye, and ways of improving it constantly in mind.

Land tenure and agricultural methods, almost static since long before the Domesday Book, alter greatly during XVIIIc. The Industrial Revolution of the latter half century draws farmers from precariously held land which they have not the will, knowledge, nor means to improve. Fewer farmers must meet an increased demand for bread and meat. Leggy animals, descended by natural selection from those that survived drowning in English mud, begin to be bred into compact meat carcasses by Bakewell of Dishley. Turnips now provide winter feed. As Chamberlayne notes, all the English wear good leather shoes. New methods of tillage, introduced by Tull, Townshend, and Coke, are taken up by rich landlords who can afford to adopt them. Arthur Young transforms the whole English system of land tenure, to aid in this production.

Spinning and weaving were home industries, bringing in cash income to self-sufficient farm people, until Hargreave's spinning jenny, Arkwright's frame, and Crompton's mule upset the equilibrium of the industry in second half XVIIIc. There is, for the first time, an excess of thread and yarn,

over workers to weave it. Weavers multiply in every vacant building. They prosper until a minister named Cartwright invents a power loom.

Nothing is more characteristic of XVIIIc. than the jealousy and competition to stifle rival trades. Now workers riot against machines, mills are burned, whole industries with their uprooted workers migrate north from river banks and depleted forests to coal-producing areas. Iron masters have learned to smelt with coke; blast furnaces, and the textile mills of Peel and Hargreaves, are worked by steam. In 1745, a druggist seeks and finds English clay to replace kaolin brought back from China as ballast; great potteries, like Wedgwood's, arise around Burslem. Steam navigation begins; bridges are rebuilt in iron; ships are plated with iron.

Country folk, unused to the sight of cash, go to work in factories and find themselves far worse off: uprooted, cramped in dark company houses, with no room to raise a pig and some cabbages, much less a cow. They are inadequately fed; fall prey to diseases to which isolated farm life has given no immunity; work 12 hours or more in factories, the air of which is filled with fine particles; they die of tuberculosis and silicosis. Drunkenness increases with misery, as gin and whiskey begin to be distilled in England. The good intentions back of the Poor Law and workhouse are horribly misused to insure a practically enslaved, immobilized labor supply. Economic pressure sends even children of five to tend machines.

The poor, orphaned, and unfortunate (whose numbers have immensely increased with war, plague, fire, and changing agricultural methods) have been neglected for the centuries since the abolition of the monasteries. Now the government, guilds and private individuals begin to be concerned with their welfare. Hospitals and asylums, free schools and workhouses begin to be built. They are still horribly inadequate, frequently heartless, and so clearly spread infection that small dispersed infirmaries are also established.

2069

2069. XVIIIc. 1702-14. English. (New York, Knoedler.)
John Marcellus Laroon.

View of the Mall in the time of Queen Anne.

The two great parks of London in XVII-XVIIIc. are St. James' with its Mall, and Hyde Park with its Ring. Both were first enclosed by Henry VIII. While the Leper Hospital was being altered into St. James' Palace, the adjoining marshy meadows were drained and turned into a deer park with a riding path, and the 390 acres of the old Hyde Manor were turned into a deer and stag preserve.

Both were improved by Charles II. The 350 foot long Ring, first used for horse races, became the fashionable drive of the late XVIIc. An enlarged St. James' Park, laid out by Lenôtre with lines of lime trees, had a long canal for the water fowl which the king loved to feed, and which still exist there.

The Ring was enclosed by "a sorry Kind of Balustrade . . . but three Foot from the Ground, and the Coaches drive round and round this. When they have turned for some time round one Way, they face about and turn t'other; So rowls the World." (Mission). During the fashionable afternoon hours, after the theatre, 200-300 coaches might be seen driving at one time, their dust kept down by watering, for which a fee of 6d per coach had been imposed in 1664. Footmen and lackeys had to remain outside the guardhouse gate, where they played rough games, and where could be bought the usual refreshments of the period: ale, spirits and syllabub, tarts and cheese-cake. After 1695, masked women and hackney coaches were forbidden. By 1712, the sale of intoxicating liquors at the gate was stopped and no stage coach, hackney coach, chaise with one horse, cart, wagon, or funeral was allowed to enter the park.

The Mall, where smoking was banned, became the fashionable promenade. During the hours between 3 o'clock dinner and 8 o'clock supper (which were also the most correct hours for making calls), Swift made his daily turns around the Mall, greeting or walking with cabinet ministers, and writing Stella (XXIII): "It is prodigious to see the number of ladies walking there." The *Spectator* (437) notes the increase of bare shoulders as he watches Gatty walking in the park at "high Mall."

John Marcellus Laroon (1679-1774) was the son of Marcellus Lauron or Laroon (1635-1702), an engraver from the Hague who lived in England.

His picture shows women of all classes wearing the fontange, which the *Spectator* (#98, June 22, 1711) says "has risen and fallen above 30° within his own memory . . . About ten years ago the commode shot up into a very great height, insomuch that the female part of our own species were much taller than the men . . . We appeared as grasshoppers before them. At present, the whole sex is in a manner dwarfed and shrunk . . . I remember several ladies who were once very near seven feet high, that at present want some inches of five." Some of these tall ladies wore masks (which are now more apt to be worn by women of poor reputation) with mantles, horizontally decorated skirts and trailing overskirts draped into bustles. They carried fans.

Although the wigs shown on the men still hang on the chest in front, they have mounted into twin peaks and have begun to rake back from the forehead. Both the waistcoat (buttoned at the waist to catch the Steinkirk), and the coat are shorter, and flare as additional width is pleated into the skirts of the coat at the sides. Pocket slits are now finished with flaps. Frogs are used, as well as buttons, for closings. Hose are rolled or gartered at the knee over close breeches, *culottes.*

The fontange is a relatively easy way for women of the lower classes to attain a fashionable look, and it has been quickly adopted by younger women. It is worn by two, walking behind the water-carrier in utilitarian, rolled-up garments (l.). Behind them, riding parties precede and follow a coach with six horses. At the end of one row of lime trees a postilion in livery and sash wears the jack boots which begin to be worn by nobody else. To the r., a sedan chair waits, while a bearer reaches for one of the buckets belonging to a woman in a cap and dark, bibbed apron.

2070. XVIIIc. 1711. English. (London, Nat. Port. Gall.)
Sir Godfrey Kneller.

Sir Christopher Wren.

Wren, who "completed the work commenced by Jones, and established the present favorite fashion of building" (Malcolm) was the most influential of the Italian-inspired English architects. Sir John Vanbrugh, the painter-architect who built the heavy, less well-scaled Blenheim and Castle Howard and the fantastic "Minced-pie" house at Greenwich, and whose theatre roof had to be rebuilt, was no such mathematician or artist as Wren, who rebuilt Jones' St. Paul's, altered Hampton Court, designed Trinity College Library at Cambridge and the brick buildings of Chelsea and Christ's Hospitals. The influence of Palladio, filtered through these three men, still influences the architecture of large public buildings. Its alternative influence in the XVIIIc. is the romantic Gothic style in which Horace Walpole rebuilt his fabulous Strawberry Hill at Twickenham and whose last remains are seen in Hudson River Gothic in America.

Wren, at 79, wears a dark wig. The first wigs in XVIIc. were of any color, often blond; now they are white or dark. Mr. Michon, a goldsmith, advertised in 1710, that he had "found out . . . a clear water" which would darken light hair. Wigs of human hair might cost 40 guineas, like Duumvir's (*Tatler*, #54); cheaper wigs had horsehair beneath, or were entirely made of horsehair. A country girl in 1700 sold her hair for £60 to get herself a dowry; a periwig-maker paid £50 for the long white hair of a woman who had died at 107. (Weekly Journal, c. 1720.)

Wren's clothing shows the trend away from Louis XIV richness, which is indicated in the garments worn at George II's birthday in 1735: "brown flowered velvets, or dark cloth Coats, laced with gold or silver, or plain velvets of various colors, and Breeches of the same." By then, "their waistcoats were either gold stuffs, or rich flowered silks of large pattern, with a white ground; the make much the same as has been worn some time, only many had open Sleeves to their Coats; their Tie Wigs were with large curls, setting forward and rising from the forehead, though not very high: the Ties were thick and longer than of late, and both behind; some few had Bag Wigs." (Malcolm)

2071. XVIIIc. c. 1712. American. (Baltimore, Hist. Soc.)
Justus Engelhardt Kühn.
Eleanor Darnall.

Kühn was a German Protestant who painted in Maryland from his naturalization in 1708 till his death in 1717.

Although Maryland was established in 1633, primarily as a colony to which Roman Catholics might emigrate to escape increasing oppression and discrimination, religious toleration was practiced there. In 1715 the proprietor turned Protestant, Catholics were disfranchised, and an influx of German Protestants soon began.

The ancestor of this five or six year old girl is supposed to have come from England in 1672. She was married, c. 1728-9, to Daniel Carroll III of Upper Marlboro, Md., whose forbears had been immigrants from Ireland in 1688. Catholic families like the Carrolls were apt to send their sons to Jesuit schools in France; their cultural relationships were as often Continental as English.

Some trace of this may be felt in Eleanor's reddish brown dress, black train, lace apron and hair arrangement, as well as in the elaborate "stock" background of gardens and balustrades which the painter probably had on hand for rich patrons. "There were no estates resembling this scene at Maryland at that or any other time," reports James W. Foster, Director of the Maryland Historical Society.

One of the products which England hoped to get from her American colonies was silk. Silkworm culture was first established by James I, bounties were offered, and from Pennsylvania southward some little silk was produced. On George II's birthday in 1735, Queen Caroline "was in a beautiful suit made of silk of the produce of Georgia, and the same was universally acknowledged to excel that of any other country."

2072. XVIIIc. 1716-8. English. (Macpherson Coll.)
Capt. Edward Teach, known as "Blackbeard the Pirate."

Teach was one of many British privateers, operating under "letters of marque" during the Wars of the Spanish Succession, who turned to piracy on their own account after the peace.

In 1717 he captured a French merchantman which he converted into a 40-gun man-of-war and renamed *Queen Anne's Revenge*. In this he harried the West Indies and the Carolina and Virginia coasts.

Piracy was hard to suppress without the cooperation of authorities, and flourished because Spain preferred pirates, to traffic with her former enemy. It was unprofitable without a partner on shore, preferably a person of standing, to dispose of the loot. Pirates were often gentlemen, although Teach happened to be a ruffian; but his accomplice and protector was the Governor of South Carolina, whose administration led to rebellion and brought S. Carolina from control of the proprietors to that of the Crown.

Two sloops, dispatched by the Governor of Virginia in 1718, captured Teach's ship, and he was shot by their commander.

Teach wore his hair and beard, which were in themselves remarkable, tied at the ears by flowing ribbons. Otherwise, he and his men

2072

2073   2074   2075   2076

2077   2078

wear the simple, utilitarian clothes with long trousers which for centuries we have seen on sailors and which, in less than a century, will be worn by most men.

2073. Early XVIIIc. English.
Waistcoat, negligée: linen, embroidered in pink, green, white and yellow silk, and silver gilt.

2074. XVIIIc. c. 1720. English.
Waistcoat: white brocade, embroidered in gold.

2075. XVIIIc. Italian.
Waistcoat: Sleeved waistcoats, with the hem patterned all around, are made for indoor wear without jacket.

2076. XVIIIc. Italian.
Waistcoat: quilted.

2077. First Half XVIIIc. French.
Waistcoat: green cut and uncut velvet, satin ground.

2078. XVIIIc. 1750-60. Italian, Venice.
Waistcoat: brocade. Brocades were especially woven for waistcoats. The Mus. of Fine Arts, Boston, has Ebenezer Storer's sleeved waistcoat, which is seen in the Metropolitan Museum's oval pastel by Copley.

Courtesy of Metropolitan Museum (2073-78)

2079. Late XVII-Early XVIIIc. French. (Boston, Mus. of
    Fine Arts, Elizabeth Day McCormick Coll.)
    Embroidered Muff: white woven-figured ground,
embroidered with gold and polychrome silk.
2080. XVIIIc. American, Rhode Island. (Boston, Mus. of
    Fine Arts.)
    Needlework Pocket Book with Silver Clasp, Hun-
garian point.
2081. Last Half XVIIIc. French. (Boston, Mus. of Fine
    Arts.)
    Embroidered Pocket Book.
2082. XVIIIc. South German. (Boston, Mus. of Fine Arts.)
    Sampler: patterns used in XVIIIc. purses.

2083. Early XVIIIc. English. (Boston, Mus. of Fine Arts,
    Elizabeth Day McCormick Coll.)
    Quilted and Embroidered Sleeveless White Jacket.
2084. XVIIIc. French. (Boston, Mus. of Fine Arts, Eliza-
    beth Day McCormick Coll.)
    Bodice of Dress: pink taffeta embroidered in straw,
giving an effect of gold embroidery.
2085. Late XVIIIc. American. (Boston, Mus. of Fine Arts.)
    Strip of Crewel Work: valance or petticoat border.
    A guest at the Princess Royal's wedding (1742)
wrote: "The Duchess of Queensbury's clothes
pleased me best; they were white satin embroidered,
the bottom of the petticoat *brown hills,* covered with

all sorts of weeds, and *every breadth* had *an old stump of a tree* that ran up almost to the top of the petticoat, broken and ragged, and worked with brown chenille, round which twined nasturtiums, honeysuckles, periwinkles, convolvuluses, and all sorts of twining flowers which spread and covered the petticoat, vines with the leaves variegated as you have seen them by the sun, all rather smaller than nature, which made them look very bright; the robings and facings were little green banks with all sorts of weeds, and the sleeves and the rest of the gown loose twining branches of the same sort as those on the petticoat; many of the leaves were finished in gold, and part of the stumps of the trees looked like the gilding of the sun. I never saw a piece of work so prettily fancied, and am quite angry with myself for not having the same thought, for it is infinitely handsomer than mine, and could *not* cost *much more*."

2086. Late XVIIIc. American. (Boston, Mus. of Fine Arts.)

Petit Point Picture: Boston Common with the old Hancock House.

When the *Spectator* (606 and 609) proposes a monumental inscription: "that she wrought out the whole Bible in tapestry, and died in a good old age, after having covered three hundred yards of wall in the mansion house," Cleora, who prefers real birds and flowers, says: "I hope to kill a hundred lovers before the best housewife in England can stitch out a battle."

2087. XVIIIc. English. (Chicago, Art Institute.)
Joseph Highmore. Pope at Twickenham.

Joseph Highmore (1692-1780), nephew of the sergeant-painter, studied art while apprenticed to the law, but became a professional painter in 1715. He was a pleasant, learned man, who painted many conversation pieces which are often mistaken for Hogarths; a number of portraits of royal or important people (including Harvard College's Hollis); and book illustrations like his twelve plates for Richardson's "Pamela" in 1744.

It was difficult for a Roman Catholic merchant's

son like Pope to get a good classical education in England in late XVIIc. By rigid self-discipline, the brilliant seventeen-year-old prodigy was eventually fitted to produce translations of Homer, subscriptions to which brought in enough money to enable him to buy a house at Twickenham in 1719. Here he laid out his famous gardens and grotto and entertained the best company of his day: Swift and Gay, Bolingbroke and Bathurst.

An illness at twelve years had been too drastically treated. Pope (1688-1744) never grew beyond 4½ feet and became deformed. Eventually he had to be laced into "a bodice of stiff canvas," and could not put on without assistance the three pairs of stockings by which he tried to conceal the thinness of his legs.

He is in negligée: waistcoat, dressing gown and cap. A wig is uncomfortable, a shaven head cold, so we find XVIIIc. literary men, and painters like Hogarth, working in a night-cap or turban, even while otherwise completely dressed.

He is receiving a letter from John Searle, for many years his faithful body-servant and gardener, who has thrown an overcoat with a round collar over the waistcoat which was probably his working dress.

William Hogarth (1697-1764), son of a schoolmaster, was first apprenticed to a silverware engraver. Hogarth was an intensely alert and curious person who so trained his visual memory that he could reproduce whole theatrical performances at which he could not make sketches. In 1725 he engraved a shop bill advertising the removal of the linen-draper's or "slop shop" of his younger sisters, Mary and Anne, to "Ye King's Arms joyning to ye Little Britain Gate, near Long Walk," which "Sells ye best and most Fashionable Ready Made Frocks, Suites of Fustian, Ticken and Holland, Stript Dimmity and Flan'el Wast-Coats, blue and canvas Frocks, and blue-coat Boys Dra^{rs}," and similar materials "By Wholesale or Retail at Reasonable Rates."

His first great work was a series of twelve illustrations for Butler's "Hudibras," in 1726. It soon became his practice to paint a picture and then make an engraving from it. His "Harlot's Progress" (1731), published by subscription, was pirated. The "Rake's Progress" (1735) was protected by an Act of Parliament copyrighting an engraving, for the passing of which Hogarth was largely responsible.

In 1729, he was secretly married, though with the connivance of her mother, to the daughter of Sir James Thornhill, at whose art school he had studied. His work for thirty-five years gives the most

minutely complete picture of a life and a period which any artist has ever attempted. Every picture is a valuable document full of allusion and satire.
2088-89. XVIIIc. 1726. English. (Metropolitan Museum, Print Room.)
Hogarth. Samuel Butler's *Hudibras*: 2088. Hudibras in Tribulation. 2089. Hudibras at the Lawyer's.

Butler's satire of "The Presbyter Knight Going to the Wars," published between 1663-78, was founded on his own experience of life in the household of a former revolutionary general, and a brief period in a law office. Hogarth depended largely on Hollar's plates for his XVIIc. women's costume.
2090. XVIIIc. c. 1728. English. (Metropolitan Museum.)
Bartholomew Dandridge. The Price Family.
2091. XVIIIc. 1742. English. (Cambridge, Fitzwilliam Mus.)
Joseph Highmore. Mrs. Elizabeth Birch and Daughter. (Late appearance of dress of 2090.)

Satin gowns, with asymmetrically clasped bodice closings; slightly supported by hoops; short sleeves (still usually without cuffs), from beneath which the ruffled shirt sleeve emerges. Women's hair in transition: Mrs. Birch's hair has lost the Louis XIV look, but is still of natural length; that of the Price women has been cut to the new three-fingers' length, and is covered by caps with lace lappets or by smaller triangular caps. High-heeled slippers.

The form of the wigs of the Price men is determined by their ages; but the front locks of the fullbottomed wig on the oldest man are knotted and thrown back over the shoulders. Coat pockets high and horizontal. Deep closed cuff; two younger men wear coat sleeves entirely without cuffs, buttoned up the out-seam, to match the breeches. Shoe toes (square on the older man), are becoming more natural in shape, as feet of younger men show.
2092. XVIIIc. 1728-32. English. (London, Sir Charles Tennant.)
Joseph Highmore, sometimes att. to *Hogarth.* The Green Room at Drury Lane.

The Drury Lane Theatre of XVIIIc. was managed by Cibber from 1704, and by Garrick after 1747. The company before which Barry is rehearsing "Romeo" consists of Miss and Mrs. Prichard; Fielding; the generous and hasty Quin, who was afraid to appear in Gay's "Beggar's Opera"; and Lavinia Fenton, who became immortal as its Polly Peachum. It is as "Polly," the duchess of Boulton, that Walpole records her death. Satiric treatment of Sir Robert Walpole and bribery in the "Beggar's Opera" brought about censorship by licensing, under which the English Theatre still operates. It closed all the theatres but the Drury Lane, Covent Garden, and Haymarket. Most of the almost numberless pleasure-gardens of XVIIIc. England flourished by evading censorship, calling performances "concerts."

An increase in the size of hoops is paralleled by greater flare in the skirts of men's coats. Coats are simple in fabric and trim, but lines of decoration, such as we see carried up the back vent of Barry's coat, reinforce its edges and prevent them from scissoring (see Ill. 2100). The long wigs of older men begin to have their front locks knotted up out of the way; in the wigs of younger men the long hair is drawn back and tied, often enclosed in a bag.

The English bodice has a long, straight, prim look, increased by the back lacing of its corset, in contrast to the more curved French *corps* which is commonly laced in front. English gowns are not much affected by the loose garments and flowing pleats of the *robe à la française* before midXVIIIc., and English gowns retain a comparatively uncluttered, circumspect look throughout XVIIIc. The edges of the bodice, finished with folds or shirred bands, scarcely emphasize the very discreet V-front.

There is no French *échelle* of laddered bows from the corset. The lace or plain kerchief over the shoulders is drawn under a bar of simple ribbon across the line of the corset-top. This may be trimmed with a bow, and another bow is sometimes seen at bottom of corset. These bars tend to multiply in number and become crossed lacings by mid-XVIIIc., but the closing does not lose characteristic simplicity.

The English skirt also remains plain, even after the round skirt changes to a laterally extended form. It is seldom split down the middle before this change makes it convenient; and when it is split, the revealed underskirt is plainer than that of France, although it is often handsomely quilted. Cuffs and the ruffles below them are also less elaborate than in France, although they become fussier by midXVIIIc.

But the English woman's head is covered long before the French. English caps are larger, more elaborate, and more enclosing. They may be tied under the chin; there are frilled mob-caps, large triangles and ovals (see Ills. 2093, 2099). Cap's long lappets hang or are pinned up, as Lavinia Fenton wears hers, to give a spreading roof-line above face.

2093. XVIIIc. 1729. English. (Metropolitan Museum.)
Hogarth. The Wedding of Stephen Beckingham and Mary Cox.

Weddings were often clandestine, usually private, and in any case small, during XVIIIc. The Marriage Act of 1753, which required public weddings to have repeated reading and publication of banns, was even considered by Fanny Burney an affront to the modesty of any women of sensibility.

The colors worn by this small wedding party in St. Martin's in the Fields are (l. to r.): f. in deep blue; m. dark gray; groom, pearl gray coat and hose, light blue vest, blue-gray breeches; bride, cream and gold; m. beige; clergyman, black, with white cassock and red hood; m. dark gray; f. shrimp pink; and f. pale yellow with blue bows.

2094. XVIIIc. 1740-50. French.
Chatelaine-nécessaire: gold and moss agate.
2095. XVIIIc. German, Regensburg.
Watch-chatelaine: gold, jewels, agate; key.
2096. Mid-XVIIIc. French.
Nécessaire: shagreen, mounted in gold.

2093

2097. XVIIIc. 1740-50. French.
Contents of nécessaire shown in Ill. 2098.
2098. XVIIIc. French.
Nécessaire: gold and enamel egg.
Courtesy of Metropolitan Museum of Art
2099. XVIIIc. English. (Metropolitan Mus., Frick Coll.)
Hogarth. Miss Mary Edwards.

The eccentric Miss Edwards, daughter of Francis Edwards of Kibworth Harcourt, Leicestershire, was a great heiress. She was clandestinely married to Lord Anne Hamilton and was painted by Hogarth with her husband, but later repudiated the marriage and declared her son illegitimate, in order to protect her fortune. She is the central figure in Hogarth's *Taste in High Life* (see Ill. 2113).

Substantially the same English cap and dress worn by the bride, Mary Cox, are shown here in an extravagant, lacy form seldom seen in England. The open V of the corsage of her brocade gown is suppressed in favor of the hanging ends of her lace-trimmed scarf. The pleats which would ordinarily finish the edges of the bodice are pushed back toward the underarm. In addition to the conventional English choker of pearls, she wears an immense, diamond pendant. A watch-chatelaine with keys and accessories is pinned at her waistline.
2100. XVIIIc. 1731. English. (London, Countess of Leicester.)
Hogarth. Indian Emperor.

Dryden had followed a series of comedies by an heroic tragedy, "The Indian Queen," in 1663. This was immensely successful because of its wonderful settings and costumes. Mrs. Marshall played Queen Zempoalla in a real Indian gown, presented by Mrs. Aphra Behn. This was followed in 1665 by "The Indian Emperor; or, The Conquest of Mexico," in which Nell Gwynn made her debut. The play had a long life. George Farquhar, who had begun as an actor in a travelling company, was so unnerved by almost killing a fellow actor in its duelling scene that he turned playwright.

Hogarth's extraordinary visual memory reproduces a performance in the private theatre of Mr. Conduit, Master of the Mint, before the duke of Cumberland, the princesses Mary and Louise, the duke and duchess of Richmond, the duke of Montague, Earl of Pomfret and Captain Pointz. The children who play wear good standard French theatrical costumes with plumed turbans, instead of Mrs. Behn's actual Indian costumes. (Sitwell: *Conv. P.*)

Men's coats are of plain material, with flaring skirts and waist-high pocket flaps. Deep cuffs, open or closed, match the waistcoat; decoration is carried up the back vent of the coat. Wigs become strongly differentiated according to the age, situation and profession of their wearers—older men wear more conservative styles of heavily curled wigs; younger men tend toward the wig with toupet and bag (worn by the duke). Caps almost universally worn by English women and girls of the upper as well as other classes.

2101. XVIIIc. 1733. English.

Hogarth. Southwark Fair.

Southwark, where Shakespeare's Globe Theatre stood, is in the heart of London at the cross-roads from Southern England. A three-day fair in September, established there in 1492, was gradually extended to two weeks. Malefactors from the rest of London went into hiding among Southwark's poverty-stricken population. The reputation of the Fair became so bad that it was abolished in 1762.

The picture teems with allusion, and with information about poor people and their fun. In front of a booth where china is sold, a bag-piper with a walking dog operates a mechanical toy with his foot. A dice game goes on under a lantern advertising Cibber and Bullock's "Fall of Bajazet."

The great sign on the roof, carrying the legend "The Stage Mutiny" refers to the complications which followed Colley Cibber's sale of Drury Lane, the year before. Revolting actors, led by Cibber's worthless son Theophilus, are gathered in Covent Garden near the Rose Tavern. Cibber sits in the left corner with a sack of money. Highmore, who had "bought into" the theatre, holds a scroll marked "6,000 £." John Ellis, who has many pugilist friends, and is the scene painter of the company, brandishes a club.

Behind him, the widow of Robert Wilks, the actor, who holds a small share, carries a banner, "We'll starve them out." In the center are Mills in the plumed costume of "Bajazet," "Doll Tearsheet," Harper as "Falstaff," and Theophilus Cibber as "Pistol."

On the slack wires are acrobats, one of whom, Cadman, was killed later by a fall.

Lee and Harper's sign in the center advertises "The Siege of Troy." "Punch's Opera" is beyond. The Union Jack, as restored by Charles II, floats above.

In front, the actors drum up trade, as a circus parade still does today. An actor in plumes and scale armor is being arrested for debt by a sheriff. A fire-swallower performs on a platform.

In back of the peep-show the inevitable pick-pocket operates on a country squire, with gloves and whip, his wife beside him. Mr. Fawkes juggles a bird. Above is the "Royal Wax Works" which shows "the whole Court of France." At the right, a broken-down horse carries a battered rider, the loose sleeve of whose sword-arm is held up by a ribbon elbow garter.

2102. XVIIIc. 1735. English.

Hogarth. Rake's Progress: plate 3.

The indispensable Hogarth plate is always an omitted one; how can one be satisfied with fewer than all eight illustrations of the "Harlot's Progress" (1731)? The eight plates of "The Rake's Progress" carry him down through Fleet Prison to Bedlam; and now one wishes one could have used the 1729 "Commissioners of the House of Commons examining the Warden of Fleet Prison" for mishandling his office.

The "leather-coat" of the Rose Tavern, Drury Lane, stands between a wench singing a bawdy ballad, *Black Joke,* and a trumpeter and blind harp-player. In back a neglected girl is setting fire to the map. All the Roman emperors on the wall have been smashed but Caesar, who is represented by a portrait of the cook—Pontiac. In front a "posture woman" is undressing for her act.

Pictures in which people are coming apart are very valuable. There is very little that we don't know about trouser buttons at fly and knee, after looking at "The Rake," or about wigs when we examine the standing man who is losing his. We see in the "posture woman's" discarded clothes the English corset, laced in back; the flaps at the bottom which hold it in place under the skirt-band; the simple laced-across placard on its front, and the ribbon bow which finishes the point as it is carried over the skirt. We understand the exact construction of her under-linen, the gores of her shoes, the clocked shaping of her torn stockings. As the curl comes out of drunken women's hair we see the three-fingers' length to which it is cut and the nasty old pad over which the hair is dressed. We see bonnet-like caps, mob-caps, and little caps dipping in the middle with their lappets pinned up. We see a girl with a narrow line of fur at the neck receiving the drunken rake's watch; (on the way he has vanquished a watchman and carried off his lantern and truncheon); a smiling Negro maid-servant; patched women in hoods and embroidered *palatines,* drunk, but still wearing their gloves.

2103. XVIIIc. 1737. American. (New York Hist. Soc.)

John Smibert. Johannes Schuyler and His Wife.

John Smibert (1688-1751), the first European artist of importance to settle in America, was born in Edinburgh, the son of a dyer. He worked as a carriage painter in London where he also copied paintings, and as a portrait painter in Edinburgh, 1714-17. He then went to Florence where he copied Venetian paintings for the Grand Duke Cosimo III. About 1720, he met his life-long friend, Dean (later Bishop) Berkeley, through whose influence he was made professor of art and architecture in a "Universal College of Art and Architecture in Bermudas," for which funds never were appropriated. His wife and the rest of the proposed faculty sailed with him in 1728 and moved to Newport, Rhode Island, in 1729, where they waited in a body for two years. In 1730, Smibert married the daughter of a school-master-physician named Williams. She had a small fortune and some valuable property. At her well-located house in Queen Street, where Bishop Berkeley visited them, Smibert painted two hundred pictures of the austere provincial aristocracy, before his sight failed c.1748. He was the designer of Faneuil Hall in Boston, and also augmented his income by an art-supply and picture-frame business which his wife carried on after his death.

The names of two of the most conservative old Dutch families of America appear here. Schuyler (1688-1747) was the sixth son of Philip Schuyler who emigrated from Holland. His wife, Elizabeth Staats, widow of Johannes Wendell, wears a mourning costume which might have come out of a Dutch portrait of XVI-XVIIc., and which is considered suitable, in any case, for a Dutch matron of her age.

The body of Schuyler's bright butternut-brown velvet coat, with deep open cuffs, has the close, wrinkled look, tight at the underarm, of a Kneller portrait of the turn of XVII-XVIIIc. He wears a long cravat, rather than the current stock and jabot of Europe. His excellent wig also has the outmoded high backward rake from a flattened part, seen in Europe a decade or two earlier.

His costume shows the time-lag of provincialism. Hers is additionally retarded by age-old, static convention. A New Yorker will inevitably be reminded of the sisters, the last of the family, who lived unseen and finally died, barricaded in the great brownstone Wendell mansion on Fifth Avenue below the Public Library, to the delight of the Sunday supplements.

2104. XVIIIc. English. (Boston, Mus. of Fine Arts.)
Doll: dark green taffeta hoop.

This "baby," as dolls were called in XVIIIc., has a complete wardrobe of gown and hat, and a set of hanging pockets which hold her needlebook and handkerchief.

"Babies" also served as fashion models. Betty Crossstich's letter (*Spectator,* iii, 277) says she has received "a French baby for the year 1712. I have taken the utmost care to have her dressed by the most famous tire-women and mantua-makers in Paris . . . The puppet was dressed in a cherry-coloured gown and petticoat, with a short working apron over it, which discovered her shape to the greatest advantage." She describes its hair, patches on the breast, and its curious necklace.

2105. XVIIIc. c. 1750. Italian. Venetian. (Metropolitan Museum.)
Hoop: linen.

2106. XVIIIc. 1750-1800. Italian, Venetian. (Metropolitan Museum.)
Hoops: linen.

"Petticoats, which began to heave and swell before you left us (Sir Roger, *Spectator,* July 27, 1711) are now blown up into a most enormous concave, and rise every day more and more . . . (What ladies) have lost in height they make up in breadth. . . . A woman's honour cannot be better entrenched than . . . in a circle within circle." He supposed the first woman he saw "thus invested in whalebone" to be "near her time . . . but soon recovered myself out of my error, when I found all the modish part of the sex as 'far gone' as herself . . . The strutting petticoat smooths all distinctions, levels the mother with the daughter, and sets maids and matrons, wives and widows, upon the same bottom. . . . Should this fashion get among the ordinary people, our public ways would be so crowded that we would want street room." This is very much what did happen.

Skirts were supported in some way during most of XVIIIc. Louise de Bussy, at 111 years of age, died in 1737 from a fall while trying on paniers. In 1742, Harlequin, disguised as a saleswoman, says, "I have corfs, hoops, *paniers,* flounces, farthingales, *sacrissins,* and *matelas piqués.* For prudes I have solid ones which cannot be raised; I have folding ones for gallants, and mixed ones for persons of the third estate . . . I have, by the grace of God, specimens of all sorts, English, French, Spanish and Italian. I make water carrier hoops for roundish waists, corfs for the thin-waisted and lanteras for the Venuses." (*Journal de Verdun.*)

The Goncourts list *paniers en gondole,* like water-carriers' yokes; *cadets* short above the knee; *à bourrelets,* which widened skirts by means of a padded band; *à guéridon,* which rested on a stand as the wearer sat; *à coudes* which were wide and supported the elbows, while describing a satisfactory oval, and were made with 5 rows of hoops (the first of which was called the *tracquenard* or trap)— 3 rows less than the English hoop; *criardes* of stiffened material which crackled, worn by great ladies and actresses; these went out of use with wicker-work *paniers* in midXVIIIc. and were replaced by whale-bone stiffened canvas skirts. In 1750, only the *janséniste* half-paniers remained, and these were ousted in 1760 by *considérations,* invented by Pamard the court dressmaker, which supported the dress without petticoat or *panier.* The idea of the hoop-skirt as an "entrencher of honor" had a long life; Marie Antoinette was accused of immorality when she began to go without hoops.

2107. XVIIIc. 1738. English. (Met. Mus., Print Room.)
G. Bickham, Jr. The Minuet, No. 5: Letting Hands Go.

As soon as XVIIIc. girls were out of a nurse's care, they were handed over to a dancing master. He was probably much like the one recommended by Madam Prim, the Alderman's Lady (*Spectator,* 376), who "besides a very soft Air he has in Dancing . . . gives them a particular Behavior at Tea-Tables and how to place Patches to the best advantage, either for Fat or Lean, Long or Oval Faces."

Eustace Budgell's worthy citizen (*Spectator,* 67), who went with his wife to a ball at Monsieur Rigadoon's school, watched the French and Country (i.e. *contra*) dances with amazement at their familiarity. "They often made use of a most impudent and lascivious Step called *Setting,* which I know not how to describe to you, but by telling you that it is the very reverse of *Back to Back*." When his daughter was "whisked round Cleverly above Ground in such a manner that I . . . saw further above her Shoe than I can think fit to acquaint you with," in a dance called "Moll Patley," he "seized on the Child and carried her home."

The first book which attempted to teach dancing by means of diagrams was published in 1588 by Thoinet Arbeau. New manuals with music and descriptions of as many as 358 figures appeared every two or three years during the first part of XVIIIc.

Typical entry in the secret diary of William Byrd of Virginia*: "I rose about 5, read Hebrew and Greek; I prayed and had coffee; I danced my dance." He must have been studying from diagrams, like the new lodger who shook the house so that the Tatler's Landlady thought he had gone mad. Addison (*Tatler,* 88) peeped in at the keyhole and saw a man "look with great attention on a book, and on a sudden jump into the air so high, that his head almost touched the ceiling. He came down safe on his right foot, and again flew up—alighting on his left; then looked again at his book, and holding out his right leg, put into it such a quivering motion, that I thought he would have shaken it off. He then used the left after the same manner, when on a sudden to my great surprise, he stooped himself incredibly low, and turned gently on his toes."

Both women's short, round skirts, and the skirts of men's coats have become very distended. The crinolined flare of the coat skirts would tend to force the sides of the vent to overlap in back; for this reason, they are reinforced by decorative bands or, as in this case, turned back double and trimmed with rows of button-holes. (See Barry, Ill. 2092.)

The knotted peruke has many forms; but when a knotted lock falls from either side of the toupet,

* Ed. Wright & Tingly, 2v. 1709-12, & 1739-41, Dietz Press, Inc. Richmond, Va.

there is always a lesser lock formed from the smooth hair in back.

2108. XVIIIc. 1738. English. (Metropolitan Museum. Print Room.)

Hogarth. Strolling Actresses in a Barn.

Through a hole in the roof of a barn belonging to the George Inn, a boy spies on the company as they prepare for the last performance of "The Devil to Pay." A handbill and list of the cast lies on the bed; a copy of the (proposed·) Act against strolling players helps support a pan of too hot pap which is set on the crown, while mother, Jupiter's eagle, feeds her squalling baby.

The barn is filled with scenery, properties, and drying wash. Cupid climbs a ladder to fetch Jove's stockings off a stage cloud. An apron, cap, underdrawers and sleeve ruffles hang on the rope walker's line.

The weeping Ganymede, wearing only a shirt and a coat with deep open cuffs, is a girl who has to take the place of a missing actor and is going to be uncomfortable and ridiculous, even if she does succeed in getting into his breeches which lie on the bed. Aurora arranges the costume of the sympathetic Siren. Flora uses the basket in which stage jewels are carried (which is about to go up in flames from the candle) as a dressing table to hold her powder-shaker and oyster-shell of rouge, as she kneels in a torn hoop-petticoat to arrange her hair. Diana stands in her shirt, her taped-together hoops and skirt collapsed about her feet. Two little demons eat, drink and smoke from the altar. A female in tumbler's tights, and an old woman with a patch over her eye, The Tragic Muse and the Ghost, let blood out of a cat's tail (to make it fierce, we are told). Juno, in her diadem and jewelled stomacher runs over her part from the book. Her leg and pretty shoe are stretched out on the wheel-barrow. The Goddess of Night, played by a Negro woman, mends Juno's stocking. A monkey plays with Jove's helmet; kittens, with the orb and lyre; and a mitre is used to carry the company's volumes of farce and tragedy.

2109. XVIIIc. 1739. Scotch. (Edinburgh, Nat. Gallery.)
Allan Ramsay. The Painter's Wife.

Allan Ramsay (1713-84) was the son of the Scotch pastoral poet of the same name, whose book-shop and lending library (the first in Scotland) was the hotbed of Scotch literature.

The virile, attractive, and cultured son studied in London in 1733, Rome in 1736, and returned to immediate success in Edinburgh in 1739.

He was made king's painter in 1767, to Reynolds' disappointment—an establishment with a number of assistants was necessary in order to turn out the quantity of presentation portraits of the King for colonial gifts. Ramsay never recovered from an accident to his painting arm and died on one of his many trips abroad.

Soon after his return to Edinburgh from his studies, Ramsay married Anne, daughter of Alexander Bayne, first Professor of Scots Law in Edinburgh University, and painted her portrait the same year. She died in 1747, and Ramsay made one of the typical XVIIIc. clandestine marriages with a daughter of Sir Alexander Lindsay in 1752.

Anne Ramsay, in her lace *palatine,* is dressed in the French, not the English style. Jacobite Nationalists opposed Hanoverian Whigs in Scotland, and demanded the repeal of the 1707 Act of Union with England. Presumably the Baynes were ardent Jacobites; in any case, Scotch culture at this period was oriented toward France rather than England, through the sympathies of a large part of the population.

2110. XVIIIc. 1739-40. English. (London, Foundling Hospital.)
Hogarth. Capt. Coram.

Thomas Coram (1668-1751) rose from common sailor to ship's captain in the colonial trade, and lived for some years in Taunton, Mass., as a ship-builder. On his return to London he was so moved by the condition of children around the docks of the East End that he worked 17 years and spent all his own fortune to get a royal charter granted in 1739 for establishment of a foundling hospital. To enter an institution, no matter how well-intentioned, during the epidemic-ridden XVIIIc., was practically a death sentence, and the privately supported Foundling Hospital was no exception. It finally received government funds and supervision. Coram was also interested in the education of Indian girls and the settlement of Nova Scotia and Georgia.

England leads in evolving many new forms of coat and topcoat with collars and double rows of buttons, by which the colored linings can be buttoned back and displayed. Coram wears shoes with the old-fashioned square toe, and his own gray hair, grown long.

2111. XVIIIc. 1741. English. (London, Nat. Port. Gall.)
J. B. van Loo. John, Lord Hervey.

Hervey had been intimate with the prince and princess of Wales and married the loveliest of the ladies in waiting. He quarrelled with George II and aligned himself with the chancellor, Walpole, whom he aided through the great influence he retained over Queen Caroline. The cushion he holds symbolizes his vice-chamberlainship of the royal household.

Hervey was involved in ugly recriminations with Pope, who was jealous of his friendship with Lady Mary Wortley Montague, and satirized him in the "Dunciad." Hervey left a valuable "Memoir of the Court of George II."

He was a fragile epileptic who died at forty-seven, two years after this picture was painted. The winter of 1741 was one of the coldest ever recorded. Hervey wears one of the first fur-lined coats, such as will be much more commonly seen after the bitter winter of 1760.

2112. XVIIIc. 1741. American. (Harvard University.)
Robert Feke.
Isaac Royall and Family.

Robert Feke (c. 1705c.-1750), the best portrait painter of his time in America, was born at Oyster Bay, L. I., New York. The son of a Baptist minister, he was listed as a "mariner," and probably came in that way to Newport, where Smibert was already established. He married a Quaker whom he used to escort to meeting-house before going to his own church. He worked in Philadelphia in 1746-50, and painted twenty portraits in Boston on visits in 1741 and 1748-9. Ill health took him to Bermuda, where he died.

Royall (1719-81), a rich resident of Medford, was high in the court and council of Massachusetts, and became America's first Brigadier General during the French wars. He gave two thousand acres of land to endow a law professorship at Harvard. Sympathetic with the mother country, he went to England at the Revolution and died there, his American estates having been confiscated.

This provincial family is a decade or so behind English fashion. The women wear asymmetrically closed satin bodices (see Ills. 2090, 2091). Their capless heads show vestiges at the temples of the little scalloped *favorites* of Louis XIV's time. There is little fullness in the skirts of Royall's coat.

The time-lag betwen London and provincial fashion was not confined to the colonies. The *Spectator* (119-120) notes: "As I proceeded in my journey, I observed the petticoat grew scantier and scantier, and about three-score miles from London was so very unfashionable that a woman might walk in it without any manner of inconvenience. The Salisbury justice of the peace's lady was at least ten years behindhand in her dress, but at the same time as fine as hands could make her." As the *Spectator* went west to Cornwall he seemed to be back in Charles II's reign. The steinkirk of 1692 "arrived but two months ago at Newcastle, and there are several *commodes* in those parts which are worth taking a journey to see."

2113. XVIIIc. 1742. English. (Metropolitan Museum, Print Room.)
Hogarth. Taste in High Life.
The eccentric Miss Edwards commissioned a picture from Hogarth for sixty guineas, as her revenge on those who had ridiculed her. The painting was never a favorite of Hogarth's, and the face he has used on the central figure, which satirizes the extremes of hoops, patches, and *robes à la française,* is astonishingly like Miss Edwards' own. (See Ill. 2099.)

The male figure is Lord Portmore, as he appeared at court on his return from France, encumbered by hat, muff, and hanging cane, and wearing a wig with a ridiculously long pigtail and a single skimpy curl before each ear. The two withered creatures express fashionable ecstasy over bits of porcelain; the great pot behind them is another expression of the craze for china.

The passion for French cooking is ridiculed by the monkey who reads a menu of absurd foods—cock's combs, duck tongues, rabbit ears, fricasseed snails and such—with a quizzing glass. His tail looks like Lord Portmore's wig; his own wig is in a square bag.

A bill for Lady Basto's gambling debt of £300 to John Pip lies on the floor by an immense stack of playing cards. A little Negro (the intelligent and beloved Ignacio Sanchez, who was painted by Gainsborough), holds one of the debased oriental figures which Hogarth ridicules without end. He is being chucked under the chin by the famous prostitute, Kitty Fisher. She lifts her hoops, since there is no space in one room for two such. A twisted scarf is buckled into place by straps at the top and bottom of her bodice; a watch and chatelaine hang from her belt.

All the pictures on the wall have significance. The dancing craze (see Ill. 2107) is noted in the figure of the French dancing master, Desnoyers, among butterflies. In the center, the Medici Venus (whose fig-leag is now half a loop); an amorino fans the flame of a burning hoop, before starting on a muff, cap and wigs; another massages a too-fat goddess. The same costume accessories are ridiculed in the adjoining picture. Below it, a girl in a pastoral hat and apron can scarcely make her way through clipped alleys in a garden; and on the fire-screen a woman in a sedan chair can hardly sit because of hoops.

2114-16. XVIIIc. 1745. English.
(Metropolitan Mus., Print Room.)
Hogarth. Marriage à la mode.

To settle gambling debts, a marriage has been arranged by their fathers between an easy-going young lord and the spoiled daughter of a rich alderman. Its course is shown by six plates: the marriage contract; breakfast; visit to the quack doctor; the toilette of the countess; the death of the earl; and the suicide of the countess.

2114. *Breakfast:* The viscount has returned to a disordered house from a night on the town; his wife's nasty little dog is much interested in a cap with ribbons which spills out of the pocket of his black and gold suit, worn with white stockings. A yawning, half-dressed manservant in olive-green coat, brown breeches and black stockings, is just beginning to straighten out the disorder of last night's cards and music. A forgotten candle is about to set fire to a chair. The lady, in a lemony dressing cape, rosy white petticoat and blue ribbons has been looking at herself in a mirror, and drinking tea. The worthy steward is leaving in disgust, with his ledger and the bills, only one of which has been paid, and that a year ago.

The room is a satire on the architect, William Kent, and the tasteless decorations of the period. The "antique" bust is all modern but the base; its nose has been chipped off deliberately. Debased oriental figurines crowd the mantel. The wall-fixture above the viscount's head is a nameless horror of clock and candles, fish, monkey, squatting eastern god, and foliage.

Hat, with wide, laced and feathered brim, cocked high; worn over a wig which has lost its curl. Coat with frog and braid trim which begins to supplant buttons. Little hood, short dressing gown; laced corset, brocade petticoat. The bald steward, with his pocket full of Methodist tracts, disdains a wig and lets what hair he has grow.

2115. *Visit to the Quack Doctor.* The viscount and a young girl have been taken to a quack doctor by an old procuress who wears black taffeta, a gold-edged red apron, flowered scarf and red ribbons. The viscount is indignant at the failure of the prescribed treatment. The quack, dressed in snuff brown with gold buttons and gray stockings, has risen from being a barber; a basin, notched to fit the neck, and a broken comb hang near a unicorn's horn, slung like a barber's pole among a collection of "rarities" and "curiosities" worthy of the would-be antiquarian, Don Saltero. Bits of clothing and armor ascribed to famous owners, a mummy,

a skeleton and a combination gallows and bottle opener "Seen and approved by the Royal Academy of Sciences at Paris."

Ruffled cap, tied about with blue ribbon; pretty, short blue and gold cape; lace trimmed apron, gold brocade petticoat, flowered in red and green, long kid gloves; enormous hoops, so large that there is a tendency to discard them altogether, around mid-XVIIIc.; watch chatelaines at waistline.

2116. *Toilette of the Countess.* The old earl is dead. The alderman's daughter is too wrapped up in the enjoyments of a fashionable countess (with coronets set on mirror and window frames) to concern herself with her baby, whose teething coral hangs forgotten on her chair. She is receiving a crowd of friends and hangers-on, while in white combing jacket, corset, yellow gown and pale brick-pink petticoat. A French hairdresser (whose coat is without cuffs, which might interfere with his work) curls her hair. A young advocate, with characteristic wig and gown, shows tickets, while pointing to a masquerade ball painted on the screen. This secret assignation, which the young earl will come upon, culminates in the earl's death in sword play and the subsequent suicide of the discredited and conscience-sticken countess, by laudanum. A fat, over-dressed Italian opera singer (dressed in putty color with dark gold brocade, flowered red and green, and a light putty-colored vest, black breeches, dark gray stock and stockings), laden with diamonds in earrings, *solitaire* pin and rings, sings to the interest of no one but a gushing lady in white with blue underskirt and ribbons. A mass of cards of invitation from such as she has spilled from his pockets. A mocking Negro servant offers her chocolate; a plain, hearty country squire plays by himself with his whip; a delicate young man, whose blue and gold coat has the new turned-over collar (in white, with a dark gray stock, brick breeches and light gray hose), sips chocolate with his hair in curl papers. A little blackamoor plays with odd lots of

fake antiques and oriental junk, which the countess has picked up at the auction of the effects of the late Timothy Babyhouse.

Wigs have entered upon the specialization, by profession and situation in life, which will eventually lead to their being given up, except by professional men. There is great variety in the form and decoration of coats worn by different sorts of people. The countess' woman friend wears the midXVIIIc. flat straw hat on top of a ruffled cap; kerchief tucked under a band across the top of the bodice, the long look of which is increased by double folds; skirt so distended by hoops that it must be slit up the front, but its edges and petticoat are untrimmed, in English use.

2117. Second quarter XVIIIc. English.
Spitalfields Silk Dress; quilted satin petticoat; cut paper lace fan.

Quilted petticoats (usually in satin, and in all colors but particularly in blue, white, greenish-white, green, and yellow) were a favorite handwork in the cold XVIIIc. An aunt in 1714 complains that her nieces, after gadding and tea-drinking, "go to bed as tired with doing nothing as I am after quilting a whole under-petticoat," and wishes they would work beds, chairs and hangings, instead of wasting their time with dress, play and visits.

2118. Third quarter XVIIIc. French.
Dress of Chinese Painted Silk. These hand-painted gowns are apt to have green, yellow, or white grounds. (M.F.A., Boston, has several.)

2119. Second quarter XVIIIc. English.
Dress of Spitalfields Brocade; in white, gold, henna and brown, worn by Lydia Catherine, duchess of Chandos.

A silk industry to rival Italy was the dream of most XVIIc. rulers. James I distributed 10,000 mulberry trees, for which the English climate was not really suited. In 1687, 13,500 Protestant refugee weavers settled at Spitalfields in N. London. When Sir Thomas Lombe set up silk spinning machines in England in 1718, (from drawings brought back

from Italy by his brother), the wool and cotton industries protested this threat to their prosperity, just as the growing Scotch linen-weaving trade had opposed the striped and checked patterns produced by the Spitalfields experts. Spitalfields silk weaving was repeatedly checked until it was moribund; then attempts were made to revive it by prohibiting any importation of silk, and exhorting everyone to wear Spitalfields out of patriotism. Queen Charlotte wore Spitalfields silk, or English calico, and embroidered her own gowns.

2120. Second quarter XVIIIc. English.
Green Damask Dress; quilted green taffeta petticoat; apron and matching hat, with polychrome and silver embroidery. Neckpiece of sheer drawn linen instead of lace.

2121. XVIIIc. French.
Hat with Appliqué Embroidery; shown with 2120.

2122. XVIIIc. c. 1785. French.
Printed Cotton Dress; straw hat.

2123. XVIIIc. 1762. (Boston, Mus. of Fine Arts.)
Sampler.
Lace developed out of fabric threads, punched or drawn, and worked. There is a return to these techniques in XVIIIc., either as an approximation of lace for those who cannot afford it, or out of the

boredom of those who have worn lace for a long time. (See Ill. 2120.)

2124-25. XVIIIc. c. 1745. English. (Cambridge, Fitzwilliam Mus.) *J. Highmore.* Illustrations for Richardson's *Pamela*.

2124. Pamela Shows Mr. Williams a Hiding Place for a Letter.

2125. Pamela Tells a Story.

Pancake-flat hats, with the lowest possible crowns, tied over ruffled caps. The English bodice has its kerchief tied in place across the top of the bodice, and drawn down to intensify the long, lean line of the bodice. The enormous hoops of mid-XVIIIc. occasionally force even English skirts to be slit up the middle, as is seen under Pamela's apron.

Severity of an Anglican clergyman in his cassock, band and solemn, deep-crowned hat, compared to the worldly dress of a French abbé; however, the typical ecclesiastical wig, in both countries, is of shoulder length, without knotted locks.

Courtesy of Museum of Fine Arts, Boston (2117-2123)

2126. XVIIIc. 1746. American. (Metropolitan Mus.)
Robert Feke. Tench Francis.

The Irish-born leader of the Pennsylvania bar wears a lawyer's wig with his brown coat and waistcoat.

2127. XVIIIc. Before 1750. Scotch. (Worcester, Severn, Stoke-Croome. Earl of Coventry.)

Allan Ramsay. George William Coventry.
A leader of the opposition, who became the 6th Earl in 1750.

2128. XVIIIc. English. (London, National Gallery.)

J. Highmore. Gentleman in Murrey-Brown Velvet.
Both 2127 and 2128 wear long, plain dark velvet coats, with very wide or deep cuffs; long, light-colored satin waistcoats. The heavily frogged and tasseled decoration of the Continent seldom appears on English coats, but the waistcoat is richly edged and may have a knotted fringe border below the last buttonhole. Wig with characteristic toupet of c. 1745.

2129. XVIIIc. Before 1748. English. (Greenwich National Maritime Mus.)

Hogarth. Lord George Graham in his Cabin.
The Navy captain, son of the duke of Montrose, who sits in his gilded mahogany cabin, was presumably painted before the establishment of uniforms in 1748.

He wears a brown velvet cap, gray-furred red gown, thrown over a turquoise-lined gray coat, white satin waistcoat, golden-brown breeches, white stockings, and red slippers. His friends are in green, with light green stockings; and in brown with gray breeches. They are attended by a cabin boy in a white apron and a Negro in a red-brown neckcloth, black coat and brown waistcoat. Graham's wig is set on the head of his dog.

The tradition of officers eating off handsome silver, even in the trenches, was established, Voltaire says, by the Marshal d'Humières in 1658, at the siege of Arras. In addition to unbreakable plate, Graham's cabin has a handsome china punch bowl.

Thomas Gainsborough (1727-88), son of a respected dissenting crêpe-maker of Sudbury, and his wife who did floral still-lifes, had painted all the scenery of Sudbury before he was ten. At fourteen he went to London, studied book-illustration with Gravelot, and returned to Sudbury for a couple of years. He removed to Ipswich in 1747, upon his marriage to Margaret Burr. Mrs. Gainsborough was charming and had a small private fortune; her real father seems to have been of very high birth. The couple were a great social success, and on the advice of Gov. Thicknesse, moved to Bath in 1759. The nobility, and the actors Gainsborough loved, like Garrick and Quin, crowded his studio and its musical parties. His fees of forty to one hundred guineas for half to full length portraits enabled him to rent Schomberg House in London in 1774. Gainsborough was one of the original members of the Royal Academy, but seldom attended its meetings after a quarrel over the hanging of his pictures in 1772, and had stopped exhibiting some years before his death from cancer. He was a handsome, gregarious, easily irritated man, who used to make up quarrels with his wife by sending his dog Fox with a charming note addressed to her spaniel Tristram. Gainsborough said that his brother Humphrey had anticipated Watts in inventing the steam-engine, and had been done out of a fortune.

Gainsborough's and Reynolds' portraits are the great English costume documents of their period.

2130. XVIIIc. 1749-50. English. (London, Sir Philip Sassoon.)
Gainsborough. The Artist, Wife and Child.

Dark coat and light waistcoat of mid-XVIIIc. The method of seaming and gathering the plain satin skirt over laterally extended hoops is clearly seen; long line of English bodice and kerchief is extended by plain narrow apron.

2131. XVIIIc. 1750-55. English. (England, Andrews Coll.)
Gainsborough. Mr. & Mrs. Robert Andrews.

Golden autumn in Suffolk when game birds are plenty and a squire carries a gun as he walks with his wife and keeps an eye on Auberies, his Sudbury estate. Mr. Andrews' buff coat, with dark velvet collar to match the breeches, is cut away and double-breasted, falling into exaggerated lapels when unfastened; the waistcoat is becoming cut away and shortened into a vest. The sparse, unpowdered wig on which a hat can be set and maintained while hunting, may even be his own hair. The hat crown is deeper, brim wider, with laced edges concavely cocked.

Over very wide hoops, the bodice of Mrs. Andrews' light, sharp blue gown is skirted like the coats of dancing girls painted by Lancret or Tiepolo. The English kerchief is usually caught across the line of the top of the corset by a ribbon, strap or pin. A wide, flopping hat is set over her cap.

2132. Mid-XVIIIc. English. (Kenilworth, Stoneleigh Abbey. Lord Leigh.)
Arthur Devis. James Brydges (1731-89), third Duke of Chandos, as a Youth.

The 1st duke of Chandos became immensely rich as paymaster of the forces abroad during the Wars of the Spanish Succession. He was Handel's and Pope's patron and lived in such style at "Canons," which cost £230,000, with his own Swiss guards lining his road to church, that he was known as "the grand duke" despite heavy losses in the African, Mississippi and South Sea crashes of 1718-20. Three

2135

2134

years after his death in 1744, "Canons" was sold for £11,000 and torn down for its materials, such as twenty-two steps each made of one piece of marble.

The 2nd duke bought Anne Wells from her drunken hostler husband, who was offering her for sale at Newbury as the duke passed through. Chandos had her educated into a charming person, and after her husband had drunk himself to death, and the duchess Mary had died, married her. When Chandos died "to the great joy of that noble family" the youth we see here became the 3rd duke. Anne Wells was not allowed burial in the family chapel where Handel had been organist.

The subject of an XVIIIc. English portrait is apt to be shown leaning against one of the classic urns, fountains or sundials with which private parks and public pleasure gardens are dotted. Great masquerades are being held, like the Venetian ridotto described by Walpole (Letter to Mann, May 3, 1749). A well known "conversation-piece" shows the con-

fusion of a couple who met at one of these balls, retired to a classic fountain in a remote part of the garden, and unmasked, only to find that they were husband and wife.

Brydges, mask in hand, cloak over shoulder, wears a waistcoat treated like a XVIIc. doublet, with lace cuffs, collar, band strings, rosettes at knees and shoes.
2133. XVIIIc. c. 1760. English. (Metropolitan Mus.)
  Francis Cotes. Harry Paulet, Duke of Boulton.
  Francis Cotes (1725?-70), a portrait painter in oils and crayon, and his brother Samuel (1734-1818), the greatest miniaturist of his day, were the children of an apothecary who, before censure by the Irish House, had been Mayor of Galway, and his wife, daughter of a high official in the Royal African Society. Francis seceded from the Society of Artists to become one of the original members of the Royal Academy; poor health sent him to Bath, where his patrons followed.

Lavinia Fenton's descendant, as an admiral, in the uniform established in 1748: blue breeches and coat with white facings and vest, laced in gold.
2134. XVIIIc. c. 1750. English. (London, A. Tooth & Sons.)
  Hogarth. The Brothers Clarke of Swakeleys Round a Table Drinking Wine.
  This picture of the brothers and their lawyers was probably painted to commemorate the purchase of their property at Ickenham, Middlesex. (Sitwell: *Conversation Pieces.*)
2135. XVIIIc. English. (London, Foundling Hospital.)
  Hogarth. March to Finchley (1750).
  Hogarth got from Hell Brueghel's *La grasse et la maigre cuisine* the idea for this canvas, which he dedicated to George III. The king, who "hated *bainting* and *boetry,* too," considered it an insult to his guards. Whereupon Hogarth ironically rededicated it to Frederick the Great.

It represents the moment in 1745 when the Young Pretender's army in Scotland seemed to threaten England; guards were marched to camp at Finchley to defend London.

With Highgate and Hampstead in the background, the crowd fills the Tottenham Court Road between the King's Head Tavern and the Adam and Eve, which at least until World War II still stood in the same place. An outdoor garden was an almost indispensable part of an XVIIIc. inn; Eden Street, to one side, now commemorates the Adam and Eve's *Paradise Gardens.*

A young guardsman starts off between sweethearts who are not only rivals for him, but represent the two political factions. The modest Protestant girl carries a picture of the duke of Cumberland and the words and music of *God Save the King* in her basket. The tough camp-follower, a cross on her cape, sells the *Jacobite Journal* and *London Evening Post,* and brandishes the *Remembrancer,* in which her banns have perhaps been printed.

From l. to r.: boy with fife; drummer; a Frenchman whispering to another, under whose overcoat shows a scrap of Highland plaid; an old woman with a baby on her back smokes a pipe; behind her, a boxing match with bare fists.

To the r. of the flag another officer kisses a milk girl in pancake hat with yoked buckets on her shoulders, from whom a boy steals milk, to the amusement of a pastry-seller, whose own wares are being stolen. In front of a very smug, proud officer, drunken soldiers fill their canteens from a keg of beer. In the r. foreground a drunken guardsman, who is losing his buttoned gaiters, reaches for a drink of gin being poured out by a woman; so does the baby on her back.

Ill. 2136 has been deleted.

2137. XVIIIc. 1754. Italian.

Canaletto. The Rotunda at Ranelagh.

The greatest of the London pleasure gardens were Vauxhall and Ranelagh.

Vauxhall in XVIIc. was called the New Spring Gardens, "a pretty contrived plantation," where one walked, picked flowers or cherries, and listened to the nightingales. Pepys ate lobster and syllabub there with his wife and Deb Mercer. Music, paintings, statues and ruins were added to its twenty acres, to its alleys and wilderness, the windings and turnings of which were "so intricate that the most experienced mothers have often lost themselves here in looking for their daughters." Swift and Sir Roger de Coverley went there, but it had become rough and disreputable when a "Ridotto al fresco," by a new management in 1732 started it on a fresh triumphant career. Season admission to its concerts was by a silver token designed by Hogarth. Everyone went; Farmer Colin recounted its delights on his return. Walpole tells a story of a mad, show-off group of the aristocracy gone by water to Vauxhall, accompanied by barges of horns and carrying with them Betty the fruit-girl with hampers of strawberries, mincing chickens in butter and cooking them in a china dish over a lamp while all the people in the gardens tried to crowd around their booth. The refreshments to be had at Vauxhall were limited to wine, beer and syllabub, meat sliced so thin you could see through it, salad, cheese and such desserts as cheese-cake and tarts.

Walpole describes the difficulties of getting to the Ridotto of 1769 (in letter to Montague, May 10), but thought little of the entertainment and illuminations. With the aid of fire-works, balloon ascensions, parachute descents, side-shows, gas lighting and concerts, Vauxhall lasted halfway through XIXc.

By midXVIIIc., skirts, while they remain plain in England, are enormously extended laterally; bodices show the front lacings common all over Europe, and the back pleats of the *robe à la française* appear on many English gowns.

Ranelagh was built at end XVIIc. by the Viscount Ranelagh, another who had found the paymastership of the army profitable. Its gardens were the finest of their size in Europe. In 1741, Walpole wrote, "an immense amphitheatre, with balconies full of little alehouses was built in rivalry with Vauxhall, and cost about twelve thousand pounds. . . . Into which everybody that loves eating, drinking, staring, or crowding is admitted for twelve pence." By 1744, he says, "it has totally beaten Vauxhall. Lord Chesterfield is so fond of it that he says he has ordered all his letters directed thither. The floor is all of beaten princes. You can't set your foot without treading on a Prince or Duke."

2137

The Jubilee Masquerade in the Venetian taste, which Walpole thought "far the best understood and prettiest spectacle" he ever saw, took place in 1749. But although everybody went there to be seen, it became a very boring place. Samuel Rogers said "all was so orderly and still that you could hear the whishing sound of the ladies' trains as the immense assembly walked round and round the room, and from time to time, as solemnly reversed."

The last superb spectacle at Ranelagh was the regatta and ball of June 23, 1775. Ranelagh finally closed in 1803.

2138. XVIIIc. 1756-61. English. (Althorp Park, Earl Spencer.)
Reynolds.
Margaret Georgiana, Countess Spencer and her daughter, later the Duchess of Devonshire.

Sir Joshua Reynolds (1723-92), with Gainsborough the greatest XVIIIc. English portrait painter, was apprenticed by his poor teacher-vicar father to a painter named Hudson, from whose stultifying influence he was rescued by a drunken artist named Gaudy, who said a picture should have rich texture "as if the colors were made of cream and cheese." He made useful friends in London in the 40's, painted in Italy, 1750-3, and was overwhelmed by society after his portrait of Admiral Keppel in 1755. His fees doubled between 1760-81, when he charged fifty to two hundred guineas for his wonderful portraits and £1500 for his dreadful historical pictures.

Reynolds was involved in the quarrels of Benjamin West and Hayman over the Society of Artists; withdrew, and was made the first president of the new Royal Academy founded 1768; his noble, detached tactfulness made him its greatest president. He was knighted and made George III's first painter after Allan Ramsay's death.

Experiments to attain a "cream and cheese" texture made many of his pictures impermanent, but they are wonderful records of costume worn by living persons, not fashion plates.

2139. XVIIIc. English. (Metropolitan Mus.)
British School (formerly attr. to Reynolds).
Portrait.
Olive costume and ribbons; tan brocade jacket.

2140. XVIIIc. English. (New York, Knoedler.)
Arthur Devis. The Putnam Family.
Arthur Devis (1711?-87) was a faithful exhibitor in the Free Society of Artists from 1762; he also repaired Sir John Thornhill's paintings at Greenwich and worked in India. His son, A. W. (1763-1822) painted a great many admirals and sea-battles.

During the 60's English upper-class dress (as seen in Ill. 2138-40) begins to show the effects of French

influences: lace ruffles, bows, shirred bands of decoration, and heads without caps on younger women. The newly-bared English head at first has a bleak, skinned-back look; then it loosens, or is studded with decoration (Putnam family) before becoming the higher, more ceremoniously dressed head shown on Queen Charlotte.

Bodices become shorter; the V-front widens into a U-shape. The kerchief is relegated to negligée, domestic dress or older women and is crossed, as though laced, by ribbons; these are sometimes caught at their intersections by flat, prim little bows (Putnam family) in place of the graduated ladder of perky bows seen on Mme. de Pompadour; the front lacing and bows come to be made of shirred bands rather than ribbon, in England, as shirred trimmings increase in use. Skirts have lost their round hoops and are unsupported; in England they are often bunched up asymmetrically, at the period when looped garlands are carried or worn (Putnam family).

Collarless coats, like Mr. Putnam's, are apt to rise high and wrinkle, as though begging for a collar.

2141. XVIIIc. 1759. English. (New York, J. P. Morgan.)
Hogarth. The Lady's Last Stake, or Virtue in Danger.

Lord Charlemont commissioned Hogarth to paint a picture on any subject he chose. The fourteen-year-old Hester Lynch Salisbury (later Mrs. Piozzi) served as the model for the young woman who, at five o'clock, as the candles burn low, has lost at piquet £500, her own jewels, and her husband's miniature and watch, to a young officer, in an unpowdered wig and uniform with cord fourragère.

English dress is becoming affected by French laciness, especially at the sleeve ruffles and neck ruche. The English bodice still retains its single bow at the top of a plain V—instead of a graduated ladder of bows. The skirt is slit over a plain petticoat, but is still untrimmed.

John Zoffany (1733-1810), a Bohemian Jew, fled his home young to study painting in Italy, and came to England c.1761. He painted dials for Rimbault's animated musical clocks, and backgrounds and draperies for portraits by Benjamin Wilson.

In Wilson's studio, the warm, gregarious, music-loving Zoffany made many friends, among them the painter Mortimer, whose acquaintanceship was wide and high, and Garrick, whose encouragement and introductions soon led Zoffany to great success as a painter of theatrical groups; he is the historian of the theatre in Garrick's time.

Zoffany's furniture, mirrors and silks had been

better than Wilson's portraits; and like Hogarth, Zoffany had the faculty of total recall, sharpened by painting seized moments in the theatre. His group portraits had such spontaneity (although the sitters might never meet in his studio), that Zoffany was soon painting "conversation pieces," as well as single portraits of the royal family and nobility. He already belonged to the Society of Artists; became one of the original members of the newly formed Royal Academy; and in 1772 showed a portrait of its members, painted, Walpole says, "by candlelight; he made no design for it, but clapped in the artists as they came to him, and yet all the attitudes are easy and natural, most of the likenesses strong."

Disappointed in his plan to make a voyage to the South Seas with Capt. Cook, the restless, extravagant Zoffany set off, c.1772, under George III's patronage, on a 2-year trip to Italy. His 2nd wife, an almost totally illiterate child of 14, was so enchantingly beautiful and sweet that she was received everywhere, and so naturally intelligent that she made up many deficiencies in her education while in Italy.

Zoffany painted everyone in the fashionable English colony in Florence, had his usual success at the Tuscan Grand Ducal court, and through its influence, went on to Vienna, where Maria Theresa created him a baron.

He returned to England, c.1774, to his intimacy with the royal family and Johann Christian Bach, to his musical parties on his barge on the Thames, served by lackeys with his new baronial crest on their magnificent liveries, and to endless portraits and conversation pieces. Among these, none is more valuable for costume than the delightful picture of the Hon. Charles Hope Vere, in the scarlet coat of the Archers, together with his two old sisters in enchanting home dress and aprons (property of Harry L. Verney).

Inspired by his friend Hodges, who did go with Cook, and who had painted successfully in India under Warren Hastings' patronage, Zoffany set off, in 1783, for a 14-year stay in India. As usual, he met, saw and painted everyone and everything: cock fights, tiger hunts, nabobs and their embassies, English governors and judges with their families, native servants and costumes, and their pets.

On the return journey, Zoffany suffered a stroke, from which he and his painting never entirely recovered.

2142. XVIIIc. 1762. English. (Kenilworth, Stoneleigh Abbey, Lord Leigh.)

John Zoffany. The Farmer's Return.

This painting, the first theatrical group exhibited at the Society of Artists, belonged to Garrick. It shows him with Mrs. Cibber in the play of that name, recounting his week in London and his visit to Vauxhall.

As many theatrically effective details of a farmer's dress as possible have been incorporated in the lower part of Garrick's costume. Soft turned-down boots are supported by straps over the knees of breeches which close by buttons and ties. Stick and clay pipe for "business" with the hands. A knotted cravat and unpowdered wig distract no attention from the face.

Mrs. Cibber wears the enclosing hood-like cap of an older woman; the young mother a cap with pinned-up lappets. Kerchiefs pinned high at the throat, their points held down by apron strings going twice about the body.

The Development of Wigs

A tendency toward baldness seems to have run through the ruling houses of Tudor, Valois and Bourbon.

As Elizabeth's red hair grew thin, it was covered by one of her eighty wigs, which ran from auburn through orange to gold, the colors which she made fashionable in her era.

Her cousin Mary Queen of Scots' own hair was black, her secretary, Nicholas White, said. In 1561 she had "perewykes," mostly red, for every day of the year, which were artfully arranged by Mary Seaton, her preferred lady-in-waiting.

It will be two centuries before the heads of royalty will be dressed by professionals. Mary's head was shaved for her flight in 1568, her French secretary, Claude Nau, said. She went to her execution "her borrowed hair a bourne (wig)." The executioner pulled it off, exposing her own hair, grown white in her forties. Women who did not have enough hair to cover high pads in late XVIc.–XVIIc. wore a "bourne."

Thomas Nash, in 1593, excoriated seekers after youth who wore periwigs, and Shakespeare mentions them in Hamlet (Act III, Scene ii).

Henry III of France began to lose his dyed hair while he was still Duke of Anjou. The fluffy hair combed up about his characteristic velvet toque was false.

His black-haired sister, Marguerite of Valois, also became bald. She selected her footmen for their beautiful blonde hair, which could be clipped when she needed a new wig.

Henry IV's hair had begun to recede long before he was murdered at fifty-three in 1610, but he was never a man who would bother with a wig.

The appearance of the Abbé de la Rivière in a long golden wig at the court in 1620, led to the use of periwigs by Louis XIII, who was growing bald, too.

Louis XIV hated wigs, but when he lost his hair in 1670, his wig-maker, Binette, provided them for him in every color and form, for negligée, walking, hunting and court wear. The most imposing wigs ever seen are the long ones, dressed high à la Fontange, in the later part of his reign.

Wigs arrived in England with Charles II, and came into general use during his reign. People had already begun to let their hair grow again during third quarter XVIIIc., though they powdered it for ceremony until the wheat famine and flour tax of 1795. The change and relaxation in fashion which began c.1784, was particularly noticeable among English men by 1790. The Crop Club, or Bedford Crops, young men of the Duke of Bedford's circle, formally gave up powder and had their hair washed and clipped in a ceremony at Woburn Abbey.

Wigs had become so specialized by professions that all but professional men, doctors, lawyers in court, clergymen and soldiers discarded them during George III's reign. As a badge of ecclesiastical dignity, they were longest worn by bishops; the summer of 1830 was so hot that bishops were excused from wearing wigs at William IV's coronation and looked to Greville very strange without them. The last appearance of the episcopal wig was on the Archbishop of Canterbury at Victoria's resplendent coronation, eight years later.

The first wigs, made on a net base, cost 50 to 80 livres and weighed as much as two pounds, before Ervais' improvements in techniques; and as much as 1,000 écus an ounce was paid for the preferred blonde hair.

Diderot's "Encyclopédie" discusses at great length the fabrication and dressing of wigs. We learn also that children's hair is too fragile. The best hair comes from beer and cider-drinking countries like Flanders, and from people between eighteen and sixty years old. Women's hair is better than men's; and that of country women (who cover it with caps and do not use powder) better than townswomen's. Goat's hair is used in cheap, provincial wigs; it has a lovely whiteness, but breaks off, as does horsehair. The paste used to set wig curls comes from the ginger-bread bakers in cities; in the country the wigmaker has to cook it up himself.

The most durable hair is chestnut; even children's brown hair can be used. Black is more desirable; *noir, petit noir,* and *noir jais,* a difficult color to find, but one which can be worn without powder. Gray tones are even better: *gris de maure,* which is *noir jais,* gone a quarter white; *gris salé,* brown hair gone a quarter white; and *blanc fond jaune,* blonde hair gone half white. Of white hair the most precious is *blanc agate,* dark hair which has turned completely white; *blanc perle* originally chestnut. *Blanc de lait,* originally blonde, or better still, red, is beyond price because of its texture and curling qualities.

The two sheets of plates under *Perruque* in the "Encyclopédie" show many forms of wig for both sexes. The ecclesiastical peruke is short and tonsured. The long, square *perruque quarrée* is, like the legal wig, persistent in English use today. It falls in two flaps with a tiny curl between them in back, exactly like a sheep's docked tail between woolly flanks. There are special pieces to extend the wigs of the legal *gens de la robe.* The *perruque à la naissance* has its back hair falling almost straight, and untied. The *perruque à la brigadière* is seen only on old-time military men by 1765. It covers the ears and has four sausage rolls carried completely around at the nape, with the back hair tied low beneath. There are wigs, both square and with knotted locks, which expose the ears. The "most modern" form is the *perruque à la régence,* the bag-wig which appeared "not forty years since" under Orleans. Wigs similarly cut to expose the ears, but without the bag, have their back hair drawn as much out of the way as possible, falling in two knotted locks, two spirally bound tails tied with small bows, or clubbed up and knotted into a *catogan.* The wig with two locks is more commonly worn at the German courts than elsewhere. "One cannot present one's self today before the King and Queen of Hungary without these two tails, young and old alike. They are also worn at great fêtes, at a *bal paré,* and by comedians in tragic roles."

There are women's wigs of two main sorts: The "modern". *chignon frisé* is a sort of cap of short curls "worn for the last twenty years, and perfected during the last ten." The fuller *chignon plein* has forms *en abbé, à la paresseuse,* and another with two curls at the ears. The *chignon relevé* has straight hair combed up high from the forehead, after the manner of Marie Antoinette's court headdresses; a sausage-like curl, *boudin,* runs vertically above each ear; for court and fête day use there are four to six extra curls which may be added, the two longest of which hang in back. The *cadinette* has a chignon of straight hair, but hangs long and square in back. There are demi-perruques to be combined with your own hair.

In England, wig-makers, few in number, worked outside the guilds until they became part of the Barbers, Bathers, Washers and Wig-makers, in 1634. Their number increased to two hundred by 1673, so that a new guild was established. Its statutes, in 1674, required that the basins which served peruke makers as signboards be white to distinguish them from the surgeon's yellow basins.

2143. XVIIIc. 1761. English.

Hogarth. The Five Orders of Perriwigs.

Hogarth's "Analysis of Beauty," 1753, was a confused treatise exposing his theories of aesthetics. In the "Five Orders of Perriwigs" he combines mockery of the as yet unpublished "Antiquities of Athens Measured and Delineated," by James Stuart and Nicholas Revett, with ridicule of a number of well-known people.

The Episcopal or Parsonic Order (equivalent to the "Encyclopédie's" abbé's wig, without a tonsure) is displayed on the Drs. Warburton and Squire, Bishops of Gloucester and of St. David's.

The Old Peerian, or Aldermanic is shown on the venial parliamentarian, Bubb Doddington, Lord Melcombe, and on the Lord Mayor, Sir Samuel Fludyer, whose full-bottomed peruke spreads over his entire back.

The Lexonic shows legal wigs, approximating the *perruque quarrée* of the "Encyclopédie."

The Composite, or Half Natural is a curlier English version of the French *perruque naissante.*

The Queerinthian, or Queue de Renard, is an exaggerated tie wig, with a distinct toupet and pigeon's wings (G.) developed into sausage-like rolls. These two last sorts have the ears exposed, like the French wigs of the same kind.

The bottom row shows Queen Charlotte with her ladies-in-waiting, their descending rank indicated by their coronets, wearing the necklock (d), which Hogarth calls the Triglyph Membretta.

In addition to the wind-blown toupet of the *Smart* (see Macaronis, 1773-4), the *London Chronicle* of 1762 describes the *"Prentice Minor-bob,* or *Hair-cap;* this is always short in the neck, to show the stone-buckle, and nicely stroked from the face to discover seven-eighths of the ears. Next, the *Citizens' Sunday Buckle,* or *Bob-major;* this is a first-rate, bearing several tiers of curls, disposed in upper, middle and lower order. Then the *Apothecaries' Bush,* on which the hat seems sinking like a stone in a snowheap. The *Physical* or *Chirurgical Ties* carry

much consequence in their foretops; and the depending ties fall fore and aft the shoulders with *secundum artem* dignity. The Scratch, or the *Blood's Skull-Covering* is combed over the forehead, untoupeted, to imitate a head of hair, because these gentlemen love to have everything natural about them. The *Jehu's Jemmy,* or *white and all white;* in little curls like a fine fleece on a lamb's back, we should say something upon, were it not for fear of offending some gentlemen of great riches, who love to look like coachmen."

The current hats of 1762 are described by the same writer. Six inch wide brims are "cocked between Quaker and Kevenhuller" (i.e in a bicorne running parallel with the shoulders). "Some have their Hats open before, like a church spout . . .; some wear them rather sharper, like the nose of a gray-hound; and we can distinguish by the taste of the Hat, the mode of the wearer's mind. There is the military cock, and the mercantile cock; and while the beaux of St. James' wear their Hats under their arms, the beaux of Moorsfield-mall wear theirs diagonally over their left or right eye. Sailors wear the sides of their Hats uniformly tacked down to the crown; and look as though they carried a triangular apple-pasty upon their heads.

"With the *Quakers,* it is a point of their faith not to wear a button, or loop tight up; their Hats spread over their heads like a pent-house; and darken the outward man, to signify they have the inner light.

"Some wear their Hats (with the corner that should come over their foreheads in a direct line) pointing into the air; these are the *Gawkies.* Others do not above half cover their heads, which is indeed owing to the shallowness of their crowns; but between beaver and eyebrows expose a piece of blank forehead, which looks like a sandy road in a surveyor's plan. . . . Hats edged around with gold binding belong to brothers of the *Turf."*

2144. XVIIIc. 1754. American. (Metropolitan Museum.)
Joseph Blackburn. Margaret Sylvester Cheeseborough.

2145. XVIIIc. American. (N. Y., Mrs. James Gore King.)
Joseph Blackburn. Mrs. John Erving Jr. (1729-1816).

Joseph Blackburn (c. 1700-c. 1765) was a contemporary of Smibert and a competent English portrait painter in the manner of Highmore and Hudson. Few facts about him are known. He painted in Bermuda in 1753, and may have come from there to America. He was working in Portsmouth in 1762, and then is lost sight of; it is surmised that he may have accompanied his patron, Sir Robert Grant, who became governor of Jamaica shortly after that date.

Both illustrations show rich provincial versions of midXVIIIc. dress.

2146. XVIIIc. c. 1760. American. (Metropolitan Mus.)
John Woolaston, Alice Christie Colden.

Woolaston painted in America, 1751-69. His portrait of Mrs. William Allen (Detroit Inst. of Arts) shows almost identical costume.

2147. XVIIIc. 1760. American. (Metropolitan Mus.)
Joseph Badger. James Badger.

Joseph Badger (1708-65), son of a tailor in Charleston, Mass., was a glazier and house painter in 1739. He was never well paid and died penniless, although between 1748-60 (the period between Smibert's illness and Copley's rise) he was Boston's

principal portrait painter. The most appealing of his earnest, rather wooden pictures are those of children.

Compromise between male and female styles used on boys who are not yet breeched: wig, cuffs, buttons on a gray coat which is prolonged into skirts, but has the low neck of woman's dress, without any linen; the *solitaire* is used in the manner of the analogous neckband of woman; (see Ill. 2148); black sash, embroidered in red and white.

2148. XVIIIc. 1761. American. (Baltimore, Gen. Lawson Riggs.)
John Hesselius. Charles Calvert of Maryland, and Negro.

Gustavus Hesselius (1682-1755) and his son John were the leading painters of portraits of the pre-Revolutionary southern aristocracy. Gustavus, born in Sweden in a learned family of clerics, was a cousin of Swedenborg. In 1711, he accompanied his brother to the Delaware parish to which he had been appointed by Charles XII. The first publicly commissioned work of art in America was probably the altar-piece he painted for a Maryland church, in 1721. As his son and pupil rose to eminence, Gustavus withdrew into his other profession of organ builder.

John Hesselius, (1728-78) "by whom the greater part of the family portraits in the old mansions of Maryland was painted, and that in respectable manner," (William Dunlop), was born in Maryland and returned there after his boyhood in Philadelphia.

2148

2149

2150

By marriage with a rich young widow of an excellent Annapolis family, he was brought into the best society of Virginia and Maryland. Despite private means, he painted steadily throughout his life, producing c. 100 portraits, although his work became lifeless and stereotyped during his last fifteen years.

The charter of Maryland was issued in 1632 to George Calvert, the first Lord Baltimore, whose descendants remained the proprietors of Maryland until the death of the last Lord Baltimore in 1771.

This little Calvert boy is in his first breeches; but like other fanciful coatless costumes his waistcoat shows XVIIc. doublet details of picadills, slashing, lace cuffs and tiny ruff, worn with an untied *solitaire* which has the characteristics of little James Badger's sash (Ill. 2147). These waistcoat costumes are always accompanied by a formless cloak.

The slave's collared livery shows patterned braid, such as has become a livery characteristic.

2149. XVIIIc. 1764. English. (London, Nat. Port. Gall.)
T. Bardwell. Maurice Suckling.

Captain Suckling (1725-78), comptroller of the navy, was a son of Chancellor Walpole's sister. His niece, Catherine Suckling, married a vicar named Nelson. It was the efforts of his Suckling uncle, not the Walpoles, which launched the career of England's greatest naval hero, Horatio Nelson.

Uniform; wig reduced to one curl.

2150. XVIIIc. 1765. English. (Met. Mus., Print Room.)
Unknown Artist. A Perspective View of the Grand Walk in Vauxhall Gardens, and the Orchestra.

No. 36 in a scrap book, "A Sketch of the Spring Gardens, Vauxhall," recently acquired by the Metropolitan's Print Room, shows the "fine pavillions, shady groves, and most delightful walks, illuminated by above one thousand lamps, so disposed that they all take fire together, almost as quick as lightning, and dart such a sudden blaze as is perfectly surprising. Here are, among others, two curious statues of Apollo the god, and Mr. Handel, the master of musick as Orpheus, by Roubillac; and in the centre of the area, where the walks terminate, is erected the temple for the musicians, which is encompassed all around with handsome seats, decorated with pleasant paintings on subjects most happily adapted to the season, place and company." (From *England's Gazetteer,* 1751.) The paintings in the booths were by Hayman and Hogarth: sports, amusements and scenes from plays.

With the milkmaid styles which are becoming fashionable everywhere, elaborate aprons are worn; the overskirt begins to be looped up behind for comfort in the manner of the *polonaise.* Hats begin to be worn outdoors, differentiated from the caps of domesticity or of formal dress.

2151. XVIIIc. 1766. English. (Metropolitan Museum.)

Reynolds. Hon. Henry Fane and his Guardians—Inigo Jones and Charles Blair.

All wear their own unpowdered hair, slightly dressed. The young heir has a red coat lined with gray; its green collar matches the waistcoat. Tan breeches, lengthened to the boot-tops, retain the strap and gold buckle of knee breeches; black boots; black hat edged with gold.

The central figure wears a white coat, embroidered in gold and lined with green to match the waistcoat; white stockings and breeches with gold buttons; black shoes with gold buckles.

The seated figure to the left wears a green uniform coat and waistcoat, with red collar, gold trim and buttons.

Fane wears soft, glove-fitting high boots, supported by knee straps.

2152. XVIIIc. 1768. English. (Mourne Park, Earl of Kilmorey.)

Gainsborough. Viscount Kilmorey.

Capt. Jack Needham, of a family which had lived at Shavington Hall, Adderly, Shropshire, since 1438, became the 10th Viscount Kilmorey. His son, later the 1st Earl of Kilmorey, served with the forces in America and was taken prisoner at Yorktown.

As Ills. 2151-53 show, waistcoats are shorter; both waistcoats and coats, military and civil, are developing lapels as well as collars. Cuffs become reduced in size, tend to be stitched flat to the sleeve, and to become a mere buttoned slit. The cuff of Fane's guardian, wearing civilian dress, is not a rectangle, but a trapezoid, spiralled about the arm.

Wigs are frequently unpowdered; by 1765 the natural hair begins to be grown and treated like a wig, with or without powder.

2153. XVIIIc. 1766-8. English. (Blockley, Northwick Park, Capt. E. G. Spencer-Churchill.)

Reynolds. Warren Hastings (1732-1818).

Hastings, an orphaned child of good but impoverished family, was shunted about among distant relatives, one of whom was connected with the East India Co. This accident sent East an honorable administrator, the eventual governor-general of India, who with Gen. Clive, established England's supremacy in India. A newly arrived council in 1773 was outraged because "Hastings might have put on a ruffled shirt" to meet them. Ancient frictions of this sort, enmeshed in the struggle between Parliament and the East India Co. for control, led to Hastings' impeachment and trial in 1788. He had never drawn a nabob's exorbitant profits from his Indian connections; his vindication in 1795 left him ruined, dependent on pensions. This portrait was painted in England during the break between his two long periods of service in India.

2154. XVIIIc. 1766. American. (Metropolitan Museum.)
Copley. Mrs. Sylvanus Bourne.

With a provincial time-lag, Mrs. Bourne wears the dress of an elderly English woman of midXVIIIc. (a grander version of Zoffany's Farmer's Wife, see Ill. 2142): enclosing, ribbon-trimmed cap; kerchief closed high and caught with the English single bow; dress of plain satin, with unexaggerated wrist ruffles; mitts.

The parents of *John Singleton Copley* (1737-1815) arrived from Ireland just in time for him to be born in Boston. His father, a tobacconist, soon died; in 1745 his mother married Peter Pelham, an excellent painter-engraver, who also taught penmanship, arithmetic and dancing. Copley, who was producing good portraits and mezzotints at fifteen, wrote Lio-

2154   2155

tard (whose chocolate girl still adorns boxes of cocoa) asking for some good Swiss pastel crayons, which Liotard sent, astonished that anyone in America had even heard of such things.

A picture of his half-brother, Henry Pelham, with a squirrel, which Copley had sent to the Society of Arts, London, in 1766, was received by Benjamin West; he encouraged Copley to come to Europe. Copley had married the gracious and lovely daughter of the agent of the East India Co., who was the consignee of the "Tea Party" tea. Copley lived in a fine Boston house and was very successful; but the riots in America shocked him; he embarked on a tour of Europe in 1774 and was joined by his family the next year.

He was equally successful in London, became an academician on the strength of one of his large historical pictures and never returned to America. "The first American flag hoisted in old England" was one he painted on a ship, in the background of a portrait in 1782.

Copley's daughter married a Boston man. His American-born son, educated in England, became the Lord Chancellor Lyndhurst, who worked for the liberalization of divorce for women, and the admission of Jews to Parliament; (his second wife was a Jewess).

2155. XVIIIc. 1766. American. (Metropolitan Museum.)
Copley. Joseph Sherburne.

Caps which protect the wigless head have changed during XVIIIc. from their gored and embroidered XVIc. form, into swathed turbans and gathered tam

2156

o'shanters of velvet or satin. Waistcoat continues to be a necessary part of negligée, and is always worn under a dressing gown. Blue turban; red waistcoat; brown brocade dressing gown with mustard lining and ·edges.

2156. XVIIIc. 1766-7. English. (Windsor, H. M. the King.)
J. Zoffany. Queen Charlotte and Her Children.

The Queen, who will eventually have nine sons and six daughters, is shown with the eldest of her present family of six: the Prince of Wales (George IV) as a Roman soldier, and the Duke of York as a Turk. Boys have been "dressed up" in exotic turbans since XVIIc. and in anachronistic XVIIc. slashings and lace during XVIIIc., just as they will be put into sailor-suits at the end XVIIIc.

They are in Old Buckingham House at Windsor; the ormolu clock shown in the background has been set near Zoffany's picture, as it now hangs at Windsor Castle.

The silver mirror of the dressing table, hung in embroidered muslin, gives a profile view of the Queen's head, dressed and studded in a decorous form of the current French style. Her double neck-ruche matches the crossed bands which trim the U-shaped front of her bodice; the sleeves have three rows of lace ruffles below elaborate self-trimmings; the petticoat has a flounce of its own satin which has been snipped and pinked into a lace-like design —the forerunner of eyelet embroidery.

2157. XVIIIv. 1769. English. (Castle Howard, Hon. Geoffrey Howard.)
Reynolds. Frederick, fifth Earl of Carlisle.

The young earl, "fond of dress and gaming—not void of ambition," but who "had but moderate parts and less application," as Walpole said, wears the gold-tasseled green robes of the Order of the Thistle. Its collar is composed of the thistle which was the Stewart badge, and the sprigs of rue of the Pict kings: all this is XVIIc. court dress, in anachronistic ceremonial use with robes.

2158. XVIIIc. English. (Birmingham, English Mus. and Art. Gall.)
Reynolds. John Thomas, Bishop of Rochester.

John Thomas (1712-93), a vicar's son who became a school-master after Oxford, married the rich widowed aunt of one of his pupils. He entered the church and rose from a living of which his brother-in-law had the disposition, to chaplain-in-ordinary to George II and George III. He became Dean of Win-

chester and received the Order of the Bath in 1768; Bishop of Rochester in 1774. He married a second rich widow and founded four Queen's College scholarships for boys whose background resembled his own.

Reynolds painted him in the red robes of the Bath, with the gold civilian form of the Grand Cross over his lawn bands and the "comely surplice with sleeves" fixed in Anglican use by Archbishop Parker in 1566; the lawn sleeves had grown immense by XVIIIc. Short episcopal wig.

2159. XVIIIc. 1772-3. English. (London, Major A. W. Foster.)
Reynolds. David Garrick and Wife.

David Garrick (1717-79) came of French Protestants who had emigrated at the revocation of the Edict of Nantes. He came to London under the wing of Samuel Johnson, and set up as a wine merchant. He was completely stage-struck, wrote poor plays, hung about theatres and acted in place of sick friends. In 1741, he made his debut as a professional in Richard III; London went mad. "There was a dozen dukes a night at Goodman's Fields," said Walpole, who, however, disliked Garrick always. Society was completely won away from its former allegiance to the opera by Garrick's vivacious modern style. As we see the end of his tradition in elderly Shakespearean actors in XXc., it does not seem as natural as it did to audiences accustomed to Quin's pompous declamations.

The opera retaliated with various pressures. Garrick alternated between London and Dublin, until he bought the Drury Lane in 1747. He had been the lover of Peg Woffington, who so became the breeches of the male parts she played. Later Garrick married a central European dancer, Mlle. Violette, "the best of women and wives," of whom even Walpole had only good to say. Mrs. Siddons made her debut, not very successfully, at Drury Lane, just before Garrick sold it to Sheridan.

The English gown keeps its specific character during about the second third of XVIIIc. The *robe à la française* to which it finally succumbs is essentially that of the second half-century. England develops its own versions, while the same gown follows a somewhat different course in France.

The English bodice retains its straighter form; its top is never so wide open and revealing as in

France, and is veiled in all sorts of scarves and kerchiefs. English sleeves become more elaborate, with much show of lace below a self-ruffle and decoration at the elbow. The characteristic pleats from the shoulder of the *robe à la française* usually flow into the back of the skirt; the overskirt is not only slit to show a triangle of underskirt, but its edges are heavily bordered with puffings and pleatings, as is the flounced petticoat.

The hair rises high over pads; the cap becomes less a separate article of dress than an arrangement of decoration related to a specific costume. England develops many forms of turban and cap of her own.

Mrs. Garrick wears a close undersleeve below the flounces at her elbow. These were more commonly seen in France in the first half of XVIIIc. than during the third quarter-century, when sleeves tend to replace ruffles by puffs at the elbow. They will reappear in France with the English styles and bonnets of c. 1784.

2160. XVIIIc. c. 1760. American. (Milton, Mass., the Misses Ware.)
Dress: of Mary Middleton Lovell, wife of James Lovell, U. S. N., Collector of the Port of Boston.
2161. Second half XVIIIc. French.
Gown: linen, wool-embroidered in chain stitch; yellow, pink, plum and green.

Courtesy of Metropolitan Museum of Art

2169.   2170   2170 A

2162. XVIIIc. 1774-93. French.
Gown: blue striped taffeta.

2163. XVIIIc. Late Louis XVI. French.
Robe *à la polonaise:* brocade of earlier date.

2164. XVIIIc. French.
Bodice and Skirt: block-printed cotton.

2165. XVIIIc. French, Marseilles.
Peasant Skirt: polychrome wood-block; possibly printed at Marseilles.

2166. XVIIIc. French.
Apron: white muslin, embroidered in gold thread, and edged with gold lace.

2167. XVIIIc. c. 1785. French, Marseilles.
Apron: polychrome wood-block print.

2168. XVIIIc. c. 1787. American. (Boston, Mrs. C. M. Stevens.)
Two dresses: yellow brocade; blue and yellow silk drouget.

2169. XVIIIc. English. (London, National Gallery.)
Francis Cotes. Mrs. Cadoux.
Mrs. Cadoux' white *robe à la française* with pink ribbons is worn over a pink petticoat. The English gown now shows flowing back pleats and is heavily trimmed with gathered serpentine bands of self material. The sleeves are finished with a pleated self-ruffle above the lace; the pink petticoat is trimmed with heavy serpentine ruffles of its own fabric.
Unpowdered hair with one of the English turbans of the 60's and 70's.

2170. XVIIIc. c. 1774-5. English. (London, Nat. Gall.)
Gainsborough. Mrs. Graham as a Housemaid.
Mary, daughter of the 3rd Lord Cathcart, was married in 1774 to Thomas Graham, later Lord Lynedock, one of Wellington's captains in the Peninsular War. This unfinished picture, painted after

the return from their honeymoon, was bought by the 5th Earl of Carlisle, who said it was perfect as it was, and must not be touched again by a brush.
A wonderful Gainsborough portrait of Mrs. Graham, now in the Edinburgh Nat. Gall., was discovered many years later, just as it had hung, at the end of their dining room, where her heartbroken husband had ordered it walled off when she died at thirty-five.
Ladies not only masquerade as housemaids and milkmaids, but styles originating at that level float up to the aristocracy. "The Ranelagh Mob, or the Hood from Low Life, a piece of gauze, clouted about the head, then crossed under the chin and brought back to fasten behind, the two ends hanging down like a pair of pigeon tails," was copied from the silk handkerchiefs which market-women tied over their ears, rolled about their throats, and then pinned up to the nape of their neck. "They were first worn in the Inner-Square of Covent Garden Market among the green-stalls. It was from there introduced into the Square or Piazzas among the stalls there. Mrs. Jane Douglas (of procuring memory) who was a very great market-woman in her way, was the first who made a Scotch lawn double neck handkerchief into the Mob above mentioned. Her females would do as the mistress did, to be sure; and after a little cut and contrivance, away they whisked them to Ranelagh. The ladies of fashion there, who sometimes dress almost like ladies of the town, immediately took the hint." (*London Chronicle,* 1762.)

2170A. XVIIIc. 1774. English.
Dickinson, after *Reynolds.* Mrs. Pelham.
English version of the loose jackets of the *caraco* sort, in a charming, completely embroidered costume.

2171. XVIIIc. 1773-1809. American. (New York Historical Soc.)

Charles Willson Peale. Peale Family Group.

The portraits for this picture, which was not finished until 1809, were painted in 1773. It shows a few members of a large and remarkably talented American family of naturalists and painters: C. W. Peale with his brothers, St. George and James; his sister Mrs. Ramsay. his first wife Rachael Brewer; his sons, Titian and Rembrandt; his cousin Margaret Durgan; his mother Margaret; the dog Argus.

Charles Peale (1709-50), of a family of English clergymen, came to Annapolis, where he taught school and married. Of his sons, Charles Willson Peale (1741-1827) and James were artists.

Charles Willson Peale married three times. By his first wife he had six children, all named after painters. Raphael and his more distinguished brother, Rembrandt (1774-1860), were artists; Rubens, a naturalist. Of his second wife's six children, Franklin was a naturalist, and his older brother Titian (named after a dead half-brother) was a naturalist-explorer, the illustrator of great ornithological and entomological works, and for many of his later years, examiner in the Patent Office.

James Peale, a miniaturist, married the sister of the painter Claypoole; he too had six children: Anna Claypoole and Sarah Miriam were well known, the one as a portrait painter, the other as a miniaturist. Margaretta painted still-lifes, and a banker son, seascapes.

C. W. Peale had a many-sided career. At thirteen he was apprenticed to a saddlemaker for seven years. He married and went into business for himself at twenty, with the backing of his employer and another Loyalist, who put him out of business when he joined the Sons of Freedom. With some instructions from Hesselius and Copley and two years study in London with West he returned to take Copley's place in Boston. Philadelphia was full of notables for the Continental Congress; he moved his family there in 1776. He painted Washington several times, and though deeply engrossed in military and patriotic activities until 1780, he managed, even while in camp at Trenton and Princeton, to record in miniature the faces of a large number of fellow officers. These he enlarged and exhibited in a gallery in Philadelphia after the war.

Then came the discovery of mastodon skeletons in Orange Co., N. Y. (still one of the richest sources). Two were excavated at his expense, and exhibited. One went to Europe in his son Rembrandt's care when he, too, studied with West. In 1802, West's gallery became the first important natural history museum in America, housed free in In-

dependence Hall; later, it entered the Philadelphia Museum. Peale was also largely responsible for the foundation of the Philadelphia Academy of the Fine Arts in 1805.

Rembrandt Peale, born on a Bucks County farm to which his mother had fled from the British occupation of Philadelphia, was a talented child of wide interests. He made five European trips before 1835, the first for study with West. He was immediately successful in whatever city he found himself: New York, Boston, Philadelphia, London, or Paris, where in 1808 he painted celebrities and naturalists like Cuvier and Count Rumford (the American-born scientist) for his father's museum, and in 1810, Napoleon. He was a more accomplished, but a less endearing artist than his father.

The Peale men (in Ill. 2171) show simplification of the wig; the stock is increased by formal folds, the jabot is suppressed. The rise at the back of the coat's neck has now rolled over into a collar.

2172. XVIIIc. 1773. American. (Metropolitan Museum.) *Copley.* Mrs. John Winthrop.

2173

Little boys show natural hair, free of cap, turban and wig.

Like the elaborately dressed Mrs. Winthrop, Mrs. Ramsay's and Rachel Peale's costume shows the gain of French influence; their hair and that of Margaret Durgan, and even of old Mrs. Peale is rising high and shows the cap in process of becoming a decoration of the hair rather than a separate object. Enclosing fichus and caps in the older, more sober English taste, on the older women.

2173. XVIIIc. 1772-75. English. (Panshanger, Lady Desborough.)

John Zoffany. The Cowper-Gore Family.

Goethe's travelled Englishman in *Wilhelm Meister* was patterned on the rich, eccentric 3rd Earl Cowper, godson of George III. He arrived in Florence on the Grand Tour, and went no further. Walpole commiserates in 1774 with Mann on the probable loss of a friend when Cowper is about to marry a Miss Gore, with whose family we see him at music. They lived in the greatest possible state, as favorites of the Tuscan Court.

Later, Cowper made one brief visit to England, and Walpole went to a concert of Italian music, not to hear the singer, but because he "was curious to see an English Earl who had passed thirty years in Florence, and is more proud of a pinchbeck Principality and a paltry Order from Wirtemberg, than he was of being a Peer of Great Britain, when Great Britain *was* something." They were introduced. "I should have taken his Highness for a Doge of Genoa: he has the awkward dignity of a temporal representative of nominal power. Peace be with him and his leaf-gold."

Lord Cowper stands in the center in a green frock-coat with small flat cuffs, white vest, breeches, and hose; and a wig with the high raked-back toupet of c. 1773. His fiancée, Miss Gore, in pink, stands before a picture which is still preserved at the Villa Palmieri. Her sister Emily, in blue, sits at the harpsichord with her father and his cello. Another sister and Mrs. Gore, in white, and in gray, listen. All show the French dress which is standard European wear.

2174. XVIIIc. English. (Parma Gallery.)

John Zoffany. Wandering Minstrels.

This picture, supposed to have been painted for Ferdinand of Bourbon-Parma, was given to the Academy of Parma by Zoffany when he became a member in 1773. A watch, probably stolen, is pinned to the vest of a dilapidated musician.

2175. XVIIIc. 1773. English. (London Museum.)

Unknown artist. A Macaroni: "Welladay, is this Son Tom?"

2176. XVIIIc. 1773. English. (New York, Mr. and Mrs. R. T. Halsey.)

John Raphael Smith. Miss Macaroni and her Gallant at a Print Shop.

2177. XVIIIc. 1774. English. (London, Duchess of Roxburghe.)

Thomas Patch. Group in Florence.

English winters were never so unpleasant, or its court life so dull as in XVIIIc. Colonial administrative posts take whole families halfway round the world. The wealth of the nabobs flows back to the mother country. Relatives remaining in England go at least for jaunts on the Continent, preferably to Italy. Art collecting is a mania. The English have money to buy Italian Renaissance paintings, or the

Canalettos supplied by Mr. Smith, the British Consul in Venice. Many return regularly to Italy. Some, like the Cowper-Gores (Ill. 2173) settle in the permanent English colony in Florence. They serve as a magnet to draw other English visitors, including painters like Tom Patch (1700-c.1774). Patch did this group picture after the manner of the caricatured Macaronis, shown in a print shop by another industrious print-maker, John Raphael Smith (1753-1812). Patch was also busy making engravings after Italian art, to be sold in such galleries.

Patch shows himself in conversation with the gesticulating Mr. Wilberforce, under a *View of the Arno* (now belonging to Mary, Countess of Ilchester). Sir Thomas Dick plays the harpsichord; Zoffany shows a drawing to Sir Henry Felton.

A picture by Zoffany of the Tribuna Gallery in Florence in 1779 shows not only Patch and his group and other regulars like Cowper and Sir Horace Mann, but more than a dozen other visiting earls, lords and notables, whom Zoffany painted in at twenty shillings a head, looking at an art collection. It includes Raphael's Madonna, unearthed by Zoffany, and sold to Cowper for a down payment and an annuity of £100 a year; and Titian's Venus, which the President of the Royal Academy, after his visit, persuaded Queen Charlotte to buy for 600 guineas.

THE MACARONIS

The "beaux" of George II's time are replaced c. 1749 by the "fribbles" of the early reign of George III. "Macaronis," extravagantly dressed, Italian-travelled young men, began to appear in the 1760's. Led by the dissolute and able Charles Fox (who will, in turn, lead the careless, neglected fashions of 1784-95), the Macaronis are at their apogee in 1772-3, when Walpole mentions them frequently: "Lord Chatham begat the East-India Co.; the East India Co. begat Lord Clive; Lord Clive begat the Macaronis, and they begat poverty." A year later, "The Macaronis, amongst whom exist the only symptoms of vivacity, are all undone, and cannot distinguish themselves by insensibility alone. They neither feel for families nor themselves."

A tendency toward extravagance in dress, already noted in the *London Chronicle* in 1762, culminates in a flood of caricatures, ridiculing the dress of the Macaronis, male and female. Their wigs, extravagantly clubbed behind, rise in a fantastically high toupet. "Every Smart . . . seems . . . to have been skating against the wind, and his hair, by the sharpness of the motion, shorn from his face." (*London Chronicle,* 1762.) A tiny Nivernois hat, tilted on the very top, is lifted, either by the point of the cutlass, or by the knob of the tall, tasseled stick, which are part of a Macaroni's equipment. Tom even carries a reticule at his wrist.

Their frock coats have small collars and are cut away to expose the whole chest. At first, they reach to mid-leg, and "are so much splashed sometimes behind," that the writer of the *London Chronicle* has "often been tempted to call out, 'Pray, dear Sir, pin up your petticoats.'" With these were worn "buttonless topcoats which only wrap over their breasts like a Morning Gown."

The linen of the Macaroni is extravagant; his very short vest is often without pockets. His skin-tight breeches finish with knee-strings. The whole costume drips with frayed-out ends of braid trimming, frogs and tassels; fobs and seals hang from pairs of watches. His shoes have high red heels and are often finished with ribbon bows and rosettes.

Miss Macaroni shows the matching height and extravagance of the headdress of the female type of Macaroni. She and her gallant wear the dotted and striped patterns to which the Macaronis were partial.

Tom's father wears the riding costume which is the uniform of a sensible old country squire.

2178. XVIIIc. Before 1775. English. (New York, Daniel H. Farr.)

John Zoffany. Dutton Family.

Mr. Dutton, who died in 1776, was born Napier, but had taken the name and coat-of-arms of his first father-in-law, Sir Ralph Dutton. He is shown in the drawing-room of Sherborne Park, Gloucestershire, with his second wife, her son James, the 1st Lord Sherborne, and fourth daughter Jane, who was married in 1775 to Thomas Coke of Holkham, later the earl of Leicester, the founder of modern agriculture and cattle-breeding in England.

Mrs. Dutton is protesting the card game which interferes with her Bible-reading. It is hot by the cannel-coal grate fire, and cold away from it. Her face is protected by a fire screen (decorated with a flower-filled urn) and she wears a long glove on her farther arm; elaborate closed cap, fichu, and black gown of an elderly Englishwoman.

Her son, dressed in grayish white with a yellow vest, wears a wig, sharply raked back in a high toupet, under "Macaroni" influence. Mr. Dutton is in purple with a conservative wig. Miss Dutton's hair is ceremoniously dressed high in the French fashion, with the ropes of pearls much used in England; black lace collar on pale green dress, worn with a quilted petticoat.

Card table of diagonally set veneer with a green baize top; floor covered, as in Queen Caroline's room at Windsor, with large oriental rug; carved and gilded girandole, set with the oval mirror of third quarter XVIIIc., will develop into circular convex bull's-eye mirrors by end XVIIIc.

2179. XVIIIc. 1776. English. (Metropolitan Museum, Print Room.)

Robert Laurie (c. 1755-1836). Scene from "She Stoops to Conquer."

The manager of Covent Garden was reluctant to produce Goldsmith's second play in 1773. But unsentimental as it was, the hilariously farcical blunders in which Tony Lumpkin and the Hardcastles were involved during the five acts of "She Stoops to Conquer" made it a tremendous success.

Stage costume contrasting conservative and sporting dress: full-bottomed wig; old-fashioned neckcloth; stockings drawn up over breeches; square-toed shoes; cloak. Fitted jockey cap; riding coat; boots with long breeches; crop; and natural locks. Hood covering large coiffure and cap, will be given supporting hoops hinged into a *Thérèse* as the head increases in size; its cape is edged with cut "eyelet" embroidery. The *caraco* has the long inner sleeve seen in English use. (Ill. 2158.)

2180-81. XVIIIc. 1777. American. (Metropolitan Museum of Art.)

C. W. Peale. Samuel Mifflin, Rebecca Edgehill Mifflin, and granddaughter, Rebecca Mifflin Francis,

The first lace, reticella, developed out of fabric threads, drawn and worked; its rectangular patterns became rounded, and then freely worked on net. Now, as we see on the edge of Mrs. Mifflin's fichu, lace patterns are again being worked on the new, extremely sheer fabrics; punched with a coarse needle, drawn and embroidered in *point de Saxe* or *point de Dresde*. Her gray-brown satin wrap is either dotted, or possibly snipped into an all-over pattern, after the manner of XVIc. doublets. This impulse, similar to the new way of producing lace, can be seen in an unmistakable form on the hem of Queen Charlotte's satin petticoat (Ill. 2156). The lace of her wrap is worked on a wide, diamond-mesh net. Quilted blue satin petticoat.

Little Rebecca's front hair is clipped. She wears a gray-brown dress spotted with embroidery; *sabots* and sash of bordered light brown gauze.

Mr. Mifflin wears his own hair, clipped into a bang and curled at the nape. Unification of costume; plain gray-brown cloth with self-covered buttons and buckled knee strap; coat creeping high and beginning to buckle at the back of the neck. Plain shirt ruffles and stock; white stockings.

2182. XVIIIc. 1777. English. (Philadelphia, Joseph E. Widener.)
Romney. William Petrie.

George Romney (1734-1802), son of a Lancashire peasant, had been a carpenter and fiddle-maker, until he began to study at nineteen, and his work was noticed by the vicar, Rev. Laurence Sterne. At twenty-eight he gave the larger part of his savings to his wife, a servant-girl who had nursed him through a fever at 21, and went off to London.

Romney was uneducated, shy, and neurotic. He had no encouragement from the English court and was never admitted to the Royal Academy. His work became fashionable, but "so many of his sitters were killed off, so many favorite ladies dismissed, so many fond wives divorced before he could bestow half an hour's pains upon their petticoats, that his unsaleable stock was immense" (Richard Cumberland). Reynolds' most important rival went mad about Lady Hamilton in 1783, and painted her in every guise. In 1799, paralyzed and ill, he returned to his wife and family, whom he had supported but seen only twice in thirty-seven years. She nursed him until his death.

2183. XVIIIc. 1776-8. English. (London, Nat. Gall.)
Romney. Beaumont Family.

The coats of Mr. Petrie and the Beaumonts show the frogs of third quarter XVIIIc., which were often grouped, turning into paired buttons set on a braid trim. Waistcoats are shorter, light in color, matching

the breeches to which they are related—in Mr. Petrie's case by delicate matching embroidery on the buckled knee strap. Increased English use of one's own hair, unpowdered and informally dressed like a wig, sometimes clipped in a bang over the forehead (left).

With draped, untrimmed, informal gowns, which with English sporting dress will so affect French fashion from the 80's, English women wear their hair unpowdered in high, rather loose piles, asymmetrically dressed with twisted scarves.

2184. XVIIIc. 1774 or 1777-8. English. (Metropolitan Museum, Frick Coll.)
Gainsborough. The Hon. Frances Duncombe.

Women's and children's dress of second half

XVIIIc. sometimes show fanciful touches of XVIIc. style. Frances Duncombe's gown, looped up as English dresses are now apt to be in some way, is inspired by Henrietta Maria's pearled satin gowns, and accompanied by a plumed version of a XVIIc. Flemish hat. "Van Dyck" styles persist into XIXc.

2185. XVIIIc. 1778. English. (San Marino, California, H. E. Huntington Art Gallery.)
Gainsborough. Juliana Howard, Lady Petre.

The English style which overwhelmed France from the 80's is worn by this Catholic Howard married to a member of one of the other traditionally Catholic families of England. Huge, high-crowned black hat trimmed with ribbon loops, which never blot out its form, worn on loosely fluffed, lightly powdered curls; puffed *bouffant* kerchief; close-waisted, long-sleeved creamy muslin or gauze jacket (shown here in a short form which makes the line of the icy-blue satin bodice below it the equivalent of a very wide belt); untrimmed blue satin skirt, veiled in sheer creamy material. Gauzy black scarf, edged with lace.

2186. XVIIIc. c. 1778. English. (Washington, Nat. Gall. of Art.)
Reynolds. Lady Caroline Howard.

Children's dress will be revolutionized by simple English muslins like this tucked gown, worn with a blue sash of the wonderful ribbons England is now weaving and will export to France, pale yellow gloves, a lace-edged black cape, and a round cap, worn over hair cropped into bangs.

2187. XVIIIc. 1777-87. English. (Washington, Nat. Gall. of Art.)
Reynolds. Lady Elizabeth Delmé and Children.

Lady Elizabeth, born Howard, was the aunt of little Lady Caroline Howard. Unpowdered hair dressed high with characteristic English negligence, wound turban-wise with a metal-threaded scarf; softly draped muslin gown, rose cloak. Boy in red coat and breeches which reach half-way below knee; collar opening out over shoulders; vest of one of the piqué-like waled and corded materials, to which matelassé forms will be added at the turn of the century for vests.

2188. Late XVIIIc. English. (Metropolitan Museum.)
British School (formerly attr. to *Romney*). John Parker.

Large plumed beaver hat, as women's hats grow large and feathered.

2189. XVIIIc. 1778. American. (Hampton Court, H. M. the King.)

Benjamin West. Queen Charlotte and the Princess Royal.

Benjamin West (1738-1820) was born in Philadelphia of Quaker parents who opposed the interest in art which he showed at seven. At eighteen, however, he was painting portraits in Philadelphia; at twenty in New York. In 1760, he was helped to go to Italy for three years. He made a great reputation there and came to London in 1763. He became a familiar of the royal family and was one of the four artists who planned the Royal Academy. In 1772, he was made historical painter to the king. "We have an American, West, who deals in high history, and is vastly admired, but he is heavier than Guercino, and has still less grace, and is very inferior," Walpole wrote after seeing the Academy Show of 1775. West was a dignified, benevolent man and an excellent teacher; he succeeded Reynolds as president of the Royal Academy. In 1802 he went to Paris to study the art of Europe which Napoleon had massed in the Louvre.

The queen disliked the English court and avoided its life as much as possible, to live with her husband (who was already deranged, although not yet confined), in an oppressive domesticity which both enjoyed, but against which a number of the dozen children already born to them rebelled with violence.

"The vivacity of the young queen of France has reached hither," Walpole wrote in 1775. "Our young ladies are covered with more plumes than any nation that has no other covering." Charlotte was unsuccessful in her opposition to plumes in a court which she did not dominate. But with her ruche-trimmed *caraco* and muslin apron (the frill of which is caught up into charming shells), she allows her hair to be dressed in a very high "head," with the scallops of a round cap appearing beneath its turbaned top.

The industrious little princess is conservatively dressed in silk with powdered hair high under a gauffered, beribboned English cap.

Greek column; helmeted antique bust.

2190. XVIIIc. c. 1779. English-American. (Washington, Nat. Gall. of Art.)

Benjamin West. Col. Guy Johnson and Capt. Joseph Brant. (*See also* Frontispiece.)

Sir William Johnson (1715-74) came to America in 1738 to administer land in the Mohawk Valley belonging to his uncle, Sir Peter Warren. Johnson established remarkable relations with the Indians; he was adopted by the Mohawks, became superintendent of the affairs of the Six Nations, and eventually of all the Indians in the province. He fought in the French and Indian Wars and with Jeffrey Amherst, kept his tribes from joining Pontiac, and was rewarded with a baronetcy and an estate of 100,000 acres at what is now Johnstown, N. Y. He lived there in a great house like an English lord, a widower with an Indian mistress called Molly Brant. His son, Sir John, succeeded to the baronetcy and became an officer.

The trusteeship of Indian affairs passed to Sir William's nephew, Guy Johnson (1740-88), whose secretary and companion in the Cherry Valley massacres was the Mohawk Chief Thayendanega, otherwise known as Joseph Brant, Molly's brother. Brant was educated by Sir William at the Indian school in Connecticut from which Dartmouth College originated. He translated the Prayer Book and part of the New Testament into Mohawk, became a missionary after the war, and raised money to build the first Episcopal church in Northern Canada, during a trip to England in 1786.

Johnson wears a fur-lined cloak, Indian-made like his moccasins, leggings and cap, together with a red coat which has a low standing collar and flaps which button back into lapels.

2191. XVIIIc. 1780-88. English. (Washington, Nat. Gall. of Art.)

Gainsborough. George IV as Prince of Wales.

The handsome Prince of Wales, in his red coat, gold epaulettes and Star of the Garter, has become "the first gentleman of Europe," in revolt against his parents' dull parsimony. He will eventually become tainted with his father's instability, descend into incredibly undignified persecution of his hated queen after he fails to have her daughter declared illegitimate, and will earn the whole-hearted detestation of his people.

2192. XVIIIc. English. (Gloucestershire, Hardwick Court, Miss Olivia Lloyd-Baker.)

John Zoffany. The Sharp Family on a Yacht.

Many upper-class families of the XVIIIc. lived like

the Zoffanys and the Sharps. Both families loved music. Sharp was Handel's doctor; Zoffany, Bach's friend. Both had houses on the river, and yachts for musical outings. Zoffany had a summer house filled with musical instruments at his boat-landing. The servants on his pink, green and buff shallop wore liveries derived from his patent of nobility from Maria Theresa: scarlet and gold faced with blue, and shoulder-knots with his crest: a sprig of clover and buffalo horns rising from a baronet's coronet. The Sharp family lived in a house and a cottage at Fulham (seen in the background, to the right of the church), which were connected by an underground passage. They often entertained George III and Queen Charlotte at tea and music on the yacht. Zoffany connected his house and summerhouse on the Strand at Chiswick with an overhead passage, in expectation of a visit from the Prince of Wales, which never came off.

Musical parties on the Thames had been loved since Tudor days. In XVIIIc. they became a passion. Those who did not keep a liveried barge could rent a barge at any landing for a ride to one of the pleasure gardens; Walpole's letters are full of such parties, which were followed by a barge of horns or other music.

The people shown include: Dr. John Sharp (1793-1758), Archbishop of Northumberland; his wife,

daughter of the Dean of Ripon, and their only daughter, Anna Jemima, in pink and green. William Sharp, the surgeon, who paid Zoffany 800 guineas for this picture, steers. He wears the Windsor uniform (blue frock coat, scarlet collar) as a member of Princess Amelia's household. (He had refused a baronetcy.) His wife sits below in a blue riding habit, holding their only child, Mary (ancestress of the picture's present owner), and her kitten. James Sharp, the eminent engineer, holds a horn called a "serpent" and wears a hat. His wife sits above in lavender, black lace and a great cap. Their only surviving child stands beside him in white muslin, pink sash and plumed cap. Elizabeth Sharp Prowse sits at the harpsichord; her sister Judith, in a brown habit beside sister Jemima, holds a lute. Their youngest sister Judith sits in profile, wearing blue moiré and holding a sheet of music. Granville Sharp, the philanthropist, holds a double-flageolet and a sheet of music. An oboe lies on the harpsichord; a theorbo stands by the cabin boy (who still lived in 1848, and gave an account of the painting). Behind him is the yacht-master, and in front lies Zoffany's dog Roma. (Information from Sitwell: "Conversation Pieces.")

Clipped hair of boy, yacht-master, and girl; bushy short wig of archbishop; reduction of other wigs to one curl. Caps giving way to plumed hats; riding costume from which walking dress of late XVIIIc. will develop.

2193. XVIIIc. 1783-90. English. (Trowbridge, Steeple Ashton, Edward Impey.)

Zoffany. Sir Elijah and Lady Impey with Indian Servants.

The Chief Justice of Bengal, Warren Hastings' friend since their school days; ayahs and servants wear Indian dress.

2194. XVIIIc. 1783-90. English. (London, Nat. Gall.)

Zoffany. Family Group.

This picture of a family with their favorite Indian servant probably came from the collection of Major-Gen. Martin, who founded a school in India, equivalent to Eton, for eighty boys.

The lady wears green and gold; her older sons, red suits with shirt collars opening wide; easy, square-cut vests, and loosening breeches, lengthening into trousers.

2195. XVIIIc. English. (Metropolitan Mus., Frick Coll.)

Gainsborough. The Mall in St. James's Park.

In one of Gainsborough's late pictures we see gauzy summer dresses, still short-waisted, frilly and looped up, under the influence of the *polonaise;* hair loosening and falling, but still powdered and caught together at the nape. Hats large, but still low and wreathed with decoration. The brim is sometimes convexly curved, intermediate between the elaborate English cap and the arrogant wide-brimmed, high-crowned hat which accompanied the pouter-pigeon kerchiefs, the long, lean waists and the plain, long skirts of the great English style.

2196. XVIIIc. 1782-4. English. (Washington, Nat. Gall. of Art.)

Romney. Mrs. Davenport.

The rigorous winter of 1784 brought large, shaggy muffs of pale furs like the white one which Mrs. Davenport wears with a fur-collared, caped *pelisse.* Such large muffs will have a life of a good quarter century, whatever the weather. Straw hat, trimmed

with bows of plain over striped ribbon, is ruched about the top of the crown, and tied under the chin.

2197. XVIIIc. c. 1785. English. (London, Nat. Gallery.)

Gainsborough. Mrs. Siddons.

A provincial actor-manager, Roger Kemble, had twelve children, many of them distinguished actors, who have passed on to their descendants, the XXc. Kemble-Coopers, the majestic carriage and wonderful nose of the family. Sarah (1755-1831) became the greatest actress of the English stage; John Philip (1757-1823), manager of Drury Lane and Covent Garden and the leading actor between Garrick and Kean.

The carefully reared girl fell in love with an unimportant actor named Siddons, by whom she had a son. In a quite ineffectual attempt to break her spirit, she was put into service as maid to a provincial lady. In 1773, she married Siddons, and eventually made a most unsuccessful debut at Drury Lane. She played the provinces, and returned to triumphant success in London in Southerne's "Fatal Marriage" in 1782. Most awesome of all was her Lady Macbeth, 1785, which is said to have frightened people into fits. Only Rachel had more passion, and she lacked Mrs. Siddons' style and tenderness. On the hem of her costume, in Reynolds' portrait of her as the Tragic Muse, Dr. Johnson wrote his name, saying, "I would not lose the honor this opportunity afforded to me for my name going down to posterity on the hem of your garment."

The accord between English fashion of 1775 and the fire and dignity of Mrs. Siddons' personal style, make this the greatest picture of proud English beauty. Immense black velvet hat with bows and crown of plumes; narrow neck ribbon, disappearing *à la solitaire* into the long loose curls of the lightly powdered curled mass. Puffed kerchief over blue-striped gown, with crossed bodice-front and long sleeves. Muff and fur-edged *pelisse.*

2198. XVIIIc. 1785-7. English. (Metropolitan Museum, Frick Coll.)

Reynolds. Elizabeth, Lady Taylor.

2199. XVIIIc. c. 1788. English. (Metropolitan Museum.)
Reynolds. Lady Smith and Children.

The hats which accompany *bouffant* kerchiefs and long-waisted, severely simple, silk, satin and cloth gowns, have plumes set on top of the crowns; neither the plumes nor ribbon loops ever obscure the form of the hat body.

2200. XVIIIc. 1786. English. (Metropolitan Museum.)
Reynolds. Mrs. Baldwin.

Pink and white turban topped with pink flowers and green leaves. Braided locks are often combined in some way with exotic turbans. A dozen ropes of seed pearls, with one blue stone, are similarly looped in graduated lengths, from Mrs. Baldwin's black velvet neckband. The ermine-collared brocade garment, in mustard and green stripes and pink flowers, appears to be a *pelisse-lévite.* Jewelled pendant on a gold chain; mustard yellow scarf in lap.

2201. XVIIIc. 1783. American. (Metropolitan Museum.)
Ralph Earle. Lady Williams and Daughter.

Ralph Earle (1751-1801) and his artist brother, James, came of a family which had lived at Newport, R. I., for four generations. Earle's career was wandering, irresponsible and drunken; he twice married and deserted both families. In 1779 he went to England, where he was very successful. He returned to America in the late 80's, and worked in New York and New England. Alexander Hamilton persuaded his wife and other ladies to sit for Earle in his cell, where he was imprisoned for debt. His son, Ralph E. W. Earle, also a painter, married Mrs. Andrew Jackson's niece and lived at the White House throughout Jackson's entire administration.

2202. XVIIIc. 1784. English. (Metropolitan Museum.)
Reynolds. Georgiana Augusta Frederica Elliott.
2203. XVIII. 1784. American. (Worcester, Art Museum.)
Ralph Earle. Man with a Gun.

English costume shown in Ills. 2201-03: Woman: cap replaced by gauze scarves; loosening, unpowdered hair; severely simple, long-sleeved satin dress; *bouffant* kerchief.

Baby: cap, bangs, muslin and ribbons.

Hunting dress: breeches lengthened to meet boot-tops; coat with collar and lapels is being sharply cut away into tails at the line of the square-cut, double-breasted vest, which also opens into lapels. High stock; small, plain ruffles.

2204. XVIIIc. 1784. English. (Metropolitan Museum, Print Room.)

John Raphael Smith, after *Reynolds.* Joseph Deane Bourke, D.D.

The de Burghs, earls of Connaught from the XIIc., were descended from William the Conqueror's half-brother, Robert of Cornwall. After the murder of the XIVc. earl, the family split into factions: the "MacWilliam Eighters" of Connaught, and the "MacWilliam Oughters" of Mayo. The viscounts and earls of Mayo, of final quarter XVIIIc., were Mac-Oughters. Joseph Deane Bourke, Archbishop of Tuan, and eventually third duke of Mayo, took inordinate pride in this descent.

Episcopal wig, band, and immense lawn sleeves.

2205. XVIIIc. 1785. English. (Hampton Court, H. M. the King.)

Copley. Children of George III.

Fanny Burney (1752-1840), the author of "Evelina," became second mistress of the robes to Queen Charlotte in 1785. Her diary gives a wonderful picture of the intimate life of the royal family. Miss Burney's superior was Mrs. Schwellenberg, who had come with the queen from Mecklenburg-Strelitz; she never learned to speak coherent English, and was "swathed in the buckram of back-stairs etiquette." This "hateful old toad-eater, as illiterate as a chambermaid, as proud as a whole German Chapter, rude, peevish, unable to bear solitude, unable to conduct herself with common decency in society" (Macaulay) had charge of the queen's wardrobe and lace-buying. The royal family kept to itself, except for a drawing-room twice a week and a court ball twice a year. The clothing of George III's children (procured by aliens who had been trained, decades before, in the traditions of small, rigid courts) is slow to show the effects of the simplicity with which English upper-class children have long been dressed.

Nevertheless, though only the baby is dressed in muslin, there is a change since the Princess Royal's powdered and dressed "head" of 1778. A sister of about the same age now goes bareheaded with natural locks. Her yellow dress is silk, but it is tucked up for play over a white petticoat. The black bead trim of her dress anticipates narrow black velvet ribbon threaded through eyelet embroidery slots. The tendency toward open collars (so clear in preceding illustrations of boys' shirts) is noticed in the little extra collar set on her fichu.

The baby, and the sister in pink, who sits above the baby-carriage, (a new invention of English coachmakers, in which no one will ever surpass them for elegance), have huge blue ribbon sashes and great white or blue hats. The covering of the underside of hats is not laid on quite flat, and within a decade the hat brim will be covered by shirred and crumpled fabric, and will have a hanging valance of lace, foreseen in the ruched edging of the hat set over the baby's cap.

2206. XVIIIc. 1787. English. (Metropolitan Museum, Print Room.)

H. Ramberg. Exhibition of the Royal Academy.

The first regular art exhibits in London grew out of the success of a show of paintings in 1758 to raise money for the Foundling Hospital. The Free Society of Artists lasted only to 1774. The longer-lived Society of Artists was disturbed by quarrels. Benjamin West, who had great influence with George III, and three of its other members, submitted plans for a Royal Academy of thirty-six members, to teach art and to give annual exhibitions. This was chartered and at work in 1769. It outgrew quarters in Pall Mall, and the King, who paid its deficits until it became self-supporting in 1781, gave it exhibition rooms in the new Somerset House in 1780, where it remained until the National Gallery was built.

Reynolds, West, and Lawrence were its first three presidents. A picture by Zoffany, belonging to the King of England, shows its life class working by candle-light in 1772. Zoffany worked on the picture without plan, inserting new-comers as they entered the room, Walpole says.

The turn in fashion has been made, but older men still cling to conservative styles, and great variety is shown in the dress of the men.

In the r. foreground a tubby man with spectacles wears a shoulder-length wig ending in two heavy rolls of hair; his coat has ample skirts, large cuffs and no collar; it is completely open, wide and quite straight up-and-down, over a long waistcoat. To his left, a man with a quizzing-glass wears boots, long elastic breeches, paired fobs, a short, striped, double-breasted vest, an open coat, much cut away, with embroidered collars and cuffs, broad-brimmed round hat, and a crop. In the center, beyond the Catholic prelate, we see hair in a *hérisson,* a double-breasted tail-coat of cloth with a high collar and lapels, short breeches, a high-brimmed cocked hat, and a stick. At the door, on the left, a cutaway coat with one high closed button. Along the wall, a man in horizontally striped stockings points to a picture; behind him stands a clerical wig. In the extreme background, behind the prelate, is a high-crowned hat, heavily cockaded, almost into a bicorne.

There is much more unanimity in the women's dress. All the hair is loose; all the hats are enormous. Either they are high-crowned, wide-brimmed and laden with plumes, or they are of the lamp-shade shape, lingerie sorts which have grown out of the elaborate English cap and mob. The skirt is very full, very plain, though it may be caught up for convenience. The bosom is enormously puffed out with kerchiefs and the effect is stressed by scarves; the bodice, below, is typically close-waisted; it may have a sash or wide belt. Its most severe form is shown in the riding coat and huge plain hat (half way down l. wall). By the door on the l. is another form: a soft, muslin dress, its fullness repeated or stressed by flounces and bands. (Also child with dog, foreground r.).

XVIIc. "Vandyck" usages continue to affect costume, through latter half XVIIIc. into XIXc.; slashed sleeves and peplum (at r. wall exh., looking up, back view).

2207

BATH AND THE "BEAUX"

Bath maintained its position as the center of the social life of England into the e.XIXc., but its greatest days were in the XVIIIc. Its baths had been used since Roman times; the Roman conduit is in use even today.

Royalty went there in XVIIc., but there were still no accommodations or roads in e.XVIIIc.; it was necessary to live in tents; Bath was full of thieves.

The supremacy of Bath can be laid to two architects, both named John Wood: father (d. 1754) and son (d. 1782); to their patron, Ralph Allen; and to the rule of "Beau" Nash.

The Woods' comprehensive plan gave Bath handsome crescents of identical, attached houses with paved roadways separating them from circles of lawn and park; and the N. and S. Parades with their shops.

Richard Nash (1674-1762) was a man of birth, taste, audacity, organizing ability, and no fortune. He managed a pageant at the Inns of Court so well that he was offered a knighthood which he refused unless a pension went with it. He lived by gambling, and was suspected of being a highwayman. He collected 50 guineas on a wager that he would not stand at the door of the York Cathedral as the congregation was leaving, dressed only in a blanket. His gambling took him to Bath, and in 1705 he became master of ceremonies of its assembly rooms, after his predecessor was killed in a duel. He became the virtual ruler of Bath and of English society. He set rules of dress and behavior at the balls and assemblies in Bath's gaming house and pump-room (from which Ernie Byfield's Chicago establishment got its name). He forbade the wearing of boots and swords and reduced dueling. Once he took a white apron off the duchess of Queensbury, as "proper only for Abigails"; watched over young women and warned them against adventurers like himself; eliminated smoking in the presence of ladies. He cleared out the robbers, paved the roads, mended the chairmen's manners, provided lodgings, and fixed a scale of prices.

Queen Anne had loved Bath; with visits from George II and Caroline in the 30's, it was established

as the most fashionable spot in England. The Germanized court offered no competition; all the painters, actors, writers, all the nobility, wealth and gaiety of England, and anyone else who could cram in, were concentrated at Bath.

Nash, in his famous great cream-colored beaver hat (which no one would dare to steal, he said), his liveried lackeys, and coach drawn by six grays, was supreme. When gambling was abolished at Bath in 1745, the town gave Nash a pension, a concession for the sale of souvenirs and snuffboxes, and eventually, a magnificent funeral.

Nash's successor as the ruler of English fashion was George Bryan Brummell (1778-1840). His grandfather was a shop-lodginghouse-keeper; his father became Lord North's secretary. The boy was known as "Buck" Brummell at Eton, where his taste in dress was already notable. He made a great reputation for wit and fashion at Oxford, became "Beau" Brummell, crony of the Prince (the Prince Regent, later George IV), came into a fortune and lost it, retired to the Continent to escape his creditors and died in a charity hospital at Caen, dirty and paralyzed. "Beau" Brummell's complete sway over society came from his sharp, amusing self-possession, and his dress, which was spectacular only in its flawless perfection and taste. The Prince of Wales "began to blubber when told that Brummell did not like the cut of his coat." (Moore: *Memoirs*.)

2207. XVIIIc. English.
Anonymous Print. A View of the Parade at Bath.
2208-11. XVIIIc. 1785-8. English Fashion Plates.

There is still a wide admixture of old and new styles in men's clothing, hair and hats. Hat brims are wider, often round. The way in which brims are cocked is turning *tricornes* into *bicornes;* the tassels which hang from either side of the hat of the wheel-chair attendant stresses this two-horned appearance, and draws the corners down in the now convex line over the forehead. These bicornes, heavily laced and cockaded, are a feature of the massively decorated court dress of Napoleon and his generals which remains embalmed in XXc. official dress of French Academicians.

Skirts become very full, bunched up into bustles, into which the waistline sinks, and becomes shorter,

Wide, plumed hats accompany tailored walking dress; hats like inverted lamp-shades, derived from caps and made of pleated and puffed fabric, are characteristically worn with muslin dresses, flounces and aprons. *Caraco* (l. side, back view); puffed *cul de Paris* (fat woman, center).

In the Parade at Bath, petticoat flounces hang free, below a projecting heading; No. 2211 shows the heading expanded and sewed down at the top into a band of shirring. The trend of the treatment of muslin is away from free-floating ruffles, in the direction of repeated, controlled bands of shirring: petticoats, No. 2208; sleeves, No. 2209; sleeves, bodice, petticoat, No. 2211. The utilitarian umbrella appears: Nos. 2208, 2210; gloves are worn or carried.

2212. XVIIIc. 1781. English.

Paul Sandby, after *Nicholas Dance*. Aquatint: "Jason and Medea," Tragic Ballet.

Even in private theatricals, English heads have become so covered with plumes by 1775 that "comedians, singers, dancers, figurantes, might all walk at a coronation." (Walpole.) European ballet costume continues to be simply a modification of the dress established by La Camargo.

2213. XVIIIc. 1787. English.

John Jones, after *Downman*. Thomas King and Elizabeth Farren.

Elizabeth Farren (c. 1759-1829) was the daughter of an apothecary turned strolling player. In 1797 she became the wife of the 12th earl of Derby. Thomas King (1730-1805) was a strolling player, picked out of a booth at Windsor, and taken to Drury Lane by Garrick; he was also a theatrical manager, wrote farces and gambled himself into poverty.

King's and Miss Farren's greatest roles were Sir Peter Teazel and Miss Hardcastle in a brilliant performance of the "School for Scandal" in 1777. It is probably as Sir Clement and Emily in Burgoyne's "Heiress" that we see them here in the exaggeration of stage costume.

Between the ruffles at the bosom, and the fullness of the skirt, rising into a bustle, the torso almost disappears, and the waistline grows shorter.

2214. XVIIIc. 1789. English.

Peter Simon, after *Downman*. Scene from "Tom Jones."

Even in the beautiful new houses at Bath, servants' quarters are in the attic, as hot and cramped as this maid's old attic is cold and bare.

The kerchief is less puffed, its ends crossed around the body, sometimes tied in back; here they are tucked into a sash which also holds the muslin apron. Figured bodice, quilted skirt; slippers with ribbon strings. Hat and striped scarf hang on a nail.

Tom, with his sleeve slit and tied over his broken arm, wears his own hair, a knotted kerchief, and a great bunch of seals. His rival shows the construction of shirt and under-drawers, and a head clipped for a wig, under his woman's disguise.

George Stubbs (1724-1806), son of a leather-dresser of Liverpool, studied and taught anatomy at York Hospital in 1746. He kept a private menagerie of animals, wild and tame, and in 1758 began eighteen months of dissection of horses, before making the illustrations for his classic "Anatomy of the Horse," first published in 1766. He began to work in enamel in 1771. Available copper plates were too small so he persuaded the Wedgwood potteries to make large plaques, thus becoming a friend of the Wedgwood family, whom he has painted riding and driving (1780). Stubbs painted such themes as the Prince of Wales' Phaeton with Thomas, the state coachman, in scarlet and gold livery (1793), and the officers, trumpeter and troopers of the 10th Light Dragoons (1793).

Stubbs is the ancestor of the English sporting print; he had worked for a year and a half at Goodwood for the duke of Richmond, painting horses and hunts. In 1790, the *Turf Review* put £9000 to the credit of the hard-working and reliable Stubbs, to enable him to record all the great racehorses; but because of the war only sixteen were finished. This is the time when the blood of three great horses, the Darley Arabian, the Byerly Turk, and the Godolphin Barb, was being fused to produce the modern race horse, which the Stud Book will begin to record in 1806. One of Stubbs' pictures is of the Godolphin Barb, a small horse which had drawn a cart in Paris, and was imported by Coke of Holkham. The blood of this great sire combined with that of the Darley Arabian in a grandson, Eclipse, one of the great racers and great studs of all time.

There is much fascinating information about the completely different horse breeds seen through the millennia in our illustrations: mean, weedy horses of little stamina in Egypt, the Italian peninsula and Rome; fast, wiry little horses of Greece, and big-boned Scythian and Manchu horses which are combined in the polo pony of India. Arabs and Barbs, combined with fine, native cart-mares, the "mad horses" of Spain, and the massive Percherons of the French Knights, into the Spanish Barb which we see rearing under Spanish royalty from XIIIc. Stallions of this breed, sent as royal gifts, improved the horse of the European knight, and were the progenitors of the coach horse. Then fleet Arab, Turkish and Barb, painstakingly bred for centuries in their native lands, arrived in XVIIc.-XVIIIc. to father the modern race-horse (James Reynolds: *A World of Horses,* Creative Age, 1947.)

Courtesy of Metropolitan Museum, Print Room (2212-14)

2215. XVIIIc. 1787. English. (London, National Gall.)
George Stubbs. Phaeton and Pair.

Under George III, English carriage-building surpassed all others. Everyone now wants to go to the
new pavilion which the Prince of Wales started to
build at Brighton in 1786. McAdam is repairing old
roads and Telford will soon begin to build new.
The Society of Arts has offered prizes for carriage-
design, one of which Elliot will win in 1804 for his
elliptical springs. These will allow the airiest of carriages to be drawn by the most sprightly of horses.
In 1787, the single horse of a cabriolet must still be
a powerful animal; the two horses of a phaeton can
be a great deal lighter. These equipages and their
riders have already evolved an immense style in
England, which no one shows better than Stubbs.

This is the English costume for riding and driving which swept over France in the 1780's and
brought English carriages of equal simplicity and
dash with it: immense plumed hat, puffed kerchief,
long fitted cloth coat-dress; men's long breeches and
boots, short vests, and round hats.

2216. XVIIIc. 1787. English. (Kenilworth, Sir Osbert
Sitwell.)
Copley. The Sitwell Family.

Left to right: Boy in blue-green coat with brass
buttons, half-long yellow-green trousers; mother
wearing muslin with green and white striped sash;
boy in red with a white sash; father in dark green
coat, scarlet lining, fawn breeches and black boots.

2217. XVIIIc. 1787-9. English. (Arlesford, Hants, Lord
Northbrook.)
Reynolds. Sir Francis Baring and Political Asso-
ciates.

Baring (1740-1810), grandson of a Lutheran minister of Bremen, founded the great English house
of Baring Bros. and became Europe's greatest merchant. We see him, wearing his own undressed hair,
with two associates at the end of the first of his
twenty-two years as a Whig in Parliament: peer in
robes, wearing the George and collar; anachronistic
wig and rabat which accompany robes of the Chancellor of the Exchequer, a post which will be held
by Baring's grandson.

2218

2218. XVIIIc. 1789-96. American. (Washington, Nat. Gall. of Art.)

Edward Savage. The Washington Family.

Edward Savage (1761-1817) was a Massachusetts goldsmith who began to paint portraits about 1789. He studied in London with West in 1791, and in Italy. He was connected with the New York and Boston Museums, which opened after Peale's in Philadelphia. He painted this portrait, finished in 1796, from sketches made in 1789.

George Washington Parke Custis, Martha Washington's grandson, born 1781, shows a boy's shirt collar opened wide over the coat, in an equivalent of the kerchief of women; women's usages often influence the necklines of boys' clothes.

The knee-breeches, which the President wears with his uniform coat and boots, have not been extended below the boot-top as in Europe.

Elinor Parke Custis' dotted muslin gown shows the way in which a wide belt or sash is raised to cover the entire torso between waistline and breasts, in the transition period from puffed kerchiefs. When the sash is eliminated, the short-waisted Directoire-Empire dress has been brought about.

Mrs. Washington, like a European woman of her age and station, continues to wear a black lace scarf, fichu, and a cap which has grown fashionably high. Her greatest conservatism, or provincialism, is shown in the pleated finish of her skirt edges.

Billy Lee, the Washingtons' favorite servant, has hair dressed in an approximation of a wig.

2219. XVIIIc. c. 1790. English. (Metropolitan Museum.)

Romney. Mrs. George Horsley.

2220. XVIIIc. English. (San Marino, California, H. E. Huntington Art Gallery.)

Rev. M. W. Peters (1742-1814). Flageolet Players.

2221. XVIIIc. 1791. English. (Hellingly, Sussex, Jack Herbert Michenham.)

Romney. Lady Hamilton as Ambassadress.

2219   2220   2221

Straw and fabric-covered hats, often decorated on the underside, are being tied down into bonnets. A favorite line, as of a crossed fichu tied about the body, is followed in the cut of Lady Hamilton's *caraco* jacket. Its edge is cut away, then the corners are tacked back; it ends in miniature tails. This bobtailed coat can be seen in the Parade at Bath, Ill. 2207. Left side, back view, woman: laced jacket with little tails (Flageolet Players).

2222. XVIIIc. 1792. English. (New York, Edward S. Harkness.)
Sir Thomas Lawrence. Miss Farren.

The cloud of the actress Elizabeth Farren's powdered hair is almost indistinguishable from the fur of her *pelisse* and great muff; gloves are now indispensable.

2223. XVIIIc. 1790. English. (New York, Racquet and Tennis Club.)
Valentine Green, after *Lemuel F. Abbott.* Mezzotint: Goffers at Blackheath. (Port. of William Innes.)

A putting-match between three players, shown in the tail-piece of an e.XVIc. Flemish *Book of Hours* (British Museum) is the earliest picture of a golf game. XVIIc. Flemish pictures continually show golf games, often played on ice, and one is shown in a Rembrandt etching of 1654. Golf had been imported to Scotland from the Low Countries long before; by the midXVc. there was legislation against it as a useless sport which was hurting archery practice. "The Royal and Ancient Game of Goff" was a favorite of many Scottish kings, before Mary Stuart was criticized for playing it soon after Darnley's murder. James II, as duke of York, was challenged to play it by two English noblemen for high stakes. He chose as his partner Johne Patersone, a shoemaker, who built a house, still standing at 77 Canongate, with his half of their winnings. Until golf clubs were formed in England in XIXc., Scotchmen living in London played, like the officer in the picture, at Blackheath.

The practical double breastedness of early military and sporting coats has been lost; the lapels are permanently and decoratively buttoned back, and the coat is held together by concealed link buttons.

2224. XVIIIc. 1790. English.
George Morland. The Squire's Door.

This is the classic example of the English riding hat and coat, with lapels, multiple capes, large but-

tons, and kerchief, which made costume history in the mid-80's and 90's. Postilion's hat replaces the traditional tricorne; it is dark brown with great brown bows, crown wreathed in orange scarlet to match gloves; coat slightly less brilliant scarlet, grayish skirt, white kerchief.

2225-26. XVIIIc. 1790. U.S.A. (Litchfield, Hist. Soc.)
Ralph Earle. Col. Benjamin Tallmadge and Son William, Mrs. Benjamin Tallmadge and Children.

Tallmadge (1754-1835), leading citizen of Litchfield, Conn., was a Revolutionary officer and member of Congress from Connecticut.

2227. XVIIIc. 1792. U.S.A. (Hartford, Wadsworth Atheneum.)
Ralph Earle. Chief Justice Oliver Ellsworth and Wife.

Oliver Ellsworth (1745-1807) was a rich lawyer who had studied theology, a member of the Continental Congress and of the Constitutional Convention. It was the "Connecticut Compromise," offered by him and Roger Sherman, which established representation by two houses of Congress. Our present Federal Court system was another of his many services, and he was the first Chief Justice. He was largely responsible for Jay's treaty with England. In 1800, Ellsworth went to France where he negotiated a treaty of free commerce with Napoleon.

2228. XVIIIc. 1793. U.S.A. (Wash., Nat. Gall. of Art.)
Gilbert Stuart. Mrs. Richard Yates.
(*See also* Frontispiece.)

Gilbert Stuart (1755-1828) went to Scotland with his teacher in 1772, returned in 1773 to his native Rhode Island; then went to London in 1775 to work with West. He painted royalty, but in 1787 fled to Dublin from his extravagant debts. He returned to America about 1792, worked with great success in New York and Philadelphia, and before his death in 1828 he painted the first half-dozen presidents, and many notables. From 1805 until his death Stuart lived in Boston.

The War of Independence changed America's traditional cultural allegiance to England. French fashions continue in sympathetic use in America long after they have been supplanted by English styles in France. The familiar time-lag between the continents is stretched by difficulties of communication at the turbulent end of XVIIIc.

American women of Revolutionary families, like Mrs. Washington and Mrs. Tallmadge, cling persistently to French ways of the 70's. The wife of conciliatory Chief Justice Ellsworth, and Mrs. Yates —depicted a year or two later, show more nearly current European styles in their long-sleeved, untrimmed satin dress, crossed fichus, and high caps.

Turkey carpets or hooked rugs, Ill. 2227, cover floors.

2229. 1785-90. U.S.A. (Providence, R.I., School of Design, Museum of Art.)

James Earle. Elizabeth and Martha Paine.

James Earle (1761-96) studied with his brother Ralph. In London he married the widow of a Loyalist who had returned to England. James Earle painted the notables of Charleston, S. C. and of London. He died of yellow fever in Charleston, on a return to America for a visit.

Short-sleeved muslin dresses are apt to be worn with long taffeta gloves which have a drawstring to tighten them about the upper arm or to have a long, taffeta sleeve set into the armseye under the short muslin sleeve. Since Elizabeth Fales Paine's taffeta sleeve is white, she has replaced the upper sleeve with a froth of ruffles, reminiscent of the edge of a frilled kerchief; blue black beads and a narrow pink ribbon at the waist. As an elderly woman, her Aunt Martha has retained the kerchief, which is tucked under the low neckline of her Directoire gown. The contrast between her long brown taffeta sleeve and her muslin sleeve is set off by a white satin ribbon tied about the upper arm.

2230. XVIIIc. 1797-1801. English. (London, Nat. Gall.)

James Downman (1750-1824). Sir Ralph Abercrombie with his son or secretary.

Abercrombie was an exceptionally enlightened and capable general who had served in Ireland and Holland and was killed in Egypt in 1801. The maps of the West Indies refer to his notable services at Sta. Lucia, St. Vincent and Trinidad, from which he returned in 1797.

At the turn of the century, there were a great many sprigged white vests, with washable forms, in heavy corded and patterned cotton, figured in silver, of which the Museum of Fine Arts, Boston, has a collection.

Hepplewhite shield-back chair of late XVIIIc.

2231-32. XVIIIc. 1794. U.S.A. (Metropolitan Mus.)

Gilbert Stuart. Josef de Jaudenes y Nebot; Martha Stoughton de Jaudenes.

The *chargé d'affaires* of Spain in the United States from 1791-96, wears Spanish official costume: dark blue velvet, with scarlet lining, waistcoat and breeches, massively embroidered in silver; white stockings; black hat with red ribbon.

His wife's froth of hair, powdered gray, is dressed with white, gray and blue-edged feathers, and the beloved pair of tall, uncurled ostrich plumes of the turn of the century; white taffeta dress, brocaded in gold, with white and gray gauze at the neck, a white corselet embroidered in gold, white and gold jewelry, chatelaine, round enamelled pendant watch and blue medallion bracelet.

ENGLISH FASHION MAGAZINES: LATE XVIII—EARLY XIX CENTURY

Nicholas Heideloff, a young German from Stuttgart, was working in Paris; at the Revolution, he fled to London where he published *Heideloff's Gallery of Fashion,* monthly from 1794-1803. It is probably the most luxurious of all fashion magazines. The copy at Museum of Fine Arts, Boston, belonged to Queen Charlotte. The plates, colored by hand, with touches of metal, show a great deal of the new outdoor life. Ladies read poetry on a stone bench by moored ships, 1795; stand in poke bonnets and wind-blown morning dress at the edge of a cliff, overlooking a beach and bath wagons, 1797. We see the blue beaver hats of 1794, the great parti-colored muffs of pale fur or eiderdown of 1794-7; the prodigiously trimmed scarves of 1795-7; the ribbon-laced sandals, high on the calf, of 1797.

Magazines of fashion, culture and information arrive in a flood with the XIXc.

Ackermann's Repository, published 1809-28, is particularly valuable for its pasted-in clippings of actual fabrics, newly produced by English and foreign firms. Its colored frontispiece is usually of the showroom of an important firm: e.g., Mr. Ackermann's art supply shop; Harding, Howell & Co., the drapers; Wedgwood's pottery. It tells of the gifts prepared for the British Embassy to the Chinese Emperor, displayed at Mr. Ross's Rooms, and shows fitted boxes and work tables, toilet sets, scent bottles

of cut and milk glass. Other articles deal with culture, science, current events, the stock market, the theatre, and show new fashions in furniture and decoration, as well as dress.

The Journal of Design, published by Chapman & Hall for a few years after 1849, continues to use actual samples, and shows swatches from the first American factories, like Dunnell in Providence. During 1850, it published serially a most valuable history of the textile industry, written by the head of the Broad Oaks firm. Such a chronology of new techniques is priceless in dating textiles and costumes. The old method of overprinting or pencilling blue on yellow to give green continued to be used long after fast green was produced in 1811. Turkey red discharge was a monopoly of Koechlin of Mulhouse until Broad Oaks got British patent rights. Machine printing of borders did not begin until 1825; color printing was slowly increased from two to six rollers by 1850. Manganese oxides date from 1827 and provide a series from yellow through orange to brown. "Fondu" and "rainbow" patterns begin in 1823-4. The ability to print on thin wool "delaines" as well as cotton coincides with the blue and brown cobalt styles of 1836. There are infinite combinations of wool with cotton and silk; "challis" becomes a favorite fabric. "Glenyou plaids" commemorate Victoria's visit to the Highlands, and are followed by "graduated rainbows" and the epoch-making "dahlia" colors which bathe everything in magenta and purple in 1844.

2233

2234　2235

2233. XVIIIc. 1794. English. (Port Sunlight, The Lady Lever Art Gallery.)
George Stubbs. Wedgwood plaque: The Haycart.
One of a series of pottery plaques, c. 30" x "40, of outdoor scenes, executed by Stubbs.
2234-35. XVIIIc. English.
Heideloff's Gallery of Fashion.
2234. (Aug., 1794.) Two Ladies, *en negligé,* Taking the Air in a Phaeton.
"Headdress: white stamp-paper hat, trimmed with a green riband and tied down with the same. One green and one yellow feather placed on the left side. Green gauze veil. The hair in small curls; plain chignon. Plain calico morning dress with long sleeves; the petticoat trimmed with a narrow flounce. Plain lawn handkerchief, green sash, lawn cloak trimmed with lace and tied behind, york tan gloves, yellow shoes."

"Headdress: straw colored hat, trimmed with orange and purple ribands, and a white lawn handkerchief, embroidered in lilac, tied down with a white riband. One lilac and white cross-striped large ostrich feather on the left side, the hair in light curls and hanging down in ringlets behind, bound with a half-handkerchief tied into a large bow in the front. Chemise of spotted muslin, trimmed with a double plaiting of broad lace about the waist, tied in front by a lilac riband, short loose sleeves, tied in the middle with the same riband. Lilac-colored sash tied behind, jonquille coloured gloves and shoes." (Text accompanying the original illustrations.)
The parasol is green, which is the usual color. The three mounting plumes, which were set in front in April (when publication began) remained there until they were moved to the l. side in August.

White horses, with black harness, yellow rosettes, and orange and yellow bands on the bridle, draw a yellow, phaeton, striped in orange.

2235. (Jan., 1799.) (Child). "The hair combed into natural curls; half-handkerchief of pink and white striped muslin, tied around the head with a bow in the front. Gray Spencer, trimmed around the waist with black velvet; muslin frock.

The hair cut short in the front, and combed straight; the hind hair in short ringlets. Bonnet of scarlet cloth, trimmed with velvet, and fur bands, bouquet of flowers of *leather* in the front. Round dress of Scotch cambric, long sleeves with Vandyke cuffs; the whole trimmed with lace, tied upon the breast with a purple satin riband. Fur belt. Mamelouc cape. Purple jean shoes, trimmed with scarlet. Gray gloves.

The toupee cut short, and combed into feather curls; the hind hair cropped. Bonnet of white satin, trimmed with purple velvet bands and cross bands, finished at the top of the crown with a small *rosette* of the same. Round satin cloak trimmed with point lace. Full muslin stock. Large gold hoop earrings. Purple Spanish leather shoes."

Muffs have grown larger, darker, more elaborate and more indispensable.

2236. XVIIIc. 1799. English. (New York, Mr. & Mrs. G. B. Wagstaff.)

Richard Westall, eng. by *C. Knight.* Fishing party.

At the Revolution and during the two following decades, "Reform" clothes for men are seen, based on workingmen's smocks, late Greek fitted tunics, and on XVIIc. doublets; they are often affected by XVIIc. slashing, especially at an upper-sleeve puff, and by "Vandyked" collars of toothed lace. This tunic and tights sports costume is its typical form, usually worn with a full beret or loose turban.

Elizabethan or "Vandyke" standing ruffs of notched lace also appear on women's low-necked dresses. These wired collars, and the *fraise* neck ruche are two opposed influences by which the composite neckline of 1820-40 will be formed. The low neck will slip to the shoulders and become horizontal. The standing and often notched collar will col-

2236

lapse into laterally jutting wings, often toothed, over leg-o'-mutton sleeves, while an inner bodice like a bertha will rise smoothly over the shoulders to the base of the throat. Then the horizontal shoulder line will weaken, leaving a high-necked gown.

2237. Late XVIIIc. French.

Bobbin lace: application d'Angleterre

2238. Early XIXc. English.

Lappets: appliqué lace

2239. XIXc. English.

Bobbin lace edgings: Bedfordshire, Buckinghamshire, Honiton, English Mechlin, Northamptonshire.

Lace-making began in England in 1567, when Flemish refugees from Alva's persecutions settled in the Midlands. Pillow lace was made in Buckinghamshire to the West of London, Bedfordshire and Northamptonshire to the N.W. Settlers from Ipswich and Suffolk, to the N.E., brought lace making to Ipswich, Mass., in 1630—41,975 yards a year were produced there by 1790. Honiton lace-making was brought to Devonshire by Dutch refugees.

Courtesy of Metropolitan Museum of Art

2237   2238   2239

XIX Century Dress: Women

THE changes in this century have been usefully charted by Cecil Willett Cunnington (*English Women's Clothing in the Nineteenth Century*. Faber and Faber. London, 1937) whose collection of 1100 costumes, 2000 accessories, fashion plates and books covering 200 years of English Women's dress has been bought by the Manchester Museum for £7000.

VERTICAL EPOCH / **EXHIBITIONISM** (1800-1821)	1800-1803	Greek ornament			
	1804-1807	Egyptian-Etruscan ornament	PURE CLASSIC		Extreme Exhibitionism
	1808-1810	Classical form. Spanish ornament.			
	1811-1813	Debased classical ornament. Slight Gothic ornament.			
	1814-1817	Debased classical ornament. Increased Gothic ornament.	DEBASED CLASSIC		Modified Exhibitionism
	1818-1821	Diminished classical form. Increasing Gothic form. Increasing Gothic ornament.			
GOTHIC CONCEALMENT (1822-1899)	1822-1864	Pure Gothic Angles	Development of the "Perfect Lady"	1822-1839	Romanticism
	1865-1899			1840-1864	Sentimentalism
		Debased Gothic Curves	Sex Re-adjustment	1865-1881	Sex-attraction by "dumb-show"
				1881-1899	Prudery vs. Emancipation

French Revolution to 1820.

The English muslin *chemise,* the basis of "classical" dress, was essentially a tube with one drawstring at a round neck, and another at a high waistline.

During the Directoire, the neck became lower, sleeves shorter, waistline higher, and the back of the skirt lengthened into a train. Tunics and slit over-dresses were added, 1803-1810; made obligatory in court use under Napoleon; and were turned into coat-dresses, *douillettes,* for domestic wear, fitted *pelisse-robes* and *redingotes* of the following periods. There are also apron-like *tablier* overdresses, open down the back.

About 1803, the full, gathered top of the *chemise* began to be covered and replaced by a tiny fitted bodice, which reached only to the armpits and the base of the breast. The front breadth of the skirt remained straight; the back breadth began to be gored and to lengthen, with its fullness massed at the center-back. The skirt of this *robe en caleçons* (to 1820) was so narrow that walking was difficult; only one petticoat was worn under it, and excessively fashionable women wore only tights; stockings were often omitted with the naked classical styles. People became so used to seeing women outdoors, dressed in muslin, during a decade of fairly warm winters, that it was feared they would ruin their health when they began to wear warm clothes indoors during the generally cold winters of 1810–1820.

About 1810-14, the neckline for daytime became higher; long sleeves were added below a puffed cap-sleeve; the skirt began to be gored wider to the hem, and to be shortened in daytime use; decoration of cord, braid, and bands of self-material replaced Greek, Etruscan and Egyptian motifs, and Hungarian, Polish and Russian frogged decoration, used on men's coats, appeared on women's riding habits, and on boys' clothing.

The favorite wraps of the Directoire and Empire were large square or oblong shawls, of the size and proportions of the Greek *chlamys* and *himation,* draped in Greek ways.

The *Spencer* (see male style) which appeared c. 1804, was a long-sleeved, short-waisted, fitted jacket, an outer garment equivalent to a bodice but differing from it in color. The Spencer, together with long scarfs and *pelisses,* remained in use through first third XIXc.

Hair was at first caught up in Greek knots, held by fillets and combs, with a hanging fringe of locks at forehead and ears. Wigs were provided in every color, quite unrelated to the wearer's natural hair and dramatic changes were made several times a day. Towards the end of the period, hair tended to be parted, drawn smoothly, and bunched into locks at the ears.

Headwear was modelled on classic helmets, oriental turbans with cock feathers, and single tall uncurled ostrich plumes. Hats with fabric tops and straw brims decorated on the underside and veiled in lace (see Ill. 1800 Ladies of Ghent) tend to become tied down into plainer bonnets: there are also hats of male top-hat shapes, and of beaver.

The classical white muslin dresses, embroidered in silver, gold or white, were worn with brightly colored long gloves and mitts; low satin or kid slippers tied with crossed ribbons; plumes, turbans and ribbons. Scarfs were often of poppy red or violet; muffs, *pelisse* edgings and neckpieces, and tippets of pale furs and eiderdown; reticules and purses of beads, straw, steel and fabric; combs, necklaces, corals, bracelets.

1821 to 1840.

Dramatic changes take place in the form of the body and of its clothing in the first years of the 20's. The waistline, which has been tucked under the breasts, drops to its normal position on a pointed or belted bodice. The gored skirt flares toward the hem and is supported by quilting or starched embroidered petticoat ruffles; it shortens, from shoe to ankle length; then it becomes fuller, first pleated at the waist; then gathered with a boned petticoat and hip and bustle pads, *tourneurs.* At the end of the period, it barely shows the point of the shoe and has reached a width of 7 or 8 breadths.

The spread at the top of the bodice is even more dramatic.

The bodice of the daytime *pelisse* is closed to the base of the throat, but it is widened by collars spread out over an immense fullness at the top of the sleeve, which assumes a leg-o'-mutton form. The round or square neck becomes horizontally cut across the shoulderline, which is further extended by wings projecting beyond the full sleeves. The fullness at the top of the leg-o'mutton sleeve slips down toward the elbow in the 30's; the wings above them droop into a dropped shoulderline, onto which are set sleeves, which are puffed at intervals around the elbow, and close-fitting below it, at the end of this period.

On the wide-winged bodice, pleated or draped decoration is laid on in a V, from points far out on the shoulder to the center of the waist belt. These decorations, like the dress itself, have dramatic form. They are made of fabric, piped, banded, folded into notched or zigzag patterns, looped into scrolls and shells, or cut into tabs, and applied, often diagonally, on repeated bands which rise horizontally on the skirt from the hem towards the knee.

Puffed flowers and leaves of gauze are also used. They tend to become flattened into spots of appliqué, as the fuller skirt loses decoration, becoming plain, slightly flounced, or edged with fringe, and often slit up the middle, at the end of the period.

The *pelisse* turns into a warm, high-necked dress, closed down the front; in its later form by bows. The neckline of the "round" dress is often raised by lingerie *chemisettes,* tuckers, widespread *pèlerines* and fichu-like *canezous,* the points of which are caught by the belt. They turn into white shirtwaists. These too, droop and become reduced as the shoulderline drops, the bodice becomes more pointed, and the longer, fuller skirt splits in the middle.

With the sloping shoulderline, cashmere shawls increase in importance. The old fitted *pelisse* goes out of style; but mantles become increasingly shaped, fitted, and hooked together into *pelisse-mantles* with long tab points and fringe trim.

The wide-shouldered dresses of the early part of the period are accompanied by enormous hats of leghorn or fabric on wire frames, laden with masses of feathers and 10–12 yards of looped ribbon, in brilliant colors. With these, the bunches of curls rise to the temples; and hair begins to stand (end first quarter XIXc.) dressed into 1 to 3 tall loops on the crown of the head supported by high ribbon loops, flowers and tortoise shell combs. About 1827, curls are often massed on left side, but less jewelry is worn. As shoulders narrow, hats are reduced into smaller, more enclosing bonnets. In evening dress, flowers are tucked at right ear.

As the shoulderline droops, the parted hair is combed in loops covering the ears; lappeted caps appear; hats of the 30's turn into bonnets and *capotes,* which surround the face and conceal it entirely from profile view.

When form and trimming become less acute, the thin merino and challis wools, muslin and silk in plain, sharp lavenders, greens and geranium pinks, become patterned into chintzes, ginghams, brocades, foulards, shot broché or striped silks and velvets of darker, heavier colors and textures; brown, violet, blues, black in violent tasteless combinations.

Fine batiste underwear was a XIXc. invention of the Empress Josephine, who changed three times a day. Underdrawers are not commonly worn by women until end first third XIXc. Then they are so long that their lace edge shows when the skirt is raised; they consist of two unconnected tubes, tied on at the waist by strings, one of which frequently becomes undone, so that one leg is occasionally dropped on the street; pantalettes had been made part of dress of English girls early in XIXc. and are worn through the 50's.

The corsets of XIXc. were long, becoming shorter by 1810; they were padded to improve the form of the 20's, and tightly laced to conform to the increasingly exuberant, plump ideal of the 30's.

All the tight bodices had to be lined; the short early forms closed by lacings, ties and buttons; the later ones principally by hooks and eyes.

Sleeves, collars and skirts require support, at first by starching, quilting and padding; then by boning and horsehair crinoline.

The earlier dress is still white with touches of brilliant color. There is a great increase in the use of silk in England—as its importation is allowed from 1824 and duties are reduced from 30% to 15%. There is even some increase in the use of Spitalfields silk. Silk lace, *blonde,* becomes immensely popular at about the time of Victoria's accession, and has its longest life in Spanish use.

Black slippers, slippers matching the costume, or white for evening, tend to replace bright-colored ones with ribbon ties around the leg. Shoes, laced up inside or front, appear, often with lighter colored silk fabric or kid tops, or buttoned gray or buff gaiters, which almost obliterate the toe. In the 30's shoes themselves are often made of fabrics, and become square-toed by 1827. Stockings are occasionally black or flesh, but are usually white.

Narrow cashmere scarfs with light grounds are replaced by darker square cashmere or paisley shawls. Gloves and mitts of kid, suede and net become shorter, embroidered and trimmed. White hats are large. Parasols are tiny, embroidered or fringed. Handkerchiefs. Hair looped or braided over the ears. Earrings hang and necklaces and paired bracelets appear; brooches at collars of day dresses.

THE 1840's.

Romanticism influenced by Scott, Victor Hugo and Dumas, fils.

The body and spirit become immobilized, sheathed and protected, drooping, helpless and meek; colors muted.

Smooth, parted hair is looped down over the ears in bands, braids or spaniels' ears of corkscrew curls, flattened with bandoline.

Large oval bonnets and *capotes,* still rather ornate and tied under the chin, prevent side glances or views; caps in daytime and evening.

Arms are imprisoned by dropped shoulders; sleeves set from that line become long and plain, then bell out; the ruffles which used to be set at the junction are reduced to folds on a cap.

Torsos are enclosed in long severe, smoothly-boned bodices over tightly laced corsets; their long points emphasized by V decorations from the wide shoulderline. Necklines do not hug the throat, at the beginning of the period, even when the bodice is cut high; and are often open a third to halfway down in a V which tends to close and rise. Evening bodices are cut straight across the shoulderline, which is surrounded by a flat valance of wide lace.

Layers of long full petticoats, banded with horsehair, support even fuller skirts, which make exercise difficult. Women drink vinegar to keep thin; good health is no longer well bred. Women do not exercise. They pile on flannel and merino underwear in the terrible cold of 1845.

At the beginning of the period there are skirts, slit in front and vertically patterned or made of vertically striped fabric, but as skirts widen their trim becomes horizontal. Borders *en disposition* are worn or printed on dress lengths and are accompanied by fashion plates, showing how to use the borders in making 3-flounced skirts and

in trimming the V of the bodice (see 2552-55). In the mid-40's the fullness of the skirt is not gathered into the waistline but pleated and gaged on.

A new impulse which will lead to the bustled dresses of the 70's is shown in the flounces of evening dresses, which are scalloped or draped up and caught with bows and flowers.

The long *pelisses* and mantles of the 30's become shorter *pardessus,* knee length, more closely fitted, with the corners of their skirts rounded off.

Both colors and patterns of fabrics are subdued and wavering. Striped and plaids are often *chiné* (the pattern, tied and dyed onto the warp, has an indistinct, irregular edge), *fondu* or blended in rainbows. There are shot taffetas, watered, *broché* and corded silks; gauzy *barèges* and *mousselines de laine* (delaines), and their various combinations with cashmere, merino and alpaca. (See *Journal of Design,* p. 791.)

Elaborate silk aprons, worn indoors, handkerchiefs; bouquets and lace; buttons, brooches, bracelets, and drop earrings; flower-wreaths on hair in the evening.

1850–1864: SENTIMENTALISM.

Talleyrand, who died in 1839, said, "He who has not lived in the years just preceding 1789 cannot know the pleasures of living."

The exhilaration of revolution was followed by a period of unprincipled venality, conscienceless acquisition, and exploitation, insistent luxury and search for distraction. Against this was set melancholy regret for grace that was gone, boredom and disgust with the crass materialism, the increased standardization and the industrialization of the present, and the future.

The Goncourt *Journals* record it: (translated by Louis Galantière, Doubleday, Doran, Garden City, 1937)

1857: "Who does not keep a carriage these days? What a society! Everybody is determined to bankrupt himself. Never have appearances been so despotic, so imperious, and so demoralizing—the thing has come to such a point that many shops now open credit in favor of their clientele, who pay only the interest on their debts."

When the first auction sale of photographs is held at the Hotel Druot in 1857: "Everything is turning black in this century, and is not photography the black vestment of the visible world?" (See Appendix).

The first commercial photography was by Daguerre's 1839 method, on silvered plates which were permanent but could not be reproduced. Daguerrotypes continued to be made long after plate photography began in the 40's. *Cartes de visite* mounted with portrait photographs first became fashionable in the 50's.

On Nov. 1, 1860, the Goncourts say, social life

is in evolution; even wives and children appear in cafés; home life is dying; the upper classes go to clubs; the lower classes to cafés. The "Universal Exposition" of 1867 is "the final blow levelled at the past, the Americanization of France, industry lording it over art, the steam thresher displacing the painting, in brief, the Federalization of Matter."

The first great International Exhibition was opened in London in 1851. It was housed in the epoch-making brilliance of the 20 acre Crystal Palace, six stories of iron-supported glass, with a swelling, vaulted glass roof, designed by the greenhouse builder, Sir Joseph Paxton. Backed by the Society of Artists which offered prizes, it drew 6,000,000 and was followed by exhibitions in other countries. The most notable were in Paris in 1855 and in 1867, which had exhibitions of machinery, the architecture of all nations, and a series of restaurants serving national foods; the Philadelphia Centennial of 1876; and the great Paris Exhibition of 1878.

The Crystal Palace was not only light and airy; its seats were comfortable. Comfortable, handsome, functional furniture and architecture could be provided by any country carpenter, after the publication of Sheraton's volumes of furniture design in late XVIIIc.-e.XIXc., and the handbooks of architecture in the early XIXc.

Against this standardization, the clear light, the bare space of the classical revival, and ingenious factory-produced cheap American furniture, was set the Romantic Gothic Revolt, from Horace Walpole's time into XIXc. XVIIIc. furniture was put into the servants' rooms. After his marriage in 1859, William Morris built his "Red House"—all brick, narrow mullioned windows and gloom. With his pre-Raphaelite artist friends, he started a firm which produced the "Beautiful" furniture, stained glass, wall-paper, and clutter of decorative objects which crammed Victorian homes; he also made a good, comfortable, functional new chair.

The sewing machine had been invented by 1830 but it became practical in 1843 with Howe's lock-stitch machine; almost simultaneous improvements were made by Wilson, Grover, Singer and Gibbs. The machine was first used in shoemaking. By the 50's, it was producing cheap, ready-to-wear men's clothing. In 1858, the great couturiers of Paris used it; and in the 60's, almost all clothing was machine-sewed and on its way to standardization.

Mass production needed mass outlets. A department store with 150 employes, the Ville de France, had been started in Paris in 1844; the Grands Halles in 1853; the Bon Marche in 1876. In the U.S.A., Oak Hall opened in Boston in 1851, and a department store at Broome St. and Broadway in 1851; A. T. Stewart's in 1863, and

the Grand Depot, in remodelled carbarns in Philadelphia, in 1876. (S. Giedion: *Space, Time and Architecture.*)

A midwestern American, Mrs. Amelia Jenks Bloomer, brought to London in 1851 her reform dress of a jacket, knee-length skirt, and Turkish trousers. In a new impatience with restraint, women begin to take over simple, masculine garments, hats, jackets, vests and boots, and invent comfortable walking and bathing costumes.

The Empress Eugenie replaces piled petticoats, c.1855, with a round crinoline skirt threaded with parallel hoops of whalebone or wire, a revival of the farthingale. With it, hoops reach their ultimate rounded width by the end of the 50's. If steps are not mincing, the hoop bounces up and the foot is seen; soon hands will catch up the skirt, exposing petticoats and shoes, boldly.

The great dressmaker of XIXc., the founder of the *haute couture* of Paris, was Worth, an Englishman who had worked in the silk-trade in Paris, before setting up a dress making establishment in 1858. He came almost immediately to the attention of the Empress Eugenie. His career as dressmaker to her white-clad court, and to the actresses and *cocottes* who have become more important than courts in launching styles, is recorded in many entries in Mme. Octave Feuillet's 4 volumes; his 30-year rule of fashion was carried on by his two sons.

During the 50's, parted hair, smooth or waved, tends to be drawn backwards and massed at the nape in curls or braids, which are often netted.

Hats appear; bonnets become smaller, made of fancy straws; caps with lappets are worn indoors by all English married women; wreaths, with evening dress.

Corsets are more elastic, and long bodices shorten as skirts become much rounder and fuller and give the waist a narrow look by contrast, not by tight lacing. Skirt ruffles multiply in number, become much narrower and project from the plane of the skirt. The hem of the skirt takes on more importance in the late 50's, and gains a wide, pleated flounce. There are also plain, full skirts, banded with zigzags in lines of velvet or braid.

Sleeves spread into wide pagoda forms, which show more of the full white sleeve of the chemisette, gathered into a tight waistband. Necklines rise to the base of the throat, and white collars become smaller.

Mantles grow shorter, in jacket or shawl-like shapes which fall into points, front and back, and are fringed.

With the invention of aniline dyes, lurid fuchsias, magentas and violets appear which appeal to the new adventuresomeness in women. Color contrasts are stronger, materials more varied: velvet, moiré, satin, and brocade are woven or used in combination with plain fabrics; there are grenadines, barèges and gauze, and new fabrics like challis and nainsook. Trimmings are made of chenille and jet, ball fringe and tassels, buttons, Honiton and Brussels lace. There are aprons, short embroidered gloves; tiny muffs; reticules of jet beads and embroidery mounted in steel, silver and gold; fans, bouquets and small parasols; gold combs, knobbed hairpins, dotted hair nets, pendant earrings; jewelry of coral, jet and hair; many bracelets. Shoes with elastic side and heels, striped stockings.

The 1860's.

During the 60's, ears reappear; parted hair is massed at the nape of the neck in chignons, curls and braids; masses of false hair are added and enclosed in spangled or chenille-dotted nets, and small hats tip forward to display the chignon's mass.

Hats tend to replace bonnets and caps, and are more laden with trimming in England than in France. Men's styles are daringly taken over by women. Ladies' tailors make jacket and skirt costumes, under the lead of the new Princess Alexandra.

The belted *canezou* grows into the white shirt-waist, worn with a separate skirt, as are red Garibaldi blouses, braided Zouave jackets and boleros.

Mid-Victorian ladies escape from enormous skirts and crinolines. Crinolines are reduced to frames of diagonally set wire, which thrust skirt fullness backwards into the bustles of the 70's. Skirts are cut in gores, and become completely smooth around the hips by last third of the decade. Princess garments appear and waistlines are lengthened by long laced corsets which, with high heels, induce the "Grecian Bend." Skirts shorten in front and drag backwards into the trains of the 70's.

Women lift skirts to show brilliant contrasting petticoats, bright colored shoes trimmed with tassels and plaid or striped stockings. English fashion, usually a year or so behind French, leads in these daring "fast" masculine and petticoat styles, which the Empress Eugenie met with on her visit to London in 1862.

The line of small ruffles on the skirt sinks toward the growingly important, pleated, petticoat-like flounces on the braided hem. Unruffled skirts have tabbed or asymmetrically shaped panels falling from the waist. Trimming is in Greek key designs, elaborate fringe, upholstery-like pleatings, lace, or even leather. On evening skirts, decoration is asymmetrically cut or looped, and puffed into bustles and polonaises.

Pagoda sleeves become plainer, showing more of the sleeve of the chemisette; then are slit and begin to enclose the wrist, making the chemisette sleeve less important. The simple closed sleeve of the tailored costume of the 60's becomes the common sleeve of the bustled 70's.

Cloaks become larger, more flowing, and cape-or-coat-like, with wide pagoda sleeves. Like everything else, they are laden with gimp, tassels, fringes, of jet, beads, bugles, and chenille. There are cashmere and yak lace shawls, elaborate filigree buttons, and a profusion of jewelry; cameos and jet medallions, chains and dog collars, earrings, brooches and many bracelets. Parasols grow larger as hats diminish in size.

Costumes continue to be made in two colors but the brilliant combinations of the beginning of the decade grow sober. With bustled dresses there is a revival of French fashions, from Watteau to Louis XV. The tailored costumes are usually cut to the base of the throat, with a small white collar. Evening necklines, slipping off the shoulders, often rise and become squares with the end of the decade. A great deal of attention begins to be given to underwear and its embellishment by embroidery.

XIX Century Men's Clothing

French Revolution to 1820.

The Revolution brought plainer cloth coats in a variety almost impossible to separate as they overlap and merge with top coats, which are turning into forms of regular coat.

There were three basic coats. The new English double-breasted, with high turn-over collar and important lapels, tended to become squarely cutaway across the waistline, while its tails retreated to the back and fell straight. Worn with knee-breeches, or more customarily with pantaloons, it becomes everyone's ordinary dress.

The single-breasted cutaway coat, with a high standing or turned-over collar, was worn with knee breeches or pantaloons, and was eventually reduced to a riding-coat (an exchange in position with the double-breasted coat, which had originated as a riding and military garment).

The court *frac,* which went out of use during the Revolution, is revived by Napoleon in court and uniform use. Its coat and waistcoat, which are sometimes related, are heavily embroidered, according to the rank of the wearer, and are usually of velvet (often violet); worn with satin knee-breeches and the *chapeau bras*—the flat hat grown out of the *chapeau à l'androsmane,* which can be carried under the arm.

During the Revolution French gentlemen are seen in the Jacobin red stocking-cap of the galley-slave, the sleeveless *carmagnole* jacket, and working men's loose blue linen trousers. From 1800–1885, there are smocks and classical tunics (see Ill. 2236) worn with long tights and loose berets.

There is an even larger number of new overgarments, some of which turn from overcoats into suit coats. The "poor devil" was a flopping plebeian coat. The *Jean de Bry* coat of 1799-1800 had a standing collar of velvet, small lapels, padded shoulders. It closed high on the breast with three large buttons and was then so sharply cut-away into short, narrow tails with pockets massed at the back, that the space between its very high waistline and the top of the breeches was filled by the vest. The ankle-length, multiple caped "Garrick" is seen throughout first quarter XIXc. There are *surtout, capote* and *redingote* overcoats which come to be worn with vests and pantaloons as forms of warm, skirted coats. They hang at levels between knee-length and half-way between knee and ankle. The "Spencer" jacket resulted from a hunting accident in 1792 in which most of the tails and sleeves of Earl Spencer's coat were torn off, and he bet that he could make his present ridiculous state a fashion. By 1804-5 it had become a very important article of women's dress; on men it was seen as a sort of extra chest-protection: a tailless or tabbed, short-waisted coat with sleeve-caps, worn over another coat. About 1807 appear braided and frogged Polish, Hungarian and Russian overcoats, the braided trim of which can be seen affecting men's, women's and children's clothes to the 50's.

Coat collars, standing or turned-over, are at first high about the ears, supported by boning; lapels are very important; and sleeves close-fitting. During the first decade, the armseye enlarges; the top of the sleeve becomes full and gathered; the cuff is often turned down or prolonged over the knuckles; the shoulder seam is drawn far down on the back of the coat; the waistline is tightened, so that the coat rolls into wrinkles around the waist in back, and tends to close higher in front. As the 20's approach, the collar, which has grown more rounded and rolling, arches away from the neck in back; the shoulder widens, the waist tightens and the chest puffs out.

The early tail coat, with collar to the ears, chin muffled in an immense cravat, enormous lapels and very long tails, in its *incroyable* form is often made of striped satin. Coat tails are customarily of knee-length or shorter to 1815; then lengthen, to the knees or longer as the 20's approach.

Throughout this period the *gilet* is cut square across the bottom; it is plain, embroidered or striped; single- or double-breasted. Two vests of different lengths and colors are often worn together, until the 30's, and one of them is apt to be vertically striped. *Gilets* are of waist length or very short at the turn of the century, lengthen to the hips, c.1812, then shorten again as bosoms puff out. While coat collars remain high the collar of the *gilet* is high, whether it is a standing or a turned over form; the *gilet* follows the lead of the coat lapels and collars as these change. Single- and double-breasted vests are interchangeably worn with either single or double-breasted coats,

but the standing collar is particularly the attribute of the single-breasted garment. Only with court costume does a waistcoat have a cut-away bottom, until the 1820's.

Breeches have a broad, front-flap opening from c.1780–1840. As they lengthen into pantaloons at the turn of the century, and grow high waisted, they come to be supported by braces or suspenders over the shoulders.

Knee breeches are worn with both single and double-breasted coats until about 1815, although they have become generally superseded by longer forms during the first decade. Elderly English country gentlemen occasionally wore them into 1870's. They are required in court costume until 1830, then become optional. Pantaloons were introduced into English army use by Wellington, c.1806, during Peninsular war, but opposition to them was still so strong in 1812 that English university students wearing them in chapel were marked as absent.

As boots appear, breeches lose their buckled band and are fastened by knee-strings below a line of buttons. By 1790 many breeches have been drawn down under the boot-top to the calf. By 1800 they are commonly of ankle length and begin to be held down by a strap under the sole of the shoe. As boots begin to be less worn, c.1815, breeches become shorter, full at the waist, wide in the leg and are generally strapless, until c.1820, when they become close fitting and strapped again until about 1840. All these tight pantaloons are made of knit stockinet or pliable doeskin, usually in lighter colors than the coat: greys, beiges, and yellows, black occasionally used with black coats; and yellowish cotton nankeen or white in summer. There are also striped forms, vertically patterned like the favorite blue and white stockings of 1770–1805, or horizontally (as seen on Goya, working in his studio, in a self-portrait). Long breeches buttoned down the entire outseam (such as we show in Alken's 1819 "Real Meltonian" series) are seen a decade earlier and are carried spatlike, over low shoes. With the appearance of Polish styles, informal pantaloons often have corded, braided or quilted patterns on the upper thigh around the flap-closings, where paired fobs used to dangle.

Either shoes or boots are worn with knee breeches. The tendency toward boots, growing throughout the final quarter century, becomes a mania from 1790–1815. There are English jockey boots with reversed tops and boot straps; Hessian, and Suvaroff boots, which have their tops scalloped into two arcs, from the joining of which hangs a tassel. There are soft boots in great variety: high and close-fitting; or short with tops flaring between ankle and calf-height, spats and gaiters in all lengths. About 1813–15 spurs are seen.

The first strapped pantaloons are worn either with boots, or with dark low shoes and light stockings. Both this type, and the shorter, wider trousers of c.1815–25 are commonly worn over soft black boots which begin to turn into shoes in the second third XIXc.

Until c.1825 collars are soft, attached to the shirt and turned up to the ears. They surround the jaw from 1800–30, and then tend to be turned down over the cravat. The kerchief which goes twice about the neck to be knotted in front is worn 1790–1830; then begins to be turned into a bow tie. It is typically white, though there are striped forms from the Revolution to 1815. Collars become detached from shirts, and starched c.1825. Ruffled shirt fronts are seen through the openings of single-breasted waistcoats until the 30's and later still in court costume. But from the 20's the frill falls at one side of a buttoned closing.

At the Revolution, hair loses its powder and is dressed in two principal fashions: the short-combed-out hedgehog, *hérisson;* its longer form *à la Titus;* or in shaggy "dog's-ear" locks, combed forward over the forehead and ears. This form developed into curly sideburns which continued to be worn when the shaggy locks become full and curlier about the ears, after 1815.

The tricorne had been pretty well replaced late in XVIIIc. by the hat turned up front and back *à l'androsmane.* The most exaggerated form of this was worn with the striped coat of the *Incroyable;* it became the hat of Napoleon's army and court. As the flat *"chapeau bras"* which could be carried tucked under the arm, or worn, but which it was never permissible to lay down, it continues in ceremonial dress use today in the costume of French academicians.

The plain English "round" hat had early Revolutionary connotations, but it was so practical that it made great strides. By 1812 it was universally worn, with conical, sugar-loaf, or spreading top-hat crown; its brim was apt to be rolled up slightly on the sides with a dip over the forehead.

Paired fobs continue to be worn, but by 1810, interest in them is transferred to the paired closing of the front flap; even this diminishes when trouser-tops become fuller, c.1815. The watch is then worn singly with a black ribbon fob, as a convenience, or with a bunch of seals.

Snuff continues to be taken; cigar smoking begins, but will not become common until practical wooden matches are invented in England in 1827. The French match of 1805 was an amusing curiosity which was ignited by dipping it into a bottle of sulphuric acid.

Sticks and quizzing glasses continue to be carried; gloves, usually yellow, are worn, especially after the bright mixed colors and patterns of the early period tend to become browns, grays, blacks, and blues, worn with lighter trousers, black hat and boots. Buttons (made of steel or pearl at the turn of the century) turn to brass or gilt.

Blue was especially fashionable and was used both in day and evening dress. The best tailor of 1816 was Weston of Old Bond Street, whose light *bleu céleste* was famous. Brummell, the arbiter of the period in England, wore carefully folded starched white cravats and perfectly tailored plain clothing. In the daytime, his brass-buttoned blue coat was worn with a buff or light colored waistcoat, buckskin breeches or pantaloons, over Hessian boots. At night, his blue coat was accompanied by a white waistcoat, pantaloons of blue stockinet, strapped over varnished black shoes worn with striped stockings. Court dress was worn at the opera and Almack's Assembly Rooms in London.

1820-40.

The corseted look for which the coat has been straining is now attained by cutting the tails separate from the body of the coat. The bosom springs open and is rounded. There are rolling shawl collars, sometimes slightly notched, which are no longer dragged away from the back of the neck. The shoulder seam moves back up into position and the shoulder line is widened with padding; sleeves become plain and close.

Coats are single or double-breasted, but are so shaped that they hold their form without being closed; double-breastedness is becoming a matter of lines of decorative buttons, as useless as the vestigial buttons on an evening tailcoat today. By 1835 the collar becomes longer, more acutely notched into prominent stitched lapels. Tailcoats are less squarely cutaway across the front and their tails hang below the knee. Blue and black continue to be dress-coat colors. In ordinary wear bottle green, mulberry and warm browns are added to black and blue coats.

But among the wonderfully individual forms of coat and topcoat, which are developing toward their culmination in the 40's and 50's, are knee-length, skirted coats with shoulder capes and sharp wide lapels, for informal wear instead of the tail coat.

Macintosh had invented waterproof cloth c. 1825; by 1830 it is used in all sorts of deeply caped travelling coats and ulsters with half-belts in back which could be buttoned to make them fit more closely. There are many very long overcoats, fitted, loose, or even full and cape-like. Until the 30's they often close by tabs. There are forms with one to four capes; fur-lined and collared *pelisses* with braid trim and frogged closings. Coats begin to be made of textured and patterned tweeds; pockets are often set in a diagonal line. Fur and long, full outer garments are usually related to the weather; they are sometimes hold-overs from the previous bad year, anticipations of another such, or mere swank like a mink-coat in Indian Summer in New York. 1820 and 1823 were rigorous winters; fur-lined Polish coats and four-collared ankle-length capes are common. The intervening years were mild, but 1830 was one of the four worst winters ever recorded. From 1830 to 1871 the weather was relatively mild, with the exception of 1838, a long winter in 1845, cold winters in 1854 and in England 1855. The short loose sports coats of the 40's and 50's could only have developed during a long run of good seasons.

Vests follow the lead of coats, and become single-breasted, or are double-breasted merely by virtue of two rows of buttons. Like coats, vests curve open, round and low, with shawl collars, the notching of which turns them into sharp lapels at the end of the period. They then begin to dip slightly at the bottom or to spring apart into points below the last button. Into the 30's two vests of different lengths are often worn together, plain over striped, or dark over light. The general trend toward variety and pattern in men's clothing is particularly shown in vests. They are made of embroidered velvet or sprigged brocade, and there are white vests which are striking with darker coats and trousers, and black neckcloths.

The pantaloon of 1820 is full about the waist even when its bottom has again become narrow and strapped under the boot. It now becomes as long as possible and narrow, following the dimensions of the limbs and narrowing at the ankle. The characteristic look of the pantaloon of the 30's comes from its tautness between braces and sole, so that the line of the thigh strains through in front, and the calf in back. About 1835 the pantaloon begins to change into trousers; it exchanges a fly-opening for the flap. Its cut becomes a little easier, so that it can be made of cloth, and the familiar grays, greens and black are enlivened by corduroy and twilled textures and small patterns.

Collars become detached from shirts and begin to be starched c.1825. The frilled shirt continues to be worn, and is required at court, but a tucked and buttoned front closing becomes more interesting.

The neckcloth becomes reduced. About 1830 it is replaced by stiffened cravats of serge, camlet, or satin, usually black, occasionally purple, and in evening dress of white satin. These buckle in back and have a bow in front. There are also "dickies" of dark stuff which are crossed and pinned and replace the shirt entirely.

Count D'Orsay, a Frenchman, who was the English arbiter of fashion in the 30's and 40's, is to be seen on the "New Yorker" magazine's original cover and in the little cut on their masthead. His fitted neckcloth of 1834 is continued into an artfully crumpled mass of satin which covers the entire breast above the rolled collar of the waistcoat. His watch chain is worn around the neck, is looped before its passes through the top button hole, and then continues into the watch pocket on the right side of the vest.

The rather full head of the 20's is cut shorter in back by 1830 and is combed up into a quiff above the forehead. About 1835, it begins to be given a part on the left side, which is continued down the back of the head. Hair is combed away from this part into locks over the ears, or bunches of curls around them. As the collar and stock come to outline the chin, rather than to muffle it, in the 20's, the sideburns are continued in a fringe of artificially curled beard, running along the jawbone and under the chin of a clean-shaven face. Moustaches, which have been reserved for the cavalry, begin to be worn by civilians in the 30's.

Soft black Wellington boots, long, narrow and square-toed, are worn under strapped trousers. Gloves remain yellowish; sticks are carried; wide-brimmed top hats of smooth black beaver with tall crowns. Caps have been worn since 1800 in peaked Orleans and Russian, Austrian and Hungarian forms of army forage cap. With the increasing individuality of men's costume during the 30's and 40's caps multiply in forms and in use with the new waterproof travelling and hunting coats.

1840-1850.

During the 40's and 50's many varieties of new coats for morning and sports wear appear, and there is an increase in the use of bold patterns, stripes, checks and plaids. There are formal tail coats, many skirted coats, developed out of overcoats, and new morning jackets in loud patterns.

The shoulder seam drops down in back; sleeves become a little fuller and longer so that they wrinkle across the bend of the elbow. The curved waist lengthens into a long torso by 1850. While this process is taking place, skirts are set on a low line, between the normal waist and the hips, in cutting the loud single-breasted morning coats, which have their front corners rounded off. Buttons are large, and button holes are sometimes set diagonally to accentuate the swing of these coats. Coat collars become wider. Lapels (which had become acute in the late 30's) are prominent, but more rounded, rolling from a lowered waistline. Coat skirts and tails fall short of knee-length; a facing of dull silk is often carried well out on their lapels; the coat tends to be buttoned higher in the 50's and 60's.

There are still many fancy silk and embroidered velvet vests as well as wash vests for summer. But the parallel between vest and coat begins to disappear in the 40's, although the vest becomes longer waisted and is then buttoned higher, as the coat makes these changes. It may now have a rolled shawl collar, while the coat collar is deeply notched; its bottom is usually spread in points below the last button.

Trousers lose their shoe-straps during the 40's. They are still very long and close-cut at the bottom, but their fit becomes much easier. During the 40's they are often made of striking plaids and of stripes used horizontally as well as vertically; the most unusual patterns are worn with the new short outercoats which are made of plain materials. Fawn and gray trousers (rather than the earlier buff or white trousers) are worn with patterned coats and with the tailed and skirted coats. In the 50's the outseam is often braided and most trousers have hip pockets in the seam.

With the 50's there is a tendency to make coats, vests and trousers match. There are plaid and fancy tweed suits with more squarely cut skirts from 1855. Many completely black costumes of cloak, coat and vest and trousers appear in the 60's.

The 40's and 50's are filled with a wonderful variety of coats and top-coats, especially for day, travel and sports. There are formal overcoats with cape and small velvet collar; fitted coats; catalonian and hooded burnoose cloaks, and heavily braided short overcoats with hoods; short, double-breasted box-coats with big buttons; tiers of pocket flaps with another on the cuff; bell-shaped and raglan-sleeved loose coats falling to mid-thigh. Coats are of black, lined with sky-blue; dark blue, green and brown; coffee, leather color, gray, and tweed mixtures; in single or double-breasted or cape forms.

The top hat changes, c.1855, from the English beaver to the silk hat which the French have learned to waterproof. Its crown takes on a cylindrical stovepipe form, with a narrow brim.

Informal felt and straw hats with low crowns and wide brims appear in the 50's, together with a wonderful assortment of visored caps for sports wear: jockey caps, caps with earflaps, caps shaped like those worn today by locomotive engineers, made of striped and plaid materials and tweed and trimmed with fur in cold winters.

Hair is still parted, but the part is often on the right side and approaches the center by 1850. The artificially curled ends of the hair of the mid-30's loosen into waves by the late 40's. In the 50's the hair is cut shorter and plastered down with Macassar oil, against which ladies pin anti-macassars on the backs of chairs.

There were a good many clean-shaven faces during the 40's; the fringe of beard below the jawbone, so characteristic of the 30's, is not continued under the entire chin, by the late 40's. Moustaches ceased to be the exclusive attribute of the English military after the Crimean War; they are seen alone on a clean-shaven face, or with the imperial worn by loyal Bonapartists in imitation of Napoleon III, whose perfect dress is even more influential than that of Victoria's consort Albert.

The new interest in the chin is related to changes in the shirt and collar. Shirts have lost their frill, and have ousted the dickey. They now have an inset bosom of tucked linen.

Made-up cravats go out of fashion before 1850. Their place is taken by a necktie, which is at first rather soft and full, becoming flatter and narrower by the 60's. Four-in-hand ties, and stocks like the Ascot worn by ushers at a wedding today appear by the 60's, worn with a stickpin. The old black stock continues in use by elderly men to 1870, with the collar turned down over it.

The choker collar of 1840 had a shaped top sewed onto a band, so that the collar curved away from the face. The edge begins to turn down; then the choker is largely superseded by a stiff standing collar. In 1848 the collar is very low, uncovering the column of the neck; it becomes higher by 1860; by the 70's the front is tabbed back or cut away to spare the adam's apple, and low, striped, turned-down collars appear.

Laced boots began to replace soft, low Wellington boots in the 50's; buttoned boots appear during the 60's; both begin to have colored uppers. Men change into wool-embroidered slippers in the house.

The use of tobacco is increasing. Cigars are elegant. Snuff loses ground; the low habit of pipe smoking gains during the 60's. Cigarettes had been brought back from the Crimean war and become as socially acceptable as the cigars; in the emancipating years of the 60's women begin to try them. But from the 50's, men retire to another room to smoke, and change there into smoking jacket and cap, which they remove before joining the ladies.

Gold watch chains, from the buttonhole to the watch pocket replace the looped neck-chain of the 40's.

THE 1860's.

During the 60's men's garments lose their shapely elegance. They are less close-waisted, more sack-like and baggy, and are made of thicker, clumsier materials.

The Empress Eugenie continued to exert an influence on costume for a longer time after her marriage in 1853 than did Napoleon III, who was ill for some years before his empire ended in 1870. Alexandra and the Prince of Wales affect fashions after their marriage in 1863; the tailored suit for women was fostered by her, and the eventual King Edward VII was always superbly turned out. But photographs of men of the 60's show a majority looking like seedy old-time American congressmen and Shakespearean actors, in battered stovepipe hats, rather wrinkled coats, and loose, flopping trousers, far removed from the fashion-plate ideal of the period.

Coats, vests, and trousers are now apt to match. Checked trousers and colored odd vests may be worn with sack coats, and striped or light-colored summer trousers with dark, matching frock coats and vests.

Single-breasted sack coats grow longer and more shapeless. Their collars and lapels are small, as coats come to be buttoned high on the chest; the lower buttons are unfastened and the edges of the coat spread or are cut away, often rounded at the corners.

Sleeves widen around the upper and middle arm and narrow toward the wrist, in fashion plates; in actuality, they are apt to appear as rather wide tubes, characterless except for wrinkles.

Frock coats are single or double-breasted, and close high. Their lapels are sometimes faced with dull silk; their tails usually fall very short of the knee.

Evening coats are cut square across the front; their tails are now more sharply cutaway and shorter.

Trousers grow wide and baggy in the middle; the fashionable trouser of the mid-60's remains wide above, but is made very tight about the calf, and there is often a line of braiding along the outseam. In actuality, trousers, especially light summer ones, appear in most photographs as flopping, shapeless and tubular. Knickerbockers appear, worn with sack shooting coats.

The most interesting men's garments of the 60's are the caped cloaks and the overcoats. Cloaks are full, and fall one third to one half way between knee and sole. They are slit at the side for the arms to pass, have a deep cape to the waist or hip line, and often a small velvet collar which hooks together at the neck. Velvet collars are no longer used on suit-coats, but are often seen on long, rather fitted overcoats which have a real elegance, and are sometimes edged with braid.

Waistcoats, fancy or matching the coat and trousers, lose shape as coats do. Double-breasted vests are seen with open frockcoats, but the usual vest is single-breasted, buttoned high like the coat but throughout its length, and is much exposed by the spreading edges of the coat.

Narrow-brimmed silk stovepipe hats, black, white or gray for the races, continue to be worn; crush opera hats appear in the 60's. But wide-brimmed, low-crowned felt hats of the "porkpie" sort become common from the 50's; round bowlers appear with the 70's. These new alternatives to the top-hat's formality reduce the popularity of the cap in the late 60's and the 70's, although there are "deerstalkers" for hunting.

Hair styles of 1860 are extremely varied. The center part of the 50's tends to become a side part from which the hair is combed away flat; however, hair is also seen combed back. The head of hair is full at the ends, which are sometimes waved; the ears come into sight in the 60's. In the beginning of the decade, hair is also rather full in back, although it does not reach the collar, and tends to spring out below the pressure line of the hard hat. But the back of the head is often trimmed as short as it is today.

There are fewer clean-shaven men during the 60's and 70's but there is great latitude in styles and combinations of face hair. Whiskers grow longer and are combed out into mutton chops and "Dundrearys"; full beards appear. Moustaches and beards may be worn alone or in any combination. With the fall of the second Bonaparte Empire, the dashing Imperial is less seen. The long reign of the yellow glove is over; now they run from grays to lavender.

2239A

2239A. French XIXc. c. 1800. (Met. Mus. of Art, Print . Room.)

Gabriel à Coblentz. Conversation piece: silhouettes on verre églomisé.

Max von Boehn's *Miniatures and Silhouettes** reproduces German cut-out pictures in white set on colored paper, made in 1631; and English examples from 1699. These cut, outline pictures were popular, even before they acquired the name under which they became a mania between 1768-80.

Through Mme. de Pompadour's influence, the post of comptroller-general of French finance was held through seven and a half months of the year 1759 by Etienne de Silhouette (1709-67), who loved cut-out pictures so much that they had been used to decorate a room in his chateau de Brie. Silhouette's popularity was destroyed by his new program of taxes on land and pensions; the nobility found themselves about to be reduced to bare essentials, and among other forms of protest and ridicule, Silhouette's name was given to these pictures of outlines.

* E. P. Dutton, N. Y., 1928, 40 col. and 200 black and white illustrations; the source of much of this information.

Their popularity was increased by the excavations of black-figured Greek pottery, and profile busts on ancient coins and cameos, and by the publication of handsomely illustrated works on *Physiognomy* by a German named Lavater, between 1775-8. The long-familiar silhouettes had occurred to Lavater as a way to collect illustrations of his theories; Mme. de Genlis did not believe in them, but interest in them was general and fashionable. Everybody was sentimental, sorrowing with *"Werther"*; Lavater was Goethe's dear friend, so they were eager to send him their silhouette, and perhaps find it used.

The most expertly cut and purest silhouettes are of last third XVIIIc. Then, they begin to be debased and set against shaded backgrounds, often less attractive than Gabriel à Coblentz' method of backing glass with drawn lines and crackled gold.

Graeco-Roman effect on form: chocolate pot and furniture; hair dressed in classical knot with classical comb, necklace and earrings set with cameos; high-waisted, short-sleeved Empire gowns. Man: long tail-coat and boots. Sentimentality: kitten playing with wool.

2240. XIXc. 1810-15. French. (Boston, Museum of Fine
    Arts.)
    Printed cotton dress; green, yellow, and red.
Plaited straw bonnet. Multicolored straw bag, woven
and glued. Handkerchief, dilute brick color and
yellow plaid. Gold necklace.

2241. XIXc. c. 1800. French. (Boston, Museum of Fine
    Arts.)
    Dress of India gauze shot with silver. Bead "bird
cage" bag; greenish-blue and white beads; floral
border, and *Ces fleurs vous parlent de moi*, worked
in beads.

2242. XIXc. 1810-15. French. (Metropolitan Museum.)
    Ball gown; white gauze, silk appliqué.

2243. XIXc. 1825-30. French. (Boston, Museum of Fine
    Arts.)
    Dress of pink and silver shot India gauze; white
mull skirt embroidered in pink, dull orange, and
black with orange leaves. Netted "miser's" purse in

silk, henna, yellow-green and steel beads, in paisley and cone pattern, with a steel ring. Fan of pierced horn leaves. Necklace and earring set, medallions and chains.

2244. XIXc. c. 1800. French. (Boston, Museum of Fine Arts, Elizabeth Day McCormick Coll.)
Spun steel bag.

2245. Early XIXc. French. (Boston, Museum of Fine Arts.)
Spun steel bag.

2246. XIXc. c. 1800-15. French. (Boston, Museum of Fine Arts.)
Folding bag of beige moiré, with steel frame and cut steel button.

New steel-making techniques in late XVIIIc. made steel jewelry possible. It provided a discreet replacement for the twinkle of diamonds, which had become dangerous in Revolutionary times, and was in any case becoming a little boring to those who could afford diamonds. Cut-steel, often combined with paste and mother-of-pearl, made handsome buttons and buckles, and catered to the desire for luxury of those who had longed for diamonds.

2247. Early XIXc. French. (Boston, Museum of Fine Arts.)
Six beaded and netted "miser's" purses.

2248. Empire Dresses: Left to Right:

French, 1805-10. Cream colored muslin dress embroidered with silver metal thread in all-over floral repeat pattern.

European, 1804-14. Spencer of light brown satin with a self-pattern.

French, 1804-10. Cap of embroidered mull trimmed with tucks and lace.

Italian(?), 1805-10. Dress of gold raw silk.

French(?), 1804-14. Turban of white satin with yellow French knots. Scarf of cream-colored sheer muslin embroidered with drawn work and gold metal thread.

Viennese, 1804-15. Dress of white muslin with vari-colored bead embroidery. Scarf of white muslin with embroidered leaf border.

Spanish(?), 1810-15. Dress of white piña-cloth with multi-colored silk embroidery and sequins.

Viennese, 1804-14. Spencer of green and pink striped satin.

French, 1804-14. Cap of embroidered mull with lace.

Courtesy of Metropolitan Museum of Art, Costume Institute

2249   2250   2251   2252

2253

2249. XIXc. 1810-30. French.

Man's court coat: Light brown uncut velvet, embroidered in chenille.

2250-51. XIXc. 1804-14. French.

Man's court costume: Coat and vest of purple brocaded velvet, embroidered in silk.

2252. Early XIXc. Italian, Venetian.

Livery coat: Olive green flannel (see Italian, 1750, Longhi).

2253. XIXc. 1810. French.

Woman's court mantle: Red velvet, embroidered in gold; worn by the Princess of Leon at the marriage of Napoleon and Marie Louise.

"COSTUMES PARISIENS"

Dated and numbered plates marked "Costumes Parisiens" come from the *Journal des dames et des modes,* founded in late XVIIIc. by the abbé de la Mésangère. Its plates were re-issued in annual volumes as *Costumes parisiens de la fin du 18e siècle et du commencement du 19e.* During more than four decades of life, it absorbed eight other fashion magazines. It is listed in the *Union Catalog of Periodicals* as *Gazette des Salons,* one of the names it bore in its later, weekly, form. Its long life, beautiful plates (of men's as well as women's fashions), and its excellent text make it one of the most important and influential of all fashion magazines.

Descriptive captions on the plates are given in translation.

2254-58. XIXc. French. (Metropolitan Museum, Print Room.)

2254. "Round embroidered *toquet,* cloth Spencer." (1800)

This *toquet* (see No. 2258) is of eyelet embroidered muslin. The combed-down fringe of hair becomes bunched in curls, high on the temples, c. 1820. Muslin dress; cloth Spencer, with sleeves extending over the hand, opens in two long points: the "Chinese" Spencer. Low-cut, heel-less slippers.

2255. "Young man's careless dress." (1802)

Top hat of beaver; wide brim curled at the sides; no hat band. Shaggy head becoming curly; hair extended down the jaw. High, turned-up collar; cravat; *jabot* ruffles are added to the shirt, as the vest opens; low striped vest with standing collar, cut square across the bottom.

The "Jean de Bry" coat, in its later exaggerations of short waist, puffed sleeve-top, and collar climbing up the back of the head, became a favorite butt of caricaturists. This is approximately its original form: a double-breasted cloth coat with three sets of buttons, cut square to show the vest hanging below; tails gradually cut away, falling short of the knee; long, notched lapels, collar climbing high in back; sleeves gathered full at the armseye, and prolonged over the knuckles. Breeches cut full into trousers, but are still very short; they have just been released from being drawn down under the boots by strings, and still have a slit for closing; stockings, low-cut heelless slippers; fob; stick.

2256. "Lace veil. Tunic. Cashmere shawl." (1803)

Indecision of the fringe of hair, which is no longer willing simply to be combed forward and down; locks oiled; veiled in a long, narrow lace scarf. Necklines are still very low, but there is a

Courtesy of Metropolitan Museum of Art

strong alternative interest in the base of the throat; a *fraise* or necklace is apt to be worn. Tunics begin to be added to classical gowns, c. 1800. As skirts shorten, the tunic is lost, but decoration is carried up from skirt hems, c. 1815, toward the point at which the tunic used to end. Cashmere shawl, patterned at the ends, with a great deal of white in its border.

2257. "Cloth redingote, trimmed with velvet." (1803)

Cloth redingote with two velvet capes and the tabbed closing taken from men's cloaks. As the warm weather of the first decade XIXc. passes, the redingote is turned into a warm, lined indoor garment, the *douillette,* which has long sleeves and is tied together at intervals by ribbon bows, or hooked together under a line of ruching. The garment and its vertical front line disappear c. 1840 as the new fullness of skirts is emphasized by horizontal trim-

mings. Taffeta hats (see No. 2258); gloves; long embroidered gauze scarf.

2258. "Trimmed hat *(chapeau),* Lingerie bonnets, *Capote* of taffeta with straw lace, *Capote* of taffeta, *Capote* of *Sparterie* and taffeta, Crepe bonnet, Hat of taffeta and straw." (1804)

The categories of e. XIXc. headcoverings overlap and merge in confusion.

Ceremonious headcoverings derive from the *pouf* arranged by the hairdresser on the ceremonious "head" of Marie Antoinette's time, although they are now usually bought ready-made: turbans, *toques, cornettes,* and triangular pinned or tied handkerchief-like arrangements.

Outdoor head coverings fall into the main headings of *chapeau, capote,* and *bonnet.*

The *chapeau* is a hat: it has a crown and a brim, as in Ill. 2257.

The *bonnet* always has a connotation of softness and of ribbon ties under the chin. It has a brim in front, and a rather important crown; it is shirred, corded and gathered into form, rather than stiffened.

The *capote* is a bonnet which consists mostly of its rigid brim, made of straw or boned into shape; it has a soft, gathered crown, and it, too, is tied under the chin. It is the ancestor of grandmother's sun bonnet.

The *toquet* of eyelet embroidery in Ill. 2254 is an intermediate: in the softness of its brim, ruffled edge, prominent crown, and its ties coming from the crown of the head, it is bonnet-like; but its brim is shaped like that of a *capote.*

2259. XIXc. c. 1801-4. Spanish. (Washington, Nat. Gall. of Art.)
    Goya. Doña Teresa Sureda.
2260. XIXc. 1805. Spanish. (Metropolitan Museum.)
    Goya. Doña Narcisa Barañana de Goicoechea.
    Spanish court dress, and even the Queen's version of national cos-
tume in 1799, is influenced by the short-waisted Empire fashions of
Europe. All the other Goya women: the duchess of Alba in 1795, the

majas, the girls in the drawings, Doña Teresa and Doña Narcisa, show the entirely different torso which is the foundation of Spanish costume: high-bosomed, with a longer, neat waist, and a swaying back line. It is this body and posture that make Doña Narcisa so triumphantly Spanish, in comparison to the Queen in not dissimilar dress in 1799. Doña Teresa's coat dress is based on the Spanish coat of Bayeu and Martinez.

2261. XIXc. 1806. Spanish. (Brooklyn Museum.)
    Goya. Tadeo Bravo de Rivério.
    Spanish lapels, collar and cut of shorter-waisted, double-breasted European coat; sword and traditional hat.

2262. XIXc. c. 1800. Scotch. (New York, Duveen.)
    Sir Henry Raeburn. Mrs. John Hutcheson Ferguson.

2263. XIXc. 1801-2. Scotch. (New York, J. P. Morgan.)
    Raeburn. Miss Rose (Mrs. Bell.)
    Triangular scarves, like those which tie on caps in Olivier's *Thé à l'Anglaise* and "half-handkerchiefs" mentioned by Heideloff were the ancestors of the *cornette* headdresses, which were worn throughout the first third XIXc. and affected bonnets into the 1860's. By the 1820's *cornettes* develop into lingerie caps, in which the point has almost disappeared,

2266

but they are differentiated from all other caps by being carried under the chin, framing the whole face in a ruffled edge. In the 30's the *cornette* may have become a mere lingerie band with a gauffered edge, tied under the chin, and is sometimes seen as a ruffle under a hat, enclosing the face.

Mrs. Ferguson's *cornette,* midway in development between the tied triangle and the made-up cap, is worn with a Van-Dyked neckline and a narrow India shawl.

Miss Rose: long black lace scarf with inner edge ruffled.

2264. XIXc. c. 1800. U.S.A. (Metropolitan Museum.)
Ezra Ames (1768-1836). Philip van Cortlandt (1749-1831).

The American patriot and statesman of the great New York family shows characteristics of first decade XIXc.: method of notching the longer, rolled collar of a plain dark cloth coat with covered buttons; striped vest with covered buttons, opened to show the sheer jabot. In this case, while the vest has a standing collar, the shirt collar has not risen above the stock. Uneven locks of hair combed forward.

2265. XIXc. c. 1802. U.S.A. (New York Historical Soc.)
C. W. Peale. Mrs. James Madison.

The fragile and scholarly Madison was married in 1794 to Dolly Todd, a plump and charming Philadelphia widow of great social aptitude.

Gauze and metal turban; uneven locks of hair combed forward; *fraise* at throat; short but not close gold chain; narrow lace-edged sheer scarf; pale satin Empire gown, as short-waisted as possible; puffed sleeves to which long sleeves are now often added, unless extremely long gloves are worn.

2266. XIXc. 1803. French. (The Louvre.)
Boilly. The Arrival of the Diligence.

A network of diligence routes now covers Europe. People begin to travel for other reasons than bare necessity. Novels are filled with details of journeys, since all novel readers have taken or hope to take just such trips as Jorrocks and the Yorkshireman set off on by "the nine o'clock Dover heavy" from the Bricklayer's Arms. Boilly's picture might serve as an illustration for Surtees: "Jorrock's Jaunts and Jollities." Only the pickpocket (who has already been seen in Boilly's *Marche incroyable*) is missing from the crowd of beggars, pedlers, cloaked and top-hatted coachmen, porters, and the soldiers who always appear among the passengers. Since luggage has to be carried on the roof of the coach or in the passenger's hands, it consists of luggage rolls, light *portemanteaux* and boxes, oddments stuffed into pillow cases or tied up in tablecloths, luncheon baskets, and umbrellas.

At the far left, an elderly man of the people wears the double-breasted, sleeveless vest which was brought to Marseilles by workers from Carmagnola in the Piedmont, got to Paris, and as the *carmagnole,* entered the dress of the people and the professional revolutionaries; it can also be seen in the *Marche incroyable.*

The hat *à l'androsmane* is turning into the rigid, flat *chapeau bras.* The officer also shows the braided openings of the front flap of long elastic breeches, through which his sash is run; the way in which these breeches are held in place at the waist when the flap is down is shown by the man who is relieving himself at the coach-wheel. The porter kneeling beside the officer's tasselled Hessian boots wears long trousers, buttoned in gaiter-fashion down the outseam.

Social differentiations are shown by the heads of women. The elderly woman of the people, and the pretty young fruit vendor with the officers, the nursemaid who kneels to blow the child's nose in the center, and the seated woman who adjusts her little girl's cap, all have their heads covered in ways appropriate to their ages. The mother and older daughter of the middle class family which clamors for father's notice are above wearing caps; their uncovered hair is twisted in Greek knots.

The most fashionably dressed people stand apart at the right. The lady is dressed with formality: long orange gloves, a pink and white *capote,* a bow of deeper pink on her white dress, which has a knot of pink ribbon appliquéd on the trailing end of the skirt she holds up, showing blue stockings and brown shoes. The early XIXc. is filled with amusing bags; hers is of a pink so deep that it is red, and consists of no more than some tassels sewn around the center of a square which has its corners knotted together. Child in peacock blue. The man, whose hair is extended well down the jowls, carries a crook-headed cane, with yellow-green coat, buff breeches, and black boots with mahogany tops.

2267. XIXc. 1804. English.

Thomas Ryder, after *Sir Thomas Beechey.* Queen Charlotte.

An elderly lady, dressed with complete suitability and complete awareness of the latest style, but no undue regard for what she finds inappropriate in it, has an aura of the 90's. She belongs to a time when short sleeves were ceremonious; neither the current very short or very long tight sleeve suits her so well as the caught and puffed sleeve of the 80's-90's. She has shortened her underskirt very slightly, and tucked up its embroidered overskirt in recognition of the draped overskirts of the first five years of XIXc., but she has retained the waistline, skirt fullness, kerchief and reinforcing long scarf knotted at the waist, trailing overdress skirt, and high-crowned cap of the 90's. She veils her cap with the current lace scarf of an imitation Roman matron.

2268. XIXc. 1804. U.S.A.

Pavel P. Svinin (1787-1839). Sunday morning in front of the Arch Street Meeting House in Philadelphia.

One of several water colors by a Russian who visited Philadelphia shows the costume of Quaker women at a time when its severity blended successfully with classical styles, and even gave their dress a startling air of advanced fashion. For all its severity, the Quaker bonnet has an exaggerated scoop which the European *capote* will not achieve for several years, and the Friends' skirts are as short as European women's are on their way to becoming in another decade.

Father with his wide-brimmed hat, long hair and XVIIIc. dress is Benjamin Franklin at Louis XVI's court, almost to the life.

2269. XIXc. 1805. French. (Boston, Museum of Fine Arts.)

Debucourt. Les courses du matin.

The passers-by and waiting crowd, making its morning round of rich patrons' houses, give a clear picture of dress suitable to many occupations.

A coachman waits for the elegant young couple which is being admitted by a servant in a powdered livery-wig. The young gentleman wears a beaver with extravagantly curled brim, cape with two cloaks, light pantaloons buttoned tight at their bottoms, some four inches above the ankle; white stockings, and slippers reduced to a minimum.

His companion shows the disintegration of classical costume. The original tubular, gathered muslin dress has been cut into a fitted bodice with the skirt fullness concentrated under it at the center back. Braids of artificial hair are worked into such an elaboration of "classical" knots and fillets that a bonnet has been achieved; it has a completely unclassical bouquet stuck in the front, and lacks only bonnet-strings; it is undoubtedly a wig.

Five categories of women's wigs are advertised *(Morning Post,* March 18, 1800) by Mr. T. Bowman's remodelled establishment in the West End: the "Tresse à la Grecque, when put over a short headdress, is a complete full dress. Price half-a-guinea, 1, 1½, 2, 3, 4, and 5 guineas." Plate 2 in Gillray's *Progress of the Toilet,* dated 1810, shows a maid about to set a wig on her mistress' clipped head.

In front of the coachman, the driver of a smart equipage decorated with Napoleonic laurel, delivers boxes for a peruke-maker. There is practically no business left in men's wigs, but women order them in all colors, and change, from red, to black, to blonde, within a matter of hours. All the boxes he carries are addressed to women; one is for Napoleon's mother, Madame Mère. At the left, two delivery-men accept snuff. One carries a magnificent pair of lacquered boots; he wears a bicorne; coat with high collar and large lapels, cut short to show the vest; long striped pantaloons; and English top boots. The other has a striped neckcloth, hoop earrings and a cropped head; he has the look of a convict, freed after long service on the galleys. He carries a bundle of new garments, tied up in the square of cloth which preceded cardboard boxes, and which is still the method by which theatrical costumes are carried.

The man from whom they accept snuff shows the plight in which the hairdressers, as well as the wig-makers, now find themselves. He clings to a powdered, tied wig; wears a striped coat and stockings, with knee-breeches, gaiters, and the apron of his trade. The box which he carries advertises the many other services by which he contrives to live, now that neither ladies nor gentlemen need the services of *Furet, artiste:*—he is also a chemist and cosmetician; he provides elastic corsets, suspenders, stockings, and is a costumer for both sexes.

Behind Furet, a dancing master, in a *hérisson*-cut tie wig, carries a rolled waltz and stands in a carefully arranged position. His collar mounts excessively high in back; his shirt ruffles reach to the bottom of his vest, which has only a button closed; his breeches are cut as high as possible, though they end with knee-strings to show his white-stockinged leg to its full advantage. Beyond him is one of the round felt hats which began to be worn in France at the turn of the century.

A tail-coat and an XVIIIc. coat, worn with knee breeches, are shown on the symphonic composer (5) and the painter (7); long stockinette pantaloons on

the bespectacled architect who carries plans and elevations for doing over an alcove in the currently fashionable Etruscan taste. Beside him, a smart bicorne is set, back to front, in the current fashion, over combed-forward locks.

During the last quarter XVIIIc., after centuries of being dressed like their parents in miniature, children finally achieved clothes designed especially for children. That independence is not maintained in early XIXc. We seldom see such literal carbon copies of grown people as are shown in this picture. Little boys of first half XIXc. do wear sailor suits, little bell-boy jackets, and plaid tam-o'-shanters. But until Dickens' day, children's dress, especially that of girls and of the littlest boys, is strongly affected by adult, especially female styles.

The mother wears an Empire gown with standing ruff and pleated hem, taffeta gloves so long that they have to be tied about the upper arm, and a turban.

The little girl's hair is fileted by a braid, and tied up in a Grecian knot; she has laced sandals, and an Etruscan scarf, sewed part way to her hem and then drawn up over the shoulder.

Her brother's costume is strongly affected by the uniform of the Empire infantryman; his beaver hat with beaked brim lacks only the brush of the Hungarian shako; his vest approximates the light-colored chest piece buttoned onto the uniform, and he wears its high-waisted breeches and boots.

The nursemaid wears the stylized cap of the region of her origin.

The extravagantly artistic amateur of antiquities, carrying a portfolio of sketches, is wrapped in a toga-like cape, and shows the sleeves prolonged over the knuckles, in its most excessive form.

The old author, with the manuscript of a new novel in his pocket, is dressed in seedy XVIIIc. wig, clothes and hat. The ordinary dress of little boys is seen on the pair building card houses, instead of peddling their papers, which are carried in a wicker-work basket, shaped like a Dutch boat.

2270 2271 2272 2273 2274 2275

2270. XIXc. 1807. U.S.A. (Metropolitan Museum.)
Gilbert Stuart. Commodore Isaac Hall.

2271. XIXc. English. (Metropolitan Museum.)
Charles Lucy. Lord Nelson in the cabin of the "Victory."

This picture, painted in 1853, shows Nelson in his admiral's uniform in the cabin of the ship on which he died at Trafalgar in 1805.

2272. XIXc. French (Metropolitan Museum.)
Ingres. Portrait of a Gentleman.

Light gray-brown overcoat; chocolate brown coat; black beaver bicorne, with white and gold decoration, carried flat under the arm.

2273. XIXc. 1805-10. French. (Philadelphia, John G. Johnson Collection.)
Ingres. Louis Charles Mercier Dupaty.

Very dark green coat; white vest and stockings, pearl gray breeches, decoration with red ribbon.

In both 2272 and 2273, we see collars to the ears; immense white knotted cravats; wide ruffles, flattened to one side, show through low opening of white vests with enormous standing collar and self-buttons. Their coats have the very high, characteristically notched lapel of c. 1810-15; full upper sleeve, forced or gathered into armseye. Locks at ears grow down the face; as the collar recedes, the line of beard will move down and follow the jawbone.

2274. XIXc. 1806. French. (New York, Cooper Union Museum.)
Debucourt, after *C. Vernet.* Aquatint: Miss Franconi performing at the Cirque Olympique, Paris.

Rosalie was the granddaughter of Antonio Franconi, the founder of the Paris hippodrome.

Sea-bathing became immensely popular by the beginning of XIXc. Theatrical people made the resort of Cabourg their own. The Goncourts, who visited it in 1863, found it a "singular place—like a fairy show," where La Franconi had a "chocolate colored chateau flanked by four towers like English privies."

Rosalie is, naturally, costumed as an amazon. Her assistants wear either a semi-military uniform with a forage cap; or a version of the poetic Reform costume seen in the *Fishing Party,* Ill. 2236.

The lady in the taffeta gloves and *capote* carries a cashmere shawl with the white ground which was at first preferred. Her muslin dress is less developed than that of the caller in Ill. 2269; its bodice and skirt are separately cut, but the goring of the back of the bodice has not eliminated all fullness.

2275. XIXc. French. (Metropolitan Museum.)
Aubrey-Lecomte, H., after *Juinne.* Mme. Récamier in her apartment.

Although this print was produced in 1827, it shows Madame Récamier in the style she made her own in first decade XIXc. Empire room with a rosebush growing in a newly excavated antique urn.

2276-79. XIXc. 1806. French. (Metropolitan Museum, Print Room.)
"Costumes Parisiens," (periodical).

2276. "Flower decorated comb; ball dress; *palatine* edged with martin."

2277. "Straw *capote;* little Scotch plaid fichu; walking dress."

2278. "*Capote* with a crown of puffs; Bagnières shawl."

2279. "Yellow straw hat, tied with an organdie fichu; dress trimmed with little tongues of cotton material."

In these four fashion plates, the new trends announce themselves. Hem trimmings have been used on gowns throughout the Classical Revival. Although any of the forms is likely to be seen at any part of the period, the trend of trimming has been a deterioration of fringe into pleating, and of pleating into gathered ruffles.

The Classical gown first lost its repetition of vertical lines in its front fullness. Pleats were massed in back and kept vertical by the weight of dragging trains; this is the time at which hems were least decorated (2266, 2280). By a new impulse, trains begin to be cut off; skirts are shortened, and pressure from the back fullness makes hems flare at the side. This new horizontal line is emphasized by ruffles and lines of notched Gothic decoration at the hem. There is a sash around the waist; the round neckline begins to turn square. More lines are cut across the body by the new short capes. The ubiquitous narrow scarf becomes squarer, and is often carried for its color, rather than worn. The bosom is still exposed, but a handkerchief is knotted about the throat or a sheer cape falls in tiers from a *fraise*.

Classical purity begins to degenerate; combs are decorated with the little bouquets which are carried

or fastened onto every costume. Curls fall down the jaw, like the sideburns of men; braids which used to filet the head slip to the forehead in an approximation of the coronet of the Napoleonic court. The classical sandal turns into a laced shoe. Greek and Etruscan patterns give way to Scotch plaids, and locally made shawls (2278) compete with oriental.

2280. XIXc. 1807. French. (Yousoupoff Coll.)
Boilly. Billiard Game.

Billiards is one of the oldest games, but it was for centuries restricted to the very rich. Public billiard halls had been licensed since mid-XVIIc, but the Revolution gave an impetus to life outside the home, and billiards, "which gives at once activity to the limbs and grace to the person" (*Morning Post,* 1809), became very fashionable at the beginning of the XIXc. both with men and women. In an age of wagers on competitions of all sorts: cocking, bull-baiting, prize fights and horse races, billiards became the favorite betting game.

Beautifully established women were another aristocratic luxury, like fine food, which the Revolution made available upon occasion, to anyone who had the price. A series of extremely elegant and business-like prostitutes help to take men away from home in XIXc. Women, curious rather than jealous about these superbly dressed and emancipated legendary creatures, also go to public places, hoping to catch a glimpse of them. (See Appendix.)

A delightful early photograph shows a gentleman of the 50's playing billiards with four cocottes who are inmates of a very grand establishment.

The whole family, including the children and dogs, goes to the billiard parlor. Mothers and grandmothers keep on the mob caps and fichus of middle age and domesticity. The gowns worn by the young girls have reached their highest point of arrogant, completely untrimmed nakedness. They are worn with a minimum of underwear; trains drag out the lines of the longest young bodies ever exhibited. But the costume, though provocative, is still dewy-fresh, uncontaminated by the shame which is about to emerge and alter it.

Hair has grown prettier; it is twisted, rather than braided and bound, into Greek knots which end in loose curls; the hair about the forehead, which was at first jaggedly fringed, then frizzed, now falls in pretty corkscrew curls.

**2280A-2281. XIXc. French. (Met. Mus., Print Room.)
Print Room.)**

"Le Bon Genre," (periodical).

The "Bon Genre's" first edition, 104 plates, appeared in 1817. The 1822 edition included eleven additional plates; a third edition was published in 1827. Its illustrations are lively and witty statements of the life of Paris since the beginning of XIXc., with a text of explanatory paragraphs, rather than fashion plates.

2280A. Lingerie bonnet-makers (1807).

2281. Grisettes getting ready for bed (1807).

These sewing girls in workshop and dormitory have learned to make clothes for themselves, as charming as the quilted capotes they turn out for the customers (2364-68). The folded scarves, colored and fringed, which they wear about their shoulders, have become the uniform of working women. They are warm and gay, and are tied around the cap to protect it in bed or out of doors, where the lower bourgeoisie (into the XXc.) do not wear hats. The deviations from the persistent cap of working women, shown in Lanté-Gatine plates of 1825, advertise wares which the hat-seller and artificial hair worker provide for their customers. Aprons, worn by working women with simple dresses of plain or printed cotton, begin to be carried up onto the bodice in bibs; but working women long retain the high waistline because of the convenience of the bibless apron set under the armpits. Hems are trimmed with narrow lines of embroidery, or braided, corded, scalloped or ruched.

The necklines of these working girls, like those of the upper classes, tend to be filled in or covered by *fraises,* multiple capes or standing ruffs. One works in long taffeta gloves, the fingers cut away to make mitts. Front laced shoes, strapped and tied slippers, heelless mules at bedtime.

**2282. XIXc. Aug. 22, 1807. French. (Versailles National
Museum.)**

J. B. Régnault. Marriage of Jerome Bonaparte and Catherine of Württemberg.

2283. XIXc. c. 1807. French. (Versailles National Mus.)

A. J. Gros. Catherine, Queen of Westphalia.

2284. XIXc. French. (Rome, Prince Scipione Borghese.)

F. P. S. Gérard. Prince Camille Borghese.

Some of Napoleon's siblings had married as they wished, before he was in a position to control their choice. He arranged marriages for the rest, and a magnificent one for himself, and set his family on the thrones of Holland, Naples, Westphalia, Spain and Tuscany between 1806-8. The costume of these courts was that of Napoleon's.

His gay and beautiful sister Pauline, widow of Gen. Leclerc, was married in 1803 to Prince Borghese. She soon left him and Rome, but friction with the new Empress sent her from the Paris court in 1810.

Jerome Bonaparte, returning from the West Indies by way of the United States, fell in love with a Miss Patterson of Baltimore and married her in 1803, when he was nineteen. Their marriage was legal in the U. S. A., and the Pope refused to dissolve it. Napoleon excluded his brother's wife from his empire; she went to London where she bore the son from whom the Bonapartes of Baltimore are descended. The marriage was annulled by imperial decree and Jerome was made King of Westphalia on his marriage to the Princess of Württemberg. Their daughter was the Goncourts' adored Princess Matilda, the center of a circle of the greatest literary men in Paris from 1850. Marcel Proust offered to act as her secretary for the memoir he could never persuade her to write, before she died, very old, in 1904.

In England, where court life had not been interrupted by Revolution, the hoop continued to be required in women's official dress. The attempt to combine contemporary fashions with hoops, and to drape an Empire dress, somehow, over a hoop that now had to start at the armpits, became so ridiculous that the use of hoops was abandoned in 1820. (See Appendix.)

The traditional cutaway frock coat continued to be worn at the English court, together with waistcoat, knee breeches, buckled shoes and sword. The coat was simple and untrimmed and followed contemporary fashions with proper dignity.

Napoleon needed for his Empire a gorgeous court costume which should be totally divorced from that of the previous regime.

He borrowed some usages from the great days of the XVIIc.; the ruff, *rabat,* rosetted shoe and plumed hat, for men. Rank was rigidly indicated by neckwear and by the amount of massive embroidery. The Emperor's costume was set apart from that of his gorgeous court by its ostentatious simplicity. His brothers' and brothers-in-law's garments are stiff with embroidery; Napoleon's coat has only the simple laced seams of the XVIIc.; he wears a plain, sheer cravat, negligently knotted, in place of their lace ruffs and *rabats.*

The men wear a slender velvet tunic or cutaway coat, reaching almost to the knee, blazing with metal in oak, laurel or palm leaves, and sun rays. It has a high standing collar, close sleeves and a sash about the waist, from which the sword hangs: a matching circular cape with an important collar; knee breeches, silk stockings and rosette-trimmed pumps.

A collar of toothed lace, like that of the XVIIc. wired ruff, is added to the contemporary white classical gown of women. Its neckline is cut square across the front; it has short puffed sleeves. The Empress' arms are bare; her ladies wear long gloves or have an additional close sleeve to the waist. The whiteness of the dress is made impressive by elaborate silver embroidery about the hem and narrow lines of vertical embroidery running up to the waistline. A narrow court train of brilliant velvet (flame, green, purple), lined with white and blazing with a border of silver embroidery, is fastened around the high waist, with a medallion closing at the center front in Napoleonic leaves, Etruscan and Egyptian patterns, (see Ill. 2253.) A glittering diadem, matching comb, earrings, and necklace accompanies the court gowns. A great many of these complete *parures* of diamonds, amethysts and other cut stones, are still to be seen, in the case specifically made to hold and display them. French court costume retained this whiteness through the last court of Eugenie, although the gown altered with the fashions.

The Queen of Westphalia's riding dress shows a combination of Napoleonic embroidery at its hem; a XVIIc. bonnet with the brush decoration which the wars of XVIIc. introduced from eastern Europe; together with lines of ermine which on the sleeve approximate XVIIc. slashings, and on the chest the horizontal braided decorations of the uniforms of XIXc. Hungarian mercenaries (which affect men's, women's and boys' coats in first half XXc.).

2285. XIXc. 1808. French. (Metropolitan Mus.)
Ingres. Lady and boy.

Drawn in Rome, with the Villa Medici and the Trinitá del Monte in the background (detail).

2286. XIXc. 1809-10. French. (Met. Mus., Frick Coll.)
David. Comtesse Daru.

2287. XIXc. 1812. French. (Germantown, Henry P. McIlhenny.)
Ingres. Comtesse de Tournon.

2288-92. XIXc. 1808-9. French. (Met. Mus., Print Room.)
"Costumes Parisiens" (periodical).

2288. *"Cornette* of embroidered muslin. Robe of *toile de Jouy."* The *cornette,* worn for day or evening, is a cap derived from a triangle. It is tied under the chin, and, in this case, also has "horns" fastened back over the crown. More figured materials, now in darker colors.

2289. "Glossy hair dressed with flowers. Decorated tulle robe."

2290. "Cossack attire."

Classical overdress turning into a long, coat-like overgarment, in which vertical lines and front closing are maintained, as in redingotes; these dresses are usually called "Circassian" or "Russian."

2291. "Coat with a single row of buttons. Leather breeches." Men's coats and women's gowns follow the same impulse toward lowered waistlines. Black hat; beige-gray coat; hose and white striped vest; white breeches; black boots with tan tops.

2292. "Hair dressed in braids. Corset *à la Ninon."* Gillray's *Progress of the Toilet,* Plate 1 (2295) shows the English corset of 1810 to be long and lank, extended below the buttocks. The French corsets define the new, longer, but much more closely laced waist; and are cut shorter, since skirts begin to spread into gores.

In 1802, "the celebrated Madame Récamier . . . created a sensation, partly by her beauty, but still more by her dress, which was vastly unlike the unsophisticated style, and *poke* bonnets, of the English women. She appeared in Kensington Gardens, *à l'antique,* a muslin dress clinging to her form like the folds of drapery on a statue; her hair in a plait at the back, and falling in small ringlets around her face, and greasy with *huile antique;* a large veil thrown over her head, completed attire, that not unnaturally caused her to be followed and stared at."

(Countess of Brownlow: *Slight Reminiscences of a Septuagenarian,* London, 1867.)

Under the influence of *huile antique,* the hair on the crown of the head becomes smooth, and is parted rather than drawn back. The fringe at the forehead is artfully arranged in little scallops and curls, which are glossy with oil. The fringe is becoming massed at the forehead in a bunch (2289), which follows the crown's tendency to become parted (2286, 2287). Little clipped tabs of hair (2290) commemorate the loose locks which used to fall at the ears (2279). Ears become uncovered, and the old dangling lock is commemorated by drop earrings (2286). Braided wigs (2292) and flowers (2286), arranged around the low line at which the court diadem had been set, begin to be abandoned; hair arrangements become more stylized, less decorated; and bunches of curls again begin to obscure the ears (2287).

The supremacy of unadorned, white, vertical dress is ended.

The skirt continues its transition into a ∧-shape, as its hem-line is reinforced by more ruffles, bands, zig-zag decorations and ruchings. The front panel of (2289) has taken its outline from the vertical lines of embroidery on the court skirt, but its net trim carries the eye from center front towards the shoulders and the side seams of the hem. The vertical lines of embroidery have begun to disintegrate in other ways. The motifs which composed the lines separate and move to right and left; all-over patterns result (2294); these become common on the new colored cottons (2288, 2290). Dark satin and velvet are used for ceremonious dresses (2287). The neckline is still wide and horizontal, but the low V-opening (2287) announces itself in the triangular *pelerine* collar of (2288); and in the diagonally folded square scarf, and the chain ending in a pendant just at the center-front of the belt of the plump Roman lady (2285).

This line will become extended into the widest shoulders ever seen, in the 30's, over leg-o'-mutton sleeves. The Countess Daru's bodice is short and square-necked; horizontal folds are already forming above the belt; and the eye is drawn to the shoulders by the crumpled subdivisions of her puffed sleeve; other short sleeves are finished with bows (2288, 2289). Then we see the waistline lengthening, and the fabric above it rucked up into deliberate folds, which are extended into the fullness of subdivided sleeves. In the gown of Madame Le Blanc (Ill. 2342) the fullness is drawn up under a corded center line which stresses the new impulse to separate the breasts.

There is an impulse to raise necklines and lengthen sleeves (2287, 2288, 2290). The standing ruff of lace on the court gown plays a part in forming both the new V-neck and the notched, toothed, or zig-zag lines of Gothic decoration (collar and cuffs in 2290; *palatine,* 2288). The "Stuart" or "Vandyke" ruffs are moved to the new, high-necked, long-sleeved dresses (2288, 2290). To some extent, the ruff replaces the *fraise,* and the long sleeve takes the place of gloves; it is trimmed at the wrist with lingerie cuffs (2290) or ribbon bows and ruching (2287**).**

The transition of lace, back into the fabric from which it originated, continues, largely in the form of eyelet embroidery.

Necklaces change character, become more massive and drop lower. The old multiple fine chains, looped to a few medallions, turn into a series of linked flat ovals of decreasing size (2282, 2286), classical medallions are replaced by cut, colored stones, often amethyst or topaz, surrounded by pearls; these in turn become outmoded as necklines rise. The old bead choker or chain grows longer and indicates the centre-front of the belt by its cross or enamelled pendant (2289). Chains increase in length and are looped up again to the watch pinned to the belt (2342).

2293

2295

2294

2293. XIXc. 1809. French. (Metropolitan Museum, Print Room.)

P. Debucourt. The Dance Mania.

The belt has momentarily become interesting; it is elaborated into corselets, which push up the breasts, define their separation, make them interesting in a fresh way. Then the corselets are forgotten. Necklines are cut excessively low to exhibit the pair of breasts; shirred up to stress their separateness. On high-necked daytime dresses, scarves are crossed to emphasize the breasts individually (see Ills. 2296, 2300-01).

Very short dancing skirts, garlanded around the hem with flowers in high relief, are much used, 1810-15 (2294). Women's hair sometimes clipped like a man's during first decade. Hair dressed with artificial braids, bouquets, close interlaced caps; bonnets; *capotes* and a hat with a crown of hinged pleats, made of diagonally striped taffeta (seated, doorway). Infantryman and man with immense decorated *chapeau bras.* Folding *lorgnon* used by man in checked vest (background, l.). Exaggerated Jean de Bry coat, with striped breeches (ext. r., foreground).

2294. XIXc. March 13, 1810. French. (Versailles, National Mus.)

Mme. P. Auzou. Marie Louise of Austria taking leave of her family.

Hair dressed *à la grecque* with braids and coronets; or parted into ringlets with flowers.

Ceremonious dress: wired XVIIc. ruff; embroidered all-over patterns; slightly gored skirts; hems edged with lace ruffle, large projecting flowers, or beaded decorations; long gold chains, looped up to a pendant or watch at belt.

Officer in court dress; tasselled Hessian or Suvaroff boots.

2295. XIXc. 1810. English. (New York Public Library, Print Room.)

James Gillray, after an amateur. Progress of the Toilet: Series of three plates. 1. *The Stays.*

2296   2297   2298

2299

The long English corset, which the French ridicule for decades to come, in the "Bon Genre."

2296-98. XIXc. 1811-12. French.

"Costumes Parisiens" (periodical).

2296. "Virginia hat. *Douillette* of Florentine taffeta." Hat crowns rise to accommodate the hair. Trimmings are bold and imaginative; here ribbon is made of strips of the bonnet's straw bound in taffeta. The second decade of XIXc. is rather consecutively cold. The *douillette* is a soft "cuddly" interlined dress, with long sleeves and a high neck; it retains the long front closing and untrimmed hemline of the whole *redingote-douillette* series of garments. Its sleeves show sectioning and puffing, which will be released to form full leg-o'-mutton sleeves. Standing collar of embroidered muslin which has completely replaced lace.

2297. "*Bandeau* of diamonds; robe of Lyons silk." Increased use of cut precious stones. Hair massed on the top of the head with tall combs. "Vandyke"

collar now two wired sections, prepared to be bent over in the fantastically projecting wings of the 20's. The looms which Jacquard introduced at Lyons in e.XIX are producing corded and textured fabrics with a minimum of the hand labor which used to be required. The classical-Napoleonic laurel leaves have now become puffed decorations; naturalistic nosegays stuck at intersections of puffing.

2298. Man: plaid cravat; striped vest; coat collar lower, thrusting out from the neck in back; waist longer; skirts less cutaway, fall rather full and short. Breeches, now recognizably trousers, still keep side-closing slit, though it cannot be closed; trousers are not yet strapped under the shoesole. Hair extended along jaw.

Woman: the sleeve seen on the *douillette* (2296) done in corded cotton on a summer dress. Scalloped standing collar and trim of eyelet embroidery which divides the breasts and is set (prophetically, see Ill. 2297) around the armseye. Tucked hem. Eyelet embroidery sash and handkerchief. When flowers are used to trim summer hats, they are like these sprays of lilac, as bold as the straw braid or feather trimmings; the character of flowers on gauzy evening garments is entirely different (2297).

2299. XIXc. 1811. French.

"Le Bon Genre" (periodical). Guessing the Kiss.

The neat braid-trimmed wigs, which came to be set over women's clipped heads and hanging locks of the first five years of the XIXc., result in natural hair, neatly and carefully dressed, smoothed and coiled. Pretty domestic dresses with necklines widened by crossed scarf and sleeves given new importance by cap or ruching around armseye.

Familiar man's dress with velvet collars.

2300   2301   2302

2301A

2300-01A. XIXc. French. (Metropolitan Museum, Print Room.)

"Costumes Parisiens" (periodical).

2300. "Open-work straw hat. Percale dress." (1812)

2301. "Hat of *gros de Naples*. Dress and pantalettes of percale." (1813)

"Women's drawers in e.XIXc. (as shown in Gillray's *Progress of the Toilet,* Ill. 2295) were knit knickers of cotton or wool. Ankle-length lingerie pantalettes came to Paris with the English fashions for active little girls, c. 1807. Their embroidered ruffles were sometimes also seen under women's short dresses, c. 1809-17. Drawers do not appear to have become an established part of women's dress until late first third XIXc. (P. Dufay: *Le Pantalon Féminin,* 1906.) Little girls wore pantalettes for about the first two-thirds of XIXc., but by 1860 they had grown shorter and plainer.

Both the girl and woman show standard summer dress: brightly colored hat of straw or taffeta; the bold outline of its high crown and curved bonnet-like brim is never confused by the imaginative trimmings, which usually give it emphasis. *Gros de Naples* is a corded silk. Lace, when made out of straw, has a character which accords well with the eyelet embroidery with which dress hems are trimmed. Colored scarf, crossed to emphasize breasts individually, and knotted in back.

2301A. "Hat of uncut velvet. Merino *redingote.*" (1813)

Textured materials (gros de Naples, lace straw, seen above) are preferred for simply trimmed, boldly designed hats, like this exaggeration of the plumed uniform hat of the infantryman, done in uncut velvet which has the texture of Turkish towel-ling. The triply collared English coat which has been in use for thirty years, is shorter and has a standing collar and ruff, and a greatly enlarged upper sleeve.

2302. XIXc. 1814. French.

Ingres. Seated Lady.

High smooth hair arrangements in braids and loops at the crown force the high crowns of the hats seen in the fashion plates above. Increasing importance, elaboration, and height of the collar; diagonal closing of bodice, influenced by crossed scarves (above). Sleeve much wider and fuller at shoulder.

2303. XIXc. 1812. French. (Versailles, National Mus.)

F. P. S. Gérard. Joachim Murat, King of Naples.

The arrogant male beauty and magnificent uniforms of one of the most brilliant of all cavalry leaders, Napoleon's companion-at-arms and brother-in-law, helped to establish his popularity as King of Naples in 1808, succeeding Joseph Bonaparte. In 1812, he is the commander of the Grand Army and is not yet quite involved in the network of treachery—his own, Austria's, and England's, which will bring him to his death in 1815. His sons lived and married in the U.S.A.; one was postmaster of Tallahassee, Florida; the other returned to France and recognition by Napoleon III during the Second Empire.

The incomparable cavalry, which Matthias of Hungary had established in XVc. to fight the Turks, spread as mercenaries and made their own hussar uniform the cavalry uniform of all European armies: a fur busby with a high brush; braided jacket; loose fur dolman hung on the left shoulder; hussar boots with tassels.

Men, women and children borrow from this idea-filled costume during first half XIXc. Especially during the period of the Napoleonic cavalry's most brilliant achievement, 1806-15, civilians wear fur-lined coats with frogged and braided chests; fur hats; breeches decorated on the thighs along the front flap opening by hussar patterns in braid, or in quilting which was very effective on leather. The braided outseam of today's dress trouser is a remnant of the hussar uniform.

2304. XIXc. 1814. French. (Versailles, National Mus.)

A. J. Gros. Duchesse d'Angoulême.

Louis XVI's daughter, the most important woman at court after her uncle's accession, shows the court

2303

2305

2304

2306

costume of Louis XVIII to be simply a development of that established by Napoleon.

The ruff has been flattened into a wide collar; sleeves are enlarged and elaborated; fabric of the bodice gathered up above the belt; increase of all-over embroidery; ermine-lined train.

2305. XIXc. 1815. French. (Versailles, National Mus.)

French School. Lazare Carnot.

The great military engineer who had voted for Louis XVI's death, offered his services to Napoleon during the Hundred Days (Spring of 1815). He defended Antwerp and was made a peer (as we see him in Napoleonic court costume) just before Louis XVIII's second restoration, upon which he emigrated to Germany. His son was an eminent French statesman; his grandson a president of the Third Republic.

2306. XIXc. 1818. French. (Versailles, National Mus.)

Théodore Géricault. Louis, King of Holland, and his son, Napoleon III.

First Empire dragoon uniform, so short-waisted that a vest must be worn with it. Hussar's uniform with braided pattern on the thighs, which are appropriated to civilian use.

2307

2307. XIXc. 1812. Scottish. (Edinburgh, National Gallery.)

Raeburn. Col. Alastair Macdonel of Glengarry.

Fashion felt the impact of Scottish national dress when it began to appear among the frock coats of the English court. Reforms in Scottish representation increased the number of tartans seen in England and their influence on fashion, after 1833.

Clan costume was a relatively late development, scarcely known before the XVIIc. Before 1600, the Gaels of Scotland "wear, like the Irish, a large and full shirt, coloured with saffron, and over this a garment hanging to the knee, of thick wool, after the manner of a cassock." (N. d'Arfeville, cosmographer to Francis I, after visiting Scotland in late XVIc.)

Moryson, who gives a great deal of information about the dress of both sexes and all classes in city and country, in both Ireland and Scotland, found the Irish in the "remote parts," c. 1600, going naked except for a cloak; the shirts of the rest of Ireland were "coloured with saffron to avoid lowziness, incident to the wearing of fowle linen." Standards of cleanliness were notoriously low in Scotland as well, but by Moryson's time, country men and "inferiour citizens" in Scotland wear "cloakes made of a course stuffe of two or three colours, in Checker worke, vulgarly called Plodan. Husbandmen" wear "gray or 'skie' homespun and blew caps very broad," he says, apparently trying to make the necessary differentiation between the dress of Highland and Lowland Scots.

The clan badge, which long antedated the tartan, was a sprig of some common plant, usually evergreen, like the oldest badge—the boxwood of the MacPhersons, holly, hawthorne, broom, yew, myrtle, club-moss; or a common flower like sunflower or foxglove.

The tartan, peculiar to the Highlands, seems to have begun as a regional distinction, and to have become differentiated between clans—men of the same name and blood, from the patriarchal chief down to his least vassal, using the same tartan, badge, and war-cry. Tartans became elaborated among clans: the chief's tartan, worn by him and his heir; the common tartan; and dress and hunting tartans.

The first clear reference to Highland tartans occurs in the bills for James V's hunting costume in 1538 for *"variant cullorit* velvet to be the Kingis Grace ane *schort Heland coit"* and some *"Heland tertane."* In 1587, Hector MacLean, heir of Duart, paid rent for the island of Islay with 60 clls of cloth in the colors of the Duart hunting tartan.

By e.XVIIc., the saffron shirt was replaced by the *breacan-féile* or belted plaid, and the *féile-beg,* or little kilt. The former was a twelve-ell length of tartan, partly pleated and belted into a kilt, with the remainder carefully draped up over the shoulder, pinned in place there, and allowed to hang down in back. The kilt was six ells long, pleated and crossed over in front; it remains in modern Highland dress, while the long belted plaid has been replaced by a coat and scarf.

Every detail of Highland costume, for all occasions, its accessories and the methods of wearing them, has become rigidly established by convention, and can only be summarized briefly: Blue bonnet, with clan badge and other decorations; scarlet garters, correctly knotted. Doublet with characteristic diamond or lozenge-shaped buttons, made of cloth, velvet, or tartan cut on the bias; kilt; shawl or long shoulder plaid (the latter always removed before entering a ballroom); plain or tartan hose (the pattern again on the bias here). All tartans used in a costume must belong to one clan. In dress use, the dress tartan must be used throughout. Low buckled black shoes; goatskin sporran; claymore and dirk. All belt and shoe buckles, all metal ornaments and mountings, must show identical Gaelic patterns, and belong to a set. Antique muzzle-loading pistol; powder-horn, carried on the right side, mouthpiece forward. (See Appendix.)

2308-09. XIXc. 1814. French. (Metropolitan Museum, Print Room.)
Vernet-Gatine. "Incroyables" (periodical plates).

Horace Vernet's "Incroyables" and "Merveilleuses," engraved by G. J. Gatine, are as good fashion plates as ever were made; the only difficulty is in deciding what to omit. Original captions are quoted in translation.

2308. "Hat with narrow, flat brim. Cravat with colored border. Gilet of matelassé piqué. Short coat with square tails set low. Boots with steel-shod heels."

The black hat now has a narrow ribbon, finished in back by a buckled bow. Red bordered cravat. Yellowish-brown vest of one of the new *matelassé* fabrics. Slate gray coat has a collar, stitched into standing (instead of boned), and therefore able to roll away from the neck, in the new impulse; shoulder seam drawn far down the back; waistline tightened and then prolonged so unnaturally low, with pockets set on the buttocks, that the coat rides up into wrinkles around the waist; cuffs with buttoned closing. Blue-gray breeches; black Hessian boots with small, high, clicking heels (after years of gliding in heelless pumps).

2309. "Breeches and gaiters of natural colored leathers. Cane-umbrella."

Green umbrella, lined with yellow-green. Yellow vest striped in green; highest possible standing collar, self-covered buttons. Vest has grown longer and more tightly fitted at the waist, so that it, too, rides up in wrinkles. Gray coat, matching buttons. Collar rolling back from the neck begins to show the rounded, bosomy curve of the coming era; low pocket-flap, spyglass. The dangling fob has grown uninteresting; seals hang at a buttonhole, through which a heavy link chain runs to the watch pocket. Leather breeches with buttoned side pocket; leather gaiters strapped to breeches.

2310-14. XIXc. 1814. French. (Met. Mus., Print Room.)
Vernet-Gatine. "Merveilleuses" (periodical plates).

2310. *"Capote* of écru percale. Scotch plaid fichu and boots. Percale umbrella."

The light brown *capote* has a brim hinged like a *calash,* in an impulse which we have already seen expressed in the crown of a hat. The *fraise* has been expanded into a flat triple ruff, since the daytime neckline must now be high; the elaboration of the lingerie collar has been moved to the sleeve-cap as its importance grows. The X-sash has grown so wide that it composes the entire red, yellow and green tartan bodice, the closing of which becomes diagonal. Yellow-green gloves; red-edged handkerchief. Notched and tucked lines of decoration mount higher as the skirt is shortened to show red, blue and yellow tartan boot, finished with red and yellow ruffles.

2311. "Velvet hat. Merino *Redingote* lined with astrakhan."

Increasing dominance of the hat; black velvet. Collar of poison-green redingote quilted, in a zigzag pattern, into standing and rolling; lined with lemon yellow. Enlargement of sleeve toward leg-o'-mutton shape.

2312. "Percale *capote* surmounted by a gauze fichu. Percale dress. Lace stockings."

The clean, severe lines of hats and bonnets deteriorate; this shirred crown is tied with a twisted pink and white fichu; the ruffle at the back of the *capote* replaces an important collar. Growing importance of the sash, especially in back, and elaboration of its pink and white ribbon. Increased use of tucks. Pink slipper with white lace stockings.

2313. "Hat *à l'Anglaise*. Spencer *à l'Anglaise*."

Plain English style. Hat with straw lace edge shows the increased mass of the ringlets on either side of the forehead. Pink-on-pink fichu tied around a sort of *fraise*. Long-waisted pink spencer with very long but comparatively narrow sleeves. Green gloves; gray parasol with white fringe; lemon yellow laced boots.

2314. "English hat. Ninon robe."

Wonderful black and white costume. Puffed bodice stresses separation of the breasts and spreads the neckline wide at the shoulders. Fullness is maintained by twisting the sheer crisp ninon of the very long, wide sleeve, and tying it at the wrist.

2315-17. XIXc. 1815-16. French.

"Le Bon Genre" (periodical).

2315. English and French Costumes.

2316. English dress.

A number of "Bon Genre" plates of 1814 and 1815 make fun of English dress. The "disgrace of English women's little flat hats, long lank corsets, and badly cut skirts" can be seen throughout the unsophisticated, dowdy illustrations of *Ackermann's Repository*. The "Bon Genre" (with No. 2315) says it is only necessary to set them beside the contrast of "our Parisiennes" to have a caricature ready-made. The text of Ill. 2316 remarks that a visit to Paris has somewhat improved the appearance of one Englishwoman (r). Her tasselled hat will appear in Ackermann in March, 1816.

The "Bon Genre" delights in caricaturing Englishmen: their long jaws; protruding rumps; uniforms; and extravagantly cut coats—too long, too short, too narrow, or too tight; and their heavily strapped squire's boots, which the French are abandoning after taking them from the English in the first place. The English now offend by a new style, shown on the officer (Ill. 2316, r.): "If one saw only *one* of these Englishmen with pantaloons over boots, one would be tempted to think he had lost his mind or memory, but among these gentlemen it is a general fashion." Within a couple of years, the French and everyone else will wear pantaloons over boots, and continue for decades to do so. It is entertaining to notice how many Paris shops will soon be run by "Mr." or "Mrs.", or be called "La Belle Anglaise."

2317. The beautiful café-keeper.

The Revolution tossed a great many chefs out to fend for themselves. They set up in whatever cellars they could afford at the only trade they knew. Aristocratic food became available, for the first time, to any passerby with the price of a meal. Such food was one of the factors which drew people from home into public places in XIXc.; fine cooking soon became generally assimilated into French existence, and the tradition of wonderful food to be found in unexpected holes-in-the-wall has never quite died out after a hundred and fifty years. But the ex-chef of a prince, prospering as a restaurant-keeper, could soon offer luxurious surroundings as well, which were as great a revelation as his food to the man-in-the-street. The throne on which the café-keeper sits dispensing lemonade had cost 12,000 francs and "passed" from an Italian palace to restaurant use after a bribe of 4,000 francs.

The seated gentleman shows the style which will be current in the 20's: hair combed forward from the crown, and up into a quiff; line of hair continued down the jaw as the collar grows lower to expose it. White collar replaced by a black satin dickey which rises into a rather high fitted collar, all cut from one bias piece or two strips folded over and pinned. Rolling collar, arched wide around the bosom. Wide, sloping shoulders, close-fitting sleeve set on a low armseye. Shaped torso with skirts separately cut, swinging in a curve over the rump, and cut away with a curve at the sides. Long glove-fitting trousers, which will soon be strapped under the elegant black boots, have a braided outseam. Top hat with slender conical crown, and narrow brim which tends to grow wider during the 30's and 40's. Boots show the new, shaped high heel.

Café-keeper's parted hair, sleek against the head, is piled in tall loops, supported by combs, on the crown of the head. Her other customer wears the high-crowned hat required by this hairdress; knotted plaid scarf between *fraise* and multiple cape-like sleeve caps of her *redingote*.

2318-20. XIXc. 1816-17. French. Metropolitan Museum, Print Room.)
"Costumes Parisiens" (periodical).
2318. "Embroidered muslin *cornette*. Morning dress."

The *cornette's* closing under the chin has been elaborated into a *fraise*, since the neck must not be uncovered; and the collar of the dress has been spread wide over the shoulders into a yoke. Shoe toes become long and square as skirts grow longer.

2319. "Hat of silk plush. *Redingote* of *levantine*."
Women have grown so used to keeping cozy during a long series of cold winters, that fashion plates load a large muff and fur-trimmed slippers on a fur-trimmed redingote of the new, twilled sarcenet called *levantine*, during what turned out to be an unusually warm winter.

2320. "Spencer of *levantine*. Percale dress."
The Spencer, with its buttoned sleeves, prophesies the wider shoulder-line and longer waist. Skirt is more gored; its hem decoration tends to become less rigidly horizontal, scalloped or edged with soft flounces; patterns turn from repeated embroidery eyelets to swinging sprays.

Courtesy of Mus. of Fine Arts, Boston, McCormick Coll. (2316); Metropolitan Mus., Print Room (2315, 2317)

2321. XIXc. 1816. French. (Metropolitan Museum, Print
     Room.)
Ingres. Gabriel Cortois de Pressigny.
   Shoulder-length powdered wig retained in ecclesiastical use, but much reduced in front, exposing
the ears.
2322. XIXc. 1815. French. (Metropolitan Museum, Print
     Room.)
Ingres. Hon. Frederic Sylvester Douglas.
2323. XIXc. 1816. French. (London, British Museum.)
Ingres. Sir John Hay and his Sister.
2324. XIXc. 1816. French.
Ingres. Mrs. Vesey and her Daughter.

Ingres' exquisite drawings of these five members
of the English colony in Rome were made possible
by Conté's wonderful new crayons. In the 30's "black-
lead pencils" will sell at 12 a shilling.
   Pencils had been made in Nuremberg by Gesner
in last quarter XVIc. from the newly discovered
English plumbago. XVII-XVIIIc. artists—Simon van
der Passe, Faithorne, Loggan, and the miniature
painters beginning with Hilliard and the Olivers,
had worked with exquisitely sharpened bits of the
graphite. The pencil business of the Fabers of Nuremberg was set up in 1760.

But like so many superior things, really good lead pencils were the result of deprivation and improvisation. When the wars cut off the supply of graphite, Conté of Paris (an artist, chemist, and inventor of the most brilliant virtuosity, who "had every science in his head and every art in his hand") combined clay and graphite in 1795.

Shoulder seams of men's coats are carried far down the back to draw the collar away from the neck. Overlong waistline and sleeves force the material to ride up in horizontal folds (Ill. 2308). Braided and frogged topcoats, inspired by Hussar uniforms.

The extremely high waistlines of 1813-8 are often dramatised, not by a Spencer, but by colored skirts worn with long-sleeved, high-necked white muslin bodices, gathered and shirred on cords like the longer-waisted *canezous* of the 40's.

The English have been twisting India scarves into turbans, as Miss Hay does, for nearly half a century. During XIXc., turbans tend to become made-up headdresses for evening wear. By the 30's they are almost the uniform of matronly mothers, massed along the sidelines at balls, and are scarcely worn by anyone else.

Reasonably plumed bonnets like Miss Vesey's are seen throughout the second decade; as hat brims flatten and spread, at the beginning of the second quarter-century, ostrich is joined by paradise, and both are prolonged and worked into fantastic swooping and swirling twisted forms. Mrs. Vesey wears a veiled *cornette*.

2325. XIXc. 1817. French. (Boston, Museum of Fine Arts, Elizabeth Day McCormick Coll.)

"Le Bon Genre" (periodical). Promenades Aériennes.

Chute-the-chutes have just been built at ruinous expense at the *barrière du Roule* (now the Parc Monceau). One rides three times around two 400-foot chutes, and then comes down a last steep fall from its 63-foot platform. A café spreads through twelve arcades and all the attendants are in uniform.

Men: the newer, narrow-brimmed, straight-crowned hat. Rounded lapels and bosom of frock-coat, now buttoned close at the normal waistline, and again cut away into slender, longer tails. These double-breasted coats, often blue with brass buttons, have extremely long sleeves covering the knuckles (c. 1815-21). The trousers which accompany them are nankeen, or other light yellowish or grayish color, expertly cut, not yet strapped under black boots. Spurs on boots, c. 1815-20.

Women: apron-like *robes en tablier* are seen during the first two decades of XIXc. Spencer with triple rows of buttons, borrowed (without braid, in this case) from the hussar uniform; the same arrangement is common on little boys' short jackets c. 1825.

2326. XIXc. c. 1817. French. (New York, J. P. Morgan.)
Sir Henry Raeburn. Lady Maitland.

Simple, unsophisticated British hair and plain long-sleeved muslin dress; wide, open collar; crossed closing; no color except square scarf.

2327. XIXc. c. 1817. French. (Metropolitan Museum.)
T. Géricault. Alfred Dedrieux.

Children have been dressed in the English way for three decades. Little boys' dress is affected by that of both women and men: parted hair, longer ringlets, very wide-open muslin collar; ankle-length trousers, slit at the bottom, buttoned high (at the line of a woman's bodice, since there is no vest; and laced fabric boots, like a woman's).

2328. XIXc. 1818. English. (Whitemarsh, Pa., George Widener.)
Ben Marshall. Weston Family.

Country clothing: soft, low-crowned felt hats; single or double-breasted coats, loose and comfortable; single-breasted vests; leather breeches and gaiters. Riding habit with cape-collar and plumed bonnet.

The Weston squires dress very much like Surtees' description of Michael Hardey, master of the farmers' hunt, at forty. "Handley Cross" was published in 1843; Hardey had died at eighty, before Mr. Jorrocks was invited to take over the pack; so the clothes described are of e.XIXc. "His hunting costume consisted of a good nut-brown coat, almost matching his complexion, a scrupulously clean white neckcloth, with a large flat-pocketed red waistcoat, patent cord breeches, and mahogany colored topboots. His undress, or home costume was the same with drab gaiters, instead of boots; and his full, or evening costume, ditto, without the gaiters." Well brushed, broad-brimmed hat. Peter, his huntsman, dressed like his master. Other members of the hunt in that day were James Fairlamb, in "a single-breasted plum-coloured coat, with large silver buttons, black boots, and white lambswool stockings drawn over his knees." Stephen Dumpling, the doctor, "dressed in orthodox black, with powder, and a pig-tail, drab shorts and top-boots."

2329-30. XIXc. 1819. English. (Gen. Cowie Coll.)
Henry Alken. "The Real M." series: *How to Qualify for a Meltonian.*

2329. *How to go to cover.*

2330. *How to take the lead.*

Those who hunted with the Meltonian were astonished to learn that "Ben Tally Ho," whose prints they admired, was the pseudonym of one of their youngest members, Henry Alken. Alken was challenged to a duel of prints by Sir Robert Frankland, which led eventually to the six plates of "The Real M." for which Alken also wrote the text, which we quote.

2329. "Be careful, even in your ride to cover, to sit with great apparent ease and grace, however uncomfortable it may be in reality. Let your horse be thoroughbred, and never ride at a less rate than 16 miles an hour. With regard to dress, I shall say but little as I have given the costume as nearly as possible in the following plates, but I must observe that Real Meltonians either are, or affect to be, a very hardy race; they disdain the frock coat used by their forefathers and appear as here represented. I shall not be surprised in the course of another season to see them (if they are not extinct) dressed in silk caps and jackets." The "Lead" shows a rider with his left hand thrust nonchalantly in his breeches pocket. "Let your attitude be extremely careless, but at the same time determinedly singular. However extraordinary the leap may be, never appear to think it of consequence."

2330. The bad sportsmanship of the Meltonian, which led Osbaldiston to withdraw his hounds from the field in protest, is mocked in the "Lead" caption. "Few sporting men arrive at this elevated situation. If, by being well laid in, you have an opportunity of taking the lead, do it at all risks. You must have no more fellow-feeling in fox-hunting than you have in your political career. . . . Should you be called upon to make your appearance before a coroner's jury, you may calculate on the pleasure you will afterwards receive . . . to hear—in an undertone— . . . *That is one of the most desperate riders in the world,* etc. . . . Do something like all this, and you may at last be taken for a *Real M.*"

Top hat crowns spread as the body begins to change form. The over-long, straight coat-body had forced the bosom of the coat upward. Douglas (No. 2322) thrusts his hand into this fullness. As the 20's approach, the torso shortens and becomes rounded. The waist is nipped in, forcing the body into hips and swelling bosom which fills out the loose fabric. The back is curved; the notched collar also becomes rounded and starts to climb back to the neck. Changes show clearly in Alken's profile views, in which the coat keeps the narrow, well-fitted sleeve (often seen 1815-18) instead of approaching the over-long, pushed-up sleeve of the 20's.

The coat is not the only practical feature of English riding dress to be taken over in France; analogous breeches buttoned along the outseam also were

borrowed; and protective panels can be seen on the street-sweeper (Ill. 2331).

2331. XIX. 1818. French. (Boston, Museum of Fine Arts, Elizabeth Day McCormick Coll.)
Debucourt, after *C. Vernet*. Passez-payez.

Getting around the muddy streets of Paris in the rain was a centuries-old problem. With the Revolution and the disappearance of sedan-chairmen, there begin to be prints showing ladies of the 90's being carried pic-a-back over rushing gutters by bare-legged men, for a fee. By 1810, skirts grow shorter, long *pelisse-redingotes* cover muslin dresses, bonnet-like hats protect heads, women wear boots and carry umbrellas. A plank and the steadying hand and wooden shoe of a street sweeper are enough, but he still collects a fee.

A decade before MacIntosh's first waterproof cloth, a street sweeper's neck is protected by a wide hat of beaver felt, his back by a deep "sailor" collar; short loose jacket; scarf wound around the waist as a French workman still wears it; trousers with heavy extra panels set along each leg and tied together in back; sabots.

2332. XIXc. 1818. French. (The Louvre.)
Ingres. Stamaty Family.

Bonnets smaller, brim arched around the face; taffeta folded over the crown; fussier trim of flowers and veils. Smoother hair, parted and braided and looped high on the crown. Neckline and collars spread wide on shoulders; crossed-over collars or ruffles; bare neck emerging; shortest possible waistline. Sleeves long and full, wide at shoulders; ruffle-trimmed around the armseye, or covered by projecting collar; tied at the wrist, and elaborated over the hand. Hem decorations narrower and less insistent, corded lines or soft ruffles.

Young boy: collar cuts a wide horizontal line across the shoulders; breeches buttoned to a high waistline; top of costume influenced by women's.

Father and son: double-breasted garments; high notched collars; straight, rugged masculine lines of 1810 rather than the new curves of the 20's. Characteristic trouser of 1818, full and spreading wide below the knees (in fashion plates, this funnelling-out trouser leg of 1818 is often much shorter than that worn by the Stamaty boy).

2333. XIXc. c. 1820. French. (Chantilly, Conde Museum.)
Boilly. Checker game at the Café Lamblin.

Male costume is becoming softer, longer, and more curved; as it loses masculinity, moustaches appear to assert maleness. Lapels roll and are rounder; coat fronts and tails are cut with swinging curves, and are longer, with tails falling to the knee or below. Sleeves have a soft, graceful leg-o'-mutton shape, and narrow toward the wrist, from which they spring wide again over the knuckles.

Mixed company and styles: old gaffers in breeches and buckled shoes, with a nightcap to keep draughts off a bald head. Man with huge umbrella wears a hat left over from the Revolution. Workmen in the identical cap, loose short jacket and neckcloth which French workmen wear today.

Pretty girl at the counter makes change by the light of a shaded oil lamp. These became practical when chimneys were added in XVIIIc., and are now common; a hanging lamp is being lit above the company by a match. Gas lamps were first used in street lighting in the 1790's. The smell was so bad and the method considered so dangerous that the use of gas, even for outdoor lighting, was ridiculed and opposed by Sir Humphrey Davy. Lamps using animal or vegetable oil were preferred for indoors, long after gas had come into use in large buildings like foundries and breweries. The gas lamp installed in Ackermann's Fine Arts Repository in the Strand in 1810 (when the Gaslight and Coke Company finally succeeded in getting a charter) made a sensation. There is a legend that "a titled lady was so pleased with the light at Ackermann's that she wanted to take it home with her in the carriage." (Ashton.)

2334. XIXc. 1818. English. (Metropolitan Museum, Print Room.)
Rowlandson. The Last Jig, or Adieu to Old England.

English sailor costume: round, low-crowned hat; short, straight, square-cut jacket, with double rows of buttons, and small lapels; knotted cravat; loose short breeches over another pair of close knee-breeches; buckled shoes. Low companions smoking the vulgar pipe.

XIX CENTURY ENGLISH CARICATURISTS AND ILLUSTRATORS

With Thomas Rowlandson (1756-1827) begins the great line of English caricaturists and illustrators of the XIXc. Rowlandson worked for Ackermann, both as a magazine and book illustrator: *Microcosm of London,* (1810); *Dr. Syntax* series (1812-22); *Vicar of Wakefield* (1817); *World in Miniature* (1821-27).

James Gillray (1757-1815), unbridled satiric plates.

Robert Dighton (1752-1812), an excellent caricaturist, (and a discriminating print collector who stole regularly from the British Museum for a dozen years before he was caught) and his son Richard (fl. 1800-27).

Henry Alken (1784-1851), described by Christopher North as "a gentleman, who has lived with gentlemen . . . feels the line that separates the true old *domini terrarum* from the *nouveau riche,* (and) not only can do what Cruikshank cannot, but he can also do almost anything that Cruikshank can." Principally, between 1813-44, he produced series of hunting and sporting prints, sketch books, sporting scrapbooks, illustrations for the *National Sports of Great Britain,* which were sold by subscription to the country gentry by travelling book agents; and Nimrod's *Life of a Sportsman,* 1842.

Isaac Cruikshank (1756?-1811?), and his sons, Robert (1789-1856) and the great George (1792-1878 often worked together. The sons together illustrated Pierce Egan's *Life in London,* and George, Dicken's *Boz.*

"Phiz" (H. K. Browne, 1815-82) was Dickens' illustrator from *Pickwick* (1837) onwards. John Leech (1817-64) worked for *Punch;* illustrated Surtees: *Handley Cross* (1854). C. S. Keene (1823-91) was the other leading illustrator for *Punch.*

2335. XIXc. 1818. French. (Metropolitan Museum, Print Room.) *Horace Vernet.* Stage Coach.

"Many alterations have lately taken place in the building of carriages. The roofs are not so round. . . . The circular springs have given way to whip springs. . . . No boots are now used, but plain coachboxes, with open fore ends. . . . During the last summer ladies were much oftener seen travelling seated on the box than in the carriage." (*The Times,* London, 1803.) On this pleasant day the stuffy interior is used for the dogs.

Young bloods, sitting on the box, began to tip the coachman into letting them handle the reins. Many became as skillful as professionals, and "Tommy Onslow," later Lord Cranford, used to wear the hayband leggings with which coachmen kept their legs warm. The Whip Club (which became The Four in Hand), Barouche Club, Tandem Club, and others, were formed, each with its distinctive uniform.

At the meet of the Four in Hand Club in Cavendish Square in 1809 (*Morning Post*) the members wore a blue (single-breast) coat, with a long waist and brass buttons, on which were engraved the words: "Four in Hand Club." Their waistcoat was of Kerscymere (a twilled fine woolen cloth of a peculiar texture) ornamented with alternate stripes of blue and yellow; small clothes of white corduroy, made moderately high, and very long over the knee, buttoning in front over the shin bone. Boots very short, with long tops, only one outside strap to each, and one to the back; the latter were employed to keep the breeches in their proper longitudinal shape. Hat with a conical crown, and the Allen brim (which even Ashton, in his *Nineteenth Century,* could not identify); box or driving coat, of white drab cloth, with fifteen capes, two tiers of pockets and an inside one for the Belcher handkerchief; cravat of white muslin spotted with black. Bouquets of myrtle, pink and yellow geraniums were worn. In May of the same year, the club buttons had already gone out of fashion, and, "Lord Hawke sported yesterday, *as buttons,* Queen Anne shillings; Mr. Ashurst displayed crown pieces."

2336. XIXc. 1818. French. (Metropolitan Museum, Print Room.) *Géricault.* Boxers.

Boxing was an XVIIIc. sport which grew in popularity as swords ceased to be worn.

Two men are mainly responsible for its rise to favor with the aristocracy. Jack Boughton (1705-89) who invented the boxing glove (for use in practice only), formulated the rules of the ring, and ran the amphitheatre in the Tottenham Court Road until 1750; and John, "Gentleman Jackson" (1769-1845) who made boxing agile and scientific. His pupil, Lord Byron, said Jackson had better manners than those of "the fellows of the College whom I meet at the high table." Both were on intimate terms with the most distinguished men of their time. John Gully, the prizefighter, was George IV's page, and became M.P. for Pontefract.

Prize fights were always fought with bare fists, pickled into toughness; fighters wore their hair long, until Jackson caught Daniel Mendoza, the Jewish fighter who owned the Lyceum, by his hair in 1790. Boxing was still a combination of wrestling and other methods; a round lasted till a man was knocked down. The fight ended when one man was unable to come to the middle of the ring when called.

The decline of boxing socially has already begun by 1818, but Géricault shows two immortals: Tom Cribb and his Negro opponent, Thomas Molyneux. Cribb wears high, loose gaiters and Molyneux, half-long breeches buttoned over striped stockings. As the coat begins to be curved in, the shape of the top hat develops swinging lines also.

2337. XIXc. c. 1820. U. S. A. (Washington, Nat. Gall. of Art, Mellon Coll.)

John Lewis Krimmel (1787-1821). Artist and family.

It would be hard to find more touchingly simple, pretty, appropriate clothes than are worn by the Krimmel family and doll.

The dressing of the little girls' parted hair with ribbons and braids is differentiated with as much loving taste as are their plain little dresses by a colored piping or yoke, bias band or scalloped hem. The women have made trimmings for their dresses from the fabric of the gown, shirred, or corded and braided; each *cornette* cap is exquisitely right.

The skirts of men's coats are only just beginning to be cut separately from the body. When, as in the case of the Krimmel men, this has not yet been done, the long, enclosing skirts of the single-breasted coat of 1818-20 fall rather straight and plain; the collar rolls; the sleeve is easy but not full at the armseye.

Mrs. Krimmel may have tailored the men's coats herself, as many a wife did in America in 1820. I think she did. It is quite impossible for any two people to put in a row of pins in the same way; anyone who has worked in a big dressmaker's or theatrical costume shop can recognize the work of different fitters. Every garment in this picture has the look of being very carefully made by a woman: one woman, or perhaps the accustomed joint work of two.

Mr. Krimmel: olive green coat. Son: gray-blue coat, black vest, fawn breeches. Mrs. Krimmel: red dress, with rose belt and bow under chin.

L. to r.: Girl in yellow dress, piped in red. Grandmother: *cornette* with striped rose and silver ribbon, brown dress, black apron. Girls: lavender hair ribbon, blue dress; black; cream dress with rose yoke; girl between her and mother: olive green dress, rose hair ribbon.

2338. XIXc. c. 1821. French.
Trade Card of *Mme. Lenormand.*
2339-41. XIXc. French.
"Costumes Parisiens" (periodical).
2339. "Chemise pleated in back, the invention of M. Styndyk; boneless corset, laced in front. Boots laced on the inside." (1822).

2340. "Gauze hat. Percale dress, corsage *à la Sévigné,* bouilloned sleeves, the hem ornamented with a lace ruffle, *entre deux,* and a band of embroidery." (1824). "Bouilloned" refers to puffing which ripples like the surface of a simmering pot.

2341. "Crepe hat banded in satin folds, ornamented with tufts of lilac. *Redingote* of *gros de Naples* trimmed with braided satin." (1821).
2342. XIXc. 1823. French.
Ingres. Mme. Le Blanc.

The trend turns from pattern towards rounded form. We have watched the appearance of the rounded breasts. Now other body curves begin to be exploited; trimmings no longer lie flat; hair becomes sculptured.

Everything is done to enhance the long plain curve of a sloping shoulder line, as it drops to a lowered armseye. In Ill. 2337, Mrs. Krimmel's shoulder seam is merely corded; in these fashion plates, we see yokes or little shoulder capes and their horizontal trimmings carry the eye towards the enlarged cap of the sleeve.

Wide shoulders help to make the longer, belted waist look small and round. The corset is gored and laced to shape the waist, but is not yet long enough to round off the hips and buttocks. These are indicated, rather than defined, by contrast with a small waist, by more definite goring of skirt seams, and by the aid of M. Styndyk's new chemise, the fullness of which helps to round out the skirt in back.

Hem decorations become much reduced and are set lower, especially on cloth and coat dresses. Trim-

mings stand out from the fabric, as roses have done, for some time on dance dresses.

The fabric itself "simmers" (see note about Ill. 2340), and boils up into puffs. Cloth dresses are trimmed with rows and braids of cord covered with fabric. The trim of lingerie dresses becomes frillier and more puffed; in addition to raised flowers and horizontal lines of puffs and ruffles, we see separate motifs applied; these sometimes reach as high as horizontal trimmings used to be carried. Mme. Lenormand's figure on the left shows a motif taken from a cashmere shawl, carried out in a froth of ruffles. The upper line in which ruffles are applied is often waved (Lenormand. l. figure); toothed edges are being rounded in scallops; color helps eyelet embroidery to rise above the fabric on which it is worked.

Hair no longer falls. It is parted, rolled, braided, and worked into standing loops.

Bonnet-like hats are a little larger; their enclosing round brims become flattened across the top as the shoulders grow wider (No. 2341). Brims are made entirely of pleating (No. 2340); or pleating is set as a lining inside straw brims; it, too, changes character, becomes softer, is gauffered into roundness, or gathered.

2343-59. XIXc. 1821. English. (New York Public Library.)
I., R. & G. Cruikshank. Illustrations for the 1821 Edition of Pierce Egan's *"Life in London:* or the Day and Night Scenes of Jerry Hawthorne, Esq. and his elegant Friend Corinthian Tom, accompanied by Bob Logic, the Oxonian, in their Rambles and Sprees through the Metropolis." (Written in 1812.)

B. Yellow paradise in a red hat, green-blue coat with yellow collar lining, over light green dress.

C. Black hat (like all), white linen and vest, dark blue coat, white pantaloons striped in red, lemon yellow gloves.

Recumbent Man. Malachite green coat, greenish yellow waistcoat, white pantaloons.

D. Blue coat, greenish yellow vest and pantaloons.

E. Yellow straw with red-tipped white ostrich, purple coat and gown, cherry scarf, brown handbag, white gloves.

F. All black.

G. Reddish plum coat with black Hussar braiding, white pantaloons.

H. White plumes, garnet bodice, pale pink dress.

I. Bright blue coat, white linen and vest, pink breeches and stockings.

J. Dark plum coat, dark gray trousers.

K. Green coat, white breeches and stockings.

L. Deep purplish-rose gown.

M. White plumes, pink gown.

N. Yellow-brown bonnet and costume, deep blue scarf.

O. Dark.

P. Dark blue coat, black pantaloons, yellow gloves.

Q. Red and yellow turban, cherry bodice and cloak trimmed with ermine, white skirt.

Courtesy of Metropolitan Museum of Art (2338-42)

2360

2361

2360. XIXc. 1821. English. (New York, Harry Peters.)
Henry Alken. "Sports of Great Britain": Fishing in a Punt.

2361. XIXc. 1823. French. (Metropolitan Museum, Print Room.)
"Costumes Parisiens" (periodical).
"Straw hat. Silk cravat. Cashmere *redingote*. Vest and trousers of piqué."
Light brown straw hat; blue gray coat; red, yellow and green plaid scarf; white vest; blue gray and white striped trousers; blue belt; violet fob and gold seals; black boots.
Male and female outlines alter sympathetically. Men's waistlines curve, and shoulders slope and widen. The sleeve is set farther out and lower; its top, which had become rather smooth, c.1818, is now eased in with more fullness over padding (2361). The lapels are rounded, even on a double-breasted coat (2360). Coat skirts tend to enclose the thighs from c.1818; *redingotes* are worn with vests and trousers as suit coats (2361). Garters are buttoned up to short sporting breeches (2360). Long trousers

have now acquired a buttoned front closing, are strapped under the boot, and probably have side pockets.

2362. XIXc. 1824. French. (Paris, Carnavalet Mus.)
Boilly. "A la santé du roi!"
Boilly's lithograph appears in colored and uncolored forms, under two titles. The version which was published, probably for political reasons, as "A la santé des lurons!" is identical except for inscriptions on door frame and shutter.
Shirts continued to be cut full, with a dropped shoulder and full sleeve, into second half XIXc.

2363. XIXc. 1824. U. S. A. (Philadelphia, Academy of Fine Arts.)
C. W. Peale. The Artist in his Museum.
The skeleton of one of Peale's mastodons shows below the curtain, and part of a lower jaw lies at his feet. Peale himself shows the persistence of the old knee breeches and buckled shoes, worn with a frock coat with velvet collar, on an elderly, conservative American gentleman.

2362

2363

2364-68. XIXc. 1824. French. (Metropolitan Museum, Print Room.)
Lanté-Gatine. Working Women of Paris.

2364. Straw hat seller: Black and green spencer bodice; shoes of light and dark blue; natural color straw hat.

2365. Cook: Red and white striped kerchief headdress, mustard yellow dress.

2366. Woman of the petite bourgeoisie: Red, green and white scarf, light pumpkin yellow redingote, green gloves, blue reticule and umbrella (edged with red and yellow), black slippers.

2367. Artificial hair worker: Black apron, yellow dress.

2368. Lady's maid: Red dress, yellow and green plaid scarf, pale blue shoes.

Superb dressmaking and millinery are becoming save work, but makes it possible to do more, in the same amount of time. They changed the bottom sheet and moved the top sheet down every two weeks, where we change both once or twice a week, and do six times as much laundry. Few of us have got around to realizing that wonderful as an electric mixer is for big jobs, about half the work we do with it can be done as fast with a fork or wooden spoon, which is a lot easier to wash up. It has interested me to realize how insidiously the process has worked during the last twenty-five years of my own life-time. Handkerchief linen, batiste and good crêpe used to be bought by the piece, and kept in a bottom drawer with carefully evolved basic patterns. It seemed perfectly reasonable to have shoes and gloves made to order, together with one perfect tailored suit. Almost everything else was made by hand at one's leisure. Suit blouses had seams hemstitched or faggoted together, cuffs and jabots of exquisitely tucked and pleated linen; they would cost perhaps

2364   2365   2366   2367   2368

the great industry of Paris in 1824. The taste and skill with which thousands of little *grisettes* have become endowed, are reflected in their own dress and in the clothes which their mothers and sisters wear at work and at marketing, twenty-five years before the sewing machine comes into use.

We look the way we do, shopping at the supermarket today, because Seventh Avenue's mass-production of clothing is New York's great industry. Our most eminent dress-making houses are infected by it; their made-to-order departments grow smaller each year. No one today can possibly afford to pay for handwork as fine as these women of a hundred and twenty-five years ago display, and no one thinks she has the time to do it herself. Women, a hundred and twenty-five years ago, were not yet the victims of labor-saving machinery, which at best does not

$125 apiece today, and one had them by the dozens in those days.

The dresses are made of the fashionable mustard and pumpkin yellows; the shoulders are widened by a gay square folded on the bias, the ghost of a Spencer, or bands of color. Their *cornettes* are delightful; and are protected at work with kerchiefs knotted high with all the art in the world. The uncovered head of the little hair worker displays the braids and curls she makes; the others can afford only an artificial curl or two at the edge of the bonnet.

There has seldom been a more comfortable, practical or attractive dress than that of c.1815. These working women have retained its plain, easy sleeve; its high waistline and its hem with low-set horizontal trim, to accommodate the aprons they must wear.

2369. XIXc. c. 1825-6. English. (Metropolitan Museum, Frick Coll.)
Thomas Lawrence. Juliana, Lady Peel.

2370. XIXc. 1826. French. (Metropolitan Museum, Print Room.)
"Costumes Parisiens" (periodical).
"Hats of Italian straw, trimmed with satin ribbon and flowers, organdy *canezous* trimmed with embroidery. One skirt of taffeta, the other of *cotepalis*."

2371. XIXc. 1826. French. (Metropolitan Museum, Print Room.)
"Petit Courrier des Dames" (periodical).
"*Redingote* of *gros de Naples* with bias-cut toothed and bow-knot trimmings. Crêpe hat with flowered gauze ribbons and *blonde*. From the shop of Mme. Mare."
Standing: lavender and black; yellow hat trimmed in black.
Seated: blue and black; rose and black hat, both trimmed with silk lace and with gauze ribbons which were either woven or painted.

2372. XIXc. 1827. French. (Metropolitan Museum, Print Room.)
"Petit Courrier des Dames" (periodical).
"*Longchamps Fashions. Gros de Naples* robe trimmed with a flounce and two rows of *chicorée*. Grenadine scarf. Rice straw hat trimmed with marabou."
Standing: lemon yellow with white sleeves and hat, marabou trimming, yellow shading to orange tips. Red, green and yellow scarf of a sheer open mesh material, usually woven of silk against wool.
Seated: white and blue.

Hat crowns have grown high to accommodate braids and loops of hair on top of the head. As shoulder lines widen, the rounded, enclosing brims of bonnets have been flattened on top. By c.1823, the round bonnet has largely been replaced by a hat with a very wide brim, made of black or violet velvet in winter, or of natural-colored straw or colored crêpe, trimmed with feathers, ribbon loops, and a few flowers. The ribbon stands in knotted loops, allied to the way in which the hair is dressed on the crown of the head. The form and trim of the straw bonnet is commemorated in the way silk lace is carried under the chin (Ill. 2371) and in the trimming on the under side of brims. A great deal of paradise like Lady Peel's is seen during the 20's and 30's. There are also flat velvet berets for day wear, and turbans (often decorated with paradise) for evening.

The *pelisse* is now either gored and fitted to a longer waistline like the *redingote* (2371), or becomes a mantle with arm slits (2369). In either case, its collar (often of white fur) has widened with the shoulder-line of dresses, and is apt to be prolonged into tippet ends in front. As skirts grow wider in the 50's, the skirts of coat and cloak have to be given up; this cape-collar with tippet ends becomes the basis for the typical outer garments of the next period.

The neckline has become established at a horizontal line across the shoulders. The space above is bare, in carriage, dress, or evening gowns; on a *redingote* or *canezou,* it is filled in by a bertha and elaborate, spreading collars.

Horizontal folds across the bodice (No. 2342) have succeeded in forming the horizontal neckline; now they turn diagonal or vertical (2370) to enhance the longer line of the torso. Sleeves are gored or gathered into rounded leg-o'-mutton tops, and now end at the wrists in small neat cuffs, or pairs of important wide bracelets (2369).

The *canezou* collar has been developed into a white shirtwaist with sleeves of its own, worn with a buckled belt over the characteristic checked or plaid skirt. Skirts are sharply gored into a smooth, tight waist in front, and are gathered into great back fullness, supported by pads.

Colors become striking and are used in combination (trim 2371, feathers 2372, skirts 2370). Brilliant checks and plaids are woven (2370) or applied (scarf 2372). Notched decorations and bows become rounder; feathers curl into fat little tips (2372); bias cutting allows toothed decorations to be puffed out (2371), and flounces to be set on in rounded rather than gathered fullness. The edges of scallops are pinked; they have the quality of the marabou trim on 2372; ruchings are frilled like the salad called *chicorée frisée* (2372).

Shoes have long narrow toes, slightly squared and gaiters or gaiter tops of fabric laced on the inside of the foot.

Short gloves are worn with long sleeves and paired bracelets.

2373-79. XIXc. 1825-8. English. (New York Pub. Lib., Print Room.)
Geo. Hunt after *Theodore Lane* (1800-28). The Rival Whiskers.

2373-2379

NERO is to be Seen

A   B   C   D   E   F   G

2380   2381   2382

To the gentleman with the spy-glass (A), the dragoon (B), the short man (C), and the Horse Artilleryman (D), with their jowls and chins surrounded by lush curls, as well as to the chimney sweep (E) and the old girl in bonnet and shawl, the wearers of the straight flowing whiskers (F and G) "look not like the Inhabitants o'the Earth and yet are on 't."

Boots are beginning to disappear, strapped under breeches. The short man wears the full hippy breeches of the 20's, loose about the leg. The taller bewhiskered man shows breeches of the earlier form closer at the knee than below; they retain a buttoned side seam although they are strapped over boots, since such tight breeches could not be got over boots in any other way. Coat skirts are cut

separately to allow a fitted waist, and pockets with flaps are set in the seam to emphasize the jut of the skirts at the hip. The square-cut *gilet* is pointing downward into a vest. Eyeglasses swing from chains around the neck; watches are worn on similar chains, which are run through the top buttonhole of the vest, then to a right hand pocket.

2380-82. XIXc. 1827-29. French. (Metropolitan Museum, Print Room.)

"Petit Courrier des Dames" (periodical).

2380. "Straw hat with knotted plumes. Moiré dress embroidered in silk. From the shop of Mrs. Guay et [*sic*] Paris, Rue de Richelieu No. 55."

2381. "Italian straw hat ornamented with birds of paradise. Robe of embroidered Palmyrienne. Pèlerine

THE BUSTLE !!!

and boa of tulle. From the shop of la Belle Anglaise, Rue de la Paix No. 20."

2382. "Robe of *gros de Naples* cut in three directions, trimmed by a deep flounce with points. From Mr. Burty's shop, Rue de Richelieu No. 89. Straw hat from the shop of Mme. Mure."

With these plates (2380-82) we reach nearly the limit of brilliant color and Gothic trimming, although not quite the limit of distortion of body form.

Shaded orange and yellow plumes are knotted into fringe. A white fabric which is already heavily patterned, like moiré, is embroidered with monstrous blue, yellow-green and purple strawberries, laid on in a serpentine line, and disappearing into full scalloped flounces.

Yellow birds of paradise, knotted with blue and yellow ribbons and long streamers of fancy gauze accompany a gown of a new shot silk and wool fabric, in what Americans would call "Alice" blue, embroidered in white, with huge puffed white sleeves. The beloved streamers of 1825-35 are further carried out in the completely absurd tulle boa. Its alternate, white embroidered in white, has pink and yellow ribbons and belt.

Flowers undreamed of in nature are wired high and veiled in lace, with yards of streaming gauze. Stripes are cut and laid over each other, every which way, in folds and tongues.

Shoes, definitely square-toed, have gaiter-like fabric tops, or cross lacings; they become increasingly

low cut by 1833. Short kid gloves disappearing under the cuff or paired wide bracelets, set with medallions. Small drop earrings.

2383. XIXc. c. 1827-9. English. (New York Public Library, Print Room.)
William Heath. The Bustle.

The *cornette* which she wears while dressing has been as wildly elaborated by bows and wired flowers as the great hat she will wear with her plaid gown; it has the bias-cut hem and skirt decoration set on in overlapping diagonal curves, which is seen in England c.1828-29.

This is probably the most informative picture in existence of the long narrow-waisted corset, and the bustle required by these gowns.

2384. XIXc. 1828. U. S. A. (New York, Harry Peters.)
John A. Woodside (1817-50). Country Fair.

Male dress in rural Maryland; Quaker in round hat and knee breeches (r.).

2385. XIXc. Published in 1844. U. S. A. (Metropolitan Museum, Print Room.)
William Henry Brown (1808-1883). John Randolph (1773-1833).

The old Republican leader, Pocahontas' descendant, who freed his own slaves, had died of tuberculosis more than a decade before this combination of silhouette and lithograph was published. He wears clothing of the 20's, with knee-breeches, stockings and boots, and keeps his handkerchief in the pocket provided in the coat tails, before the days of side pockets in trousers.

2386. XIXc. 1825-30. English. (Metropolitan Museum, Print Room.)

Augustin Edouart (1788-1861). Cut-paper silhouettes, painted ground: The Magic Lantern.

The silhouettes suggest a date c.1826. The elderly gentleman seated with his peg-leg stuck out, still wears a wig; short wide pantaloons, and low shoes with a bow. So does the operator of the magic lantern, whose shirt collar still stands, but is not excessively high. The gentleman to the right has a full, rounded head of hair and coat with a high collar, but the tendencies of the 30's appear in his sloping shoulder, smooth sleeve, long swinging lines and long fitted trousers. The lady has the mounting hair of 1825-30, and the short waist and bell-shaped flounced skirt of England c. 1826.

2387. XIXc. c. 1825. U. S. A. (Metropolitan Museum.)
Chester Harding (1792-1866). Mrs. Thomas Brewster Coolidge.

Mrs. Coolidge wears a favorite English hat of e. 1825, which has a swinging black velvet brim, many plumes, and is worn over a lacy *cornette* which frames the face. Grey *pelisse*-mantle with a small ermine collar, and lemon yellow gloves, all of which appear to be of about the same date.

2388. XIXc. c. 1830. Spanish. (Madrid, Prado.)
V. Lopez y Pontaña. Queen Marie-Christine de Bourbon.

Spanish court costume, after Goya, is accurately painted by Lopez y Pontaña (1772-1850). He shows the wife of Ferdinand VII in a wonderful jewelled *parure:* hair ornament worn with bunches of diagonally-set sausage curls (1825-30's), earrings, necklace, and wide belt; embroidered gown with horizontally pleated bodice-top (1825-30's).

2389-90. XIXc. 1829. French. (New York Public Library.)
"Costumes Parisiens" (periodical).

"Polish *redingote* with interlaced embroidery. Pantaloons of Balkan earth color. Cloth coat with velvet collar. Silk gilet over gilet of piqué. Cashmere pantaloons."

There are excellent plates of men, especially of their outer garments, in the "Costumes Parisiens" of 1828-31.

The Polish redingote, of military inspiration, has a standing military collar; standing collars become a feature of the dress of the 30's. Coat collars and lapels are at their most prominent and rolling, 1825-30; during the 30's, coats tend to close high, often by two rows of buttons, and lapels either jut wide, high on the chest or are suppressed altogether. The jut of the hip, 1825-35, is apt to be stressed by a pocket flap set in the waistline.

Trousers worn over boots are longer and wider than those worn with striped stockings and pumps. The latter type, which has a rather persistently stressed outseam, will prevail; cutting becomes more expert, and the trouser which follows the proportions of the limb (though it may be a great deal wider in actual use than in fashion plates) becomes longer in the 30's, and is usually strapped under the boot.

2391-92. XIXc. e.1830's. German. (Metropolitan Museum, Print Room.)

William Alexander Wolfgang von Kobell (1766-1853).

Pencil and white chalk on blue paper. Sketches of horsewomen:

Classic riding dress of 1830-3; collar grows higher; sleeve tops have reached their ultimate balloon-fullness; skirts begin to be pleated and gathered onto the bodice.

2393. XIXc. c. 1830. French. (Met. Mus., Print Room.)
Achille Devéria. Dumas, père.

The elder Dumas was the son of a Napoleonic general who was himself the offspring of a Santo Dominican Negro woman and a French marquis. When the Goncourts met him at the Princess Matilda's in 1865 his negroid hair had turned pepper and salt, and he had grown enormous, with a moon-like face and the "tiny eye of a hippopotamus, bright, cunning and watchful, even when veiled; his voice was hoarse, his facts flabbergasting, his memory immense"; the "sober athlete of the *feuilleton* and of copy," had no wit, color or nuance, and never touched wine, coffee or tobacco.

In one of Devéria's many lithograph portraits Dumas wears boots with long squared toes and small, low heels, and one of the alternative trousers of the period: tight, widening toward the bottom, and ending well above the ankle. By 1833-4 this trouser will become longer and very wide, shrinking again by 1835. Another pantaloon of the period is so long, that it breaks across the instep as it is strapped down under the boot.

The standing collar of the shirt barely shows above fitted cravat, which is becoming tied with a flat bow. Dumas' vest has the high, standing collar which has reappeared with the 30's, together with a coat collar, which is again carried high in back. This is a preliminary to the wide, very sloping shoulder-line of the mid30's, which will slide into a close, narrow sleeve finished with a small turned cuff. Dumas' shoulder is still narrow; his sleeve still puffed at the top and extended over the hand. Watch on chain around the neck.

The variety of cut and fabric in men's clothes during the 30's defies any brief summary. The *Journal des Tailleurs,* (at Metropolitan Museum Print Room), published from the office of the *Petit Courrier des Dames,* 1830-40, provides not only hand-colored plates of monthly new fashions, but exact patterns, and pages of explanatory text about coats, redingotes, pantaloons, vests, mantles, uniforms, women's riding habits, boys' and girls' clothing, dressing gowns, masquerade costumes, and men-servants' liveries.

Similar information, for the mid-40's, may be found in Joseph Conts: "A Practical Guide for the Tailor's Cutting-Room," Blackie & Son, London (after 1844), which also contains "clerical and forensic" dress, military, naval, and Highland costume, directions for cutting for "disproportioned persons," and liveries for page, footman, postillion, tiger, groom, coachman, and jockey. (M.M.A., Print Room.)

2394-95. XIXc. 1830. French. (New York Public Library.)
"Costumes Parisiens" (periodical).

"Cloth *pelisse* with a shawl collar of velvet, closed by bordered tabs. Coat with velvet collar. Cashmere pantaloon."

The pelisse is brown with a gray collar and brilliant blue-green lining. The coat beneath is bright blue; vest gold and white. The immense white cravat forces the shirt ruffles to lie flat as they are pinned by a brooch. Black pantaloons and pumps; white stockings dotted in black.

2396-98. XIXc. 1834. French. (Paris, Bibliotheque Nationale.)
H. Daumier.
2396-97. "Un rentier des bons royaux, un rentier des Cortes."
2398. Cartoon from *L'Association mensuelle.* "Ne vous y frottez pas."

Fashion plates and fashionable portraits have a wonderful antidote in Daumier: haranguing parliamentarians, bored judges, suspect lawyers with widowed clients, people who live well or badly off their dividends, kings, generals or class-conscious young printers.

Hat crowns are straighter, the brims less curved. Collars, often of velvet, mount high in back and are more important than lapels, as many coats and overcoats close higher, often by two rows of rather closely set buttons. The small figure with outstretched arms shows the velvet-collared, double-breasted tail coat of the 30's, cut across at a line somewhat lower than the fitted waist.

2399. XIXc. c. 1830. French. (Metropolitan Museum.)

Wedding dress: embroidered India muslin.

2399

2400-03. XIXc. c. 1830-35. U. S. A. (Metropolitan Museum, Costume Institute.)

2400. Child's rose and tan changeable silk dress. (c.1830)

2401. White silk wedding dress in fancy weave with moiré stripe (1831-34). Cream-colored blonde lace veil (c.1830).

2402. Hanging on stand: a printed cotton dress with floral pattern on a cream ground (c.1835), found in Maine. Cream-colored silk dress (Viennese 1833-34) of fancy twill with an all-over self-pattern in leaf design.

2403. Tan silk taffeta dress with self-trimming (c.1830), found in Connecticut. Natural leghorn hat.

2400   2401   2402   2403

2404. XIXc. c. 1830. English.
    Pelisse of quilted striped silk.

2405. XIXc. c. 1833. U. S. A.
    Wedding dress: white satin embroidered in white silk.

2406. XIXc. c. 1836-7. English.
    Visiting dress: dark red moiré.

2407. XIXc. c. 1845. U. S. A.
    Brocade dress.

2408. XIXc. Probably English.
Corset: quilted white sateen.

2409 Mid-XIXc. French.
Man's straw hat.

2410. XIXc. (early) English?
Buskins: elastic sided blue kid.

2411-12. XIXc. U. S. A.
Shoes and slippers.

2413

2414

2415

2416

2417

2418

2415. Breeches: white cotton sateen; waist buttoned down center back; drop seat fastened to waist.
2416. Sock: knitted cotton.
2417. Linen shirt.
2418. Shoes: black leather.

2413-18. XIXc. 1837. U. S. A. (Boston, Mus. of Fine Arts.)

Boys' clothing: worn at the age of 5 by Henry Augustus Thompson of Charlestown, Mass. (b.1832-d.1837), cousin of Benjamin Thompson, Count Rumford.

2413-14. Coat: front and back. Black wool broadcloth, black velvet collar, tan cotton fancy piqué attached waistcoat front.

2419. e.XIXc. French or Spanish. (New York, Cooper Union Mus.)

Gloves: white kid, printed and painted in wavy green lines; medallions of Liberty on back, crossing bands with flowers on wrist.

2420. XIXc. c. 1840. Spanish.

Gloves: yellow kid, printed in black; design of ovals; scene of gentleman giving a present to lady seated under a tree (back); chain with links of lozenge shapes and floral forms (wrist); tops scalloped.

2419   2420   2421

2422

2423   2424

2421. XIXc. c. 1820. English?
  Gloves: suede, printed in black; leaf design at thumb piece; country scene with boy and girl (back); three bands with medallions of boys' heads (wrist); inside mark undecipherable. "Patent," with crown and shield supported by lion and unicorn.

2422-24. XIXc. German and Austrian. (Metropolitan Museum.)

2422. French comb, gilt brass and ruby glass beads.

2423. Three German tortoise shell combs.

2424. Sides. Austrian, Salzburg, silver hair ornaments.

2425. XIXc. English.
Floral polychrome: roller-printed cotton.

2426. XIXc. after 1837. English.
Simulated patchwork: printed cotton: medallions from scenes in "Pickwick Papers."

2427. XIXc. 1830. Alsatian Mulhouse.
Wool challis.

2428. First half XIXc. U. S. A. (Metropolitan Museum.)
Patchwork quilt. Calico, and later, silk, from used garments, make quilts invaluable costume documents. A quilt in the Philadelphia Museum, made by daughters who used to work in the shop of John Hewson, the first calico printer to work in

America, undoubtedly contains samples of his work; it would be interesting to eliminate as many of its recognizable imported pieces as possible. Another important quilt in the Staten Island Museum (gift of Miss Yetman) is made up of homespun, obviously locally printed, and undoubtedly the work of the Old Staten Island Print Works, which opened early in second decade, XIXc.

2429. Mid-XIXc. English.
"Giroflé-girofla": roller-printed cotton, purple and mauve on buff.

2430. XIXc. 1830's. French. (Versailles, Nat. Museum.)
C. E. Champmartin. Mme. de Mirbel.
Portrait of a fashionable portrait miniaturist, (wife of a distinguished botanist) who enjoyed the patronage of Louis XVIII in his old age.

2431. XIXc. c. 1835. U. S. A.
J. J. Audubon (1780-1851). Mrs. Anna Cora (Ogden) Mowatt.
Mrs. Mowatt (1819-70) married at fifteen, and three years later went to Europe for some time. In 1845 she wrote a play, *Fashion* (which was delightfully revived in the 1920's by the Provincetown-Greenwich Village Theatre). She then turned

actress, toured America and Europe with E. L. Davenport as her leading man. Her blameless life, charm and intelligence did a great deal to improve the social standing of the profession. The artist is the great ornithologist.

2432-33. XIXc. 1830's. French.
Paul Gavarni. "Les Français peints par eux-mêmes": 2432. *Woman sketching,* 2433. *Chasing butterflies* (detail).
Sulpice-Guillaume Chevalier (1804-66) who signed himself "Gavarni," the brilliant and cultivated satirist of Louis-Philippe's epoch, was born poor,

2432   2433

and began as a fashion artist for *La Mode;* the success of *Charivari* was due to his caricatures, and he became the most prolific and sought-after book illustrator of his day. In addition to those for Sue and Balzac, he made many of the illustrations for "Les Français peints par eux-mêmes." He did a score of series of pictures of *lorettes,* students, and young people's gaiety; then turned to bitter, grotesque denunciations of humanity in general, and family life in particular.

"Les Français peints par eux-mêmes," L. Curmer, Paris, 1840-43, consists of five volumes about Paris, and four on the Provinces. Gavarni, H. Monnier, Gagniet, Cousin and others illustrate articles of hundreds of authors, who describe people of every category; duchesses, sisters-of-charity, actresses, mothers, boarding school girls, midwives; the army, national guard, and even the camp followers; jails and their inmates; occupations as varied as cemetery gardener, sailor, phrenologist, and travelling salesman; the different provinces, with their customs and dress.

As dress in 2430 to 2433 indicates, angularity can no longer be maintained. The width of the costume begins to slip and soften. The wide, level hat brim again begins to curve around the face into a bonnet. The sharp projections of the collar, below a deep yokes, are softened into yoke-shaped cape collars (2433), or are given up altogether (2431, 2432). The sleeve cannot be made any larger, and its decline is foretold. Its fullness begins to slip down the shoulder, as the disappearance of wings brings the armseye into sight; the first inches of the sleeve top are pleated or shirred into the equivalent of the

dropped shoulder into which the bodice of the 40's will be cut. There is a further tendency to reduce the sleeve by tightening the lower arm (2431). By 1836 the *gigot* sleeve will have been demolished.

Mrs. Mowatt shows the transitional skirt, between the gored form, smooth at the hips and full behind and the full round skirt, made of straight lengths sewed together (2430).

As jutting wings, made of the same fabric as the dress, tend to disappear, the lingerie collar on the yoke grows more important; it is sheer and soft, set well down to show the column of the neck (2432).

Mme. de Mirbel's costume shows the simultaneous softening of color and line. The variation which we have seen in the orange-to-yellow feathers (2372) is commemorated in her warm purplish-pink bonnet tied with yellow-pink ribbons. Her short-sleeved white dress is finished with wide, gold-buckled black bracelets. Its tab ends are crossed under a white belt, narrowly lined with orange and blue. Black slippers laced over white stockings.

During the 30's, the hair is often parted on either side, the center section combed back, the sides combed down smooth, turning into locks or ringlets in front of the ears, and the long hair braided, coiled, or built up into loops on the crown (2431, 2432).

The imaginative colored aprons of working girls have begun to be incorporated into dress (2280A-2281). This practical fashion has been taken over in the delaine sketching costume; pretty silk aprons are on their way to becoming fixed in the domestic dress of gentlewomen in the 40's.

2434

2436

2435

2437

2434. XIXc. 1831. French.

"Costumes Parisiens" (periodical).

"Cashmere turban executed by Mr. Alexander. Robe with flat embroidery in silk. Cashmere mantle edged with crushed astrakhan."

2435, 2437. XIXc. 1833. French-English.

"Le Follet Courrier des Salons" (periodical).

This periodical, subtitled "Ladies' Magazine," had both French and English offices. The introductory words of the captions (which we italicize) are in English of a sort. In translating the balance of the text, we have followed the orthography of the period, rather than make it conform to modern usages.

2435. *"Morning-dress:* coiffure executed by Mr. Mariton, Rue St. Honore, 244. Robe of chiné gros de Naples, with a lace guimpe and trimming, from the workshop of Mme. Neuette-Larcher, dressmaker to H.M. the Queen (Rue Vivienne, 4)."

2437. *"Valking dress*: straw hat, crown of gros de Naples, from the workshop of Mlle. Bonté, Rue des fossés Montmartre. Pelerine-mantelet of plain mousseline lined with gauze, from the shop of Mme. Chaigneau-Popelard, Boulevart Bonne-Nouvelle, No. 4."

2436. XIXc. c. 1835. French.

A. Devéria. Mlle. Amigo of the Théâtre Italien.

The smooth sloping shoulder, bare or covered with a guimpe, has become paramount. Peaks over sleeves have turned into widespread smooth collars, which either stress the dropped armseye, or are eliminated altogether.

As outlines soften, so do fabrics and trimmings. Eyelet embroidery and projecting ruffles give way to flat embroideries of silk (2380) which are now applied on the skirt itself (2434). Fabrics are patterned all over in small printed and often indistinctly woven patterns in moiré and chiné silks (2434-35). Lace returns in small patterns; net gloves.

The fullness of the sleeve is being crushed down from the shoulder, and up from the wrist, into a puff set on a dropped armseye.

Elaborately dressed hair, which in 1833 **requires** the services of Mr. Mariton, becomes smoothed down to the ears and simplified by 1835 (2436). Hat brims become smaller and more enclosing; crowns and trimming are reduced in unison with hair.

2438. XIXc. 1833. English. (New York Public Library, Rare Book Room.)

Henry Alken. "Jorrocks' Jaunts and Jollities" by Surtees: Mr. Jorrocks Renounces the Acquaintance-ship of the Yorkshireman.

Robert S. Surtees (1803-64) came of an old Durham family. He helped found, and was the first editor of, the "New Sporting Magazine." In 1833 he wrote for it a series of stories about a sporting cockney grocer, and his adventures with the Surrey Hunt and Stag Hounds, shooting, betting at the Newmarket races, aquatics at Margate, his trip to Paris, and a dinner party at home. It was from these stories that Dickens got the idea for "Pickwick Papers." The collected stories were published in 1838 as "Jorrocks' Jaunts and Jollities," with pictures by *Phiz;* Ackermann republished it in 1843 with fifteen colored plates by Alken. In "Handley Cross," 1843, illustrated by John Leech, we have a continuation of Jorrocks who has now become a M. F. H.

"Jorrocks" is a mine of information about English sporting life and dress, which Surtees differentiates in detail by age and position in life. His trip to France with Stubbs is equally full of fascinating stuff about manners and clothing.

Jorrocks and the Yorkshireman have started on their autumn trip to Paris. We ride with them toward the Channel, learning the colors of all sorts of smart new turnouts, their horses and accompanying liveries. We see how people dress, and pack in hat-boxes, carpet-bags, with the last-minute left-overs done up in a red handkerchief.

The captain of the French mail packet is "dressed much like a new policeman, with an embroidered collar to his coat, and a broad red band around a forage-cap."

Men travellers wear a "sable-collared frockcoat," or "a blue camlet cloak, green travelling cap, with a large patent-leather peak."

Customs-house officials in France are dressed in green coat, white trousers, black sugar-loaf "caps," and have swords by their sides.

Jorrocks runs into Thompson, with "mustachios, in a hussar foraging cap stuck on the side of his head, dressed in a black-velvet shooting jacket, and with half a jeweller's shop about him in the way of chains, brooches, rings, and buttons." The traveller is offered a cigar from a box of "beautiful Havannahs," and promised a clean towel every third day, at the inn favored by the British colony of Boulogne. He flips his Hessian boots clean with his handkerchief, combs out his whiskers, calls on the British consul, who wears green spectacles. (Astigmatism began to be corrected with cylindrical lenses c.1827. Book illustrations are increasingly filled with spectacle-wearers.)

The travellers take a diligence for Paris. The conductor wears "the usual frogged, tagged, and embroidered jacket and fur-bound cap." Among the other passengers are an Englishman in "a dark blue camlet cloak, fastened with bronze lion-head clasps, a red neckcloth, and a shabby, napless, broad-brimmed brown hat"; a "red-trousered dragoon, in a frock-coat and flat foraging cap with a flying tassel";

an Englishwoman "either an upper nursery-maid or lower governess," old and ugly enough to travel alone, dressed in "a black beaver bonnet lined with scarlet silk, a nankeen pelisse with a blue ribbon, and pea-green boots"; and a very well "got-up" Frenchwoman. "Her bonnet was a pink satin, with a white blonde *ruche* surmounted by a rich blonde veil, with a white rose placed elegantly on one side, and her glossy auburn hair pressed down the sides of a milk-white forehead, in the Madonna style. Her pelisse was of 'violet-de-bois' figured silk, worn with a black velvet pèlerine and a handsomely embroidered collar. Her boots were of a color to match the pelisse; and a massive gold chain around her neck, and a solitary pearl on a middle finger, were all the jewellery she displayed."

Mr. Jorrocks, who had "caught a glimpse of her foot and ankle as she mounted," opens up his English-French phrase-book, Mme. de Genlis' "Manuel du Voyageur," and goes to work to pick up the Countess.

She has hung her bonnet from the roof of the diligence and tied a "broad-brimmed cambric kerchief over her handsome lace cap"; she falls asleep on Mr. Jorrocks' shoulder, and the Madonna *front* slips to show her own graying hair. We learn, incidentally, during this part of the trip, that gloves, handkerchiefs, gowns and reticules in Paris have lately been affected by the "giraffe mania."

Alken's illustration above shows a Sunday afternoon in the Tuileries gardens, which is filled with "emigrating English" and "Parisians returned from their chateaux." Mr. Stubbs has "indulged in six sous worth of chairs—one to sit upon and one for each leg—and, John Bull-like, stretched himself out in the shade below the lofty trees, to view the gay groups who promenaded the alleys before him."

"First, there came a helmeted cuirassier, with his wife in blue satin, and a little boy in his hand in uniform, with a wooden sword, a perfect miniature of the father. Then a group of short-petticoated, shuffling French women, each with a greyhound in slips, followed by an awkward Englishman with a sister on each arm, all stepping out like grenadiers. Then came a ribbon'd chevalier of the Legion of Honour, whose hat was oftener in his hand than on his head, followed by a nondescript-looking militaire with fierce mustachios, in shining jack-boots, white leathers, and a sort of Italian military cloak, with one side thrown over the shoulder, to exhibit the wearer's leg, and the bright scabbard of a large sword, while on the hero's left arm hung a splendidly-dressed woman." It is "Monsieur le *Colonel Jorrockes,*" done up in a great pair of false mustachios, accompanied by the Countess, with whom he is now living.

The Yorkshireman calls on them at one o'clock. He is admitted by a half-dressed Negro serving man, into a messy room full of red velvet chairs. The Countess is "of course . . . still *en déshabille,* with her nightcap on, a loose robe de chambre of flannel, and a flaming broad-striped red-and-black Scotch shawl thrown over her shoulders, and swan's-down-

2438

lined slippers on her feet. Mr. Jorrocks had his
leather pantaloons on, with a rich blue and yellow
brocade dressing-gown and blue morocco slippers to
match."

Mr. Jorrocks goes to dress and returns "en grand
costume—finely cleaned leathers, jack-boots and
brass spurs, with a spic and span new blue military
frock-coat, hooking and eyeing up to the chin, all
covered with braid, frogs, tags, and buttons." Jorrocks complains that "it is rather tight—partiklarly
around the waist," but thinks the Yorkshireman
should have one too. The Countess suggests that he
also get "some of those things—not pantaloons—not
those sacks of things called trousers" (which the
Yorkshireman is wearing). It turns out that she
means black satin breeches.

It is arranged that Mr. Stubbs will accompany
them to a *soirée-dansante* given by the Countess de
Jackson, a *marchande de modes,* married to an English horse dealer. At nine o'clock that night, he toils
back up the dirty stairway to the Countess' apartment on the third landing (see Paris apartment
house: Ill. 2489), and is received by the Negro Aga-
memnon, who has now got into "a roomy uniform
of a chasseur—dark green and tarnished gold, with
a cocked hat and black feather, and a couteau de
chasse, slung by a shining patent-leather belt, over his
shoulder. The "Colonel" is "extremely smart: thin
black gauze-silk stockings, black satin breeches; well-
washed, well-starched white waistcoat with a rolling
collar, showing an amplitude of frill; a blue coat
with yellow buttons and a velvet collar, while his
pumps shone as bright as polished steel." . . . "Rouge
and the milliner had effectually reduced (the Countess') age from five-and-forty down to five-and-
twenty. She wore a dress of the palest pink satin,
with lilies of the valley in her hair, and an ex-

quisitely wrought gold armlet, with a most Lillipu-
tian watch in the centre." Off they go to waltz. This
is the sort of invaluable information with which
Victorian novels are packed.

2439. XIXc. 1834. French.
"La Revue des Modes de Paris" (periodical).

"Ladies' riding habit in zephyr cloth with a velvet
collar. Merino pantaloons, morocco boots. *Panne*
coat, velvet collar, corded gray-white velours pantaloon."

Dark blue habit; pale lavender hat, with pale
gray-green scarf and matching green gloves; yellow
boots.

Bottle-green coat, black collar, yellow gloves.

The riding habit has developed extremely sloping
shoulders and a longer waist. It is worn with long
breeches strapped under the boot, like men's pantaloons. The small figure shows the lapels of the habit,
three rows of buttons, standing collar and stock tied
in a bow, and a pleated and ruffled shirt.

The man is a typical figure of the 30's: tall, slender
silk hat; bunched curls at male as at female temples;
jaw framed by sideburns and standing collar. What
is essentially a double-breasted overgarment has been
turned into a tail coat with a smooth, close sleeve.
Its double row of buttons is set in a V to stress its
narrow-waisted torso; the skirts are cut away at a
point below the exaggeratedly fitted waist, and are
rounded off to outline the hips' roundness before
falling in long, straight square tails. Striped pantaloons strapped over boots with long, narrow, square
toes and spurs. Tasselled stick.

2440. XIXc. 1837. French.
Gavarni. Court dress.

The court coat has had a standing collar throughout the century. It is roundly cutaway, tight-waisted,

and rounded over hips and buttocks like coats in
general; worn with knee breeches and *chapeau bras*.

Ladies' hair in spaniels' ears at the side, with the
knot on the crown slipping lower down during the
30's. The customarily rather plain skirt of the 30's
is looped up over flounces of the lace which is used
in court dress. Long kid gloves, since the arm and
hand are pretty consistently covered during the 30's.
2441. XIXc. 1835. French.
Henri Monnier. The composer Zérézo.

The composer shows the vast difference between
the fashion-plate ideal and the pantaloon under the
actual stresses of thigh, knee and buttocks.
2442. XIXc. 1835. French.
Town dress: The wide, flat, deliriously trimmed
hats of 1827 turn into bonnets with strings coming
from far back on the neck, a bow set on the under
side of the brim, and paradise or ostrich trimming.
By mid-30's the bonnet starts to enclose the face and

for a year or so scoops high in front. By 1840 it becomes smaller and more rounded—a frame for the
face. Its brim drips with lace which is carried under
the chin like a *cornette;* or a lingerie frill like that
of a cap is set around the crown opening under the
brim. Short kid gloves, disappearing into long
sleeves; lace handkerchiefs.

Mantles have bow-tied *pèlerine* collars and huge
open sleeves which are given form by several tucks
across the elbow.

Men's collars large, high in back, often of velvet;
coat with reduced lapels buttoned high on chest;
tall, rather straight-crowned top hat; fringe of beard
outlining chin.
**2443. XIXc. 1836. English. (New York, F. Ambrose
Clark.)**
James Pollard. Manchester-Liverpool Mailcoach.

Courtesy of Metropolitan Museum, Print Room (2439)

Floating veils on enclosing bonnets as well as top-hat of riding habit (2439).

Dark dickey and coat, separated by a line of white vest, worn with a forage cap and light-colored (probably waterproofed) topcoat. Colored cravats; light and dark toppers.

2444. XIXc. 1836. Danish. (Frederiksborg Museum.)
Conrad Blunck. Danish Artists in a Roman Inn. The seated figure in the foreground is the sculp-tor Thorwaldsen. Dark cravats; shirts with full sleeves; vests have a skeleton back of plain fabric; trousers require suspenders, and have side pockets into which the handkerchief can be stuck. The fashion plate figure of the mid1830's seems rather remote, and there is little difference between the comfortable clothes shown here and those which a similar group would be wearing a century later, with the exception of hats,

2445-46. XIXc. 1838-39. French-English.
"La Mode" (periodical).

2445. Hair parted, waved and curled. Moustache with beard or hair surrounding chin. Collar turned down over a crumpled dickey of dark satin; separated by line of white vest, which parallels the coat collar; wide jutting lapels, set rather high, on short, double-breasted coat. Characteristic short, fitted topcoat of 30's; narrow, glove-fitting trousers strapped over delicate boots.

Standing stock and cravat, with ruffled shirt, the cuffs turned back over the shallow coat cuff; fitted frock coat; fancy brocade vest; trousers strapped but cutaway over instep to show striped stockings and low bow-trimmed shoes.

Coat collars are set low on the neck and lie flat. Single-breasted coats are worn open; their fronts cannot be closed, and the roll of the lapel is carried down almost their entire length. Top hat crowns taller and heavier.

2446. "Dressing gown in Persian taste from Doucet. Little lappeted bonnet from Mme. LaSalle. Redingote with pelerine of Tulasne Ledoux. Divan from Maigret. Embroidery frame, canvas and wools from Serré Delisle."

Victorian domesticity rampant. When her husband has worn out his complete Persian outfit from Doucet, which is the favorite gift of the 30's and 40's, the lady (who wears kid gloves even while embroidering), will undoubtedly make him a pair of wool-embroidered slippers. Hair, smooth to the ears, then falling in long bunched curls, is covered at home by a cap with long lappets. The skirt front has begun to be split and its edges decorated, in e. 30's. In late 30's the hem of the underskirt is trimmed; by the 40's, the slit overskirt disappears, and the remaining skirt may have several rows of ruffles. At the turn of 30's-40's, cartridge pleating is a favorite method, both of trimming and attaching the skirt to the waistband.

Courtesy of Metropolitan Museum, Print Room

2447-48. XIXc. 1838. English. (New York Public Lib.)
"Court Magazine," Vol. 2 (periodical).

Descriptions which accompany plates are quoted, without modernization of orthography.

2447. *"Toilette d'Intérieur:* Fashionable morning costume. Redingote of pearl grey silk. Corsage half high, made tight to fit the bust, and crossing in front. The skirt is likewise made to cross, and is rounded at the lower corners. The trimming consists of a single *bouillon* round the corsage, and a double round the skirt, with a tolerably deep lace at the edge. The sleeves are quite plain at the shoulder, the remainder full, and the wrist plain and deep. At top are two *bouillons* and a lace frill. Blonde cap, ornamented with flowers and ribbons. The border is deep; it is quite plain across the brow and full at each side of the face; bows of pink ribbon are placed underneath the border at the right side, and a full-blown rose at the left. Hair in bands; white kid gloves; black shoes."

2448. Sitting figure: "The dress is made in a similar fashion to the one just described. The cap is also like the other, with the difference of two half-wreaths being put at the back of the border instead of the trimming underneath."

2449-50. XIXc. 1839. English. (New York Public Library.)
"Court Magazine," Vol. 4.

2449. Seated figure: *"Toilette d'Intérieur. Home Morning Dress.* Dress of white muslin: corsage *demi-décolletée* (half high); the back has a few gathers at the waist; the fronts cross and are in large set folds on plaits; round the neck is a narrow lace. The sleeves are short and do not even cover the elbow. They are quite tight and have double tucks (which are cut the cross way) put on as plain as possible and close together so that the upper tuck covers the putting on of the one below it, and so on. The skirt has rather a deep flounce, at the very bottom. Aprons of *broché* silk with a flounce of the same all round and a double one at the bot-

tom; the pockets are on the outside, rather pointed at bottom; they are put on with a narrow flounce all round except at top. The cap consists of a mere *cornet à la paysanne;* the crown is like a half handkerchief plaited into form at the back; the lappets in front descend below the ears and are turned up again and fastened amidst the plaits at the back of the cap; they are considerably stiffened and in three or four deep plaits on folds. A coloured ribbon, after forming a rosette-bow in front, encircles the cap and finishes in a bow with long ends at back; a small bouquet of rose is placed at the left side. Hair in smooth bands, the ends braided and turned up at each side of the face. Bow of coloured ribbon fastening the corsage in front. Hair chain. Half-length black netting mittens."

2450. "Redingote of *poux de soie, couleur cendre.* The corsage is made to fit perfectly tight to the bust, and without a waistband. The back is plain, the fronts *en chale,* like a gentleman's waistcoat, with collar turned over and lapels turned back; it merely meets at the waist in front. It will be perceived that the collar and fronts are lined with buckram or some other stiffening to make them sit as in the plate. The sleeves are tight at top, confined in plaits toward the wrist, the remainder full. The skirt, which is very long and very ample has five *rouleaux* down each side of the front, which are continued round the bottom of the skirt. These *rouleaux* are put in a bunch close together at the waist, but occupy a wider space as they go down. The chemisette is of cambric, the front in set plaits, and *à sabot,* or small plaited frills down the front; round the neck is a lace or cambric frill. The ruffles are cambric trimmed with lace. Hat of *paille de riz* lined and trimmed with delicate pink *crepe lisse.* A bunch of roses is placed as low as possible at the right side, and a light wreath of the same crosses the brow and descends a little at each side under the front of the hat. Hair in bands. Pale yellow gloves. Black varnished leather shoes."

2451. XIXc. 1830-40. French. (Boston, Museum of Fine Arts, Elizabeth Day McCormick Coll.)

Silk apron: embroidered in "ribbon work" in brilliant colors; one apron on plum, another on brown ground, in same collection.

Aprons reappeared in the latter half of the 30's, and increased in use. "Never was there a greater rage for aprons," of satin or shot silk for morning or afternoon, than in 1847.

2452. XIXc. c. 1842. French. (Metropolitan Museum, Print Room.)

La Sylphide Corset.

From which of the magazines published by the *Société des Modes Réunies* this loose plate comes has not yet been determined. Hottenroth dates a re-drawing of it as 1850, which is so nearly a decade too late that it may be a misprint. We are not much helped by its name; the incomparable grace of La Taglioni in *La Sylphide* (Thackeray: "The New-

combs") had caused costume accessories to be called by that name long before and after she chose that ballet from her repertoire for her New York début in 1838. There is a *La Sylphide* parasol in England in 1846.

Sleeve puffs on a dropped shoulder-line (which the little boned shoulder caps would support) were passing fast by the 40's. Dark bows at the collar are seen throughout the 30's and most of the 40's. But the collars of these chemisettes have lost all lateral spread; they are small and round, and the chemisette is designed to fill in the deep V-opening of the early 40's. Hair has the coronet braid of end 30's. As curls grow longer and looser at the beginning of the 40's, their earlier bunched form is commemorated in the ribbons at the ears of small caps. The museum sets a tentative date of c. 1842.

2453. XIXc. 1839-40. French. (Versailles, Nat. Mus.)

F. X. Winterhalter. Marie of Orleans, wife of

Prince Alexander of Würtemberg, and their son, Philip.

Louis-Philippe's daughter, who died at about this time, holds the son born in July 1838.

Until 1840, a full sleeve is still occasionally seen; it is finished by a turned-back, ruffled cuff, and has a deep, shirred upper section, which is concealed here by the spreading, ruffled, crossed and pinned collars, into which the old shoulder caps have sunk. Hair is looped smoothly at the ears; the cap again begins to cover the daytime head, and its lappets or trim replace bunches of falling curls.

2454-55. XIXc. 1840. U.S.A. (Metropolitan Museum.)

Nelson Cook. James Merrill Cook, Anne Cady Cook.

Slight provincial time-lag, more apparent in Mrs. Cook's dress: see neck and sleeves (2431) and coarse mesh net and lace morning dress (2435). Hair looped above the line of the ears in the simplest way of the 30's. Good band of deep lace, which she has no intention of ruining by cutting, has been pleated together in a fan to give it play.

2454. Black satin stock; rounded opening, tight, high waist and enclosing skirts of 30's; velvet lapels have the more rounded form, and the sleeves the buttoned seam opening of the late 30's-40's; braid-covered buttons, white cuff emerges as sleeve shortens.

2456. XIXc. 1840. U.S.A. (Charleston, S. C., Coll. of City.)

C. Meyr. Firemasters and officers of the Volunteer Fire Company.

Much less distortion of male body form and cut of clothes in U.S.A. Strapped pantaloons, longer and easier in the lower leg; many long tubular trousers. The new jacket of the 40's, buttoned above the waistline, cut away below; diagonal pocket with flaps (2 from r.).

High silk toppers and lower-crowned light-colored hats.

2457. XIXc. 1841. U.S.A. (Washington, Mellon Coll.)

Henry Inman (1801-46). Charles Fenno Hoffman (1806-84).

The author, editor and lawyer shows hair parted at the side, waved and curled, as is the longer fringe

of hair along the jowls. Fitted stock and tied cravat. Shoulders wider and sloping; sleeve plain, shorter, shows a line of shirt cuff; lapels wider, their edges stitched and often (from c. 1835) faced with velvet. Coats, which have largely been worn closed during the daytime in the 30's, open to show vests; these are noticeable in satin, brocade or embroidery (c. 1835-60). Pantaloons (pleated fullness at waistline c. 1838) are also covered with pattern; diamonds, checks, loud stripes, even embroidered sprigs on light summer pantaloons when worn with plain coats (c. 1835-60). Coat, vest, pantaloons and cravat are usually of different color and fabric during the 40's; all are capable of being loudly patterned, but only one patterned garment appears in each outfit, as: a dark brown coat and white vest with yellowish striped trousers, or white pantaloons and a leather vest with a checked coat. The exception is the patterned cravat, but this is separated from a fancy coat by a plain vest.

The watch-chain, which in D'Orsay's time was worn around the neck, has now dropped into the opening of the vest; it will grow shorter and be carried from a lower buttonhole to the vest pocket.

2458-59. XIXc. 1841. French. (Met. Mus. of Art.)
Gavarni. "Les Lorettes."

2458. *Mon petit homme, faut être raisonnable . . . c'est mon parrain qui veut absolument me faire un sort, dans son bien des Bouches-du-Rhône pour l'éducation de sa petite . . . je vais te laisser la mienne.*

2459. *Mon adoré . . . dis-moi ton petit nom.*

The *lorettes,* shown in a wonderful series of color plates, were the little lights o'love who practically filled the new apartment building near the church of Notre-Dame de Lorette in 1840.

Men: top hat wider brimmed and curving; parted and curled hair; beards; collar turned down over cravat; rounded male shoulder, torso and hips; tight-waisted patterned pantaloons, full at hips, pleated into waistband, narrow below, strapped under boots and cut away over instep.

Women: wide shoulder abandoned for wide hips; an enormous amount of ungored width was gathered into fashionable skirts. Gloved hand and long sleeve connected by pairs of wide bracelets; plaid umbrellas.

2460. XIXc. April 1842. U.S.A. (New York Public Lib.)
"Godey's Lady's Book" (periodical).

Godey's, the most influential American fashion magazine, was published from 1830-98. Its plates are both in color or black and white, like this one. The chief defect of *Godey's* is that plates seldom have an explanatory text, at this period, and that the quality of the plates, during its long life, is variable.

These ladies, wearing short gloves under all circumstances show (l. to r.) the mitred folds seen in 2449-50 becoming simplified and drawn down a lengthening bodice, while the V-neck begins its rise to a high, closed line by the addition of embroidered collars.

Bonnets close by knotted, scarf-like ties, often patterned, rather than ribbon bows and streamers. (See plaid cravat, like those of the men in 2474, knotted like these bonnet-ties, at the throat of lady in 2475.)

Frogged and corded trimmings increase in use on women's clothes, and on men's top-coats and dressing gowns during the 40's.

Curls become fewer in number, longer and more spiral (like shavings) during the 40's; the sides of evening caps lengthen with them. Curls and evenings caps tend to become eliminated; the evening head of the 50's may show a curl or two, but is decorated with flowers, rather than a cap.

Black net and lace scarves with long, knotted fringe ends. Cords threaded with small bead-like ornaments are seen across foreheads in afternoon and evening dress during latter half of 30's and first half of 40's (third from left).

Skirts continue to show inverted V openings to mid-40's; are edged with puffed cordings (Ills. 2447-48) or unhemmed ruchings with pinked or frayed edges and are frequently caught together down the front with knots or frogged ornaments.

Fabrics in combinations of heavy and light stripes are used especially in 1841-2 in combinations of diagonal against vertical. Sleeves becoming plainer and closer during first half of 40's, and are finished by a small tight cuff.

There is a great deal of lace during the 40's, but

2460

2461

2462

it tends to be superseded by fringes and frogs, running designs in cordlike braids, and by rosettes and appliquéd roses, on bonnets and evening dresses; all in very much debased taste, according to general midXXc. opinion.

2461. XIXc. 1843. French. (New York Public Library.)
Grandville. "Les petites misères de la vie humaine," by E. Forgues:

"*Je traverse le boulevard, où vingt fumeurs effrontés m'obsèdent de leur attention quêteuse.*"

"Grandville" was the pseudonym of a strangely talented artist named Jean Ignace Isidore Gérard (1803-47).

His illustrations for "Les petites misères de la vie humaine," which follows the trend set by "Les Français peints par eux-mêmes" are straightforward enough. His really astonishing surrealistic productions show the metamorphosis of women into bright flowers ("Les fleurs animées," 1847), and of people into frightful animals ("Scènes de la vie privée et publique des animaux," 1843).

Top hat crowns and brims are more insistent; great variety in hair: cut full all around, or combed down and under smoothly—in a way related to women's oiled loops of hair; or clipped short; moustaches, beards or mutton chops, alone or combined. Great variety of topcoats, sometimes caped or hooded in latter half of the 40's, with larger buttons than in the 30's; single-breasted topcoats often closed by tabs or frogs; diagonally set pockets in the skirts of topcoats. Many men carry sticks during the late 30's and the 40's. The unaccompanied lady is bothered by a score of men puffing on cigars and urchins smoking the still vulgar pipe.

2462. XIXc. 1844. French. (Hendecourt Coll., Southeby Sale 1925.)

Ingres. Mme. and Mlle. Reiset.

The descent of the *canezou* blouse from the sleeveless *fichu-canezou* is clear in this illustration. The points of the corded and gathered fichu hang over the belt.

The *canezou* was, strictly, a white blouse, but its corded and puffed treatment affected other pale colored garments (2468-9). V-necklines are filled in with chemisettes, collars and cravats, the ends of which are shaped like rabbit ears, rather than flat ribbons. Curls, longer and lanker, start higher on the head.

2463. XIXc. 1842. French. (Metropolitan Museum, Print Room.)

Grandville. Poster: "Fables of Florian."

Women's hair has been looped madonna-fashion during 30's to cover the ears. The natural tendency of the ears to break through is especially exploited in the 40's. A loose tress separates from the rest of

the hair, and is worked around the ears, as a frame, or in a loop above the ear. The rest of the hair is braided. On girls it falls in two ribbon-tied pigtails, which are sometimes wound spirally over the ears. But ribbon knots decorate women's coiled braids also, and they wear necklaces, lace collars, brooches, and scarves similar to the girl on the poster (who undoubtedly wears pantalettes and a rather long skirt.) The bonnet brim surrounds the head so closely, that the back must be cut away. Coiled hair may fit into the tiny crown, or is concealed by the ruffle which covers the back of the neck.

Everybody can now have imitation paradise feathers made in Paris from cock feathers, and very durable. Miss Jelly, the dressmaker, took hers off her Sunday bonnet, in costuming her lodger, Capt. Doleful, as the Great Mogul, for the Handley Cross fancy dress ball.

Long hanging ends are loved in the mid40's; they become shawl-like and pointed, in the 50's, but they are now still band-like in France—long narrow scarves which are held tight around the shoulders; scarves and ribbons on hair, hats, and hanging sashes (2458).

2464. XIXc. 1845. Swedish. (Stockholm, Hallwylska Collection.)

Unknown painter. Brothers Hans and Walter J. Hallwyl.

Boys' clothes have been apt to show the influence of sailors' or soldiers' uniforms from final quarter of XVIIIc. The chests of fitted jackets or full blouses are decorated with two or three rows of buttons, which draw together towards the waist; or the same pattern is braided or laced across the chest. Long trousers. Low laced shoes.

2465

2465. XIXc. 1844. English-French. (New York, Daniel H. Farr.)

E. H. T. Pingret (1788-1875). Arrival of Louis-Philippe at Windsor.

Mme. de Genlis' pupil, Philippe-Egalité's son, earned his living as a teacher in Switzerland, after the Revolution, with which he had been in complete sympathy. He travelled with his brothers in America for three years, and then settled in England at Twickenham. When a brother became tubercular, Louis-Philippe went with him to Italy. There he married a granddaughter of Marie Thérèse and Charles IV in 1809, and lived until Louis XVIII's accession brought them back to immense estates in France. He sent his eight children to public school, and because of liberal leanings was forced to live in England again in 1815-17. At the Revolution of 1830, he walked through the streets to the Hôtel de Ville, and was proclaimed king. Victoria and Albert visited him in France in 1843, and in 1844 he returned their visit. With age, he became more Bourbon and reactionary; in 1848, he and Queen Marie Amélie found it advisable to slip away, as "Mr. and Mrs. Smith," to England, where he died.

Small round bonnets; flowing veils; *pèlerine-mantelets* with long tab ends, shawls, shorter *pelisses,* over long, full, round skirts, some with the vertical front trimming, which appeared briefly, mostly plain, tending towards horizontal flounces.

Girls in pantalettes under seven-eighths-long dresses, pair of long braids; tiny boy in rather long dress with pantaloons.

2466-71. XIXc. March 1843. U.S.A. (New York Public Library.)

"Godey's Lady's Book." (periodical).

This plate, in soft, pale colors, shows l. to r.:

2466   2467   2468   2469   2470   2471

2472

2466. Boy: black top hat, bright blue blouse, and trousers with some of the fullness of a woman's skirts.

2467. Boy: because younger, shows even more female influence, combined with a man's tasselled green forage cap; green dress over white, lace-edged pantalettes.

2468. Lady: pink and blue flower-trimmed bonnet; gray gown with the shirring seen on so many *canezou* blouses of the 40's. Gloves and embroidered handkerchief.

2469. Lady: scarf-tied pale blue bonnet and gown. Her yellow *palatine* or *pèlerine-mantelet* shows the roses which are embroidered or applied on many evening dresses of latter half of the 40's; combined with foliated embroidery, lace, and tabbed rosettes.

2470. Girl: white bonnet, lined with dark and light rose shirrings; brown cloak; white dress and pantalettes.

2471. Girl: rosette-trimmed pink bonnet tied like a cravat; blue-green pardessus. The borders of outer garments are increasingly edged with running corded patterns, which will become fancy braids and fringes by the 50's.

2472. XIXc. 1843. French. (New York Public Library.)

E. L. Lami. "The American in Paris in Summer." Lami's illustrations for Jules Janin's two books, translated as "Summer in Paris" and "Winter in Paris," give enchanting pictures of Paris existence in home, street and park.

The dry comment of a very old man in the country a quarter of a century ago, when a guest of mine set off for a sun bath, was: "There used to be a style if a sun-ray hit you, it'd kill you." His provincial childhood had been lived under the tra-

dition, at least, of tightly constricted Victorian ladies, doing a little needlework in a dark-papered room behind heavily curtained windows, and drinking vinegar against the "green sickness" or living on toast and tea to enhance a white skin. It was protected out of doors by a completely concealing bonnet, long sleeves and wide bracelet to insure no dark line above the short glove. The glove protected the whiteness of a hand which was (ideally at least) never seen, because it was never ungloved.

Between the hysteria and tuberculosis induced by this sort of life, we see a great many convalescing ladies, slightly propped up, surrounded by rewarding solicitude.

Men's hair was parted on the side and cut full all around. Shaped collar, set on a curved band, arches around the face or begins to turn down over the dark cravat or dickey fastened with a brooch. Soft, curved shirt cuff turned back over cuff of dark suits, with matching coats and trousers. These are cut with great elegance in long, less closely fitted lines, and are worn with white vests of piqué or corded cotton. Flower in lapel; rings, gloves. Top hat of the visitor is carried after the tradition of the court *chapeau bras* which is never set down.

It is after ten by candlelight. The ladies wear simple home evening dress, with uncluttered skirts, masses of lace at the elbows, in the sleeve elaboration seen especially in France; and lace scarves or collars at comparatively high necks. The visiting lady wears more ceremonious evening dress, with a valance of lace around a low neckline and no sleeve trimming below it. She wears a cap, but caps are beginning to lose ground already.

The invalid wears an informal cap, but like the other ladies at home here, bare heads are often trimmed instead with twists and loops of ribbon or cord.

2473

2474

2473. XIXc. 1843-4. English.

"Phiz" (H. K. Browne). Dickens' "Martin Chuzzlewit." Pleasant Little Family Party at Mr. Pecksniff's.

The strong-minded widow of a deceased brother of Mr. Martin Chuzzlewit, and "her spinster daughters, three in number, and of gentlemanly deportment . . . so mortified . . . with tight stays . . . that . . . sharp lacing was expressed in their very noses," show skirts slightly less developed than those in Louis-Philippe's 1844 visit, still full in back only. But the pelisse is already having difficulty in covering them, and is being shortened; veiled bonnets; V-necked, long-waisted bodices, rather large collars.

Sitting by Mr. Pecksniff (is it Mrs. Spottletoe?): bows in hair and chain with pendant.

Mr. Spottletoe: beard without moustache; black dickey-cravat; watch chain around neck, velvet collared coat, differing in color and fabric from vest and breeches.

George Chuzzlewit, the "gay bachelor cousin" . . . so overfed "that the bright spots on his cravat, and the rich pattern on his waistcoat, and even his glittering trinkets, seemed to have broken out upon him," shows another version of the quiff of hair beside Mr. Pecksniff's. Mr. Chuzzlewit's "very dark and very hairy" grand nephew sits with a bell-shaped top hat on the knee of his horizontally striped pantaloons, with one of the light-colored short topcoats hanging on his shoulders: all pantaloons still strapped under boots.

2474. XIXc. Early 1840's. Scotch.

David Octavius Hill. Chalmers Family at Merchiston.

Wedgwood, the potter, had produced fugitive silhouette images on sensitized paper by the turn of the century. Research from 1814 enabled Nicéphore de Niepce to make fixed pictures on silvered plates. His process was refined after his death in 1833 by his son Isidore, in partnership with Daguerre, and published in 1839. Photography began to be practiced, almost immediately, all over the world.

David Octavius Hill (1802-70), a Scottish portrait painter, was the first great photographer, and remains one of the greatest.

The dresses are made from a fabric which was extremely fashionable in England in 1841. Solid stripes are crossed by almost invisible lines, between which blocks of chiné pattern or flower motifs form a broken stripe. The stripes are effectively used here with the spreading collars of the late 30's to exploit construction shown in the 1839 plates. They replace mitred folds in cutting the bodice; they form diagonal closings and panels under the split skirt front, and are used in sleeves which become increasingly plain and close-fitting—1840-45.

Men's top hats grow more massive and belled. Parted hair grows longer in back. Cravats are colored, or patterned in stripes or plaids, and almost conceal the collar, which begins during the 40's to turn down over the cravat. Coats and topcoats are worn open and have grown longer, ending below rather than above the knee.

Vests end in points, are often made of brocade, and are usually lighter or darker than the rest of the costume.

Trousers are lighter in color than coats, have become more tubular, and have lost the strap under the boot.

2475. XIXc. Mid-1840's. Scotch.

David Octavius Hill. Lady in a Flowered Dress.

In England, in first half of the 1840's, the sleeve is apt to be simple, close and finished with a cuff. During the latter 40's, it shortens, and begins to bell out over a shirred and puffed white inner sleeve. Necklines grow higher and collars closer in latter half of 40's. The bonnet of first half of the decade is roundly enclosing and is fastened under the chin in knotted ties (like the plaid cravat worn by the lady), rather than by a bow of flat ribbon.

Hair has been worn smoothly looped (as an alternative to ringlets), sometimes exposing the ear, from the early 30's.

Hill's photograph of Margaret Fuller in 1846 shows an almost identical hair-do, worn by the American feminist who was drowned on her return trip when her ship went down off Fire Island.

Watch on cord around neck, pinned at waist. Cashmere shawl with long, knotted fringe.

2476. XIXc. Mid-1840's. Scotch.

David Octavius Hill. Lady Ruthven.

The close bonnet of first half of 40's becomes wider spread at the bottom in 1845-6. Horizontal lines have been used in opposition to vertical since the late 30's, but do not begin to prevail until second half of 40's. After the wide embroidered collars of the 30's, lace and net reappeared and were used for a decade or two in pèlerines and flounces; a great deal of it was black like Lady Ruthven's folded shawl.

2480

2482

2484

2481

2483

2485

Courtesy of Metropolitan Museum of Art

2477-79. XIXc. 1840-48. U.S.A. (Metropolitan Museum, Print Room.)

Southworth and Hawes (fl. 1840-62).

2477. John Quincy Adams (1767-1848).

2478. Harriet Beecher Stowe (1811-96).

2479. Emerson School.

Southworth and Hawes were in partnership from 1840-62. These photographs are difficult to date accurately because they show, seated, people who are not concerned with the latest fashion.

Mr. Adams wears clothes one would expect to find on an elderly man at any time between the beginning of the photographers' partnership and the subject's death: a double-breasted tailcoat with velvet collar; unstrapped trousers; laced shoes instead of boots.

Fringed black lace and net scarves and high-necked bodices, shirred horizontally like Mrs. Stowe's, are seen throughout the 40's, but the high mounting of her corkscrew curls makes mid-decade to second half decade seem probable, despite her apparent youth.

The Emerson School for young ladies in Boston was run by the son of the minister of the Unitarian church; Ralph Waldo Emerson, another of his sons, taught there for several years after his graduation from Harvard. There were decades during which schoolteachers could look like this one, but his laced low shoes and collar, full back hair, combined with the small collars on his pupils' high-necked bodices, the shirred band attaching sleeves to a dropped shoulder, and the increasing width of the bottom of sleeve of the dotted dress, the spiraling of braids around the ears, make a guess of 1846 reasonable.

2480. Early XIXc. French.

Bobbin lace veil: sprays of bobbin lace appliquéd on machine net.

2481. XIXc. French.

Shawl: needlepoint and point de gaze.

2482. Mid-XIXc. Flemish, Brussels.

Handkerchief: Brussels lace.

2483. XIXc. French.

Parasol cover: black Chantilly.

2484. Mid-XIXc. French.

Embroidered panel: part of 4-piece muslin dress.

2485. XIXc. German.

Square of embroidered china silk.

2486. XIXc. 1844. Spanish. (Madrid, Museo Romantico.)
Vincent Lopez. Marquis de Remisa.

Lapels roll back throughout the length of an open coat and become wider. They are connected to a wider collar at a deep notch, from which a seam runs down, piecing the lapel with a strip of even width. This is the vestige of the center seam which was necessary to make coats which overlapped fit over a globular chest. Sleeves slightly longer. Tied cravat, important shirt and vest buttons; chain from second buttonhole to watch pocket. The Marquis' trousers are still strapped under patent leather boots.

2487. XIXc. 1845. French. (New York, Frick Coll.)

Ingres. Countess d'Haussonville.

Hair looped above the ears and drawn back into a braided bun, dressed with ribbon loops.

Neckline rising on all dresses, day or evening. Interest is being transferred, in evening dresses, from a horizontal neckline with a lace valance or rigidly pleated band, to a V-line leading from the point of a shorter-waisted bodice to the sleeve. Sleeves, which have scarcely been seen, are elaborated in the new way—by manipulation of fabric into gathered and corded puffings. Skirt fullness is increased by gathered flounces, which begin as one flounce at bottom, increase to three in the 50's.

2488. XIXc. Mid-1840's. French. (New York, Cooper Union Museum.)

Constantin Guys (1805-92). The New Fashion.

Guys, son of the chief commander of the French Navy, was born c. 1805 in Flushing where his uncle was the French plenipotentiary. He was in Greece with Byron in 1824, and travelled all over Europe, the Near East and North Africa. He served in the Dragoons and lived the life of a dandy, until indignation at his father's remarriage to a sixteen-year-old girl sent him to London to "live by his wits." Nobody quite knows when he began to draw his better-known pictures; there is little information about their dates. By 1848, he was a staff artist for the *Illustrated London News* and covered the Crimean War for them. He fell on ill days, and consorted with the Baudelaire coterie and with gutter characters whom he drew wonderfully as he had done blooded horses, elegant carriages and fashionable women. In 1885, he was run over and was

taken to a hospital where he died seven years later.

Shop girl peers out to look at fashions seen c. 1845; long, loose *pelisse-mantles* with fur edging and long cylindrical muffs; bonnets with veils and wide loops and strings hanging down in back.

2489. XIXc. 1845. French.

Bertail (pseudonym). "Le Diable à Paris": Cross-Section of a House in Paris, Jan. 1, 1845.

2490. XIXc. French.

Constantin Guys. Sketch: Pen ink, and water color.

Hair longer, waved rather than curled (second half of 40's) moustache; very full hair on jaws, with moustache. Evening dress: white bow tie; pleated shirt front, now without ruffle, exposed by low-cut white vest, the skirts of which spring apart below the last closing (lapped over, as are some bodice-closings); wide trousers, no longer strapped over boots; long narrow squared toes; straighter stove-pipe hats.

Coronet braid high on head (late 40's); the slit-skirt line of e. 40's persists to 50's in hanging sash ends in front; long lace scarf; short gloves; fan.

2491. XIXc. 1849. German.

August von Kreling (1819-76). "Alte und neue Kinderlieder": Christmas Eve.

Husbands now change into dressing gown, cap and slippers at home; pipe smoking is rising socially.

Small loop of hair at ears; braids set as a coronet in the Guys illustration tend to slip lower into a coiled bun, c. 1850.

Wonderful German toys at the holiday, which was especially developed in Germany.

2492. XIXc. 1843. French. (The Louvre.)

Théodore Chassériau. The Artist's Sisters, Adèle and Aline.

Bodices partly or entirely corded in this way are

seen from the late 30's through the 40's and are the basis of the shape of the *canezou* into the 60's. Hair is often waved and drawn back, dressed with small, gold-edged combs and coiled in back, rather than looped or with bunched curls.

2493. XIXc. 1845. French. (Versailles, Nat. Mus.)
F. X. Winterhalter. Marie Caroline Auguste de Bourbon, duchesse d'Aumale.

2494. XIXc. 1845. French. (Versailles, Nat. Mus.)
F. X. Winterhalter. Marie Clémentine d' Orléans, princesse de Saxe-Coburg-Gotha.

2495. XIXc. c. 1850. French. (Metropolitan Museum, Print Room.)
Achille Lefèvre, after *Winterhalter*. Marie-Amélie, wife of Louis-Philippe.

Winterhalter's portraits, which royalty loved, are scarcely portraits at all, but the period of the lovely lace-flounced gowns painted by this German has come to be called by his name.

The duchesse d'Aumale's ceremonial gown is veiled in black lace. Its bodice is drawn down into a long point, but the waist is actually shortened in the way of the 50's. Its neckline combines and elaborates the two favorite finishes of evening gowns: a wide band of pleated fabric, mitred at center-front like picture-frame moulding; and a lace valance. Here the lace bands are doubled, and finished with a pleated heading which may be said to sketch the third flounce of the 50's (Marie-Amélie). The gown also shows the new interest in manipulated self-fabric in the deep pleats by which the skirt fullness is obtained.

With these new trends, the gown also shows the persistence of shaded color. It allies a rosy pink with a yellower pink, used under the lower flounces of lace on the skirt, down the point of the bodice, and on the folds under the first lace valance. The favorite roses of the mid40's and 50's help to alter the horizontal line of the valance in the direction of the bodice cut *en coeur* of the 50's. Ubiquitous trailing black lace scarf of mid40's.

The princess of Saxe-Coburg-Gotha's less formal summer muslin evening gown, its shirred heading threaded with ribbon, shows the formal folds deteriorating into gathers, laid across the bodice in a diagonal closing line.

Elaborated puffings are seen, particularly in France, on evening gowns which do not carry a lace valance.

When curls are worn, they are larger, longer and more spiral, and start higher on the temples. The back hair is set in a braided coronet which tends to slip into a bun at the nape.

The cap loses favor with younger women, who now dress their hair with flowers, loops and puffs of ribbon, and feathers.

With her long, aging face, Marie-Amélie retains the diagonally set sausage curls of the 30's.

Caps have for a long time been worn by any woman who has been married long enough to have a baby, and the queen is the mother of eight.

The buckled belt of the 30's continues to be worn in the 40's on bodices which do not finish in a point. Elaborate French sleeve. Bracelets increase in im-

2496

portance—not the pairs of wide band bracelets at the wrist of long-sleeved gowns, but elaborate single bracelets worn higher on the arm; gloves slightly higher, with XVIIc. slashed cuffs.

2496. XIXc. Jan. 15, 1848. English. (New York Public Library.)

"The Ladies' Newspaper" (periodical, later called "The Queen"). Quotations are from original text accompanying the picture.

"Costume for a little boy between six and seven years of age. Hat of black felt, the crown round and the brim turned up on each side. Instead of a band, a cord passed twice around the hat, and tied in the back, where it is finished with two tassels. Paletot of gray cloth, edged all around with embroidery in gray soutache. Trousers of blue cloth, gathered on a band at the waist. Black glazed leather shoes and garters of chamois leather.

"Carriage dress. Bonnet of pink therry velvet, trimmed with white lace, and a white voilette attached to the edge of the bonnet. Dress of Pekin with satin stripes, green and rose color. The skirt with three flounces, each edged with green silk fringe, headed by two rows of green velvet. The corsage is high and plain, and the sleeves tight to the arm and fastening closely to the wrist, where they are finished by turn-up cuffs. Gloves of pale yellow kid.

"Walking dress. Bonnet of embroidered velvet, with pale green satin, and a demi-wreath of velvet flowers on the outside. Strings of green satin ribbon, the same colour as the lining and undertrimming of bows of ribbon and velvet flowers in variegated hues. A pardessus of rich brown satin, of the paletot form, and thickly wadded, so that, with an appearance of lightness, it combines a sufficient degree of warmth for the promenade, even on the coldest day. The pardessus is finished at the bottom, up the two fronts, and at the ends of the sleeves, by a deep row of quilting. The dress, which is of the same material as the pardessus, is also quilted up the front. Slate-coloured kid gloves."

2497. XIXc. 1848. U.S.A. (Baltimore, Walters Art Gall.)

R. C. Woodville. Sailor's Wedding.

Bride: *canezou* with shirred sleeves and shoulder worn with round skirt trimmed with three rows of tucks.

Sailor: after the quiffs of the 30's and the curls of the 40's, hair grew longer. It was sometimes set carefully around the ears in what we would call a "page-boy bob." Shiny patent-leather sailor's hat, low-crowned, wide-brimmed; "sailor" collar, worn with neckerchief, open over short jacket; wide trousers.

Best man: collar turned down over knotted, fringed kerchief-tie first worn, knotted like bonnet-strings, by women (2475); pleated shirt front; horizontally striped vest.

Older men: stock or standing collar; double-breasted vest; felt or stovepipe hats in light colors.

Mother: standard bonnet-and-cashmere-shawl costume.

2498. XIXc. 1848. U.S.A. (Baltimore, C. Morgan Marshall.)

R. C. Woodville. Politics in an Oyster House.

Booth in oyster house: jet for gas light. Beards begin to appear. Man, with crêpe mourning-band on tall, cylindrical top hat, wears shoes with light-colored buttoned uppers. Side pockets in trousers.

2499. XIXc. 1849. English.

"Phiz." Dickens: "David Copperfield": After Mr. Waterbrook's Dinner-Party.

There are still many variations of excessive collars (like the host's), stocks and ties, and comic heads of hair (like Tommy Tucker's, in the back-ground) for Dickens to make fun of, among Mr. Waterbrook's refined guests of Bank and Treasury, all "iced for the occasion . . . like the wine." Pantaloons have lost their straps. Some have grown long and wide, into trousers; others, like those of the bespectacled man, are extremely short and tight, to exhibit his shoes with the fashionable light-colored tops.

2500. XIXc. July 1850. French. (Metropolitan Museum, Print Room.)

Lacouchie. "Le Parisien" (periodical).

The 50's bring an extraordinary and inventive assortment of short coats, designed for specific purposes and times of day; the first real "three-piece suits;" and breast pockets on coats.

Low-crowned, wide-brimmed hats, in light colors, edged with braid, appear in informal use. There are light-colored silk toppers, tall and cylindrical, as well as the more formal black.

Hair had been comparatively flat in back, though long and curled at the ears during the 40's. It turned smoother and longer in back in the late 40's. With the 50's, it fluffs out full all around. The hair along the jowls also fluffs out into mutton chops.

The newest collar is turned down very low over a loose bow tie, exposing a bare column of the male throat for the first time in three centuries. Shirt fronts are pleated and obviously buttoned. Loose

2499

bows are tied around standing collars in more formal dress.

The new complete, matching suit, worn by the fisherman, has a longer waist and lapel, and rounds off into cutaway skirts over a rounded rump. Although it has not been found necessary in this case, these bob-tailed skirts are often cut separately and seamed on to a waistline, which is cut on a diagonal line to correspond with the slanting breast pocket.

The most characteristic thing about all these new garments is an interest in parallels. This line is most carefully maintained in the relationship between the line of vest and coat openings; the white piping on the vest of the stage or movie banker is a last vestige of this elegance. Edges are stitched, piped or faced, and the silk lining of topcoats begins to be displayed.

Vests lengthen with coats, and are prolonged and spread apart below their last button, from which a short chain is carried to the watch pocket.

When striped fabric is used in vests, it is cut on a diagonal to enhance the new piped and diagonal lines of the rest of the garments.

Trousers are much easier in cut. The more ceremonious pantaloons are pleated into the waistband, braided along the outseam, and inconspicuously held down by a wide band under the boot. The trousers worn by the fisherman have matching spats, which mask all but the tips of shoes. His companion's frankly short, unstrapped trousers are worn with bow-trimmed pumps. The shoes of the young fisherman have buttoned, light-colored tops.

The young servant with clipped hair who carries the fish, shows livery anachronisms in stock and knee breeches (worn with gaiters), together with a smart new coat with flap pockets, a line of striped vest, and a forage cap.

Pince-nez glasses on a cord around neck as women carry watches (Ill. 2475).

2500

2501-03. XIXc. Spring and Summer 1850. U.S.A. (New York, Harry T. Peters.)

T. S. Sinclair. Fashion Plate for S. A. and A. F. Ward of Philadelphia.

Most men's fashion plates seen in the U.S.A. before the end of the Civil War are frankly French. This is one of the early American-made ones. No doubt it is based on French sources, just as the identical French gown turns up in English, German and French magazines, as fast as it can be copied.

The elegant European silhouette loses some of its ease in crossing the Atlantic.

The Marquis de Remisa (2486), the men in Lami's illustrations (2472) are European gentlemen; The *Parisien* fashion plate (2500) shows mannequins of gentlemen. Sinclair's plate is charming, but there is something provincial, self-conscious and sententious about it. The men in the top row all look as though they had just been elected to their first term in the House of Representatives, and were taking a deep breath in their new outfits, to say a few words at a farewell reception.

They show, however, the same new sloping shoulder, longer waistline and shorter skirts, on clothes which have under consideration the idea of closing again across the chest, and of becoming unified suits of one material. This is least obvious in summer fashion plates which show trousers in light colors and stripes. Hair is not curled artificially, but is full at the sides and nape. Collars turn down over dark or fancy tied cravats. Fancy vests, very chesty and full of buttons and watch chains. Sports clothes are shown on men's fashion plates everywhere, with low-crowned sports hats, in straw, for summer, and light-colored toppers for riding and the races. The American frontiersman's outfit for hunting is seen in European fashion plates.

Flat-crowned, wide-brimmed hats, like the Amazon's (2545), appear in the 50's and will be common by the 60's.

Caps are retained by ladies, but they are small, set on the back of plain hair which is parted and drawn up; they are trimmed with flowers and streamers of fancy ribbon falling down behind.

Bonnets, as in Europe in 1850, jut far out in back, and are rose-trimmed; their brims are drawn around the chin and are tied with small bows and streamers of ribbon with a fancy edge.

The bodice shown in *Godey's*, April, 1842, was cut in a few large sections, with gored panels set over. The 1850 bodice takes over the gores while getting rid of the decoration. It is shorter, carefully curved and fitted, and is trimmed with narrow bands of ruched, quilted and shirred fabric along a V-opening. The shoulder is smoothly rounded; the sleeve is easier and shorter, and flows wider at the bottom. The bare lower arm is loaded with bracelets in the evening. A full sheer white chemisette sleeve, gathered onto a close band at the wrist, flows from the short bell sleeve in daytime. Skirts are wide and become increasingly gored as their size increases.

Pardessus are smoothly fitted and untrimmed around neck, shoulders and waist. Their short sleeves and skirts both bell out and are heavily edged with flounces, lace or fringe.

Gowns, like that worn under this pardessus begin to be made of brocades and flowered stuffs, reputed to be in the style of one of one or another of the Louis' of France, between Louis XIII-XVI.

Riding habit with rather long basque worn with a full, round skirt and wide-brimmed, low-crowned hat.

2504-21. XIXc. 1851. English.

"Townsend's Magazine" (periodical).

Plates in color, with little or no explanatory text.

Nothing is more characteristic of the late 40's and the 50's than the variety of short outdoor coats for both sexes. There are short, loose sacque-like jackets, shaped *visites,* paletots and pardessus; and cloaks, mantelets and *sorties de bal,* which are usually founded on shawl and scarf shapes and increase in use as skirts spread too wide for the straighter forms of jacket.

Another fashion magazine of the period says: "How we contrived to exist before the pardessus was invented seems now a difficult problem to solve; a lady of fashion needs at least five: (1) of cashmere or merino for the morning; (2) of velvet for calls; (3) of silk or satin trimmed with lace for dinners; (4) of lace, for full dress; (5) one lined with fur for going to a ball. For (1) the "Louis XV," stiff with rich facings; for (2) the "Mousquetaire," coquettish; (3) the "Duchess," magnificent in ornament; (4) the "Puritan," elegantly simple; (5) the "Hungarian casaweck," richly trimmed with fur.

("Townsend Magazine" description of Ills. 2504-21:)

"Pardessus of the Pompadour style, of coloured silk heavily fringed; demi-long sleeves; some open, over the chest and fastening with two buttons, others hanging loose and only closed at the neck."

"Louis" styles are potent influences; the belling *pagoda* sleeve of Louis XIV with its rows of lace flounces (2508, 2511) as the entire silhouette becomes pagoda-like (lower center); Louis XV brocades and flowered cottons (lower, c.); which will be followed by Louis XVI *caracos* and *polonaises.*

Bonnets have round brims which tend to spread wider; they are shaped like a present-day peach basket, and are set well back on the head, projecting behind and exposing the face completely. There are bonnets of straw, velvet, silk, or lingerie capotes; the inner brim usually lined with color or shirring; trimmed according to the season with flowers, fancy ribbon, or winter feathers.

With the bloomer begins the whole series of "fast" styles, masculine adaptations which accompanied the "women's rights" movement, and the beginning of cigarette smoking by women.

The waistcoat (2510) was the fashionable sensation of 1851. It was often elaborately embroidered or brocaded, but we see it here in its most audacious plain form, complete with little watch pockets, and accompanied by a pair of pockets in the skirt, analogous to the new side pockets in trousers. Another such style is the plain little jacket (2506) with buttoned tab closings and pocket flaps.

The Scotsman represented in Cruikshank's "Bloomer" (2531) is an allusion to the popularity of plaids which are seen in fabrics and ribbons in women's and boys' clothing (2505) and (2520).

Pantalettes grow shorter, and like everything else white, are covered with embroidery, eyelets and notched edges. They are not only worn by girls, but by boys of astonishingly large size.

2504. Pink bonnet, violet gown.

2505. Blue and green bonnet, brown and black dress.

2506. Tan bonnet, dull lavender jacket and skirt.

2507. Pink bonnet, blue jacket braided in black.

2508. Yellow-green bonnet, rose mantle, braided in black, over a white skirt.

2509. Lavender bonnet, green mantle with wide collar.

2510. White bonnet, yellow ribbons, braid patterned white skirt, white vest, dull brick pink jacket and skirt.

2511. Black bonnet with pink flowers, leaves and ribbons, with the last remnants of the cornette tied under the chin; gray-blue patterned dress.

2512. Girl: flat yellow straw hat, pink ribbons and dress with horizontal lines of flounces, blue buttoned shoes.

2513. Little girl with pink parachute: flounced white raised embroidery, blue fringed sash, and blue shoes with a pleated cuff.

2514. Little boy: tabbed blue jacket and dress; striped stockings and green shoes.

2515. Girl: white bonnet, pale salmon-tan dress, white boots with black toes.

2516. Mamma: pink straw bonnet, green and black "Persian" percale redingote; matching mantelet with a capuchon hood (seen also on men's short sports coats).

2517. Big boy: tan tie, black coat; brown and black plaid trousers, striped stockings and black shoes.

2518. Swinging girl: wide yellow straw, pink ribbons, white blouse made like a man's shirt, pink skirt, black shoes.

2519. Boy: straw hat with streamers; short-sleeved tan blouse, white shirt and trousers, brown shoes.

2520. Boy: white cap—black and white plaid band; blue and black plaid dress, gray and black buttoned shoes.

2521. Boy: cocoa brown, embroidered in white roses and leaves; long pantalettes, and high brown gaiters.

2522. XIXc. 1851. French. (London, Nat. Gallery.) *Ingres.* Mme. Moitessier.

Women break out of rigid, concealing clothes in the 50's, as out of constricting convention. In another year, bloomers will appear in Hyde Park, and women will speak publicly on female rights.

Mme. Moitessier shows luscious bare shoulders, arms covered by handsome bracelets, and hands without gloves holding a fan (in which the renewed interest of the late 40's continues). Hair is no longer curled, or dankly looped; it looks very clean and well brushed, and is drawn back, under the scrap of lace which the evening cap has become.

There are a great many wide triangles in the costume of the 50's, especially on the outer garments, like the *mantillas* and *sorties de bal* which grew out of folded shawls. The fringed corner which finishes the bodice of her brocade gown is of that nature, and is combined with the wonderful, flowered and bordered fancy ribbons of the 50's.

Tiny cords are worn about both men's and women's necks (2475, 2500).

Courtesy of Metropolitan Museum of Art

2523. XVIIIc. (end Directoire.) French.

Fan; paper and wood; 5 groups representing *les jarretières, la danse, la folie, le colin maillard, la main chaude;* French verses at top of leaf.

2524. e.XIX. Empire. French.

Fan: brisé; horn engraved with floral design, embossed with gold, and spangled.

2525-26. XIXc. c. 1835. French.

Paris fan: probably made for the Spanish trade; by Coustellier; carved ivory stick, leaf, engraved and painted with episodes from Rossini's *Barber of Seville,* and part of score.

2527. XIXc. 1840-50. French.

Fan: sticks of pearl matrix, silver gilt; painted mount.

2528. Late XVIII-e.XIX. French.

Fan-lorgnette: brisé; ivory, carved and inlaid with mica.

2529. XIXc. c. 1850. Spanish?

Fan: Chantilly lace, 2 colors, mounted on pearl matrix sticks. (See Appendix.)

2530-31. XIXc. 1852-53. English. (New York Public Library, Print Room.)

George Cruikshank. "Comic Almanack" (periodical).

2530. "The Rights of Women, or the Effects of Female Enfranchisement."

2531. "The Bloomers in Hyde Park, or an Extraordinary Exhibition for 1852."

Cruikshank was a most vital and prolific illustrator and cartoonist. Born into a family of artists in 1792, he was at work by 1811. He and his brother Isaac illustrated in color the invaluable compendium which Pierce Egan had written in 1812 as *Life in London.*

Cruikshank lived to 1878, but his period of extraordinary usefulness for costume ends at about the time when the *Comic Almanack* (begun in 1835) ceased publication in 1853. For all their interest, the two frontispieces we reproduce are inferior to hundreds of black and white vignettes of the earlier decades.

2530

"THE RIGHTS of WOMEN" or the EFFECTS of FEMALE ENFRANCHISEMENT

2531

The "Bloomers" in Hyde Park, or an Extraordinary Exhibition for 1852

2532. XIXc. 1854. English. (New York Public Library.)

John Leech. "Handley Cross": Sir Thomas Trout and the Bloomer.

The influence of the sensational garment brought from the U.S.A. by Mrs. Amelia Bloomer spread to the provinces and caused Surtees to write a supplementary chapter for the 1854 edition of "Handley Cross." In Leech's colored plate, Constantia, lovely daughter of Mrs. Mendlove, hostess of the Turtle Doves Hotel, is shown in the entrance hall, in 1854, in "the full-blown costume of a Bloomer."

Constantia, very much the blonde soubrette, lets her curls flow over a fitted gray jacket with short perky skirts, a tiny white collar and a large, deep rose bow at the throat, a short but very wide hoop skirt, with three tiers of rose-bound flounces, and white muslin pantalettes gathered around the ankles.

In the five-fold colored frontispieces to the later *Almanacks,* Cruikshank amuses himself with the bell crowns and exaggeratedly curved brims seen in the Gavarni and Grandville illustrations, and the extraordinary variety of new hat shapes in the fre-

quently battered condition never seen in fashion plates and portraits, and seldom even in photographs.

Odd trousers, and men's suits with bob-tailed jackets and large pocket flaps are now seen in the loudest patterns ever known. "William the Conqueror" (right) wears a short cocoa brown jacket with huge buttons, patterned in a dark brown plaid, four units of which cover his back, plain cocoa brown trousers, a brown hat of a low-crowned bowler shape, a shirt collar dotted in red spots nearly as large as a dime, and a red cravat. Its ends are so widespread that in our back view of William we see their ends projecting on either side of his luxuriant brown beard, almost as Cruikshank caricatures them in the "Bloomer."

Versions of the wide flat hat seen on the Sinclair Amazon appear in Hyde Park on every age and sex, and on a woman riding sidesaddle in bloomers.

Small parasols, canes with horn handles, fringed shawls patterned in garlands of flowers; a Scotsman (in reference to Highland fashions), and every sort of bloomer Cruikshank could think of.

2533. XIXc. 1852. U.S.A. (Metropolitan Museum.)

Samuel Waldo and *William Jewett*. Portrait of an old lady.

Samuel L. Waldo (1783-1861), son of a Connecticut farmer, painted either signs or portraits until he was taken to South Carolina by the Hon. John Rutledge. Money he made there enabled him to study in England with West and Copley in 1806. He returned to New York, where he painted "scores of heads . . . of dignified, benevolent gentlemen, with white hair and white chokers, or of ladies in wonderful caps and shawls."

William Jewett (1792-1874) was grinding colors for a Connecticut carriage maker when Waldo finally succeeded in releasing him from his apprenticeship. He lived with the Jewetts for nearly two decades, and from preparing Waldo's paints, became his co-worker. He lived in New Jersey after 1842.

Elderly provincial lady—under less compulsion than Queen Marie-Amélie (Ill. 2495) to make any concessions at all to new fashions—retains the comfortable dress of the 30's which she knows to be extremely becoming and suitable. Her wonderful cap and *fraise* are, however, edged with the new padded and raised embroidery.

2534. XIXc. 1853. U.S.A.-French. (New York Public Library, Art Room.)

Jules David and *Compte-Calix*. "Monitor of Fashion," No. 1 (periodical).

"The Monitor of Fashion," with plates by two French dress designers, Compte-Calix and Jules David, was published from Sept. 1853 to 1854 in New York by Genio G. Scott. It has lovely delicate plates of extremely elegant gowns, and of embroidery patterns. The colors in which it was printed have sometimes altered, and often stain the opposite pages.

The fastidiously gloved visitors show embroidered white costumes which have grown entirely high-necked.

L. to r.: Deeply notched eyelet and raised embroidery flounces *à disposition,* like the ready-made dress lengths of printed or brocaded materials especially produced to be made up into flounced dresses, and sold with accompanying plates to show how the patterns may be utilized; tiny cap with a long fall of crisp, sheer ruffles and blue ribbons.

Cord-embroidered jacket-like bodice; pink ribbons at small collar and volants of raised and eyelet embroidery on the pagoda sleeve.

Green bodice, edged with embroidery.

Cap with lavender and brown ribbons, gray Louis XIV coat, laced in gold, worn with an embroidered white vest and lingerie sleeves, and a lavender and white skirt in a fragmentary plaid pattern.

2535

2535. XIXc. 1854. French. (Montpellier, Musee Fabre.)
Gustave Courbet. "Bon jour, M. Courbet . . ."

The fine provincial museum at Montpellier had been founded in 1837 with the collection of a M. Fabre. Another local art-lover, who intended to leave his pictures to the museum was a M. Bruyas, who got every artist he knew to paint his portrait.

Bruyas and his servant have gone out to meet Courbet, who is arriving on foot for a four months visit.

All show the wonderful beards which have reappeared for the first time in over two hundred years.

Courbet wears the shirt of his period, still wide and shapeless, with a small turned-back cuff. His trousers are tucked into the cloth tops of buttoned boots, after the manner of infantrymen's gaiters.

With a soft cap, Bruyas wears one of the wonderful new short country coats, lined throughout with a striped material which is rolled over the edge as a binding. Similar coats can be found through the 60's, with contrasting piped or braided edges. Their influence could still be seen in smoking jackets and dressing gowns in e. XXc., which were often made of reversible material, one side chocolate brown, perhaps, and the other a light snuff, finished with an edge of twisted silk cord.

2536-40. XIXc. 1854. U.S.A., Philadelphia.

F. Mahan. Paris, New York and Philadelphia fashions for Spring and Summer, 1854.

The fertility of invention shown in dress, particularly men's dress, during the 50's, was only one expression of the ferment and excitement of a tense decade.

Authors, artists, workers and women are all stirring in revolt. Formal religion is losing its hold, but the effort to synthesize a variety of new ideas and feelings has the force of a religious revival.

The aristocracy is being supplanted by the rich. Wives with money arrive in England from America and the outposts of Empire. Industrialization is shifting populations as never before in England; new inventions are constantly being made, especially in America, which has small manpower for the utilization of great resources.

Wide casting about for bases can be seen in the clothes and backgrounds of these fashion plates.

After a return to the Gothic, style has marched ahead chronologically, Louis by Louis, through the XVIIc. and XVIIIc.; in details of men's clothing shown here, it has arrived at a period scarcely more than a generation before its own time.

The New Gothic Masonic Temple is flanked by traditional XVIIIc. brick houses with small-paned windows, on one side; on the other, by office buildings of the new sort. The cotton goods district in downtown New York is still largely housed in buildings of this type built just before and after the Civil War. Castiron allows buildings like A. T.

Stewart's store of 1863 (now Wanamaker's), which was based on an Italian model, to provide more air and light than most offices built between the 70's and the most recent decades.

The lacings and hanging ends of ribbon on the jacket of the lady (2537) are of XVIIc. inspiration. The braided riding habit with wide cuffs and plumed hat (2540) is Louis XIV; the parlor furniture and hangings, Louis XV and XVI. An attempt is being made to reintroduce lace at the wrist of a gentleman (2539); his shirt has the ruffles and brooch, and another man (2536) the notched lapels of e. XIXc.

A great effort was made in mid-50's to popularize elaborately embroidered trousers (2536-2538); it was not very successful, although trousers did become loudly and enormously crossed with plaids. There are also a great many fancy vests, which will go out of use rather abruptly in first half of the 1860's.

Shirt bosoms are pleated; curved collars, set on a straight band, can stand or be turned down; with patterned vests and trousers, cravats are of plain satin, tied in thick wadded bows.

Shoulders are sloped by drawn-back seams; waists are long; skirts separately cut; sleeves usually have button-trimmed cuffs. Pockets, finished in many ways, are set in all sorts of new positions. One man (2539) has a diagonal pocket on the left chest; a tiny change pocket above the waist on the right, and a flap pocket set in the waist seam. Corduroy hunting outfit with jockey cap and gaiters (2539).

2541. XIXc. 1854. French. (Metropolitan Museum, Print Room.)

A. L. Noël, after *Winterhalter*. Empress Eugénie.

The Napoleonic tradition of white gowns with colored velvet trains is continued in the gowns of the court of Napoleon III.

The lovely evening gowns which Worth made for the Empress remain one of the classic forms of evening dress in our own XXc.—probably the most graceful in movement and the most universally becoming that has ever been contrived.

Gowns made of lace flounces are almost entirely a court fashion, but designs of white lace edgings on colored silk grounds are provided in the dress lengths *à disposition*.

Soft, natural parted hair is drawn back into a coil (which swells in size, so that the shape of head coverings will have to be changed to accommodate the mass). Quantities of important bracelets.

2542-44. XIXc. 1855-56. French.

E. Guérard.

2542. The Tuileries Gardens.
2543. The Boulevard des Italiens.
2544. The Palais d'Industrie.

2542. Nursemaids in trim uniform or the dress of their native province. Children in variations of the clothes seen in Ill. 2512-21: skirts with many ruffles, belted blouses, open jackets, trimmed with scallops, braid, buttons and Scotch tartan; worn with pantalettes or trousers; folding Scotch caps with streamers, forage caps, soft round hats, or in the case of girls, very small caps or mere hair ribbons.

2543. Smartly turned out equipages stop at the curb of Tortoni's establishment for a word with a gentleman who has been having one of its celebrated ices.

2544. Mixed crowds, drawn by the great Industrial Exposition of 1855.

The skirt of 1850 might have three gathered flounces of approximately the same depth worn over horsehair-stiffened petticoats. By latter half of the 50's, the flounces have multiplied in number, and are often of varying depth. Each flounce is now backed by stiffening and is ruffled on, so that it stands out from the body of the skirt. Its edge is scalloped, sprigged or edged to enhance the irregular protruding look. The increased size and weight of the skirt has been made possible by the new artificial crinoline petticoat, stiffened by whalebone, wire or watch-spring steel.

The body now appears triangular (2542). The tiny head has, paradoxically, been brought about by the increased bulk of the hair at the back of the

2543

2544

head (2541). Peach-basket-shaped bonnets cannot be set over it, and are replaced by little tied-on triangles, the old cornette come back (2544). Smooth shoulders spread into pagoda sleeves, and skirts below them become so distended that it is increasingly difficult to cut a fitted outer garment to cover them (2544). Shawls, or flowing mantles based on the triangular form of a shawl, also try to avoid crushing down skirts which it is hard enough to hold out; their use increases.

Tiny parasols; flat hats with streamers (like that on little girl, in 2544), which, it is felt, still give the complexion some protection, now that women are unwilling to be caged in a bonnet.

Wonderful details of omnibuses; flower seller and tied apron (2543, ext. right).

2545. XIXc. 1856. French. (Metropolitan Museum.)

G. Courbet. Amazon.

Habits of dark cloth are high necked, with narrow mannish sleeves, short basques tabbed in back, and scantier gored skirts, with most of the fullness drawn toward the back. Ribbon-trimmed black silk hat. The sleeve of the habit has been shortened to show a shirt sleeve and cuff, as in the current gown. The cuff-button is set low, although the turn-back of the cuff has deepened.

2546. XIXc. 1857-62. French.

Pierre Petit. Delacroix.

This photograph, taken in Paris in 1862, shows the painter with the same beard and hair, collar and stock, and the identical trousers and topcoat he wears in an 1857 photograph. The exception is the suit coat, which in 1857 has a velvet collar and braid-edged lapel. The trouser pocket, more clearly seen in the 1857 photograph, is not a straight slash, but is pointed like an envelope flap; fly closing now well established.

2547. XIXc. 1858. English.

John Leech. Illustration for "Ask Mamma."

There are not many surviving examples of the orange paper covers in which Victorian novels, like Surtees' "Ask Mamma" were published serially, in parts, at 1s. each.

Leech gives us a rare opportunity to see a Victorian gentleman in embroidered suspenders and flaring, turned back cuffs, tying a stock, while a maid gets her mistress into a ball gown. Women's hair, massed lower in back, is now apt to be waved.

The trim of an evening bodice is set on the line of the old lace valance, but in the general tendency toward scalloped edges, the material is apt to be caught up in front and at the shoulders. Skirts are apt to be trimmed by similar swags of material caught by flowers, bows, or both. A tendency towards asymmetry is shown early in the 50's in the placing of garlands of flowers across the bodice, running down the upper section of the skirt of an evening gown. Hair dressed with trailing flowers at the ears; many bracelets.

2548-49. Early XIXc. French. (Boston, Mus. of Fine Arts.)
   Two pairs of embroidered suspenders.
2550. XIXc. English? (Metropolitan Museum.)
   Man's silk handkerchief: red and yellow.

2551. Early XIXc. French or German? (Metropolitan
   Museum.)

   Pair of braces.

2552. XIXc. 1852-9. French.
Lithographed fashion plate.

2553. XIXc. 1858. French.
Calling costume; fawn taffeta brocaded in brown velvet in a lace design.

The elaborately bordered fabrics of the 50's and 60's were woven in special dress lengths, *à disposition*. They were accompanied by fashion plates showing how dresses might be cut from the available pattern, and the proportions to be used. Here we see the identical fabric, in suggested use as an evening dress, and made up into an actual visiting costume.

2554-55. XIXc. 1858. French.
"Nouveautés de Paris" (periodical fashion plate).

2554. Robe de mousseline à volants de coté.

2555. Robe d'organdi à deux volants doubles.

Materials were also printed in different patterns in allied colors (like the brown, beige, dull yellow and white seen here), so that they could be used together in alternating flounces of the newer sort: larger in number, and apt not to be identical in depth or pattern. The rise, multiplication and increased fullness of the skirt are paralleled by the sleeve; both its pagoda shape and the skirt outline become formless. With the approach of the 60's, the clutter begins to be cleared away. Sleeves are less trimmed, or are close in toward the wrist, or made plain and close, or so shortened that the shirt sleeve takes over. Horizontal decoration is pushed down toward the hem in small ruffles, velvet bands or braid. The front of the crinoline flattens and the skirt is often panelled with a ruched or pleated edging. In this muslin robe, panels are cut from a pattern which at least recalls rows of small ruffles.

Materials, we find from reading such advertisements as those in the "Illustrated London News" in 1858, are sold by the dress length. King's of Regent St. lists "the new autumn silks: striped and checked £1 2s 6d the Full Dress, Shepherd's Plaid Silks, Gros de Afriques & Gros Royals, Brocaded Poult de Soies; three-flounced silks: £2 2s 6d, two-flounced silks £2 18s 6d, velvet flounced silks £5 10s 0d, Moirés antiques £2 18s 6d, and Lyons silk velvets 7s 6d per yard" (for the favorite trimming).

Dresses can be bought partly finished: "Shepherd's-check flounced dress, made up in all colours, (the skirt) lined and richly trimmed with velvet with materials for Bodice, price 14s 9d; with our new Paris Jacket made and trimmed to correspond, 18s 6d the Dress complete. Drawings and patterns free. For country orders, size around the shoulders and waist, with the length of the skirt."

Courtesy of Metropolitan Museum of Art (2553); Print Room (2552, 2554-55)

2556   **2557**

2556-57. XIXc. 1857. German. (New York Public Lib.)

"Der Bazar" (periodical). Nov. 15. Parisian Modes.

Left. Robe of violet grenadine with three volants checked in darker color and trimmed with narrow silk fringe. Smooth bodice with *bretelles* and collar of notched lace; full mousseline sleeves with double cuffs of valenciennes.

Right. Robe of green rep with a double skirt, trimmed with matching tassels and braid. "Medici" sleeves with five puffs; ruffs at wrist and throat. Grenadine velvet hat trimmed with black lace.

2558-61. XIXc. 1857. German.

"Der Bazar," Dec. 1. Parisian Modes.

These French plates are found recopied in English and American magazines at about the same time.

The new long cloaks with oriental names, resulting from the Crimean War, have open sleeves, pèlerines and capuchon hoods, tassel and braid trim.

Flounced skirts are being replaced by plainer skirts, often à *tablier,* with apron-shaped panels in front, patterned in small squares or diamonds, narrowly cross-hatched in lines of self-colored velvet or satin, and dotted with vertical lines of buttons or passementerie.

2558. Gray taffeta dress: apron-shaped panel in velvet linen edged in buttons. Mantle of blue and black *drap mousaya* with blue wool trimming and tassels. Hat of field-gray taffeta and velvet, trimmed with a tuft of lace on one side, grape tendrils on the other, tulle ruche under brim and band of velvet in back.

2559. Gown of fancy material. Dark brown *Caid* mantle trimmed with galloon Brandenbourgs; the burnous has a capuchon hood. Red velvet bonnet, trimmed with three rolls of velvet, curled plume, tulle or blonde.

2560. Steel gray cashmere dress. Mantle à *l'hongroise.* Corded green silk hat with velvet leaves and flowers under the brim. Compromise between triangular, flattened bonnet and the oncoming hats; curtain of bonnet turning into a rumpled brim in back.

2561. Wool dress; apron panel diapered in narrow satin bands trimmed with lines of passementerie. *Pultava* mantle in brown plush, striped in white. White satin hat with a lace ruffle and garnet lining.

2562. XVIII-XIXc. India.
Cashmere shawl.
2563. Early XIXc. India.
Cashmere shawl: brick red ground, embroidered border.
2564. XIXc. India.
"Paisley" shawl: black center; palm leaf border in red, blue and green.
2565. Early XIXc. English.
Printed handkerchief: *Declaration of Independence.*
2566-67. XIXc. c. 1840. Alsatian, Mulhouse.
Two cotton calicos: "paisley" shawl designs and colorings; impure, degraded derivatives.

2568-70. First half XIXc. Alsatian, Mulhouse.
Three cotton calicos: designs particularly popular in black, gray, lavender and purples.
2571-74. XIXc. French.
"Le Moniteur des Dames et Demoiselles" (periodical). 2571-72. Plate by *Jules David:* Church (1857); 2573-74. Plate by *F. C. Compte-Calix:* Country (1858).

Hats and coats are reestablished in everyday use but, as in late XVIIIc., they are informal. Church and calling costumes still require bonnet and shawl.

2576   2577

2575

Jules David shows children dressed for first communion:

2571. Mother: small white bonnet over a tumbling chignon. Hair is frequently clubbed into a net in the late 50's. The usage will increase and the nets become dotted with chenille. Chocolate-brown and black plaid gown, and India shawl. As both women show, shawls or shawl-like coverings have largely replaced fitted overgarments: the shawl adds to the triangular body outline, protects the chest and shoulders without deforming the distended skirt, which offers plenty of problems as it is. A fine India shawl was light but extremely warm; it was also a luxury comparable to mink or sable today; its cost could rise into the thousands.

2572. Daughter: increasingly fussy lower sleeve of late 50's, often in repeated puffs, with the new interest in panels expressed in wide ribbon tabs.

2573. The hunter wears a wide-brimmed brown hat, green corduroy coat and white trousers.

2574. His lady: wide flat brown hat with red flowers, green leaves, and black streamers; black and white shawl, with a capuchon hood bordered in plaid, tasseled and fringed in red, blue, green, black and white; gown with white ground, bands of blue plaid and beige flowers.

2575. XIXc. 1858. U.S.A. (New York Public Library.)
"Graham's Magazine" (May), Philadelphia.

Calling costumes follow the trend already set by walking dress. Skirt flounces are less rumpled; their numbers are reduced, and the outline of the costume becomes more clearly defined than in Ills. 2556-57. The division by plain and checked material combined on one flounce in 1857, is now made on alternating flounces. The flounces are laid on flatter; a scalloped edge commemorates the actual projection of the 1857 flounces.

Apron-shaped panels, cross-hatched and studded into diaper-cloth patterns, are characteristic of the late 50's (2558-61).

The apron is used here on a coat-costume allied to that worn by the Empress Eugenie. This fashion plate shows the new smoothness of the bodice and shoulder-line, which is emphasized in the captions of fashion plates, as bretelles are eliminated. Sleeves of dresses and chemisettes also become less complicated.

Hats worn with walking dress are still apt to carry the flowers, lace and strings of the bonnet from which they are just becoming differentiated. By the 60's they will become plainer and their brims smaller. White walking dress; brown hat and strings, with trimming of white lace and pink and white flowers.

Casaque for visiting, heavily trimmed with black lace, worn with the required bonnet, over a blue and black gown; small parasol of white lace.

Boy in white dress, magenta jacket and gaiters, plaid stockings.

2576-77. XIXc. 1858. German. (New York Public Lib.)
"Der Bazar," Aug. 8.

Clearer bell-shaped outlines and reduction of clutter; fewer horizontal lines; projecting flounces replaced by bands of pleating.

2576. Dress of horizontally striped gray taffeta, trimmed in gray taffeta with puffings of violet taffeta. "Horn of plenty"-shaped sleeves with shoulder caps and a "jockey" of violet puffing. Sleeves of embroidered mull. Rice straw bonnet trimmed with white tulle and violets.

2577. Black barège gown, with two skirts; pleated trim à la vielle, like the edgings of XVIIIc. skirts. Ruched bretelles; sleeves a yard wide at the bottom. Black crêpe bonnet trimmed with black taffeta braids, black dahlias with salmon-colored glass centers, and black silk lace (blonde). The inevitable lace parasol of ceremonious dress. This French design appears in fashion magazines in England and U. S. A. as well.

2578-80. XIXc. 1858. English. (New York Public Library.)
"Illustrated London News," Oct. 2.

Original text quoted.

2578. "A dress in the new style called *à six lis*. It has a double skirt—the upper one consisting of six breadths of silk of two different kinds; the one being plain rose colour and the other having a light gray checquered with rose.

"The breadths of these two different silks are disposed alternately, and the upper skirt is edged with white and rose-colored fringe, having a head of passementerie. The corsage is three-quarters high, and over it is worn a small fichu Antoinette made of white tulle, disposed in flat plaits, each one headed by a plisse of narrow, rose-colored ribbon. The sleeves, which, like the upper skirt of the dress, are made of two different silks, are wide and do not descend lower than the elbow. They are trimmed with fringe like that which edges the skirt, under-sleeves of plain tulle in three puffs, between each of which there is a ruche of rose-colored ribbon with a small bow in front of the arm. The lower skirt is composed of chequered silk, edged by a broad band of rose colour. Bonnet of paille-de-riz, with crown of rose-colored tulle, encircled by a wreath of small roses and foliage. Undertrimming, a cordon of the same."

2579. "Dress with double skirt of green silk, of that bright marine hue to which the French have given the name of vert d'Azof. The corsage is plain, high to the throat, and pointed at the waist both in front and at the back. The sleeves are slit open in front of the arm, and edged round with tassel fringe. The same trimming edges the upper skirt of the dress.

The scarf mantelet of black silk is trimmed with very rich chenille fringe. Bonnet of white silk, trimmed with mauve color. The bavolet (or curtain) is made of mauve-colored ribbon, and the wide strings are edged with a narrow plisse of mauve color. The undertrimming consists of a demi-wreath of white daisies, placed on the upper part of the forehead, under-sleeves of plain muslin, confined at the wrists by coral bracelets."

2580. "Evening Costume. Dress of white muslin with three flounces, simply edged with broad hems. The low corsage has a berthe of maltese lace, and the sleeves are trimmed with the same. Sash of tartan ribbon, fastened in front of the waist in a bow, and long flowing ends. Bows of the same ribbon on the shoulders. Collarette of black velvet, fastened in front of the throat by a pearl brooch. Head-dress: bows of black velvet fixed in pearl-headed Italian pins. Black velvet bracelets with pearl snaps."

2581-87. XIXc. 1858. French-U.S.A.

"Le Progrès: Bulletin of Fashion," No. 98, New York (Feb.).

An American publication shows the fashions of Paris hat, shoe and shirt makers.

There is still great variety in hat crowns and brims; they will become much less romantic with the 60's, and turn into plain stovepipe hats, most resembling the central example shown here.

Hair is still full, but there is a tendency (shown by the same man) for the back of a gentleman's head to be trimmed short, as only servants' hair has been cut in the fashion plates of the last decades. Beards, dundrearies, mutton chops and moustaches continue, but more clean shaven faces appear in the 60's. Shoe heels become much higher, and heels begin to appear on women's shoes as well.

The cut of clothes still has a romantic elegance, but the approach of the long, heavy, shapeless clothes of the 60's can be sensed, except in the trousers. These are still made from checked cloth and show no signs of baggy knees, whereas the shapeless trousers of the 60's are plainer, sometimes braided down the outseam, striped rather widely, or patterned in small checks.

Vests decline in importance, as coat fronts begin to button, or, in the case of frock and tail coats, are cut to meet. The waistline slips lower; coat skirts are longer and straighter; sleeves widen throughout; overcoats for city wear are much longer and straighter, with breast pocket flaps, smaller buttons, and edges "enhanced by the application of a peculiar

and neatly stitched binding." (Adv. in *Illus. London News,* Oct. 23, 1858.) Capes have been worn through the romantic period; the 50's are full of cape-like coats and coat-like capes. There is, if anything, an increase in frogged and tasseled closings on short, informal topcoats, and on smoking jackets and dressing gowns, all of which have shawl collars.

Footmen in XVIIIc. court livery and fourragères, heavily braided. The young son of the house in a military looking belted blouse and braided kepi.

Interest is working back through the Renaissance to the Gothic; massive carved furniture with coats of arms.

2588. XIXc. 1858. U.S.A. (Boston, Mus. of Fine Arts.) *Winslow Homer.* Boston Common.

Round crinolines and hoops were hard enough to manage without wind. Feet and legs inevitably begin to show just before the crinoline starts to be

2588

flattened in front into greater manageability. The struggle to conceal the feet is admitted to be a lost cause. Shoes come to have heels and decoration and stockings are made in colors, stripes and plaids. In Boston in 1858, there are heels on shoes, but the only plaid legs are the gaiters of the little boy who has lost his plumed straw hat.

Top hat with straight brim and crown; long, less fitted coat; cuffs a little longer over the hand; checked trousers. Canes have horn or metal heads bent at a right angle.

2589-95. XIXc. 1859. U.S.A.-French.
"Le Progrès: Bulletin of Fashion," No. 110, New York (Feb.).

Increase of costumes for sports, indoors and out, and for comfortable leisure at home. A great deal of pattern is still used, but it tends to become smaller and to be used on all three pieces of the suit. Trousers and sleeves are wider; coats straighter, longer, buttoned higher, with great attention to edges; these are stitched, piped or braided. Bows and four-in-hands better tied; cravats crossed and stuck with a gold pin. Watch chains with massive links. Back hair trimmed shorter.

The Gothic revival brings a renewed interest in fencing; suits of armor stand about and crossed swords decorate dark, gold-scrolled wallpapers. There are half a dozen advertisements weekly in the *Illus. London News* of Heraldic Offices where family arms, crests and pedigrees can be obtained. Coats of arms begin to be seen again.

Heavy velvet curtains, divans and comfortably upholstered chairs, button-tufted and fringed. Anything for which a beadwork, crochet or cross-stitch cover can be made now has one, and the band about the upholstered chair was undoubtedly some of the hostess' woolwork. All the weeklies and fashion magazines now publish fancy-work patterns, but they are probably seen at their most wonderful in the huge plates (of tea-cosies, netted bottle cases, paper flowers, and every article of wearing apparel of the whole family) found in "Der Bazar, Illustrirte Damen-Zeitung," published in Berlin from about 1854 (New York Public Library).

Black enamel and gold decorated furniture, some inlaid with mother-of-pearl. Machine-produced ingrain carpets in quantity in the latter half 50's cover the floor from wall to wall.

2596. XIXc. 1859. French. (London, Nat. Port. Gall.)
Winterhalter. Albert, Consort of Victoria.

2597. XIXc. 1859-60. French. (Vevay, Musee des Beaux-
Arts.)
Courbet. Dr. Max Bouchon.

A good deal of slope-shouldered elegance is retained, but trousers are more tubular. Albert's head
is conventionally fluffy, but Dr. Bouchon's hair,
beard and moustache are uncurled and smoothed
down in the new way. Heavier, wider-toed shoes.

2598. XIXc. c. 1859. U.S.A.
Thomas Read. The Children of Marcus Ward.

Boy's hair slicked down. Baby boys in the U. S. A.
appear in underwear-like outfits, completely white
and much tucked and embroidered. They are bow-
tied at each shoulder of a low slipping neckline like
that of a woman's evening dress. A very amusing
American primitive in the New York Hist. Soc.
shows a boy with a small dog and a huge drum,
similarly dressed with knee-length drawers and no
petticoat. Victorian Gothic furniture. Round tables
with circular velvet or broadcloth covers to the floor,
edged with fringe and embroidered in colors on
gold.

2599. XIXc. 1859. French. (Delphine Ramel Coll.)
Ingres. Mme. Ingres.

Mme. Ingres' bodice elaborates the use of fringed
shawl borders and corners seen on Mme. Moitessier
(Ill. 2522). The flowered brocades of the periods of
the various Louis' are passing, and the ribbon
streamers at Mme. Moitessier's shoulders have be-

come complicated by the 60's into dipping caps, set
over puffs. In evening gowns, a line of lingerie rises
from under the neckline of the shorter-waisted bodice. Hair returns to smooth loops over the ears.
Lappets with rounded ends hang from caps and
bonnets, and are tied under the chin. The rounded
and trimmed ends of bonnet strings may spread
over most of the bosom of a cloak in the 60's.

2600. XIXc. 1858-60. English. (London, South Kensing-
    ton Museum.)

D. G. Rossetti. Elizabeth Eleanor Siddal.

The beautiful Miss Siddal, who married Rossetti
in 1860 and committed suicide in 1862, had been a
milliner's assistant and a model for the Pre-Raphael-
ites. She is shown here in the sort of esthetic garment with which they attempted to reform women's
crinolined and corseted dress. Rossetti, a friend of
William Morris since Oxford, joined with him,
Burne-Jones, and others in founding the firm of
Morris, Marshall & Faulkner in 1862, for the reform
of architecture and interior decoration as well.

2601

2601. XIXc. 1860. English.

John Leech. Surtees: "Plain or Ringlets." The Gipsy's Prophecy.

Little round hats with a feather are worn over hair caught in chenille-dotted nets. Older women wear small triangular bonnets fastened with long, wide bonnet strings tied in a substantial bow. Tiny frilled parasols. Man (background, l.) in a white summer suit and round-crowned hat; low-crowned bowlers are common by mid60's. Riding habit (backgr. r.) short basques; gored skirt cut longer and fuller in back than in 1850.

2602. XIXc. c. 1860. English. (Metropolitan Museum, Print Room.)

W. M. Thackeray. Mr. T. Visiting Mrs. W. H. Brookfield.

This very amusing combination of silhouette and water color, supposed to be by the novelist's own hand, is so full of contradictions that it may very well be a forgery. Mrs. B. was married in 1841; the little girl of perhaps six might be well along in a series; Mrs. B.'s three skirt flounces could scarcely lie so flat after the mid50's, nor her skirt have become so distended much before that time; it is probably a rather uninspired cutting of the dress of the turn of the 50's and 60's. Thackeray died late in 1863, but the firm of *Morris, Marshall, Faulkner & Co.* founded in January, 1862, had scarcely had time to become an extremely potent influence or to have developed its own style to this extent. In any

case, the architecture and decoration shown here are pure "artistic" 1870's:

Small-paned windows set over narrow, herringbone panelling; dado, lined with china; lamp set on a bracket; Eastlake furniture; bric-a-brac filling a what-not; photographs and pictures in easel frames; Chinese jardinières and umbrella-stands filled with cactus, dried pampas grass, and palm leaf fans. Similar panelling in my grandfather's very "elegant mansion" of the period, in U. S. A., was done in strips stained alternately light and dark, which gleamed, cherry and lemon-colored, under mirror-like varnish; the window was in red, blue, green, yellow and purple glass.

2602

2603. XIXc. c. 1847. English. (Metropolitan Museum.)
  Victorian wedding dress: pale gray satin with moiré stripes.

2604. XIXc. c. 1854. U.S.A. (Museum of the City of New York.)
  Wedding dress: cream taffeta.

2605. XIXc. 1860. U.S.A. (Metropolitan Museum.)
  Dress for a 13-year-old girl: Alsatian-made challis.

2606. XIXc. c. 1860. U.S.A. (Brooklyn Museum.)
  Walking dress: apple green and white figured silk.

2607. XIXc. 1860. U.S.A. (Museum of the City of New York.)
Ball dress: lavender silk, brocaded in gray velvet. Worn at the 1860 ball for the Prince of Wales.

2608. XIXc. 1861. U.S.A. (Museum of the City of New York.)
Victorian ball dress: white moiré and turquoise blue velvet.

2609. XIXc. c. 1863. U.S.A. (Metropolitan Museum.)
Victorian ball dress: blue taffeta, brocaded in black velvet.

2610. XIXc. 1863. English-Scottish. (Toronto, Capt. James W. Flanagan.)
Ball dress: Stuart tartan; made by Elise of London for Alexandra, Princess of Wales, for a ball at Balmoral Castle.

2611. XIXc. c. 1860. French.

Pink taffeta ball gown, trimmed with ruching of self material, and frills of cream-colored lace.

2612. XIXc. 1860-64. English.

Ball dress of lilac ribbed silk trimmed with ruching of lilac taffeta and black and cream lace. Black lace mitts and shawl.

"What-not" with shells and china souvenirs; artificial flowers under a glass bell.

2613. XIXc. c. 1864. Viennese.

Purple faille silk visiting dress trimmed with applied feather motive done in black chenille and velvet ribbon.

Cap of black and white net trimmed with purple ribbon bows.

2614. XIXc. 1865. English.

Cherry red satin visiting dress trimmed with red velvet and black lace. Black lace coat (American c.1865). Hat of natural colored straw trimmed with black lace and red flowers (European c.1865).

Courtesy of Metropolitan Museum, Costume Institute

2615

2615. XIXc. U.S.A.

"Illustrated London News," Nov. 24, 1860. Grand Ball given at the Academy of Music, N. Y., in honor of His Royal Highness, the Prince of Wales.

The greatest social event which had ever taken place in the United States was the ball for the Prince of Wales. He arrived as "Lord Renfrew" and is the slender young man in the middle, the Ribbon of the Garter with which he had been invested in 1858 across his chest. It took the democratic United States more than half a century to recover from its interest in nobility, which got worse before it got better.

Women's clothes are still influenced by XVIIIc. court styles. The photograph of gown (2607) worn at this ball shows a bordered silk *à disposition* in a French lace pattern. The girl with whom the Prince dances has an XVIIIc. overskirt over a common form of underskirt made of narrow rows of puffings. Necklines dip toward the parting of the breasts. The decoration of the top of the bodice, usually puffed, is elaborated at the shoulders, sometimes over a puffed sleeve.

2616 – 2620

2621 – 2625

2616-20. XIXc. 1862. French. (Metropolitan Museum, Print Room.)

"Les Modes parisiennes" (periodical). Petticoats, corsets, and skirt-lifter.

2621-25. XIXc. German. (New York Public Library.)

"Der Bazar," Oct. 1, 1864. Crinolines from 1858-1865.

2626. XIXc. French.

Photograph of street. Shops exhibiting crinolines.

Crinolines, when they appeared in mid50's, were a great improvement over piled-on petticoats. But they had many disadvantages. They were inflammable. "Not a year passes but in this country alone hundreds suffer death by burning through crinoline." Eventually, women of all classes wore crinolines, and could burn up while cooking dinner in a sweeping skirt, as well as while waltzing in a skirt puffed with tulle.

"Eugénie hoop skeleton skirts" and "Vigoria crinoline petticoats," advertised in "The Queen," 1858, were largely replaced by cages of hoops made of watch-spring steel "so flexible that they can be wound around the finger," covered with "lace yarn." (Advertisement. Godey's, 1858.)

Douglas and Sherwood's "new expansion skirt" was an improvement for flexibility and support over their patent adjustable bustle and skirt of fine cloth, whalebone, and eyelets; its expansion adjustments and slides are silvered against sticking, as the rubber-

covered ones do. Gutta-percha covered hoops, on the other hand, were washable. All forms of uncased metal hoops were likely to catch in the shoe.

Every month in every magazine read by women for nearly two decades, new patents are advertised which positively obviate some complication attendant on hoops. A unique method, in each case, keeps them from being heavy, weak, inflammable, dirty, rusty, menacing traps, or causes of embarrassment. One does "not cause accidents"; another "allows a lady (to) ascend a steep stair, throw herself into an armchair, etc., without inconvenience to herself, or provoking the rude remarks of the observers." (Quoted by Cunnington.)

Mme. Demorest, who published the "Mirror of Fashion" in New York in 1862, also had an emporium which sold sewing machines (with extra self-tucking and quilting attachments at $5), eagle talon hooks and eyes, and her "Prize Medal Skirt," which "Godey's" speaks of as superior:

"These graceful, durable and economical skirts possess and combine every desirable quality. The standards are very numerous, and being passed through the covering, prevents the possibility of their slipping on the springs or GETTING OUT OF ORDER, and as their peculiarity has been patented, they cannot be sold by other parties generally. The size is very moderate, and the shape that which is best adapted for giving a graceful and undulating flow to the fullness of the dress. The materials of which the springs are composed has been wrought and tempered to an exquisite nicety. The strength is equal to any emergency to which it is likely to be subjected." You also got twice as many springs for half the price of former wire supports, in Mme. Demorest's wire skirt.

By 1850, little whalebone was used in corsets. They were elaborately gored, with set-in gussets of elastic. Front closings with spring latches were first shown at the 1851 exhibition. George Roberts' showrooms had "500 real linsey-woolsey and patent steel petticoats and 5000 pairs of stays to choose from" in 1858. (Ill. London News.)

Corsets become shorter-waisted with the approach of the 60's; they close in front or back, with a steel busk in front, few bones, and many elastic gussets. As the crinoline diminishes, the corset becomes more tightly laced.

The round crinoline of 1858 becomes flattened in front by 1862, and has been made much smaller above. From then until the return of the bustle in the 70's, the crinoline is progressively skeletonized. By latter half 60's, it has usually returned to the form of a gored petticoat of fabric with a flat panel in front and a few steels threaded through slots in the bottom; or it may be held out by rows of horsehair-filled puffings. It may simply be a steel-threaded hem hung on tapes from the waist.

With summer dresses, two white petticoats were worn over a crinoline, or one white petticoat over a "steel petticoat." With other dresses, the crinoline was covered by one colored petticoat of silk or wool.

English women are becoming physically active by the 60's. They walk and participate in sports for which special clothing will have to be provided.

Crinolines bounce; English women become less perturbed by what is revealed, and early in the 60's, begin instead to exploit it. Petticoat hems become as elaborately trimmed as the hems of dresses, and are made in brilliant colors: red, plaids, or stripes, as are stockings. English walking boots are trimmed and made in bright, eye-catching colors. Methods of hitching up the skirt mechanically are contrived, by which the petticoat is permanently displayed.

England, usually a year behind France, leads France by a year in these matters of striking shoes, stockings and petticoats; English colors are more violent and English hats and bonnets are overtrimmed by French standards.

The English petticoat with hitched-up skirts was notice by Eugénie on a visit to England; by the summer of 1862 French fashion plates show skirts which exploit what is underneath. Skirts hitched up by mechanical devices come quickly into general French use, and can be seen on Manet's *Street Singer* (1862, Ill. 2736).

During the 60's, hips are made increasingly slender; skirts are gored and petticoat fullness is set further down on deeper yokes. By 1865, the problem of keeping the hem of the skirt hitched up for active wear is solved by making the skirts of walking dresses shorter than the petticoat.

Mechanical lifting devices had begun to be advertised in second half of the 50's. "Nicolls' Patent Highland Cloak for ladies," says the Illus. London News in 1858, "somewhat resembles the old Spanish Roquelaire and has an elastic Capucine Hood. It is not cumbersome or heavy and measures 12 to 16 yards around the outer edge, falling in graceful folds from the shoulder, but by a mechanical contrivance (such being a part of the patent) the wearer can instantly form semi-sleeves, and thus leave the arms at liberty; at the same time the cloak can be made as quickly to resume its original shape. . . . The price will be two guineas and a half for each cloak, but with the Mecanique and a lined Hood, a few shillings more is charged."

Mme. de Plument's method (2616-20) of catching up her handsome petticoats is no doubt a specialty of her corset shop.

This interest in conversion and mechanical devices is not restricted to clothing. "Der Bazar," that catch-all of the latest gadgets, shows patent folding bent-wood chairs in 1864. America, with her great resources and small population, had been forced to invent labor-saving devices during the 50's. "The only substructure capable of supporting the drawn-up skirt gracefully" in 1863, is the *"cage Americaine."*

The American sewing machine, with special attachments (like Mme. Demorest's) is used to finish the already partly-made women's dress. Men's and boys' clothing becomes almost entirely factory-made during the 60's.

American folding beds, mechanical devices and wonderful tools, shown at the Philadelphia Centennial Fair in 1876, will fascinate English people, who have relegated to the attic or servants' rooms, and long ago forgotten, the ingenious convertible furniture invented by Sheraton (*Designs for Hunting Furniture,* 3rd edition, 1812).

Women's clothing, sold ready-made or semi-finished in the 50's, becomes almost entirely machine-sewed by the 60's. During this decade, women's clothing becomes subdivided into more special categories than had ever been known before, or seen since the 70's. There are clothes for the house alone, for walking on the street, for walking at the beach at Brighton; for playing tennis or bathing; clothes for church, for making calls; for different sorts of evening wear. Some are made by tailors, others by dressmakers. Hats may be worn with some; others require the more formal bonnet; all take different shoes, coats and wraps.

This makes it possible for a large part of women's clothing to be factory-made, as boots and shoes, and men's and children's clothes already are. By the final quarter-century practically all inexpensive everyday and work clothes of both sexes will be factory produced.

2627-32. XIXc. 1860. French-English.

"L'Illustrateur des Dames" (periodical). Plates of fashions shown at the London Exposition.

Crinolines bounce; feet show; shoes acquire heels and are made well worth looking at.

2627. Bottine de Dames (Angleterre): black with green uppers.

2628. Bottine-Eugénie (Angleterre): copper brown.

2629. Soulier de Boudoir (France): white, lined with blue; blue and white trimming.

2630. Descente de lit (France): white, lined with a light sharp blue to match heel, and touches in its white trim.

2631. Mule, Louis XIV (France): cerise.

2632. Bottine de Bal (France): black boot with a silvery-gold heel and appliquéd stars and moon; gold, silver and white fringe.

2633-41. XIXc. 1864. German.

"Der Bazar," Dec. 1.

Higher and more elaborate boots, which, the cap-

tion explains, follow the trend toward masculine styles.

2633. High boot of Russia leather; Cossack embroidery in black and white silk; black ball fringe, buttons and velvet bow.

2634. Boot checkered in black and gray leather lozenges; toe of patent leather; closed by gray cord and large white mother-of-pearl buttons; notched top finished with black lace.

2635. High boot of brown morocco, edged with black patent leather; dark brown taffeta laces and three brown chenille tassels.

2636. Pansy purple velvet shoe, gray border, flower appliqué in gold satin, purple cord and tassel.

2637. Young girl's half high boot of brown rep, trimmed with a bunch of flowers made of black lace or passementerie.

2638. Black patent leather shoe, lined with red morocco, red cord edge and tassel.

2639. Boot of Romany leather and elastic, trimmed in patent leather with jet ball buttons.

2640. Black grosgrain shoe, checkered appliqué in white and purple; rosette of black chenille with a white mother-of-pearl center.

2641. Black satin boot. Three rolls of gray plush at the top represent the stalk, and gray leather trim on the boot, the leaves, seed pods, and flower of a reed-plant; gray pearl buttons.

2642

2645

2644

2643

2646

2647

2648

2649

2650

2651

2652

2653

2642-63. XIXc. 1862. German. (New York Public Lib.)
"Der Bazar," April 1.
2642, 2645. Collars: man.
2643, 46. Pinafores: girl, 3-5 years; girl, 5-7 years.
2644. Shirt: man.
2647. Corset: girl, 4-6 years.

2648-49. Shirt: boy.
2650. Petticoat: girl, 3-5 years.
2651. Drawers: girl, 6-8 years.
2652. White blouse: girl, 9-11 years; blouses of
the elaborate *canezou* type are extremely popular
with women as well.

2653. Nightgown: girl, 10-14 years.
2654, 55. Nightcap; Zouave chemisette: lady.
2656. Shoes: baby, 6-12 mos.
2657. Embroidered bee (actual size), for cashmere shawl.

2658. Embroidered cashmere scarf.
2659. Bed jacket: lady.
2660. Collar and chemisette: lady, negligée dress.
2661. Sleeve with cuff: lady, negligée dress.
2662, 63. Chemise, gauffered trim; nightshirt: lady.

2664-69. XIXc. First half 1860's.

Cartes de Visite.

2664. George Becks (New York c.1860).

2665. Man and 2 women (unknown).

2666. Husband and wife (St. Johns, New Brunswick).

2667. Man in checked suit and leggings (Provenance unknown, April 8, 1862).

2668. William Byron (Provenance unknown, April 16, 1863).

2669. Photographed by Southwell Bros., London, Photographers Royal.

Courtesy of Culver Service

2670-75. XIXc. French.
Cartes de Visite.

2670. Empress Eugenie (French, latter half of 50's).

2671. H. R. H. the Princess Alice, Mother of the Czarina (English, 1862).

2672. The future Edward VII and Alexandra, about the time of their marriage (English c.1863).

2673. Black pillbox hat with feathers (Provenance unknown, 1862).

2674. Ermine trimmed jacket (unknown).

2675. Embroidered tabs on chest (unknown).

The passion of the 1850's for Louis XIII-XVI dress and furniture is most familiar to us now in the horsehair-covered rosewood or mahogany chairs which the Victorians evolved out of Louis XVI forms, and which we see in so many of these *cartes de visite.*

Women began to assume men's coats and vests by 1850. Jackets, such as the Empress wears, based on French court coats, with basques equivalent to one of the standard three skirt flounces, are typical of the 50's. The Empress appears to have liked this coat-style very much; she is shown in photographs of the 60's wearing it, with cuffs and a much reduced peplum edged with long fringe.

The Empress, who led in replacing layers of flounced petticoat by the crinoline in 1856, was beautifully dressed by Worth in perfect rather than extreme taste, but is apt to be years in advance of the usual photograph.

Other elements of her dress are seen in French fashion plates of latter half of the 50's. These plates are first redrawn in English magazines; a few weeks later they appear in *Der Bazar,* and the month after that in *Godey's.* By the time an American girl has been photographed in a dilution of the style, in her best, but not absolutely new dress, several years have passed. The English time lag is about one year.

With the crinoline, skirts can afford to lose their puckered flounces and turn full, round, simpler and more becoming. Trimmings alter in the same way; puffed bands become formalized into cartridge or flat pleated self-trimmings—which will become standard in the 60's. The Empress wears this sort of trimming at a time when the partly made up dresses advertised in English newspapers are all banded in velvet, and many are still cluttered with flounces. Sleeves also become simplified, together with their undersleeves; the Empress wears high close cuffs, just before the close sleeve begins to reappear as an alternative to pagoda and bishop sleeves, in the last years of the 50's; white undersleeves also become simplified, and high cuffs appear on plain sleeves. Instead of bretelles, a slight fullness is carried down her bodice from each shoulder.

Square India shawls, folded into a triangle, are supplanted by long, scarf-like shapes (2671) before they (and similar lace shawls) disappear altogether with the advent of the bustled dress.

The reduction of the crinoline begins first at its top by the beginning of the 60's. English girls who, in 1865, are "brave enough to be seen without crinolines" are "remarked for their extremely forlorn appearance." There is only a band of bottom support on the skirt of (2675). The young girl of Nancy in 1865 (2679) is lank indeed.

At the turn of the 50's-60's, in France, and in 1860 in England and America, begins a series of bolero-like jackets: gold braided red Garibaldi jackets, zouave jackets, the Spanish braided velvet jackets, Figaros and the "Alexandra" which appears at the time of her marriage (2672). White blouses of the lingerie canezou type, or scrolled in corded patterns, and loose red Garibaldi shirts trimmed in black soutache, are worn with colored skirts, belts and fitted corselets, throughout first half of 60's. Large buttons run up dress fronts from late 50's through the first years of the 60's. Black velvet ribbon with pendant at throat (2671, 2672) and Manet, 1866, *Woman with Parrot* (2739).

Round skirts of even length tend to become flattened in front, and to drag out in back, with the front and sides gored, and fullness massed toward the back. By mid60's crinolines are worn by women of all ages and classes. Active young women appear in skirts well off the ground, during the daytime. Skirts are no longer drawn up mechanically for walking, but are made in distinct categories of short skirts and bustled trained skirts for calling and evening. London tailors and habit makers begin to make women's daytime clothes of the sort in which Alexandra looked particularly well.

Curls were worn bunched behind the ears *à l'hongroise* for a couple of brief years at the end of the 50's, and began to be seen again in daytime use at mid60's. As the head becomes squarer bonnets are largely replaced by hats, but their bows and wide strings are continued in round embroidered tabs at the throat (2675). Designs for their decoration appear in pattern books for several years before 1865.

Edward (2672), one of the best dressed of kings, wears a standing wing collar, dotted tie, run (like Dickens', 1857) through a ring, matching vest and coat with braided edges, and gray trousers.

2676-81. XIXc. 1860-67. French.

2676. Woman seated among fuchsia plants.

This dress, which shows analogies with Ill. 2670 in its cartridge-pleated trim and fullness of the bodice from the shoulders, is set, by a fascinating chance, against a background of fuchsia plants. The beloved colors combined in fuchsia flowers were among the first coal-tar dyes to be produced: mauve, 1856, followed at the end of the 50's by magenta and solferino (fuchsia), Hoffmann's Violet, Iodine Green, Bismarck Brown, and Aniline Blue and Black. We see costumes carried out largely in these new aniline colors, by 1863-4, in the strongly contrasted costumes characteristic of the 60's.

2677. Rigolboche, Queen of the Can-Can.

Rigolboche was not one of the elegant cocottes like Cora Pearl or the prodigal Anna Deslions, although she had diamonds and carriages to match theirs. She danced at the Mabille Gardens in the 60's, where the Prince of Wales and the greatest figures in French society and the arts could be found on Tuesdays and Saturdays. Rigolboche was ugly as a death's head, smoked like a chimney, and yelled out anything that came into her head, in rough, audacious slang and a voice like broken glass. She danced with a uninhibited frenzy which nearly dislocated her wonderful legs. Instead of dying bankrupt at forty-four like Cora Pearl, she retired early to the Côte d'Azur where she finished her days running a most respectable boarding-house for ladies.

2678. Cape and lace scarf (1863).

2679. Young girl from Nancy (1865). Skirt without crinoline.

2680. Veiled head (1865).

2681. Plumed hat, lace scarf (1867). Black lace and tulle squares and triangles reduced from shawls to scarves and veils. Hat brim rolled up at sides; pendant earrings, as hair is drawn up; masses of artificial hair in chignon.

2682-83. XIXc. 1860-65. Italian. (New York Public Library, Picture Coll.)
Garibaldi.

The triumphs of the Italian liberator in the summer of 1860 and the enthusiasm with which he was received in London in 1864 gave a long life to fashions inspired by his pill-box cap and blazing shirt.

Young women were adopting men's styles, from jockey cap to boots, and taking pleasure in violent contrasts. Nothing pleased them more, for half a decade, than these Garibaldi styles. They wore the pill box, scrolled with braid, exactly like the versions in which he was photographed; it also affected the shape of other hats. His bloused red shirt is always full and buttoned down the front, with a loose sleeve and tight cuff; it is often plain, but in its character-

2682

istic form has a tucked bosom and is more elaborately decorated with gold or black soutache than
the shirt he wears here. "Garibaldi striped silks" appeared in 1860 in England.

**2684. XIXc. 1863. English. (New York Public Library,
Picture Coll.)**
Edward VII as Prince of Wales.

2685. XIXc. 1867. English. (Culver Service.)
Charles Dickens.
On his second American lecture tour, the English
author is dressed to knock his provincial audience
cold in admiration of his elegance. It still has a
certain force.
The degradation of the patchwork quilt had begun by the 50's, but quilting was still a technique
in which many women were proficient, despite
Mme. Demorest's sewing machine attachment. *Der
Bazar* in the latter half of the 50's shows the first
turned down shirt collars for men, elaborately patterned in quilting over cord; very attractive they
are, too.
During, and for a few years after each excessively
cold winter: 1830, 1845, quilting reappears. There
was a series of rigorous winters in the mid50's. By
their end, the emancipation of women had begun;
they start to walk instead of being driven in a

closed carriage. Until quilting is ousted by sealskin
in the 70's, it makes comfortable muffs and linings
for short walking coats. Quilting was taken over
by men in the cold winters of 1860-61-65. The vest
worn by T. M. Fay, Union College Class of '60, is
handsomely quilted in a basket-weave pattern. The
shift to plain or braid-edged vests has already begun
in 1860; quilting moves to the handsome linings of
men's loose coats and capes, which wearers have
been holding back and displaying since the latter
half of the 50's.
For all the velvet and quilting shown by Dickens,
men's clothing is turning fast, from 1860, into forms
familiar to us now. Dickens wears a plain turned-
down collar, pleated shirt front, and straight cuffs.
Like the Prince of Wales (Ill. 2672) he wears his
necktie hanging like a modern four-in-hand; it is
not yet knotted, but is drawn through a seal ring,
as fussy gentlemen still wore theirs in e.XXc. His
waistcoat is of velvet, but is plain; by 1860 the
watch chain of large links is commonly caught by
a bar through one of the buttonholes between the
middle and the bottom of the vest, and dangles a
bunch of seals and trinkets.
In the engraving of the Prince of Wales (after a
photograph of 1863), we see the formal afternoon
dress of the next half century established in essentials.

2683

2684

2685

Men's Dress: As Shown in College Photographs of Early 1860's

The early 1860's is the turning point in men's dress.

Until you have examined photographs of the graduating class of—say Union College, Schenectady, N. Y., in 1860, it is difficult to believe how much variation will be found in head and facial hair, collar and tie, vest and coat details. Culver Service has a number of war-time sets from Amherst, Hamilton, etc., which usually include favorite professors and the college janitor. Their examples from Union have been used because they show the widest range, and are accurately dated.

Some of the best-dressed young men appear in clothes such as their fathers have worn through the 50's; others, in buying their first suit of "store clothes," have happened to hit on new trends which lead to the 70's. The direction in which styles move are seen on the handsome, fashionably dressed Hamilton boy (2694), on Prof. Root, in his matching coat and vest of textured material, and on the Union class of 1868, in their freshman year.

Hair may be as short as Ingham's, rather like a farm hand's today, or fall in locks like Custer's scouts (Pitt, Fargo); there is a good deal of involved work with a comb about the ears (Campbell).

The long-haired Fargo and short-haired Ingham are completely shaved; moustaches are combed down like Gleason's, or twisted wide like Pitt's. Green has a complete beard. A fellow who looks like Gen. Grant has hair on the jowls and a shaved chin; McElroy has the same pattern, long and fluffed; Flick and Morrison (who also has an imperial) have their jowls shaved.

Collars stand, high and overlapping (Van Winkle), or low and flat as a choir boy's, exposing the neck (Fargo), or are turned over and stiffly starched (Green); there is often a three-inch gap in front, to show off an enormous tie, like Pitt's soft, thick bow, or "Grant's" fringed satin.

Bow ties of whatever form in 1860 have a common characteristic: they are tied with affected negligence, with an end and loop under the vest and coat collar, and the other side out and over. The most characteristic tie of 1860 is a narrow ribbon, striped across the end, often in red or black. Gleason's, striped lengthwise in velvet, merely dangles from a knot. Morrison's is patterned diagonally. Σ Φ's wear their pins in huge cravats, like Campbell's plaid, tied and twisted over to cover the shirt front. Other shirt fronts are closed by large, dark pearl studs (Gleason, Van Winkle).

There are many fancy, brocaded vests with long lapels, opening low (Flick, Green, Campbell, and Fay's handsome quilted vest), in the manner of the 50's. These are worn with coats with long lapels, worn open, with fronts parallel. There are other vests which compromise between the old open front and the new impulse to button up high, shown by Gleason and McElroy. Fargo's checked vest, which would choke him if closed, has in fact a loop from the fourth buttonhole for catching it together. Over it appears the diagonal strap which is seen on many young men in the early 60's (2694); its use is not confined to America, but where it goes and what it carries I do not know. Gleason's coat, without lapels, follows this same open and closed bulge, into which the hand is sometimes thrust as in a sling.

McElroy's suit is actually the latest thing. Its bound edge is buttoned high, once, and then spreads open; small lapels expose the chest on which a breast pocket is set on the level of the button. Campbell's suit, though it still carries a velvet collar and is worn with a waffle-patterned vest, also shows new trends: a rough textured and patterned fabric (Prof. Root), in place of broadcloth; small, short lapel with its buttonhole set diagonally; piped pocket edge. Gleason's coat may be compared to Ill. 2706; and the clothing of the handsome Hamilton boy, with Ill. 2712.

2686

2687

2686-2700. XIXc. 1860. U.S.A. (Culver Service.)
2686. Alburn I. Fargo, Monterey, Mass.
2687. Unknown.
2688. Edgar B. Van Winkle, N. Y.
2689. Unknown.
2690. W. H. McElroy, Albany.
2691. E. C. Morrison, Modena, N. Y.

2692. W. H. Pitt, Granger, N. Y.
2693. Douglas Campbell.
2694. Edgar W. Crowell (Hamilton College, 1865-68).
2695. Weston Flick, Great Valley, N. Y.
2696. Prof. E. W. Root, brother of Elihu (Hamilton College).

2697. T. M. Fay, Pavilion, N. Y.
2698. William Green.

2699. George T. Ingham, Salem, N. J.
2700. A. Will Gleason.

2701. XIXc. Mid-50's. Provenance unknown.

Seated Woman with Fur Stole.

Hair form, wide collar, large brooch, and short, wide, lace-flounced bell sleeve of mid50's. Sealskin, which everyone will wear in the 70's, begins to be advertised in the 50's, and is proudly shown off here in an interesting form. The stole, related in shape to the many fichu collars with tab ends, is accompanied by a pair of cuffs which have no connection with the dress. They are obviously intended to be worn, out of doors, in reversed position, over the conventionally clasped hands of the period to form a cylindrical muff.

2702. XIXc. Mid-60's. U.S.A.

Stereopticon View at Saratoga Springs.

Happy middle class crowd at Saratoga at about the end of Civil War. Crinolines are still wide at the bottom, but the cylindrical form of the 1858 crinoline has become pyramidal. Decoration sinks toward the hem which begins to drag out in back. Loose paletots and mantles. There are still wide-brimmed hats plumed around the brim, and plain small banded hats. But brims are rolling up at the sides, and begin to dip forward, with decoration massed on top.

Light-colored top hats are more sporting than black; many pork pie, boater and incipient low-crowned bowler shapes. The young man (l. of c.) shows the characteristic light trousers of the 60's, often with matching vest (Ill. 2712), worn with knee-length topcoats; sleeve characteristically clumsy and over long. Behind him, l., a widely-spaced turned-down collar.

2703. XIXc. c. 1860. U.S.A.

Niagara Falls.

Summer dresses of the small shepherds' checks and dots of the late 50's. Plumed hat, with swinging brim; bodices, losing crossed fichus, have in their place a shoulder cap, often fringed, or a sleeve gathered full onto a dropped shoulder-line; fringed shepherds' check shawl; smaller white collars. Men's coats long; sleeves wider, baggy, sagging at elbow. Pork pie hats.

Courtesy of Culver Service

2704

2704. XIXc. 1865. U.S.A., Schenectady.

Freshman Class of 1868, Union College.

The Union College class of 1860 showed all sorts of extravagantly long or roached-out hair, beards, mutton chops and moustaches.

In 1865, the freshmen are uniformly clean shaven. Their hair has none of the wild tumbled look of Flick (2695) and Fargo (2686). It is slicked down, much closer to the head in oiled waves. The roached-out hair back of McElroy's (2690) and Campbell's (2693) ears is reduced to a turn-up like a drake's tail, and the part moves a little closer to the center.

Turn-over collars no longer show the wide gap seen on Flick, or on the very "hick" character in the Saratoga stereopticon picture. String ties, bows, and ascots are all less noticeable. The only patterned tie shown here is seen on the boy (back, 5 from l.) who wears the only silk vest; his coat most nearly resembles the 1860 form, with its longer lapels, worn open, with more nearly parallel edges (although the edges are somewhat cutaway here).

The 1865 coat follows the trend indicated by McElroy in 1860: short lapels, buttoned high on the chest, with edges sloping away below. The thick clumsy sleeve of e.60's (in Saratoga photograph) remains wide at the elbow but narrows toward the hand and is shorter. As on McElroy's suit and in Ill. 2712 there are many contrasting bindings and buttons, but the high pocket, which was set at the level of the first button on McElroy's suit, has dropped toward the second, or (in the case of the double-breasted suit), as low as the breast pocket of Ill. 2712.

Matching vest and trousers in plaid (instead of light color, as in Saratoga photo) on seated figure, r. Fancy vests have been almost entirely replaced by plain tailored vests, with no decoration except the fashionable contrasting bindings and buttons; watch chains from a bar in a middle buttonhole to vest pocket. Trousers are wide and tubular. There are many round-crowned hats with slightly curling brims, the binding of which is often contrasting. One cap.

The seniors, in 1865, do show more fantasy in facial hair, with which they have more to experiment than the freshmen. But they are notably less lush than the class of '60.

Courtesy of Culver Service

2705

2706

2707 - 2708

2705-16. XIXc. 1860-62. Portuguese. (New York Public
Library.)

"O Mensageiro das Damas" (periodical).

It is during the 60's that the present-day dress of
men becomes universally established. Clothing, for
both men and women, is being subdivided into categories suitable for one occasion and inappropriate
for another. Fancy vests and light trousers agreeing
with neither coat nor vest pass out of fashion rapidly after 1860 (compare Union College and photos
of 1860 with group of 1865). There are widely
striped trousers; but the strongest tendency is towards
agreement of at least two pieces of the suit, and the
matching three-piece suit for morning wear comes
into use (2716). The new trend of 1861 is for vests
and trousers to match, as we see they do commonly
by 1865 (Ill. 2712 and group photo, Union College).
The bound edge, which is seen from the late 50's
is particularly noticeable on vests (Ill. 2712, and
1865 group Union Coll.).

Suits and loose finger-length topcoats have plenty
of pockets and all trousers have fly closing. Straw
hats, shaped much like modern panamas (2706) and
boaters (2716) are worn with informal clothes, together with turn-down collars. These have grown
high (2706, 2716) and are accompanied by well-tied
bows, or long ties in the nature of four-in-hands,
although they are still apt to be folded over or
passed through a ring, rather than knotted.

The tendency of the 50's to show off handsome
coat linings increases with the quilted linings of the
60's (2713 and 2685).

The more enclosing brims of women's bonnets
are trimmed on the under side with a row of flowers

above the hair; ruches of tulle at the cheeks; full
projecting curtain of lace, straw or fabric behind;
bonnet strings still important.

Women's dresses are usually machine-sewed. The
boned bodices, smooth and slope-shouldered, are
often without shoulder caps; bretelles are barely recalled in occasional ruched decoration down the
front of the bodice; the wide bottom of the sleeve
tends to close in, altering the bell into a bishop
sleeve, as wide or wider at the elbow than at the
bottom.

The skirt, gored into a more slender hipline, remains very wide below. It is much plainer, with its
trimming (when horizontal) concentrated on the
hemline or lower third of the skirt. When flounces are
used they are narrow, repeated, frilly, (often with
a pinked edge) and are made of plain-color materials; though on an 1860 skirt (2705), two colors
continue to be alternated.

Borders à disposition pass with the beginning of
the 60's. Cartridge pleated and ruched trimmings
often agree in fabric and color with the body of
the gown. But in the main, decoration is now contrasting, both in color and texture (fur, 2708; lace,
2715; velvet bands, 2723-24). It often has an irregular edge (2708, 2711). A tendency of the skirt to be
notched, cut or drawn up to show the petticoat
(2711) will increase.

2705. White bonnet with a scarlet edge, scarlet
flowers set under brim, white ruching below the
hair-line, black lace curtain and cream-colored ribbon. Lavender dress patterned in black; alternate
black and lavender ruffled trim.

2706. (June, 1860) Straw hat, black band. Turned-down collar with stitched decoration, garnet tie, gray coat, white trousers, black shoes, blue-gray gloves.

2707. (March, 1861) Dark gray topcoat; cool gray vest; standing collar with black tie; blue gray breeches and boot tops; yellow gloves.

2708. White bonnet and plume, purple edge and curtain in back, cerise bows. Gray gown, appliqué of brown fur; lemon yellow gloves.

2709. Bonnet of yellow straw, violets and leaves, with violet ruching and bonnet strings. Light cocoa-colored gown.

2710. (July, 1861) Gray top hat, vest, and breeches. Black stock, gold pin and heavy watch chain. Brown coat with stitched collar, lemon yellow gloves.

2711. White bonnet and strings and black lace

fall, lined with cerise and trimmed with grapes and roses. Malachite green dress.

2712. (Sept., 1861) Blue tie with striped ends. Off-white vest and trousers, bound and banded in black; black coat displaying satin lining and binding. Black top hat.

2713. (Nov., 1861) Black top hat. Turned-over collar, purple tie. Brown cape with velvet collar, and quilted light gray lining. Striped gray trousers; lemon gloves.

2714. White bonnet, strings and fall, trimmed with lavender and white flowers. Greenish-gray dress, lavender ruchings.

2716. (Aug., 1862) Yellow straw hat, black binding and band. Turned down collar, scarlet tie. Gray mixture three piece suit, lavender gloves, black patent leather pumps; gold watch chain. Cigarette, coming into more common use with the Crimean War.

2717-22. XIXc.
Cartes de Visite, 1860-65.
2717. San Francisco?
2718. Bridgeport, Conn.
2719. Bridgeport, Conn.
2720. Liverpool.
2721. Pittsfield, Mass.
2722. France: Empress Eugenie.

Hair, which has been brushed down from a part for decades, begins in the 60's to be brushed sideways from it, squaring the crown of the head and the forehead. The old crescent of braided back hair, which had helped to form the oval head (2718) falls or is netted into a chignon of more oblong shape, parallel with the neck (2719, 2722). Details of every step in hairdressing (as well as in every branch of sewing and fancy work) between mid-50's to mid80's, can be studied in the huge plates of "Der Bazar, Illustrirte Damen Zeitung" of Berlin.

One of the sleeves to appear in the late 50's, as fichu-like bretelles lose ground, is basically close fitted, but covered with a series of puffs. Mrs. James Gordon Bennett wears the *canezou*-like sleeve as she welcomes the Japanese envoys in 1860 (Frank Leslie's *Illustrated Newspaper*). Flowing sleeves continue to be seen on summer dresses and bolero jackets. On heavy silk dresses this sleeve, set under an epaulette at a dropped shoulder-line, tends to close in toward the wrist (2718-19). This sleeve form is exactly paralleled by the shape of men's sleeves, sagging toward a baggy elbow (Ill. 2669).

By mid60's, there are many completely smooth, untrimmed bodices and sleeves (2722). Braided zouave jackets and Spanish bolero styles affect the bodices of dresses with which they are not worn. Their outlines are sketched in braid or buttons (2719, 2721), on bodices which are rising into little standing collars. The points of vests are elaborated into tabs and trimmed with upholstery-like pleatings (2719).

Emphasis is shifting from sleeves. The skirt will become looped up to show the petticoat, on its way to becoming bustled in late 60's. The line of the bodice, down the front or across at the height of the epaulettes, will become stressed by pleating. In second half of the 60's these trimmings outline a round or square yoke; it may be filled in by lingerie chemisettes, or be continued in the fabric of the dress, to a standing collar.

2723-26. XIXc. 1861. French. (New York Public Lib.) "Moniteur de la Mode," January.

2723. Hair dressed with pink and blue morning glories and green leaves, and ostrich tips in two shades of pink. Pink bodice, banded in deeper pink with bouquets matching hair decoration. Skirt of pink puffs, edged in black and white lace. White scarf, fan, gloves, and single but important bracelet on each arm.

2724. Cerise bonnet, strings, and puffs under the brim; white ruching at the cheeks; black lace at back of crown, and curtain. Tan gown trimmed in black velvet.

Many diagonal lines and diamond patterns, which tends to become less geometric and regular within a couple of years. The double skirts of the late 50's have become united; what was the lower skirt is trimmed, and its pattern is carried up at the sides in a line established by decoration or long tabs in the late 50's. This placing of decoration had given

the outline of the skirt à tablier. The diamond patterns with which the apron front had been cross-hatched continue in favor, but are more broadly executed in velvet straps. Zigzag, notched and diamond effects seen everywhere cause the ends of the straps to be cut in points.

2725. Straw hat trimmed with a rose and white ostrich plume. Shirt with mannish standing collar and tie, and deep, turned-back cuffs. Severe walking costume in yellowish-fawn (with matching gloves); black trim in bolder lines; bolero jacket (favored through first half of the 60's) with notched sleeves; row of buttons up front (late 50's-e. 60's).

2726. White bonnet and strings; roses under brim, and rose plumes. Mole brown gown edged in garnet. Bell sleeves gathered into bishop sleeves; tabs replaced by sash ends, cut off diagonally. Saw-toothed hem of the upper skirt has the bold contrasting edge used also in men's dress. The small crisp ruffles of the petticoat-like underskirt are set on with an upholstered finish. (July, plates by Jules David.)

2727. XIXc. 1861. U.S.A.
"Godey's Lady's Book," March.

The diagonal line of 1861 is applied with the new bold simplicity on a dress prophetically cut on princess lines.

2728-35. XIXc. 1862. French.
"Moniteur de la Mode" (periodical). Plates by *Jules David*.

2728. (March.) Evening costume in two shades of yellow: light combined with pumpkin, worn with a white ostrich plume, and trimmed with white lace. The skirts of evening and calling gowns all tend to be shortened and cut up in some way to display the underskirt.

2729. Costume of Diana for one of the many costume balls of the 60's. Red crescent and flowers; red and yellow bow and quiver. White gauze shirt and harem trousers. Leopard skin; skirt of shaded green leaves over pink. Gold shoes (see 2632).

2730. (March.) Diagonal lines becoming spiral as they lose force. Red and white flowers, green leaves, with a taffeta dress of a sharp aniline green, between jade and malachite, trimmed with white lace.

2731. Quilted bonnet, white lined with rose; blue-black bows set under and on top of brim; black fall with a white line and white lace border; white bonnet strings with black lines. Purple gown, boldly patterned in black squares set on their points; bodice springs apart below the last button into the tabs of a vest.

2732. (June.) Gauzy summer bonnet: the old line of flowers under the brim has been forced out by the rise of ruching (which used to be set at the cheeks), and flowers are reduced to a red, yellow and green posy, with daisies scattered over the crown; white bonnet strings. The favorites among all the aniline colors appear in the lavender gown, the skirts of which are deeply cut up and turned back to show narrow violet ruffles.

2733. Like her companion's, the under brim of the yellow and white bonnet is entirely filled with ruching, and merely set with a small green and white bouquet; white strings. Full white shirt with scarlet collar and cuffs. Princess gown of brilliant blue-green trimmed with bright, deep blue; skirt permanently drawn up under its braid and tassel decoration, to show the white skirt beneath.

2734. (July.) The straw hat which accompanied walking dress in 1861 had acquired an ostrich plume, but was narrower-brimmed than the hat of 1858. By 1862, the brim has become much smaller and the plume (here shaded in deep rose) is accompanied by ribbon bows (dark blue) rather than flowers.

The costume shown here is composed of all the favorite items of informal dress of first half of the 60's. When not so insistently braid trimmed, it is apt to be accompanied by Garibaldi's little braid-patterned pill-box hat.

In this case, the costume is of greenish putty color, with the ubiquitous soutache braid trim of the period, in black. The shirt, with its little mannish collar, and full sleeve gathered into a tight cuff, is white. The enormously popular red Garibaldi shirt is made in the same way, and is usually braided on the bosom. Zouave and bolero jackets with simple funneled sleeves are enormously popular; so is the "Swiss corselet" or belt seen here, which is often notched, above and below, into two points instead of one. The same is true of loose paletots and capes, reaching a little below the hips, which are seen on many cartes de visite of first half 60's.

2735. Bonnet (filled with ruching), plume, and fall are white; crown and strings, arsenic green; white shirt with a magenta bow tie. Gray gown with a waistcoat-like bodice and lapels; strap trim in arsenic-green.

2736. XIXc. 1862. French. (Boston, Mrs. Montgomery Sears.)

Manet. Street Singer.
Pill-box hat; loose paletot with bound edges taken

2736

2737

2738

2739

over from men's dress. Skirt hem caught up mechanically.

2737. XIXc. 1862-3. French. (Louvre.)
Manet. Luncheon on the Grass.

2738. XIXc. c. 1864. French.
Photograph of Gustave Courbet.

2739. XIXc. 1866. French. (Metropolitan Museum.)
Manet. Woman with Parrot.
Dressing gown; medallion on black ribbon at throat.

2740. XIXc. 1863. German.
"Der Bazar," May 8.
Mantles and mantillas for summer. The loose

jackets, hanging to just below the hips, become longer and more closely fitted. The gowns beneath them are laced in through the torso, gored into smoother hips, and are often cut in a princess line. There are "fast" little mannish topcoats (upper left) worn with severe hats. Collars, cuffs and lapels increase in importance; sleeves are more tubular. Trim more resembling that used on dresses; running "Greek" key designs replace the familiar soutache braiding. Burnous and Talma cloaks continue; cloaks are caught together in back, rather than actually hooded.

Plain little bowlers, taken over from men, and high-crowned hats with ostrich and a ribbon band,

2740

supplement the familiar wider forms, which are trimmed with plumes or a nosegay, and often have a valance of lace all around the brim.

Bonnet brims stand high and squarer, behind hair dressed high above the temples; back hair falls low, clubbed into a *catogan,* often supplemented with false hair, and set with elaborate combs. Lower left: skirts and cloaks made of material in small repeated patterns.

Plaid stockings and brightly colored boots worn by women, as well as children.

2741-42. XIXc. 1863. German. (New York Public Lib.) "Der Bazar," May 15.

Acute patterns of squares and diamonds are becoming curved, or are mitred into running band and Greek designs.

The trim of boned and fitted bodices outlines a yoke or bertha. Necklines are higher, with standing collars, ruches and bow ties. Sleeves either return to a long, simple form of the bell sleeve, which preceded the bishop sleeve, or become tubular. White undersleeves are reduced. Buckled belts.

Der Bazar gives illustrations in actual size for setting on these decorations and for laying out the pleating, which is done by the methods of an upholsterer of our day.

The wide-sleeved dress is in the fashionable new "tourterelle," a turtle-dove gray, tinged with brown; pleated hem of black taffeta; trim of white lace and

black velvet. The curled hair is more elaborately dressed with black lace and a hanging veil.

The other dress, of violet poplin, is trimmed with violet taffeta and black velvet. Cap of mousseline, black velvet ribbon and rosettes of violet ribbon. Hair rolled back from the temples, full, square and high.

2743-49. XIXc. 1863. U.S.A.
"Godey's Lady's Book," September.

Women have a great deal more hair, elaborately arranged in a multitude of ways: coronet braids, combs, flowers and ribbons, caps and catogans; but always rolled or drawn away from the face, higher and squarer at the crown, and massed longer and fuller in back. A center part is far from absolute now, and the hair is often waved or curled.

The variety which had been instituted by skirts, is now surpassed by bodices. They are elaborated by both cut and trim. It is no longer inevitable that they button up the front, and it may be difficult to decide just where they do close. Most of these gowns have been so affected by the Zouave jackets of the e. 60's, that they give at least the appearance of a skimpy fitted jacket (cut well away from the neck) worn over a plain, high-necked bodice. The return of the pagoda sleeve (in a longer, more tubular form) is also an effect of the jackets, on which wide, simple sleeves appeared, while dress sleeves inclined toward elaborate bishop shapes.

2743. Brown dress, on which a long, fitted, open-front coat has been sketched in black lace; large elaborate bow at throat.

2744. Mother exhibiting puppet show: blue gown, trimmed in black, with dark blue ribbons. Wide, low neckline; shoulders covered by a white bertha finished by a ruche at the throat.

2745. Child on lap: white bertha; low-necked white dress embroidered in red.

2746. Girl on hassock: dark gray, trimmed in dark red with ball fringe.

2747. Flowers in hair. Dress in two shades of gray, trimmed with black lace; its bodice juggles the themes of bolero and the Swiss belt so often worn with it.

2748. Green, braided by black soutache into a coat-dress with important cuffs. Return of cap; white with green trim. Chairs (often folding), made of bentwood or reed in rounded form, are advertised by 1861.

2749. Pink jacket dress, with pink frogged and buttoned lapels and collar.

2750-54. XIXc. June, 1864. U.S.A.

"Godey's Lady's Book," June.

Return of the lace cap; bonnets; informal hats, trimmed with plumes and ribbon, rather than flowers; brims dip forward, in the line on which hats will come to be tilted. Gloves white to pale lemon yellow.

The amount of applied trimming is being reduced as more patterned materials, in relatively modest, inconspicuous patterns, are used.

Scale patterns and careful instructions have to be given in all the fashion magazines for laying out and constructing the decorations which are used. Interlaced diamond patterns in simple velvet bands have become short tabbed straps, elaborately bordered and braided (2754). The small ruffles and banded cartridge pleatings of e. 60's have been combined into ruffles cut on the bias, and laid on with upholstery-like regularity. Even these tend to be replaced by deep scallops and fringes.

2750. Small ruffled and tasseled parasols. Rose-red bonnet; white mantilla caught with tassels at a bertha top. Magenta gown with small dark figures.

2751. White hat and plume, red bow. Dark gray dress with self-color fringe and tassels, lighter gray pipings and carved pearl buttons; corselet front and apron give princess form to gown; underskirt in narrow, lighter gray stripes, with piped scallops.

2752. White hat with bright cobalt-blue bow. Black and white costume of patterned and plain fabric. Round corselet (another step in the transition to the princess cut); skirt slashed to show small frill of the underskirt.

2753. White hat, red trim and strings. Buff coat-costume, strap decoration done in black braid.

2754. Black lace Figaro jacket with epaulettes cut with a bertha top. Cobalt blue gown with elaborate black-braided tabs; ruching with a pinked edge set over a carefully pleated bias-cut flounce at the hem.

2755-56. XIXc. 1864. German.

"Der Bazar," July 15.

2755. Swimming suit for ladies. The long, loose, ambiguous chemise in which women have bathed, is replaced during first half 60's by bathing suits in which it is possible to swim.

2756. Gymnastic dress for young girls. Pantalettes have practically disappeared, but their advantages are retained in loose trousers in dresses specifically designed for athletics.

2757. XIXc. 1863. Swedish. (Stockholm, Hallwyl Coll.)

Agnes von Hallwyl, age 7.

2758. XIXc. 1866-7. French. (Louvre.)

Edgar Degas. Portrait of his cousin's family.

High boots and pinafores. Pantalettes coming to the end of their use during first half 60's.

2759-64. XIXc. 1864. U.S.A.

"Godey's Lady's Book," November.

The earlier two-skirted or coat-skirted effects (2743-49) are being broken up and shortened, especially in front.

Bodices are no longer bolero jackets, but are carried down, in a fitted princess line, into postilion's tabs and tails. Interest is being focused on the back of the skirt over the buttocks, where skirts will soon be caught up into polonaises and the bustles of the 70's. There are points, jagged tabs, heavy mixed and ball fringes. The scrawlings of soutache (hem, 2759) are being supplanted by more parallel patterns in wide braid or cord elaborated into Hungarian loops and frogs, and trimmed with braid-covered wooden moulds, hanging like tassels (2764; sleeves and waistline of coat, c. figure).

Bonnet brims rise high in front and are trimmed with jutting quills (2763); the curtain in back edged with ball-fringe or jet pendants.

Back hair clubbed into coarse-meshed chenille nets or ribbons, when not covered by bonnet curtains.

2759. Red and green hair decoration. White jacket and black skirt, both banded in ruby red, scrolled in black soutache.

2760. Gray hat, malachite green and white ribbons, white bouquet; black hair net. Black jacket, jet studded. Dulled malachite green tabs, edged with black lace, over a plain skirt of a dirty pink.

2761. White bonnet with strings and fall narrowly striped in black and white. Gray coat and skirt; self colored frogs; ruby red vest.

2762. White bonnet and falls; lavender crown and puffed brim, trimmed with red roses and pointed green leaves. Salmon-buff gown, trimmed with black lace; hem of skirt caught up to show petticoat, tabbed alternately in white and cobalt blue, both with a line of black braid. Pocket in skirt front.

2763. White bonnet, jet trimming, black feather and green spray. Light violet gown, trimmed in black and violet.

2764. Kneeling girl: red-purple hair ribbons and white chenille net. Shirred white blouse with Medici sleeves; pinafore dress of stone-gray trimmed with red-purple velvet in a Hussar pattern.

2765   2766   2767   2768   2769

2765-69. XIXc. June, 1865. U.S.A.
"Godey's Lady's Book," June.

Narrow stripes, small all-over repeats, more "made" trimmings, scalloped, folded over, and set with tassels and pendants. Closer sleeves. The long, clear princess line is disturbed, as waistlines shorten under Empire influences in France, and hips spread. Skirts are much narrower and rounder at the hem, fuller and less gored at the waist, and begin to be caught up about the hips (2769) as well as in front to show petticoat flounces (2767). Forward rake of hats continues.

2765. Hair trimmed with violets and white lace. White gown, banded in light violet with white tassels.

2766. Black and white fabric, trimmed with black lace, and cobalt blue bands and tassels; red fan.

2767. Light brown straw with white plumes. White blouse, black embroidered. Cocoa brown costume, Figaro jacket and Swiss belt, trimmed with black braid and pendants; white petticoat flounces, banded in red.

2768. Black lace cap; light violet overdress, edged with buff braid, patterned in red and green, and skirt-pockets; white underdress.

2769. White straw hat with red and white plumes. Black and white striped dress; sash ends and scallops in dull cherry red.

2770. XIXc. 1865. U.S.A.

"Frank Leslie's Chimney Corner" (periodical). Grand Reception of the Notables of the Nation at the White House.

Hair dressed with elaborate combs of gold filigree and jet, chains and ornaments, flowers and ribbon. Bead necklaces, earring, important gold bracelets, fans, lace handkerchiefs.

Shorter-waisted evening dresses with trains, showing Empire and "Pompadour" influences. Double skirts, the uppermost with battle-mented or scalloped edges; increased interest in the back of the skirt —basques, tabs, sashes, the ends of which sometimes catch up the overskirt.

The familiar small flounces and strap decorations are used below tabbed and scalloped overskirts. Newer gowns have underskirts which might have been executed by an upholsterer: draped and caught in a scale pattern, with an overskirt inspired by XVIIIc. French court styles (2 from r.): button tufted with train and sash knotted over buttocks (background, l. of center).

2771-76. XIXc. Nov., 1865. U.S.A.
"Godey's Lady's Book," November.

2771. White hat, violet quills and streamers; violet paletot and skirt with matching cord trim.

2772. Hair banded in tan. Black coat trimmed with braid and jet. Tan striped skirt.

2773. Tan bonnet with lavender tassels and lining, white ruche, green and lavender trim; stone gray bonnet strings with border in lavender, green and white. Greenish-blue dress with wide buckled belt, skirt pockets and a yoke banded in stone gray.

2774. Pale gray hat and costume, trimmed in dull malachite green.

2775. Seated girl: black hair ribbons with long streamers; black boots. Dull red-violet costume edged with black and white braid and white cord fringe.

2776. White blouse; warm blue violet jacket and taffeta skirt, trimmed with jet.

2777. XIXc. 1865. French.

Dollfus Mieg & Cie. Robe trianon.

Fashion plate published by the great Alsatian firm of cotton printers to show the use of one of their bordered fabrics.

Flounces patterned *à disposition* in 50's were followed by half a decade in which plain colored fabrics predominated, and decoration and edgings were largely made of fabric and applied: cartridge pleating and ruchings; or bands of color laid on in straps, or outlining invected and tabbed borders of upholstery-like skirt hems.

Now there is a return to small overall patterns; as in this gown in the lavender and black combination which becomes popular with the advent of aniline dyes. A tabbed, strap-like, repeated belt-closing is used on the border of a plain morning dress, which is cut with the new (and transient) simplicity which preceded the bustle. Parasol. Hair rolled high and square at the temples, with a large chignon, curls behind the ears. Long dangling earrings. The neckline is raised by a ruche which replaces the small collar. More pattern is used on bodice, the bosom of which rounds as the waistline is tightened; sleeves plainer and closer; skirt fullness drawn toward the back and lengthened, soon to be caught up in a bustle.

2778. XIXc. 1867. French. (Paris, Luxembourg.)

J. F. Bazille. Family Reunion.

Appendix

The way in which this book has been put together, the sort of material to be found in this Appendix, and its organization, have been discussed in the Introduction.

No bibliography of costume books is attempted here. Any Library equipped for costume research will have such comprehensive works as:

Hilaire and Meyer Hiler: *Bibliography of Costume*, H. W. Wilson Co., 1939.

Isabel Munro and Dorothy E. Cook: *Costume Index*, H. W. Wilson Co., 1937.

These supplement older works like:

René Colas: *Bibliographie générale du costume et de la mode*, 2 vols., Librairie René Colas, Paris, 1933.

Katalog der Freiherrlich von Lipperheide'schen Kostümbibliothek, 2 vols., Lipperheide, Berlin, 1896-1905.

The standard dictionaries of costume words are:

Victor Gay: *Glossaire archéologique du moyen-âge et de la renaissance*, 2 vols., Paris, Société bibl., 1887-1928.

Camille Enlart: *Manuel d'archéologie française*, III, *Le costume*, Auguste Picard, Paris, 1916.

Guidance, and leads to source material and to the most important books on every aspect of life in all periods of history, can be found in publications of the Clarendon Press, Oxford, and of the Cambridge University Press. For instance, the Cambridge Ancient (6 vols), Mediaeval (8 vols), and Modern (13 vols. and Atlas) Histories; J. E. Sandys: *Companion to Latin Studies;* Barnard's *Companion to English History (Middle Ages); Shakspere's England*, 2 vols., Clarendon Press, Oxford, 1916; and so on, to and beyond the 2 vols. of *Early Victorian England*.

Wonderful bibliographical material on the whole mediaeval period will be found in:

Louis Jean Paetow: *A Guide to the Study of Mediaeval History*, F. S. Crofts & Co., N. Y., 1933, prepared under the auspices of the Mediaeval Academy of America.

There are, however, some books which are cited because their illustrations are entirely documentary. Others are so useful that reference is frequently made to them in our text or appendix. If they are not found below, look for them under the Chapter Headings to which they relate, in the Appendix. They have been given key abbreviations for the sake of brevity.

[Leloir] Maurice Leloir: *Histoire du costume, de l'antiquité à 1914*, H. Ernst, Paris, is the most sumptuous and ambitious of modern books on costume. Its illustrations are frequently in colored facsimile, always documents or photographs of actual garments. Its publication, interrupted by World War I, was never completed. Few libraries have its 5 volumes, but it is worth communicating with the Union Catalog of the Library of Congress, to find whether it is available in your city, and where. Many patterns and outline drawings of details.

[von Boehn] Max von Boehn: *Die Mode, La Mode*, or *Modes and Manners*. I do not suppose that there has ever been anything to compare, in quantity, quality and modest price, with these 8 little volumes. The text is good in all languages. The quality of reproduction is best in the German edition. The chronological arrangement is good, from the first Christian centuries through the XVIIIc. Wonderfully chosen pictures are jumbled with infuriating carelessness in the 4 volumes which cover 1790-1914.

[Hottenroth] Frédéric Hottenroth: *Le Costume chez les peuples anciens et modernes*, Armand Guérinet, Paris, gives outline drawings of European dress, armor and jewelry, and some patterns, from IVc. B.C. to 1870, with special emphasis on German peasant dress, to which Hottenroth devotes another classic work in German.

Despite my distaste for books illustrated by line drawings, I cannot deny that the "little" Hottenroth is part of the foundation of a costume library. You could no more design imaginative costumes from it than you

could create a very spirited fish from inspecting a plate of its boiled bones, but it is a valuable skeleton on which to hang accumulated information.

[Köhler] Carl Köhler and Emma von Sichart: *A History of Costume*, David McKay, Philadelphia, gives patterns and photographs, together with some outline drawings, of costume from the Ancient Orient to 1870.

[K. & S.: Short Hist.] Frances M. Kelly and Randolph Schwabe: *A Short History of Costume and Armour, chiefly in England, 1066-1800*, Scribners, N. Y., 1931.

[K. & S.: Hist. C.] F. M. Kelly and R. Schwabe: *Historic Costume, a Chronicle of Fashion in Western Europe, 1490-1790*, Scribners, N. Y., 1931.

The exceptions to my feelings about line drawings are found in these two admirable books, covering all too limited a field, in which documentary illustrations in color and half-tone are supplemented by unimpeachable line drawings by Mr. Schwabe, Slade Professor of Art at University College, London. They provide good glossaries of the most important words relating to costume and armor. I consider them the best one-vol. books ever published on costume.

[Norris] Herbert Norris: *Costume and Fashion*. Vol. I, *The Evolution of European Dress Through the Earlier Ages*, 1924. Vol. II, *Senlac to Bosworth, 1066-1485*, 1927. Vol. III, parts 1 & 2: *The Tudors, 1485-1603*, E. P. Dutton, N. Y. Vols. IV: *The Stuarts* and V: *The Hanoverians*, are to come. Vol. VI: *The Nineteenth Century*, written with Oswald Curtis, was published by J. M. Dent, London, 1933.

A great deal of research went into these volumes, to which I am indebted for facts, quotations and color notes. His illustrations are entirely redrawn.

[Piton] Camille Piton: *Le costume civil en France, du XIIIe au XIXe siècle*, E. Flammarion, Paris, has wonderful illustrations and a very poor text.

[Hirth's Form.] Georg *Hirth's Formenschatz*, 35 vols., Munich, 1877-1911, is a wonderful photographic compendium of the art of all ages. His other great compilations of engravings are listed under *Culture Moves North:* XVIc.

[Leggett] William F. Leggett: *Ancient and Mediaeval Dyes*, Chemical Pub. Co., N. Y., 1944, is a very useful small book.

[D'All. Acc.] Henri D'Allemagne: *Les accessoires du costume et du mobilier*, 3 vols. Schemit, Paris, 1928, gives photographs of XII-midXIXc. objects: jewelry, purses, fans, combs, buttons, snuff boxes, etc. Like all his books, it is invaluable, of impeccable scholarship, and superbly illustrated.

[Forrer] R. Forrer: *Die Kunst des Zugdrucks*, Schlesier & Schweikhardt, Strassburg, 1898, has fine reproductions of textiles of XII-XIVc.

[Lacroix, A. M. A.] Paul Lacroix: *The Arts in the Middle Ages, and at the period of the Renaissance*, Chapman & Hall, London, 1870.

[Lacroix, M. C. D.] —: *Manners, Customs and Dress during Middle Ages and during the Renaissance period*, 1874.

[Lacroix, M. R. L.] —: *Military and Religious Life in the Middle Ages and at the period of the Renaissance*, 1874.

[Lacroix, S. L.] —: *Science and Literature in the Middle Ages and in the period of the Renaissance*, Bickers & Son, London, 1878.

Dorothy Hartley and Margaret M. Elliot: *Life and Work of the People of England*, a pictorial record from contemporary sources, G. P. Putnam, N. Y., is an admirable series of books. Volumes on the XIV, XV, XVI, XVIIc. have been published. Conquest to 1300, and XVIIIc. were in preparation, and have probably been published.

The Ancient Orient

[Heuzey] L. A. and J. Heuzey: *Histoire du costume dans l'antiquité classique, l'Orient, Egypte, Mesopotamie, Syrie, Phoenicie,* ed. "Les Belles-Lettres," Paris, 1935. is the most scholarly work on the costume of this period.

[H. & H.] Mary G. Houston and Florence S. Hornblower: *Ancient Egyptian, Assyrian and Persian Costume,* London, 1920.
Köhler also gives patterns for this period.

[Pope] Arthur Upham Pope: *Survey of Persian Art, from Prehistoric Times to the Present,* 6 vols., Oxford University Press, London, 1938-9. We are much obliged to text and illustrations of these sumptuous volumes.

[Enc. ph.] *Encyclopédie photographique de l'art: Musée du Louvre,* 3 vols., ed. Tel, Paris, 1935-38; Parts 1-5, *Egypt;* 6-12, *Ancient Mesopotamia (Sumer, Babylonia, Elam)* ; 13, *Seals and Cylinders;* 14, *Canaan (Phoenicia, Judea, Arabia)* , is the source of many fine illustrations.

[Louvre] Louvre. *Antiquités orientales; Sumer, Babylonia, Elam.*

[Hall] H. R. H. Hall: *Babylonian and Assyrian Sculpture in the British Museum,* 1928.

[Sarre-Herzfeld] F. Sarre and Ernst Herzfeld: *Iranische Felsreliefe,* 3 vols., Berlin, 1912.
Among other useful books are:
Albert Neuberger: *The Technical Arts and Sciences of the Ancients,* tr. by Henry L. Brose ,Macmillan, N. Y., 1930: antiquity through the Roman period.
G. Rawlinson: *The Five Great Monarchies of the Ancient Eastern World,* 3 vols., 1871. (Re-issued, 190-? by Dodd, Mead & Co.)
G. Maspéro: *Life in Ancient Egypt and Assyria,* 1892.
O. M. Dalton: *The Treasure of the Oxus,* London, 1926, and E. Herzfeld: *Am Tor von Asien,* Berlin, 1926.

SOURCES OF OUR ILLUSTRATIONS:
1. (Louvre) .
5, 6, 7, 9, 11, 12, 33. (Enc. ph.) .
18, 19, 26. (Hall) .
29-33, 35-37. (Pope) .
34. (Sarre-Herzfeld) .

The Nile

Egyptian costume is treated by Heuzey, Houston and Hornblower, and by Köhler.

[Riefstahl] Elizabeth Riefstahl: *Patterned Textiles in Pharaonic Egypt,* Brooklyn Museum, 1944, 56 p. and 56 photographs.
Pagan and Christian Egypt, 1-10 Century A.D.—the catalog of the Brooklyn Museum's great exhibition in 1941. It has notes by John D. Cooney and Elizabeth Riefstahl, an excellent bibliography, 86 p. of text and 105 more pages consisting of about 170 large photographs. We are largely indebted to these two volumes for our information about Coptic dress. Cooper Union, Victoria and Albert, and Berlin Museums also have rich Coptic collections.
Etoffes byzantines, coptes, romaines, du IVe au Xe siècle, A. Guérinet, Paris, 16 pl., partly col.

[Ency. ph.] The Louvre's *Encyclopédie photographique de l'art,* and

[A. A. E.] *The Art of Ancient Egypt,* Phaidon Press, 1933, are rich sources of photographs.

[N. deG. D.] Wall paintings in Egyptian tombs have been reproduced in sumptuous color facsimile in N. de Garis Davis' *Ancient Egyptian Painting,* 2 volumes, and others devoted to specific tombs, published by the Metropolitan Museum of Art.
Cairo Museum: *Catalogue générale des antiquités égyptiennes,* and publications like those of Chicago University's Oriental Institute, and Berlin Museum, are useful.
General works like Sir W. M. Flinders Petrie: *Arts and Crafts of Ancient Egypt,* and his *History of Egypt;* A. Erman: *Life in Ancient Egypt,* Macmillan, 1894; G. Maspero: *Life in Ancient Egypt and Assyria,* Appleton, 1892; and Sir J. Gardner Wilkinson: *Manners and Customs of the Ancient Egyptians,* Dodd, Mead, 1879, are full of costume information.

SOURCES OF OUR ILLUSTRATIONS:
55-72, 92-94. (N. deG. D.) .
73, 74. Schiaparelli: *La Tomba dell' Architetto Cha.*
79-87, 95-98. (A. A. E.) .

The Greek Sphere

[Bieber] M. Bieber: *Entwicklungsgeschichte der Griechischen Tracht,* Berlin, 1934: scholarly text, illustrated by photographs.

[Repond) Jules Repond: *Secrets de la draperie antique,* Les Belles-lettres, Paris, 1931: photographed reconstructions of Greek dress; as well in Heuzey, Houston and Hornblower and Köhler.
Schuchardt: *Studien zur Altgriechischen Tracht.*
Studniezka: *Beitrage zur Geschichte der Altgriechischen Tracht,* Abh. des Arch. Epigr. Seminares der U. Wien, Vienna, 1886.
Sir William Ridgeway: *The Early Age of Greece,* 2 vols., Cambridge, 1901-03.
T. D. Seymour: *Life in the Homeric Age,* 1908.
Chadwick: *Heroic Age,* 1911.

[Zervos] C. Zervos: *Art en Grèce,* Cahiers d'Art, Paris, 1936, and Enc. ph. provide beautiful photographs.

SOURCES OF OUR ILLUSTRATIONS:
130-31. Matz: in "Antike," XI, pl. 179, 14.
132, 136. Also information about 138: Arthur J. Evans: *Palace of Minos,* 4 vols., 1921-35: a rich source of information about Aegean dress and decorative motifs, architecture and life.
135. Enc. ph.
139. Zervos.

ETRUSCAN

[Marthe] J. E. Marthe: *L'Art Etrusque,* Firmin-Didot, Paris, 1889: deals with Etruscan dress.
The best way to learn about Etruscan costume is to look at pictures. Since Celtic, Phoenician, Greek and many other cultures met in rich Etruria, there are quantities of well illustrated works which deal with her art, from the Early Iron Age down. Among them are:
Della Seta: *Italia Antica.*

[R. MacI.] D. Randall-MacIvor: *Early Iron Age in Italy,* 1927, and *Villanovans and Early Etruscans,* 1924, both pub. by Clarendon Press, Oxford.
C. Q. Giglioni: *L'Arte Etrusca.*
P. Ducati: *Storia dell'Arte Etrusca.*

[Weege] F. Weege: *Etruskische Malerei,* which reproduces the tomb paintings from Corneto.
Loukomski: *L'art étrusque.*

For Etruscan helmets and the transition into European helmets see:
Léon Coutil: *Les Casques Proto-Etrusques, Etrusques, et Gaulois,* W. Sifter, Gand, 1914.
Sir Guy Francis Laking: *A Record of European Arms and Armour through Seven Centuries,* 5 vols., London, G. Bell & Sons, 1920-22.

For Greek armor see:
Franz, Freiherr von Lipperheide: *Antike Helme.*
Reichel: *Homerische Waffen.*
R. Burton: *The Book of the Sword.*

SOURCES OF OUR ILLUSTRATIONS:
148. Also information: R. Maci I. He gives a line drawing of the entire pattern of the Certosa situla, and descriptions of the other situlae mentioned.
149. *Notizie degli Scavi,* 1938, p. 240, fig. 10.
145-46, 151-53, 203, 214-16. Enc. ph.
161. Hinks: *Catalogue of Greek, Etruscan and Roman Paintings and Mosaics in the British Museum,* 1933.
170, A, B. British Museum: *Guide to the Early Iron Age.*
195-97, 229-31, 233. Scheffer: *Die Kultur der Griechen.*
204-06. Picard: *La vie privée dans la Grèce classique.*

SCYTHIAN

SOURCES OF OUR ILLUSTRATIONS:
250. Bulletin, Russian Archaeol. Commission (in Russian) , 49, pl. 2, fig. 3.
252. M. Rostovtzeff: *Animal Style in S. Russia and China.*
254. M. Rostovtzeff: *Iranians and Greeks in S. Russia.*
256-57. "Revue archéologique," 4th series.
259. Dimitrescu: *L'art préhistorique en Roumanie.*

Romans and Barbarians

[Wilson] L. M. Wilson: *Clothing of the Ancient Romans,* Johns Hopkins Univ. Studies in Archaeology, No. 24, Johns Hopkins Press, Baltimore, 1938. Also see Heuzey, and Repond.

SOURCES OF OUR ILLUSTRATIONS NOT ACKNOWLEDGED IN TEXT:

273, 274, 278. Enc. ph., and text.
276. *Dura: Preliminary Report, 1933-5,* Yale University.
277. M. Rostovtzeff: *Dura-Europos and its Art,* Clarendon Press, Oxford, 1938. [Rachel Wischnitzer: *The Messianistic Theme in the Paintings of the Dura Synagogue* (rep. of the 30 panels), Univ. of Chicago Press, 1948].
279-87. Hayford Peirce and Royall Tyler: *L'Art Byzantin,* 2 vols., Librairie de France, Paris, 1932-34. [Peirce-Tyler.]
288. A. Kingsley Porter: *Spanish Romanesque Sculpture,* 2 vols., Florence, Pantheon, 1928. [Porter: *Sp. Rom. Sc.*]
289-90. Hans Achelis: *Die Katakomben von Neapel,* Leipzig, Hiersemann, 1935-36.
291-92. Hartel and Wickoff: *Wiener Genesis.*
293. Testo: *Il Rotolo di Giosue.* (Latter 2 are in Morgan Library.)
297, 298, 302. Photos by Prof. Karl Lehmann-Hartleben.
307, 308. W. A. Ritter von Jenny: *Germanischer Schmuck des Frühen Mittelalters.*

BARBARIAN DRESS

Köhler; Norris, vol. I; and such volumes as the book and museum reports on Jutland finds, mentioned in footnotes, our p. 89. I am indebted to Mr. William H. Forsyth, Assistant Curator of Mediaeval Art at the Metropolitan Museum of Art for information on jewelry of the Migration periods, shown on our pp. 71, 72, 91 and 92.

The Roman Catholic Church

Father Joseph Braun: *Die Liturgische Gewandung,* Freiburg-in-Breisgau, 1907 is the greatest authority.
Catholic Encyclopaedia, N. Y., 1907 on.
English and Protestant vestments can be seen in works by Druitt; Bloxam; H. J. Clayton: *Cassock and Gown,* Oxford, 1929; P. Dearmer: *Linen Ornaments of the Church,* Oxford, 1929.
I am obliged to the Very Rev. Msgr. Thomas J. McMahon for the chart of ecclesiastical vestments and colors on our p. 94, drawn from C. F. Du Cange: *Glossarium ad Scriptores Mediae et Infimae Latinitatis.* To it should be added colors of the "church cassock" for choir wear: priest, black; bishop and archbishop, purple; cardinal, scarlet; pope, white; deacon and sub-deacon, black; monks, color of order.
The dalmatic and tunicle distinctive of deacons and sub-deacons are never worn by priests, unless officiating as deacons or by papal privilege; worn under the chasuble, never under the cope; and over the stole. The Pope's tiara is the symbol of his office and jurisdiction; his ordinary head covering is the *pileus,* skull cap.
Ills. 327-30 are taken from A. W. Pugin: *Glossary of Ecclesiastical Ornament and Costume,* 1868.

The Dark Ages, VII-XIc.

[Barnard] Barnard's *Companion to English History: Middle Ages,* Clarendon Press, Oxford, is an excellent one-vol. guide to English life and dress, of and after the Conquest.
[Bede-A-S Chron.] *The Ecclesiastical History of England* by the Venerable Bede, b.673, and the *Anglo-Saxon Chronicle* (Caesar to midXIIc), are the source books of the period preceding the Conquest; published together in I vol., George Bell & Sons, London, 1903.
[Malmesbury] The *Chronicle of the Kings of England* by William of Malmesbury, b.1095/6, same publisher, 1895, is a fine costume source for the years 449-1142, especially for the Conquest which had taken place during his parents' time. Anglo-Norman warfare is discussed in Chap. III of
[Round] J. Horace Round: *The Commune of London,* Archibald Constable & Co., Westminster, 1899, which is a miscellany of fascinating scholarly information about the early Mediaeval period in England.

[Wright] Thomas Wright: *The Celt, the Roman, and the Saxon,* a history of the early inhabitants of Britain, down to the conversion of the Anglo-Saxons to Christianity, Arthur Hall, Virtue, & Co., London, 1852, with some engraved illustrations by Fairholt, is obviously not the latest work on the subject, but I have found its one vol. useful, ever since it was given me in my childhood, together with most of the books mentioned above, and Henry Sweet's *Anglo-Saxon Primer,* by my aunt, Frances G. Davenport, the historian.
Eric Millar: *La miniature anglaise du Xe au XIIIe siècle.*

SOURCES OF OUR ILLUSTRATIONS:

331-33, 337, 351-354. Westwood: *Miniatures and Ornaments of Anglo-Saxon and Irish Manuscripts.*
334. H. F. Blunck: *Die nordische Welt.*
335. G. Hirth's *Formenschatz.*
336. Raimond van Marle: *La peinture romane au moyen-âge.*
From bound volumes of photographs, belonging to the Pierpont Morgan Library:
338-39. Valenciennes Ms. 99, 38 photos.
340. Gerona Ms. 60, 173 photos.
341. Codex Aemilianensis, 42 photos.
344. Trier Stadtbib. Ms. 31, 76 photos.
360. Burgo de Osma 2, 2 vols. photos. Also in T. Rojo Otcajo: *El "Beato" de la catedral de Osma,* ed. de Cluny, Paris, 1942, 29 col. plates.
361-363. Bib. nat., lat. 8878, photos, but endlessly reproduced.
342, 347, 349, 350. Adolph Goldschmidt: *German Illumination:* Harcourt Brace, N. Y., 1928: vol. 1. Ottonian [Goldschmidt: Ott.]. 343. vol. 2. Carolingian Period. [Goldschmidt: Carol].
345, 348. Merton: *Buchmalerei in St. Gallen, IX-XIc.* Columban's hermit followers had an immense but short lived prestige. The Benedictines, the only other monastic order existing in Europe, entirely supplanted them by VIIIc. and were the only religious order until the great Xc. rise of Cluny. St. Gall, taken over by the Benedictines, remained for three centuries one of the greatest monasteries in Europe.
355, 366. Bastard: *Portraits de Nicéphore Botaniate, empereur d'Orient et de l'impératrice Marie sa femme.*
357, 358. Max Hauttmann: *Die Kunst des Frühen Mittelalters,* Berlin, Prophyläen, 1929.
359. Porter: *Sp. Rom. Sc.*
364-365. Basserman-Jordan: *Bamberger Domschatz.*
366-369. *Miniature sacre e profane del anno 1023 illustr. l'Enciclopedia medioevale di Rabano Mauro,* Monte Cassino, 1896, 133 col. pl.
372-374. *The Tapestry of Bayeux,* Society of Antiquaries, London, 1819-23.
375-78. Swarzenski: *Salzburger Malerei.*

Knighthood in Flower, XIIc.

HERALDRY

Arthur Charles Fox-Davies: *A Complete Guide to Heraldry,* Dodge Pub. Co., N. Y.
Woodward: *Treatise on Heraldry, British and Foreign,* 1896.
Joseph Edmonson: *Complete Body of Heraldry,* 1780.
Mrs. Bury Palliser: *Historic Devices, Badges, and War Cries,* S. Low Son and Marston, London, 1870.
In blazoning, color is never applied on color, nor metal on metal. The fur *vair* is *argent* and *azur* unless specifically blazoned. *Gules* (red) and *azure* (blue) come from the Persian *gûl* and *lâzurd* (lapis-lazuli), and show Arab influence from the Crusades. The *field* (background) may be *semé* (sown or powdered) with fleurs-de-lys, as in the old arms of France, crosslets, lozenges, etc.
Establishment of bearings:
In 1047, Geoffrey Plantagenet, grandfather of Geoffrey II of Anjou, "Martel," described in a rage "the color of his horse and the arms he meant to use" in a specific combat. (Malmesbury.) In 1160, Matthieu I de Montmorency bore no arms on his shield; the shield of Matthieu II de Montmorency, in 1177 bore the early Montmorency arms.
In XIVc., when the arms of France changed from the small fleurs-de-lys semé, of *France ancient* to the 3 large ones of *France modern,* the led coursers of the French Lord de Coucy were richly caparisoned with housings which mixed the ancient arms of Coucy with those he now bore. Frois-

sart records the rage of Sir John Chandos at finding his arms borne by the Marshal of the French, Lord John de Clermont. Because of the truce they had to wait until the next day's battle to settle the matter by arms. By 1386, Sir Richard le Scrope sued, rather than fought Sir Robert Grosvenor concerning the right to use a certain coat of arms. (Rickert: *Chaucer's World* gives excerpts of the testimony.)

SOURCES OF OUR ILLUSTRATIONS:

386. *Canterbury Psalter*, introduction by M. R. James, Humphries & Co., London, 1935.
387. Tancred Borenius and E. W. Tristram: *English Mediaeval Painting*, Pegasus Press, Paris, 1927, 101 pl. [Borenius-Tristram.]
396. *Congres archéologique de France*, Angers & Saumur.
402. Oskar Wulff: *Altchristliche u. mittelalterliche Byzantin. u. Italien. Bildwerke*, 2 vol. Berlin, 1909-11.
403. *Miniature del Registro di S. Angelo in Formis*.
405-408. Albert Boeckler: *Das Stuttgart Passionale*, Augsburg, 1903.
409. *Miniaturen des Kupferstichkabinetts der Staatlichen Museum, Berlin*.
410. Gantner: *Kunstgeschichte der Schweiz*.
411, 420, 421. H. F. Blunck: *Die nordische Welt*.
412, 413. *Die Regensburg Prüfeniger Buchmalerei des XII-XIIIJ*.
414-417. *Hortus Deliciarum*, Schlesier & Schweikhardt, Strassburg, 1901.
422-425. Brit. Mus. Add. 11695, from 2 bound volumes of photographs in the Morgan Library:
426. J. Dominguez Bordona: *Spanish Illumination*, 2 vols., Harcourt Brace, N. Y., 1930. [Bordona]
4313-434. Porter: *Sp. Rom. Sc.*

Feudal Lords and Kings, XIIIc.

Sources of information: Arms and Armor, 650-1650 A.D.:
The preeminent collections and catalogs of armor are those of the *Vienna Historical Museum;* of the *Armory of the Castle of Churburg*, the personal collection of the armor of generations of the ancestors of Oswald Graf Trapp (trans. with notes by Sir James G. Mann); the *Metropolitan Museum of Art*. The armor of the *Wallace Collection* has been catalogued by S. J. Camp; that of Madrid's *Armeria Real*, by Count Valencia de Don Juan; that of various Swiss collections, by Charles Buttin.
I have relied mainly on publications by the Curators of the Metropolitan Museum of Art (listed below), and on the following:
Germain Demay: *Le costume d'après les sceaux*, Paris, 1880.
Auguste Demmin: *Arms and Armour*, London, Geo. Bell & Sons, 1877.
C. C. ffoulkes: *The Armourer and his Craft* (from XI to XVIc), 1912.
J. H. von Hefner-Altenneck: *Waffen* (from beginning of Middle Ages to end of XVIIc.), 1903.
F. M. Kelly & R. Schwabe: *A Short History of Costume and Armour, chiefly in England*, 1066-1800.
Sir Guy Francis Laking: *A Record of European Arms and Armour through Seven Centuries*, 5 vols., London, Geo. Bell & Sons, 1920-22.
Sir James G. Mann: *Notes on Armour of the Maximilian Period and the Italian Wars*, "Archaeologica," LXXIX, 1929.
Viollet-le-Duc: *Dictionnaire raisonné du mobilier français*.
In describing illustrations of armor in the Metropolitan Museum of Art, I have drawn heavily, by quotation or abstract, from Bashford Dean: *Catalog of Arms and Armor*, M.M.A., 1930; Stephen V. Grancsay: *Historical Armor*, a picture book, M.M.A., 1946; ibid: *Mutual Influences of Costume and Armor*, a study of specimens in the M.M.A., Bulletin, vol. III, 1930-31.
Ills. 435-436 are charts prepared under the direction of Bashford Dean, former Curator of the Arms and Armor Collection of the M.M.A., and of Stephen V. Grancsay, the present Curator. We are greatly indebted to Mr. Grancsay for permission to use them. They were executed by Stanley J. Rowland, Hashima Murayama, and Randolph Bullock, the Assistant Curator.
We reproduce photographs and drawings after rubbings of monumental effigies and brasses (referred to under chapter headings, XIVc. on, by key names), taken from:

[Boutell] Charles Boutell: *Monumental Brasses and Slabs*, London, Cogswell, 1847.
[Cotman] J. S. Cotman: *Engravings of Sepulchral Brasses of Norfolk and Suffolk*, 2 vols., 1839.
[Creeny: I. S.] Rev. W. F. Creeny: *Incised Slabs on the Continent of Europe*.
[Creeny: M. B.] —: *Monumental Brasses on the Continent of Europe*.
[Crossley] F. H. Crossley: *English Church Monuments*, London, 1921.
[Dunkin] Edward E. H. W. Dunkin: *Monumental Brasses of Cornwall*, London, 1882.
[Haines] Rev. H. Haines: *A Manual for the Study of Monumental Brasses*, Oxford, 1848.
[Photol.] *Photolithographs of Monumental Brasses*.
[Stothard] C. A. Stothard: *The Monumental Effigies of Great Britain*.
[V. & A. R. of B.] *Victoria and Albert Museum: Catalogue of Rubbings of Brasses*.
[Waller] J. G. Waller: *Monumental Brasses*.
There are many others such as:
Frederick Chancellor: *Ancient Sepulchral Monuments of Essex*.
A. Hartshorne: *Recumbent Monumental Effigies of Northamptonshire*.
T. and G. Hollis: *Monumental Effigies*.
E. S. Prior and Arthur Gardiner: *An Account of Mediaeval Figure Sculpture in England*.
An excellent picture of XIIIc. life, amply backed by research, can be found in William Stearns Davis: *Life on a Mediaeval Barony, a Picture of a Typical Feudal Community in the Thirteenth Century*, Harper & Bros., N. Y., 1923.

SOURCES OF OUR ILLUSTRATIONS:

465. (Piton).
466. (Hirth).
467. Henri Focillon: *Peintures Romanes des églises de France*, Paul Hartmann, Paris, 1938.
438-86. M. R. James: *Drawings by Matthew Paris*.
487. O. E. Saunders: *English Illuminations*, 2 vols. Firenze, Pantheon, 1927. [Saunders]
488-90. *Rutland Psalter*: int. by Eric George Millar, Roxburghe Club, Oxford, 1937.
491. *La Estoire de Seint Aedward le Rei*, ed. by Montague Rhodes James, Roxburghe Club, Oxford, 1920.
492. Saunders: v. II.
493. Victoria and Albert Museum: *Catalogue of Rubbings of Brasses*.
494. Antonio Morassi: *Storia della Pittura nella Venezia Tridentina*, Rome, Libreria dello Stato, 1934.
499. C. Zervos: *Catalan Art*, from the 9th to the 15th century, W. Heinemann, London, 1937. [Zervos, C. A...
501-06. Bound vol. of photos at Morgan Library: *Book of Chess*.
Page 181, top col. 2. *The Disk of Theodosius* can be seen in Peirce and Tyler.
The many *Book of Chess* mss. show Negroes, Jews, monks, pharmacists, and the identical tents used throughout all the wars of Mediaeval Europe.
507-12. Bordona: shows many other mss. of the *Cantigas* and *Book of Chess*.
Page 184. Glove as gage: When Maurice de Prendergast is accused of treason, in the XIIIc. Anglo-Norman *Book of Howth*:
"E Morice a sun guant plie
A son seignur lad baille" and in XIVc., "He shall wage his law with his folded glove (de son guant plyee), and shall deliver it into the hand of the other, and then take it back and find pledge for his law" (Round: *Commune of London*.)
513-15, 522-23, 525-26, 529. Hauttmann; Patterns in Hottenroth and Köhler.
517-20. Bound vol. photos in Morgan Lib., but beautifully reproduced in *Heinrich von Veldeke: Eneide*, ed. Albert Boecklin, Otto Harrasowitz, Leipzig, 1939, 91 pl., part col.
524. Georg Swarzenski: *Die lateinischen illuminierten Handschriften des XIII J., in den Ländern am Rhein, Main, Donau*, Berlin, 1936.
527, 530-31. Erwin Panofsky: *Die Deutsche Plastik des XI bis XIII j.*, Munich, K. Wolf, 1924.
528. *Deutsche Kunst*, Bremen, Angelsachsen Verlag, vol. 8, No. II.

The Rising Bourgeoisie, XIVc.

Sir John Froissart (1337/8-1410/20): *Chronicle of England, France and Spain,* is of course the greatest XIVc. European source. Unlike Chaucer, who must have talked to everybody, his French contemporary and acquaintance, Froissart, spoke only to gentlefolk. But no man in his time even approximated Froissart's acquaintanceship among all the nobility and gentry between Scotland and Venice, nor his charm and gusto.

Other rich English sources, in addition to those given on our p. 196, are:

Geoffrey Chaucer: *Canterbury Tales.*

Ralph Holinshed: *Chronicles of England, Scotland and Ireland,* 1578, from which Shakespeare drew his material for Macbeth, Lear, and the historical plays.

John Stow: *Survey of London,* 1598: ed. Henry Morley, George Rutledge & Sons, London, 1890: full of information about earlier days and ways.

Joseph Strutt: *Sports and Pastimes of the People of England,* London, Methuen, 1903.

Eric G. Millar: *English Illuminated Mss. of the XIVth and XVth Centuries,* Paris & Brussels, G. van Oest, 1928.

Sources of monumental brasses and effigies are listed in appendix of chapter: *Feudal Lords and Kings.*

SOURCES OF OUR ILLUSTRATIONS:

Full titles of Brass sources are with Armor in appendix of previous chapter.

532-33. *Rows* Roll by John *Rous;* in the *Paston Letters* we find this name variously spelled, even in the same letter, as: Rowse, Rouse, Rows, Rus, Russe. The *Rows Roll* has disappeared; copy in College of Arms, London.

534, 536. *Two East Anglian Psalters at Bodleian,* Oxford, described by Sidney C. Cockerell and Montague Rhodes James, Roxburghe Club, Oxford, 1926. (*Ormesby Psalter,* 34 pl., 3 col.; *Bromholme Psalter,* II pl., I col.).

535. *Gorleston Psalter; library of C. W. Dyson Perrins,* described by S. C. Cockerell, Bernard Quaritch, London.

537-38. *The Antiquities of Westminster Abbey.*

439-52. *Tickhill Psalter,* D. D. Egbert, N. Y. 1940, 111 pl.

553. Boutell.

554-55. Waller.

556, 557-58. V. &. A., R. of B.

560. The *Ellesmere Chaucer,* reprod. in facsimile, Manchester, the Univ. Press, 1911. Some in color.

561. The *Treatise of Walter de Milamete,* Oxford, Roxburghe Club, 1913.

562. Crossley: *Eng. Ch. Mon.*

563. Boutell: *Mon. Br. and Slabs.*

564-74. *Luttrell Psalter;* int. by E. G. Millar, London, British Museum, 1932, 183 monochromes and 2 col. pl.

575-84. *Romance of Alexander;* int. by M. R. James, Oxford, Clarendon Press, 1933.

585. *Photolith. of Mon. Brasses.*

586. Cotman: *Sepul. Br. of Norfolk and Suffolk.*

When Jeanne de Navarre (d.1304) travelled to Bruges and Ghent with Philip the Fair, she was astonished at the wealth she saw: "I thought I was the only queen there, but I saw more than 600." A rich trader of Valenciennes, at the French court, end XIIIc., was offered no cushion. He sat on his pearl and gold embroidered cloak, lined with fur, and left it, saying to the servant who reminded him of it, that it was not the custom in his country for people to carry their cushions away with them. (Lacroix: Middle Ages.)

588-89, 590. Borenius and Tristram: *E.M.P.* The sculptured effigies of the 2 daughters and 3 sons (Ills. 588-89) in ordinary dress, c.1380, from Edward III's tomb in Westminster Abbey, are shown in K.&S.: *Sh.Hist.,* Pl. XII.

591. V.&A.: *R. of B.*

592-93. Boutell.

594. Cotman.

595-96. *Photolith. Mon.* Most of the names on these Norfolk brasses appear in the *Paston Letters;* Stapleton helps John Paston settle a lawsuit between their cousins, Brian Stapleton and Elizabeth Clere.

597.] Boutell.

598-99. V.&A.: *R. of B.*

600-01. Boutell.

602. Color repr. of "Wilton House Diptych," in K.&S.:

S. H. "Sion Cope" rep. in *Enc. Brit.,* 11th ed., Embroidery, pl. II, fig. 9. Effigies of Edward III's sons, York Minster and Anne of Bohemia; rep. in line drawings, S. R. Gardiner: *Student's Hist. of Eng.* p. 237, and 267. "Atchievements" of Edward, the Black Prince, photos in *Vetusta Monumenta,* vol. VI.; embroidered robes of Richard II, vol. I.

603. The Rev. Thomas J. McMahon, as a professor at Dunwoodie, had been kind enough to help in ecclesiastical research. As the Very Rev. Msgr. McMahon, he told me about the tiaras, but lacking the facilities of the college library, was unable to give a final answer on the other Papal vestments, nor have I found anyone else willing to commit himself.

627. Chantilly, Musée Condé:*Cabinet des Mss.,* vol. I.

628. H. M. R. Martin: *Les Joyaux de l'enluminure à la Bibl. Nat.,* Paris et Bruxelles, G. van Oest, 1928.

637-41. *Manessa Codex,* Leipzig, 1925-27, 320 col. facs.

642-47. *Rohmfahrt Kaiser Heinrichs VII* ed. Georg Irmer, Weidmannsche Buchhandlung, Berlin, 1881, 39 pl., part col.

648. *Das Soester Nequambuch, das buch der Freuler Stadtbuch,* pub. by Hist. Comm., Prov. Westphalen.

649. Photos in Morgan Lib., of Ms., which in 1933 was in hands of the dealer Weiss of Munich.

650-52. Creeny: *Mon. Br. of Eur.*

653. Floerke: *Das Weib in der Renaissance.*

654. Boutell.

657. [Vitry-Brière] P. G. Vitry-Brière: *Documents de sculpture française,* 3 vols., D. A. Longuet, Paris, 1906-11.

658. Gaignières Coll. Many rep. in Piton.

660-61. *Les principaux mss. à peintures de la Bib. Roy. de Belgique,* ed. Father J. van den Gheyn.

662. Couderc: *Album de Portraits,* enluminures des mss. du moyen-âge, VI-XVc., Bib. Nat., Paris, ed. Gazette de beaux-arts, 1927.

668-70. Goury and Jones: *Plans, Elevations, Sections and Details of the Alhambra,* 2 vols., London, 1842-45.

The Renaissance Begins, XVc.

G. F. Young: *The Medici,* Modern Library, N. Y., 1930.

Jacob Burckhardt: *The Civilization of the Renaissance in Italy,* Oxford Univ. Press, N. Y., 1945.

J. A. Crowe and G. B. Cavalcasse: *History of Painting in Italy, Umbria, Florence and Siena from the second to the sixteenth century,* J. Murray, London, 1903-14, among innumerable works on Italian painting.

Much material in Vasari's delightful yet reliable biographies of artists refers to XVc. although written in XVIc.

Eric Millar: *English Illuminated Mss. of the XIVth and XVth Centuries.*

Paul Durrieu: *La miniature flamande au temps de la cour de Bourgogne,* Bruxelles et Paris, G. van Oest, 1921.

Religiöse Kunst aus Hessen und Nassau: Verlag des Kunstgeschichtlichen Seminars, Lahn, Marburg, 1932, 2 vols. of pl., I of text. Is invaluable for illustrations, not only of pictures and sculpture, but of embroideries, tapestries, printed textiles, and many other articles in secular use.

G. J. Demotte: *Tapisserie Gothique,* Paris & N. Y., Demotte, 1924.

Philippe de Commines (c.1445-c.1511): *Memoirs,* by the father of modern history, who served Charles the Bold and Louis XI, is valuable for the years 1464-1495.

SOURCES OF OUR ILLUSTRATIONS:

674-77. Photographs in Frick Art Reference Lib.

678. Ignaz Seelos: *Fresken-Cyclus des Schlosses Runkelstein bei Bozen,* Plan 29, Tafel XIX, col. rep.

705. *Die Tarocchi.*

708-10. A. M. Hind: *Early Italian Engraving,* vol. II. In 4 vols. (vol. 2-4 are plates). Quaritch, London, 1938.

711: Schubring: *Cassoni,* vol. I.

717-18. Musée Condé, Chantilly, has many Pisanello sketches. Shoulder plates like those of St. George: Boccacino's "Procession to Calvary," rep. in J. Starkie Gardner: *Armour in England,* part 2 (Foreign Armour), p. 32, Macmillan, N. Y., 1892.

720-23. Pietro Toesca: *La pittura e la miniatura nella Lombardia,* U. Hoepli, Milan, 1912.

741-42. I am much indebted to research by the Art Division

of the N. Y. Public Lib. for information about these two pictures.

753, 756, 757, 759. Photographs courtesy of Henry Varnum Poor.

784. I am grateful to Fern Rusk Shapely, Research Division of the National Gallery of Art, Washington, for this information. In Mrs. Shapley's *A Portrait of Francesco Sforza,* (15 p., 13 ills.) "Arts Quarterly," Winter, 1945, the *spazzola* is seen in relief on Sforza coats-of-arms, and on the lance rest of the interesting armor worn by Francesco in the N.G.A. portrait.

789-92. Liebreich: *Claus Sluter.* Information on Ill. 790 from Rev. T. J. McMahon.

793. Troescher: *Claus Sluter.*

795. Vitry-Brière.

796-98. Camille Couderc: *Livre de Chasse par Gaston-Phoebus, Comte de Foix,* imp. Berthaud frères, Paris, 1909, 87 pl.

799-803. Henri Martin: *Boccace de Jean sans Peur.*

Page 295. Domestic Architecture:

S. F. Markham: *Climate and the Energy of Nations,* Oxford University Press, London, 1924.

S. Giedion: *Space, Time and Architecture,* Harvard University Press, Cambridge, 1943, a book of major importance—a history of architecture, its materials, and its underlying philosophy, since the Middle Ages, with excellent photographs.

Louis Mumford: *The Culture of Cities,* Harcourt Brace, 1938, and *Techniques and Civilizations,* 1934, both well-illustrated, outline the changes in cities: mediaeval, baroque and industrial.

A. Newberger (see app., *The Ancient Orient*) reveals the extent of the degradation of techniques in Europe, after Roman times.

Cooper Union, started in 1854-5, and eventually raised to 7½ stories, would have been the first steel-skeleton building, had Peter Cooper not decided that he could improve on the beams he had already prepared and sold them to Harper Bros. The first iron bridge was that over the Severn in 1775-9, and at about the same time, iron was used in factory roof construction in England.

804-06. Camille Couderc: *Album de portraits.*

807-10. *Très-riches heures,* ed. Durrieu, Plon Nourrit, Paris, 1904.

812-15. The figure from Foxton, Trinity College, Cambridge, is reproduced in K.&S.: *Short Hist.,* as are more figures of the counts and countesses than the Victoria and Albert Museum was able to supply, immediately after the war.

823. Boutell.

826. Quotations from Chamberlayne: *The Present State of England,* 38th ed., 1755, and Stow: *Survey of London,* 1598.

827-28. Frick Art Reference Library photographs.

829. Information about this illustration is largely taken from Margaret Scherer: *About the Round Table,* Metropolitan Museum of Art Bulletin, 1945.

There was very little open space in a mediaeval walled town. In 1395, London Bridge was the scene of the joust between David, the Scots Earl of Crawford, and the English Lord Wells. At that time the bridge was coped and "was not replenished with houses built thereupon, as it hath since been, and now is," Stow tells us (1598). He describes the bridge of his day as "having with the drawbridge 20 arches made of squared stone, of height 60 feet and in breadth 30, distant from one another 20 feet, compact and jointed together with vaults and cellars; upon both sides be houses built, so that it seemeth rather a continual street than a bridge." The early bridge, without houses, therefore offered a long, wide space and sound foundation for a joust.

830-31. Reproduced under same title; at Morgan Library.

832-35. *Ystoire de Helayne,* ed. J. van den Gheyn, Vromant et cie., Bruxelles, 1913, 26 pl.

839-46. Fouquet. *Grandes chroniques de France,* imp. Berthaud frères, Paris, 1906, 51 pl.

847-48. *Oeuvre de Fouquet: Heures de Maistre Etienne Chevalier,* ed. M. l'Abbé Delaunay, L. Curmer, Paris, 1866-7, 2 vols., col. pl.

849-50. Couderc: *Album de portraits.*

851. Bib. Nat.; *Portraits des Rois de France.*

873-76. *Les Sieurs de Gavres,* Van Dale, Bruxelles, 1845.

880. Metropolitan Museum of Art photograph.

893-98. Good color reproductions of the "Charlatan" and others in Jacques Combe: *Jerome Bosch,* ed. Pierre Tisne, Paris, 1946.

899-902. François Courboin: *Histoire illustrée de la gravure en France,* vol. 2; 4 vols. Paris, Le Garrec, 1923-28.

904. Courboin: *Album de portraits.*

906. In such matters as the bells worn by the Hero, garters, gloves, and accessories, as well as civil, military, and ecclesiastical costume, Enlart: *Manuel d'archéologie française,* vol. 3, *Costume,* is invaluable.

907-8. Frick Art Reference Library photographs.

911-12, 915, 918-20, 932-33. Waller.

913-14, 916, 921, 928, 930-31. Boutell.

917. Dunkin: *Mon. Br. of Cornwall.*

922-25, 939. *Catalogue of an Exhibition of British Mediaeval Art,* Burlington Fine Arts Club, London, 1939.

934-38. *The Pageants of Richard Beauchamp, Earl of Warwick,* in facsimile, Roxburghe Club, Oxford, 1908.

940. Mrs. Poole's *Catalogue* is an extremely valuable work which gives color and biographical notes.

941. Creeny.

942-43. Cotman: *Sep. Br. of Norfolk.*

945-52, 960. C. Zervos: *Catalan Art from 9th to 15th Centuries,* W. Heinemann, London, 1937; superbly illustrated like all Zervos' books.

953-54. See Ill. 922.

955, 961-68. Bordona: Sp. Ill., vol. II.

972. *Chantilly: Cabinet de mss.,* vol. I.

975. *Hirth's Formenschatz.*

976-79. Max Lehrs: *Katalog der im Germ. Mus. befind. Deutschen Kupferstiche d. XVj.,* Nuremberg, 1887.

981. Creeny: *Mon. Br. of Cont. Eur.*

982-83. Hans Thalhofer: *Livre d'Escrime,* ed. Gustav Hagsell, Prague, 1901.

984-86. H. T. Bossert and W. F. Storck (publishers): *Mittelalteres Hausbuch,* by Master of the Amsterdam Cabinet, Leipzig, 1912.

995. Lippmann facsimiles, Metrop. Mus. Lending Coll.

Culture Moves North, XVIc.

Sources of information about Tudor costume:

Edward Hall (c.1498-1547): *Chronical,* 1542; complete ed., 1809; *Henry VIII,* 1904. Hall was a lawyer and member of Parliament. His eyewitness accounts of the reigns of Henry VII-VIII are rich in glamorous detail.

William Harrison (1534-93): *Description of England,* published in 1578, together with:

Ralph Holinshed (d.c.1580): *Chronicles of England, Scotland, and Ireland;* 6 vols., 1808. Harrison's work is the basis for *Shakespeare's England,* 2 vols., Clarendon Press, Oxford, 1916; Shakespeare got the material for his historical plays, Macbeth, and Lear from Holinshed; Sir Walter Scott is another debtor to Holinshed.

Philip Stubbes (c.1555-c.1610): *Anatomy of Abuses,* 1583. Absolutely nothing is more informative, nor more wonderful reading, than the revilings, item by item, of every excess of Elizabethan fashion by a very eloquent Puritan of whom Nash said: "It is a great pity for him, that, being such a good fellow as he is, he should speak against dice as he doth." The 3rd ed. of 1585 was reprinted by W. Pickering, London, 1835.

John Stow or Stowe (1525-1605): *Survey of London,* 1598; amended in 1603, 1618, 1633, 1720 and 1754; reprints of 1598 ed. in 1842, 1846, 1876. Any page references I may have given are from the H. Morley ed., George Routledge & Sons, London, 1890, which has no index.

Stow was a tailor's son turned antiquarian; the facts he amasses were fascinating in themselves, and his expression of them quaint and appealing. The number of editions gives some indication of the book's importance, but it was also the begetter of many similar and invaluable books in XVIIc., such as *L'état de France,* and Chamberlayne's *Present State of England.*

John Speed (1552-1629): maps, particularly the *Theatre of the Empire of Great Britain,* 1611, contain delightful costumed figures in the cartouches and borders.

William Camden (1557-1623): *Brittanica,* written in Latin, trans. in 1610, and *Annals of the Reign of Elizabeth,* trans. 1635. He was the antiquarian after whom the Camden Society, publishers of so many important books, was named.

Thomas Coryat (1577-1617) : *Crudities,* 1611; 2 vols., James MacLehose, Univ. of Glasgow, 1905, and

Fynes Moryson (1566-1630) : *Itinerary,* 1617; 4 vols., same pub., 1907, were two observant young Englishmen's records of what they saw during years of travel in Europe and the Orient, at the turn of the century.

Arthur Ponsonby: *English Diaries,* Methuen, London, 1922, provides excerpts from diaries, and a bibliography of those available in reprint.

Pictures of Tudor dress:

The best portraits of Elizabeth are by the Flemings, Marc Gheeraerts, the elder, b.1525, and his son Marc, the younger, b.1561, who came to England with his father in 1568. He married into the family of another dynasty of Flemish painters domiciled in England, the de Critz, and died in England in 1636. Federigo Zuccaro (1542-1609) was an Italian who worked in England from 1574-82. Indigenous English painting begins at the end of the XVIc. with Isaac Oliver and Nicholas Hilliard.

Good reproductions are to be found in:

Walpole Society publications, especially the article on *Gheeraerts,* vol. 3, 1913-4.

Collins Baker and Constable: *English Painting, 16th and 17th Centuries,* Harcourt Brace, N. Y., 1930.

Miniature Painting: see list in appendix ref. to Ill. 1546.

Sir Lionel Cust (editor) : *Catalogue of the Pictures, etc. in the National Portrait Gallery,* London, 14th ed., 1909.

H. K. Morse: *Elizabethan Pageantry,* Studio, London, 1934, is based on beautifully chosen illustrations, accompanied by text taken from contemporary authors.

Kelly and Schwabe: both volumes, and Norris, vol. III, Books 1 and 2, are particularly useful at this period, together with the old and always good F. W. Fairholt: *Costume in England,* 1896 ed., and John Hewitt: *Ancient Armour and Weapons,* 1859-61.

London Museum: The Cheapside Horde of Elizabethan and Jacobean Jewelry, Cat. 2, 1928, illustrates and describes what was probably the stock of a XVIIc. jeweller, dug up in 1912 at the corner of Friday St. and Cheapside: XV-XVIIc. jewelry and Roman cameos and intaglios.

Information: Horace Walpole: *Anecdotes of Painting in England,* 6 vols., 1782.

European sources:

Benvenuto Cellini (1500-71) : *Autobiography,* of the Florentine goldsmith, soldier, and adventurer, who spent much time in France in the service of Francis I.

Giorgio Vasari (1511-71) : *Lives of the Painters* (1550) , himself a painter, studied the painters of Italy under Medici patronage, and is our principal source of information about them.

Pierre de Bourdielle, Seigneur and Abbé de Brantôme (c.1540-1614) : *Memoirs* (12 vols., ed. Lalanne, Soc. de l'Hist. de Fr., 1864-96) . Brantôme was familiar with the court of Marguerite of Valois, in which his mother and grandmother had served, travelled in Scotland with Mary Stuart, knew Elizabeth, and Charles IX, journeyed in Italy, Spain, Morocco, and wrote his memoirs at the end of his life.

Fugger News Letters; 1568-1605, John Lane, London, 1924; see Ill. 1053.

Christopher Weiditz: *Trachtenbuch von seinen Reisen nach Spanien,* 1529, *und den Niederlanden,* 1531-2, ed. Dr. T. Hampe, Museum, Nuremberg, 1927; rep. partly in color, text in English, Spanish and German. (N. Y. Pub. Lib., Art Room.)

Dimier: *Histoire de la peinture de portraits en France au XVIe siècle,* 2 vols. Paris et Bruxelles, G. van Oest, 1924-26.

Georg Hirth: *Les grands Illustrateurs,* 1500-1800, 6 vols., Munich, 1888-91.

Hirth & R. Muther: *Kulturgeschichtliches Bilderbuch aus drei Jahrhunderten,* XVI-XIX. G. Hirth's Verlag, Munich, 1923-5: the greatest collection of woodcuts and engravings of Europe. Vol. III: Costumes.

SOURCES OF OUR ILLUSTRATIONS:

1003-04. Creeny: *Mon. Br. of Cont. Eur.*

1010. Costume of Nuremberg: shown in plates by Hans Scheuffelein, 1530, available in reproduction; in Holbein's colored drawings of day, church, and dance dress (Vienna, Albertina) ; and in the *Weisskunig* (Ills. 1035-36)

1023-26. Lippmann facsimiles, Met. Mus. Lending Coll.

1035-36. Emperor Maximilian I: *Der Weisskunig,* ed. by Marx Treitzsaurwein, Vienna, 1775.

1038. Oskar Fischel: *Chronisten der Mode,* Muller, Potsdam, 1923; an assortment of fresh, finely selected and reproduced documentary illustrations, carried into the XXc.

1046-47. Roblot-Delondre: *Portraits d'Infantes,* XVI siècle, Paris: G. van Oest, 1913.

1049. *Les dessins de Hans Holbein,* le jeune. Publ. par Paul Ganz, Genève, Ed. d'art et de science, 1939.

1050. *Bilder-katalog zu Max Geisberg, Der Deutsche Einblatt-holzschnitt,* (first half XVIc.) , Munich, H. Schmidt, 1930.

1058. Color rep. in K.&S.: *Hist. Cost.,* p. 49.

Page 403. Clocks and Watches: Sources of Information:

G. C. Williamson: *Catalogue of the Collection of Watches, the property of J. Pierpont Morgan,* Cheapside Press, London, 1912.

G. H. Baillie: *Watches,* their history, decoration and mechanism, Methuen, London, 1927 (many color pl.) .

Collection of Watches loaned to the Metropolitan Museum of Art by Mrs. George A. Hearn, privately pr., 1907.

Wade: *British Chronology,* Bohn, London, 1847; this is, by the way, a very useful book, which lists new usages and laws, many relating to dress; statement about 1288 clock. Coryat gives much information about clocks. Norris, vol. 3, gives the inventory of Henry VIII's clocks.

Page 414, and Ills. 1107-11. G. Glück: *Pieter Brueghel the Elder,* Hyperion Press, Paris, 1937. Reproduces his paintings in color with enlargements in offset.

1115. Blunck: *Nordische Welt.*

1122, 1126. Hirth: *Kult. Bild.*

1123-24. (at N. Y. Pub. Lib., see Ill. 1113) .

1125. Lippman facsimile.

1128-29, 1131-32. My embarrassment at my ignorance of these Netherlands symbols has been considerably relieved by a very kind letter from Mr. Edgar Wind of Smith College, who says there is little he can tell me. The figure 1128 is a bird-catcher, as the inscription says, but he seems to have been generalized into a catcher of animals of all kinds—a pied piper. The monkeys and rabbits probably have their usual connotations of sensuality and fertility. In connection with 1129, he indicated the Clutton article, p. 287 ff, from which Ills. 1131-32 and their text were drawn. Lorraine is, of course, adjacent to Flanders.

1135, 1137. Exh. Br. Med. Art.

1138. *Handzeichnungen Schweizerischer Meister,* (XV-XVIII Centuries) .

1139. Cotman.

1152-53. *Les dessins de Hans Holbein.* (See Appendix on Ill. 1049.)

1161-62, 1172. Collins Baker and Constable: *Eng. P.,* 16-*17th c.*

1164-66. Waller.

1171. Quotation from the *Literary Remains of Edward VI,* Clarendon Historical Reprints, 1884, which ends after "I fell sick of the measles and small-pox," of which he died at 16. I am obliged to Norris for the information about "La Pelegrina."

1172, 1178, 1207. Collins Baker and Constable.

1176. See London Museum: Cheapside Horde.

1184. Hirth: *Kult. Bild.,* vol. 3.

1190. Lippmann facs.

1193. For more information, see A. W. Kendrick: *English Embroidery,* and *Book of Old Embroidery.*

Page 448. European Textile Design, see Henri Cluzot and Francis Morris: *Painted and Printed Fabrics,* a history of the manufacture at Jouy and other ateliers in France, 1760-1815, Met. Mus., N. Y., 1927. Has a good bibliography. The finest book on Jouy toiles, with notes by Cluzot, appeared later: Henri D'Allemagne, *La Toile imprimée, les indiennes de trait,* Gründ, Paris, 1942, 2 vols., 1 of text, 1 loose plates, many col.

Page 455. Covered faces, Moorish women: earlier instances shown in Ruth M. Anderson: *Pleated Headdresses of Castile and Leon, XII-XIII c.,* "Notes Hispanic," Hisp. Soc. of N. Y., 1942.

1213-15. Full title of rep. given in XVIc. Eur. sources.

1228. Engraving with spectacles, rep. in Hind: *Early Italian Engs.,* pl. 74.

1230. *The Hispanic-American Review,* Duke Univ. Press, Nov., 1943, has culled from ships' registers of the

House of Trade in Seville an extremely informative list of the merchandise carried by Spain to America, 1534-87, and the provenance, by countries and cities, of many articles. Dolls came from Flanders, chessmen from France. The largest proportion of goods from outside Spain was clothing from France and Holland, then Portugal, England, Italy and Germany, in order. Certain Spanish cities specialized in clothing production.

1233-35. Tailor shop of 1588, master and 2 assistants, and all equipment, shown in James P. R. Lyell: *Early Book Illustration in Spain*, Grafton House, London, 1926, fig. 140. Lyell gives 1 page of each of the most important books published in XV-XVIc. Early Spanish engraving was largely in German hands; and tends to show standard European dress of the period before their migration to Spain. Striking Spanish dress is shown in the 1502 ed. of *La Celestina*, Seville, 1502, by Jacob Cronberger (Lyell, fig. 120). All publication was censored in advance by the Church. Wonderful tasselled Cardinal hats, significant of patronage, appear on title pages (into XVIIIc. in Manila); shown in Fr. Vindel: *Manual gráfico-descriptivo del Bibliofilio Hispano-Americano*, 1475-1850, Madrid, 1930.

1247, 1249. Couderc: *Album de portraits*.

1248, 1254. Martin: *Joyaux d'enluminure*.

1258. Bib. Nat.: *Port. des Rois de France*.

1259. Meurgey: *Principaux mss. à peintures du Musée Condé, Chantilly*.

1263-64. Crêpe: excellent example in the hats of Isaac Oliver's *Three Brothers Brown and their Servant*, 1597 (Earl Spencer Coll.); see *Burlington Mag.*, Feb. 1917, vol. 30, p. 57c; *Connoisseur*, July, 1937, vol. 100, p. 28; and K.&S.: *Sh. Hist.*, pl. XVIII.

1280. *Chantilly: Cabinet des mss.*, vol. I.

1296-99. Mediaeval Paris, before alteration by Louis XIV, can be seen in the enchanting bird's-eye map in an extremely useful book, *Cosmographie universelle*, Nicolas Chesneau, Paris, 1575 (Met. Mus., Print Room). Much help in early history, vanished or altered locales, can be had from it. Also from the Marquis de Rochegude: *Guide pratique à travers le vieux Paris*, Champion, Paris, 1923; and Henri Sauval (1620-70): *Histoire et recherches des antiquité de la ville de Paris*, 3 vols., Paris, 1724.

1303. Bertelli's *solana* brim, shown in C. Yriarte: *Venice*, Geo. Bell, London, 1880, p. 242.

1311. *Illustrated Catalog of Pictures of Siena*.

SOURCES OF INFORMATION ON COSTUME:

Stubbes, Coryat and Moryson are useful for the early part of the century in England.

The greatest sources of the Restoration are, of course, the diaries kept by the dignified John Evelyn (1620-1703), which covers his life span; and that by the contemporary whom he characterizes as a "worthy, industrious and curious person": Samuel Pepys (1633-1703), who kept his indiscreet diary, in shorthand, from 1660-69.

Evelyn, a well-born, cultivated, and much traveled courtier, sought and was sought by most of the persons of the artistic, architectural, scientific, and literary worlds of his age. He visited great houses, and gardens (of which he was himself a notable designer), was the intimate of the greatest virtuosi and antiquarians of Europe, particularly Arundel, Cotton, founder of the Cottonian Library, and Ashmole. Evelyn established Grinling Gibbons' career by his introductions to Charles II and Sir Christopher Wren; consulted the great engravers: Bosse, Perelle, Hollar, Nanteuil and Prince Rupert, and published a *History of Chalcography*. He investigated new scientific discoveries, as well as every sort of amusing curiosity.

Pepys, of yeoman stock become gentry with good connections, rose high in the Admiralty service by his industry. He willed his fine library to his college of Magdalen at Oxford. His secret diary is full of wonderful gossip and the most minute, shameless and vital accounts of daily life, with details on his wife and servants, meals and hangovers, clothes and amusements, his contemporaries and their manners. There is nothing dull about Evelyn's diary, but that of Pepys is certainly one of the most honest and entertaining ever written.

Other valuable sources are:

Jonathan Swift: *Journal to Stella*, (1710-13), Methuen,

London, 1901. *The Life and Times of Anthony Wood*, antiquary of Oxford, described by Himself, 5 vols., Oxford Historical Soc., 1891-1900, is a masterpiece of editing on the part of Andrew Clark. Its 5th vol. is made up of 6 separate and incomparable indexes. Anthony à Wood (1632-95), whose diary and recordings of Oxford life are the best and often the only information we have, kept daily accounts of his expenditures.

[Mrs. Reginald Lane Poole: *Catalogue of Portraits in the possession of the University, Colleges, City and County of Oxford*, 3 vols. Clarendon Press, Oxford, 1925].

Thomas Fuller (1608-61): *History of Cambridge*, pub. 1655; and *Worthies of England*, 1662.

Lucy Hutchinson: *Memoirs of the Life of Colonel Hutchinson*, (1615-64); and the various satires of William Prynne (1600-69), give the Puritan side.

Gramont's *Memoirs of the Court of Charles II*, ed. Sir Walter Scott, Bohn, London, 1864, includes in the same volume Charles II's own account of his escape, as dictated to Pepys, and the *Boscobel Tracts*. Gramont (1621-1707) was a French nobleman who served under Condé, was an intimate of Louis XIV, was temporarily exiled to London, where he married the beauty Elizabeth Hamilton, and lived at intervals during Charles II's restoration. From information given by Gramont at 80, his brother-in-law, Anthony Hamilton, wrote one of the most frank and vivid of memoirs.

Bishop Gilbert Burnet (1643-1715): *History of His Own Time*, pub. 6 years after his death. Burnet was an intimate of William and Mary. Chamberlayne's *Present State of England* (see app., Ill. 1415). *Memoirs of the Verneys: Hatton Family Correspondence*. Account books kept by the thrifty Quakeress, Sarah Fell (pub. 1920). And the *Household Book* (1663-66) of the Scots Archbishop Charp.

English Diaries, ed. Arthur Ponsonby, Methuen, London, c.1922, gives a chronological list of English diaries, XVI-XIXc., and excerpts.

Horace Walpole: *Anecdotes of Painting in England*, 5 vols., 1782. Splendid examples of e. XVIIc. portraits will be found in Morse: *Elizabethan Pageantry*; and of whole century, in Collins Baker and Constable: *English Painting in the Sixteenth and Seventeenth Centuries*, Harcourt Brace, N. Y., 1917; and the same authors' *Lely and the Stuart Portrait Painters*.

For books on miniature painting, see Appendix on Ill. 1546.

Works devoted to *English Conversation Pieces*, such as those by Sacheverell Sitwell, or G. C. Williamson, are excellently illustrated and informative.

Of later books, see:

John Heneage Jesse: *England Under the Stuarts*, 3 vols., Geo. Bell & Sons, London, 1893. It is rich in well documented quotations, and illustrated by engravings from original documents; much costume information, and leads to other sources.

John Ashton: *Social Life in the Reign of Queen Anne*, taken from Original Sources, Scribner & Welford, N. Y., 1883, is extremely valuable.

Some French sources are listed in text of Ills. 1427, p. 547, or like Saint-Simon and Mme. de Sévigné, are described in detail under other captions. *Memoirs of the Duchess of Orleans*, Chatto & Windus, London, 1904; Barbier: *Journal*; Saint-Evremond; and some information about this period in later memoirs, like those of d'Argenson and d'Heziques. *L'Etat nouveau de la France* (see App., Ill. 1415). Sainte-Beuve: *Causeries du lundi* is full of precious information about XVII-XVIIIc., as are Racinet, Lacroix, and D'Allemagne, and Hippolyte Roy: *La vie, la mode et le costume au XVIIe siècle. époque Louis XIII*.

J. E. Farmer: *Versailles and the Court under Louis XIV*, Century, N. Y., 1906, is a useful book to which I am much indebted.

Moreau-Nélation: *Les Clouet et leurs émules*, 3 vols., and Hirth's vols. of prints.

SOURCES OF OUR ILLUSTRATIONS:

1354, 1356, 1357, 1407, 1417, 1430. Bouvy: *Gravure de portraits et d'allégories*.

1355-57. The movements of the early theatres from one to another *jeu de paume* can be followed in Rochegude (see Ills. 1296-99).

1369. André Blum: *A. Bosse et la Société française au XVIIe siècle,* Morance, Paris, shows all the plates.

1388. Color rep. in Piton.

1389-90. *Chalcographie du Mus. Imp., vol. 32, Ch. XII: fêtes et cérémonies,* (Met. Mus., Print Room). *Courses de Testes et de Bague faites par le Roy.* Denkmäler des Theatres, Nat. Theatre, Wien, pub. by R. Piper, Munich, is also good.

1415. Edward Chamberlayne (1616-1703), later secretary to the first Earl of Carlisle, while travelling on the Continent during the civil wars, came upon *L'Estat nouveau de la France,* published in Paris in 1661. On it he modelled his equally valuable *Present State of England,* first published anonymously in 1669, of which there were 3 editions in the next year, and 36 by 1755. They are mines of information.

Guy Miege (1644-1718?), a scholarly Swiss who came to England at Charles II's coronation, was Carlisle's secretary during his 1663-5 embassy to Russia, Sweden, and Denmark, and published his *Relation of Three Embassies* in 1669. Miege later taught geography and French, published a number of grammars and dictionaries, and in 1691, a *New State of England,* which Chamberlayne resented as a plagiarism. It was inferior, except in geography, but went through 18 editions by 1748. With the uniting of England and Scotland, the editions of both men's works, after 1707-8, were called *The Present State of Great Britain.*

Page 547. A. Savine: *Un séjour en France sous Louis XV, Lettres du baron de Pöllnitz,* Louis-Michaud, Paris, 1909. Princess Palatine by Rigaud, rep. in von Boehn: *Die Mode,* XVIIIc., p. 7.

1437-39. F. Libron and H. Clouzot: *Le Corset dans l'art et les moeurs du XIII-XXs.,* Paris, 1933.

1447. Quotation from Ashton: see above.

Page 558. Information on trades from George Unwin: *Industrial Organization in the 16th and 17th Centuries,* Clarendon Press, Oxford, 1904; Stow: *Survey of London,* 1598; Anthony Wood: *Life and Times;* and Diderot's *Encyclopédie: Tailleurs.*

1463-65. *Trou-madame* plates in Museum of Fine Arts, Boston, Elizabeth Day McCormick Coll. See Henri D'Allemagne: *Histoire des jouets,* 1902; *Récréations et passe-temps,* 1905; *Les Cartes à jouer du XIV-XXe siècle,* 1906, all pub. by Hachette, Paris (Cooper Union Museum).

1466. "Ranelagh Mob," *London Chronicle,* v.XI, p. 167 seq., 1762; long quotation by Malcolm: *Manners and Customs of London,* 1810, v.2,p.338, a very useful source.

1467. R. Whyte quotation from Morse; white beaver inf. from Beau Brummell: *Male and Female Costume.* Norris, vol. III, lists the personages in this picture, and describes alterations in costume, under different sovereigns, of these bodyguards. Quotations from Chamberlayne, 1755 ed., p. 107. Various editions list officers of the government and all Crown establishments, give incumbents by name, down to the lowest ranks, giving duty, pay and dress.

1468. A series of contemporary engravings of the funeral procession of Queen Elizabeth in 1603, showing people of every degree in mourning costume, is reproduced in "Vetusta Monumenta," Vol. III. The diary of the undertaker, Henry Machin, from 1550-63 (pub. by the Camden Society, 1848), describes funerals, ceremonies, revels, pageants, trials and executions under Edw. VI, Mary and Elizabeth.

1469. Colvin: *Engraving and Engravers in England.* Anne's use of Elizabeth's wardrobe, from Kendrick: *English Embroidery.*

1467, 1475, 1529-30. Collins Baker and Constable: *Eng. Painting,* 1500-1700.

1515-17. Waller.

Page 583-4. Tobacco and Snuff information from: John Ashton: *Social Life in the Reign of Queen Anne,* taken from original sources, Chatto and Windus, London, 1904.

Jonathan Swift: *The Journal to Stella,* Methuen, London, 1901.

Max von Boehn: *Miniatures and Silhouettes,* E. P. Dutton, N. Y., 1928 (40 col., halftone pl.)

Richard and Martin Norton: *History of Gold Snuff Boxes,* Phillips, London, 1938.

Henry Nocq: *Tabatières, boites, étuis, XVIII-XIXe s.,* de la collection du Musée du Louvre, van Oest, Paris, 1930.

H. D'Allemagne: *Les accessoires du costume,* Schemit, Paris, 1928.

1546. Miniature Painting sources:

Charles Holme (ed.) and H. A. Kennedy (text): *Early English Portrait Miniatures in the collection of the Duke of Buccleugh,* Studio, London, 1917.

G. C. Williamson: *History of Portrait Miniatures,* 1531-1860, George Bell, London, 1904, 2 magnificent vols., largely English.

Ernst Lemberger: *Portrait Miniatures of five centuries,* Hodder and Staughton, N. Y., no date; 75 col. pl.

A Collection of English Miniatures by Hilliard, Oliver, Cooper, Cosway, Smart, Plimner, and other artists of the 16th, 17th, and 18th centuries; plates and text, no author, date or publisher (Frick Art Reference Library).

Max von Boehn: *Miniatures and Silhouettes,* E. P. Dutton, N. Y., 1928, 40 col., 200 halftone.

The Morgan Collection.

1547. Charles' own account, and the *Boscobel Tracts* are included in Gramont's *Memoirs of the Court of Charles II,* ed. by Sir Walter Scott, Bohn, London, 1864.

1555. (omitted, because permission for its use had not been received by our deadline) should have been *Gilles van Terborch,* The Tichborne Dole, 1671, belonging to Sir Anthony Doughty-Tichborne, Alresford, Hants, England. It can be seen at the Frick Art Reference Library. It is one of the most important costume documents of Restoration England. In 1150, the tenderhearted lady of Alresford, lying on her death-bed, renewed her pleas to her husband to give part of his rich wheat lands to the hungry villagers. Lord Tichborne said grimly that she might give away as much of his property as she herself could walk around. She contrived to get out of bed; on her hands and knees, she encircled in one day a 23 acre plot which is still called "The Crawls," and laid a dying curse on the Tichbornes. The manor house would crumble; there would be seven generations of sons, and seven of daughters; then the name would end, unless the family gave a gallon of flour to every grown person and half a gallon to every child in the village of Alresford on every Lady Day. The dole was given, until the family left England 600 years later. The curse was then fulfilled in every detail, the lordship finally failing on a Tichborne who had changed his name to Doughty. In 1947, the current master of Alresford got permission from his government to buy flour, with ration points given up by the villagers, in order to fend off the Tichborne curse. ("Time," March 17, 1947).

1557-58. These, and many other fine early portraits appear in the Worcester Art Museum: *XVIIc. Painting in New England,* 1935. Permission to use the Freake portrait has been refused by the new owners to James Thomas Flexner: *First Flowers of Our Wilderness,* Houghton. Mifflin & Co., Boston, 1947 (an admirable book), and to us. Fortunately the former owners allowed it to be reproduced, and its delightful vermillion, lemon yellow, and sage green costumes can be seen in a fine color reproduction by Max Jaffe.

1559-78. Anthony Wood: full title in sources, above.

Mrs. Poole's *Cat. of Oxford Port.* (full title above) supplies information, including color notes, about portraits of every sort of person connected with Oxford, from the earliest times to 1925, including such characters as Mother George, an old female servant of Wadham College in XVIIc. Unfortunately, another Oxford character is missing: "Mother Louse," the innkeeper mentioned by Wood, "probably the last woman in England that wore a ruff." An engraving of her does, however, exist; as I remember, by Faithorne.

1581-82. Lady Newdegate: *Cavalier and Puritan,* diaries and newsletters of Sir Robert Newdegate (1644-1710), Longmans Green, N. Y., 1901, gives an idea of XVIIc. prodigality. He lists the foodstuffs used during the 12 days of Christmas, 1668; equivalent amounts were given away:

<table>
<tbody>
<tr><td colspan="2">By the Cook.</td><td>Dairymaid</td></tr>
</tbody>
</table>

By the Cook.

2 Beefes
6 Muttons
6 Veales
18 Turkeys
50 Geese
16 Ducks
42 Capons
2 Pullets
3 Chickin
3 Pigs
1 Swan
1 pay Bird
  (peacock?)
100 Rabbits
100 strikes
  of Wheat

Dairymaid
140 pounds of
butter

Beer
17 Hogsheads
  of Beer
3 Hogsheads
  of Ale
1 Barrel of
  March Beer

1585-86. Details photos in Preston Remington: *English Domestic Needlework of the XVI-XVII-XVIIIc.*, Metropolitan Museum of Art, N. Y., 1945.

1591. Hirth: *Kult. Bild.*

1595. Thomas Kellie: *Military Instructions for the Learned*, q. by Morse.

1596. Hirth: *Kult. Bild.* For its history and alterations in costume, see Col. Repond: *Le costume de la garde suisse pontificale et la renaissance italienne*, Rome, 1917. The origin of their parti-color uniforms is given under the Ill. by Vasari, end Italian XVIc.

1624. Tobacco: a Presbyterian minister like Henry Newcombe continually tells his diary, 1661-3: "How tobacco doth too much fill my thoughts and selfe denial about such a stinking thing might do well . . . I doe see my slavery with . . . this base tobacco." (Ponsonby: *Eng. Diaries*).

1648. Holland, in the second half of the XVIIc., abounds in group portraits of volunteer militia companies, men and women board members of guilds and hospitals, and other civic associations. Hals, from 1615, and Rembrandt during the 30's painted dozens of them, as did other artists like the Dutch Jan de Bray (1607-97), and the Flemish G. Flinck.

1654. Hirth: *Kult. Bild.*

1681. Ward: *The Electress Sophia and the Hanoverian Succession.*

Page 630. Europe Grows Colder: Mr. Benjamin Parry, Chief of the U. S. Weather Bureau in New York, became interested in my intuitions about the change in climate, and was good enough to help me substantiate them by indicating the Hildebrandsson article.

The "Frost Fair" is mentioned in *A Young Squire of the Seventeenth Century*, from the papers (1676-86) of Christopher Jeaffreason, 2 vols., Hurst and Blackett, London, 1878.

Page 634. Knitting by Hand and Machine: quotation from George Bryan Brummell: *Male and Female Costume*, Doubleday, Doran, N. Y., 1933. "Beau" Brummell's book was pieced together verbatim, from other writers, without acknowledgements. Mary's entire costume is described with obvious accuracy by a contemporary, but in this case, I do not happen to recognize the source.

1716. G. Yriarte: *Venice*, George Bell & Sons, London, 1880; he also wrote a useful *Vie d'un Patricien de Venise au XVIe siècle*, illustrated by unusual woodcuts by Bertelli and Franco. Coryat; full title given in XVIc. sources.

1723. Colored cuffs: *Peter Candid's* Countess Palatine Magdalena von Neuburg (Schleissheim Gallery), with a silver doublet sleeve, has lace cuffs worn over a flaring cuff of the scarlet of her overdress (in color in von Boehn: *Die Mode, XVIIc.*, opp. 14).

1733-38. See Lucien Duchartre: *Italian Comedy*, John Day, N. Y., 1928; Allardyce Nicoll: *Masks, Mimes and Miracles*, Harcourt Brace, N. Y., 1931; and George Freedley and John Reeves: *A History of the Theatre*, Crown, N. Y., 1941, with an excellent bibliography.

1739. For information on methods of staging, consult Lee Simonson: *The Stage Is Set*, Harcourt Brace, N. Y., 1946, which carries the history of theatrical design to our own times: and Allardyce Nicoll: *Development of the Theatre*, Harcourt Brace, N. Y., 1927, both beautifully illustrated.

Page 644. Court Dwarfs: see Alice Jane McVan: *Spanish Dwarfs*, "Notes Hispanic," Hisp. Soc., N. Y., 1942, p. 97-129. Ciba Simposia: *Dwarfs*, is one of that wonderful series of monthly pamphlets, issued and sent to physicians by the Ciba Pharmaceutical Products, Inc., Summit, N. J. They are illustrated by beautifully chosen documentary pictures or by photographs, and cover such a range of subjects as Twins, Shoes, Clothing and Hygiene, Cities and Houses.

1760, 1762. *Société de l'histoire du costume*, Bulletin.

The Revolt of Minds and Men, XVIIIc.

From the beginning of the XVIIIc., we are almost overwhelmed by the rich flood of primary source material.

In England, the *Spectator, Tatler* and their many imitators, and half a hundred newspapers at a time could be read free in the coffee houses. Information can be had from the *Gentleman's Magazine;* from plays, poems and novels by Gay, Pope, Swift, Defoe, Fielding, Goldsmith, Boswell and Johnson. Defoe's *Tour* tells much about all classes in the provinces in 1724; there are Arthur Young's *Tours* (1768-80) and his *Travels in the Kingdom of France*, 2 vols., published in Dublin in 1793. Swift's *Journal to Stella* is precious, as are the *Journals* and *Letters* of Walpole. There is no end to the memoirs, letters and journals: Lord Hervey's *Memoirs of the Court of George II*, Lady Mary Lepel Hervey's, Lord Chesterfield's, John Wesley's; those of Mrs. Delaney, Maria Edgeworth, Fanny Burney (Mme. D'Arblay), and endless others.

In France there are fewer periodicals or great writers but quantities of wonderful memoirs: d'Argenson's (1694-1757) which cover 1725 and 1756; those of dukes like Luynes and Lazun; of Mme. Campan who is painstaking and reliable in matters of court routine and dress, if nothing else; of Mme. de Genlis, etc., never forgetting the usefulness of Voltaire. This would be beyond our powers of assimiliation. Fortunately there arises, especially in France, a series of great writers, all stemming from the period they describe, who have done it for us. These secondary source books, well documented and reliable, include Taine's *Ancien Régime;* Sainte-Beuve's *Causeries du Lundi;* the Goncourts' *Woman of the 18th Century;* Chateaubriand's *Mémoires d'outre-tombe.* Even Michelet is invaluable, as is Lacroix: *Eighteenth Century.*

In the XIX and XX centuries all the XVIIIc. courts and kings and mistresses will be described in quantities of books by later writers such as Pierre de Nolhac: *Le château de Versailles sous Louis XV:* Count Fleury: *Louis XV et les petites maitresses;* and a great series by the industrious Imbert de Saint-Amand on courts and court ladies.

In England we have precious source material in such books as later editions of Chamberlayne; in James P. Malcolm: *Manners and Customs of London during the Eighteenth Century*, 2 vols., Longmans, Hurst, Rees and Orme, London, 2nd ed., 1810 (book written in 1807); and John Ashton: *Social Life in the Reign of Queen Anne*, Taken from Original Sources, Scribner and Wellford, New York, 1883. All give a wonderful mass of information from contemporary sources about dress, manners and amusements.

Sacheverell Sitwell: *Conversation Pieces* and C. G. Williamson: *English Conversation Pieces*, reproduce beautifully (often in color) and describe the less formal group pictures by Copley, Cotes, Davis, Gainsborough, Hayman, Highmore, Morland, Patch, Stubbs, Zoffany and many others of XVIII and XIXc. I am greatly indebted to both books. Lady Victoria Manners and C. G. Williamson: John Zoffany, John Lane, London, 1920; magnificent book. Warwick Wroth: *London Pleasure Gardens of the Eighteenth Century*, Macmillan, London, 1896.

The best biographies of American painters are to be found in the *Dictionary of American Biography*, Scribners, 1931, published under the auspices of the American Council of Learned Societies; from it I have drawn most of my material on Smibert and his successors.

Page. 654. Women's heads and caps: The French Night Cap; Ranelagh Mob, or the Hood from Low Life; Mary Queen of Scots Cap; and the Turban Roll worn around Mecklenburgh Caps, are described in the "History of Costume," *London Chronicle*, 1762, v. X, p. 167 seq. quoted by Malcolm, v. 2, p. 338.

Page 656. "Joseph": Advertisements of stolen goods (liberally quoted by Malcolm, v. 2, Chap. VIII) give names, descriptions and colors of articles of male and female dress of XVIIIc. England.

SOURCES OF OUR ILLUSTRATIONS:

1770. "Oeuvre de Watteau."

1816, 1818-20. Another equipage was a *brouette*, a sedan chair on two wheels, drawn by one chairman: Gillot's *Vinaigrettes ou Brouettes* (Louvre), is produced in Hilaire Belloc: *The Highway and its Vehicles*, Studio, London, 1925.

1862-63. Mme. d'Epinay wears a dark collar of this sort in her portrait by Léotard (Louvre), reproduced in Helen Clergue: *The Salon*, G. P. Putnam's Sons, N. Y., 1907, opp. p. 120. I think I remember one on Julie de Lespinasse, in one of Carmontelle's many drawings at Chantilly.

1871-74. The yellow coats worn by Fersen and his colleagues masquerading as coachmen, at the flight of the royal family, were part of the Condé liveries for which Longprix was highest bidder, at the suppression of privilege in 1789 (G. Lenotre: *The Flight of Marie Antoinette*).

1940. These Sèvres medallions were sold in the booths which cluttered staircases and corridors of Versailles, to the disgust of Marie Antoinette's brother, on his visit. *Benjamin Franklin and His Circle*, Metropolitan Museum of Art, N. Y., 1936, reproduces a great many medallions, designed by Flaxman for Wedgwood, which are invaluable for the information they give on wigs, neckwear and all the new collars appropriate to men of different professions, like Sir Hans Sloane, Dr. Henry Pemberton, the physicist, William Penn, or the elder and younger Pitt.

1997. Breeches held down by criss-cross ties are shown in a caricature of Col. Duff, afterwards Lord Fyfe, rep. in John Ashton: *The Dawn of the XIXth Century in England*, T. Fisher Unwin, London, 1906, p. 252. (This contains many excellent contemporary quotations, though it is not so good as his enchanting *Social Life in the Reign of Queen Anne*).

2021. Karl Mayer Sammlung: *Wiener Porzellan*. This famous collection (illus. cat. in M.M.A.Lib.) belonged to the father of Francis G. Mayer, the photographer of so many museum collections, who made the Kodachromes of the Brunias buttons (Ill. 1946-63), despite their fixed bull's-eye covering of glass.

Page 741. Of many studies on the content of Hogarth's work, I am perhaps most indebted to *The Works of William Hogarth*, 10 vols., George Barrie & Sons, Philadelphia, 1900.

Pages 761-63. Wigs: Kelly and Schwabe: *Hist. Cost.*, p. 201, shows 4 wigs from the *Encyclopédie*. Fig. 89-A, B, *perruque à noeuds*; C, D, the soldier's *perruque à la brigadière*; fig. 90 A, B, the *catogan*; C, *perruque à deux queues*.

2223. *Sporting Prints and Paintings*, Metropolitan Museum of Art, N. Y., 1937.

The Mills Rise, XIXc.

Source material is too plentiful and too easily available for listing.

Page 796. Claude Blanchard: *Dames du coeur*, éd. du Pré aux clercs, Paris, 1946, shows 17 of the first photographs ever made. Some are of great cocottes like Cora Pearl, and the Goncourts' neighbor and friend, Anna Deslions, who dressed with great elegance and launched styles. There are also actresses and dancers in costume, among them Mogador in male dress; Rigolboche, queen of the can-can; and Alice la Provençale, high-kicking and showing her long white drawers.

Early photographs form only part of the superb illustrations in color, and black and white, of *Un siécle d'Elégance française*, éd. du Chêne, Paris, 1943.

Page 806. *Costumes Parisiens*. The life histories of these early XIXc. fashion magazines can be traced with the help of G. Vicaire: *Manuel de l'amateur des livres du XIXc.* 1801-93; Paris, 1900.

2280. See Appendix reference for page 796. *Dames du coeur.*

2283. Empire dress with hoops: A drawing of an English court dress of 1810 will be found in Norris and Curtis: *Cost. and Fashion*, vol. VI, pl. 31, Dent, London, 1933.

2307. d'Arfeville quotation, from a most useful small book on Scottish dress, badges and war-cries, illustrated by many colored plates of tartans. All editions of *The Scottish Clans and Their Tartans*, W. and A. K. Johnston, Edinburgh, are not as good as the 11th, of 1913, to which I am indebted.

2329-30. Walter Shaw Sparrow: *Henry Alken*, Scribners, N. Y., 1927, is full of useful things like the front and back views of lines of spectators at the finish of Squire Osbaldiston's legendary wager of 200 miles against time, mounted on Tranby.

2440-42, 2627-32, 2676, 2678-81. *Siècle d'Elégance française.*

2444. Blunck: *Nordische Welt.*

2474. Not many of the Metropolitan Museum's wonderful collection of photographs by Hill have as yet been photographed. The Print Room was kind enough to select the Chalmers Family as the next to be done, because of its varied costume. The male portraits show many wonderful cravats, vests and coats. Brady's Civil War photographs are also in the Print Room. As we go to press, I have just discovered that one of their newly acquired early photographs by Braun, shows the Countess of Castiglione holding the identical black and white lace fan in the Museum's collection, shown in our Ill. 2529.

2488. Cooper Union has many of his pen, ink and water color studies of ladies and gentlemen, walking and driving, at balls and operas, in the 40's and 50's. Others are reproduced in *Constantin Guys, The Painter of Victorian Life*, ed. Geoffrey Holme, Studio, London, 1930.

2501-03. From Harry T. Peters: *America on Stone*, Doubleday Doran, 1931. Valuable illustrations of American lithographs.

2589-95. Gothic Revival handiwork: In *Der Bazar, Illustrierte Damen-Zeitung*, on top of my favorite tea-cozy sits a stuffed dog, carrying in his mouth a miniature of his mistress' bead bag. I once had to sit for some time on a green velvet couch-cover, the work of a Victorian needlewoman who was so in love with her really superb technical capacities that she had carried life-size acorns (in full relief, done in real gold thread) from the border onto the top, in lieu of tuft-buttons. One of the most amusing by-products of research for this book was to come across what must have been the source of her design: the set of jewels, furnished by Ball, Black & Co. for Mme. Oviedo's diamond wedding, shown in *Frank Leslie's Illustrated Newspaper*, vol. 8, 1859, p. 363.

2677. Claude Blanchard: *Dames du coeur.*

INDEX

The Index is meant to guide the reader to the elements of costume. To have entered every possible reference to each item would have resulted in an unwieldy, impractical mass. Therefore, an attempt was made to select representative examples of each of the elements. Roman numbers refer to page entries in the text; italic numbers refer to illustrations; CP refers to Color Plates.